Doctor Who
in Time and Spac

GW01458822

CRITICAL EXPLORATIONS IN SCIENCE FICTION AND FANTASY
(a series edited by Donald E. Palumbo and C.W. Sullivan III)

Doctor Who in Time and Space

Essays on Themes, Characters, History and Fandom, 1963–2012

Edited by GILLIAN I. LEITCH

CRITICAL EXPLORATIONS IN SCIENCE FICTION AND FANTASY, 39
Donald E. Palumbo *and* C.W. Sullivan III, series editors

McFarland & Company, Inc., Publishers
Jefferson, North Carolina, and London

LIBRARY OF CONGRESS CATALOGUING-IN-PUBLICATION DATA

Doctor Who in time and space : essays on themes, characters,
history and fandom, 1963–2012 / edited by Gillian I. Leitch.
p.   cm. — (Critical explorations in science fiction and fantasy ; 39)
[Donald E. Palumbo and C.W. Sullivan III, series editors]
Includes bibliographical references and index.

ISBN 978-0-7864-6549-1
softcover : acid free paper ∞

1. Doctor Who (Television program : 1963–1989)   2. Doctor Who
(Television program : 2005–)   3. Science fiction television programs — Great
Britain — History and criticism.   I. Leitch, Gillian I., 1967–
PN1992.77.D6273D625 2013   791.45'72 — dc23   2013003027

BRITISH LIBRARY CATALOGUING DATA ARE AVAILABLE

On the cover: Billie Piper and Christopher Eccleston in the first season
of the revived *Doctor Who* series in 2005 (BBC/Photofest)

Manufactured in the United States of America

*McFarland & Company, Inc., Publishers
Box 611, Jefferson, North Carolina 28640
www.mcfarlandpub.com*

Table of Contents

Introduction

GILLIAN I. LEITCH

It is doubtful that either the BBC or producer Sydney Newman knew, when they first developed the science fiction television series *Doctor Who*, that it would still be in production fifty years later, or that it would garner such a large and international fan base. Initially developed as an educational program which would fill a gap in the BBC's schedule,[1] the series holds two Guinness world records as the most successful science fiction series and the longest running science fiction series.[2] It not only remains a mainstay in the world of science fiction television, but can be considered a cultural phenomenon. It has spawned books, audio plays, comics, action figures, games, DVDs, clubs, fan websites, fan fiction, and conventions. *Doctor Who* stands out among its peers because of its place in science fiction television as among the earliest of the genre, by its longevity (as celebrated by Guinness), and from the culture of its fan base, now spanning several generations of viewers.

In compiling this book it was my intention to include essays which represented the many aspects of the series, from its fans, to its narratives, themes, and its characters. Its evolution over the last fifty years, with changes in production, production values, creative personnel, audience, technology, and the society in which it was made, make it a fascinating subject of study. Clearly no book can do *Doctor Who* justice, but it is my hope that this collection presents a diverse reading of both the series itself and its influence.

I will lay out my colors right away, and declare that I am a huge fan of *Doctor Who*, and have been for a long while. I began watching the original series, kept the faith during the many years when it was not produced, and am now following the new series avidly. In this I am not alone. Fans have come to be an essential element in *Doctor Who*.

In an interview in 1982, Matthew Waterhouse, who played the companion Adric, said that he kept his membership in the Doctor Who Appreciation Society secret at his audition in order to be taken seriously for the role.[3] But fans are taken seriously, and it is in the faithful fan base that the seeds of the series' rebirth in 2005 were planted. A huge fan of the original series, Russell T. Davies was asked by the BBC to revive the series.[4] Other members of the series' creative team like Steven Moffat and Paul Cornell were also fans of the original series. *Doctor Who*'s fans have elevated the program from a science fiction television series to a cultural phenomenon

It is from the fan's perspective that this book begins. In "Event TV: Fan Consumption of Televised *Doctor Who* in Britain (1963 — Present)," Andrew O'Day explores the ways in which the original series of *Doctor Who* was watched and experienced by its British audience. Early fans, without the benefit of PVR, VCRs, DVDs or Internet downloads, had to dedicate time to watch the series when it aired. The act of watching, then, was as important as the show itself. *Doctor Who* viewing was a part of the phenomenon itself. As technology has caught up with the desire to re-watch the program, fans have adapted their viewing behavior. Watching *Doctor Who,* new and old, was and is an event for its fans.

The idea of the fan as part of the phenomenon of *Doctor Who* is continued by O'Day in "Social Spaces: British Fandom to the Present," which examines how the series has brought people together. *Doctor Who* has caused fans to socialize, through fan groups, fanzines, the Internet and conventions. It is a large and varied group of people who enjoy the series and identify themselves as fans. Their interactions with the series and other fans are just as diverse, creating different kinds of communities and social spaces.

The series was cancelled in 1989, leaving fans to their own devices. Hopes for its resurrection were fueled then dashed by the ill-fated BBC/Fox co-produced television movie in 1996. Fans had to depend instead on their imaginations, reruns of the series, fan productions and novelizations. Aaron Gulyas' "Don't Call It a Comeback" discusses the production of *Doctor Who*–related material during these "wilderness years." This fifteen-year period saw *Doctor Who* fans shape and reshape the storyline to their own design. Gulyas considers the material which was produced, how it was received by fans at the time, and the thorny question of what to make of this wealth of production when the new series began in 2005.

As in the previous essay, the thorny question of "Whose Doctor?" is addressed, here from the perspective of the Canadian fan. The series has attracted from its earliest years an audience outside of Great Britain, particularly in the Commonwealth, which enjoyed a favored position in obtaining BBC programming. Canadians are especially connected to the series, beginning with its creator Sydney Newman, who was a Canadian. J.M. Frey discusses the connection between *Doctor Who* and Canadian fans, and their identification with the series, the characters, and its production.

Such a dedicated fan base comes from a large and inventive corpus. The concept of a time-travelling Doctor, his unusual ship shaped like a British police telephone box, and his various enemies and monsters captured the viewers' imaginations. And while it has evolved over the decades, with changes in cast, production, and production values, it has maintained its essential core.

Time travel is the main premise of *Doctor Who* and has been a constant throughout its production. "In and Out of Time: Memory and Chronology" explores the concept of time as used in the series. Time and timeliness, according to Kieran Tranter, is at the core of the success of the series. The Doctor is a time traveler, and the show itself has endured a long time, being then both about time and situated within various time streams. Time is variable, as are the perceptions of it and its presentation in the series. Continuing with the theme of time in the following essay, "Effecting the Cause: Time Travel Narratives," Paul Booth discusses the use of time travel as narrative, and the paradox of time travel. The series has, over the years, explored the contradictions of time travel, cause and effect, in different manners, in the old and the new series.

Doctor Who, over its long run, has used journalists and media as a narrative tool and to further the action in its episodes. This is particularly true of the new series, which has frequently presented television news broadcasts and broadcasters as narrative devices, and media sources as elements of danger. Racheline Maltese's "Narrative Conflict and the Portrayal of Media, Public Relations and Marketing in the New *Doctor Who*" demonstrates how such characters who work in media are portrayed as both suspect and trusted, a conflicted position, which adds a dynamic to the audience's acceptance of truths and ideals presented in the stories.

Nostalgia is another important element in the series. Maura Grady and Cassie Hemstrom, in "Nostalgia for Empire, 1963–1974," show how time travel allowed for the portrayal of a British past, where the Empire still existed, and Britain was great. Traveling to the future likewise allowed for a vision of a British future where, while the Empire is gone, the British essence and identity remain strong. Grady and Hemstrom highlight a critical period in British history, when society was undergoing great change, and the traditional British identity was being challenged.

It is an oft-quoted statement that *Who* fans hid behind the sofa during many of its scariest scenes. Peter Davison, the fifth incarnation of the Doctor, admitted to being frightened watching the series as a child, and that his "sister cowered behind the sofa or hid her head beneath the cushions."[5] Violence is an integral part in the portrayal of conflict and the creation of the sense of menace. In "A Needle Through the Heart: Violence and Tragedy as a Narrative Device," Lindsay Coleman discusses the uses of violence in the original series, and the critical reactions that resulted in the British media. *Doctor Who*, developed originally as a children's series, was a prime target. It was in this period that Mary Whitehouse and others criticized television for portraying violence and stressed the negative impact it had on children.

Death follows the Doctor throughout his travels, and while he can regenerate his form in a physical crisis, and has lived over nine hundred years, those he surrounds himself with have no such crutch. They are mortal, and as such, can and do die. In "Everything Dies: The Message of Mortality in the Eccleston and Tennant Years" Kristine Larsen looks at matter of death. The Doctor must deal with the mortality of his companions, those he meets on his travels, and the overwhelming sense of loss he feels as the last Time Lord. Death is not wished for, and it inevitability is fought by both the Doctor and those around him.

Apocalypse is another recurring theme in the series. The Doctor and his companions often have to deal with events or characters which threaten the very existence of life, be it life on Earth, or in the universe as a whole. In "'Ready to outsit eternity': Human Responses to the Apocalypse," Andrew Crome demonstrates that apocalypse acts as both a problem to be resolved and an idea that has ramifications for the characters within the story. And as with other elements of the series, the portrayal of the apocalyptic has changed over the run of the series.

Doctor Who is a very British television series. And as remarkably simplistic and broad this statement is, it is an important part of its narrative. In "A Country Made from Metal? The 'Britishness' of Human-Machine Marriage in Series 31" by Kate Flynn, the ideas of mechanization, love and British identity are inextricably linked. Identity takes on many forms. Rory and Amy as married companions demonstrate the complex inter-relationship of identity, romantic ideals and the construction of a British life, and the perpetuation of it even when the life itself is artificial through a choice of symbols and ideas.

One of the most creative aspects of *Doctor Who* is the wide variety of aliens the Doctor encounters in his travels. From the Daleks to the Ice Warriors, these aliens have acted as threats to the peace of the universe. Of the many alien foes that have been introduced into new series of *Doctor Who*, the Weeping Angels have by far been the most fascinating. At once seemingly harmless and inanimate, they are fierce and utterly scary. David Whitt, in "'Whatever you do, don't blink!' Gothic Horror and the Weeping Angels Trilogy," shows how the program borrows successfully from other genres. The Weeping Angels and the stories in which they feature are prime examples of gothic horror, yet at the same time are science fiction.

In the episode "The Next Doctor," Jackson Lake tells Rosita that the companions must always do what the Doctor says. An interesting perspective, but one based mostly on illusion. On the death of Caroline John, who played companion Liz Shaw, Steven Moffat, producer, more accurately stated that "the Doctor's companions should never be his assistants — they're the people who keep him on his toes and that's what Caroline did."[6] Companions are the foil to the Doctor, asking the questions that the audience want answered, and getting into situations which propel the action of the episode forward. The Doctor rarely travels without a companion, and it is through them that the audience understands his character.

Of the forty-three companions who have traveled with the Doctor over the series, twenty-eight have been women,[7] and so the final three essays are dedicated to the experience of female companions. Antoinette F. Winstead's "*Doctor Who*'s Women and His Little Blue Box: Time Travel as a Heroic Journey of Self-Discovery for Rose Tyler, Martha Jones and Donna Noble" demonstrates that the companions experience internal changes as they forsake home and family to travel through time and space with him. Their journeys as companions act as metaphors for their spiritual journeys as women.

Of all the companions, it is Sarah Jane Smith, who first appeared in *Doctor Who* in 1973 with the third Doctor, who has enjoyed the strongest connection with the series' audience. She left the series in 1976, but returned again in 1983 for the 20th anniversary special "The Five Doctors" and in the new series in 2006 with "School Reunion," and then "Stolen Earth" and "Journey's End" in 2008. In the time between, she was offered not one but two spin-off opportunities, the last, *The Sarah Jane Adventures,* being the most successful. Sarah Jane is unique among the companions for the recurrences of her character, and her popularity. What was it about her life as a companion which informed her decisions post–Doctor? Sherry Ginn's essay title, "Spoiled for Another Life: Sarah Jane Smith's Adventures with and Without Doctor Who," addresses that question.

The last essay, Lynnette Porter's "Chasing Amy: The Evolution of the Doctor's Female Companion in the New *Who*," deals with the most recent companion Amy Pond, and how the nature of being a companion has changed over the years. Amy marks a departure on many levels from the Doctor's previous companions. More than any other in the new series, her sexuality and wearing of more overtly suggestive costumes have been pointed out and critiqued. Her relationship with the Doctor is also portrayed differently from that of the other companions.

Doctor Who has been in production for thirty-three years, and on the air as new episodes and repeats for almost fifty years. It represents a long history of creative writing, production and performance. This science fiction phenomenon has taken its viewers on travels through time and space in over 200 story arcs. The cast, including the main character of the Doctor, has changed numerous times, as have the producers, the writers, and the production teams. British society and the corporation that commissioned the series have also changed, as have the budgets and the technology involved in the productions. Despite this, the series has kept to core idea of time travel with an alien in an implausible machine, with quirky and interesting companions, solving problems and defeating scary and devious enemies. Along the way the series has also managed to keep a core group of fans interested in its characters and adventures. *Doctor Who* exists, then, as a corpus of science fiction writing and production, and a sustained cultural phenomenon.

The problem with such a long and interesting history as that of *Doctor Who,* if there can be said to be one, is the passage of time, and the inevitable passing of those associated with the series. The recent deaths of Elisabeth Sladen, Nicholas Courtney, Caroline John and Mary Tamm have underscored this. The sense of loss and nostalgia, particularly for the original series, has given their fans good reason to revisit their incredible performances. I would like to dedicate this book to the actors, producers, writers and others responsible for the production of *Doctor Who*, past and present, who inspired me and the contributors to this book.

NOTES

1. Jim Leach, *Doctor Who,* TV Milestones Series (Detroit: Wayne State University Press, 2009), p. 1.
2. http://www.doctorwhonews.net/2011/09/dwn150911135512-dalek-collector-enters.html (8/19/2012).
3. Alan Road, *Doctor Who: The Making of a Television Series* (New York: Puffin, 1983), p. 17.
4. Andrew Cartmel, *Through Time: An Unauthorised and Unofficial History of Doctor Who* (New York: Continuum International, 2005), p. 188, and http://tardis.wikia.com/wiki/Steven_Moffat (8/19/2012).
5. Alan Road, *Doctor Who: The Making of a Television Series* (New York: Puffin, 1983), p. 11.
6. http://www.bbc.co.uk/news/entertainment-arts-18531461 (7/28/2012).
7. For the sake of clarity I have counted Romana once although she was played by two different actresses.

1

Event TV

Fan Consumption of Televised Doctor Who *in Britain (1963–Present)*

ANDREW O'DAY[1]

The first episode of *Doctor Who*, "An Unearthly Child," aired on Saturday, November 23, 1963, on BBC1. Popular writers and academics have provided suitable histories of the program itself and it is not my intention to replicate these here.[2] Similarly, it is not my intention to trace the development of *Doctor Who* fandom in Britain to the present day since the scope would be too broad. I am also not interested in looking at the ways in which fans make value judgments and analyze the program, which have been subjects widely discussed elsewhere.[3] My aim is to trace the different ways in which fans have consumed the television episodes of *Doctor Who*, as this process is more complex than that of sitting at home and watching the television set and the BBC1 first transmissions. Such a study involves looking not only at technological factors but also at institutional, economic, and social ones and the ways these interact.

This essay will demonstrate that consuming *Doctor Who* has always been an "Event" for fans. The label "Event TV" has been employed in two contexts. The first of these is by scholars like Daniel Dayan and Elihu Katz who "have proposed the idea of media events — the live televising of official ceremonies which embody a society's values" (e.g., royal weddings, funerals, and sports tournaments).[4] The second usage of the term by scholars like Mark Jancovich and James Lyons refers to "must-see TV ... shows that are not simply part of a habitual flow of television programming but ... have become 'essential viewing.'"[5] This essay will show that the notion of *Doctor Who* as an "Event" for fans goes further than that of "must-see TV" and has, over time, worked in different ways. The chapter will also show that the notion of 'Event TV' in new *Who* operates alongside industrial practices.

The essay will not only make use of secondary sources to contribute to this developing picture, and theorize, but will also draw on primary archival material, such as newsletters, and fanzines, as well as, very importantly, interviews with fans, conducted in person and by email. My methodology is mostly qualitative. As far as space permits, an attempt has been made to reproduce some material in lengthy quotations to give a sense of the different voices at work. In conducting these interviews, I did not ask very broad questions, but specific questions. Therefore, the slight possibility exists that respondents may have occasionally said what they felt I wanted to hear. But because these people knew they would be quoted they would have been careful as to what they said.

1960s and 1970s Consumption of Doctor Who

In addition to there being *Radio Times* covers and features, and events within the program's diegesis, such as the return of old monsters and changes in Doctors, *Doctor Who* was consumed differently by fans of yesteryear as a consequence of the technology of the time. Once an episode had been shown fans had no expectation of seeing it again, and, as these comments by fans illustrate, one had to be there on time to see *Doctor Who* on a Saturday evening, forsaking, where one could, any other type of special events. The program fits in with what Jancovich and Lyons call "date" or "appointment" television.[6] We see the anxieties experienced by fans to make sure that they saw the episodes on first transmission, anxieties that continued throughout the 1970s and into the early 1980s, as well as their taping the audio-soundtrack of episodes for listening to again, and savoring repeats:

> TONY CLARK: There's iPlayer today. Back in the '60s and '70s you had to see it on transmission, you had to watch it. I entered a competition to design an egg ... the judging was on Saturday. *Doctor Who* was on that evening.... Time was getting on...and they were about to announce the judging of the competition ... I wanted to get back to watch *Doctor Who* ... my neighbour drove us back ... and as I'd read the time wrong I was actually an hour early for *Doctor Who*! If you didn't see *Doctor Who* on transmission you were never likely to see it again.
>
> JAN VINCENT-RUDZKI: That's why I taped it. I recorded the first two episodes of the first Dalek story and then off and on, when I could afford the tape ... I listened and re-listened to them. I listened to Inferno on the way to school.
>
> TONY CLARK: It was something like March 1980. JN-T was being interviewed ... I came to London to see Michealjohn Harris. I got my sister to do an audio recording. I remember standing outside a window seeing images on a television. When I got home I listened to the recording and put the sounds to the images in my memory.
>
> J. JEREMY BENTHAM: The repeat of "The Deadly Assassin" in 1977 coincided with one of the One Tun [pub] "do's." There was a television above the bar. We asked the landlady if she could put it on but she said no as it would probably upset some of the regulars![7]
>
> TONY CLARK: By the mid–1970s we were getting summer repeats of *Doctor Who*, but that would only be two stories out of five or six, and as an avid *Doctor Who* fan, it would be impossible to guess which ones they were likely to be. As a child, a few months between series seemed a very long time ... the repeats filled the gap nicely.[8]

Because there was no expectation of seeing *Doctor Who* again, rather than picturing all fans as "hiding behind the sofa" (although Peter Gilman speaks about being half in the room, half out of it in fear),[9] it is fair to assume that fans viewing of the actual episodes treated them as more of a special event and were in many cases more attentive, and a few comments made to me testify to this type of viewing:

> JAN VINCENT-RUDZKI: I valued the viewing experience more. The audios were merely a memory reflection of what I'd seen, or rather experienced. Just like the cinema, I wouldn't have looked from the screen because "I was there." I was absorbed in the story.[10]
>
> TONY CLARK: Like most fans, I wasn't even able to make audio recordings of the episodes, so everything that was viewed lived only in the memory. There was no way of viewing the episode again.... The need to commit the episodes to memory became a must, so I was keen not to miss a minute. I wanted to make sure I didn't miss anything that I had the chance to see ... being as I was too young to remember the start of the series in 1963 I was hooked from Jon Pertwee onwards (having seen some Troughton as a youngster). I remember that I hated anyone making a noise or even talking when the show was on, there was no chance to rewind and watch something again. I hated it if we had any visitors to the house when *Doctor Who* was on ... my parents would make me turn the volume of the TV down.[11]

JAMES SPENCE: I had to absorb every frame as there was never any chance of a repeat unless the BBC were kind to us. I recorded the audio from "Death" ["Death to the Daleks"] onwards and so had the audio to assist my memories. My memories of the B/W are/were way better than the reality (the memory DOES cheat). When I got my first VCR (1981) it was *Star Trek* rather than *DW* which got played the most but when it came to, the pre–VCR days, *DW* audio tapes were played more than *ST*. Guess, *DW* had better stories but *ST* had better visuals.[12]

TIM HARRIS: Before the advent of videotapes the experience of watching Doctor Who on TV consisted of regimentally checking for when it was on and then not missing it. I tended to watch it more avidly as a result, although never to a point where my family and I were fully quiet during a broadcast.[13]

Regular color transmissions had begun on BBC2 July 1, 1967, and another feature in the history of *Doctor Who* was its being broadcast in color from the first Jon Pertwee episode onward in 1970. Some were fortunate enough to see this, although, as suggested by one fan, the program's being transmitted in color was not necessarily an event:

J. JEREMY BENTHAM: I did see "Spearhead from Space" in colour on 3 January 1970. BBC2 had already been broadcasting in colour for a few years and my father decided to rent a colour set in time for the Mexico Olympics in 1968. The first series of "*Star Trek*" had been running in *Doctor Who*'s slot, in black & white, throughout the summer and autumn of 1969, and right after the last episode of its run was shown, BBC1 trailed the return of *Doctor Who* by screening a compilation of clips from the last episode of "War Games" before launching into an excerpt (in full colour) from the first episode of "Spearhead."[14]

JAMES SPENCE: My parents got a colour telly in time for episode 2 of "Death to the Daleks." It wasn't a big event as a few months before when a neighbour got a colour TV ... by looking out my kitchen window I saw a bit of "Spock's Brain"— Mr. Spock wasn't green which surprised me. Seeing *DW* in colour wasn't any big deal for me (quite disappointed colour-wise in comparison to the two movies).[15]

These were some of the ways in which fans consumed *Doctor Who*. Apart from listening to audio recordings and watching repeats, the only other way of experiencing *Doctor Who* stories again (or indeed for later fans for the very first time) was by reading the hugely successful Target novelization range. David J. Howe (who, born in 1961, would have been one of those captivated by these books) provides a detailed history of these elsewhere and points out that "for many viewers, the novelisations were their first opportunity to relive old adventures" as "this was ten years before the advent of *Doctor Who* on commercially available video."[16] What began as a modest endeavor of a few titles in 1973, once Richard Henwood had spotted a few out-of-print *Doctor Who* hardbacks from the 1960s when visiting the offices of publishers Frederick Muller in Tottenham Court Road[17], really took off with speed in the late 1970s. Between 1973 and 1994, there were 153 Target *Doctor Who* novelizations, over 800 individual printings and re-printings, with over 13 million copies in print.[18] These novelizations differed in their level of fidelity to the original broadcast episodes. Fan enthusiasm surrounding these novelizations is, for instance, evident through letters between J. Jeremy Bentham and the assistant to the children's book editor for Target, who, before the advent of many *Doctor Who* news sources, would send Bentham a list both of forthcoming *Doctor Who* publications and novelizations that they hoped to release in the near future.[19] As Tony Clark puts it, "The Target books were a boost, but they didn't start appearing until 1973, and even then they were not that frequent at first."[20] Listening and reading would continue to be a fan practice from the 1980s onwards when fans discovered how many of the 1960s William Hartnell and Patrick Troughton episodes had been wiped from the BBC archives. Prominent fan Ian Levine saved much material and launched searches for missing material.[21] Today, the soundtracks of missing episodes have been commercially released, while there have also been series of fan reconstructions (e.g., by *Loose Cannon*) of these episodes where the soundtracks are accompanied by existing stills.

While writers like David J. Howe, Mark Stammers, Stephen James Walker, and, more recently, Brian J. Robb, have debunked the myth that organized *Doctor Who* fandom did not really get off the ground until the mid–1970s,[22] and that, in fact, from 1965 onwards, there was activity in the form of the *William Hartnell Fan Club*, and the *Doctor Who Fan Club* (run by Larry Leake and Philip Jon Oliver, then by Graham Tattersall and then by 14-year-old schoolboy Keith Miller).[23] It was the mid–1970s that would see fans like Jan Vincent-Rudzki (from Westfield College), Gordon Blows, J. Jeremy Bentham (from University College) and Stuart Glazebrook making contact and forming the Doctor Who Appreciation Society (DWAS). Just as the 1980s would see fans desperate to obtain copies of *Doctor Who* stories on video, the 1970s was when fans came together as a group, and corresponded with one another about making audio copies of older and contemporary episodes, as is evident, for example, in a series of letters between J. Jeremy Bentham and Gordon Blows in 1976, and between Bentham and Stuart Glazebrook in 1976 and 1977.[24] Later, in the *Doctor Who Appreciation Society Yearbook* for 1978–79, David Owen revealed that the Liverpool local group listened to tapes of old *Doctor Who* episodes, which foreshadowed local groups watching old videos in the 1980s. It must be borne in mind, however, that not all fans had access to these audio tapes. Fan Tim Harris, for example, recalls having had the audios of episode 6 of "Planet of the Daleks" and episode 3 of "The Time Warrior" recorded for him when he had no choice but to attend weddings (as well as having missed episode 1 of "Genesis of the Daleks") but notes: "I didn't have enough money as a kid to record the audios en masse but in later years when Kroll was taking up valuable screen space I'd often regret not having a copy of the odd classic episode or two to listen to. Target Books filled a hole but I regretted not having the audios."[25]

1980s "Event TV" and the Shift of the 1990s and 2000s Consumption of Doctor Who

By the 1980s *Doctor Who* had a long and secure past. This decade brought with it a new producer for the program, John Nathan-Turner, whose idea of event TV would be to continually bring back elements from the program's history in a postmodern fashion, so much so that after awhile it seemed commonplace rather than a special occasion. Indeed, Nathan-Turner was responsible for overseeing the program's 20th anniversary season where each story featured an element from the series' past, and the 90-minute 20th anniversary special "The Five Doctors," which was marked as even more of an "event" than the 10th anniversary special "The Three Doctors," by way of its being screened separately from a main season. "The Five Doctors" was also rare for '80s *Who* in that it was given a *Radio Times* cover.

This was not the only strategy used to resurrect (sometimes unsuccessfully) the past. Up until 1981, repeats of *Doctor Who* had tended to be of the current Doctor, so the announcement that BBC2 would screen *The Five Faces of Doctor Who* season in the fall was, as fan Peter Gilman puts it, an "event."[26] In the summer of 1982, there was another repeat season called *Doctor Who and the Monsters*.[27] These institutional decisions were mirrored by screenings at *Doctor Who* conventions.

Old episodes were, for example, screened at DWAS conventions, following a tradition begun in the late 1970s.[28] The quotes reproduced here reveal how special these occasions were where, in one instance, a year's wait for a story was deemed worthwhile:

TREVOR WAYNE [on PanoptiCon III]: Having secured all four episodes of the first Doctor Who story, the organisers had something very special to build a convention around.[29]

GARY RUSSELL [on Interface I]: Immediately afterwards they ran an excellent DWAS title sequence ... followed by episode one of "The Rescue" ... the first episode of "Beyond the Sun" was shown.... It was pleasant to see Dick Mills turn up and ... a showing of "Unearthly Child."[30]

PAM BADDELEY [on PanoptiCon IV]: A main highlight of Panopticon's is the screening of old episodes, as those who saw "The Tribe of Gum," "Beyond the Sun" and "The Rescue" for the first time at previous gatherings will testify. We all had high hopes of seeing the programme's second serial, "The Dead Planet," at Panopticon IV, but unfortunately, it was not to be.[31]

DOMINIC MAY [on PanoptiCon V]: On stepped Mr. Howe in an immaculately pressed suit and launched into his spiel, before long introducing the first item. An item which was most unexpected too: "Prisoners of Conciergerie," which is episode six of "The Reign of Terror." ... David Howe came on stage again ... and immediately led us into ... "The Dead Planet," which was greeted by warm applause considering it was a year later than promised, but in my view the wait was worthwhile.[32]

ROBERT MOUBERT [on Inter-face II]: Not even the prospect of giving me money could dissuade those present from hastening upstairs to watch the first of the old episodes.[33]

In 1983, *Doctor Who* celebrated its 20th anniversary and was enjoying immense popularity. To mark the occasion BBC Enterprises held a mammoth event on the grounds of Longleat House in Wiltshire over the Easter weekend. Longleat had housed a *Doctor Who* exhibition since 1973. But the sheer number of people who actually turned up was not foreseen. Heavily advertised not only by the DWAS, but also nationwide in the *Radio Times* (after *Doctor Who* billings) and through trailers on BBC1 itself, and on the Radio 2 *Ed Stewart Show*, it was calculated that around 20,000 people would show up, but the reality of the situation was that nearly three times as many came (from different parts of the country and from different parts of the world), so that radio announcements had to be made advising people not to go unless they had tickets and police in helicopters had to turn people away.

The event was the first time British fans had seen so many *Doctor Who* stars together in one place, and featured all surviving Doctors (including the very private Patrick Troughton who was persuaded to come, making this one of only two convention appearances in Britain). William Hartnell's wife, Heather, also appeared. There were tents for the Radiophonic Workshop (itself 25 years old), for Visual Effects, and for Merchandise, while autograph sessions took place in the Orange Room, with some queues lasting 4½ hours, meaning that some guests would come out and talk to attendees in line. Photo opportunities were available at the inside exhibits, including the sets for the then unseen special "The Five Doctors," and of people pretending to drive the Doctor's car Bessie or be pictured with monsters or stepping out of the TARDIS.[34] But photos of the guests had to be taken by attendees. It is telling, therefore, that with all these other attractions, the main lure for some was the *Doctor Who* cinema.

It was an event for many that a large marquee tent was devoted to showing one story from each Doctor over the course of the Easter weekend. These were "The Dalek Invasion of Earth," "The Dominators," "Terror of the Autons," "Terror of the Zygons" and "The Visitation." Paul Winter, now coordinator of DWAS, notes that it was the *Doctor Who* cinema he was looking forward to most of all and that he was excited to be going to see "The Dalek Invasion of Earth." His not being able to get in spoiled the rest of the day for him. Robin Prichard reveals that he queued for some time to see "The Dominators" as he had not seen it since its first transmission. And Nicholas Briggs, who now ironically provides the Dalek voices for the new *Doctor Who* series, states that the main thing he wanted to do at Longleat '83 was to see old episodes and to tape the soundtrack. He was quite annoyed that John Leeson's K9 voice over the Longleat announcement service drowned out the sound. He said that he would have cut the wire with his pen knife had he not been afraid of being electrocuted.[35] This era also saw the Video Room become a feature of *Doctor Who* conventions, such as at Mary Milton's two Leisure Hive events held at the Wiltshire Hotel in Swindon where videos would not only play during the day but also all through the night.

For those wanting to see old episodes, there was also the National Film Theatre's (NFT's) weekend on October 29 and 30, 1983.[36] Bentham remembers the weekend fondly:

> "Doctor Who — The Developing Art" was unquestionably a huge highpoint in what had already been a very eventful year for *Doctor Who* fans. The project came about simply because Manuel Alvarado, one of the authors of the Media Studies book *Doctor Who, The Unfolding Text*, was a close friend of Richard Patterson, a director of programming at the NFT. Manuel was keen to have some kind of launch event for his book, and Richard liked the idea of staging something big to mark Doctor Who's looming 20th anniversary — which might just happen to fill the NFT to capacity along the way as well. I'd worked extensively with Alvarado and his co-author, John Tulloch, during their writing of *The Unfolding Text*, providing what you might call the "hard *Who*" facts and figures stuff, so it was one of those "Boy, oh boy, yes!" moments when they then asked if I'd like to be involved in selecting the NFT programming schedule, and producing the accompanying sleeve-notes booklet. Here for one weekend only was an opportunity to present more than 30 individual episodes, many of them unseen by the public since their original transmissions, as well as several full stories (at least one per Doctor) on the big screens of the NFT. We'd had Longleat back in April, of course, but the logistical problems encountered by that event have become legendary. Only a couple of hundred attendees at best had been able to squeeze into that cold, drafty marquee tent to view a muzzy copy of "The Dalek Invasion of Earth." The NFT's two cinemas could provide comfortable seating for several hundred at a time, and offer all of the seating, food and bar facilities normally associated with fan conventions. With a lot of help from Ian Levine a hugely impressive list of material was prepared for screening.[37]

It is telling that so much of this "launch event" involved the screening of old episodes, although many of Bentham's own memories are of the special guests:

> I doubted Richard Patterson's claim that the NFT had successfully booked Patrick Troughton to appear on the Sunday. That doubt persisted right through to the Sunday morning of the weekend itself—indeed right up to the moment when, without flurry or fanfare, the great man himself abruptly ambled into the NFT cafe and proceeded to order a coffee. The sound of jaws hitting the floor in shared astoundment was almost audible. And there were so many others: Heather Hartnell with her sharp mind full of memories, the ever-entertaining double act of Barry Letts and Terrance Dicks, Anthony Ainley — all gush and froth — Dalek creator Raymond Cusick, and for me personally a last chance (not that I knew it then) to talk and listen to that grand master of Doctor Who directing, Douglas Camfield, before his sad death some months later. It was an amazing weekend with a great many special and irreplaceable memories for me. I think my personal favourite is still the Tex Avery-style double-take that one fan performed during the presentation of "The War Games" when he suddenly realised the voice of the Doctor on screen was identical to the voice he could hear murmuring away in the seat behind him.[38]

In a 1984 review in the fanzine *Cloister Bell* that may appear very odd to us today, none other than Robert Shearman, writer of the new series episode "Dalek" (2005), commented on the event, and although he too had stories of the special guests he gives a description and analysis of the stories and episodes, many of which he had not seen for many years:

> NFT seemed like paradise ("Such stuff as dreams are made of") ... I very carefully selected those sessions of episodes ... which I wanted to see most.... "The Demons" may be my favourite *Who* story, and its impression was heightened by the retrieval of the colour episodes and by Barry Letts' opening speech.... Pure nostalgia rolled through me as I shared the audience's obvious enjoyment of the story.... My memories of Pertwee and Delgado were rekindled with the next session, which was the "Third Doctor's Selected Gems" ... Terrance Dicks had warned us about the Dinosaurs in "Invasion of the Dinosaurs" 6, but they were worse than I had thought.... I saw "Dalek Invasion of Earth" 1 for the second time, after I had managed to see the Longleat farce. "Dalek Invasion" always remained rather dim in my memory because of the crowd and the cries of John Leeson.... "Ark in Space" is probably the best-remembered Baker story ... I had seen many of the Troughton selected gems at various conventions, but as he is my favourite Doctor I came to see this interesting group.[39]

One can see the reasons for these screenings being events. The early 1980s marked a technological shift which would have implications for the whole of *Doctor Who* fandom since this was the age that ushered in the home VCR. A special documentary on the recent DVD release of "Revenge of the Cybermen" discusses the topic of the advent of VCRs at some length. Bentham states elsewhere that "during the 70s and well into the 80s it was quite common practice to rent TV equipment rather than buy it outright" and that he rented his first VCR in the summer of 1978 "just in time to catch the reruns of 'The Invisible Enemy' and 'The Sun Makers'" with the tape being "virtually bald" from over watching before the Key to Time season started in September.[40] Vincent-Rudzki "started taping off-air from the repeat of *Deadly Assassin*."[41] In the DVD documentary, one fan, Paul Jones, talks about later viewing and how a three-hour VHS tape cost £10 so that one had to record over the tape once one had watched it a few times.

A poll was carried out at the Longleat 1983 convention to discover which *Doctor Who* story the fans would most like to see released in commercial videotape form. The story most selected was the first Tom Baker season offering from 1975, which was subsequently released (with episodes edited together, no special features, and an incorrect design of a Cyberman pictured on the video's cover) at a staggering price of £39.95. As pointed out, taking into account rates of inflation this was eight times more than a *Doctor Who* DVD costs today. Nevertheless, Paul Jones tells of how his best friend got the video and he went to this friend's house to watch it. The stories were also released very intermittently with episodes edited together and their purchase costs high until the recommended retail price became standardized at £9.99 in 1987, with many more releases from around 1990.[42]

During the 1980s video piracy was ripe. For example, the Jon Pertwee stories were repeated in a loop in color on Australia's ABC channel, whereas repeats from this era were rare in America where stories from the Tom Baker era were rescreened on a regular basis. The Australians, meanwhile, complained about the fact that the more recent *Doctor Who* stories, starring Peter Davison, were not screened there, so British copies of the newer stories were exchanged for the older Australian material. There still existed the problem of how to obtain copies of the William Hartnell and Patrick Troughton black and white episodes, since these were not repeated in Australia. However, a solution was found which was that people had friends who worked in the BBC archives willing to make copies. In order to obtain copies of these stories, however, fans found that they had to have something to bargain with and swap such as merchandise. Otherwise, one had to rely on the black market which normally charged about £5 an episode. But a really rare story such as "Doctor Who and the Silurians" in color (taken from an off-air USA recording) would cost between £350 and £800. The picture quality of these videotapes was often extremely poor: the more times it was copied down the worse the picture and sound quality got (the picture could appear grainy, could start to lose its color, could feature drop-outs, and there would be a hissing sound on the tape where there was supposed to be silence).[43]

Activities within DWAS local groups during the 1980s could differ from those in the 1970s since in the 1980s members could sit in the dark watching old episodes of *Doctor Who* on videotape, and members of one local group could bargain over videotapes with members of another. All this activity was long before the weekly 6 P.M. repeats of the beginning of the Tom Baker era on Superchannel, which were enthusiastically taped by those lucky enough to have a satellite dish or cable, or before Galaxy and the 1990s repeats on U.K. Gold (when there were also many more commercial tapes out). Fan Tim Harris notes:

> We already had cable by the time Superchannel came along but I stocked up on videotapes ready for showings of Tom Baker stories. I left it to my mother to record the episodes and sometimes she would even remember to do so, albeit that occasionally there would be the odd missing five minutes or so. Having stocked up on tapes it was disappointing that Superchannel disappeared from our cable service very quickly and I was envious of another friend who still got the channel by satellite, and who didn't seem to care about recording it. When BSB came along and it was announced that *Doctor Who* would appear on a channel called Galaxy I phoned up and got BSB installed well in time.[44] I thought Galaxy was excellent and [friend] James and I spent one particular weekend in one room at my house with multiple video recorders recording a special weekend of *Doctor Who*–related programmes that Galaxy broadcast. It didn't last, BSB was swallowed up by SKY and non–BBC broadcast *Doctor Who* was lost to me yet again and I could only look at yet another redundant pile of blank tapes and sigh. It was with a sense of "Yeah, so what?" when I heard U.K. Gold was going to be broadcasting *Doctor Who* because it seemed to promise the same as Superchannel and BSB and I thought, "Yeah, but it won't last."[45]

Writing for the fanzine *Frontier Worlds* in the early 1980s, John Bok raises a great number of the issues that we have considered thus far, and employs terminology of watching "old" *Doctor Who* as having been an "event":

> When I first saw an "oldie" I sat there desperately, and unsuccessfully, trying to memorise visually every individual scene, since it was such an event to view an old story.... Who can recall the tremendous feeling of excitement and expectancy prior to "An Unearthly Child" being repeated on BBC2 in 1981? Excitement because we were being given a chance to obtain a first-class copy of this undoubted classic which previously had been unobtainable to the majority of us. Yet now it is nothing ... I would guess that, thanks to video, there is now a more relaxed attitude in relation to watching the programme when actually transmitted. Before the advent of video it was unheard of to miss an episode unless there was some major catastrophe such as a wedding. Unheard of, because that person knew that he would never be able to see that episode again.... Yet now, there is no qualm whatsoever about missing an episode since, if they don't actually have a video-recorder themselves ... they will know someone who does have one.[46]

This issue of what is or is not event TV is also apparent in the 1990s, when *Doctor Who* was off the air as a regular television program, as well as in the 2000s. One can detect a notable shift. Disappearing at conventions of the 1990s were the typical video rooms of the 1980s' conventions. These had been made redundant by advances in technology whereby most fans owned a home VCR, and where all existing *Doctor Who* episodes had been released by the BBC in commercial videotape form. Fans still had to pay to attend these conventions and therefore would expect more for their money than an experience they could just as easily get at home. The only exceptions to this rule are when an episode is recolourized or when a missing episode is recovered and premiered as an event, as was the case at a DWAS convention in 2004 when the until-then missing episode from "The Daleks' Master Plan," "Day of Armageddon" (1965), was screened. It is telling, for example, that when asked what place the DWAS has in the Internet-age, current coordinator Paul Winter pointed to these screenings:

> I guess that the Internet has meant that the market for our services has shrunk.... The provision of *Doctor Who* news, both officially ... and also from fan-run sites ... has meant that the place of a monthly news magazine has been supplanted.... This is not an issue for *CT* [*Celestial Toyroom*, the DWAS monthly newsletter]. Some twenty years ago the then-Society executive took the decision to move *CT* away from being a newsletter and into the realm of a magazine proper and that remains the case today ... the Society also attempted to establish itself as an event organiser in its own right ... I think that we have done that although I would still like us to be a bigger player in the field.... We have always sought to follow the guidelines on *Doctor Who* events, the most significant one of all being the requirement to be non-profit making.... We keep our conventions to one or maybe two per year and we have been rewarded in our approach by the provision of material and also guests that might not otherwise have been available. For example, in 2004 we screened the then-recently-recovered episode "Day of Armageddon" months before its DVD release and in 2009 we were given access to the re-colourised part 3 of "Planet of the Daleks".... DWAS is not just a monthly magazine — it is what you want it to be — you can get discounts on events, access to signed items ... and more.[47]

Similarly, the discovery of episode 3 of "Galaxy Four" (1965) and episode 2 of "The Underwater Menace" (1967) was announced at the British Film Institute's Missing Believed Wiped day on December 11, 2011, and the episodes screened there and on 2 December 2012, which were events.[48]

However, the release of *Doctor Who* on DVD now may tell us about the way most old episodes have lost their event TV status. Because the stories have been seen by many of the fans so many times, and have all been released at least once in a commercially-available format, the episodes have been repackaged with a host of special features, including the option to listen to an audio commentary over the episodes by actors from the stories and members of the production team, as well as watch specially-made documentaries, the option to read production notes subtitles over the episodes, and sometimes the option to watch episodes with updated effects or to listen to an isolated musical soundtrack. It is not unreasonable to assume that for many older fans, it is these special features that have assumed the role of the event rather than the episodes themselves, except, for instance, where the missing episodes of "The Invasion" (1968) and "The Reign of Terror" (1964) have been animated or stories have been re-colorized like "The Ambassadors of Death" (1970). Indeed, as Peter Gilman notes, he has become "more selective in purchasing" and will "only buy certain stories on DVD." He has not bought "Time-Flight" or "Meglos."[49] However, recent times have seen the emergence of Tweetviews which are "an organized viewing of a particular *Doctor Who* story on DVD, where everybody can participate by tweeting comments as they watch the show simultaneously."[50]

In the 1990s and 2000s there was also a shift from old televised *Doctor Who* episodes being an "event" to experiencing new *Doctor Who*— in different media (the Virgin New and Missing Adventures books and particularly the licensed Big Finish audios), where fandom became something other than being a fan of televised *Doctor Who*. Tellingly, the Big Finish *Doctor Who* range was announced at a fan event, the convention *Battlefield II* in 1999, suggesting that the target audience were fans. What is so significant about these audio dramas, unlike those of BBV or Magic Bullet Productions, is that they feature the Doctors and companions from the original series, played by the original actors. Rather than old episodes of *Doctor Who* being screened in the main hall as in the conventions of old, after the celebrity dinner at the beginning of the evening's entertainment, the announcement about these new audios took place in the main hall for maximum exposure and clips were played from the first audio "The Sirens of Time." However, while *Doctor Who* as event TV may have appeared no more, developments in the early 2000s would mean that this was certainly not the case.

The 2005 Revival of Doctor Who *and the Redefinition of "Event TV"*

The return of *Doctor Who* has always been a type of "event" for fans, something to be anticipated with enthusiasm, but this was never more so than with the program's return to BBC1 in 2005. When *Doctor Who* returned, it did so in an industrial context where "must-see TV" exists as a category, and is publicized and promoted as such. New *Doctor Who* exists in a TVIII environment of brand-centric event TV drama. Having been off-air as a regular series since 1989 — some 16 years earlier — with only the controversial 1996 TV movie starring Paul McGann (loved by some, loathed by many) to fill the void, a massive publicity campaign was launched to herald the program's 2005 comeback, including giant billboards promoting the series. On the day of transmission of the first episode "Rose" (March 26, 2005), a palpable sense of excitement was generated on BBC1, with a documentary about the new series airing shortly before the first episode and with even news presenters and weathermen referring to the program's imminent return. New *Doctor Who* is given constant event status through, for instance, numerous *Radio Times* covers (including at the launch of a season as well as after the first few episodes once the initial excitement has died down), through specials aired every Christmas Day, and is even inscribed into the diegetic world of narratives. Following the success of this first season, it seems that producer Russell T. Davies and now Steven Moffat have sought every opportunity to give *Doctor Who* the status of event TV with the notion of an event inscribed in the diegesis of the first episodes of seasons. In each year of a new season since the program's return, the program has been given a fresh "catch," as it were, which has indeed been picked up on each occasion by the mainstream press. So, for example, the 2006 episode "New Earth" (April 15, 2006) marked the beginning of the first full-length season to star David Tennant in the leading role; the 2007 and 2008 episodes "Smith and Jones" (March 31, 2007) and "Partners in Crime" (April 5, 2008) introduced the full-time companions Martha Jones and Donna Noble, respectively; while the 2010 season and the episode "The Eleventh Hour" (April 3, 2010) marked the start of Matt Smith's first full-length season as the Doctor.

The excitement of the 2005 return of *Doctor Who* was indeed felt everywhere, but nowhere more visibly than at a London pub on the Farringdon Road, then called The Printworks. It was here that J. Jeremy Bentham and his wife Paula (with the assistance of their good friend Tony Clark) held the first of what has now become a tradition of *Doctor Who* launch parties, screening season premieres live. This had been done before when, on September 6, 1986, the first episode of "The Trial of a Time Lord" was broadcast live on a big screen to some 500 attendees at the DWAS Panopticon convention, and at the first DWASocial on February 28, 1981, which coincided with part one of "Logopolis."[51] However, those were conventions not devoted solely to these screenings. Organizing the first of these parties brought with it its own set of challenges for the team. For one thing, they had to settle on an appropriate venue (one which was not concerned about throwing out regulars, and with a huge screen which everyone could see). For another, they had no idea how many fans they would attract, with advertising initially taking place through flyers, through word-of-mouth at The Fitzroy Tavern, and through publicity on the Internet. They also had to determine when the transmission of season premieres would be, as BBC program planning always kept this a closely guarded secret.

A long-time watering hole for *Doctor Who* fans, The Fitzroy Tavern itself was immediately dismissed as a possible setting for these parties as it lacked a permanent screen. January 2005, however, brought a solution to the team's dilemma when Peter Gilman's suggestion of The Printworks, which boasted a big screen, had other smaller screens around the bar, was relatively quiet on a Saturday, and which welcomed families, seemed ideal. Fortuitously, the landlord was enthusiastic and the Benthams certainly need not have worried about whether fans would turn up to these parties. Although some fans preferred to stay at home and watch the episodes in solitude with the curtains drawn, many gathered around the screens at The Printworks in 2005.[52]

The idea of the transmission of the first episode "Rose" as event TV can be seen in a different manner to the launches of subsequent seasons. As Douglas McNaughton points out:

> The official BBC1 premiere ... was treated as a live broadcast ... so the *simultaneity* of the viewing experience was important, connecting fans to a diaspora of similar audiences. A pirate copy of "Rose" was leaked onto the Internet several weeks before transmission, opening up a dilemma for fans: watch immediately or wait for the official transmission date?... For some, the chance to delay this event added to the pleasure of anticipation... Fans constructed "Rose" as a media event to conform to the producers' injunction that the show needed big ratings to succeed.

McNaughton cites one viewer who states:

> I turned down the chance to see "Rose" last Sunday when a journalist friend of mine rang me to say she had [a] preview [copy]. Last night another friend phoned to say he'd managed to download it from the internet and did I want to go round and see it? Again, I declined ... I want this to be a Wonderful event, not some little secret to be watched over a PC monitor and "enjoyed" alone as if it were a guilty pleasure.

This viewer invited a few friends to his house to watch the episode, with "everyone ... bringing a 'buffet' item" while he would "be getting a bottle of champagne."[53] J. Jeremy Bentham, meanwhile, stated to me:

> I did not see the episode in advance of the live BBC1 TX. There were copies ... of "Rose" ... doing the rounds, following the press launch a week or so earlier, but they were incomplete/alternative edits, and I was passionate about wanting to see it "live" on the big screen.[54]

Each of the Benthams' subsequent launch parties got bigger, with most fans returning the next year, and fans coming from as far afield as the United States, Canada, Australia and even Sweden to attend. The team also relates the story of one person who came from the North East of Scotland, leaving for London on the coach the night before. The maximum number of people allowed under health and safety regulations was approximately 300 and the team were receiving over 500 requests for admission, meaning that names had to be drawn from a hat (in one case the party was publicized in *Doctor Who Magazine*). For the year of "specials" a smaller party of around 150 people was held at the One Tun pub on New Year's Day 2010 to mark David Tennant's swan song as the Doctor.[55]

By the time of the 2010 launch party, Wetherspoon had sold off *The Printworks*, which had been refurbished in a Goth style and renamed Ghost. Despite initial anxieties of whether people would still turn up for a new Doctor (a lot of female fans had gone before to see David Tennant) it is telling that for their 2010 launch party the team went to The Crosse Keys, one of London's biggest pubs, located on Gracechurch Street, near Leadenhall Market, which has an extremely wide projection screen and monitors around the bar. The Benthams had been initially anxious that they would not be able to fill The Crosse Keys with a required number of around 750 people, but it soon became apparent to the team that even with the amazing capacity of the pub, the most recent of their launch parties was massively over-subscribed, and that not everyone could be accommodated. Furthermore, at The Crosse Keys, the doormen were required to check the IDs of people who looked younger than 18 and, as this had not been anticipated, people unable to prove their age were refused admission. Those people were redirected to the gay establishment the Retro Bar near Trafalgar Square, which broadcast episodes of the new series on a regular basis. In this instance, the team had been able to post information about the party on the Internet sites Gallifrey Base and *Doctor Who* Online.[56]

While it is important to realize that the experience of watching *Doctor Who* live on a big screen with other fans is an "event" in itself, the team sought to make the days even more special.

> TONY CLARK: We wanted to keep people interested before the episode started. If young people had come a long way we wanted to give them a day to remember.
>
> J. JEREMY BENTHAM [taking a sip of beer]: We wanted to give people that bit extra ... and show that we're not just a whole bunch of alcoholics watching an episode of *Doctor Who* for an hour.

So, for example, special guests were in attendance. Writers Steven Moffat, Paul Cornell, Rob Shearman, Gareth Roberts and Nev Fountain were present at the first; Nicholas Courtney at the second; and Katy Manning, Philip Madoc and Toby Hadoke were present at the 2010 launch (although Katy Manning did not stay for the actual episode, preferring to watch it at home). Many fans had mistakenly believed Matt Smith would also attend. As these are not licensed BBC events the guests were not paid, and were not interviewed in the manner of conventions but attendees would buy people like Nicholas Courtney free drinks, and over the course of the day would seize the chance to get autographs. At the first 2005 party, the guests were given a rose to wear since the episode being shown was "Rose." J. Jeremy Bentham provided a small introduction at each party to thank everyone for coming, and Toby Hadoke did some emceeing at the 2010 launch. In addition to this, not only were the venues decorated with posters (brought by Paula Bentham) and filled with K9 and Dalek props (enabling photo opportunities) but Bruce Campbell of TV and Film Memorabilia and The Stamp Centre also had stalls at various of these parties, which were in some cases not only covered in Wetherspoons' newsletter, and in the Metro and on BBC Radio London but were webcast to other fans by *Doctor Who* Online.[57]

J. Jeremy Bentham was keen to stress the fact that these parties were an extension of the notion which lay behind the One Tun and Fitzroy Tavern gatherings which was to bring fans together and get them networking.[58] *Doctor Who* fan gatherings took place at the One Tun pub in London from 1976 onwards, and were subsequently promoted in the DWAS newsletter *CT* and fanzine *TARDIS*.[59] A falling out with the landlord meant that the gatherings were shifted to The Fitzroy Tavern in Charlotte Street, where they continue on the first Thursday evening of every month to this day.[60] Tony Clark also commented that there would be people at these launch parties who would not know other *Doctor Who* fans in person, including shy and younger people. Clark relates his own experience of growing-up and his feeling of being "the only *Doctor Who* fan in the village" and states of the launch parties that he hopes "people will leave having made new friends, new contacts."[61]

There have also been non–London based parties, including a "Journey's End" screening party in Liverpool at the Adelphi in 2008 and a Glasgow event.[62] Elsewhere, Gareth Kavanagh held screening parties at his pub The Lass O'Gowrie on Charles Street, in Manchester's city center, which were free to attend but were on a first-come, first-served basis. Under 16s were allowed to attend until nine o'clock as long as they were accompanied by an adult. Not only are season premieres of the new *Doctor Who* series events but so are the climax to seasons. Hills concentrates on the story-arc escalation which acts as an equivalent to the "increase in narrative stake ... structured into reality TV and talent shows that progress towards a final" with which new *Doctor Who* has had to compete.[63] While there was no regular series of *Doctor Who* in 2009, the year was marked by three specials, the last of which was the start of a two-part adventure, shown on Christmas Day, and which concluded with David Tennant's much anticipated swan song, broadcast on New Year's Day 2010. The Lass O'Gowrie pub was also the setting for the launch of "The Eleventh Hour." A color publicity poster was designed for each of the screenings, with the witty captions "END OF TIME AT THE BAR! Join us for David Tennant's final adventure, The End of Time, Part Two, LIVE on the big screen!" and "'Time, Please'—Join us for Matt Smith's first adventure, The Eleventh Hour, LIVE on the BIG SCREEN!" running along the top, lending the gatherings "event" status. Kavanagh notes to me that in terms of attendance about 60 people showed up for "The End of Time Part Two" and about 40 for "The Eleventh Hour" and that he was "pleasantly surprised" with the figures for the former "as it was New Year's Day and public transport is pretty limited."[64] Kavanagh reveals that "there was an interesting mix of Who fans from the Manchester area and North West (with many in fancy dress), a limited number of kids accompanied generally by 'fan dads,' a good number of gay fans (with the screening promoted selectively in nearby Canal Street) and a huge number of 20 and 30 something female fans" including his female staff.[65] In talking about the origins of the screenings, Kavanagh did not have the same problems as the Benthams in having to search for a suitable venue with a big screen, and he compares the *Doctor Who* screenings to pubs showing sporting events and *The X Factor* which is interesting in light of Hills' above comments that story-arc escalation leads up to a final in *Doctor Who* much in the same way as talent shows:

> We show various bits of live sport like the football, rugby and big tournaments like the World Cup so are already set up with big screen projectors ($1 \times 100"$ and $1 \times 140"$) and dedicated sound system, so technically we were a go.... The Lass is my pub which also gives me carte blanche to indulge my whims like *Doctor Who*, original comic art and classic arcade games. We'd also run two *Doctor Who* conventions by then so I was beginning to see how the pub could host more niche events, if only we could conjure up the confidence to have a go. I mean, pubs up and down the land regularly show *The X Factor* on a Saturday night (especially in and around Canal Street where it is practically an institution!), so why not *Doctor Who*—especially the end of the rudely popular Tennant era?[66]

Indeed, Kavanagh goes on to remark;

> it's ... worth considering the reactions of non-fans, especially on "The Eleventh Hour" as this was an Easter Saturday with people already out for a pint. Although some people did come in and end up watching, I had purposely emptied the pub of footy fans earlier on and retained a bouncer

(a crunch Premiership game — Manchester United v Chelsea has been on earlier in the day) to manage punters as I had decided not to show Burnley v Manchester City opposite *Who*. Predictably, the City fans failed to understand that their game had been bumped for *Who* as in their mind, *nothing* is more important than Manchester City.[67]

Like the Benthams, Kavanagh comments on how these *Doctor Who* screenings can be friendship-building and even notes how they have sparked further pub gatherings:

> The specialness of the end of the Tennant era and a new Doctor were vital though to get people out the house and make them feel part of something bigger, communal as being a Who fan can be a relatively solitary experience in my experience with the majority of friendships conducted via forums and round-robin emails.... As for the role of alcohol, I suspect there's a whole paper to be written about the propensity to over-consume when faced with a room of fellow fans that probably has its roots in shyness and overcompensation!... These event are friendship builders.... They have also enjoyed a positive legacy at the Lass to boot, through our facilitating of a regular, mainstream "open invite" meeting of *Doctor Who* fans in the snug of the pub held in on the last Saturday of the month, since January 2010 and in rude health.[68]

Kavanagh continues to note about audience reaction:

> The die-hards were probably the most negative, giving people talking "the look" and scuttling out at the end without stopping for a chat. I suspect these fans did not return for "The Eleventh Hour" screening. However, the majority of fans appeared to have made a day of it making friends, enjoying a drink and sharing opinions in a more human forum than is usually allowed.[69]

Indeed, Kavanagh's screenings were not attended by special guests from the program, largely for the practical reason of not being able to get them.

Matt Smith's second season as the Doctor did raise interesting questions about the notion of event screenings since it was split into two halves, one screened in spring 2011 and one in fall 2011, and therefore in effect had two premieres and two concluding points. The hook of the first episode "The Impossible Astronaut" was that one of the main characters would die, while the first episode of the second half "Let's Kill Hitler" would continue the season. As early as January 2011, Kavanagh was thinking about the season split, stating to me:

> More screenings would definitely be considered although the scale would depend solely on what else was going on in the pub at the time. One of the great difficulties in arranging these is that the BBC often holds back the transmission time and date until relatively late in the day, meaning planning becomes tricky and last minute in nature. The split seasons also offer great possibilities, as I assume the end of the first half will be a dirty great big huge cliffhanger that people will be salivating to see resolved![70]

Since that comment was made, there was indeed a live screening of "The Impossible Astronaut" (April 23, 2011) at the Lass, publicized by posters, with a turnout of about 40, with Kavanagh noting assertively, "I think we'll do one for the first half series finale and also the second half debut and finale."[71] As it happens, however, such was the popularity of the events that regular screenings of every episode from the second half of the 2011 season beginning with "Let's Kill Hitler" took place at the Lass.[72] J. Jeremy Bentham, meanwhile, held a screening party for the episode "The Impossible Astronaut." Such was the fan demand that a Little Light Launch for roughly 170 fans was held at the One Tun pub, including a buffet.[73] Fans turned up wearing Stetsons (a wink to the episode filmed in the U.S.) and some drank champagne to celebrate, with there being a noisy build-up to the start of the episode. There was a communal feeling with a clap at the onscreen dedication to Elisabeth

Sladen and much laughter at the episode's humor. However, there was not a follow-up screening during the 2011 season. In addition to these screening parties, the BFI has started premiering episodes of the new series (with special guests in attendance) including Christmas specials, and "Let's Kill Hitler" (August 15, 2011), and "Asylum of the Daleks" (August 14, 2012), the latter of which had as its hook the appearance of all different types of Dalek from the program's history.

Back in 1982 — some thirty years ago — John Ellis theorized television as an intimate medium, watched in a domestic setting on a very small screen, with the characteristic mode of viewing being the glance as opposed to the gaze, with people watching while involved in other household activities or while talking to one another. Conversely, watching films involved people making a specific effort to leave the home and go to the cinema, paying an admission fee, where, as Ellis pointed out, viewers would watch an enormous screen in darkness and in silence, employing an attentive gaze.[74] It has, however, long been recognized that there are other ways of watching television, even in a domestic setting. Ellis' characteristic mode of television viewing is what Jeremy Tunstall would classify as either "secondary" or "tertiary" involvement with media, where one pays only momentary attention to the television set, being engaged in another activity ("tertiary"), or pays attention some of the time, listening to the sound, while pre-occupied ("secondary"). However, Tunstall recognizes that there is also "primary involvement" where one gives the television one's full attention.[75] This is where viewers make a conscious selection of a specific program that is viewed faithfully from week to week, and are engaged in what Bob Mullan calls "ritualised viewing."[76] John Thornton Caldwell has indeed described "glance theory" as "the *myth* of distraction" (my italics).[77] "Ritualised viewing" is employed by *Doctor Who* fans generally. We have already seen how back in the 1960s, '70s, and '80s, fans did not watch *Doctor Who* incidentally but actually went to great pains to record and listen to the narratives repeatedly. As fan James Spence's response earlier to the question of whether he watched more attentively in the pre–VCR days, that he had to "absorb every frame," indicates the fact that fans thought they would not see these *Doctor Who* episodes again, meant that they watched in a way opposite to Ellis' "glance theory." Furthermore, Tony Clark's comment that he "hated anyone making a noise or even talking when the show was on" stands in opposition to Ellis' notion that television is watched while involved in other household activities or while talking to one another. Jan Vincent-Rudzki indeed compares his viewing experience to that at the cinema, where he "wouldn't have looked from the screen," while Ellis drew a distinction between viewing television and cinema spectatorship. In the 1980s fans also went to great lengths to obtain pirated video copies and gaze at them even when their picture quality was poor. The "launch parties" for the BBC Wales series can, furthermore, be seen as an extreme type of "ritualised viewing" which, in part, replicates the cinematic experience even more and extends that where fans come from other countries to watch the episodes. *Doctor Who* fans make a decision to leave the domestic setting and travel to a particular venue to specifically watch an episode of *Doctor Who* on an enormous screen. Catherine Johnson has challenged the notion that telefantasy is unsuited to visual spectacle[78] and the episodes screened at these "launch parties" would sometimes boast visual style. For example, the pre-credit sequence to "The Eleventh Hour" can be seen as analogous to the opening special effect of "The Trial of a Time Lord" that elicited a gasp from viewers at Panopticon back in 1986. Indeed, it is telling that J. Jeremy Bentham compares these new series launch parties with "going to the cinema and seeing a film."[79] Furthermore, the BFI premieres of episodes remind one of film premieres.

Conclusion

The ways in which fans consume *Doctor Who*, as traced in this essay, have evidently varied over the program's long history, in relation to institutional, social, economic, and especially technological factors. For example, we have seen that before the advent of the VCR fans used to tape the soundtrack of episodes and read the Target novelizations of stories; that copies of these tapes used to circulate and be played at local group meetings; that with the arrival of VCRs, pirated copies of stories used to circulate among fans; and that with the advent of the BBC Wales series fans grouped together to watch episodes live on a big screen, showing how the notion of *Doctor Who* as event TV has become redefined in the 21st century and that there is a very visible fan culture. This chapter may seem to have traced a history of "technological determinism." But, in fact, this has not been the case. While changes in technology have indisputably altered the ways in which fans have consumed *Doctor Who*, the social network of fandom has been just as important: the ways that fans used to make copies of the soundtracks for one another in the 1970s when the Doctor Who Appreciation Society was formed and listen to them at local group gatherings; the ways in which pirated videos circulated in the 1980s including at local groups; and the way in which old episodes and new have been screened at different types of events. Without the social network of fandom, history would not have progressed in the same way. Furthermore, economics has played a role in this developing picture since the release of *Doctor Who* on commercial videotape (and now on DVD) has affected the landscape of fandom, where the typical convention video room of the 1980s has become a dinosaur. While the attention of this chapter has been on the consumption of *Doctor Who* in Britain, we have also seen how globalization is important since pirated videos from the United States and Australia came onto the British fan network. There are other avenues of investigation to be covered in relation to *Doctor Who* fandom in future. For instance, with the program's 50th anniversary on the horizon (Saturday, November 23, 2013) it will be interesting to see what events take place to mark this, whether there is a special 50th anniversary episode, and in what setting this is consumed by fans. One thing is certain: as the Doctor's travels continue, so too is this history ongoing.

NOTES

1. In addition to all those who agreed to be interviewed, I would like to offer my sincere thanks to J. Jeremy Bentham for organizing interviews and providing archival material; to Tim Harris for providing a wealth of research material; to Dr. James Spence for advice; and to Dr. Matt Hills for his encouragement with the project.

2. See James Chapman, *Inside the TARDIS: The Worlds of Doctor Who* (London: I.B. Tauris, 2006); David J. Howe, Mark Stammers, and Stephen James Walker, *Doctor Who: The Sixties* (London, Virgin, 1993); David J. Howe, Mark Stammers, and Stephen James Walker, *Doctor Who: The Seventies* (London: Virgin, 1994); David J. Howe, Mark Stammers, and Stephen James Walker, *Doctor Who: The Eighties* (London: Virgin, 1996).

3. Work has been done on this by, for example, Alan McKee, "Why Is 'City of Death' The Best *Doctor Who* Story?" in David Butler, ed., *Time And Relative Dissertations in Space* (Manchester: Manchester University Press, 2007); pp. 233–45.

4. Daniel Dayan and Elihu Katz, *Media Events: The Live Broadcasting of History* (Cambridge: Harvard University Press, 1992), discussed in Douglas McNaughton, "Regeneration of a Brand: The Fan Audience and the 2005 *Doctor Who* Revival," in Chris Hansen, ed., *Ruminations, Peregrinations, and Regenerations: A Critical Approach to Doctor Who* (Newcastle upon Tyne: Cambridge Scholars, 2010): pp. 200–201.

5. Mark Jancovich and James Lyons, *Quality Popular Television* (London: BFI, 2003): p. 2.

6. Ibid.

7. J. Jeremy Bentham, Paula Bentham, Tony Clark, Peter Gilman, David Miller, and Jan Vincent-Rudzki, interview at The Fitzroy Tavern, London, 8 January 2011.

8. Tony Clark, interview by email, 17 February 2011.

9. Bentham et al., interview.

10. Jan Vincent-Rudzki, interview by email, 20 February 2011.

11. Clark, interview.

12. James Spence, interview by email, 14 February 2011.

13. Tim Harris, interview by email, 18 February 2011.

14. J. Jeremy Bentham, interview conducted for a fan website, 4 January 2011.

15. Spence, interview.

16. David J. Howe, *The Target Book: A History of the Target Doctor Who Books* (Tolworth: Telos, 2007): pp. 11–12.

17. Ibid., p. 17.

18. Ibid., p. 12.

19. Letters to Jeremy Bentham, dated 6 September 1973 and 24 January 1973.

20. Clark interview.

21. For further reading see Richard Molesworth, *Wiped! Doctor Who's Missing Episodes* (Tolworth: Telos, 2010). Also see fan publication *Nothing at the End of the Lane* for details of episode junking, reconstructions, and tele-snaps taken of the missing episodes.

22. Howe, Stammers, and Walker, *Doctor Who: The Seventies*; Brian J. Robb, *Timeless Adventures: How Doctor Who Conquered TV* (Harpenden: Kamera, 2009).

23. Stephen James Walker, *Talkback, Volume One: The Sixties* (Tolworth: Telos, 2006.) Howe, Stammers, and Walker, *Doctor Who: The Seventies*, pp. 273–4.

24. Letters, for example, from Gordon Blows to J. Jeremy Bentham dated 11 February 1976, 16 February 1976, 27 February 1976, 25 July 1976, 29 September 1976, and 3 October 1976, and from Stuart Glazebrook to J. Jeremy Bentham dated 26 August 1976, 6 September 1976, 24 October 1976, 22 November 1976, 1 December 1976, 1 March 1977, 16 September 1977, and 24 October 1977.

25. Tim Harris, interview by email, 14 February 2011.

26. Bentham et al. (interview; The repeat season comprised of "An Unearthly Child," "The Krotons," "Carnival of Monsters," "The Three Doctors" and "Logopolis." For program information see Videography.

27. This season comprised of "The Curse of Peladon," a heavily-edited "Genesis of the Daleks," and "Earthshock."

28. Trevor Wayne, Panopticon 78, *The Doctor Who Appreciation Society Yearbook 1978–79*, pp. 10–17.

29. Trevor Wayne, Panopticon III, *The Doctor Who Appreciation Society Yearbook 1979–81*, pp. 15–20.

30. Gary Russell, Interface I, *The Doctor Who Appreciation Society Yearbook 1979–81*, p. 43.

31. Pam Paddeley, Panopticon IV, *The Doctor Who Appreciation Society Yearbook 1982*, pp. 4–7.

32. Dominic May, Panopticon V, *The Doctor Who Appreciation Society Yearbook 1982*, pp. 20–4.

33. Robert Moubert, Inter-face II, *The Doctor Who Appreciation Society Yearbook 1982*, pp. 32–3.

34. This information has been taken from Keith Barnfather, prod., *Longleat '83: The Greatest Show in the Galaxy?*, Reeltime Pictures, 2007.

35. Information up to this point in paragraph taken from Barnfather.

36. See National Film Theatre October/November 1983 booklet.

37. J. Jeremy Bentham, interview by email, 13 February 2011.

38. Ibid.

39. Robert Shearman, "The National Film Theatre: A Weekend Through Space And Time," *Cloister Bell* 8 (1984): pp. 35–41.

40. Bentham interview, 4 January 2011.

41. Jan Vincent-Rudzki, interview by email, 9 December 2010.

42. Information in paragraph taken from the DVD special feature, Ed Stradling, prod., "Cheques, Lies, and Videotape," *Doctor Who: Revenge of the Cybermen*, 2entertain, 2009.

43. Information in paragraph taken from the DVD special feature Ed Stradling, prod., "Cheques, Lies, And Videotape," *Doctor Who: Revenge of the Cybermen*, 2entertain, 2009.

44. BSB stands for British Satellite Broadcasting.

45. Harris interview, 14 February 2011.

46. John Bok, "Get It Taped?" *Frontier Worlds* 17 (1983): pp. 17–19.

47. Paul Winter, interview by email, 21 January 2011.

48. James Hoare, "Doctor Who Galaxy Four and The Underwater Menace Missing Episodes Found," *http://www.scifinow.co.uk*.

49. Bentham et al. interview, 2011.

50. Chuck Foster, "Tweetview3: The War Machines," *Doctor Who News Page,* 17 February 2011, *http://www.doctorwhonews.net/.*

51. David Brunt, and Keith A. Hopkins, *Doctor Who Appreciation Society: 20 Years of the DWAS,* p. 12.

52. Information here supplied by J. Jeremy Bentham, Paula Bentham, and Tony Clark in Bentham et al. interview, 2011.

53. McNaughton, "Regeneration of a Brand," in Hansen, ed., pp. 200–201.

54. J. Jeremy Bentham, Interview by email, 11 April 2011.

55. Information in this paragraph supplied by J. Jeremy Bentham, Paula Bentham, and Tony Clark in Bentham et al. interview, 2011.

56. Ibid.

57. Ibid.

58. Bentham et al. interview, 2011.

59. See, for instance, "Fan Scene," *TARDIS* 9(3): p. 13.

60. Lea, "The Fitzroy Tavern Doctor Who Fan Gatherings," *Fish Fingers and Custard* 3 (2010): pp. 40–42.

61. Bentham et al. interview, 2011.

62. Paul W, 7 March 2010, *http://gallifreybase.com/forum/showthread.php?t=37779.*

63. Matt Hills, *Triumph of a Time Lord: Regenerating Doctor Who in the Twenty-First Century* (London: I.B. Tauris, 2010): p. 97.

64. Gareth Kavanagh, interview by email, 13 January 2011.

65. Ibid.

66. Ibid.

67. Ibid.

68. Ibid.

69. Ibid.

70. Ibid.

71. Gareth Kavanagh, interview by email, 25 April 2011.

72. "Lass O'Gowrie News," *http://www.thelass.co.uk/news.php.*

73. J. Jeremy Bentham, interview by email, 26 April 2011.

74. John Ellis, *Visible Fictions: Cinema, Television, Video* (London: Routledge and Kegan Paul, 1982).

75. Jeremy Tunstall, *The Media in Britain* (London: Constable, 1983): p. 135.

76. Bob Mullan, *Consuming Television* (Oxford: Blackwell, 1997): p. 65.

77. John Thornton Caldwell, *Televisuality: Style, Crisis, And Authority In American Television* (New Brunswick: Rutgers University Press, 1995): p. 25.

78. Catherine Johnson, *Telefantasy* (London: BFI, 2005): 147. Johnson is challenging critics such as Noel Carroll, *Engaging the Moving Image* (New Haven, Yale University Press, 2003): p. 270.

79. Bentham et al. interview, 2011.

Social Spaces

British Fandom to the Present

ANDREW O'DAY[1]

Over the years it [*Doctor Who*] has brought people together in a positive way.... It gives an emphasis to friendship that will fossil boundaries (politics, religion).... It's a very positive force and the characters within the programme give off a very positive force.

— Peter Gilman[2]

While the previous essay examined the different ways in which *Doctor Who* fans have consumed the television program, and at how the concept of "event TV" has been redefined over the decades since the program's start, it also raised the issue of the importance of social gatherings in watching *Doctor Who*. This essay will investigate further the social spaces of fandom. I will concentrate on the spaces opened up for fans by conventions and local groups, by the Internet, and by different types of fan production (the fanzine, fan fiction, podcasting, and "fanvids"). Changes in technology have in some cases changed the form of fan production like the fanzine, but its primary goal has not changed. It will also demonstrate how Matt Hills was correct when he stated that the "community support model" of fandom must actually be interrogated,[3] since fandom, like everyday life, is made up of different people with clashing personalities. The essay will conclude by arguing that rather than being a homogeneous mass, fandom is made up of different types of people (e.g., of different genders, races, and sexualities), and will investigate the way in which diversity is acknowledged and the way that sometimes separate spaces are produced. The methodology employed and its potential pitfalls are the same as in the previous essay.

Conventions, Excursions and Local Groups

On one level, *Doctor Who* conventions provide a space for fans' devotion to the series and its performers. The first Doctor Who Appreciation Society (DWAS) convention, Convention '77, was held on August 6, 1977 at Broomwood Church Hall in Battersea, a year after the Society went nationwide. According to Jan Vincent-Rudzki, the organizers "knew *Star Trek* had conventions in America" and they wanted to "see if they could get anyone from the program."[4] This they managed to do with Graham Williams, Tom Baker (sporting his old raincoat), Louise Jameson, Jon Pertwee, and Matt Irvine attending. As Vincent-

Rudzki enthusiastically remembers, "the atmosphere was electric" and that night they decided to do another one the following year.[5]

The next year, was renamed, and *PanoptiCon '78* took place at Imperial College, London, on August 12 and 13, 1978.[6] They had, as Vincent-Rudzki puts it, a "guest list that you would struggle to get professionally" with guests wandering around the bar and chatting to attendees.[7] At this point, the actors were not paid fees (that came later as a result of the American influence),[8] so only a small admission fee was charged at the first for hiring the church hall, while the university settings with their student rooms were ideal for attendees.[9] PanoptiCon would continue throughout the 1980s, alongside other DWAS events such as Inter-Face and DWASocial, with these events organized by a variety of people, but facing competition. The DWAS's most ambitious convention would be A Voyage with the Doctor on March 21, 1987, set on the ferry to Holland.[10]

The 1990s and 2000s (with conventions such as Manopticon; Dominitemporal Services events, including Panopticon; Battlefield; Vortex Events conventions; Dimensions on Tyne; Dimensions; Invasion; and Regenerations) continued this trend where events were centered in a "main hall" and guests from the program would be interviewed over the course of the day. Autograph sessions would typically take place in a separate room. At Longleat '83, access to the stars of the program was highly restricted and photographs show not only the stars from the program but also crowds of other people with their cameras. But in these conventions of the 1990s and early 2000s a new feature was "the photo studio." With information posted on a board about the times different photo sessions would occur, attendees would pay to have their photo taken with a guest or guests from the original series and Big Finish, and the queues for these sessions were relatively short. While at Longleat '83 there was no real opportunity to have one's photo taken posing with a guest, at some of these conventions Anthony Ainley (the Master), for instance, did a back-to-back pose in the manner of publicity stills of him and Peter Davison from the 1982 *Doctor Who* story "Time-Flight." These photographs were taken by professional photographer Robin Prichard (other than at Ian Burgess events in Weston-super-Mare where Burgess, also a professional photographer, would take the photographs himself) and might include a photo of an attendee dressed in the sixth Doctor's multi-colored coat, standing by Colin Baker himself. There was also ample opportunity for one to get one's photograph taken with guests for free by giving someone nearby one's own camera.

10th Planet introduced the idea of "Coffee Clubs" where attendees would bid on tickets to enable them to sit and have coffee or tea and biscuits with a special guest. The evenings for these conventions also often started with a "Celebrity Dinner" where one could pay to sit and eat with one or more of the special guests. One either sat or ate with a guest or guests for an entire meal (sometimes one had a choice of whom to sit with), or the guests were rotated across the different tables over the courses of the meal. As in the 1980s, the evenings would typically then feature some type of entertainment (cabaret by guests from the series or comedy sketches by The Off Stage Theatre Group), followed by a knee-breaking disco, and there was also opportunity then (and indeed during the day) to sit and converse with guests in the bar area.[11] With the series now back on air there are also Fantom Films and Starfury conventions; queues for photo sessions can be longer, and access to guests like Matt Smith restricted.

But *Doctor Who* jaunts and conventions also provide a literal space for fans to meet, and cement friendships with, one another. We saw in the previous essay how gatherings at the One Tun and The Fitzroy Tavern provide such spaces. Furthermore, the Blackpool

Doctor Who exhibition had opened in 1974, a year after that at Longleat, and the DWAS (including J. Jeremy Bentham) went on a mini-bus trip known as "BLACKPOOL JAUNT 1979," which involved them looking at the exhibits, and after dinner having a social gathering with their North DWAS comrades. Moreover, as Vincent-Rudzki reveals, at the first DWAS convention in 1977 there were people who were there to "pick on people standing at the wall because they were so nervous" with the idea being to "bring people together."[12] Even from the mass scale Longleat '83 there are stories of fans who met in the endless autograph queues who have remained friends to this very day. A feature incorporated into the television program *Landladies* on *Doctor Who* conventions (filmed at a 1999 Ian Burgess event at the Playhouse Theatre) not only depicts fans humorously interacting with guests from the program, but also a series of comments by fans. One fan states, "We see each other 4 times a year ... it's always same group who go to every convention," while another notes, "I've made some nice friends and we just like being together. It's wonderful." Still another fan states that conventions are "about meeting old friends and new friends, getting together and indulging in one's interest."

DWAS local groups have been a feature of the landscape of fandom since the late 1970s when the first local group was set up by John Keung of Stoke-on-Trent. The main purpose of these groups was "to provide members of DWAS with a social platform close to their own home"; initially, the local group leader had to be a member of DWAS but today any one member can be the DWAS representative, and the groups were promoted in *CT*.[13] As the following quotes from the 1978–79, 1979–81 and 1982 *Doctor Who Appreciation Society Yearbooks* as well as other interview material reveal, groups ranged in size from half a dozen or less, to 40 members, were held at people's homes, or at pubs, or at larger facilities, and included special guests or special outings:

> DAVID J. HOWE [North Surrey/South London]: We held our second meeting. We were lucky enough to have Mr Terrance Dicks along as a special guest.... As a result of the publicity given to us and the meetings by the local press we received a number of offers for fetes and other special "do's".... Our first event of 1979 ... was extremely well attended by over thirty people who came to enjoy the usual mixture of talks, discussions and visual entertainment.[14]
>
> MARK FRANCOMBE: The Cardiff Local Group, or Cardiff Time Lords, began in a pub on August 13, 1982, with the attendance of six. Since then our number has risen to eleven.... We have been able to obtain a room in the centre of Cardiff where we hold meetings nearly every week.... October saw the appearance of Peter Davison as the Doctor, in Cardiff.... Members of the group went along to see him and were allowed to talk with him for quite some time ... other members paid a visit to London, including the BBC Photographic Library, Madame Tussauds and Heathrow Airport. Other activities include quizzes ... visual goodies and general discussions.[15]
>
> STEPHEN P. BOA: The members of the Derby local group of the DWAS are a small but keen collection of fans of the programme.... The meetings and outings ... are held at one another's homes or at a local pub in Derby itself.... The first DWAS meeting that some of the members attended was the Blackpool weekend in May 1982, arranged by the Reference Department.... Shortly after this, I organised our first major meeting — Event One. Our guests were Jeremy Bentham and Sue Moore.... The best was yet to come... Event Two ... with ... guest ... Uncle David Saunders.[16]
>
> LIAM RUDDEN: 1982 saw a lot of changes in the Lothians Local Group.... Meetings were held in a number of locations, the most suitable of these being the Wester Hailes Education Centre.... June saw several members of the Group travelling to Dundee for a joint-meeting.... Membership ... increased to 40 ... making it the largest LG in the country.... One of the highlights of the year was the appearance of Terrance Dicks at the Edinburgh Menzies store.

A very large number of LG members were there, and a video of the event was made by one member.[17]

MARK CHALONER [Manchester]: 1982 was an exceptionally good year, and membership now runs at approximately one dozen members.... We are hoping in the New Year to have one or two guest speakers, such as one of the writers of the *Doctor Who* scripts who lives locally.... We attended PanoptiCon V and Inter-Face II, and we hope to get to Blackpool and Longleat, so 1983 looks like another exciting year.[18]

JACKIE MARSHALL: It was ... in *Celestial Toyroom* [the DWAS monthly newsletter] that I found out about the Norwich Local Group when it was formed. My memories of that time are a little hazy — possibly due to alcohol. Ahem! As I recall, there were probably between about twenty and thirty members ... and the meetings were held (I believe) fortnightly. It was a very active group, which was part of the appeal. It held at least two conventions, and tracked down *Who* celebrities whenever they appeared in the area — such as Fraser Hines at Blofield Summer Fair. Panopticon (the main Doctor Who Appreciation Society convention) was both expensive and only held yearly. The local group meetings were, therefore, very important socially. A lot of chat (and drinking, by those of age) went on, and guest speakers were invited. Back then, the only ways you could connect with other fans were phone conversations (not always practical as homes then tended to have one line centrally positioned in the house), letters (slow!) and physically meeting each other (expensive!). Setting up and maintaining any sense of community in a fandom took a lot more effort pre the Internet![19]

However, some reports indicate the absence of special guests from the program (and sometimes their unimportance) and, held at people's homes, how they were simply a platform for social interaction (as well as in some cases first playing the audios and later the videos of old episodes):

DAVID OWEN [Liverpool]: This is one local group that doesn't raise money for charity, publicise the programme, produce an absorbing fanzine or invite members of the production team to meetings — all we do is regularly get together ourselves, and occasionally bring in an outsider to brighten things up. Isn't that what it's all about?[20]

PETER BAINES: 1982 has been a very quiet year for the Reading Local Group. Although we have met several times, these meetings have been social get togethers rather than business conferences.... All that can be said is that the local group is fulfilling its function of bringing *Doctor Who* fans together, which from the feedback I receive, it performs admirably[21]

TIM HARRIS: On Sunday, 8 June 1986, I was invited to a meeting of the Oxford *Doctor Who* local group by my oldest friend: I hadn't really been aware of any local group in Oxford at that time, although I had been a member of DWAS since 1983. Up to that point it was only this friend and my own brothers that I could converse with regarding *Doctor Who* so it was a nice experience to meet other people. I was made welcome by those present and it felt very comfortable to be there ... I realised ... that my own interest in *Doctor Who* was ... nothing as shown by the collections of other people. They seemed a good bunch and I enjoyed those early meetings in particular ... it was a worthy way of meeting like-minded people, and it made me more focused in my appreciation of the series.[22]

The Internet as Social Space

During the 1990s, fans at first clustered on Internet newsgroups, notably rec.arts.drwho, which were divided into various topic threads. A sister site, rec.arts.drwhomoderated, was primarily used to post announcements. Later in the 1990s, fans were to be found frequenting the Outpost Gallifrey forum which was more heavily (though not entirely) policed, leaving the rec.arts group largely barren. Created and administered by an American fan, J. Shaun

Lyon, and launched on December 11, 1995, Outpost Gallifrey was primarily created to promote Lyon's own convention Gallifrey One, held annually in Los Angeles. In addition to an entire section devoted to this (featuring not only news about the upcoming convention and how to register but also an archive of photographs from previous years' events), the site contained other sections such as an episode guide, a reviews section, feature articles, and a news page. Traffic frequently went to the Outpost Gallifrey *Forum*, popular with fans worldwide. On December 1, 2006, the news page, which Lyon was no longer interested in updating, was to be re-launched with Lyon as editor, with reports made by an international committee. At the end of August 2007 Lyon announced that save for the Gallifrey *One* pages, the news page (to be called the *Doctor Who* News Page), and the forum (to become the *Doctor Who* Forum), the rest of the site would no longer be updated. Except as a portal for the Gallifrey One convention, the site was to close completely on July 31, 2009, at which time the forum had 40,000 registered members, 15,000 of which were considered active.

It was replaced by Gallifrey Base, which now exists alongside Sebastian J. Brook's *Doctor Who* Online (DWO) forum.[23] DWO had begun life in 1996 as *Doctor Who:* The REGENERATIVE Website and, having changed its name in 2000, in April 2003 opened a forum similar in design to Outpost Gallifrey's with some 32,000 members, while, in July 2012, Gallifrey Base had 60,237 members. There are other discussion forums including Custard's *Doctor Who* forum on Roobarb's Forum, and the *Doctor Who* forum at Digital Spy and some devoted to particular aspects of the series like Ian Levine's Planet Kembel but the above are the most frequented.

Outpost Gallifrey, *Doctor Who* Online, and Gallifrey Base illustrated predictions that were earlier made about the future of online communities. In J. C. R. Licklider and Robert W. Taylor's 1968 essay "The Computer as Communication Device," the authors envisaged that future "online interactive communities ... will be communities not of common location but of common interest,"[24] while, in 1987, Howard Rheingold coined the term "virtual community" to describe the new experience where "a group of people who may or may not meet one another face to face ... exchange words and ideas through the mediation of computer bulletin boards and networks."[25] These writers may as well have been predicting the arrival of the Outpost Gallifrey forum and later *Doctor Who* Online's and Gallifrey Base's with their bulletin-like design. As Brigid Cherry explores in detail, today, forums such as Gallifrey Base can be used to discuss the new *Doctor Who* series.[26] There are, however, disadvantages to the Internet, as these comments made to me, by current coordinator of DWAS Paul Winter, and one-time convention organizer Les Hollis, reveal:

> PAUL WINTER: One of the downsides the instant nature of the 'Net has had on fandom has often taken place in these discussion forums. Any kind of social community whether it is real or virtual is going to spawn conflict and *Doctor Who* fandom already had that in abundance. The Internet came along and made things 10 times worse. Some of the things I see posted online range from ignorant to absolutely vitriolic. And some of that is about DWAS and occasionally me personally![27]

> LES HOLLIS: There is no "form" to online forums.... People hide behind keyboards and post knee jerk reactions without due consideration for the people behind the avatar. I currently have my ex's online friends sending me abusive messages after hearing her side of a story. The protective anonymity of an Internet connection.[28]

Although the Internet has been critiqued by many for its lack of regulation, there were types of regulation at work on Outpost Gallifrey which can now be seen on Gallifrey Base, put in place to avoid the type of "flame wars" found on rec.arts newsgroups. There are sets of rules which members must follow with moderators (to an extent) policing threads. Members who do not obey the rules risk being expelled from the community. However, as with other uses of the Internet, a great deal of self-regulation is required, where members exercise their right to choose not to participate in such threads.

It is not only these forums that have seen social interaction between *Doctor Who* fans, but also today social networking sites (SNS) such as MySpace, Facebook (launched at around the time of the new *Doctor Who* series) and now, as Benjamin Cook notes, Twitter (used by more than 200 million people worldwide).[29] Sites like Facebook enable more privacy than that to be found, for instance, on Gallifrey Base, as one can share messages on one's "Wall" and photos with one's chosen "Friends." On Twitter fans are able to create threads amongst themselves as well as follow prominent *Doctor Who* names (writers for the new series, producers, and actors), who may reply to some messages, and follow the creation of new episodes.[30] In this way, Sarah Lacy points out that while "the dotcoms of the late 1990s created more wealth, jobs, and public companies," and while "the Web 2.0 companies of the mid–2000s may never have the same financial impact ... it's hard to imagine they won't have a far greater social impact," even though there are harmful uses of such sites such as the presence of pedophiles.[31]

Fan Production: Fanzines, Fan Fiction, Podcasting, and "Fanvids"

The *Doctor Who* fanzine had its roots in the newsletters of the 1960s, designed to bind fans together. The William Hartnell Fan Club, run from a base in Stoke-on-Trent, produced an irregular single A4 information sheet. In late 1966 or early 1967, the Doctor Who Fan Club sent out autographed postcards and a more regular stapled A5 newsletter including not only story previews but also contributions from members (like artwork and short stories). In the late 1960s, Graham Tattersall, who had taken over the running of the club, produced a newsletter and a more substantial magazine, which also looked at other science fiction programs, before being replaced by 14-year-old Scottish fan Keith Miller at the end of 1971.[32] According to David J. Howe, Mark Stammers, and Stephen James Walker, Miller was responsible for producing (on his school equipment) a monthly A5 newsletter, the *Doctor Who Fan Club Monthly*, sent out free of charge to members. In April 1973, the newsletter *DWFC Mag* went bi-monthly. When membership grew and it became impractical to produce the newsletter at school, Sarah Newman arranged for the newsletter to be produced on a BBC duplicator and sent to the club's members at the BBC's expense. After the *DWFC Mag* folded, in July 1976 Miller would go on to produce his own short-lived fanzine *Doctor Who Digest*, priced at 35p per copy.[33]

In June 1975, Andrew Johnson (a fan of both SF and comics) started a fanzine called *TARDIS*. He quickly lost interest (after only two issues), so Gordon Blows took the fanzine over, and soon began to have meetings with a couple of fans from the University of London's Westfield College. One of these was Vincent-Rudzki, who had written an article for the second issue of *TARDIS* and who, with his friend Stephen Payne, at the suggestion of Tom Baker, went on to found the DWAS. The society's newsletter *Celestial Toyroom* (CT) was at first a "bonus" to the A5 *TARDIS*, which became the society's fanzine, and from March 1977 was merged to its inner pages,[34] while from January 1978 the society published fan fiction in *Cosmic Masque*.[35]

Fanzines could also be produced by local groups[36] and cement the relationships between members. In an article for the DWAS fanzine *TARDIS*, Gavin N. French shows through a quantitative study of the number of fanzines produced between 1976 and 1985 (based on advertisements in the DWAS newsletter *CT*) dramatic increases at the end of the 1970s and again in 1983, following the Longleat '83 convention, and a full-page advertisement for the society in *Doctor Who Monthly* Issue 88 (see Fig. 1).[37] French points out that 1983 saw DWAS membership rise by a third to more than 1,500, and that this upward trend continued with membership figures reaching 3,000 during 1984 and settling at 3,200 in 1985. According to French, after 1979, editors had to pay for advertisement space but that at one point almost two thirds of *CT's* content was made up of adverts with the eventual introduction of *CT Advertiser*,[38] which lasted from January 1985 to March 1986.[39] Notable fanzines of the late 1970s and '80s were David J. Howe's *Oracle*, Simon Lydiard's *Skaro*, Gary Russell's *Shada*, Peter Ware's *Chronic Hysteresis*, Owen Bywater's *Cloister Bell*, Simon Black's *Spectrox*, and Brian J. Robb's *The Highlander*. It was in this genre that Paul Cornell first came to prominence, writing for other fanzines and organizing Fan Aid, before he would go on to write for Virgin's New Adventures. These fanzines were typically in A5 format, though the later 1980s saw the launch of the A4 magazine *The Frame* with glossy paper and clear black and white and color photographs. Not only did fanzine editors pay to advertise in *CT*, but they would also pay to have a fanzine table in the dealer's room at conventions and for many of them their presence at these events would strengthen their bonds with other fanzine editors and with customers. A comment by Brian J. Robb in his fanzine's convention report for 1985's *PanoptiCon VI* underlines this:

> It was during the Saturday that everyone had the chance to buy past issues of "The Highlander" in the fanzine room. They sold very well, and if you bought one there — thanks, and I hope you enjoyed it. Also, "hello" to all the other fanzine editors I met there and had a chat with.[40]

Interestingly, some fanzine editors of the 1970s and 1980s have gone on to do work on *Doctor Who* professionally, and a couple of them were available to comment on the fondness with which they remember their fanzine roots:

> DAVID J. HOWE: I do have fond memories of doing The Frame (and my earlier fanzine Oracle). Creating a fanzine back then was a labour of love as there was no technology to help you — we're talking typewriter, correction fluid and dry transfer lettering! Also there was nothing else like the fanzines out there where you could express yourself freely, and gain readers by doing so. In many ways the art of the fanzine has been all but killed by the Internet, where anyone can put anything on view to others in seconds. It ... all helped contribute to the social aspects — meeting friends, discussing articles and interviews, finding talented artists, writers and photographers to work with, then of course selling them at conventions and events, meeting other fanzine editors and contributing to their work as well as they contributing to yours ... it was all a breeding ground for talent and friendship really.[41]
>
> PETER ANGHELIDES: Fanzine publishing in the 1970s and 1980s was our "internet." I got together with my pals from school and put together something that was an excuse to reach out to other *Doctor Who* fans all round the world. Of course these days you can do that at the click of a mouse. But back then, it involved writing or commissioning material, designing and printing, advertising, posting copies out to people, corresponding with subscribers, and flogging the fanzines at conventions.[42]

Furthermore, tape 'zines such as David Howe's *The Oracle Speaks*, and *Time Listener*, *Zero Room*, and *Sonic Waves*[43] illustrate how different type of fanzines were produced, while the unlicensed *Audio Visuals* plays (1984–1991) are a precursor to the licensed Big Finish audios.

Figure 1. Fanzines produced between 1976 and 1985.

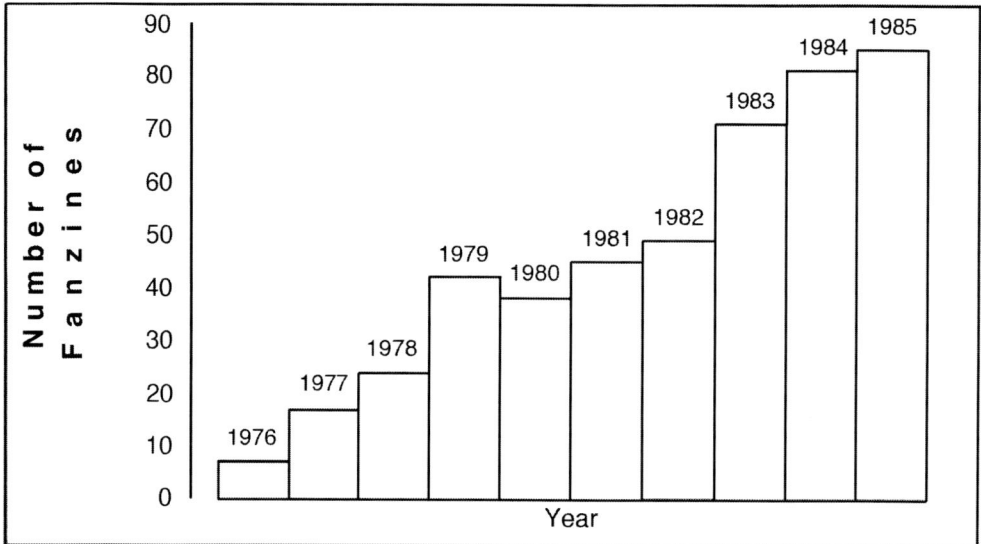

The motives behind the production of the monthly news publication *Doctor Who Bulletin* (*DWB*) were more dubious. Edited by Gary Levy, it began life in 1983 in the smaller format of most fanzines, but after only eight issues turned into a glossy A4 magazine, featuring increasing uses of color, and supplying advertising space to other fanzines. While *CT*, like *Doctor Who Monthly*, had to follow guidelines for news reporting set out by the *Doctor Who* production office, limiting what could be said, *DWB* was under no such restrictions, and quickly resembled a tabloid newspaper, with sensationalistic stories on the front cover, which were to be continued within its pages. Towards the end of *Doctor Who*'s run, *DWB* was redefined as *Dream Watch Bulletin*, covering other fantasy television, and then became *Dreamwatch* magazine. However, its early sensationalist style certainly drew fans to purchase the magazine and to talk about it amongst themselves.

There was a distinct lack of fanzine tables in the convention dealers' rooms of the 1990s and early 2000s, where fanzine editors had been replaced by, and (as in the case of Gary Russell) had turned into "professionalized fans" selling officially licensed Big Finish audio dramas, which, like *Doctor Who Magazine* of the period, helped bind fans. This aspect of social interaction was reduced. But there were fanzines, like Colin Brockhurst's *Circus*, a new look *Skaro*, and the Seventh Door fanzines as well as *Yak Butter Sandwich* and *Spaceball Ricochet* in which Lance Parkin and Tat Wood respectively came to prominence. *Doctor Who Magazine* featured an occasional column called "The Fanzine Trap" compiled by John Ainsworth. There has also been a fanzine devoted to *Doctor Who Magazine*, *Vworp! Vworp!*, and today one which revolves around the Big Finish audios called *The Finished Product*, showing how fandom not only centers around the televised *Doctor Who*.

A feature of *Doctor Who* fandom since the program's return has been what many call "the fanzine renaissance." Some of the concerns of fanzine editors today have differed from their 1980s counterparts. While writers like David J. Howe and Peter Anghelides have drawn a distinction between fanzines of old and the Internet of today, one can see that rather than meaning the death of the fanzine, the Internet is employed as a tool. While there is the Canada-based *Doctor Who* Information Network print magazine *Enlightenment* which began in 1984 and continues to this day, the Canadian *Doctor Who* fan magazine *Whotopia*, launched in 2003, became a free downloadable magazine with its 17th issue in July 2009. However, *Eyepiece*, produced in Britain, is billed as having been the first online fanzine. It was edited by Matthew Harris from North Cornwall. In the FAQ section to his website Harris writes:

> Apart from the cost, and the love thang, the great advantage of doing an online magazine is that it ... means we've got a circulation of potentially billions of people — if we attract enough contributions, we can be the Fanzine of the World, reaching out and touching Doctor Who fans throughought the entirety of human civilisation.[44]

Other groups such as Reverse the Polarity Publications began with the online fanzine *Wibbly Wobbly Timey Wimey*. There are also fanzines which are available in two formats, a strategy utilized by the newspapers of today. One can choose between a print or electronic version. One such fanzine was *Shooty Dog Thing*, edited by Paul Castle, which was launched in 2007. Castle explains on his website:

> The fanzine is available in two different editions. The idea of the issue was to produce as a 48-page A5 fanzine, but the handicap there is that you have to spend money on printing and posting, and ask people for money, and that's where the last fanzine failed. I didn't really want to go down the webzine road as I'm not that keen on them ... so I compromised. *Shooty Dog Thing* will be published in two editions: one as a simple PDF file you can read on the computer screen, the other as a pair of PDFs you can print out, fold and staple.[45]

Another fanzine which makes use of new technology is Daniel Gee's *Fish Fingers and Custard*, which, as the title alluding to the Matt Smith *Doctor Who* episode "The Eleventh Hour" suggests, was launched much more recently. As Gee explains in the editorial to issue one:

> The late 80s/early 90s is considered to be the "golden age" of Doctor Who fanzines. Today, what with the Internet, plenty people consider that the fanzine is a thing of the past. But why? Surely the Internet can be used as a tool to make fan-publications even more popular than they were? ... I was browsing a fanzine section of a *Doctor Who* message board, looking at the various downloadable PDFs and I just thought to myself—"I love writing. I love fanzines and I love *Doctor Who.*" The idea hit me in the head as hard as a woman does, when I drunkenly try to chat them up in a club! I would do a *Doctor Who* fanzine and prove, first to myself, that I could do it and secondly, that my theory of the Internet not being the end of fanzines but a useful tool instead was right...
>
> I'm a huge supporter of the printed medium, simply because I lack the concentration of being able to read anything online for more than 10 minutes! So I decided upon doing the fanzine on paper, but I thought back to my "internet theory" and realized that I could not exclude those who like to read stuff online. We are supposed to be embracing new technology, after all! A free-downloadable fanzine or a paper copy (with glossy covers!) for a tiny production cost would be the way that I present the fanzine.... The sun hasn't yet set on the age of fanzines![46]

What the above quotations by both Castle and Gee indicate, is that these editors were wrestling with the issue of how to produce a *Doctor Who* fanzine in the Internet-age, as they saw potential problems with a printed magazine.

Gee's decision to produce a printed fanzine, while making a downloadable copy available, can be probed further. Gee observes to me:

> A lot more people download the fanzine than those who bought a paper copy. I only print 50 paper copies and the download figure is about 20 times that! I suppose the free download helps to promote the paper copies.... Plus the paper copies are very good and well worth 2 quid (including

postage!). A few people have commented that they purchased the paper copy after downloading, so I think it's well worth doing.[47]

Reactions on the *Fish Fingers and Custard* Facebook site, used, along with a Facebook page, a Twitter account, and its own forum, to promote the fanzine, also reveal the benefits of using both formats. One reaction to the printed copy of *Fish Fingers and Custard* by fellow fanzine editor David MacGowan reads: "Incidentally that paper version looks sexy as fuck ... wish I could afford colour printing."[48] Furthermore, reader Annabel Graham states "Keep your copies well looked after.... This could be the start of something big."[49] Another reader, James Beckwith, stranded by snowfall, comments, "I took issue 3 with me to read on holiday. Sadly my flight got cancelled and I'm stuck in the U.K. for another week. I did read bits of the 'zine whilst waiting at the airport and loving what I've read so far. Saving the rest for when (touch wood) I actually get to go away."[50] Meanwhile, in response to a question that I put on the Facebook group asking members whether they preferred to download a copy or buy a printed copy and their reasons for this,[51] Tim Jousma comments: "Personally, I download it. Working at an electronics store has gotten me used to staring at words on the screen all day so it's nice to be able to have something I can check out during downtime at work. Plus, with the next issue, I can read my first submission!!!!"[52] David MacGowan again pops up, stating: "Printed for me ... I like to stroke things lovingly."[53]

It must be noted that not all current fanzine editors have gone down this route of making a downloadable copy available. David MacGowan edits *Rassilon's Rod*, which was launched before *Fish Fingers and Custard*, at the live screening to "The Eleventh Hour," held at the Lass O'Gowrie pub in Manchester. Similarly, between June 2010 and January 2011, Grant Bull edited what is described as "an old-school paper 'zine," *Blue Box*. In July 2010, Oliver Wake's *Panic Moon* was launched in A6 format, lasting until January 2012. And Reverse the Polarity Publications have now released the printed fanzine *The Eleventh Hour*. MacGowan and Wake talked to me about their choice of the printed medium:

> DAVID MACGOWAN: Interestingly, many people reacted with genuine confusion about being asked to actually send ... an S.A.E. and had trouble finding envelopes. If the Rod reminds just one person how to write an address on a rectangular piece of paper with a gluey flap, I will have contributed positively to society.[54]
>
> OLIVER WAKE: I love hardcopy fanzines. Something you can hold in your hand and read in bed. Naturally, the Internet has taken over many of the functions of fanzines, enabling anyone to share their thoughts or artwork. But fanzines still have some advantages. Most fan content on the Internet is unedited and appears piecemeal in blogs or off-the-cuff forum postings. Often, but not always, it's badly written or represents a knee-jerk reaction. Fanzines offer a space for edited, considered articles, which have been honed for publication. There are websites that do the same, of course. Personally, I don't like screen-reading, and I believe many people feel the same, which leads to a lot of skim reading on the Internet.... It's hard to get readers to engage if they're only skimming through your text. A fanzine is also a great showcase for original art, albeit with certain constraints, which will nearly always look better printed than on a screen.... I love hardcopy, producing something I can physically give out and people can stuff in their pockets or throw across the room in fury.[55]

However, while some concerns may be different from those of the 1980s fanzine editors, reasons for the fanzines being produced remain similar. These fanzines are produced by people from a variety of professions for pleasure, with small print-runs (for example, *Panic Moon* had a print run of about 200 copies per issue, except for the mini–Christmas "freebie" of which there were only 50 copies in existence),[56] and advertised on *The Doctor Who News*

Page. While many fanzine editors and contributors from the late 1970s and 1980s have gone on to professional work of some sort relating to *Doctor Who*, this is not what first motivates the production of a fanzine, as illustrated in these comments taken from the Internet and specially-conducted interviews:

> MATTHEW HARRIS: Magazine-writing is fun. And doing it online means I don't bleed money getting it printed. I make it for the love of it, give it away for the love of it, and if it's read, it's read for the love of it.[57]
>
> PAUL CASTLE: I created the fanzine because I love *Doctor Who* in all shapes and forms, and miss the old days of fanzines. Paul Cornell edited a book called *Licence Denied* back in 1997 after Virgin Publishing lost the licence to publish original *Doctor Who* fiction. As a kind of last word on the subject Paul Cornell closed the Virgin era by editing a collection of the very best fanzine articles. Inspired by this I edited my first fanzine, *Eye of Orion*, which ran for seven issues over the next four years, but real life intruded as my university days came to an end and it all went pear-shaped. And then, last summer, I picked up *Licence Denied* from the bookcase as I was rushing out the door, and in the pub and on the train throughout that afternoon I found myself falling in love with the idea of producing a fanzine again. Both my mum and my girlfriend had suggested I get a hobby as my cycle of work-sleep-work-sleep was getting me down, and it was the latter who suggested I start writing fanzines again. And there the fun began.[58]
>
> DANIEL GEE: The key to doing one is being excited when you're writing it. If you aren't having fun, then you shouldn't be doing it.... It's a dream to be [professionally] involved with *Doctor Who*, certainly, but that's where it ends.... I think those days of fans like myself getting to be involved with *Doctor Who* are over. I do get the feeling that the production team are distancing themselves away from the fans these days.[59]
>
> DAVID MCGOWAN: I got three 'zines/related publications in the post in one week (the book of *Shooty Dog Thing*, *Time Unincorporated 1*, *Vworp!Vworp!* and realised that as well as being excited tremendously by the content, I was also excited at the idea of doing a print fanzine, now, today, because I never did back in the day, that fanzines didn't have to be a nostalgic thing fans recalled wistfully in between posting on an online forum. I wasn't worried about a print fanzine reaching a lesser crowd than a PDF 'zine — if the readership of the *Rod* trickles to three people and I'm scrawling it on backs of envelopes and shoving them physically into people's coat pockets I'll still get the sense of fun and enjoyment that putting out the 'zine gives me. There is a tangible thrill to printed matter. I'm not too worried about not reaching a zillion readers.... I want to edit a *Doctor Who* fanzine not become the next Rupert Murdoch ... there are a lot of books and mags out there, but my attitude has always been why should they have all the fun? This is my 'zine, reflecting my views on the series, me having my say (and my writers having theirs). The benefit is that it is fun!... Other than the *Rod* I work full-time in the care industry and stare wistfully into the distance as I dream of one day being the editor of *DWM*, which I know will never happen. It's important to state that for me a fanzine isn't an attempt to show people how good I am at designing or writing or editing (that should be pretty obvious anyway!), merely that I am a fan and I want to spread the love, as young people don't say.[60]

The fanzine increases social interaction, and indeed the form of the fanzine in, for example, the printed medium, may be designed to contribute to this:

> PAUL CASTLE: *Shooty Dog Thing* was born from a desire to be more sociable at *Doctor Who* conventions. I wasn't one of life's go-up-to-random-strangers-and-start-a-conversation people, even within a situation where you've got loads in common. What I needed was something to pre-empt me, something to make a little bit of a name for myself so that I wasn't shy.... *Shooty Dog Thing* has now gone professional, with a first volume (which collected the best of the ten-issue run) selling out of reprint after reprint, and a second volume of totally new material going to print next month. I now travel the country and even the world promoting

it, with conventions in Los Angeles, Swansea, Birmingham [U.K.] and Newcastle-upon-Tyne, meeting many people who are now firm friends.[61]

DANIEL GEE: It can be too easy to post on a forum, write a blog or whatever. I feel that these things miss that sense of belonging, which is what makes a fandom what it is. A fanzine is something that people do together — I know that I couldn't put this thing together without the talents of others.[62]

I've not yet met anyone, as I've not been out on the convention circuit as of yet, although I do think the Internet is a separate community of its own. I've made a few "friends" because of them sending me stuff.... But that's where it ends, I mean I've got readers who live thousands of miles away, so I'm hardly going to see them down the local for a beer!... The [Facebook] Christmas party was a way of trying to connect and have some banter with readers.[63]

DAVID MACGOWAN: It's something that's passed round friends.... The online fandom world feels too weird and virtual and disconnected. I can see the attraction for those not of pub-going age but for me fandom is a real world activity.... I meet a lot of my contributors in person, at regular fan meets, trips down the pub, one-off conventions, etc. Many of us meet outside the *Doctor Who* fan world. Being part of fan culture, and fanzine culture, means a lot to me. Debates and arguments are much more measured, and if anyone disagrees it's easy to just buy another round of drinks and move onto something more sociable, like discussing the merits of Matt Smith's weird skeletal structure. And most people are very agreeable when discussing if their article, or part of it, doesn't fit the ethos of the 'zine. I very rarely take my editor's hat with me to fan gatherings. (This is an actual hat, by the way. It's an old baseball cap with the words "Chicago Bears" replaced by a picture of Clay Hickman, for inspiration.)[64]

OLIVER WAKE: Whilst a fanzine is an egotistical project I believe it is still a team effort.... For this reason I don't give myself an editor credit in the 'zine, for example, although it's no secret that that's my role.... A few of the contributors are friends and I've met a few others face-to-face but most of it is done via email. ... I'm trying to encourage more interaction via the letters page, and for this purpose I've also set up a facebook page for the 'zine.... We often contribute to each other's 'zines.... I haven't attended any conventions with the 'zine but have made a few visits to the Tav [the Fitzroy Tavern] and tried selling a few there.... Some are very enthusiastic but others are used to the previous Tav culture of free 'zines and disapprove of selling 'zines.[65]

These comments illustrate that the aim of the fanzine now is little different than it was in the 1980s. The difference is that some see that the community evolves on the Web, while for others it takes place in person, and that there can be those who disapprove of fans selling fanzines.

Another highly active area of contemporary fan cultural productivity is podcasting which also encourages social interaction. A podcast is a series of either video or audio files which can be downloaded from a main site and which appears on a feed. The *Doctor Who Online* site, mentioned earlier, features the "DWO Whocast" section. This section contains, for instance, downloadable audio reviews of the latest DVD releases, as well as audio reviews of episodes from recent seasons of the program. Listeners are invited to discuss these podcasts in the main forum. Similar in nature are the American *Doctor Who: Podshock*, which British fans can follow, and *The Doctor Who Podcast.Com*. *Doctor Who* podcasting therefore ties in with Internet discussion forums (since the listener is invited to discuss the podcast in the main discussion area) and develops out of 'zines (especially those audio 'zines, like the 1980s *Sonic Waves*, which contained reviews of then-contemporary stories).

Moreover, just as since the 1970s fans have become what Henry Jenkins calls "textual poachers" writing fan fiction[66] (first for fanzines and then on the Internet),[67] they also engage in the practice of making *Doctor Who* fan videos (known as "fanvids"). In the 1980s, for example, when the technology became available, Local Groups could engage in this social activity, as was the case with the Oxford local group's very short video *The Revenge of Zeg*, copied onto VHS tape, which led to their making a variety of other longer productions based on programs like *The Champions*. However, Jeremy Sarachan notes that different types of fanvids are made today, and in the age of Web 2.0, where there is a democratization of the public sphere, as outlined by Jürgen Habermas, they are shared on sites such as YouTube, free of charge and without censorship.[68] These fanvids differ from *PanoptiCon's* comic sketch *The Few Doctors*, as that has been made commercially available. Although these fanvids are illegal they are tolerated, and include creating new up-to-date title sequences, placing a musical track over mixed footage to provide a certain meaning (as was indeed also done with ironic effect for the *PanoptiCon* conventions), bridging continuity gaps (by, for example, using effects to show Paul McGann's Doctor regenerate into Christopher Eccleston's), and solving plot inconsistencies by creating new scenes.[69] Unlike the videos of the 1980s, when these videos are posted to YouTube, people can join an ongoing discussion about them. These videos not only bind people together but also magnify their dedication to the program, and, as Paul Booth would argue, are fun to make.[70]

Spaces for Race, Gender and Sexuality

It is also important to recognize that *Doctor Who* fandom can open up spaces for diverse people, including peoples of different genders, sexualities, and races. Prominent women in *Doctor Who* fandom, for example, have included 1980s *TARDIS* editor Ann O'Neill; 1980s convention organizer and editor of the fanzine *Paradise Lost* Mary Milton; Val Douglas; Jackie Marshall (cited earlier); Brigid Cherry (who edited her own fanzine *The Rocky Doctor Picture Show*); feature writer for the new-look *Skaro* fanzine Vanessa Bishop; and Karen Davies of DWAS.

For some of these women, gender is not really an issue. Val Douglas and Jackie Marshall, for instance, edited the fanzine *Queen Bat* after *Space Rat*. *Queen Bat* lasted for 10 issues and had an average print run of 100 copies per issue. They also contributed to other fanzines. Their comments to me are much the same as those of their male contemporaries and more recent male fanzine editors. They see themselves as part of a *Doctor Who* community:

> VAL DOUGLAS: I used to write letters to other fanzines saying what stories or articles I'd particularly enjoyed because everyone appreciates ... feedback. I also contributed to other fanzines because many of the people who contributed to *Queen Bat* produced their own 'zines. It did create a sense of fandom community as well a providing the practical benefit of getting more 'zines to read because contributors received free copies.[71]
>
> JACKIE MARSHALL: Producing a fanzine was a way of both cementing and establishing new friendships; I'm still in touch with some people I got to know at that time purely because they sent in contributions. There was a big sense of community inherent in producing a fanzine: by its nature, it was a collaborative act. Fans created them as a labour of love and sold them to their friends, commenting on and contributing to their friends' 'zines at the same time. The reciprocal nature of this was probably inevitable: we were all sharing an interest and wanted to be as involved as we could. Fanzine work was just as important as any published work to me.[72]

I wondered, however, whether they might be making some gender statement with the title *Queen Bat*, in addition to its rhyme with *Space Rat* and its alluding to the *Doctor Who* story "The Caves of Androzani" (1984). But I am informed that this was not so:

VAL DOUGLAS: We weren't making any gender statement with the *Queen Bat* title. Our *Space Rat* logo was a gun-wielding rat in a spacesuit and we just thought it would be nice if the 'zine's successor also had an animal title and logo. "The Caves of Androzani" was one of our favourite stories so we took the queen bat from there and called our letters page "Spectrox Nest" to continue the "Androzani" theme. I was aware that the majority of *Doctor Who* fans were male but I've always considered the gender of fellow fans to be irrelevant. The only gender-related issue for me was having a horror of writing something which others would dismiss as a girly, Mary Sue fic but this had nothing to do with male dominated *Doctor Who* fandom.[73]

JACKIE MARSHALL: I was aware that women weren't as visible in fandom but I never (at that time) saw myself as on a mission to make women more visible. Although maybe I should have: my friend Jacqui went with Brigid Cherry to the Tavern in London once and when she introduced herself, they all automatically assumed she was me! Because, clearly, there couldn't be two women in *Doctor Who* fandom with the same name! She played along with it for the duration of the evening without any of them suspecting.[74]

Leslie McMurtry, however, although not a radical feminist, tells me that while she never sets out with a women's issues agenda in mind, in her short stories, radio plays, and poetry, she often finds herself "attracted to certain historical subjects/stories/personalities because of their relation to women" as well as their stories being untold,[75] and in the editorial to issue one of *The Terrible Zodin*, she invokes a different set of concerns which went into producing the e-zine than those raised by her near contemporaries like Daniel Gee:

What I like best about the *Doctor Who* community is its diversity.... I'm a 20-something-year-old female — and as you'll see the authors and artists involved in this ... run the gamut. We are a cross-ocean network.... Some of us are new *Who* fans, while others have been watching the show since the '70s and '80s. Importantly, many of the contributors ... are female. While *Doctor Who Magazine*'s latest poll still showed the men outnumbering the women 2 to 1, we are an undeniable presence and growing. I was tempted to make *TTZ* a fan magazine for women, by women, but that's obviously missing the point. I wanted to show diversity, so why close off half the population? Certainly we can all co-exist in this crazy *Who* world! But that's another area of diversity — I've tried to include pieces on the new series, the "classic" series and everything in between. There's poetry, paper dolls, personal essays, scholarly essays, reviews, art, comics, and sheer silliness.[76]

McMurtry's original temptation to carve out a space for women may seem like a precursor to Lynne M. Thomas and Tara O'Shea's 2010 edited volume *Chicks Dig Time Lords: A Celebration of Doctor Who by the Women Who Love It*, although McMurtry decided against producing an exclusively gendered 'zine. McMurtry did not even start off with this agenda in mind: she wanted to produce a 'zine since her work was at first rejected by Paul Castle of *Shooty Dog Thing*.[77] "The Terrible Zodin" is a female villainess alluded to but not seen in "The Five Doctors" (1983). But McMurtry's choice of a villainess for the title of the 'zine was, as she tells me, not a conscious gender statement:

I didn't pick up on Patrick Troughton muttering about "The Terrible Zodin" in *"The Five Doctors"* — while reading *Shooty Dog Thing* I came across the name in one of the cartoons by Mike Morgan and was told by editor Paul Castle about Zodin's "appearance." So, while I'd like to say there is deeper significance ... that isn't strictly true ... I chose the name for its distinctiveness and the fact it would make a snappy acronym and also because it would intrigue new series fans to discover who she was/where she was from. I do find it interesting I chose a *villain*'s name rather than one of the female companions or supporting characters — I'm a big fan of the *Batman* universe ... and my favorite characters within that are villainesses like Catwoman and Harley Quinn. So I wonder if a propensity for strong, albeit non-law-abiding, females did come into it unconsciously.[78]

McMurtry reveals that while there are now more female *Doctor Who* book authors (like Kate Orman, Lloyd Rose, and Una McCormack), with there now being books for the more recent Doctors, and a female director Alice Troughton, there are less female writers for televised *Who* (for which she would one day like to write). Asked whether she is achieving her stated aim with *The Terrible Zodin*, McMurtry notes:

> I think *TTZ* can improve, and we need to seek out even more female writers, as a rather surprising sector of our contributors are male. We also need to interview more women who are involved in *Doctor Who* in some way (dream interviewee is Jacqueline Rayner) ... I'd like to attract diversity in every respect.... For the record, two of the contributors I have met in person are black (and male).[79]

Recently, Rebecca Williams has drawn attention to the diversity of *Doctor Who* fandom and examined female fans responses to David Tennant on the Internet *Doctor Who Forum*. Williams writes that "the advent of the Internet and the relaunch of 'new Who' in 2005 has led to wider fragmentation of the audience and the formation of often disparate groups who read the show through different 'filters' such as the long-standing history of the show, the auteur figure of Russell T. Davies, or various characters or actors."[80] Williams notes that "female fans [called "fangirls"] are often dismissed as silly or trivial and those who express overly sexualized desire for celebrities or characters are frequently devalued" with such expressions "often ... only ... articulated in 'safe' female spaces such as women-only message boards or online list-servs."[81] More feminized fan spaces include Live Journal. This idea builds on Rhiannon Bury's work. Bury provides a book-length ethnographic study of two all-female online communities founded to discuss science fiction television programs and their male actors.[82]

The Yahoo Internet group Gaywhovians, meanwhile, is a specific freer queer space "for gay and lesbian *Doctor Who* fans to discuss the best Sci-Fi show ever." Previous work in fan studies on gay fandom includes Henry Jenkins' famous chapter on the *Star Trek* group Gaylaxians, founded in 1987, which, as well as seeking queer representation within the program, "sought to increase gay visibility within the science fiction fan community and 'to help gay fans contact and develop friendships with each other.'" To this end, Gaylaxians hosted a national convention Gaylaxicon.[83] Gay men are similarly a very visible group in *Doctor Who* fandom, lesbians less so. Founded on February 29, 2000, the Gaywhovians group is classified as an adult one, which, as of July 10, 2012, has some 547 members. From the main page, one can access a list of members, one can look at photographs of members who have uploaded images of themselves, and one can look at the results of playful polls that members have participated in. Threads are started on the group and members contribute to these threads by posting messages, which members can decide to access on the main site or receive in their email inboxes. The group is moderated so as to prevent "flame wars" within these threads. A reading made in July 2012 showed around 37,000 posts having been made, with the peak being in July 2005 (at the end of the first Russell T. Davies season of the program), during which 1,264 posts were made. In the past, threads have concerned value judgments of all parts of the *Doctor Who* universe, including the Big Finish audios and the new BBC Wales series, and they have dealt with the sexuality of performers, and sexuality within the program, with the posters' own sexuality coming to the fore. Members contribute to threads debating whether a certain performer is gay, stating that he must be "one of us," a common gay phrase indicating group solidarity. Threads concerning the new series deal with Captain Jack and John Barrowman, as well as other guest stars, and an extremely witty thread from

May 2006 deals with that year's episode "Rise of the Cybermen," parts of which are reproduced here:

> Mickey tied to a chair in just his boxer shorts, "Ricky" dressed in black interrogating him and Andrew Hayden-Smith on his knees at Mickey's feet.........no wonder the Cybermen were "rising"
>
> I would be on my knees too, mind you I am always nearly on my knees LOL
>
> Nothing wrong with that ☺ Incidentally what was it that Mr Hayden-Smith was scanning Mickey's very smooth legs with? It looked like a sonic screwdriver......
>
> Maybe it was a sonic razor? ☺
>
> His eyes ☺ For a brief moment as they cut away during that scene you can see young Hayden-Smith staring quite obviously at Noel's crotch. And who can blame him?...
>
> I think it was a dildo...
>
> He's a dirty bitch! And that's fabulous

Another thread, called "Varying Replies," deals with the following episode of this two-parter, "The Age of Steel," to which a member humorously writes:

> Lovely emotional stuff, Rose is rejected by her father and then Mickey runs out on her in favour of a twinky blond (I'm sorry, but he carries poppers around with him and then Mickey offers to take him to Paris as they drive off into the sunset together...). Thought the emotional stuff was very well handled.

Evidently these fans are poaching the text in their own way. The group enables its members to engage in witty banter without hostility about sexuality and the posts draw on a vocabulary which is particularly understood by the LGB community (e.g., "dirty bitch," "twinky blond," "poppers"). Posters have also been known to make references to their "bf"s (short for "boyfriend"). Furthermore, there are regular postings to inform members of the traditional Fitzroy Tavern gatherings and some of these members are friends who do not solely rely on groups such as this or the Facebook *Doctor Who* Gay Fans Group, but who also meet in person.

Conclusion

This essay has not examined what Hills calls the "'lone fans' of today operating outside of" a "specific strata of fandom." There are further avenues of investigation into *Doctor Who* fandom in Britain. For example, the topic of news reporting can be traced with regard to *Doctor Who Monthly, CT, DWB,* and now the Internet. Moreover, the notion of the specialist store (Forbidden Planet, Galaxy Four, Kulture Shock, 10th Planet, and The Who Shop), with their signings of merchandise, can be probed in relation to economic concerns such as their not wanting fans to buy DVDs and books off the Internet (Amazon.com and Play.com) or the local high street. Furthermore, Hills' comment that "fandoms can be 'tangled' up with and between an intertextual range of objects" where "to even nominate a fandom as 'belonging' to one show or individual can sometimes be problematic,"[84] has become especially true with the arrival of the *Doctor Who* spin-offs *Torchwood* (2006–) and *The Sarah Jane Adventures* (2007–11). Finally, a broadened study could interview important names in American and Australian *Doctor Who* fandom such as J. Shaun Lyon, Lucy Zinkiewicz, and Dallas Jones.[85]

NOTES

1. In addition to all those who agreed to be interviewed, I would like to offer my thanks to J. Jeremy Bentham for organising interviews and providing archival material; to Dr. Brigid Cherry for putting me in touch with some interviewees; to Tim Harris for providing a wealth of research material; and to Dr. Matt Hills for his encouragement with the project.

2. J. Jeremy Bentham, Paula Bentham, Tony Clark, Peter Gilman, David Miller, and Jan Vincent-Rudzki, interview at Fitzroy Tavern, London, 8 January 2011.

3. Matt Hills, "Gender and Fan Culture," 2007, http://www.henryjenkins.org/2007/08/gender_and_fan_culture_round_t.html.

4. Bentham et al. interview, 2011.

5. Ibid.

6. For further details see Wayne, Trevor, "Convention '77," *The Doctor Who Appreciation Society Yearbook* 1977–78, 27–31; Trevor Wayne, "Panopticon 78," *The Doctor Who Appreciation Society Yearbook 1978–79*, pp. 10–16.

7. Bentham et al. Interview 2011.

8. This would first occur at DWASocial V, see David Brunt and Keith A. Hopkins, *Doctor Who Appreciation Society: 20 Years of the DWAS*, p. 15.

9. Bentham et al. Interview, 2011.

10. Brunt and Hopkins, *Doctor Who Appreciation Society*, p. 23.

11. Karen Louise Hayward has written about her experiences at conventions and meeting the stars. Hayward, Karen Louise, *Un-conventional: 13 Years of Meeting the Stars of Doctor Who* (Andover: 100 Publishing, 2010).

12. Bentham et al. Interview, 2011.

13. Cate Caruth, "Local Groups," in Brunt and Hopkins, *Doctor Who Appreciation Society,* pp. 20–21.

14. *Doctor Who Appreciation Society Yearbook 1978–79, 1980–81.*

15. *Doctor Who Appreciation Society Yearbook 1982.*

16. Ibid.

17. Ibid.

18. Ibid.

19. Jackie Marshall, interview by email, 5 February 2011.

20. *Doctor Who Appreciation Society Yearbook 1979–81.*

21. *Doctor Who Appreciation Society Yearbook 1982.*

22. Tim Harris, interview by email, 14 February 2011.

23. Information in this paragraph taken from http://en.wikipedia.org/wiki/Outpost_Gallifrey.

24. David Kirkpatrick, *The Facebook Effect*, (London: Virgin, 2010): p. 66.

25. Ibid, p. 67.

26. Brigid Cherry, "Squee, Retcon, Fanwank and the Not-We: Computer-Mediated Discourse and the Online Audience for Nu Who," in Chris Hansen, ed, *Ruminations, Peregrinations, and Regenerations: A Critical Approach to Doctor Who* (Newcastle upon Tyne: Cambridge Scholars, 2010): pp. 209–232.

27. Paul Winter, interview by email, 21 January 2011.

28. Les Hollis, interview by Facebook, 11 February 2011.

29. Benjamin Cook, "40 People Every *Doctor Who* Fan Should Follow on Twitter," *Doctor Who Magazine* 430 (2011): pp. 60–63.

30. Ibid, p. 60.

31. Sarah Lacy, *The Facebook Story* (Richmond: Crimson, 2009): p. 306.

32. Information to here taken from Stephen James Walker, *Talkback, Volume One: The Sixties* (Tolworth: Telos, 2006). For information on the early years of *Doctor Who* fandom Keith Miller has recently released *The Official Doctor Who Fan Club, Volume 1.*

33. David J. Howe, Mark Stammers, and Stephen James Walker, *Doctor Who: The Seventies* (London: Virgin, 1994).

34. Brunt and Hopkins, *Doctor Who Appreciation Society,* pp. 4–5. This would change when *TARDIS* was included in *CT.*

35. Ibid., p. 7; editors of *Cosmic Masque* included John Peel and Stephen Evans, Ian McLachlan, and Jonathan Way.

36. See "Local Groups" in *The Doctor Who Appreciation Society Yearbook 1979–81, 1982.*

37. Brunt and Hopkins, *Doctor Who Appreciation Society*, p. 14.

38. Gavin N. French, "Fanfare for FANZINES," *TARDIS* 10. 4 (1985): pp. 24–26.

39. Brunt and Hopkins, *Doctor Who Appreciation Society*, p. 22.

40. Brian J. Robb, "Panopticon VI — Report (1)," *The Highlander* 4, pp. 11–13.

41. David J. Howe, interview by email, 25 January 2011.

42. Peter Anghelides, interview by email, 26 January 2011.

43. French ,"Fanfare for FANZINES," p. 25.

44. Matthew Harris, "The Eyepiece Homepage," http://www.angelfire.com/zine2/bobthefishmagazines/faq.html.

45. Paul Castle, "*Shooty Dog Thing*— Issue One" *Brax's Shooty Dog Thing*, 7 March 2007, http://brax-zine.blogspot.com/search?updated-max=2007–09–06T21%3A49%3A00–07%3A00&max-results=7 .

46. Daniel Gee, "The Sun Hasn't Yet Set ... An Editorial," *Fish Fingers and Custard* 1(2010): pp. 2–3, http://viewer.zoho.com/docs/gNbfdg.

47. Daniel Gee, interview by email, 23 January 2011.

48. 27 June 2010, 15:54, http://www.facebook.com/home.php#!/group.php?gid=120375671317475 .

49. 14 December 2010, 03:46, http://www.facebook.com/home.php#!/group.php?gid=1203756713 17475.

50. 20 December 2010, 10:34, http://www.facebook.com/home.php#!/group.php?gid=120375671317 475.

51. 10 January 2011, 00:38, http://www.facebook.com/home.php#!/group.php?gid=120375671317475.

52. 13 January 2011, 01:23, http://www.facebook.com/home.php#!/group.php?gid=120375671317475.

53. 14 January 2011, 21:06, http://www.facebook.com/home.php#!/group.php?gid=120375671317475.

54. David MacGowan, interview by email, 11 January 2011.

55. Oliver Wake, interview by email, 22 January 2011.

56. Ibid.

57. Harris interview, 2011.

58. Castle interview, 2007.

59. Gee interview, 2011.

60. MacGowan interview, 2011.

61. Paul Castle, interview by email, 10 February 2011.

62. Gee interview, 2010.

63. Gee interview, 2011.

64. MacGowan interview, 2011.

65. Wake interview, 2011.

66. Henry Jenkins, *Textual Poachers: Television Fans and Participatory Culture* (London: Routledge, 1992).

67. There are still fan fiction 'zines online such as *Inferno Fiction*.

68. Jeremy Sarachan, "*Doctor Who* Fan Videos, YouTube, and the Public Sphere," in Chris Hansen, ed., *Ruminations, Peregrinations, and Regenerations: A Critical Approach to Doctor Who* (Newcastle: Cambridge Scholars, 2010): pp. 249–61.

69. Ibid.

70. Ibid; Paul Booth, *Digital Fandom: New Media Studies* (New York: Peter Lang, 2010).

71. Val Douglas, interview by email, 29 January 2011.

72. Marshall interview, 2011.

73. Douglas interview, 2011.

74. Marshall interview, 2011.

75. Leslie McMurtry, interview by email, 24 January 2011.

76. Leslie McMurtry, "Editorial," *The Terrible Zodin*, 2008, http://dl.dropbox.com/u/15011735/The%20Terrible%20Zodin/TTZ1%20The%20Terrible%20Zodin%20Issue%201%20Winter%202008.pdf 1: 2.

77. McMurtry interview, 2011.

78. Ibid.

79. Ibid.

80. Rebecca Williams, "Desiring the Doctor: Identity, Gender and Genre in Online Fandom," in Tobias Hochscherf and James Leggott, eds., *British Science Fiction Film and Television: Critical Essays* (Jefferson, NC: McFarland, 2011): p. 177.

81. Ibid., pp. 167–68.

82. Rhiannon Bury, *Cyberspaces of Their Own: Female Fandoms Online* (New York: Peter Lang, 2005).

83. Henry Jenkins, "'Out of the closet and into the universe': Queers and *Star Trek*," in John Tulloch and Henry Jenkins, *Science Fiction Audiences: Watching Doctor Who and Star Trek* (London: Routledge, 1995): p. 237.

84. Matt Hills, "Gender and Fan Culture," 2007, http://www.henryjenkins.org/2007/08/gender_and_fan_culture_round_t.html, Fanzines and conventions such as Infinity in Cardiff and the Cult TV Festival were devoted to numerous series.

85. See John Nathan-Turner, "Who's America?" *Doctor Who Magazine* 117 (1991): pp. 11–15; Chris Noll, and Debbie Glienke, "Doctor Who in Chicago," *Doctor Who Summer Special* (1984): pp. 28–33; Kathleen Toth, "Doctor Who American Style" *Cloister Bell* 10/11: pp. 15–21; Sarah Prefect, "...And Aussie-Style Too!" *Cloister Bell* 10/11:pp. 21–4; Kathleen Toth, "TARDIS 21," *Cloister Bell* 12: pp. 32–3. A call was made on the Doctor Who News Page on 30 July 2011 for contributions to a book on American *Doctor Who* fandom titled *Red White and Who: The Story of Doctor Who in America.*

3

Don't Call It a Comeback

Aaron Gulyas

Since *Doctor Who*'s high-profile return to television, the "wilderness years" from 1990 through September 26, 2003, when BBC1 controller Lorraine Heggessey announced the return of the show, have begun to take on the appearance of a variegated yet distinct era of the show's history. Virgin's *New Adventures* (featuring Sylvester McCoy's seventh Doctor) and subsequent line of "past–Doctor" spin-off novels dominated the literary sector of *Doctor Who* fandom. Independently-produced videos presented actors from the show's past in science fiction adventures that — for some — partially sated the appetite for televised *Doctor Who* adventures.

During those wilderness years there arose an oasis — a television movie on American network television. Co-produced by the BBC, it was intended to serve as a "backdoor pilot" for a potential television series. This oasis, however, proved to be a mirage. Ratings (in the United States, at least) were disappointing and a new series did not materialize. Spin-off media continued (now somewhat more tightly controlled by the BBC) with new novels and audio adventures featuring television's eighth Doctor Paul McGann. As the dream of a new *Doctor Who* series on television became a reality with Heggessey's 2003 announcement, the memory of 1996 lingered; would the show vanish again? Whether it survived or not, what would the place of the new series be within the vast panoply of *Doctor Who*?

That question "Where does it fit?" was one which dominated discussion of both the 1996 movie and the 2005 series. The argument over what did or did not constitute "proper" *Doctor Who* was one that extended beyond the criticism of television. During the 1990s and early 2000s, fans applied the "real *Doctor Who*" test to the spin-off materials as well. At its heart, this argument concerns the notion of audience. Who, in the end, is *Doctor Who* for? *Doctor Who* fandom, collectively, struggled with this during the "wilderness years." Fan fiction, licensed novels, tangentially-related spinoff videos, and debates on Internet discussion groups filled the gap left by the end of the original run of the series. Fans — amateur and professional — used these media to shape *Doctor Who* in their own images. Fans, for a time, possessed a greater degree of ownership than they ever had before. This ownership meant that creators charged with resurrecting the show for a new audience had to be aware of these expectations of the fans and speak to those expectations in some way. The 1996 Fox movie and 2005's "Rose" both bore this burden. The manner in which producers shaped their respective "comebacks" sparked fan reactions that reflected how well or poorly the resurgent programs had met those fans' expectations. These expectations revolved around the stories' places within the broad *Doctor Who* narrative as well as questions of tone and production.

It is certainly imprudent to try to define a generalized "fan reaction" to these productions. Like most science fiction fans, *Doctor Who* fans are a diverse group with myriad opinions. Additionally, those individual fans' opinions of specific *Doctor Who* episodes changed over time. There is no "pulse" of *Doctor Who* fandom. What this essay will do, rather, is discuss how fans framed the discussion of these two new iterations of *Doctor Who* in terms of its place in the history of the show and how their reactions to new, televised *Doctor Who* changed between 1996 and 2005.

As *Doctor Who* reached the end of its original television run in 1989, it had evolved from a popular children's show to a national institution. It was a show that many commentators believed had lost its way. While increasing call-backs to the series' past kept fans intrigued, the general public began to move away from the series. *Doctor Who* had made the transition from family viewing to "cult" television. In volume 5 of their *About Time* series of books, Lawrence Miles and Tat Wood summed up the transition the show made in the 1980s:

> If you switched on halfway through an episode there was no incentive to sit back and see what would happen. In the '70s it was written and directed so that anyone could pick it up at almost any point. Many commentators singled this out as the defining quality of the programme's appeal.... By 1981 ... this was not a program for casual viewers. But that didn't matter, because there was a fandom, guaranteed to watch anything with a police box in it.[1]

Doctor Who in the 1980s featured a heavy reliance on references to the series' past. Thirteen out of twenty serials during Peter Davison's tenure as the Doctor, from 1982 to 1984, featured some character or concept which appeared previously in the series. During the subsequent era under Colin Baker, this trend increased (six of seven serials contained material from, or reference to the series' past). This focus on "continuity" abated somewhat during Sylvester McCoy's years on the show (1987–1989). By that time, however, ratings had declined to roughly half the level they had been earlier in the decade. *Doctor Who*, the BBC felt, needed a rest.

Doctor Who fandom continued to grow even after the BBC ceased production of the series at the end of its 26th season in 1989. *Doctor Who Magazine* continued to publish on a monthly basis; fanzines continued to appear and were sold at the continuing *Doctor Who* fan conventions. The expanding home video market in the 1990s led to classic *Doctor Who* serials making their way into fans' VCRs, sparking new debates and discussion on the burgeoning Internet, with usenet groups like rec.arts.drwho connecting fans to each other from around the world. During this time, there was an increasing sense among some fans of a collective ownership of the series and its legacy. In the words of *Doctor Who* fan and author Tat Wood, during this time, "1990, 1991, 1992 ... it was obvious that there wasn't going to be a new series, so it was ours, Virgin [Books, publishers of the *New Adventures* series of spin-off novels] hadn't taken it away from us yet."[2] Tensions existed within that fan community which revolved around varying interpretations of *Doctor Who*'s purpose. Was it serious science fiction television, in the same vein as *Star Trek*? Was the show best considered family tea-time entertainment with science fiction overtones? Or was *Doctor Who* something unique and indefinable?

> Fan culture seems to thrive on conflict. Derek Johnson argues that there exists a constitutive centrality of antagonism and power to television fandom.... Ongoing struggles for discursive dominance constitute fandom as a hegemonic struggle over interpretation and evaluation through which relationships among fan, text, and producer are continually articulated, disarticulated, and rearticulated.[3]

Doctor Who fans in the 1990s certainly participated in what Johnson calls "fan-tagonism." The frequency and ferocity of their arguments heightened when Virgin Books received permission from the BBC to create original *Doctor Who* novels. The *New Adventures* series of novels promised to present stories "too broad and deep for the small screen."[4] Thus was born two of the great fan debates of the 1990s. One of these was the question of *Doctor Who*–ness. The other was the struggle over the "canon" or, put another way, what items constituted entries into the official, accepted list of "real" *Doctor Who*, as opposed to items and products which fans considered spin-offs, and not necessarily part of the accepted continuity.

The *New Adventures* began publication in 1991 with the *Timewyrm* series of four linked novels. From the beginning there were fans who asserted that this constituted, in essence, "season 27" of *Doctor Who*, as the books featured the Doctor in his seventh incarnation, accompanied by his companion Ace, continuing their televised adventures which had concluded at the end of 1989. The first three novels in the range, written by established *Who* writers John Peel, Terrence Dicks, and Nigel Robinson were traditional — if lengthy — *Doctor Who* adventures. The fourth, *Timewyrm: Revelation* by newcomer Paul Cornell, took the series in a different direction. Cornell's book used the Doctor's subconscious as the setting for a good part of the story and battling against the story's villain (the eponymous Timewyrm) was more about psychology and dialogue than spaceships and technobabble. *Revelation*'s storytelling was non-linear and, significantly, was the first of the novels that could not, in all probability, be producible as a television serial. From that point on, traditional, linear *Doctor Who*–style storytelling would be the exception in the *New Adventures* rather than the rule.

Fan critiques of the *New Adventures*, unsurprisingly, often centered on how well they continued to convey the spirit of *Doctor Who*, in terms of characterization, continuity, and tone. One early *New Adventures* installment that particularly polarized readers was *Transit* by Ben Aaronovich. Aaronovich had previously written two *Doctor Who* serials, *Remembrance of the Daleks* and *Battlefield*, and, thus, readers had expectations that his first original *Doctor Who* novel would be along the same lines as the television show. On the contrary, *Transit* pushed the limits of the "adult" in literary *Doctor Who*. The Doctor's companion utters the word "fuck," among other transgressions. Matthew Sadler, writing in the *New Adventures* fanzine *Broadsword*, commented:

> The reader is left wondering who the author thinks his audience is. There is swearing in the dialogue throughout the book, and the sexual encounters in the story made me wonder if the author was either acting out an adolescent fantasy, or desperately trying to appeal to a teenage audience.... One wouldn't be the slightest bit prudish to be of the opinion that this is not *Doctor Who*, William Hartnell would be spinning in his grave at the thought of this ever being acceptable for Who. It was also disappointing to read about the Doctor being drunk, even if he was only harmlessly singing happy birthday to the universe.[5]

While many *New Adventures* readers were turned off by this, and vowed never to read another ever again, some were thrilled by *Transit*'s presentation of *Doctor Who* with a more harsher edge to it. Responding to Sadler's comments, Richard Prekodravac defended Aaronovich's approach to *Doctor Who*:

> Transit reveals itself as slick fast paced and powerful. It kicks hard and it moves fast. It's hip and intelligent and confronts with a harsh reality. Sex. Death. *Transit* is not just words and does not just tell a story and it does not depict a society. It is a society created not just represented. The people aren't characters for a story but are part of something beyond the confines of a novel; they're not lifelike but living.[6]

"Hip" is a word that few applied to *Doctor Who* during the 1990s but the authors of the *New Adventures* relished the opportunity to drag the *Doctor Who* mythos into the future. The *New Adventures* authors, certainly, were conscious of the burden to make sure their new *Doctor Who* stories were of their time. Paul Cornell, interviewed in 1995, stated this as his "philosophy" of where the *New Adventures* needed to take *Doctor Who*:

> Well for a start we've got to push this envelope. Doctor Who is dead, the New Adventures is all that is left, we've got to change things we've got to take that format, make it relevant to the times we are in now, and keep going forward with it to innovate.... We're now in the situation where the New Adventures are tremendously different to where we left Doctor Who on television.[7]

The notion that *Doctor Who* was dead lurked in the backs of many fans' minds. When the show's 30th anniversary, in 1993, passed without an announcement about a new, ongoing series, they feared the worst—which was that the show was never coming back to television.

The fear that *Doctor Who* was finished on television did not, however, mean that fans automatically assumed that the *New Adventures* were the successor to the show. While it is incredibly difficult to know what percentage of *Doctor Who* fans were *New Adventures* readers (and even more difficult to determine how many of those readers actually liked the books, rather than reading them out of a "fannish" sense of completion), one of the most significant indicators of the *New Adventures* penetration into fandom was the ongoing development of *Doctor Who Magazine*'s long running comic serial. Initially, after the show ceased production, the seventh Doctor and Ace continued their adventures in the pages of *DWM*. In 1992, however, editors made the decision to tie the comic continuity to that of the *New Adventures*. References to and characters from the novels appeared; *New Adventures* writers scripted some of the comics. By 1995, however, the magazine decided to "de-link" the comics continuity from that of the *New Adventures* citing reader polls indicating that a minority of *DWM* readers followed the novels with any regularity.[8]

Thus, divisions appeared within the *Doctor Who* fan community over what constituted actual, real, accepted *Doctor Who*—what was, to use fandom's adjectivized term, "canon"? Before the television series ended, this was not a significant debate. What was televised was "real" *Doctor Who* and what wasn't, wasn't. Thus, if a conflict existed between the televised version of the story and the novelization of that story, the television version won. Comic adventures were fun, but not televised and, thus, not real. The two films from the 1960s, based on television adventures, were not "real." The stage plays from the 1970s and 1990s? Not really *Doctor Who*. One could certainly enjoy them, but one should never try to settle an argument with evidence from a piece of *Doctor Who* that was "non-canon."

One of the forums in which fan discussion increasingly took place in the 1990s and into the 2000s was the Internet usenet group rec.arts.drwho. Usenet groups, while declining in recent years due to competition from web-based discussion forums, were once the centerpiece of online fan discussion. As Sascha Segan of *PC Magazine* wrote in 2008, "The eye candy of the Web and the marketing dollars of Web site owners helped push people over to profit-making sites. Usenet's slightly arcane access methods and text-only protocols have nothing on the glitz and glamour of MySpace."[9] What helped, according to Segan, to decrease the appeal of Usenet discussion groups is also what makes them a valuable resource for examining the development of online *Doctor Who* fandom.

Usenet groups like rec.arts.drwho exist as a decentralized, unmoderated space largely free from outside manipulation. Multiple potential sources for fan opinion exist, including web pages, fanzines, and the pages of *Doctor Who Magazine*. Rec.arts.drwho has advantages over all of these. First, is the unmoderated, unedited, and uncensored nature of Usenet. The system is decentralized, with no one person or group of people able to restrict what people say. While this did tend to draw conversation thread toward ad hominem flame wars, it also meant that no one opinion could artificially dominate the proceedings. Another advantage of rec.arts.drwho for the researcher is the fact that through Web gateways and archives such as DejaNews and, more recently, Google, Usenet is indexed, searchable, and complete in a way that transient websites and transient fanzines are not. Longevity also favors the Usenet groups as a resource — their unbroken chain of existence from the early 1990s to the present providing a view of long-term development that is not available with other resources.

Of course, there are disadvantages to using resources like rec.arts.drwho as well. It is representative of a relatively small group of fans, limited not only to those who had Internet access, but a smaller subset who spent the time and effort to use this "slightly arcane" system. However, as this particular study is concerned with change over a relatively long period of *Doctor Who* time —1996 to 2003 — rec.arts.drwho represents and excellent opportunity to study the changes in attitudes of fans in a particular discursive space over that span of time. Usenet groups such as rec.arts.drwho aren't perfect sources, but they are, thanks to careful archiving and easy searching, complete.

Once the series was off the air, the notion of canon expanded. Some fans posited that since the BBC licensed the *New Adventures* and some of them were written by established *Doctor Who* television writers such as Terrence Dicks, Marc Platt, and Ben Aaronovich, then couldn't they also be considered canon? Other fans replied that *only* the televised adventures were canon and, thus, the novels didn't count. Still others compromised, such as rec.arts.drwho poster "The Admiral":

> If something really interested me in one of them, I might include it in my personal picture of the Whoniverse. That doesn't mean I would expect future TV endeavours to respect those elements — I can separate "true" canonity [sic] from my own.[10]

The notion of a personal canon of what was *Doctor Who* and what wasn't was a key development in fan conception of "real" *Doctor Who* in the 1990s. *Doctor Who* could be whatever any particular fan wanted it to be.

The fan wrangling over canon, while often tedious and pedantic, is crucial for understanding the reaction to the 1996 Fox television movie. The "canonicity" debate revolves around fans' conflicting understandings about what *Doctor Who* was and, just as importantly, what constituted *Doctor Who*. Even fans who did not read all (or any) of the books had opinions about whether they constituted real *Doctor Who*. Real *Doctor Who* was televised, created by the BBC, and remained true to the tone and spirit of the original twenty-six seasons of the series, even if that tone varied wildly over the course of that original run. Arguments over tone, canonicity, and fidelity to the original series would play a major role in fans' reception of the 1996 movie. Fan conversations in the early 1990s laid the groundwork for the arguments which would occur once their beloved show returned to the screen.

The 1996 Fox network television movie *Doctor Who* had a long, convoluted path to television screens. Although an in-depth examination of the various scripts and treatments is beyond the scope of this study, it is useful to explore one of the key decisions made in the production process. It was not a foregone conclusion that the Fox *Doctor Who* would, in fact, be a continuation of the television show which ran on the BBC from 1963 to 1989, which had inspired a line of mature, thoughtful novels, and which had a global, ready-made fan base. The movie as televised was the third script commissioned for the project. The earliest treatment and script rebooted the series. The central concept of the Doctor as a Time Lord from Gallifrey remained, but the characters goals and motivations changed. No longer would the Doctor be a curious wanderer in time and space. Rather, he would be on a quest to find his lost father (named Ulysses in some versions) and have adventures along the way. Familiar *Doctor Who* figures such as the Master, the Daleks, and the Cybermen would appear but would be drastically altered. The second draft, according to producer Phillip Segal, "was just too straight-ahead. It didn't have the quirky Whovian elements to it."[11] The final version of the script would strive to continue the story of *Doctor Who* as it had been left in 1989.

This type of revamp is not unheard of—*Battlestar Galactica* went through a similar change—but in the case of *Doctor Who*, producers made the decision to continue the series rather than reinvent it. Some aspects of the earlier versions would seep in. The Doctor makes a non sequitur reference to his father, for example, and—as was the case in an earlier iteration of the story—the Doctor reveals that he is half-human. For the most part, however, the 1996 *Doctor Who* was a continuation of the classic series. This decision to continue the series, not reinvent it, raised the stakes with regard to fan expectations. In the months preceding the premiere, fans on the Usenet group rec.arts.drwho (the largest and least-moderated fan forum of the 1990s) discussed how the movie would fit into established *Doctor Who* continuity. These expectations serve as context for the eventual disappointment in the movie among some fans. In the months leading up to the airing of the movie, scriptwriter Matthew Jacobs did outreach work with *Doctor Who* fan outlets such as *Doctor Who Magazine* and the *Doctor Who* Online area of America Online. He sought to assure fans that the aspects of *Doctor Who* important to them would be preserved. Segal stated to *Doctor Who Magazine*:

> Our final writer, Matthew Jacobs, loves this who; he loves the character and understand the Doctor and it shows on the page in every detail.... The sonic screwdriver, the yoyo, and jellybabies—bits and pieces that Sylvester [McCoy] had never had in the series but told us he would have loved to have played with.[12]

Segal referred to these continuity touches as "kisses to the past"[13]—present for no other reason than to reassure the view that they were, in fact, watching *Doctor Who*. Despite these reassurances, many fans had strong reservations about the prospects of reviving *Doctor Who* on television.

Expectation and fear existed side by side on rec.arts.drwho during late 1995 and early 1996 as bits and pieces about the forthcoming movie began to filter into the public. The greatest area of concern was how the movie would fit into the already established continuity of *Doctor Who* as established in the television series and through the *New* and *Missing Adventures* lines of novels. There was equal concern that the over-reliance on continuity touchstones would alienate new viewers and limit the movie's chances of success. This tension between innovation and tradition was similar to that which surrounded the development of the *New Adventures* in the early 1990s. Once again, the question of *Doctor Who's* audience—longtime fans versus casual readers/viewers—was paramount. This time, however, the stakes were higher. This was *Doctor Who*, back on television after seven years. Many fans saw this as a make-or-break moment for the show.

Robert G. Cole was a poster to rec.arts.drwho who expressed great concern about the place of the television movie in *Doctor Who's* continuity. On June 8, 1995, he posted:

There seems to be a lot of talk about continuity (or the lack thereof) in the proposed new movie. I know that I for one greatly fear the movie. Not because of continuity issues themselves (at least, that isn't my main concern) but what the use of continuity would mean in terms of the future of Doctor Who.

Cole outlined what he saw as the possible impact the movie would have on established *Doctor Who* continuity. If the movie followed continuity and failed, then continuity would be "forever altered." If the movie broke continuity and was a success, "then the original continuity would be lost forever."[14] In order to prevent such alteration, Cole recommended that the BBC bring back Sylvester McCoy and Sophie Aldred (the seventh Doctor and his companion, Ace) and pick the show up precisely where it left off in 1989. Among those who replied to Cole's thread, Ian J. Davenport and his comments were typical of those who took a more relaxed view of continuity:

> You can't load tons of continuity onto a general audience and still hold their interest. The time to be worrying about linking that in is when (if) the series comes along, and the regeneration can be handled in it's own story in flashback. A gradual series of revelations about the main character and history avoids overloading casual viewers, and may even intrigue new regular viewers as a hook.[15]

Thus, in the months leading up to the movie there was a split between those who believed the show should fit tightly and demonstrably into established continuity and those who believe the show should reach out to new viewer first, and then tie into storylines and characters from the show's long history once an audience firmly supported the show.

Fans' expectations, fears, and concerns about the movie and how it would fit into established *Doctor Who* continuity also encompassed a number of specific areas. Would the TARDIS still be a police box? Would the Doctor be explicitly identified as a Time Lord? One example of the way in which expectations were framed by the classic series involved how the movie would introduce the new Doctor. The concerns of a person posting to rec.arts.drwho as "Davros" was typical in his post entitled "Will the movie with the new dweeb include a regeneration?" He wrote, "In order to preserve continuity (something that Hollywood rarely cares about); will they provide a McCoy to Dweeb regeneration sequence?? Anybody know?[16] Another poster, Andy Williams, speculated on how the regeneration sequence might be used to provide continuity with the original run of the series:

> I was thinking last night about how the regeneration sequence will be handled and who if any, will feature. In both Tom Baker's, Peter Davison's and Colin Baker's regenerations there have been flashbacks to previous companions and also the Master. So it got me wondering if they will use small clips of previous companions with maybe the Ainley Master saying "Die Doctor, Die." Or perhaps they might include a clip of each of the earlier incarnations in some sort of video montage? What does everyone think?[17]

Doctor Who, for fans, means a regeneration sequence from one actor/incarnation to the next. If the movie didn't provide that, could it truly be a continuation of the series? During the 1980s, the series (in "Logopolis/Castrovalva," "Caves of Androzani"/"Twin Dilemma," and "Time and the Rani") conditioned fans to expect a sequence of events in which the Doctor is injured, regenerates into a new persona, and spends a few episodes suffering from post-regenerative instability of some sort. Even in "Time and the Rani," when Colin Baker was unavailable to reprise his role as the sixth Doctor, a regeneration was accomplished with incoming Doctor Sylvester McCoy dressed like his predecessor. Although viewers were unlikely to actually think that the Colin Baker was on the screen, the tactic preserved the tradition of the regeneration sequence within the larger *Doctor Who* narrative. By bringing Sylvester McCoy as the seventh Doctor into the plot to pass the torch to the new eighth Doctor, the producers would cement the place of the movie within the larger picture of *Doctor Who* continuity.

The regeneration sequence was only one example of the call-backs to the classic series that fans expected. The Doctor, consensus claimed, must be British and they hoped that the creators would remain true to the character, often ignoring that the character of the Doctor had changed over the course of the original series and the movie must not be too "glossy" or "American." There must be a companion-type character. Countless posters and commentators had their say in what constituted real *Doctor Who*. Since Philip Segal was active in courting the online *Doctor Who* fan community, it stands to reason that his vision for the show, those "kisses to the past," would tend to cater to these fan concerns.

When the movie premiered in May of 1996, it welcomed fans with continuity references such as the sonic screwdriver, jelly babies, a lavishly re-designed TARDIS console room, the fourth Doctor's scarf, and the Master. Strikingly, it also contained elements (some exceedingly picayune) that seemingly flew in the face of established *Doctor Who* continuity. The Doctor is a Time Lord from the planet Gallifrey but he is also half-human (on his mother's side). The seventh Doctor actually died before the regeneration into his eighth persona took place. The TARDIS's malfunctioning chameleon circuit is renamed a cloaking device. The TARDIS contains an Eye of Harmony—an artifact thought to exist only on Gallifrey. The Doctor himself engages in several romantic kisses with Grace Holloway, the companion character in the movie. Online and off, fans created laundry lists of continuity touches and gaffes; the kisses to the past were balanced out by changes, errors, and actual kisses.

From its opening shot and line of dialogue, the movie set out to establish a connection with existing *Doctor Who* fans. With the camera zooming in on a planet, a voiceover intones, "It was on the planet Skaro that my old enemy the Master was finally put on trial."[18] For *Doctor Who* fans, this makes sense. Skaro is the home planet of the Daleks, who chatter their trademark "EX-TER-MIN-ATE!" as the Master is executed. The action shifts to the Doctor, whose voice is clearly different than the Doctor narrating the beginning of the film. Fans know that this is the seventh Doctor before the narration reveals it. The beginning of this movie, at least, seems directly targeted at fans. The subsequent film is peppered with continuity touchstones as the seventh Doctor dies, becomes the eighth Doctor, and proceeds to defeat the Master in his plan to steal the Doctor's body. The character of the Master, as well, hearkened back to that with which fans might be familiar. Like the Master of the 1980s, the Master in the Movie requires a new body and his machinations revolve around that goal.

The question for fans was whether the continuity-filled movie, even with its errors and additions, fulfilled their expectations of what *Doctor Who* could and should be in the 1990s. As was the case with the *New Adventures* spin-off novels, fans found themselves differing on what *Doctor Who* should be, regardless of genre. The reaction to the movie would highlight these diverse views of the show.

Fan reaction to the 1996 movie was mixed, and has continued to evolve over time. One aspect of *Doctor Who* fandom which has persisted from the 1980s onward is the continuous re-assessment of stories thanks to their presence on video, fan-produced audio (in the case of episodes junked by the BBC), and DVD. As new generations of fans experience the stories, they reclassify them from classics to clunkers, or vice-versa. In some cases, entire eras of the show's history are re-examined with a new eye.

The 1996 movie has gone through a similar phase of re-evaluation; in fact it may have undergone more scrutiny than any *Doctor Who* story up to that point in time, due to the perception that the future of the show depended on its performance. As fan and writer Lance Parkin said in 1996, "It's already clear that 'fan opinion' of the McGann movie depends on whether it spawns a series or not. If it fails in that basic task, we'll all start the inquest: the script was weak, the ending was rubbish, no time travel, no monsters, poor continuity."[19] One of the most noticeable trends in the earliest reviews of the movie was that writers seemed to go out of their way to accentuate the positive. Alan Toombs, on rec.arts.drwho, posted, "As an introduction for Paul McGann it worked perfectly and on first impressions I'm finding him to be charming and charismatic. Sylvester McCoy got a better send-off than any fan could have hoped for. Daphne Ashbook provided an excellent foil to McGann's raw energy."[20] Sean Gaffney, posting just days after the movie aired, said, "I had a few niggles, but not enough to make me complain. This was a really good pilot. I'm sad that it didn't get the ratings. Who deserves a new chance with Paul McGann."[21]

Despite the enthusiasm, even positive reviews were conditional. The aspects that concerned rec.arts.drwho fans the most were drastic departures from what had come before. Replying to the Sean Gaffney post quoted above, Angus Gulliver stated,

> A cautous [sic] thumbs-up from me. We've got a great Doctor, and a very promising companion (if she returns). Some glitches need to be ironed out, but bringing in script-writers who are familiar with old Who (Mr. [Terrence] Dicks where are you?) will help. All the ingredients [sic] are there, they just need mixing together a little more carefully and in different quantities. Segal-Who has potential, and I watched this pilot knowing that most involved had not worked on the old show.[22]

Often, fans saw problems with the movie as being the result of creators who were unfamiliar with the original program. Gulliver's mention of Terrence Dicks is particularly interesting. Dicks was the script editor of *Doctor Who* during the early 1970s and wrote several scripts for the series as well as the majority of the popular novelizations published by Target books. In fan circles, Terrence Dicks' work was representative of "traditional" *Doctor Who*. Gulliver's comment not only critiques the movie, but also indicates a very specific vision of what kind of *Doctor Who* any future series should be, but also plays a role in the wider debate over what does or does not constitution "proper" "classic" or "good" *Doctor Who*.

Other critiques of the movie were more specific. In particular, what some fans saw as excessive violence. Poster "GLC" complained:

> I knew we were in trouble as soon as the Uzi's [sic] came out. I don't know what kind of sick people Hollywood marketing moles think we are, but they lately cannot resist giving imported cultural products their own coat of fashionable violence.... And Doctor Who must be taken down in a hail of bullets without saying a word because it fits someone's idea of "gritty" and "realistic." The hero I admired for saying, in a previous incarnation, "Show people that you mean them no harm and they won't hurt you ... nine times out of ten.... Where was the whimsy and the fun?"[23]

Although these concerns are about media violence in general, GLC specifically criticized the violence in the *Doctor Who* movie in terms of its discontinuity with the show as previously perceived. GLC saw *Doctor Who* as whimsical, fun, and nonviolent. Like Angus Gulliver's invocation of Terrence Dicks as the type of writer *Doctor Who* producers should bring on board to work on a potential new series, GLC's conception of *Doctor Who* was limited to a particular kind of *Doctor Who*. One could hardly characterize "The Caves of Androzani" (1984) as whimsical nor "The Massacre of St. Bartholomew's Eve" (1966) as fun. The 1984

"Resurrection of the Daleks" had far more gunplay than the 1996 movie and lacked whimsy. GLC would, in all likelihood, identify these stories as proper *Doctor Who*. As part of the original "canon" the 26 seasons of the BBC television show are, seemingly, exempt from scrutiny as to their *Doctor Who*–ness. Not all the criticism of the movie was blind to the need for *Doctor Who* to change over time. Lynn Eades had problems with the movie, but felt it was worth continuing as a series:

> I too had trouble with the plot, the half-human bit, and especially the kiss! But as has been said, this is a pilot and your [sic] talking to an American audience many of whom have no idea who the Doctor is and why they should care! Unfortunately a little Americanization was necessary, I feel, to gain the American audience. What made me the happiest was that they didn't cater to the non–Whovian. Explinations [sic] of what a Time Lord is and what the TARDIS is were precise and they didn't rehash it over and over. I loved the film, except for the stupid, too long commercials!!!!!!!!!!!!![24]

The future of *Doctor Who*, Eades argued, would be best served by pushing forward, gaining a new audience while retaining the old. If some aspects of this meant that long-term fans felt disenfranchised, then that was part of the cost of the show continuing.

Just as fans online commented on the movie's level of *Doctor Who* fidelity, fanzine and magazine writers also weighed in on the issue. Edwin Patterson, writing in the November 1996 issue of *Time Space Visualizer,* argued, "Doctor Who has undoubtedly lost its roots. It has become what many fans feared in the early nineties—A police box and a Time Lord but not truly Doctor Who."[25] While online critiques focused on the characterization of the Doctor as one of the few things right with the television movie, some magazine writers believed that characterization to be as emphatically wrong—if not more wrong—than other aspects of the production. One of the significant aspects of the Doctor's character was his newly apparent heterosexual tendencies, as evidenced by the kisses with Grace Holloway. Although online commentators had a variety of reactions to the kiss, ranging from rationalization (Susan Foreman was the Doctor's granddaughter, so he obviously had sex at some point), to dismissal (it was post-regenerative trauma so it doesn't *really* define his characterization any more than the fourth Doctor's donning of a Viking helmet in "Robot" defined his), these writers saw these kisses—and the alteration of the Doctor/Companion dynamic in a romantic direction as being a significant shift in the character's—and the show's—development.

That shift was toward presenting the Doctor and the show from a heteronormative point of view. Heteronormativity, a term coined by Michael Warner in 1991 is a cultural mindset in which heterosexuality is assumed to be the proper human sexual orientation. Such a worldview considers people who engage in sexual practices that transcend the heterosexual norm to be deviant. Warner argued that the persistence of heteronormative ideals contributed to the marginalization and oppression of non-heteronormative actions and expressions.[26] While one could argue that a thread of heteronormativity persisted in classic televised *Doctor Who,* the character of the Doctor himself had been consistently asexual. The television movie altered that perception. Writing in *Doctor Who Magazine,* Matt Jones lamented this change in the Doctor's characterization:

> To make the Doctor heterosexual only serves to make him more ordinary, more like all the other heroes. His curious asexuality has always given him a childlike quality. Sex and romance seem to baffle him. It is as if they are outside his comprehension.... What makes the Doctor unique and alien is that he loves on a different level and in a different way to us mere mortals. His is a big love for big things. To make him a half-human heterosexual turns him into just another "guy with two hearts."[27]

For those fans for whom the Doctor was a heroic adventure figure whose goal was not to "get the girl," a demonstrably heterosexual Doctor was a change too many. Like the commentators who focused on the movie's violence, "American-ness" or lack of whimsy, those who questioned the romantic aspects of the movie did so because they found it utterly at odds with what they believed *Doctor Who* represented. Some non-heterosexual fans viewed the kiss with Grace Holloway as a fundamental shift in the character of the Doctor.

Doctor Who fandom has traditionally had a sizable GLBT constituency. In 2007, Ed Hagan, writing for *The Guardian* online, speculated as to why:

> The Doctor, standing up for the persecuted and the oppressed, is an attractive figure for a young person growing up and feeling a little different from everyone else. He's always been a little bit anti-establishment too; unlike Star Trek, the Doctor would be more likely to topple a Federation than endorse it.[28]

Doctor Who, for many fans — especially those in the U.K. — existed outside the traditional science fiction/cult television world. Its hero was iconoclastic, non-violent (mostly), and resolutely asexual. The Doctor's asexuality and willingness, across 26 seasons of televised adventures, to befriend those whom society marginalized appealed to many, but was especially meaningful for GLBT fans. For the television movie to undermine that asexuality threatened the foundations of the show that provided a haven for fans who may have wished for a hero like the Doctor in their own life. As Matt Jones suggested, such a move would make him "more like all the other heroes." This fundamental change to the character of the Doctor may lead to a fundamental change in the nature of *Doctor Who* fans and fandom. Guy Wigmore, writing in the fanzine *Silver Carrier* shortly after the television movie aired, conveyed this fear in a tongue-in-cheek poem. The first and second stanzas set out the situation in which some fans found themselves following the Fox movie:

> *Fellow fans, all hail the day*
> *McGann appeared as Doctor Who*
> *Our new Doctor has led the way:*
> *Girls and women, we want you!*
> *No more will menky lives be grey.*
>
> *Fans were once a sexless breed.*
> *That changed with Paul McGann's first snog.*
> *Our blood was stirred we found the need*
> *To love and live like our new god:*
> *As love-loctors we would succeed.*[29]

Fans attach meaning to the Doctor's actions. He is an aspirational figure; his righteous actions, his championing of underdogs and those subject to persecution serve as goals for fans to achieve in their own lives. If one of this new Doctor's actions is to engage in heterosexual romantic activity (or *any* romantic activity), where did that leave fans?

Fan reaction to the 1996 *Doctor Who* television movie was varied, but a common thread running through them was a distinct impression that something fundamental was missing from the series. Whether this was whimsy, humor, a vital link to the series' past, or the character of the Doctor himself differed from one fan to another. Even fans who appreciated the movie as a continuation of the classic series which they loved so much often had reservations about some aspects of the show. Although the 1996 movie did not spawn a series, the character of the eighth Doctor continued to appear in licensed spin-off media such as novels and audio dramas. Significantly, as Lance Parkin points out, these media "have been characterized by their lack of any building on *The TV Movie*. The eighth Doctor isn't half-human, he doesn't kiss girls, he doesn't see people's future when he meets them, he doesn't think about Grace."[30] The *Doctor Who* spin-off world, being an outlet for fan creativity, cannibalized the 1996 movie, remolding the eighth Doctor into the characterization they wanted him to have and — perhaps — what they felt it should have been from the beginning.

The Fox movie's failure to launch a *Doctor Who* revival dampened fan enthusiasm for another comeback for the show. The BBC was, apparently, unwilling to undertake a new series without a partnership with an American production company (with the accompanying American broadcast and merchandising outlets). Stories continued to circulate — as they had since the late 1980s — of a theatrically released *Doctor Who* feature film. *Doctor Who* on television, which many fans considered to be its natural environment, seemed to be a lost cause. This was not the end of the continuing *Doctor Who* story but rather a point at which the show's fans began to fear that the show might never return to television. This led to the flourishing of *Doctor Who* in media other than television.

Although the Fox movie did not lead to a new televised *Doctor Who* series, this one-time adventure of the eighth Doctor spawned a variety of spin-off media, carrying the character into the future. Unlike the development of *Doctor Who* in the early 1990s, the direction of the show's continuing non-canonical narrative splintered into different strands which revolved around Paul McGann's brief — but generally well received — performance. The eighth Doctor appeared in BBC licensed audio plays from Big Finish productions. The BBC, snatching the baton from Virgin, began publishing a series of novels featuring the eighth Doctor. *Doctor Who Magazine* began featuring the eighth Doctor in its monthly comic section. Crucially, none of these three strands were connected to each other in any way. A fan could follow the audios without following the books, or the comics, or any combination of the three. The adventures of the Doctor and Sam, the Doctor and Izzy, or the Doctor and Charley each existed in hermetically sealed universes, cut off from each other, cut off from the Virgin New Adventure line of novels and, in most cases, cut off even from the narrative and character tropes of the TV movie that had launched the eighth Doctor.

In the years after the 1996 TV Movie, following the continuing adventures of *Doctor Who* became a multiple-choice proposition for fans. If they chose to follow new stories rather than rely on the original twenty-six seasons for their *Doctor Who* fix, they had a number of options. Between novels, audios, and comics, the eighth Doctor would go on to have the longest tenure of any current incarnation of the character, resulting in even more arguments about the *Doctor Who* canon than in the days of the Virgin *New Adventures*. Emerging fights went beyond the basic and well-worn argument over whether or not fans should consider anything but the televised adventures as part of the canon. Subsets of the canonicity argument pitted the BBC-published novels against the Virgin *New Adventures* against the audios against the *Doctor Who Magazine* comics in a fierce battle over "real" *Doctor Who*. Despite the novels' and audio plays' officially licensed status, some fans refused to acknowledge them as part of *Doctor Who* proper. As one rec.arts.drwho fan stated, "My view is that both the books and the audios take the show into areas it has not really gone to and there is nothing wrong with that but they are most definately [sic] not canon. Merely fan fiction of a variable quality."[31]

Some fans, of course, became concerned about the increasing splits within *Doctor Who* fandom, and some urged the adoption of a unified canon as a step toward ensuring the continuation of the *Doctor Who*. Rec.arts.drwho user John L. Beven II, in a thread entitled

"Firing the Canon," stated, "I think for DW to survive that there's going to have to be some criteria that most people can look at and say 'That's true DW!' The more objective (and thus more defendable) the criteria is the better. Otherwise, every new change in the series will just serve to further factionalize fandom."[32] Other fans saw the variety in *Doctor Who* media as the narrative equivalent of biodiversity — there was some *Doctor Who* available for anyone who wanted some, regardless of their desired media format. Print, audio, comic — all media were represented except, of course, television.

With the prospects of televised *Doctor Who* looking ever more remote, creators sought ways to move the narrative forward. The BBC eighth Doctor novels saw Gallifrey and the Time Lords destroyed and the Doctor's memory erased. This jettisoned years of continuity, both from the novel series and the television show, and returned the character of the Doctor to a mysterious wanderer in time and space. While this is a major shift for the show, BBCi, the online arm of the BBC, went even further in 2003.

Broadcast in November and December 2003, *Scream of the Shalka* was a Flash-animated adventure that starred Richard E. Grant as the Doctor. In early promotions for the Web adventure, the BBC indicated that the story would launch the Doctor's ninth incarnation and that there would be further adventures. Although *Doctor Who*'s televised return would render *Scream of the Shalka* an anomaly — relegating Grant's Doctor to the same not-the-real-Doctor category as, say, Peter Cushing — it serves as an example of the distance from 1996. The BBC, seemingly setting aside the possibility of a televised continuation of *Doctor Who*, moved on to a new incarnation of the Doctor — something the Virgin *New Adventures* had been expressly forbidden to do by the BBC. Even the format, Internet animation, signaled a shift in thinking. BBCi's production was not television or a fully-animated cartoon, not a fully-produced straight-to-DVD adventure, but rather a hybrid creation designed for the new-media web. It went beyond television, moving *Doctor Who* into the future of media and entertainment.

In 2004, as anticipation built for the rebooted BBC series, author Lance Parkin, writing in the Canadian fanzine *Enlightenment,* summed up the culmination of the eighth Doctor's era:

> The books and audios have diverged to the point that they now have fictional reasons for the fact they seem to operate in entirely different universes. The fact that the boos and audios have *different* explanations for the divergence is as clear proof as you need that McGann's return to the role has done nothing to unify *Doctor Who*.[33]

Doctor Who had no master narrative during the 1990s. Novels, audio plays, comics, and Webcasts all competed for fan attention and fan money. If the 1996 Fox movie launched a series, there might have been a unified, accepted, canonical narrative as during the series' original run. However, that did not happen, and it would be up to a new series to establish an accepted unity and continuity.

When Lorraine Heggessey announced, in September 2003, that Russell T. Davies would be taking the helm of the reborn *Doctor Who* series, fans once again engaged in fevered speculation about the future of their show. Two key concerns shaped online fan expectations of the 2005 revival of *Doctor Who*. First there was the perennial fear that producers, in seeking to appeal to new viewers, would jettison *Doctor Who* continuity and history. Second was the fear of Davies going too far in attempting to make the show relevant to a twenty-first century audience, particularly in the realm of politics and sexuality. Despite the growth of World Wide Web forums such as Outpost Gallifrey taking some traffic from the venerable rec.arts.drwho usenet group, RADW remains a valuable source for checking the pulse of unorganized *Doctor Who* fandom in the twenty-first century.

Continuity was, in the twenty-fist century, just as important as it was to the *Doctor Who* fan base as it had been in 1996. One significant difference, however, was that fans saw the impact of the 1996 film's continuity overload and realized that the show still had to appeal to a wide enough audience to guarantee continuing support. Thus, there was among some fans the willingness to accept some changes. Fans still, however, considered some areas of Doctor Who to be sacrosanct. One example was fear that the new series would be a reboot rather than the latest chapters in the saga that began in 1963. Rec.arts.drwho poster Aaron Pynn worried about this:

> As a series starting now will it be restarting the series as if the other doctors never exsisted [sic] because if so I have a serious problem with anyone dumping 30 years of history to give it a fresh new start. If they are just going to start it and go ahead as if it had never gone off the air but update it for a broader audience then thats [sic] fine and to be expected. Will the doctor be meeting everyone for the first time again? I certainly hope not... No one really wants the whole history of Doctor Who washed over and restarted do they. Can't they just continue it and make it fresh. Buffy The Vampire Slayer wasn't like the horrid film but at least they had the decency to acknowledge it.[34]

The fate of the 1996 film had demonstrated that a fan audience was not large enough to guarantee success. Any new *Doctor Who* needed to appeal to the masses while maintaining enough continuity with the past to assure loyal fans that they were truly watching *Doctor Who* and not some new series that happened to simply be called *Doctor Who*. Russell T. Davies was able to assuage fan fears that his *Doctor Who* would be a reboot in his "Production Notes" column in *Doctor Who Magazine*. In issue 344, Davies assured fans that the new Doctor would be *their* Doctor: "He's the same man who fought the Drahvins, The Macra, The Axons, The Wirrn, the Terileptils, the Borad, the Bannermen and the Master in San Francisco on New Year's Eve 1999."[35]

Despite these assurances, some fans felt that the BBC resurrection of the series should continue the adventures of the eighth Doctor as played by Paul McGann. Some, even, pointing to Christopher Eccleston's starring role in another Russell T. Davies drama, *The Second Coming*, thought the fix was in. One rec.arts.drwho poster was happy that filming would not start until July 2004 because it meant there was, "plenty of time to 'sabotage' things so that we get a TV series with the brilliant 8th Doctor, and not the unnecessary 9th Doctor. Is Chris' casting just nepotism? While I'm sure that Russell knows and understands Doctor Who, I find it hard to think of Chris as being even remotely Doctorish."[36] Subsequent posters to this thread pointed out that few of the previous actors who portrayed the Doctor appeared "Doctorish" before their stories aired. Most fans on rec.arts.drwho were enthusiastic about Eccleston's potential as the ninth Doctor.

Russell T. Davies's previous work was also a stumbling block to some fans as they anticipated the return of *Doctor Who*. The 1996 movie had been the product of a vast number of creative minds — multiple scriptwriters, storyliners, and producers from the Fox network and BBC. The 2005 revival, on the other hand, was under the creative control of Davies. Davies had a high media profile from his television writing, leading to an enormous amount of scrutiny of this past work. Not surprisingly, fans set to analyzing Davies's 1996 *New Adventures* novel *Damaged Goods*, scrutinizing this novel for clues to how the new series might develop. Mark Gary, writing on rec.arts.drwho, expressed worry at what the novel suggested for the future of the show:

> I just recently re-read "Damaged Goods" and found it largely enjoyable, but was uncomfortable with some of it, as it did go outside of some of the Doctor Who boundaries. I therefore hope that the BBC keep some sort of control on what Mr. Davies is going to write. I don't want a Doctor Who story with "politics" and "issues" in the mistaken belief that makes it somehow relevant to the audience. Leave that for the books. I want a superb Doctor Who romp in time and space with aliens, baddies and mad scientists getting their collective buts [sic] kicked (not literally though) by the good Doctor.[37]

Mark Gary's argument is framed, as many are many positions that concerned fan expectations for the future, in terms of a specific vision of what *Doctor Who* is, or should be. *Doctor Who* is a "romp"—lighthearted and fun—with specific, predictable goals. There should exist a clearly defined villain who should, of course, fall victim to the Doctor's cunning and wit. Further along in the same discussion thread, Gary pointed to a scene in *Damaged Goods* which hint at homosexual activity between two characters (one of whom is the Doctor's companion, Chris) and also to Davies's work on the groundbreaking series *Queer as Folk* as warning signs that his *Doctor Who* revival would not be in the proper vein.

Fans also scrutinized Russell T. Davies's own sexual orientation — seemingly showcased in *Queer as Folk*. Quoting an interview in which Davies warned fans, "Don't assume that the Doctor can never have sex. I'm not saying anything and you will have to wait and see how he develops. But he can always change. We shouldn't assume the character cannot change in some ways." Alan S. Wales, posting on rec.arts.drwho, argued:

> Now, this is absolutely the wrong direction to take the Doctor, IMO. It doesn't matter if the Doctor has sex with a woman, a man, or Sil, it would be wrong. The asexual nature of the Doctor is one part of his character that should not be tampered with. I understand that Davies is gay. In light of this fact and his statement above, I sincerely hope that this facet of his personality doesn't make an appearance in the new series, especially with regards to the Doctor's character.[38]

Even apart from the dismissal of Davies's sexuality as "a facet of his personality," there is an undercurrent of homophobia surrounding this critique of an aspect of a television series that did not yet exist. Wales believes that the one of the crucial aspects of the Doctor's character is his asexuality. What threatens that status quo is not simply Davies's assertion that the Doctor could be a sexual creature but Davies's own homosexuality. Further along this same discussion thread, user "Andy" questioned Wales's motives in posting, writing, "What is it about being gay that disturbs people so much? Why does it make you think Davies will insinuate sexual propaganda into a family show? Why don't you think straight writers will do the same thing?"[39] From that point, the thread descended into a flame war over the original poster's homophobia and becomes less useful as a source of fan opinion on the new series.

Like the previous revival of *Doctor Who*, fan concerns over the BBC's 2005 relaunch (at least as reflected in postings at rec.arts.drwho) tended to revolve around notions of what "*Doctor Who*" meant — what makes the show *their* show? Unlike the situation in 1996, many fans were more willing to loosen the reins on specific connections to the original 26 seasons of the show. This is unsurprising since, by 2005, there were a number of narrative strands that fans could consider the rightful heir to the *Doctor Who* story. The search for a new *Doctor Who* master narrative might end with the new series, but only if it was successful. The show needed a fresh start, connected to the past, but not fannishly enslaved to it. Another significant difference between the anticipation for new *Doctor Who* in 1996 and 2005 is the degree to which fans believed they could get inside the mind of Russell T. Davies, through scrutinizing his previous work and even his sexuality.

Fan reaction to "Rose," the first episode of the Russell T. Davies–produced *Doctor Who*, reflected many of the same concerns that appeared in the months leading up to its broadcast such as the new series' place in the *Doctor Who* world, the suitability of Christopher Eccleston to the lead role, and the infiltration of sexuality and politics into the show. Although the concerns of fans during the period between the announcement and the broadcast of the show, were similar to those expressed as the 1996 Fox movie approached, there were some significant differences in the reactions.

One of the crucial differences between 1996 and 2005 is that the new *Doctor Who* was launched as a series — no matter what happened, there would be something coming after "Rose." Unlike 1996, there was no drawn-out suspense over whether or not there would be new *Doctor Who* with the new Doctor. The 2005 incarnation was not a one-off but rather a fully-fledged series. Many fans, such as rec.arts.drwho poster "Nightspirit," whose post "My Review of Doctor Who 27x01," sets "Rose" as the new series, a direct continuation of the old, down to the subject line, which imagines the new series as the next season of *Doctor Who*, as if the gap between 1989 and 2005 was a routine hiatus. Nightspirit's review of "Rose" bore out the position that the new series and the old series were contiguous parts of the narrative, claiming that "even though this episode is rushed it shows there is a good faith effort to be true to the original."[40] Assessment of entertainment-value, in fan reviews of "Rose," is sublimated to determinations of the episode's place in the *Doctor Who* saga. Often, as with the 1996 Fox movie fan-reviewers judge actions, characters, and bits of dialogue in terms of their relation to what has come before.

Nightspirit's review of "Rose" does just that in its assessment of Christopher Eccleston's ninth Doctor: "When he peeked back outside the TARDIS at the end and said to Rose 'Did I mention it travels in time?' I laughed because that was a Baker moment if there ever was though his expressions made him look more like Peter Davison than Baker."[41] While, on the one hand, defining character touches such as this in terms of previous *Doctor Who* stories may serve to cement the series in a hidebound past, it is also a way of designating a kind of "fannish" cache. This, the fan seem to say, is worthy of being called *Doctor Who*, because this line is just the sort of thing Tom Baker would say. Also worth noting is Nightspirit's use of "Tom Baker" rather than "the fourth Doctor." Just as the show becomes sublimated to its own legacy, actors become sublimated to the roles they play. Unlike Nightspirit, rec.arts.drwho poster L. Ross Raszewski claimed that "Eccleston plays a very interesting and fun character. But he's not yet the Doctor, and I'm not convinced that he *can* be."[42] Thus, in the mind of Raszewski, and other fans, an actor does not portray the Doctor but rather becomes him. While a disinterested critic of the show might have argued that Christopher Eccleston became the Doctor as soon as the appropriate contracts were signed, fan critics tended to meld the production, actors, and legacy of *Doctor Who* into a whole.

Adding to the concern over continuity with the classic series as well as the 1996 Fox movie was the question of regeneration. As noted above, many fans questioned how the show would introduce the new Doctor. When "Rose" aired with no overt indication of how, viewers looked for signs that the show's creative team had bent the narrative knee to the fundamental *Doctor Who* convention of regeneration. One rec.arts.drwho poster wrote, "I think [the Doctor] must have very recently regenerated. Throughout the episode he seemed like he was still a bit delierious [sic] from the transformation — like Tom Baker was after he was introduced."[43] Another poster agreed, saying, "I also got the impression that he'd only recently regenerated. Apart from seeing his reflection for the first time, there was also the bit with the cards, where he first thinks he has become an expert manipulator, then loses them." Russell T. Davies left a deliberate and noticeable gap between the 1996 television movie and "Rose." While the Doctor shown on screen is the ninth Doctor, a direct continuation of the character and narrative that has come before, this gap allowed fans to slot in whichever of the eighth Doctor's post-movie activities they liked. If the fans did not follow the eighth Doctor spinoff adventures, then they could just assume that the Doctor had regenerated at some point. Crucially, however, the unreferenced regeneration lowered the barrier for casual viewers whose appreciation was vital for the continued success of the show.

Production decisions (as opposed to issues of characters and narrative) such as the design of the opening titles also served as a base of comparison to the original series. Poster "The Unnaturalist" found the new title sequence graphics to be inferior to those of the past:

> First of all we have the new titles, which I found slightly unoriginal in that it is just an updated version of the old slit scan going down a tunnel idea (apart from the brief moment where the TARDIS materialises into real space), presumably showing the TARDIS' flight through the time/space vortex. I might have preferred something more abstract; weird shapes that morph, like a constantly evolving Rorschach inkblot. Something more like the original "howlaround" titles from the 60s maybe.

Interestingly, "The Unnaturalist" criticized the new title graphics as being derivative of those of the 1970s while expressing the belief that the titles should have been derivative of the 1960s. Similarly, fan Mike Morris found "Rose" to look "reassuringly cheap; for all the protestations to the contrary, the fact remains that 'Rose' ... doesn't look any more expensive than, say, 'Ghost Light' or 'The Curse of Fenric.'" *Doctor Who*'s budget restrictions and the oft-ridiculed visual deficits that resulted are a mark of quality, of true *Doctor Who*–ness. While this is a conscious call-back to the atmosphere of the original series, one could also read it as a veiled criticism of the 1996 Fox movie. Glossiness and special effects, traditionally, were not things most fans associated with the show. The restraint producers used in the style of "Rose" allowed them to emphasize what *Doctor Who* has always been best at. As Morris said, "Part of the reason that Doctor Who works is that it can't rely on visuals — it has to rely on good storytelling and dialogue."[44] *Doctor Who*'s hallmarks are story and character. "Rose" had these, while the Fox movie was lacking.

This notion of viewer accessibility was also a concern of *Doctor Who* fans leading up to "Rose." The 1996 movie had failed to catch on with viewers to the degree necessary to launch a new series. The compact, 45-minute quick paced "Rose" would prove more successful. Not all fans thought this was an appropriate format for the show. One fan wrote

> I realise that they wanted to eliminate the episodic format and go for a more Star Trek pace, but I think they lost something in the process. There is no build up of the story, no time for atmosphere or setting the scene (which the Episode 1s of the old series were adored for).[45]

Other fan reviewers privileged accessibility over intricacies of plot. Mike Morris's comments, written two weeks after "Rose" reflects this view, comparing the episode to the fourth Doctor's swan song, "Logopolis":

> Yes, Logopolis has a very rickety plot. Yes, Rose barely manages to tell a coherent alien invasion story. And the truth is that neither of those things matter all that much. They aren't the primary purpose of those stories. In truth, this was a salutary lesson in how to re-establish the Doctor as a character. Just as the telemovie fell into almost every trap imaginable, this one neatly avoided all of them.[46]

These traps included starting the show with a regeneration and over-explaining every aspect of the show's history — similar to the charges some fans laid against the Fox movie after it failed to launch an ongoing series.

"Rose" was a success, as were the subsequent episodes of that first series of Russell T. Davies's *Doctor Who*. The series ended on a regeneration introducing the tenth Doctor and would continue to high ratings, critical acclaim, awards, and, for the most part, fan satisfaction. Fan *dis*satisfaction would often stem from a conviction that the show played too strongly for a casual audience, providing loosely plotted stories and whiz-bang paciness to keep people watching. Like "Rose," subsequent episodes of the show were not designed with fans exclusively in mind. Continuity with the original run of *Doctor Who* was kept to a minimum and enjoyment of the over-arching plot of the new series did not depend on prior knowledge of the show's decades-long history. Unlike the 1996 Fox movie, the Russell T. Davies series, from its beginning in "Rose" was able to adequately address fan concerns — continuity with the past in particular — while establishing a strong collection with the viewing public of Britain.

Throughout the period from 1990 to 2005, unorganized *Doctor Who* fandom, in particular, the fans inhabiting discursive spaces on the Internet, attempted to define a cohesive master narrative for the show. Spin-off novels, comic strips and, later, officially licensed audio dramas featuring cast members from the show failed to unify the multiple strands of *Doctor Who*'s narrative and provide a unifying force for fandom as had the show's original twenty-six seasons of televised adventures.

During these fifteen years in the wilderness, an opportunity arose to unify fandom under a new Doctor and new ongoing television adventures. The 1996 Fox television movie failed to do so despite superficially catering to many of the concerns fans held about new *Doctor Who*. The story featured a regeneration scene from the seventh to eighth Doctors; it had numerous references to the previous history of the show; the new Doctor's personality seemed appropriately "Doctorish." There were problems, of course, the most glaring being the Doctor's newfound heterosexual tendencies. The 1996 movie, for the most part, fit. It was *Doctor Who* — updated, a bit American, perhaps, but still recognizably the show the fans loved. During the period following the news that this "backdoor pilot" would not be continued as an ongoing series, *Doctor Who* fandom split further between book fans, audio fans, comic strip fans, and fans who eschewed all the spinoffs in favor of re-evaluating the increasingly available classic shows on VHS and, later, DVD.

In contrast, "Rose," the premier episode of the 2005 BBC relaunch of the show, sacrificed tight continuity to *Doctor Who*'s direct past in order to lower the bar of accessibility to casual viewers. The 2005 *Doctor Who* revival positioned the show self-consciously as family viewing rather than a cult/science fiction show. While some fan reviewers lamented the advent of self-contained 45-minute episodes, the new series fit into television of the twenty-first century. Commercially and critically, the new series has been a success and has done far more than the 1996 Fox movie to unify fandom under a new master narrative. The BBC novel series ended, then rebooted in 2005 with stories featuring the current Doctors in stories which slot in between the televised adventures. The audio adventures featuring the fifth, sixth, seventh, and eighth Doctors from Big Finish productions continue but are firmly entrenched as fan-targeted as opposed to attempting to appeal to a wide audience.

Doctor Who is, indeed, back. In different ways, the 1996 Fox movie and 2005's "Rose" both met and confounded fan expectations, carrying on a delicate balancing act between appealing to fans and appealing to a wider audience. "Rose" succeeded where the previous effort failed by appealing to casual viewers while leaving enough tantalizing gaps that long-time fans kept watching, longing for the show to fill in those missing links in the narrative. It was recognizably *Doctor Who*, but it was also recognizably modern, entertaining, and engaging enough to ensure that viewers would return in numbers great enough to guarantee success.

NOTES

1. Lawrence Miles and Tat Wood, *About Time: The Unauthorized Guide to Doctor Who,* volume 5 (Des Moines: Mad Norwegian Press, 2005): p. 315.

2. TachyonTV Podcast, 30 August 2007.

3. Derek Johnson, "Fan-Tagonism: Factions, Institutions, and Constituitive Hegemonies of Fandom," in Gray, et al., *Fandom: Identities and Communities in a Mediated World* (New York: NYU Press, 2007): pp. 285–286.

4. This tagline appeared on the back cover of *New Adventures* from *Timewyrm: Genesys* (1991) to *Cat's Cradle: Witchmark* (1992).

5. Matthew Sadler, "Controversy: Against," *Broadsword,* Issue 6, http://web.archive.org/web/1997010 1125834/modjadji.anu.edu.au/steve/broadsword/issue6/debate6.html (12 January, 2011).

6. Richard Prekodravac, "Controversy: Positive" *Broadsword,* Issue 6, http://web.archive.org/web/ 19970101125834/modjadji.anu.edu.au/steve/broadsword/issue6/debate6.html (12 January 2011).

7. Nathan Bottomley, "Interview with Paul Cornell," *Broadsword,* Issue 3, http://www.sorddin.com/broadsword-old/issue3/interview3.html (12 January 2011).

8. "Letters to the Editor," *Doctor Who Magazine,* Issue 240, 23 October 1996: p. 34.

9. Sascha Segan, "R.I.P Usenet: 1980–2008," *PC Magazine,* 31 July 2008, p. 2 (8 May 2011).

10. "The Admiral," "re: Canonical New Adventures?" 9 December 1993. Online Posting. Newsgroup rec.arts.drwho. Usenet (13 January 2011).

11. Gary Gillatt, "Executive Decisions," *Doctor Who Magazine,* 3 July 1996, pp. 6–10.

12. *Ibid.*

13. Fans would quote Segal as using this phrase throughout the months leading up to the May 1996 premier. Segal himself used this phrase first during a panel at Gallifrey One convention in Los Angeles in February 1996. Rec.arts.drwho poster "TaylorCSUN" supplied one of the most compete reports of this appearance ("TaylorCSUN," "NEWS from Mr Segal/Gallifrey One (SPOILERS AT THE END)," 17 February 1996. Online posting. Newsgroup rec.arts.drwho. Usenet (3 August 2011).

14. Robert G. Cole, "Continuity — New Movie & BBC Series," 8 June 1995. Online posting. Newsgroup rec.arts.drwho. Usenet (12 January 2011).

15. Ian J. Davenport, "Re: Continuity — New Movie & BBC Series," 20 June 1995. Online posting. Newsgroup rec.arts.drwho. Usenet (12 January 2011).

16. "Davros," "Will the movie with the new dweeb include a regeneration?" 14 April 1996. Online posting. Newsgroup rec.arts.drwho. Usenet (12 January 2011).

17. Andy Williams, "The new regeneration: who/what will feature?" 27 February 1996. Online posting. Newsgroup rec.arts.drwho. Usenet (12 January 2011).

18. *Doctor Who,* Fox, WFTT, Fort Wayne, Indiana, May 14, 1996.

19. Lance Parkin, "The Nth Doctor," *Matrix,* No. 54, Summer 1996, in Parkin, *Time Unincorporated: The Doctor Who Fanzine Archives,* volume 1 (Des Moines: Mad Norwegian Press, 2009): p. 126.

20. Alan Toombs, "Style and Content," 2 June 1996. Online Posting. Newsgroup rec.arts.drwho. Usenet (13 January 2011).

21. Sean Gaffney, "The Movie: Review by the Happy Guy," 20 May 1996. Online Posting. Newsgroup rec.arts.drwho. Usenet (13 January 2011).

22. Angus Gulliver, "Re: The Movie: Review by the Happy Guy," 23 May 1996. Online Posting. Newsgroup rec.arts.drwho. Usenet (13 January 2011).

23. "GLC," "The Kiss Fine But Opening Absolutely Unpleasant." 15 May 1996. Online Posting. Newsgroup rec.arts.drwho. Usenet (13 January 2011).

24. Lyn Eades, "The time to act is NOW! (warning long posting, no spoilers!)," 16 May 1996. Online posting. Newsgroup rec.arts.drwho. Usenet (13 January 2011).

25. Edwin Patterson, "Re-Evaluating the TV Movie," *Time Space Visualizer,* No. 49, archived at http://nzdwfc.tetrap.com/archive/tsv49/tvmovie.html (10 January 2011).

26. Michael Warner, "Introduction: Fear of a Queer Planet," *Social Text* 29 (1991): pp. 3–17.

27. Matt Jones, "Not Even Close....," *Doctor Who Magazine*, Issue 240, 23 October 1996: p. 43.

28. Ed Hagan, "Why does the gay community love Doctor Who?" 25 June 2007. Web (22 February 2011).

29. Guy Wigmore, "William Keith's Ministry of Love," *Silver Carrier*, Number 9, in Paul Cornell, ed., *Licence Denied: Rumblings from the Doctor Who Underground* (London: Virgin, 1997): p. 60.

30. Lance Parkin, "A 40 Year Adventure in Time and Space," in Parkin, *Time Unincorporated*: p. 63.

31. "'Flatley, my Dear, I don't Riverdance.' Can the Original Stories and Big Finish be considered Canon." 17 March 2003. Online Posting. Newsgroup rec.arts.drwho. Usenet (24 April 2011).

32. John L. Beven, "Re: Firing the Canon," 7 October 1998. Online Posting. Newsgroup rec.arts.drwho. Usenet (24 April 2011).

33. Parkin, pp. 157–158.

34. Aaron Pynn, "Is the new seies [sic] a continuation or a Reinvention???" 29 September 2004. Online Posting. rec.arts.drwho. Usenet (6 May 2011).

35. Russell T. Davies, "Production Notes #4: Think of a Number," *Doctor Who Magazine*, Issue 344, 23 June 2004: p. 45.

36. Duncan Corps, "Re: Ecclestone says," 2 April 2004. Online Posting. rec.arts.drwho. Usenet (1 May 2011).

37. Mark Gary, "Russel T. Davies," 27 September 2003. Online Posting. Rec.arts.drwho. Usenet (1 May 2011).

38. Alan S. Wales, "The New Doctor and Sex," 17 March 2004. Online Posting. Rec.arts.drwho. Usenet (1 May 2011).

39. "Andy," "Re: The New Doctor and Sex," 17 March 2004. Online Posting. Rec.arts.drwho. Usenet (1 May 2011).

40. "Nightspirit," "My Review of Doctor Who 27x01," 26 March 2005. Online Posting. rec.arts.drwho. Usenet (4 April 2011).

41. *Ibid.*

42. L. Ross Raszewski, "Re: My Review of Doctor Who 27x01," 27 March 2005. Online Posting. rec.arts.drwho. Usenet (4 April 2011).

43. Sean Huxter, "Re: In-Depth analysis of Rose (Spoiler City!)" 27 March 2005. Online Posting. rec.arts.drwho. Usenet (4 April 2011).

44. Mike Morris, "He's Back and It's About Right," Collection of Rose Reviews. 1 April 2005. Web. http://www.pagefillers.com/dwrg/rose.htm (21 May 2011).

45. Andrew Feryok, "We've Missed You!" Collection of Rose Reviews," 4 April 2005. Web. http://www.pagefillers.com/dwrg/rose.htm (21 May 2011).

46. Mike, Morris, "He's Back and It's About Right," Collection of Rose Reviews. 1 April 2005. Web. http://www.pagefillers.com/dwrg/rose.htm (21 May 2011).

4

Whose Doctor?[1]

J.M. Frey

One of the things that first struck me upon watching the new *Doctor Who* was the fact that when the Doctor visited North America, it was generally to grace with his presence New York. The Doctor completely ignored Canada, my home and native land. The question that I asked myself was "Why?" for a unique relationship exists between the Land of the Maple Leaf and *Doctor Who*. Canadian television benefits from its commonwealth relationship with Great Britain and vice versa: they import and export each other's programs and documentaries, films and filmmakers, post-graduate students and teachers, techies and technology.[2] The Canadian Broadcasting Company and the British Broadcasting Company occasionally work in tandem on a single project, co-producing series or films, or offering tax breaks for on-location productions to each other. For the first three seasons of Russell T. Davies' *Doctor Who* series and the first season of *Torchwood* a percentage of its funding was provided by the Canadian taxpayers, enough to earn the Canadian Broadcasting Corporation a co-production credit.[3] But the unique relationship with Canada goes back further: the Doctor may be half human and half Gallifreyian, but the human side is at least partially Canadian.

Sydney Cecil Newman, a Canadian-born film and television producer, was the BBC head of drama in April of 1963, when *Doctor Who* first aired, and played an integral part in its inception. Also, in the 2006 episode "Army of Ghosts," Yvonne Hartman, head of the Torchwood Institute, explains to Jackie Tyler that Torchwood exists to protect Queen, Country, and the British Empire, which could be interpreted to mean that the Empire secretly still exits — and considering the colonialist narratives with which *Torchwood* is rife, it is distinctly possible.[4]

But if a Canadian put the dream on the screen, Canadian money pays for it, and Canada is still a part of the imagined British Empire, where is the Canadian talent? None of the current characters, actors, or artistic team on BBC's most legendary sci-fi series is noticeably Canadian, and the Doctor never visits Canada. Also, treatment of the Canadian heritage of *Doctor Who* by both the BBC and academia to date has been seasoned with colonialist slant: the "Canadianness" of the series is generally ignored, silenced, written out, or subjugated. In fact, the colonialistic writing out of Newman and any Canadianness in the genesis narratives of the program are mirrored in the colonialism displayed by the Torchwood institute and the new production: while Canada remains a source of resources (natural for the Empire, monetary for the BBC), it is still marginalized and unrecognized for its contributions, and nearly completely fails to be portrayed.

I propose to acknowledge this slant, and highlight the Canadian contributions in the origin narratives and on-screen stories and in doing so attempt to break the colonialist hold on the program. To that end, this essay investigates the toque-clad history of *Who*, the colonialism that the new *Who* propagates, and how the essence of *Doctor Who* conforms to the agreed-upon popular definition of "Canadian art" in terms of its narratives. In short, how it would be a benefit for everyone on both sides of the pond if there was a little more maple syrup in the *Doctor's* tea.

Canadian by Birth: Sydney Cecil Newman

Canadian-born Sydney Cecil Newman was the producer in charge of the BBC's drama department in 1962 when he was informed that a program had to be created for the teatime slot between *Grandstand* and *Juke Box Jury.*[5] Newman wanted a family-oriented program that would keep the viewers who had tuned in for the football scores to stay, and to get those intent on the pop music to tune in earlier. While the BBC had commissioned earlier investigations into producing a science fiction serial,[6] even so far as to establishing the archetypal quartet of main characters optimal for inspiring a "loyalty" audience of continuous viewers, it wasn't until Newman that the program came into being. This program, he decided, should be quintessentially Newman-esque. That is, like his previous serials, this new program should be educational, but painlessly so; entertaining but with high moral standards; reflect contemporary issues and ethics; dramatize history; make science fun and fascinating; speculate on the future of human society, and evolve with the television technology as it became available; a series that reflects the viewer back at him or herself. And, as a twist, it would be a series about a "crotchety old man ... at least 745 years old."[7] This was *Doctor Who*.

To understand how absolutely vital to the shape and mandates of *Doctor Who* the experiences and opinions of its creator were, we must understand Newman's career, his artistic aims, and the work he did that led up to laying the foundation for *Doctor Who*. It is a program that reflects the 1960s Canadian broadcasting ethic so perfectly it is almost a wonder that time and circumstance made it a British program at all.

Newman was born in Toronto, Ontario, in 1917,[8] and worked his way up through the ranks at the Canadian Broadcasting Corporation, apprenticing "under documentary film pioneer John Grierson at the National Film Board of Canada before moving onto the role of supervising producer of Drama at the [CBC] in the 1950s."[9] There, he worked as an on-staff producer, supervising writing for both topical and commercial drama anthologies, focusing mainly on adapting stage plays to the camera.[10] He also supervised the creation of new anthologies that fulfilled his preference for increasingly contemporary-slanted work.

It was an effort to retain and define the Canadian voice in an era when television was new and there was a scramble to fill time on the airwaves. American programming was beginning to leak north of the border, threatening Canada's embryonic attempts to define its own broadcasting culture, and its inspiration for forming, the BBC, had already set a high precedent in quality standards. Newman believed that representing Canadians on television, or in dramatic situations, seemed to be the best way to make the CBC attractive to Canadian viewers,[11] which eventually became a central tenant of the CBC's broadcasting mandates. Like many practitioners in early Canadian television culture, Newman preferred original stories written directly for television rather than rehashing tired classical of the stage and literature, and championed the development of new talent. Newman had a veritable shopping list of preferences for his productions: he preferred Canadian characters and settings and Canadian key creative personnel, including writers; he favored fledgling producers, directors, and actors in an effort to develop and work-shop new talent, as well as new technicians and techniques; he offered these newcomers chances to experiment beyond the American filmic formulae.

Newman's approach to his broadcasting ethos closely mirrors that of John Reith, the first general manager and director of the BBC; it is probable that Newman's own dedication to education, quality and entertainment may stem directly from Reithianism, though it could have as easily been the result of a cultural zeitgeist in television creation.[12] Either way, as many television critics deride the Reithian model for being elitist and monoculturalistic, if Newman actually did pattern his own preferences on Reithianism, it surly was with Canada's multicultural social landscape in mind.

At this time the original CBC programs, such as *The CBC Television Theatre* (1953–57), were considered adventurous and bold in their steady weekly creation of new material, and also for setting stories outside of the familiar "drawing room drama" theatrical convention. Impressed, the BBC began purchasing CBC kinescopes, sight unseen, for airing in Great Britain.[13] While at the CBC, Newman contributed heavily in the development of the "docu-drama" genre: period stories based on actual events, persons and situations, but dramatized in such a way as to be entertaining, informative and educational.[14] Newman also helped devise and was partially responsible, as supervising producer, on *Space Command*, a series fusing science fiction with education, staring a pre–*Star Trek* James Doohan and William Shatner.[15] (*Space Command* could feasibly be called *Doctor Who's* older, albeit less successful, brother.) By the time *Doctor Who* was conceived, Newman had previous experience fusing sci-fi, historical, documentary and educational genres. Already the roots of *Doctor Who's* mandates were germinating: entertain and educate, make history come alive, make knowledge accessible and intriguing, and give new artists a chance to prove themselves.

Newman's reputation as a desirable, innovative producer spread and Granada, "most innovative of British commercial television networks" at the time, imported Newman to spice up their programming in 1958.[16] Newman next transferred to the Associated British Corporation, an offshoot of ITV, and produced the wildly popular *Armchair Theatre* and *The Avengers*. According to rumor, he was then offered the role of head of drama at the BBC while drinking in a pub. Shaun Sutton inherited the BBC's head of drama position from Newman decades later, and says that when he arrived at the Station, Newman was "redoubtable, rambunctious, full-blooded ... [Newman] burst into BBC drama at its moment of expansion, seized the opportunity and set a match to a dramatic bonfire that has warmed us all since."[17] British television drama reached its peak after its Canadian counterpart, and Newman is directly credited for the success. In part, because Newman introduced new theatrical and playwriting voices to the camera, voices like Alun Owen, Harold Pinter, and Clive Exton.

BBC writers under Newman enjoyed an influence over their scripts and a collaboration with the creative processes that was virtually absent in the other broadcasting models of the era.[18] Newman's desire was to tap into the growing audience of middle class working families. They were purchasing television sets in fantastic numbers, and Newman sought to find a way to speak to the audience as a whole despite cultural and class differences, as he had with multicultural Canada. Newman provoked dinner table conversation with programs that were recognizable and relevant, but innovative and entertaining enough to keep people tuning in week after week.[19] In *Doctor Who,* the audience-surrogate characters, Susan Foreman, Ian and Barbara, hail from Coal Hill School, a familiar and unlovely building "uniquely like the schools the bulk of *Doctor Who*'s young audience actually attended. The [Coal Hill] sequences anchor [it] in a reality" that spoke to its viewers on their level.[20] Former *Doctor Who* supervising script editor Andrew Cartmel suggests that Newman may even have had a direct hand in the creation of the eerily and effectively alien opening scenes of the first episode.[21] Filming also required significant technological advancements or work-arounds in order for each story to be televised or created realistically enough to convince the audience that they were indeed on Mars, in pre-history, or anywhere beyond a studio or quarry. As an example — multi-track recording and playback systems had to be invented and engineered specifically to record *Doctor Who*'s theme.[22]

Of course, any *Doctor Who* enthusiast worth his or her salt knows that while *Doctor Who* did achieve all of Newman's broadcasting aims, the largest reason for its popularity can be reduced to one word: Daleks.

One such enthusiast, and member of the Doctor Who Information Network, Graeme Burk explains that "the original conception of *Doctor Who* was to be something that taught kids something about history and it taught kids something about science. And that quickly broke down, [in the] the first season, after Verity Lambert took over."[23] In the documentary *The Planet of the Doctor*, Lambert explains that she first worked with Newman at ABC on *Armchair Theatre* as a Production Assistant. When he transferred to BBC, Newman offered Lambert a chance to produce *Doctor Who*. Lambert admits that Newman

> used to get quite cross at [her], because the serials from the future were supposed to be scientific, and have some kind of scientific basis. And since science was not one of [her] best subjects at school [she] think[s] they were more imaginative than scientific. In fact, when [they] did the first Dalek serial, Sydney was really quite furious. Because he had said to [Lambert] at the beginning, "Now Verity, the one thing I do not want are Bug Eyed Monsters."[24]

Airing for the first time the day after the assassination of John F. Kennedy, *Doctor Who* became an international phenomenon, and the longest running science fiction serial in the history of television,[25] partially because of those very Bug Eyed Monsters. Burk explains that the "first Dalek Story pretty much signaled [the educational factor's] abandonment," and the popularity of the BEM was a "damning indictment of the show Newman wanted to produce. The one that caught on with the British public. And Newman got that. He told Lambert, "you obviously understand this better than me," and let her get on with it.[26]

While the Daleks are considered the main reason why *Doctor Who* initially garnered a large fanbase, the "key to [its] longevity ... has been its format, which has proved malleable enough to respond flexibly to both changing broadcasting ecologies and to cultural determinants from inside and outside the BBC."[27] It became a text of its time, an "arena for exploring emerging issues in British life"[28] (as Newman had done with *The CBC Television Theatre*), offering commentaries on the present by addressing current issues in futuristic settings, as classic sci-fi must.

Newman returned to Canada in 1970, but his return marked the beginning of a period of decline in his career. For a few months in 1970 he was the director of the Canadian Radio Television and Telecommunications Commission (CRTC).[29] The CRTC is a governing body that defines and regulates Canadian content laws, dictating what percentage of content aired in Canada must be written, produced, presented, or otherwise contributed to by Canadians and in which amounts, or feature cultural and creative content that is definitively Canadian. But Newman's tenure was mired in controversy, especially over his inability to connect to French Canadian filmmakers.[30] He was head of the National Film Board[31] from 1970 to 1978, and from then on he changed positions frequently in the next decade. On October 6, 1986, he was asked for advice by then-controller of BBC 1 Micheal Grade on how to regenerate the lagging *Doctor Who*. Newman asked to be put back in control of the series as executive producer. The subsequent meeting with the BBC head of drama Jonathan Powell did not go well, and Newman withdrew his request.[32] Newman also requested to have his name added to the series credits acknowledging him as the creator, but was denied by the acting head of series and serials, Ken Riddington, as department heads at the BBC aren't given such acknowledgements.[33] Burk says that "there is a lot of Newman's DNA in the show that can be celebrated and connected. The audience surrogate figure of the companion is down to Newman (and can be seen as a dramatic hook he took from his other work: the original *Avengers* uses a similar fish-out-of-water audience identification figure). The secular, inquisitive attitude to science and value of intelligence. And, in suggesting a 'cosmic hobo' character for Patrick Troughton's Doctor he helped foster the difference in incarnations of the Doctor. But *Doctor Who* hasn't been the program Newman created since December 1963 otherwise, I think."[34]

Whether fans believe the program still lives up to its original mandate or not, the genesis of *Doctor Who* in Newman's original blueprints cannot be denied. Therefore, I posit that *Doctor Who*'s popularity is due to those very things which only Newman and his particularly Canadian ethos could have imparted to the program[35]; the docu-drama quality, its artistic and technological experimentation, its edutainment mandate, and its willingness to reflect the audience back at themselves "series the revered placed [sic] in the pantheon of science fiction it enjoys.... By constantly whisking viewers away to weird and wonderful realms of imagination, *Doctor Who* continues to serve as a complex forum for advancing revolutionary ideas about life, the universe, and everything."[36]

Perhaps even the Doctor's desperate need to heal the universe and rebel against his Time Lord upbringing can be traced back to Newman, who resisted the lure of televising stodgy classics, just like the Doctor resisted falling in line with his homeworld's laws and traditions. Newman wielded his programs like scalpels, cutting into the heart of society, urging his audience to analyze what was revealed, to use the tools provided by his instruction question, just as the Doctor urges his Companions and viewers to explore the world, live life with eyes open, and fix what needs fixing, to help heal a wounded universe. Newman's uniquely Canadian views informed not only CBC and BBC programming during the height of their respective Drama Department's glory days, but served as the very foundation of *Doctor Who*, perhaps the foundation of the very Doctor himself. Like Newman, the Doctor revels in making education fun and interesting, in science, in meeting historical figures and humanizing them, in encouraging new thought, in training up new talent like Sarah Jane Smith the reporter, or Rose Tyler the freedom fighter, and in playing with new technologies.

One might even go so far as to stretch the metaphor and suggest that the Doctor is Sydney Newman's perfect fantasy avatar: his Mary Sue. Even the Doctor himself is Canadian in a way. From another culture and place, he has adopted Earth in general, and the United Kingdom in particular, as his home ground. His story —finding love, family, a place to take pride in, and something worth fighting for — closely matches the experience of many new Canadian immigrants. While Canada has a less than spectacular record in regards to the treatment of its First Nations Peoples, there is an ever growing effort to make amends and preserve the history of the land. Canada is still a place where multiculturalism is valued, and every Canadian — whether their ancestors traveled here in an airplane, steam or sailing ship, or along the Bering Strait — is encouraged to honor the customs and traditions of their heritage while finding a home under the colors of the Maple Leaf. The Doctor, too, chooses to be associated with Earth while keeping his Gallifreyian upbringing, and does his utmost to respect Earth's pre-established cultures.

Despite the gregarious relationship between the CBC and the BBC and the consistent swapping of writers and producers, no more Canadians followed in Newman's footsteps. Newman was awarded the prestigious Order of Canada in 1991, and passed away in Toronto in 1997.[37]

Unbeknownst to Newman, he did later get his creator's credit: in the 2007 episode "Human Nature" by Paul Cornell, the Doctor, as John Smith, tells Nurse Joan Redfern that his father's name was Sydney.

Canadian by Production: Canadian Interest, Locations, and Funds

Doctor Who's ties to Canada do not end with its creator. The program has benefited from Canadian co-production money, has been filmed on Canadian soil, and has had the support of not only Canadian fans, but also CBC staffers. Yet, overwhelmingly, the above ties are ignored or written out of production narratives, to the point where the exclusion resembles a sort of broadcast colonialism.

Accounts of the history and relaunch of *Doctor Who* overwhelmingly cite the locus of production as solely in the U.K., with the exception of a few location shots elsewhere in Europe. Yet, the rebooted program was not only funded by Canadian taxpayer money, there are also two other instances where the program was physically — if not narratively — within Canada itself. In the first instance, Canadian production company Nelvana, famous for animated children's edu-tainment television programs, pitched the idea for an animated steampunk-esque series after the 1989 cancellation of *Doctor Who.* However, after a year in development, the BBC withdrew rights, and both broadcasting corporations were left without its staple science fiction series for over a decade.[38] In the second instance, the 1996 made-for-TV-movie was filmed in Vancouver, BC (though set in San Francisco), and co-produced by Universal Television, BBC Television, BBC Worldwide, and Fox. It also failed to revive the series in England or attract new audience from the United States, where it was set and targeted. As a point of interest, television series, and overwhelmingly science fiction series such as *Highlander, Supernatural,* the *Stargate* franchise, etc., are set in the United States but are often filmed in the Vancouver area.

As well, the majority of press surrounding Davies' *Doctor Who,* significantly locate the production at the BBC Wales studio, and the production capital as coming from the BBC alone. Yet when Russell T. Davis sought to relaunch the *Doctor Who* franchise in 2004, the CBC provided him with funding in order to produce the program. The amount — which hearsay puts at approximately $1.3 million Canadian per season — was sufficient to earn the CBC a minority co-production credit for the first to third seasons of *Doctor Who,* and the first season of *Torchwood.* The money provided annually to the CBC comes from internal revenue and federal funding taken from taxes. Thus, each Canadian taxpayer imparted approximately $0.06 towards the show per season. The rebirth of *Doctor Who,* as with its genesis, was therefore supported by Canadians.

And, for the first season, the CBC's employee in charge of the property was Slakaw Kylmiw. A *Doctor Who* fan, Kylmiw oversaw a huge and successful advertising drive on the program's behalf in 2005.[39] The reintroduction of the Doctor to the CBC occurred at just the right moment for the Corporation: the National Hockey League had gone on strike and the CBC's viewership ratings were suffering as a result. Burk notes that "the ratings which were huge in 2005 and better than much of the CBC's domestic programming even in 2006 (200,000 viewers switched off after Doctor Who when the much bigger hyped *Rumours* came on)."[40]

However, even the CBC seems to be uninterested in toting its own co-pro show as Canadian. Once the NHL was back, and when Kylmiw left his position, the program slipped quickly into obscurity. "The level of enthusiasm from the CBC," says fan Andrew Gurudata, "was already visibly less than it had been the previous year. [There was] less promotion, less energy. And most disappointing for fans, perhaps, less information flow and contact between the CBC and [the fans] who were supporting the show."[41] Episodes were aired at new times with no advertising to indicate the change, with a six-week gap between "The Impossible Planet" and "The Satan Pit," and by the third season almost all advertising had ceased and the airing dates were so far behind the BBC that even the American broadcasting companies for whom the program was merely an acquisition had aired episodes before the CBC.[42] Rob Salem, entertainment correspondent for the *Toronto Star,* says that *Doctor Who* fans "regularly overflow [Salem's] email with desperate inquiries about when the CBC will get around to airing the reborn British sci-fi series' fourth season, particularly since it has already been seen in the States. Not to mention the fact that the Mothercorp actually owns a piece of the show."[43]

Eventually the "mothercorp" did begin airing the fourth season; September 9, 2008, but failed to air the cross-season Christmas episode "Voyage of the Damned." Any inquiries from viewers into this behavior was met with silence or a response that *Doctor Who* is an acquisition, not a co-production, and therefore no special attention to the program is obligated. Yet the episodes of seasons 1–3, when aired in Canada, continued to note in the credits that the program was a co-production, as did the Canadian press releases. Episodes aired in Britain do not note Canada's co-production status.

As a co-producer of the program, the CBC was entitled to air the episodes before its rival broadcasting corporations, an entitlement of which they were not taking advantage. There is a large fan base for the show in North America, a fan base that the CBC was not only failing to appease — though they had the means — but in mismanaging the property, actively alienating. This mismanagement went so far that when *Doctor Who* won a Constellation Award in SciFi Excellence for its contribution to Canadian science fiction in both 2007 and 2008, the CBC failed to send a representative to either ceremony — even though actor John Barrowman was in the city at the time under contract to the CBC for the Canadian version of *How Do You Solve a Problem Like Maria?* The CBC then failed to send the trophies to the appropriate persons at BBC Wales, instead forwarding them to BBC Worldwide, where they vanished.[44]

The bigger problem of the CBC's indifference to the program was that they had a ratings winner on which they had already spent a lot of money, yet aired as solid schedule filler instead of a program that could earn ratings and drive up advertising revenue. Canadian fans feel a special connection to the program because its *pater famillias* was a Canadian, and because they were informed during the end credits of every episode that it was their taxpayer money that partially funded it. Fans felt the CBC owed them to advertise and air the program to the best of its ability.[45] That there was (and still is) also no response from the CBC when fans, scholars, and critics attempt communication on the subject only furthers the frustration that fans feel with the CBC's handling of *Doctor Who*. Were the program to fall under Canadian content laws,[46] then the CBC would possibly have been more reliable in its advertising and airing of *Doctor Who*. However, even with funding from the CBC, a co-production credit, and a Canadian father, the *Doctor* does not qualify as "CanCon," and could not possibly do so without replacing the whole of the key creative staff with Canadians. Canadian fans, then, must turn their eyes back to the BBC and the Doctor for the acknowledgement for which we yearn.

Curiously, when the SyFy Network in the United States purchased the series in 2006 for airing, the BBC *Doctor Who* website featured a splash page featuring the Doctor and Rose in front of the American flag while the "Star Spangled Banner" played. "Admittedly, the purchase was important to American fans who had been clamouring for the series," Burk points out, "but it also felt like pandering to some level."[47] Di Rocco responded to the sale and SyFy's advertising by saying on his blog:

> Already we've had Executive Producer Julie Gardner mention on BBC radio how thrilled she was that Doctor Who has at last "made it across the pond" with the sale to the U.S. This has followed countless comments from fans (unfortunately, mainly British fans) to the effect that the series had not yet been seen across the Atlantic, not to mention a program that has never had a story set in Canada, on TV, radio, audio or even a full novel (this gives Canada the unfortunate distinction of being the only country that has had a Doctor Who story filmed on its land, but never had one set there). There has barely been any explicit Canadian characters in Doctor Who, leading fans to desperately clutch at characters like Mr. Huckle from Terror of the Zygons and proclaim them to be Canadians in a last-ditch effort to prove that Canada as a country exists in the Doctor Who world.[48]

Seeing as the Doctor is half–Canadian, and a portion of Davies' funding came from Canada, it may be expected that a Canadian serial would air. Yet, in all of his nine hundred-plus years of temporal and spatial wanderings, the Doctor has not visited Canada, nor has it been even shown in its entirety. There seems little indication from this vantage point of pre–*Torchwood: Miracle Day* that this serial, though shot and set in America, will ever venture to Canada either.

In an informal tally of which countries were visited, referred to, and shown, and their frequencies in the 2005–2008 series (both *Doctor Who* and *Torchwood*), I noted that the only references to Canada — six in total — were glimpses of the northern tip of Quebec during zoom-ins. Beyond the six brief glimpses in the rebooted series, there are also only six mentions of or references to Canada in the Classic series (see Appendix), and in *The Sarah Jane Adventures*, a program that does not receive funding from the CBC, there is an Ontario provincial license plate mounted on the wall of her attic lab,[49] and a mention to the "Dominion of Canada" in "Children of Earth: Day Four."

Professor James Chapman explains that this writing out of Canada is in all probability not deliberate, and that the real seed of the issue comes from

> the quaint convention of classic *Doctor Who* ... that alien invasion of the Earth invariably centres on London and the Home Counties — though the reason for this probably has more to do with production economies than it does with the strategic significance of south-eastern England.[50]

Davies further inflates this anxiety about the U.K.'s prestige by shifting the center of several important alien invasions and occurrences from Britain to the United States (New York

City, specifically) in the new series, effectively undermining not only Britain's role as a great power in the world, but solidifying it as a poor number two when Britain's own particular hero abandons them to save the citizens of NYC—in all its incarnations—instead. In the interest of balance, I do have to admit that *Doctor Who* has not exclusively privileged British history. Early episodes "The Reign of Terror," "The Myth Makers," "The Aztecs," and "Marco Polo" had the Doctor traveling the world.[51] Yet, this can be taken as further proof that the Doctor only seems interested in visiting places from which he did not hail: not only was Canada forgotten, but while the Doctor traveled Spain and Mexico, it would be several seasons before Gallifrey was named, let alone visited. This Britain-centric attitude reflects the Cold War tensions present at the time of the classic series airing, the sense of paranoia that accompanies a "nation vulnerable to alien ... invasion [which] proves unable to resist a technological superior force,"[52] and it also suggests a "perverse sense of national self-importance and prestige: as long as alien invaders deem in necessary to take over the British Isles as a prelude to their conquest of the Earth, the illusion of Britain as a great power is maintained."[53] The very Canadianness of the series, therefore, threatens this attitude and thus is erased in order to maintain this illusion.

I argue, however, that reincluding this missing element would not weaken the appeal of *Doctor Who* or its importance as the pinnacle of British science fiction, but rather add a facet of experience that more accurately reflects the program's genesis for its audience, and more directly reflects the Commonwealth from which it was born. The Doctor can be the timeless iconic symbol of British sci-fi *and* a hero on a quest to truly embrace the multicultural ethic that he champions amid the stars.

Canadian by Colonialism: Prejudice in New Who and Torchwood

This aggressive colonization of *Doctor Who* and the Britain-centric revisionist creation narratives also invade the episode texts. That *Torchwood* deals overwhelmingly with colonialist narratives supports Newman's prerogatives to both entertain and educate, and to promote multiculturalism. The question that arises, however, is how are these "other" people that these programs portray structured? Who, in *Who*, are the subalterns, who the colonizing force, and who the postcolonialists? *Doctor Who* continually challenges the binary of "us" and "them"; just as the Doctor challenges Rose, and therefore his audience, to open up and accept all species into her definition of "people" in the 2005 episode "The End of the World."[54]

Yet, there is continued evidence that, whether purposefully or not, instead of challenging the colonialist hegemony, both *Doctor Who* and *Torchwood* are in danger of reinforcing it. In the 2006 episode "Army of Ghosts," Yvonne Hartman regards the Doctor as the noble yet ignorant "Other," the colonized subaltern who, once captured, requires teaching, purifying, and initiation into the way things are done within Torchwood's Empire: the "right way." In the same episode, Hartman explains to Jackie Tyler that Torchwood exists to protect Queen, Country, and the British Empire. "There isn't a British Empire," Jackie protests. To which Hartman replies, "Not yet." What I think Hartman meant to say, if I may assume, is "There was, is, and will be again."[55] Hartman's behavior and attitude are positioned as negative—the Doctor and therefore the audience dislike her heavy handedness and ignorance—and yet there is no moment when Hartman is actually called out. And in Davies' *Who,* the colonies are narrowed to their most iconic city, New York, which stands in as not only a representation for the United States, but of the entirety of the North America. In colonialist literatures, the "New World" was often portrayed as a home to either the "ignorant, exotic redskins" or of the "quaint, moronic, low class colonial immigrants," "criminals," and "disgraced high society." The New York citizens of Davis' *Who* reflect this lingering colonialist stereotyping: low class burlesque dancer Tahllulah, the ragtag group of the Hoovervillians in Central Park,[56] the sociopath Luke Rattigan who poisons the sky with Atmos,[57] and even the con man Captain Jack Harkness. American in accent and despicable in ethics when he's first introduced, Harkness is a potential murderer, oversexed, morally loose, and in possession of a name and identity which he has stolen from a dead man,[58] and whose actions in the future towards exposing the original Harkness' homosexuality in front of his squad are, in all probability, what got him "accidentally killed" in a training exercise the next day.[59] All of these instances just further reinforce the colonialist narrative, whether intentionally or not.

As well, the original Torchwood Institute featured in the new *Who* was a colonizing, imperialistic force that forces its presence in situations with no contextual understanding with little concern for the culture, taboos, or conscious of the "other" which it colonizes. "If it's alien, it's ours" is the motto of the organization.[60] As an example: in the 2008 episode "Fragments," Torchwood Cardiff agents Emily and Alice capture time traveler and more importantly *American* Captain Jack Harkness—an exotic "other"; eroticized and attractive yet pitiable and ignorant—and forcibly indoctrinate him into employment at the Institute.[61] A "colonial discourse" is enacted upon him, a "discourse of colonial power which creates the world in which a colonized subject lives and acts ... denying agency to the native subject."[62] Harkness is, in essence, enslaved and brainwashed. It isn't until the eve of the year 2000 that Harkness is given back his agency. Director of Torchwood Cardiff, Alex, says it is his "gift for one hundred years service as a field operative" before blowing out his own brains.[63] Harkness, liberated, then retakes his agency and forces the organization into a period of post-colonialist restructuring. He explains that when "the old regime was destroyed at Canary Wharf. [Harkness] rebuilt [Torchwood], [he] changed it, and when [he] did that, [he] did it for [the Doctor], in [his] honour,"[64] in the Doctor's spirit of healing and multiculturalism. To be glib, Harkness attempts to force Canadianness back into the program.

Harkness is not, however, entirely successful. He pushes Torchwood away from its imperialistic past and into a binary-free future. Yet despite his best efforts, in the first episode of the series, his new team is shown to be shockingly imperialist—Toshiko Sato pillages technology for her own use, Owen Harper metaphorically rapes a pair of subalterns, and Suzie kills "meaningless" and "nobody" people in the pursuit of science and justifies the murders with her own moral and intellectual superiority.[65] This leads to a very different tone for *Torchwood* than Newman intended for *Doctor Who,* one that struggles in a more mature and realistic way with the multicultural, post-colonialistic affirmation of life that sprang from the Commonwealth ethos, but clashes with real world reaction to hegemony and culture. It is only with the addition of Gwen Cooper to Torchwood Cardiff that the lingering miasma of colonialism begins to dissipate fully. Her demand that the rest of the team see the victims and perpetrators as people, as human, sets her up as the "The Doctor" of the series and *Torchwood*'s Newman surrogate.

Torchwood begins down the road of Said's "contrapuntal" texts, where colonizer and colonized—Torchwood and Aliens and Colonialists—are considered together, deconstructing the binary opposition of "us" and "other" and creating a new multicultural "we" of mutual understanding and consideration.[66] Schuster and Powers say that "*Doctor Who* recognizes itself as a television program and is therefore capable of critiquing not only itself but its viewers as well ... it holds a mirror up to our ... lives and challenges us to prove ourselves better ... than the people we're watching"[67] which is a direct legacy of Newman's desires when it came to creating programming that makes the audience talk about what the audience lives. If only its very "Canadianness" could be similarly valued.

Maple Syrup in the Tea: Defining Canadian Art, and Proposing Its Presence in Doctor Who

Canadians have done great things for the world: we invented hockey, basketball and icewine, Velcro, snowmobiles, and telephones. Canada was at the helm of the Peacekeeping Corps, and won major battles for the allies in both world wars. Canada has given the world Celine Dion, Jim Carrey, Michael J. Fox, William Shatner, Christopher Plummer, Margaret Atwood, Margaret Laurence, and a hundred more singers, dancers, actors, artists, and writers that the world assumes are American. Joe Balsillie's Canadian tech company Research In Motion has changed the way the world accesses the internet and took the office to the street. And yet, in some small corner of our minds, Canada seems to us Canadians to still be the also-ran little brother; sweet, honest, forthright, but ultimately too polite and soft spoken to be capable of being a major player on the world stage. We live in constant fear of dribbling on our shirts.[68] That is why Canadians also fight so hard to point out what *is* Canadian and successful, to prove that we have what it takes to earn the same sort of respect as our self-important southerly neighbor, and to come out from under the shadow of our Commonwealth mother.

As a country filled predominantly with peoples whose own ancestors originated in another country and culture, and only a small handful of its First Peoples still practicing their own cultural and beliefs in the modern day, Canada has no singular "culture" on which to build the ramparts of its personal identity — rather, Canada is a miscellany of hundreds of belief systems, values, languages, cultures, and people and therefore cannot clearly define what "Canadian" is. Ask a Canadian, and he or she will give you a string of answers which are *nots*: Canada is not solely a nation of lumberjacks and beer drinkers, Canada is not the U.K. but it is also not the U.S. Canada is not a nation solely of First Peoples, but nor is it solely a nation of immigrants. Canada is not white. Canada is not colored. Canada is not solely one religion. Canada is a nation which defines its identity by what it is *not*, as it is impossible to pin-down, due to the surging and vibrant multiculturalism alive in the country, what it *is*.

I propose that Canada, therefore, can be defined as possessing what I call the Identity of Absence. If the Canadian national identity does exist, it is currently germinating, and that the identity of absence is a stop-gap measure for the present which allows Canadians to define themselves to the rest of the world while simultaneously attempting to cipher just how to describe itself to itself. Tentative about assigning labels and restrictions, Canada is also attempting to merge complete multiculturalism with national pride. It is unfortunately in a position where the only solid definition of Canada as a nation must rely on absence. What Canadians *are* has not yet had the opportunity to blossom. The dilemma is that in being everything to everyone Canada at the same time becomes a symbol of no one.

While Canada as a whole cannot possibly now, while the Nation is still in its first fledgling stages of life at a mere one and a half centuries old, have a firm grasp of its own self-image (unlike many of the great European or Asian Nations who have had dozens of centuries to develop and define themselves, or the United States, which chose a national identity for itself in the first years of its existence and has reinforced it with a "melting pot" approach to multiculturalism), it is possible to create and art which speaks to the human existence. While Canadian theater and film will remain fractured and regionalized until the day arrives that Canada has had enough birthdays and been through enough joys and suffering to understand its own identity, Canadian art can still speak of the human condition: to humans, from humans. For now, Canadian theater and film, regionalized as it may be, is concerned less with national identity, and more with exposing the truths of the human heart, and speak to the entire population *only* if underneath the regionalism lies universally recognizable humanistic struggles and characters.

Canadian art can be therefore said to be mainly about the suffering of Man vs. Nature/Society/Self, focusing on an individual's experiences in Canada's extreme climate, the stresses of inter-cultural negotiation, or personal comedies and tragedies. If we follow this thread of logic then, *Doctor Who* is already intensely Canadian. As I mentioned earlier, the aliens offered in *Doctor Who* and its spinoffs are intended as surrogates for audiences who fear the "Other," and the Doctor is meant to be a teacher of the importance of tolerance and acceptance; the struggles of these "Others"—the Doctor himself included—are then meant to represent the human animal as a whole.

Another general Canadian trope is that any film/ television show/ play that is "Canadian" has the tendency to not actually fully conclude, either in action, plot, or in character journey.[69] This may be a reflection of the never-ending toil of living in a part of the world whose climate is not necessarily conducive to "easy living" six months out of twelve, or of the evolutionary process that Canada as a nation and identity is undergoing even now. In that way, again, *Doctor Who,* with its constant retellings of history, its never-dying hero (and villains), and its time travel, is intensely Canadian.

Lastly, Canadian actor and playwright John Gray (best known for his role as the pianist in the two-man play *Billy Bishop Goes to War)* points out that, on the whole, "Canadians don't much like listening in on other people's conversations. They think it's impolite. This plays havoc with the basic convention of the theatre itself, so what do you do? Well, you drop the fourth wall and simply talk to the audience."[70] Thus, Canadian theater and film, or rather, the successful pieces, for the most part, avoid the conventions of naturalism and either are structurally unique, or contain such elements as direct address, multiple characters played by few actors, or song and dance. That is, Canadians like to be entertained, to be told stories, but not to eavesdrop or be told what to think. Canadians seem to prefer art that talks *to, about,* and *with* them—not *at* them. Again, set in the U.K. for predominantly British audiences, this makes *Doctor Who* very much a canonical Canadian work as it is not meant to speak directly to the Canadian audience, but does reflect many Canadian values.

Perhaps, then, my personal yearning to see actual Canadiana within the program is not related to an acknowledgement of Newman and Canada's contribution, but to a national inferiority complex.

John Gray remarks that it is "really amazing, the extent to which [foreign] acceptance affects Canadian prestige."[71] As an example, he speaks of his time with *Billy Bishop Goes to War* on Broadway. There were interviews and fame for Gray and his partner within the American and Canadian press, but there was never a word about the show itself; no interest in what it meant, what it was trying to say about heroes, about Canada, about life. All that mattered was that we were going to Broadway ... would we cure or confirm the National Inferiority Complex? ... Canadians have long existed with the suspicion that we have something missing in our chromosomal make-up when it comes to art; that there is some wishy-washy component in our gene structure that makes us incapable of strong artistic statement. This is our colonial heritage at work. We export natural resources, we import culture. This is our lot in life.[72]

Academic Jerry Wasserman also states that one "of the distinguishing features of modern Canadian drama has been the tendency to give a voice to the dispossessed ... George F. Walker, Judith Thompson, Tompson Highway and others have continued to write plays dramatizing the 'Canadian other.'"[73] That is to say that perhaps Canada addresses its national inferiority complex by exploring the marginalized, the minorities, exoticfied, the colonialized, and the uncertain. For what are Canadians but colonists, minorities, marginalized in the Empire and exotic-ized by American and British media and literature. Regionalist art therefore may write from the specific locale and point of view yet it is applicable to humanity as a whole as well. Canada, as stated before, is country where our early ancestors had to struggle to survive, where the First Peoples have to fight to maintain their culture, and where Mother Nature has no qualms about piling our major urban centers under ungodly amounts of snow. Canadians, as a whole, are used to fighting for comfort and all over the country they can share in the feelings of frustration of cross cultural and language communication. As much as Canada has its multicultural and geographical barriers, one thing Canadians do share is our strong will to survive, even if it's a menial and repetitive existence. This, also, can be very clearly seen in the character and motivations of the Doctor. In fact, as ephemeral as a final definition of just what a Canadian is, I hazard to put forth that the Doctor is the perfect example of a Canadian.

Perhaps then, Canadian identity is less one of absence, and more an identity of shared experience. The Doctor, therefore, already offers Canadians a lot of themselves within his own makeup, and within the themes and struggles within *Doctor Who,* as he also does to the intended British audience, and also to viewers from elsewhere. But as to specific Canadiana itself? Canadians are given a Doctor who represents Canadian interests but does not visit, a national broadcasting corporation that utilizes taxpayer money to fund but not successfully deliver the program, and a spin-off that smacks of colonialist narratives. Di Rocco echoes my pleas for Canadianism in *Who:*

> A Canadian created Doctor Who. We were the first country on this side of the Atlantic to buy the original series, and the first country anywhere to buy the new series. A plethora of missing colour Pertwee episodes were recovered in Canada. Doctor Who has been filmed here and we [were the] "co-producers" of the new series. Canadians usually don't ask for much, but I think we are entitled to the acknowledgement of our existence. Can the TARDIS not land here once?[74]
> So what can our beloved Doctor do to save the day?

I would be remiss if I led the reader to believe that there have been absolutely *no* references to Canada in the half a century that *Doctor Who* has touched our imaginations, that there has been *no* connection to Canada within the *Doctor Who* canon.

- British ex-pat and Hartnell-era writer John Lucratti did later work for the CBC, and one of his CBC radio stories was rewritten as the 1964 episode "Marco Polo."[75]
- McCoy-era script editor Andrew Cartmel grew up in Canada, though he wasn't born in the country.

- Only Lucratti, unsuccessfully, pitched a Canadian-set story, meant to take place in the Bay of Fundy and featuring a story about Leif Eriksson — which then later became a short story published in *Doctor Who Magazine*, entitled "Who Discovered America?"[76]
- During David Tennant's second appearance on the talk show *The Friday Night Project*, the first question in a quiz show portion that Tennant had to answer was "What French Canadian superstar turned forty this week?"[77]
- In the 2009 *Torchwood* series "The Children of Earth,"[78] there were several mentions of Canada: in "Day One," the General mentions that he too wishes he could "bloody well get assigned to Vancouver."[79]
- In "Day Two," the government official John Frobisher's wife Anne exclaims, "It's affected Don and Wendy's kids too, and they live in Canada!"[80]
- And in "Day Three," as Frobisher is listing countries at 48:00, he says, "The Provinces and Territories of the Dominion of Cana —," at which point he is cut off by a jump cut, though the remainder of the word obviously must be "-da."[81] He does say "Canada" in full later in the episode.[82] It is an interesting and needlessly formal way of referring to Canada, and one that reinforces the notion that in the *Torchwood* universe, the British Empire still secretly exists — Canada is not a nation to the Torchwood Institute, but a colony.
- There is also the matter of Frobisher's name — Frobisher Bay is a port of historical significance in Canada, made popular by the James Gordon song "(Frozen in) Frobisher Bay." Whether this was an intentional reference is unknown.

And while these are significant mentions, when compared with those of other countries featured in *Doctor Who*— Italy, Spain, the United States of America, etc.— they are relatively slim pickings. Going forward, Canadian fans would like to see a tighter connection, and to aid current executive producer Steven Moffat and the creative team, I suggest the following.

To dispel the lingering Imperialism of the Torchwood Institute, and disperse the colonialist taking of resources without a giving back to the colony as the BBC has done with Canadian taxpayer money, creators and producers could send either *Torchwood* or *Doctor Who* to Canada. A series or episode serial based in Canada would not only help burst the remaining colonialist stereotypes of the country, but also pay homage to Newman, reward the North American fans whose tireless work to get *Doctor Who* on the air in Canada was partially the reason the CBC was airing the Davies episodes to begin with, force the CBC the to strengthen its ties to the program, repay the tax dollars Canadians have invested in the series, and boost fan tourism to the shooting locations. This is unlikely, however, because Canada's valued multiculturalism has also created a nation nearly void of those iconic stereotypes that can make it instantly recognizable to British viewers. Icons like the Statue of Liberty immediately put viewers in mind of the U.S. and New York; it establishes location in a split second, preserving precious minutes of dialogue and scene-setting for storytelling, which makes cities with such iconic emblems appealing story locations. Unfortunately, there is no such iconic intersect of place, era, and icon for Canada. At least, not famous enough for young British audiences.

Then perhaps a Canadian companion? Peri the American has already served her term in the TARDIS. This would also allow the show to move beyond the stereotyping of the Canadian national identity that programs such as *Due South* or *South Park* rely upon, and consequently help the evolution of the Canadian national identity itself.

The program could also fall back on Newman's other artistic aims and give new talents a chance to expand their portfolios and experiment in professional broadcasting by establishing a sort of exchange program between the CBC and the BBC; CBC film school students could spend semesters working for the program, or Canadian writers could be contracted on episodes for the upcoming seasons. Canadian actors could be hired to play characters on the program. This could all serve to provide the program with vaunted "CanCon" status, which would bring the Canadian contributions to greater attention, and inevitably Canadian artistic values would make their way onto the screen and again, aid in the evolution of the Canadian national identity beyond beer-commercial stereotypes.

So far, *Doctor Who* has been widely regarded in academic discourses surrounding the program as being thoroughly "British" science fiction. Highlighting Newman's Canadian heritage and devotion to the early CBC artistic ideal should be highlighted in future academic works and origin narratives, and doing so will not, I believe, impact negatively or threaten such a well established cultural institution as the Doctor, but rather give him more dimension and offer a new and fascinating aspect for fans and program creators to explore.

For that matter, why aren't there Torchwood teams scattered all over the world? It's not as if Great Britain has cornered the market on "phantasmahoojits" for the Doctor, or Torchwood's operatives, or even Sarah Jane[83] and K9 to face. And Torchwood does have a chartered edict to protect the British Empire. So where, then, is Torchwood Sydney, Torchwood Johannesburg, or Torchwood Hong Kong? To some, the very "Britishness" of *Doctor Who* is to some the most appealing aspect of the program; then, perhaps, to preserve this "Britishness," a spin-off series similar to *Torchwood: Miracle Day* set in Canada could explore Canada's multiculturalism, develop Canada's artistic voice and identity, and still preserve the essential aspects of the program that makes it valued by viewers. Torchwood Four went missing, Jack says,[84] and the Torchwood bases have a penchant for being hidden under large phallic structures, so I know exactly where it's gone.

It's in Toronto, just down the street from the CBC studios headquarters, beneath the CNTower.[85] And think of what a glorious tip of the hat to Sydney that would be.

APPENDIX

Mentions of Canada in the Classic *Doctor Who* Series and Spin-Offs Compiled by Gian Luca Di Rocco[86]

Episode/Series Title	Doctor Incarnation	Mention
"Seeds of Death"	2nd	Reference to Toronto and Ottawa.
"Enemy of the World"	2nd	Reference to "the wheat plains of Canada."
"Frontier in Space"	3rd	Reference to the city of "New Montréal."
"Claws of Axos"	3rd	The city of Ottawa is sent one unit of Axos (relatively low, compared to the 4–6 units sent to other cities that are not national capitals).
"Ambassadors of Death"	3rd	Reference to Algonquin Park (in northern Ontario).
"Mysterious Planet"	6th	Reference to the nesting habit of a Canada goose.
Doctor Who, the Movie	8th	Filmed in Vancouver, though set in San Francisco.
The Sarah Jane Adventures	10th	Sarah Jane's attic lab has an Ontario license plate mounted on the wall

Episode/Series Title	*Doctor Incarnation*	*Mention*
		(white, with blue lettering and the motto "Yours to Discover!").
Other	1st or 2nd	John Lucratti, a writer for the series in the 1960s, expressed a desire to write a story set at the Bay of Fundy (in Nova Scotia, Canada), where the tide is has the greatest flow of water in the world. His pitch was never developed.

Notes

1. This paper was first presented November 14, 2008, to the Whoniversal Appeal Academic Conference.

2. Mary Jane Miller, *Turn Up the Contrast: CBC Television Drama Since 1952* (Vancouver: University of British Columbia Press, 1987); The Canadian Broadcasting Corporation, *CBC.ca*, http://www.cbc.ca (March 06, 2009).

3. Gun Akyuz, "BBC Sci-fi Thriller Finds Partner," *C21Media*, http://www.c21media.net/news/detail.asp?area=4&article=29877 (October 27, 2008).

4. "Army of Ghosts." For program details see Videography.

5. David J. Howe, Mark Stammers and Stephen James Walker, *Doctor Who—The Eighties*, 1st ed., London: Virgin,1996; Graeme Burk, "CanCon Who: Half Canadian, on His Father's Side," *Enlightenment Magazine*, Issue 97 (March/April 2000): "The Doctor, Eh?" http://www.dwin.org/article.php?sid=67 (September 30, 2008).

6. James Chapman, *Inside the TARDIS: The Worlds of Doctor Who* (New York: I.B. Taurus, 2006), pp. 16–17.

7. Kim Newman, *Doctor Who: A Critical Reading of the Series* (London: British Film Institute, 2005) p.15.

8. Miller; *Turn Up the Contrast*; Burk, "CanCon Who."

9. Robert J. Sawyer, in Johnny Kalangis, dir., *The Planet of the Doctor,* 2005, Canadian Broadcasting Corporation http://www.cbc.ca/planetofthedoctor/videos.html# (September 30, 2008), Part 1, min 4:30–5:16.

10. Miller, *Turn Up the Contrast*, p. 188.

11. Ibid., p. 197.

12. Una McCormak, personal correspondence (October 12, 2009).

13. Miller, *Turn Up the Contrast*, p. 194.

14. Ibid., p. 258.

15. Robert J. Sawyer, in Kalaingas, dir., *The Planet of the Doctor,* 2005. Canadian Broadcasting Corporation. http://www.cbc.ca/planetofthedoctor/videos.html# (September 30, 2008), Part 1, min 4:30–5:16.

16. Miller, *Turn Up the Contrast*, p. 194.

17. Ibid.

18. Ibid., p. 203.

19. Ibid., p. 206.

20. Newman, *Doctor Who*, p. 12.

21. Andrew Cartmel, *Through Time: An Unauthorized and Unofficial History of Doctor Who* (London: Continuum International, 2005), p. 8.

22. Kalangis, dir., Part 6, min 1:15.

23. Graeme Burk, in Kalaingas, dir., *The Planet of the Doctor,* 2005. Canadian Broadcasting Corporation. http://www.cbc.ca/planetofthedoctor/videos.html# (September 30, 2008), Part 1, min 5:16–5:28.

24. Verity Lambert, in Kalaingas, dir., *The Planet of the Doctor,* 2005, Canadian Broadcasting Corporation http://www.cbc.ca/planetofthedoctor/videos.html# (September 30, 2008), Part 1, min 5:28–6:40.

25. Cartmel, *Through Time*, p. 10.

26. Graeme Burk, personal correspondence (August 12, 2010).

27. James Chapman, *Inside the TARDIS: The Worlds of Doctor Who* (New York: I.B. Taurus, 2006), p. 3.

28. Ibid., p. 6.

29. Canadian Radio-television and Telecommunications Commission, Canadian Content for Radio and Television Fact Sheet http://www.crtc.gc.ca/public/old_pubs_e/G11.htm (September 30, 2008).

30. Burk, personal correspondence.

31. Miller, *Turn Up the Contrast*: Burk, "CanCon Who.."

32. Howe, Stammers and Walker, *Doctor Who—The Eighties.*

33. Ibid., p. 92.

34. Burk, personal correspondence.

35. Marc Schuster and Tom Powers, *The Greatest Show in the Galaxy: The Discerning Fan's Guide to Doctor Who* (Jefferson, NC: McFarland, 2007).

36. Ibid., p. 7.

37. Matthew Kilburn, "Newman, Sydney Cecil (1917–1997)," *Oxford Dictionary of National Biography* http://www.oxforddnb.com/view/article/68398 (January 26, 2010).

38. Kalangis, dir., Part 6, min 4:30.

39. Andrew Gurudata, "CanCon Who: Rage Against the Machine," *Enlightenment Magazine,* Issue 147 (September 2008), pp. 24–25.

40. Burk, personal correspondence.

41. Gurudata, "CanCon Who" p. 24.

42. Ibid.

43. Rob Salem, "Some Good News From Who-ville," *The Toronto Star.com* http://www.thestar.com/entertainment/article/501961 (October 3, 2008).

44. Gurudata, "CanCon Who," pp. 22–24.

45. Gian-Luca (John) Di Rocco, "January 16, 2006 — Attn: Uk — Canada Exists!" *The Doctor Who Blog* http://www.dwin.org/expressionengine/index.php/site/attn_uk_canada_exists/ (January 15, 2010).

46. Canadian Radio-television and Telecommunications Commission, Canadian Content for Radio and Television Fact Sheet http://www.crtc.gc.ca/public/old_pubs_e/G11.htm (September 30, 2008).

47. Burk, personal correspondence.

48. Di Rocco, "January 16, 2006."

49. Gian-Luca (John) Di Rocco, interview (October 2, 2008).

50. Chapman, *Inside the TARDIS*, p. 5.

51. Ibid., p. 32.

52. Ibid., p. 5.

53. Ibid.

54. "The End of the World."

55. "Army of Ghosts."

56. "Daleks in Manhattan."

57. "Poison Sky."

58. "The Empty Child."

59. *Torchwood*: "Captain Jack Harkness."

60. "Army of Ghosts."

61. *Torchwood*: "Fragments."

62. Jonathan Culler, *Literary Theory, A Very Short Introduction* (Oxford: Oxford University Press, 1997), pp. 188–189.

63. Chibnall.

64. "The Sound of Drums."

65. *Torchwood*: "Everything Changes."

66. Peter Brooker, *A Glossary of Cultural Theory, 2 ed.* (London: Arnold Hodder Headline Group, 2003), p. 183.

67. Schuster and Powers, *The Greatest Show in the Galaxy*, p. 19.

68. John Gray, "Billy Bishop Goes to War: Forward," *Modern Canadian Plays*, vol. 1 4, ed. Jerry Wasserman, (Vancouver: Talonbooks, 2000).

69. Kieran Keohane, *Symptoms of Canada* (Toronto: University of Toronto Press, 1997); S.M. Crean, *Who's Afraid of Canadian Culture?* (Don Mills, Ontario: General, 1976); Mary Jane Miller, *Rewind and Search: Conversations with the Makers and Decision-Makers of CBC Television Drama)* (Montreal and Kingston: McGill-Queens University Press, 1996).

70. Gray in Wasserman, *Modern Canadian Plays*: vol. 4, p. 294.

71. Ibid., p. 295.

72. Ibid.

73. Jerry Wasserman, "John Gray with Eric Peterson," *Modern Canadian Plays,* vol. 1 4, ed. Jerry Wasserman, (Vancouver: Talonbooks, 2000), p. 321.

74. Di Rocco, "January 16, 2006."

75. Burk, personal correspondence (August 12, 2010).

76. Shannon Patrick Sullivan, "The Lost Stories," *A Brief History of Time (Travel)* http://www.shannonsullivan.com/drwho/lostunt.html, 1995–2010 (February 10, 2011).

77. Steve Smith, *The Friday Night Project—"David Tennant,"* Justin Lee Collins, Allan Carr, feat. David Tennant, http://www.youtube.com/watch?v=cAYuHbHJmr0&feature=related (September 6, 2008).

78. An anecdote: I was in Cardiff presenting the early version of this very paper during the filming of "Children of Earth"; there has been the suggestion that those staffers who heard me present the paper went back to the BBC to requested references to Canada be added to the script. As much as I wish this was the case, it cannot be, alas. For the day I presented the paper was the cast's final day of shooting— unless a certain mad fellow with a blue box was also in the room as I presented, the timeline just doesn't mesh.

79. *Torchwood:* "Day One."

80. *Torchwood:* "Day Four."

81. *Torchwood:* "Day Two."

82. *Torchwood:* "Day Five."

83. When I wrote this essay in 2008, Elizabeth Sladen had not yet passed away. I struggled with removing this reference to Sarah Jane, but decided to leave it in both as an homage to Sladen and because Sarah Jane the character still continues in the *Doctor Who* universe, in my mind, even though her actress does not.

84. *Torchwood:* "Everything Changes."

85. J.M. Frey, *Where Is Torchwood 4?* dir. Karen Wood, feat. J.M. Frey, http://www.youtube.com/watch?v=mULMXxztIGw (March 3, 2011).

86. Di Rocco, interview.

5

In and Out of Time

Memory and Chronology

Kieran Tranter

> What, then, is time? I know well enough what it is, provided that nobody asks
> me; but if I am asked what it is and try to explain, I am baffled.
> — St. Augustine, *Confessions*, Book XI, 14[1]

This essay responds to an obvious question that critics face when presented with the sheer cultural phenomenon that is *Doctor Who*: What has made this show — the basic elements of which were settled during Patrick Troughton's tenure (1966–1970)[2] — endure? What about it has sustained 26 years of episodes before its 1989 "production halt," sustained an active fan community, and commercial output during the sixteen-year interregnum, and then led to such a successful return in 2005? Indeed, this post-millennium success must be seen in the context of a hostile television market for science fictions over the 2000s, where many critically well-received science fictions (for example, *Farscape* [1998–2002], *Star Trek: Enterprise* [2001–2005], *Firefly* [2002], *Terminator: The Sarah Connor Chronicles* [2007–2009], *Dollhouse* [2009–2010] and *Caprica* [2010]) were prematurely cancelled by the networks. This essay argues that the success of *Doctor Who* lies in the core thematic of the show. The unfolding text of *Doctor Who* is about time. This timeness of the show seems obvious. After all it has, for a long time, charted the adventures in time and space of a particularly active Time Lord and his idiosyncratic blue time machine.

What is specifically argued is that the show's engagement with time involves the intertwining of *timelessness* and *timefullness*. In presenting these two divergent accounts of time — and their combination in memory and chronology — the show can be seen as being performative of Western accounts of time. In this it not only traces the tensions within Western time, but significantly offers hope; a way of living as beings gifted with memory and chronology.

This argument is in two stages. The first stage looks in more detail at one of the classic responses to the question of the success of *Doctor Who*: its characterization as an unfolding text. It is argued that central to this flexibility has been the TARDIS and the timelessness — the not belonging to any time, and the primacy of the present — that is an essential feature of the show. However, this timelessness is immediately contradicted. The Doctor has a personal history; he has aged, notwithstanding the illusion of some more youthful regenerations. In this the show is actually *timefull*. For fans the *timefullness* of the series is deeply personal. Generations of television audiences have demarked moments of their life by which Doctor was adventuring in the evenings. What emerges is that the show projects both *timelessness* and *timefullness*.

The second stage places this timelessness and timefullness into the context of the Western tradition of time. It is argued that the enigma of time lies in the co-positioning of timelessness and timefullness. Chronology begins with timelessness to give meaning to timefullness. While the locus for the experience of time, memory begins with timefullness to give meaning to timelessness. It will be shown how the Doctor's "ethics," the complexities between his "liberal humanist" orientation of nonviolence, and live and let live, and his "Gallifreyian" tendencies of a will to power and maker of "terrible" decisions, can be mapped temporally. Not surprisingly as a face changer the Doctor possesses a dimorphic being grounded in chronology and memory. In manifesting these two ethics within a likable, eccentric, alien lead character, *Doctor Who* is critically performative towards received notions of Western time. Memory, the storehouse for a life lived full of time and chronology, the technical carving of time into standing reserve so as to resource the will to power and necessitate terrible decision, become, in the Doctor, intertwined. In so doing *Doctor Who* has spoken to its audiences of the tension — and more importantly the hope — from living as a being gifted with memory *and* chronology.

Timelessness and Timefullness

Doctor Who has been a remarkable cultural phenomenon. Rapidly approaching fifty years of cultural life, *Doctor Who* is more than a set of known television shows produced by the BBC from 1963 to 1989 and then from 2005 on.[3] A decade before George Lucas allegedly "pioneered" tie-in merchandizing with a science fiction text,[4] British and Australian audiences were eagerly buying yearly annuals, novelizations, and Dalek wallpaper.[5] It sustained active fan societies even during the sixteen-year programming break, augmented by some broadcasters, the Australian Broadcasting Company (ABC) particularly, re-running the back catalogue over the 1990s and 2000s.[6] Key terms associated with the show — TARDIS, Dalek, "bigger on the inside" — are now deeply engrained in the popular lexicon of the U.K. and Australia.[7] The interaction of fandom and absence of televised stories from 1989 to 2005, led to a massive amount of quasi-canonical, and sometimes BBC-sanctioned, radio plays, novels and comics, and non-commercial fanfic.[8] Then there is the mainstream success, both within its traditional markets and in North America, of its post–2005 BBC Wales regeneration (new *Who*); which in turn has spawned an avalanche of tie-ins, almanacs, novels, merchandising, DVD sales, iTunes downloads, and two spin-off shows, *Torchwood* (2006–) and the *Sarah Jane Adventures* (2007–2011). In recognition of this cultural phenomenon, *Doctor Who* in 2009 was recognized by the Guinness Book of World Records as the most successful science fiction series "of all-time."[9]

A central component of the success of *Doctor Who*, both classic and new *Who*, has been its status as "mainstream" television. Obscured a little by the beast of Who fandom and by critics following John Tulloch's emphasis on fan cultures, and the interaction of fans and producers,[10] there has been the recognition that the show's success has been its broad audience appeal and following. *Doctor Who* is, and was, a prime-time family show.[11] As Matt Hills observes that one of the many, slightly ironic fan criticisms of the John Nathan-Turner period of the 1980s was the over-use of self-referential "fanwank" in the screened episodes that made the texts more cultishly opaque to non-fan audiences.[12] BBC Wales's *Doctor Who*, while clearly sharing much in common with "quality TV," including homage to that definitional quality-cult television, *Buffy the Vampire Slayer* (1997–2003), with "School Reunion,"[13] has been successful because beyond the fanzines, discussion boards and blogs of fanboys *Doctor Who* has been discussed, critiqued, even reenacted, in school yards, workplaces and pubs for nearly fifty years.

In this context of mainstream success, critics have attempted to identify the features within the *Doctor Who* mega-text that have ensured its longevity. The touchstone for this direction in Who-studies is Tulloch and Manuel Alvarado's cultural studies classic *Doctor Who: The Unfolding Text*. They argued that "Doctor Who ... [is] an 'unfolding text' subtly shifting its ground in response to social and professional pressures, yet vindicating television's recipe for success: something different but something the same."[14] Their thesis is essentially that the basic premise of *Doctor Who* is remarkably open-ended. So while they chart how various periods of the show can be explained as a complex manifestation of personalities (actors, writers, and especially producers), institutional influences internal to the BBC, and wider cultural pressures, their message is that *Doctor Who* remained different yet same.[15] Unlike other science fictions whose mega-text constrains diversity in story-telling, for James Chapman, following the "unfolding text thesis," the essential open-endess of *Doctor Who* has allowed it to first move in the 1960s from a family-history-quasi-educational show to a more strongly themed science fiction, and then to regularly reinvent itself every few years with the change of producer, lead actors, aesthetics and mood.[16] In can be suggested that in *Doctor Who* the BBC hit upon the "perfect science fiction premise."[17]

In all this change one of the few visuals that has not changed much over the life of the show has been the TARDIS.[18] While the interior of the TARDIS, always "bigger on the inside," changes,[19] its exterior has remained inspired by the Gilbert MacKenzie Trench London Metropolitan Police telephone boxes that were first commissioned in 1929. The TARDIS' visual continuity as a blue police box, notwithstanding the occasional operation of its "chameleon circuit," is the defining element of *Doctor Who*. Indeed, the new-in-2010 logo heralds the "Steven Moffat" era with a stylized TARDIS. In this context Chapman has described the TARDIS' exterior as "sacrosanct."[20]

The TARDIS is first and foremost a time machine, the Doctor a Time Lord, and it seems plausible that the show is about time-travelling.[21] Hills has cautioned of the danger for scholars from making these jumps from unfolding text to time machine to the essence of *Doctor Who* as time-travelling. His concern with essence-ing *Doctor Who* would be the construction of categories, as can be seen in the fan realms, of authentic and inauthentic elements within the Who-verse; of good Who (adult, horror, science fictional) and bad Who (childish, comic, fantasy).[22] He argues that if *Doctor Who* is defined as time-travelling, the historicals of the early years, and their importance in the foundation of the show, would be left off the cultural studies horizon.[23]

However, Hills makes a jump too far. *Doctor Who* is not quite about time-travelling. There are only a few stories that feature the Doctor utilizing the TARDIS inter-text to move within times.[24] The general model, set by the historicals, is that the TARDIS arrives in a time and space, the Doctor and companion emerge, there is adventure-action-triumph within that locale, and then post-climax the Doctor and companion enter the soon-to-vanish TARDIS while the episode ally looks on incredulously. However, notwithstanding that there are only nine story lines that feature time in the title,[25] it is the many and multiple representations of time that can be seen as dominating the show.

Hills seems to agree. His book moves rapidly to a consideration of the time thematic within new *Who*.[26] The TARDIS frees *Doctor Who* from any specific time. The temporal backdrop of episodes range from the various ends of the universe,[27] the creation of Earth[28] to its solar obliteration.[29] The Doctor has witnessed and participated in most major events within Earth's history, some of them more than once. He has saved from various interferences a who's who of European historical figures — Robespierre,[30] King John,[31] Queen Victoria,[32] H. G. Wells,[33] Van Gogh,[34] Dickens,[35] Churchill,[36] to name but a few. The Doctor has looped back on the lives of companions[37] and jumped forward to show the future consequences of non-interference.[38] He has messed with the history of the Daleks to such a point that continuity-junkie fans need to generate parallel Dalek histories. From these narratives the Doctor emerges as *timeless*, as beyond time, materializing within event only to vanish again with a grinding whir.

This timelessness presents a dynamic conception of events-within-time. Time is repeatedly shown to be in flux. What is at stake in the Doctor's adventures is the very nature of time. History can be changed. The Doctor's universe can be appreciated as one without lineal history and fate. Various invasions of Earth by Daleks, Cybermen, Sontarans et al. are to be actively repelled.[39] In this, the series bumps continually into the often observed time-traveler paradox, or "Grandfather paradox."[40] Stated briefly, if time-travel was possible, could a time-traveler go back and kill his own grandfather, thus preventing his own future birth? The logic spirals out into a "chicken and egg" infinity. At a more pragmatic narrative level it creates the "Groundhog Day" scenario — reminiscent of a platform computer game — of being able to return to a past point with future knowledge, in order to successfully navigate the obstacles ahead. This "common sense" critique of *Doctor Who* — "If he has a time machine, why doesn't he just go back in time and prevent any of this from happening in the first place?" — was wonderfully parodied in Steven Moffat's scripted 1999 comedy special *Doctor Who and the Curse of a Fatal Death*[41] where the Doctor and the Master engage in one-upmanship on who went back earlier in time to place booby-traps. What Moffat highlights is how the possibilities of timelessness is corrosive to narrative. As a consequence a variety of script devices, such as Barry Letts' and Terrance Dick's "Blinovitch Limitation,"[42] the Time Lord's policy/principle/dictate of non-interference, or so-called Laws of Time, have attempted to limit the Doctor's timelessness.

However, these external constraints have proven weak. Breaking the "Blinovitch Limitation" just seems to create paradoxes, sometimes comic,[43] sometimes tragic, as in the new *Who* episode "Father's Day."[44] The second Doctor convinces the Time Lords that a pure policy of non-interference is unwise, and while still sentenced to regenerate and exiled on Earth, his species appears much more interfering as the '70s proceed.[45] And the grandiose "Laws of Time" appear to be technically mutable. The Master can transform the TARDIS into a "Paradox Machine" allowing the Grandfather paradox to be a planet-wide phenomenon,[46] and the tenth Doctor can claim to be a "Time Lord Victorious" and sort of change the outcome of the 2059 destruction of the Mars colony.[47]

The final image, the fading retina imprint of a vanishing TARDIS, in this incomplete bounding of the Doctor is a reaffirmation of the Doctor's timelessness. The Doctor is bound within a narrative sequence, within the linear unfolding of timespace, either because he has lost the TARDIS, as in "The Impossible Planet,"[48] or because he simply chooses to be. It is this act of restraint that is the most common. The first Doctor would admonish companions not to "change history,"[49] and would actively defeat the history changing plans of the "Time Meddler,"[50] yet would often get involved himself as seen in the "Gunfighters."[51] The Doctor presents himself as arbitrator of history. The mystical explanation from new *Who* that sensing the distinction between "unchangeable" events and more "wibbly-wobbly timey-wimey" history is something deep within a Time Lord's being not only infuriates fans who hold that *Doctor Who* should have a hard science fiction essence, but reinforces the primacy of present over other temporal dimensions. The Doctor's *now* is what matters with both past and present dematerializing into a haze of now-choice.

This *now-ness* as an implication of the timelessness of the show can be seen within the stories from new *Who*. The re-occurrence of "Bad Wolf" through season one — as graffiti and public announcements[52] — is revealed in "Parting of the Ways"[53] as messages that the time vortex infused Rose has sent back to herself. This temporal circularity (Rose becomes the Bad Wolf because she prompted her past self to do so) places the now of self-creation as a timeless act that "authors" the past. Similarly, "The Lodger"[54] has the note that leads the Doctor to the alien-spaceship inflected tenement as contrived by himself, post-adventure. In both, present re-configures past.

The implications of the Doctor's timelessness are a particular feature of Moffat's contributions as a script writer and more recently producer. Moffat's stories — especially the BAFTA- and Hugo-winning "Girl in the Fireplace,"[55] "Blink,"[56] the introduction of Professor/Dr. River Song (Alex Kingston) in "Silence in the Library,"[57] the "cracks in time" narrative arc for season five, and the River/Amy/Doctor, child-parent conundrum of the mid-season six finale — play with the timelessness of the Doctor. The tragedy of "Girl in the Fireplace" is that years pass for Madame de Pompadour in 18th century Versailles compared to mere minutes for the Doctor. "Blink" is resolved through the Doctor meeting Sally Sparrow (Carey Mulligan) multi-chronically (that is, after she had survived the Weeping Angels, but before he had). This temporal displacement is also evident in the humor and mystery of River Song who kept meeting the Doctor across seasons four and five "too soon," and her fan pleasing resistance to "spoilers." The 2010 season presents the unwinding of time, of a specific event rendering creation to nothing. Further, the revelation in the mid-season finale of season six that Amy's and Rory's (Arthur Darvill) kidnapped child is River combined with time and space jumping as the Doctor recruits his army to go "to war"[58] almost excessively emphasizes the confounding of linear, normal, time by the Doctor. In these Moffat can be seen, more than any other contributor to *Doctor Who,* as bringing into the texts the possibilities and paradoxes of time-travel of the show's mega-text. But, paradoxically, in doing so, his stories challenge the timelessness of the series.

Moffat, like Russell T. Davies before him, presents the Doctor with a history. The Doctor might dance timelessly across this and parallel universes, but he has a personal past. The Doctor has aged since the BBC first started broadcasting his adventures, from 450 years old (the assumption is Earth years, not Gallifrey's) as the second Doctor to around 900 for the seventh to eleventh. There are all those young women (and men, and robotic dogs) that he has consecutively traveled with. There is a linear continuality, the Doctors seem to number-off intra-text, taking William Hartnell as "One,"[59] and in the few multi-Doctor episodes there is disparaging of the "younger" self.[60] The Doctor continually remembers. He remembers old foes and past adventures, indeed, often remembering, distastefully, past personalities, much to fan joy/anguish. There are events in his past. There was the impervious Time War occurring during his eighth or ninth incarnation. He was a parent, possibly referring to Susan Foreman, his "granddaughter" from 1963.[61] He remembers the times he has thwarted the Daleks. However, in this remembering of past there is an openness to the future. As Moffat has made clear with River Song and the season five story arc/cliffhanger into season six, the Doctor is not omnipresent. He might dip across linear time in his wanderings and he might have a past, but he doesn't know his future. The sixth Doctor wonders if his current regeneration is truly his last, as faces his tombstone in "Revelation of the Daleks."[62] Meeting Sally Sparrow in "Blink" is "complicated," but it is only complicated because the Doctor, like the human Sally Sparrow, is *timefull*. The Doctor continually asks River who she is. He is full of time, existing in a personal time-stream, in which there is a past to remember, a present to experience, and an unknown future.

This timefullness of the show manifested elsewhere. It is evident in the spaces of the show. Notwithstanding having the full gamut of the universe to visit, the Doctor keeps returning to Earth, the United Kingdom, and particularly London, from the mid–1960s to the first decades of the twenty-first century. Even the first Doctor as the most "historical," and the fourth Doctor as the most "spacey opera," kept returning to the broadcast "present" U.K. to save the day. Whether this is because the BBC's budget was unable to sustain the high cost alien/SF sets as wag fans suggest, or, as Hills has argued, through a conscious decision of producers, especially the fan-producers of new *Who*, to keep the mainstream audience through maintaining contemporary story links,[63] is at one level immaterial. What it does reveal is a *timefullness* to the show that undercuts its immediate suggestion of timelessness. *Doctor Who* has a location in time and space. It is post-war British.

The majority of the Doctor's companions have been broadcast-contemporary Londoners, with only the occasional non-human, non-contemporary, or very occasionally non–English companion. Indeed, the Doctor, putting to one side the 1996 tele-movie, has only traveled with two non–U.K. contemporary companions, the American Peri Brown (played by English actor Nicola Bryant) and the Australian airhostess Tegan Jovanka (played by Australian actor Janet Fielding). It is London that is seemingly forever under threat, even in the Cardiff-filmed new *Who*. For Chapman, various eras of the show can be seen as reflecting the cultural anxieties of the U.K. Early 1970s concerns of the sinister state, Cold War fear, and nostalgia for "Pax Britannia" can be seen in the conspiracy, alien invasions repealed in the Letts-Dick era by Jon Pertwee's James Bond–like athleticism and gadgets, Brigadier Alastair Gordon Lethbridge-Stewart's (Nicholas Courtney) loyal Tommies,[64] and the fragmented violence of Thatcher's 1980s England in Colin Baker's aggressive sixth Doctor.[65] This carries over to guest stars that chart the range of U.K. actors and cultural figures — from BBC newsreader Kenneth Kendall[66] to comedians John Cleese[67] and Alexei Sayle,[68] to character actors Sir Derek Jacobi[69] and Bill Nighy,[70] to pop princess Kylie Minogue,[71] and companion-marrying (Romana II [Lalla Ward]) Professor Richard Dawkins.[72] The Doctors themselves tend to articulate around the Byronic hero of aristocratic and knowing,[73] while referencing various British masculinities: action-dandy (Pertwee), responsibility shirking younger-son-to-nobility (Tom Baker), Edwardian upper-class man of action (Peter Davison),[74] working-class damaged everyman (Christopher Eccleston),[75] mod (David Tennant),[76] and eccentric inventor-type (Troughton, Sylvester McCoy, Matt Smith). And while the Doctor was allowed to leave BBC enunciation behind with McCoy, subsequent Doctors, the "every planet has a north"[77] Eccleston and the RSC-trained Scot Tennant, have kept the accent located in the British Isles.

This sense of time and space is core to fan remembering of the show. The cultural phenomenon of *Doctor Who* is intertwined with my personal biography. Like many of the current generation of *Doctor Who* aca-fans[78] and the current fan-producers,[79] I have early memories of glimpsing terrifying rubber suits from behind the sofa and still have a childish sense of anticipation and excitement whenever I hear the theme music. I can strongly identify with Pertwee-era *Doctor Who* that the Australian Broadcasting Company re-ran before the evening news in the mid–1980s, motivating me to finish my homework by 6:30 P.M. The third Doctor probably explains the early life desire to complete a Ph.D. so as to legitimately be called Doctor. Like David Tennant my childhood forays into acting always had a self-image of playing the Doctor; alas unlike Tennant, the closest I come is the persona I adopt in jurisprudence lectures. I can, and with apologies to Moffat, recall my family's dislike of "that twit Tristan" from *All Creatures Great and Small* (1978–1980) replacing the definitional Tom Baker in 1982. Then there is the restorative nostalgia[80] of Davies' stint at new *Who* with its intra and inter-textual referencing, and with Tennant, an ego-ideal, trench-coated Generation X Doctor. But most deeply there is something fabulous about watching my own daughter grow into the show, from hiding behind the sofa to having detailed plot discussions and Daleks on her school books. Here the Doctor, like many in the U.K. and Australia, commingles with the linear narrative of my life.

Doctor Who does this because the show has that remarkable broadcast continuity. It was shown (and re-shown) at specific times. Generations can demark, as I can, childhood, adolescence, and adulthood by which Doctor was adventuring in the evenings. Here the experience of *Doctor Who* has a particularly temporal quality. There is an aligning of times and an ordering of events that, although experienced, lend themselves to cross-referenced timelines of personal and Who. This tendency returns to fanwank. Talk of continuity and fans cannot go past the mountains of fan energy gone into mapping the Doctor's travels against the wider timelines of the Who-verse; and the debates and intricacies that attempting such a project generates regarding the multiple histories of the Daleks, the history of the Time Lords, or attempting to explain changing aesthetics of the Cybermen in terms of newer or older models.[81] Episodes become pinpoints on an imagined linear history, which seems to be completely at odds with the initial timelessness of the Doctor.

What emerges is that *Doctor Who* is about time, but its times are enigmatic and paradoxical (My giddy Aunt! An enigmatic time paradox! Run!). The time-traveling motifs and the sense of timelessness suggest nonlinear time, a time of now-events that resonate across a fluid, dynamic timespace. In this context the narrational revealing of time and the order of history seem to be located more by the Doctor's ethics, in his leaving alone or choosing to change, rather than an inherent property of the universe. This prioritizing of present against an ordered narrated time is at once complicated. The Doctor remains time-full. He has a personal past and an uncertain future. More specifically, he has a place within the U.K. of the broadcast "present" from 1963 onwards, that can be mapped and appreciated within the lives of fans who in-turn map the Doctor's universe in complicated linear schemas. This paradox is performative. In prioritizing time as timelessness and timefulness, *Doctor Who* materializes within Western tradition on time.

Chronology and Memory

Time is the "gift" of the West. From Plato onwards the Western philosophical tradition has attempted to reason time. As in any good *Doctor Who* episode, the tradition twists and turns, and occasionally faces death just as the theme music intrudes. It has involved two divergent accounts of time, reflecting classic disagreement. The first, identified originally with Plato, is a locating of time as the definition of the world of semblances. In this material world time flows; while in the metaphysical realm of forms, there is no time, just existence.[82]

This becomes in Augustine the notion of time versus eternity, God versus man, with the soul the locale for the experience of time.[83] The second follows Aristotle's rejection of a dualistic reality and its speleological metaphors. For Aristotle the world of semblance is the world of philosophy, and time is a succession of now-events. The past was the now, while the future is the now-to-come.[84]

Contemporary "philosophy of time" remains to a large extent locked into the perimeters of classical thought. J. M. E. McTaggart's 1908 essay gave the uninspiring terms A-series and B-series to what the tradition had come to define as the two meta-accounts of time.[85] The A-series presents a tensed account of time; this happened, then that. With the A-series objects move through time, a semblance in motion comprehensible in its change and decay by reference to an eternal pure form. As such in the A-series, it is sensible to talk of the experience of time passing.[86] The B-series is without tense.[87] Events are described as earlier, later or simultaneous.[88] There is order, but not movement. In both, the present acts as a "privileged" location. In the A-series it is the magic moment when future becomes past. In the B-series it is the cipher for the tenseless ordering. Another way to describe the difference is A-series time is subjective, while B-series time is objective.

Positions within the orthodox tradition of time are not directly manifested within *Doctor Who*; after all, the Doctor has not visited, adventured with, or saved Plato or Aristotle (although one of them might be dazed and confused in the background of "Time and the Rani").[89] However, what can be seen is that the recurring concepts that bounce around the vortex that is the philosophy of time are animated within *Doctor Who*. The identified notion of the Doctor's timelessness, of being outside time, resonates with the B-series idea of objective time, of now-events that are later, earlier or simultaneous. Yet as was identified this now-ness gave the Doctor a potentially limitless present that overshadows past and future, similar to the possibility of presentism that is strongly present in the A-series.[90] Further, the recognition of the Doctor's timefullness — of his intra-text history, his remembering, and his post-war to present-day Englishness — and the co-locating of the show with the lives of fans strongly suggests the experience of the linear movement of time from the A-series. Yet the tendency to then map the times of the Doctor by fans enacts the objective time of ordered events of the B-series.

What these manifestations of elements from the tradition of time in *Doctor Who* suggest, beyond a complex unity between the A- and B-series that is acknowledged intra-tradition,[91] is how timelessness and timefullness are integral to being in time. Timelessness suggests objective time — it gives rise to *chronology*—yet it is chronology that grounds the fan experience of *Doctor Who*. Chronology becomes meaningful in the context of being timefull, of reflecting on the past-now in the present so as to anticipate the future (i.e., when the next episodes of the Doctor are to be screened). However, parallel with this movement of time-lessness to timefullness, there is the movement from timefullness to timelessness. Timefull-ness discloses an unknown future and an insubstantial present (to say this is now, means now has passed, for what is the duration of now?)[92] leaving only the past to remember. This prioritizes *memory*. Yet memory of the experience of the past cannot relive the past. Watching late–Tom Baker episodes ("Nightmare of Eden,"[93] for example) with adult eyes thirty years after they were first broadcast, I can reluctantly agree with the criticisms that his clownish improvising was undermining the show.[94] Yet those exact moments of off-cue humor I can remember as key to liking T. Baker's Doctor as a child. What is suggested is that being in time involves chronology and memory, and the question becomes how to live caught between these two seemingly incompatible times.

Chronology is the way of the machine. Chronology is the dividing of time so that time can be used.[95] Chronology guarantees the routine ordering of Western life; the reduction of the timefull anxiety of an unknown future through the fixing of structure and expectations. For Martin Heidegger the defining characteristic of technology was temporal. The essence of technology was the dividing of the world into standing reserve that could be deployed.[96] This ideal of deployment suggests a making ready for the future. It is pure B-series time. The future can be ordered and known, actively anticipated and prepared for, while the past can also be known, recalled, evidenced in diaries, notes, and all the other evidential paraphernalia that accumulates to witness the past. It is unsurprising therefore that in *Doctor Who* chronology comes with technology. The classic image of chronology is the chronometer.[97] The many clocks associated with the Doctor point to this. It is a pocket watch that seemingly can contain a Time Lord's essence in "Human Nature,"[98] "Family of Blood"[99] and "Utopia,"[100] and then there is the pocket watch holding a publicity shot of Paul McGann for the 1996 movie. This is also attested in the interiors of the TARDIS. The TARDIS' interior, notwithstanding changes, references machine. From the stylized regular "egg-crate/honeycomb" walls to the Hartnell/Troughton console resembling the control room of a 1950s nuclear plant, to the Nathan-Turner period's rapidly outdated early '80s computer parts,[101] to new *Who*'s steampunk meets alien tech mishmashes, the TARDIS has mostly been presented as a technical object. Even the fabulous season six episode "The Doctor's Wife"[102] where the TARDIS's essence becomes embodied by Idris (Suranne Jones), this transposing is unstable and mortal; Idris needs to be reunited with her proper form — the mechanistic TARDIS hardware. The Doctor is not the first male to feminize his conveyance as "sexy old girl." Ultimately, this prioritizing the technical is reflected in the Doctor. He is a technologist; the various regenerations confidently claim to fix, meddle or reprogram alien and Earth technologies.

In contrast memory is more organic. The machine suggests pure technical reproduction, yet memory can never reproduce. Memory occurs against the possibility of forgetting,[103] and the tactile imprints from emotions and the senses. A feeling, a smell, a distressing thought can be a mnemonic trigger. Memory is soft; chronology is hard. It is tempting to juxtapose chronology and machine with memory and flesh. Memory is personal. It is A-series time of a present that can only but dwell in the past. The debates within fan quarters on remembering the best episode, the best Doctor, the best monster, the best villain, the best whatever, represent this. So too does the Doctor's continual claim to remember, and his privileging that memory against whatever reality the TARDIS doors have opened up to. "This isn't right," more than one Doctor has said to more than one companion as the precursor to making it right.

This clarifies a tension identified by Who-studies concerning the Doctor's ethics. The Doctor seems to possess a dimorphic sense of ethics.[104] The Doctor clearly stands for certain principles over others.[105] Repeatedly he takes up the cause of individuals against oppressive collectives, with most of the reoccurring "big bads," the Daleks, Cybermen and Sontarans, portrayed as anti-individual, hierarchical despots.[106] Aside from some well-documented notorious examples to the contrary,[107] the Doctor's preferred method of engagement involves reasoning and non-violence. The Doctor rarely kills in person; he talks, he offers peaceful solutions, and in doing so he routinely has let the Master get away. He respects what could be called benign cultural diversity. Provided a society mirrors the ethics of peaceful coexistence, nonviolence, and talk, it will earn his protection. In this the Doctor appears to be the paradigmatic liberal humanist.[108] This manifests within his strange/estranged attraction to humans. Repeatedly the Doctor has suggested that humans' modest living, their loving and their simple deaths when their time is due, are what attract him to them. This tendency was placed in the forefront in Paul Cornell's scripted new *Who* double episodes "Human Nature/Family of Blood" where a humanized Doctor falls in love with school nurse Joan Redfern (Jessica Hynes), and the reluctance of the Doctor to leave the possible middleclass life of work, children and scarlet-dressing-gown-comfortable-old-age. These values of domestic life, of peace and reproduction are in the storehouse of memory, not the Doctor's but John Smith's memory-to-come. The significance is that the temporal ground for these values — values of living-with and getting along, values of the importance of the every-day — is timefullness.

However, the Doctor is *not* a liberal humanist of live and let live. John Fiske's fabulous 1983 structuralist reading of "The Creature from the Pit"[109] argued that behind the Doctor's liberalist veneer lay the violence and oppression of capitalist system where conflict is man-aged.[110] In "Family of Blood" the Doctor chooses to be the Doctor, and not the human school teacher. The Doctor has always been surrounded by death. Not an episode goes by without a body count, especially during the "high gothic" Philip Hinchcliffe era. The Doctor's proximity to this death was firmly established in Davies' new *Who* opening episode "Rose" where Clive (Mark Benton), in a parody of *Doctor Who* fandom, tells Rose (Billie Piper) that the only certainty if the Doctor is about is that people are going to die.[111] The Doctor is repeatedly the locus of "terrible decision." The Doctor makes, programs or facil-itates death. This dimension to the Doctor was made very explicit in the final seasons of the original run, in episodes like "The Cures of Fenric"[112] and "Silver Nemesis,"[113] where the clownish superficiality of McCoy became transposed by an alien, manipulative personality. The Doctor in action and inaction, through deciding to stay or to leave in his blue box, through helping or, as Tennant played with firm features and fiery eyes, refusing to aid, dic-tates the fates of the mere time and space bound creatures he lords over. This Doctor is not the liberal humanist of cosmopolitan values, but rather a primal figure of pure violence — a sovereign in the Schmittian sense — who guards the everyday through the terror of the exception.[114] This is the ethics, or, more precisely, proto-ethics, of the timeless being; past, present, future are known, mapped and are to be technically manipulated. This is the being that is responsible for the unfolding of time, rather than subject to its flows.

So the Doctor manifests both temporal ethics. He, after all, has two hearts; one heart is the liberal humanist heart of memory, and letting live in-time; the other heart the will to power of chronology, timelessness, and terrible decision. This binary circulatory system places the essence of the Doctor in both ways of being in time. The earlier suggestion of the technicity disclosed by chronology and the organic-ness of memory suggests a cyber-netic-ness to the Doctor. The alien, time-traveling Doctor, in community with the Daleks and Cybermen, can be considered a cyborg. There is clearly a symbiotic relationship between Doctor and TARDIS. Most of the regeneration scenes occur inside the TARDIS; and the Doctor would not be a Time Lord — with the timeless technicity of the will to power that the species name suggests — without his "Type 40 Time Capsule." For Anne Cranny-Francis and Tulloch this hybridity of the Doctor makes sense of the Doctor's complicated ethics. For them the Doctor is logical *and* emotional; and as such "the series explores the nature of embodied human subjectivity as a mixed, and muddled sensory, emotional and intellectual complex, not a simple linear Cartesian."[115] Whereas the Daleks and Cybermen fail through a prioritizing of the rational and technical, underpinned by chronology, over the emotions and memory, for the Doctor "ethical judgments ... [are] not based on intellectual or rationalist judgments but on a fully embodied, emotional, sensory and intellectual engagement with the context of judgment."[116] And this, like the TARDIS' Emergency Program One, returns this chapter to an earlier moment in timespace; namely its opening question.

"What has made *Doctor Who* enduring?" is because it is an "unfolding text," and it is because it is about time. But it, specifically, has endured across time because the Doctor — likeable, mysterious, eccentric, sometimes handsome — is critically performative of what it means to live Western time. For Martin Heidegger, the English analytical distinctions of A-series and B-series did not feature in his rejection of the received as the "vulgar" account of time.[117] For Heidegger the Western tradition missed what he saw as the specific human significance of time.[118] Being is temporal; and this temporality is assured by being thrown into the world, with the certainty of the finitude of death.[119] Yet Being is aware of its own being; its primal futurity safeguards past and present. In this Heidegger's Being exists across times while simultaneously it can only be in a linear time that ends in death. To be human in the West is to be timefull *and also* timeless.[120] For Heidegger the challenge is to be "res-olute"[121] in the present and grasp the unity of the three temporal dimensions — the ecstases[122] — as the ground for free action; that is action that does not unthinkingly reflect the has-been of the past, or frantically avoiding the will-be of the death-that-awaits.[123]

The Doctor endures because the time-travelling being that was birthed by Sydney Newman and Verity Lambert in 1963 appeals across the age-brackets because of his res-oluteness. The Doctor, and not the Master, *is* the master of time. This is what Western time calls the beings of the West to be. The Doctor is a paradigm of what it means to be a being gifted with memory and chronology. The Doctor is not infallible in his actions. He regularly makes mistakes, sometimes, as in "The Ark,"[124] "Face of Evil,"[125] and "Bad Wolf,"[126] discovering his earlier involvement has necessitated further involvement. "I am sorry, I am sorry" became one of the tenth doctor's verbal cues. But what the Doctor shows, time and time again, is that the timelessness of chronology empowers the making of change; while the timefullness of memory is the touchstone for this making of the world.

The Doctor is not a "hero" in the Joseph Campbell tradition; he is no farm boy of mysterious parentage, who through coincident quests into a wider universe where his true identity and mythic *conserving* role can be revealed.[127] The Doctor, possessor of chronology and memory, is the changer of worlds. Although Fiske's use of the term "conservative" has a specific pedigree within his neo–Marxist orientation, the Doctor is not, intra-text, a con-server of the status quo. For every invasion story where the threat from without is repulsed; there is another story of social and political change. To remain within the Campbell oeuvre the Doctor is much more a "trickster"[128] character than the hero. Humans might want to declare that he is neither "trickster nor goblin," but at the very moment he acts remarkably trickster-like, magically appearing on stage as the anti–Doctor army chants for courage.[129] A more experienced foe seems to know more. "Gandalf" taunts the Master (John Simm) to the aged tenth Doctor in "Last of the Time Lords." In community with J. R. R. Tolkien's definitional fantasy wizard, the Doctor through technics of talk, wand (sonic screwdriver), and magic cabinet (TARDIS), and with the confidence of memory and emotion, discharges a responsibility to the becoming of the world.

This calling to safeguard becoming, through the interplay of memory and chronology is what was played out in the Moffat penned 2010 season-ending "The Big Bang"[130] where memory — Amy Pond's (Karen Gillan) and the Doctor's — is the locale for the rebooting of creation. Moffat, the most time conscious of new *Who*'s fan-producers, could be seen bring-ing exactly to the forefront what is enduring about *Doctor Who*. In the West our tendency to timelessness witnessed by our power to make the world through technologies of time (our diaries and calendars of known futures), and all our time saving devices (our transport, information and domestic technologies) coexists with our timefullness of memory and finitude. The Doctor speaks not just to the complexities of this dimorphic being, but the calling to this being to be responsible for the becoming of the world.

NOTES

1. Saint Augustine, "Confessions" (Harmondsworth, Middlesex: Penguin, 1961), Book XI, 14: p. 264.
2. Piers D. Britton, and Simon J. Barker, *Reading Between Designs: Visual Imagery and the Generation of Meaning in the Avengers, the Prisoner, and Doctor Who* (Austin: University of Texas Press, 2003): p. 135.
3. Lance Parkin, "Truths Universally Acknowledged: How the 'Rules' of *Doctor Who* Affect the Writing," in *Thirdperson: Authoring and Exploring Vast Narratives*, ed. Pat Harrigan and Noah Wardrip-Fin (Cambridge: MIT Press, 2009).
4. John Shelton Lawrence, "Introduction: Spectacle, Merchandise, and Influence," in *Finding the Force of the Star Wars Franchise*, ed. Matthew Wihelm Kapell and John Shelton Lawrence (New York: Peter Lang, 2006).
5. Jonathan Bignell, "The Child as Adressee, Viewer and Consumer in Mid–1960s *Doctor Who*," in *Time and Relative Dissertations in Space: Critical Perspectives on Doctor Who*, ed. David Butler (Manchester: Manchester University Press, 2007): pp. 51–53.
6. Alan McKee, "Is *Doctor Who* Australia," *Media International Australia*, no. 132 (2009).
7. Parkin, "Truths Universally Acknowledged," p. 19.
8. C.B. Harvey, "Canon, Myth, and Memory in Doctor Who," in *The Mythological Dimensions of Doctor Who*, ed. Anthony Burdge, Jessica Burke, and Kristine Larson (Cawfordville, Kitsune Books, 2010): p. 24.
9. Liz Shannon Miller, "'Doctor Who' Honored by Guinness: Sci-Fi Series Considered Most Successful of All-Time," *Variety*, 26 July 2009, http://www.variety.com/article/VR1118006512?refCatId=14 (8 February 2011).
10. John Tulloch and Henry Jenkins, *Science Fiction Audiences: Watching Doctor Who and Star Trek* (London, Routledge, 1995). See also Matt Hills, "The Dispersible Television Text: Theorising Moments of the New Doctor Who," *Science Fiction Film and Television* 1, no. 1 (2008).
11. Parkin, "Truths Universally Acknowledged," p. 15.
12. Matt Hills, *Triumph of a Time Lord: Regenerating Doctor Who in the Twenty-First Century* (London: I.B. Tauris, 2010): p. 60.
13. "School Reunion"; Anne Cranny-Francis and John Tulloch, "Vaster Than Empire(s), and More Slow: The Politics and Economics of Embodiment in *Doctor Who*," in *Thirdperson: Authoring and Exploring Vast Narratives*, ed. Pat Harrigan and Noah Wardrip-Fin (Cambridge: MIT Press, 2009): p. 346.
14. John Tulloch and Manuel Alvardo, *Doctor Who: The Unfolding Text* (London: Macmillian, 1983): p. 3.
15. Ibid., pp. 4–5.
16. James Chapman, *Inside the TARDIS: The Worlds of Doctor Who a Cultural History* (London: I.B. Tauris, 2006): p. 3.
17. Stan Beeler, "*Stargate SG-1* and the Quest for the Perfect Science Fiction Premise," in *The Essential Science Fiction Reader*, ed. J.P. Telotte (Lexington: University Press of Kentucky, 2008): p. 267.
18. Britton and Barker, *Reading Between Designs*, p.167.
19. Ibid., pp. 184–189.
20. Chapman, *Inside the TARDIS*, p. 103.
21. Alec Charles, "The Ideology of Anachronism: Television, History and the Nature of Time," in *Time and Relative Dissertations in Space: Critical Perspectives on Doctor Who*, ed. David Butler (Manchester: Manchester University Press, 2007): p. 113.
22. Hills, *Triumph of a Time Lord*, p.5–6.
23. Ibid., pp. 7, 90.
24. As obvious, recent, exception was the 2010 Christmas special "A Christmas Carol."
25. "The Time Meddler"; "The Time Monster"; "The Time Warrior"; "The Invasion of Time"; "Time-Flight"; "Timelash"; "Time and the Rani"; "Last of the Time Lords"; "The End of Time." For program details see Videography.
26. Hills, *Triumph of a Time Lord*, pp. 88–115.

27. "Utopia."

28. "The Runaway Bride."

29. "The End of the World."

30. "The Reign of Terror."

31. "The King's Demons."

32. "Tooth and Claw."

33. "Timelash."

34. "Vicent and the Doctor."

35. "The Unquiet Dead."

36. "Victory of the Daleks."

37. "Father's Day."

38. "Pyramids of Mars."

39. Hills, *Triumph of a Time Lord*, p. 94.

40. David Lewis, "The Paradoxes of Time Travel," *American Philosophical Quarterly* 13, no. 2 (1976): pp. 149–152.

41. John Henderson, "Doctor Who and the Curse of Fatal Death," in *Doctor Who*, United Kingdom, BBC, 1999.

42. "Day of the Daleks."

43. Ibid.

44. "Father's Day."

45. "Genesis of the Daleks."

46. "Last of the Time Lords."

47. "Waters of Mars."

48. "The Impossible Planet."

49. "The Aztecs."

50. "The Time Meddler."

51. "The Gunfighters."

52. Neil Perryman, "*Doctor Who* and the Convergence of Media: A Case Study in 'Transmedia Storytelling,'" *Convergence: The International Journal of Research into Media Technologies* 14, no. 1 (2008): pp. 27–28.

53. "The Parting of the Ways."

54. "The Lodger."

55. "The Girl in the Fireplace."

56. "Blink."

57. "Silence in the Library."

58. "A Good Man Goes to War."

59. "The Eleventh Hour."

60. "The Three Doctors"; "The Five Doctors."

61. "The Doctor's Daughter"; "The Unearthly Child."

62. "Revelation of the Daleks."

63. Hills, *Triumph of a Time Lord*, pp. 212–214.

64. Chapman, *Inside the TARDIS*, p. 82.

65. Ibid., p. 157.

66. "The War Machines."

67. "City of Death."

68. "Revelation of the Daleks."

69. "Utopia."

70. "Vicent and the Doctor."

71. "Voyage of the Dammed."

72. "The Stolen Earth."

73. G. Todd Davis, "The Eternal Vigil: Captain Jack as Byronic Hero," in *Illuminating Tourchwood: Essays on Narrative, Character and Sexuality in the BBC Series*, ed. Andrew Ireland (Jefferson, NC: McFarland, 2010): p. 85.

74. Chapman, *Inside the TARDIS*, p. 142.

75. Hills, *Triumph of a Time Lord*, p. 154.

76. Mark Bould, "Science Fiction in the United Kingdom," in *The Essential Science Fiction Reader*, ed. J.P. Telotte (Lexington: University Press of Kentucky, 2008): p. 225.

77. "Rose."

78. Chapman, *Inside the TARDIS*, p. 11.

79. Hills, *Triumph of a Time Lord*, pp. 213–214.

80. Svetlana Boym, *The Future of Nostalgia* (New York: Basic Books, 2001): pp. 41–42.

81. See for example Lance Parkin, *Ahistory: An Unathorised History of the Doctor Who Universe* (Des Moines: Mad Norwegian Press, 2006).

82. Plato, *Timaeus and Critias*, trans. Desmond Lee (London: Penguin, 1965): pp. 51–52 [37–38].

83. Genevieve Lloyd, *Being in Time: Selves and Narrators in Philosophy and Literature* (London: Routledge, 1993): p. 15.

84. Aristotle, "Physics," in *The Complete Works of Aristotle: The Revised Oxford Translation*, ed. Jonathan Barnes (Princeton: Princeton University Press, 1984): pp. 369–378 [218ᵃ-224ᵃ].

85. Richard M. Gale, "The Static Versus the Dynamic Temporal," in *The Philosophy of Time: A Collection of Essays*, ed. Richard M. Gale (Highlands, NJ: Humanities Press, 1968): p. 66.

86. John McTaggart and Ellis McTaggart, *The Nature of Existence*, vol. 2 (Cambridge: Cambridge University Press, 1927): p. 11 [307].

87. Ibid., p. 10 [306].

88. Craig Bourne, *A Future for Presentism* (Oxford: Clarendon Press, 2006): p. 3.

89. "Time and the Rani."

90. Bourne, *A Future for Presentism*, p. 10.

91. Louis E. Wolcher, *Law's Task: The Tragic Circle of Law, Justice and Human Suffering* (Aldershot, Ashgate, 2008): pp. 176–177.

92. Robin Le Poidevin, *The Images of Time* (Oxford: Oxford University Press, 2007): p. 79.

93. "Nightmare of Eden."

94. Tulloch and Alvarado, *Doctor Who*, pp. 160–168.

95. Bernard Stiegler, *Technics and Time, 1: The Fault of Epimetheus*, trans. Richard Beardsworth (Stanford: Stanford University Press, 1998): p. 213.

96. Martin Heidegger, "The Question Concerning Technology," in *The Question Concerning Technology and Other Essays* (New York: Harper & Row, 1977): p. 24.

97. Martin Heidegger, *The Concept of Time*, trans. William McNeill (Oxford: Basil Blackwell, 1992): p. 2E.

98. "Human Nature."

99. "The Family of Blood."

100. "Utopia."

101. Britton and Barker, *Reading Between Designs*, 184–189.

102. "The Doctor's Wife."

103. Stephen David Ross, *Un-Forgetting: Re-Calling Time Lost* (New York: Global Academic, 2009).

104. See generally Lindy A. Orthia, "'Sociopathetic Abscess' or 'Yawning Chasm'? The Absent Postcolonial Transition in *Doctor Who*," *The Journal of Commonwealth Literature* 45, no. 2 (2010); Alan McKee, "Is Doctor Who Political?" *European Journal of Cultural Studies* 7, no. 2 (2004).

105. Nicholas J. Cull, "'Bigger on the Inside...': *Doctor Who* as British Cultural History," in *The Historian, Television and Television History*, ed. Graham Roberts and Philip M. Taylor (Luton: University of Luton Press, 2001): p. 100; Peter R. Gregg, "England Looks to the Future: The Cultural Forum Model and *Doctor Who*," *Journal of Popular Culture* 37, no. 4 (2004): p. 652.

106. Bould, "Science Fiction in the United Kingdom," p. 217.

107. Tulloch and Jenkins, *Science Fiction Audiences*, p. 160.

108. Orthia, "'Sociopathetic Abscess' or 'Yawning Chasm'? The Absent Postcolonial Transition in *Doctor Who*," p. 216; Dee Amy-Chinn, "Rose Tyler: The Ethics of Care and the Limit of Agency," *Science Fiction Film and Television* 1, no. 2 (2008).

109. "The Creature from the Pit."

110. John Fiske, "*Doctor Who*: Ideology and the Reading of a Popular Narrative Text," *Australian Journal of Screen Theory* 14–15 (1983): p. 96.

111. "Rose."

112. "The Curse of Fenric."

113. "Silver Nemesis."

114. Carl Schmitt, *Political Theology: Four Chapters on the Concept of Sovereignty*, trans. George Schwab (Cambridge: MIT Press, 1922): pp. 5–7.

115. Cranny-Francis and Tulloch, "Vaster Than Empire(s), and More Slow: The Politics and Economics of Embodiment in *Doctor Who*," p. 354.

116. Ibid.

117. Pierre Keller, "Heidegger's Critique of the Vulgar Notion of Time," *International Journal of Philosophical Studies* 4, no. 1 (1996): pp. 45–46.

118. Martin Heidegger, *Being and Time*, ed. Dennis J. Schmidt, trans. Joan Stambaugh, (New York: State University of New York Press, 1996): p. 217 [235].

119. Ibid., pp. 227–231 [245–249].

120. Ibid., p. 384 [419].

121. Ibid., p. 274 [298].

122. Ibid., p. 321 [350].

123. Ibid., p. 319 [348]. See Carol J. White, *Time and Death: Heidegger's Analysis of Finitude* (Aldershot: Ashgate, 2005): pp. 107–108.

124. "The Ark."

125. "The Face of Evil."

126. "Bad Wolf."

127. Jospeh Campbell, *The Hero with a Thousand Faces*, 2d ed. (Princeton: Princeton University Press, 1968).

128. Joseph Campbell, *The Masks of God: Primitive Mythology* (New York: Penguin, 1959): p.273.

129. "A Good Man Goes to War."

130. "The Big Bang."

6

Effecting the Cause

Time Travel Narratives

PAUL BOOTH

"Time travel—you can't keep it straight in your head"

In "The Big Bang" (2010), the final episode of the fifth season of the new *Doctor Who* series, the Doctor, while completely encased in a giant vault called the Pandorica, also appears in front of a surprised Rory, who recently watched the Time Lord get locked in the vault. This newly-appeared Doctor and the understandably-shocked Rory have the following head-hurting conversation:

DOCTOR: "You need to get me out of the Pandorica."
RORY: "But you're not in the Pandorica."
DOCTOR: "Yes I am. Well, now I'm not, but I was back then ... which is *now* from your point of view, which is *back then* from my point of view. Time travel — you can't keep it straight in your head."[1]

Rory's bewilderment is palpable, as the Doctor's appearance to Rory comes as a result of the Doctor's time manipulation. Namely, the Doctor traveled from the future, in which he *has* escaped from the Pandorica, to tell Rory how to help him escape from the Pandorica. Confusing? It only gets more so.

Doctor Who's audience must have gotten used to the dynamism of time travel narratives throughout the temporally-complex fifth series of *Doctor Who*. The notion of time travel, as arguably the central focus of the 2005–present "new *Who*" series of *Doctor Who*,[2] and as a component of the 1963–1989 classic *Who*, has become a singular *narrative device* which presupposes a number of assumptions about the nature of time, history and memory, all of which *Doctor Who* skillfully — but playfully — negotiates and synthesizes through the travels of the Doctor and his companions. Although there are many differences between the classic *Who* and the new *Who* series, I believe none is more intrinsic to helping understand larger shifts in the cultural consciousness than those that highlight temporal displacement as a narrative focus.

From its start as a historically-themed children's show through today's action-adventure multi-media experience, *Doctor Who* has thrilled audiences with bizarre aliens, macabre humor, larger-than-life villains, strange worlds, and time travel mechanics. Noticeably, however, in the traditional 1963–1989 series the actual concept of time travel is rarely explored — a few mentions of the *fact* of time travel usually serve as plot constructs to propel the Doctor from story to story. The actual philosophy of time travel is often ignored, slighted, or elided, often through the Doctor's well-timed witty banter or through televisual slight-of-hand. For example, in the classic serial "Genesis of the Daleks" (1975) the Doctor philosophizes about his ability as a time traveler to commit genocide of the Daleks in their own past:

> Do I have the right? Simply touch one wire against the other, and that's it. The Daleks cease to exist. Hundreds of millions of people, thousands of generations can live without fear, in peace ... and never even know the word "Dalek."[3]

His qualms are justified, for the ultimate destruction of the Daleks would not only "wipe out a whole intelligent life-form," but would also cause an unmentioned problem — namely, a bilking paradox, wherein the destruction of the Daleks would cause a break in the timeline so large that there would be no reason for the Doctor to go back in time to destroy the Daleks.[4] Instead of dealing with this paradox, the serial postpones the decision of the Dalek's destruction for a later date, which wraps up the cause/effect narrative without exploring any of the larger time travel implications or causality loops involved in the process.

The traditional series' elision of time travel, however, shifts in the new series to a fascination for it. Take, for example, the new *Who* episode, "Smith and Jones." The first shot the audience sees is of new companion Martha Jones walking down the street in London. She is approached by the Doctor, whom she has yet to meet. He takes off his tie and exclaims, "Like so, see?" The audience is presented with time travel before they even experience a plot. At the end of the episode, when Martha doesn't believe the Doctor actually is a time traveler, he hops in his TARDIS, dematerializes, and returns a few seconds later holding his tie. It is another neat ending, and exists as a moment of narrative excitement to subvert the audience's conventional expectations for cause/effect plotlines. This subversion becomes major focus in the new *Who*.

Indeed, I wish to deal most directly with causes and effects; the title of this chapter reflects the necessarily awkward parlance one must take when exploring effects that emerge before causes. If we take the definition of *effect* as "to produce ... bring about; accomplish; make happen," then we must assume that causality itself is solely uni-directional.[5] Causes lead to effects. Yet, our very human ability to think outside this causal notion is what separates us from the animals.[6] As Suddendorf and Corballis argue, the human "ability to travel mentally in time — an ability that is itself characterized by generativity and combinatorial flexibility," is the primary way we understand the relationship between our environment and ourselves.[7] In this essay, I examine time travel as a narrative device within the world of *Doctor Who*, and argue that time travel as television trope serves as a facilitating heuristic for contemporary, complex narratives. This assessment stands alongside Matt Hills's book, which states that the time travel motifs in new *Who* reverberate with new readings of traditional *generic* expectations.[8] I agree with Hills in this regard, that genre is equally mutable in new *Who*, but I think that the narrative implications of time travel deserve attention as well.

Using a narratological assessment of *Doctor Who*, therefore, I examine the implications of time travel for illuminating issues of narrative theory. Although obviously not a factual science program, and the actual mechanics of time travel would assumingly be not as exciting to most viewers as the latest Dalek design or Sontaran invasion plan, the notion of time travel is central not only to the plot of the new *Doctor Who*, but also to the structure of its narrative. In order to develop this idea further, I use Richard Walsh's conception of a "rhetoric of fictionality" as a heuristic for examining the evolution of narrative in *Doctor*

Who.[9] Then, I cull from *Doctor Who* illustrations of complex narratives, and use the example of time travel to further explore this narrative trope in terms of our quotidian media usage.[10]

Time Travel and Narrative Structure: "The TARDIS is exploding right now"

As a concept as well as in practice, time travel as a trope offers a useful heuristic for examining narrative theory. One of *Doctor Who*'s most important contributions for a scholarly investigation lies in its exemplar treatment of changing narrative tropes.[11] It should come as no surprise, then, that time travel in fiction offers a useful way of renegotiating what narrative scholar Richard Walsh calls the "complex relations between narration (whether authorial or not) and fictional representation."[12] Through these relations, audiences take meaning from narratives and apply it to their own lives to learn about and discover aspects of their selves. For Walsh, this distinction, between what a narrative says and what an audience takes from it, forms the basis for a number of explorations of the power of narrative. Narrative both offers meaning and allows audiences to create meaning. From the earliest narratology studies of Propp to more contemporary models of active reading espoused by Fiske and Jenkins, the dichotomy between a narrative's *motive* and its *interpretation* hinge on the meanings that audiences create from it.

Time travel offers a mode of storytelling that highlights the divide between the narrative *story* from a narrative *discourse*.[13] The story describes what happens in a narrative, while the discourse represents how that story is told to the viewer. That is, what we see on the screen is a discourse, in whatever chronological order in which it is presented, and our mental reconstruction of those images into a chronological order is the story. Traditionally, our culture reinforces the notion that a story is privileged over a discourse, as it is the story that the audience seemingly uncovers.[14] Yet, this privileging exists within a logical impossibility: namely, if the discourse is what reveals the story to us, then the *story* must be inherently secondary to the *discourse*. In fact, taken to its logical extreme, the fictional story literally *cannot exist* without an accompanying discourse. The telling of the story must precede the story itself.

As Ricoeur reminds us, all narrative takes place within a prescribed time, an "uncriticized temporal framework."[15] As his narrative philosophy describes, therefore, the main function of a narrative is to *construct* and *order* events in a timeframe. Time travel highlights this role by creating two separate but connected time frames. In the first timeframe the time traveler ventures outside his/her timescape. In the second timeframe the series of events that the time traveler leaves structures its own timescape, from which the time traveler is now removed. In *Doctor Who* terms the Doctor exists "outside" of time, but that doesn't mean that he himself is not affected by time — he ages, but he ages in a way counter to the rest of the (linear) universe. As an audience we follow his story, but the discourse could just as well illustrate Rose's, Sarah Jane's, Donna's, or Amy's.[16] It is in the show's choice to follow the Doctor that our experience of *Doctor Who*'s narrative becomes destabilized.

Specifically, the effect of time travel highlights the separation of the experience of the story from the story itself. The audience follows the Doctor's timescapes, and the underlying story of the (linear) universe is constructed from the audience's fragmented experiences with the Doctor. In this subjective frame of reference, the audience uncovers the story from the exposition of their flight with the Doctor. But the Doctor acts and causes acts to happen across time. Therefore, to understand time in this manner means that the audience must recognize that any decisions the Doctor makes *must have already been made*. Everything that has, will have, or continues to happen, has already happened. The audience views what is "now" to the Doctor, but which is always necessarily "past" in the specific story of the universe. While the discourse of *Doctor Who* must therefore contain the events and elements that make up the story of *Doctor Who*, it is only through a combination of the linear and nonlinear telling of the discourse that the audience sees the story. The 2010 Christmas special "A Christmas Carol" represents this linear/nonlinear discursive style, as the majority of the discourse takes place in the *now* with the Scrooge-like Karzran Sardick, but the Doctor also travels to Sardick's past and interacts with his past self in the *now* of the discourse in order to elicit changes in the present/future. By presenting his present self with images of his past, the Doctor changes Sardick's present memories, and affects his future decisions.

To time travel within a narrative, therefore, presupposes the separation of discourse and story, but also hinges on the fact that these two descriptors are inextricably linked. Time travel changes the story by adjusting the discourse. We can see this dual nature of narrative in "The Pandorica Opens" and "The Big Bang." The Doctor has just learned that the Pandorica—a mythical prison which was built to trap a wizard ("the Pandorica? Ha! That's just a fairy tale," exclaims the Doctor in "Flesh and Stone")—turns out to be his own prison, and he is the "wizard" in his own Time Lord fairy tale. Surprised at this revelation, he screams, "No! Please listen to me! The TARDIS is exploding right now and I'm the only one who can stop it!"

Indeed, in the discourse the timing of the opening of the Pandorica in the year A.D. 102 matches the precise point in time in which the TARDIS disappears in the future (A.D. 2010—the palindromic match to the Pandorica's opening). But when exactly is "*now*" for the Doctor in the story? These two points, separated by thousands of years, are linked in the discourse, as the *now* in the Doctor's sentence seems to be referring not to a linear progression of time, but rather to a construction of time as *simultaneously co-existent* linearities. What the Doctor implies, therefore, is that time is not uni-linear, but rather multi-linear: multiple perspectives on the timeline exist *at the same time*. This temporality is mirrored in the relationship and the dichotomy between the Doctor's narrative story and discourse. We see the events as simultaneous *and* causal, even if in linear time they are not. This bifurcation of meaning, this contradictory yet inseparable divide in narrative theory, is reflected back at the audience, for the audience sees both events happening simultaneously in the discourse, although of course the opening of the Pandorica occurred two thousand years prior to the explosion in the story.

Similarly, the Doctor was sent back to that point in time *precisely because* the Pandorica was opening. Cause and effect—the central tenets of narrative itself—are thrown into confusion, as the opening of the Pandorica signaled the end of the Universe precisely because the Pandorica was opening in order to prevent the end of the universe. The Pandorica's opening is timed perfectly from this one event: the explosion of the TARDIS and the locking up of the Doctor. The only way this could happen is if we imagine that time travel in *Doctor Who* assumes that time is multi-linear, and that all points emanate from an ever-changing "now." This solution points to the necessity of believing that time from any event must be measured from itself as a zero point and moving outwards in multiple directions equally (in the way we measure B.C. in a numerically similar, but directionally opposite manner than we do A.D.).

As Hills suggests, the use of time in *Doctor Who* may be "more fundamental to the series' narrative construction" than anything else.[17] For a show like *Doctor Who,* which projects contemporary issues into science-fiction settings,[18] the way it deals with narrative complexity is a reflection of an increased temporal complexity in our own lives.[19] Therefore, just as we can examine the narrative of *Doctor Who* to elucidate issues of narrative sustainability, so too should we examine the implications of complex narratives on our quotidian selves. The increasing complexity of the time travel narrative of *Doctor Who* emerges during a period in time when our own subjective lives are under constant scrutiny. In short, we "time travel" every time we glimpse our Facebook news, our RSS feeds, and our wiki trends. Like Sardick in "A Christmas Carol," we literally watch our immediate past/present flow before our eyes, affecting our present/future. In his authoritative book about time travel, physicist Paul Nahin illustrates this flow by quoting H. B. Franklin: "When one says time travel what one really means is an extraordinary dislocation of someone's consciousness in time."[20] It is this dislocation which is so significant to today's complexity in terms of the *Doctor Who* narrative.

Our use of hypermediated digital technology has only increased this sense of timelessness in our lives: according to Andrew Gorman, "there is a pervasive uneasiness about our present and an uncertainty about our future, along with a concurrent nostalgia about our past" all functioning at the same time in our postmodern media usage.[21] Take, for example, the use of "tabs" on today's Internet browser windows. Instead of opening a new browser window for every webpage one wants to view, browsers such as Internet Explorer, Apple Safari, Mozilla Firefox, and Google Chrome allow the use of tabs: multiple windows which open on the same browser. One could hypothetically open a Facebook page, a Google search, an email program, a Netflix streaming queue, and so on. Each of these windows forms a multi-linear experience of the web. Each opens onto a particular time; a particular space. Indeed, the use of these hypermediated windows interacts with our own experiences online, such that each window appears to have a different time frame. We may not be traveling in time like *Doctor Who* while we sit at our computers, but we peek into a different time frames, different temporal situations. Our single browser becomes a vehicle for the exploration of the temporal displacement of our selves. For example, I may have my email set to refresh every minute, my Facebook feed set to refresh every ten, and my Google news set for updates every five. My *linear* experience of these media does not reflect the *multi-linear* existence of the browser's windows; but these windows reveal a *multi-linear* slice of my life. Like the Doctor, we can return to the past and "refresh" the present. I certainly don't mean to insinuate that *Doctor Who* is the *cause* of our hypermediated life, nor do I indicate the opposite; rather, I merely contend that the paradoxes at the heart of new *Who* become symbolic of our narrativized experiences as "a particular way of meaning, a particular kind of contribution to cultural discourse at large."[22] *Doctor Who,* in this way, is both an exemplar of, and a comment on, quotidian changes in our cultural life.

Memories, Paradox, and the Pandorica: "I'm rubbish at weddings ... especially my own"

Time travel narratives question our most cherished ideas about narrative coherence and structure, but this transgression of linearity is far more than mere escapist entertainment (although much of it can be pleasurable). These narratives often present a serious look at the issues affecting the everyday lives of its viewers, for when stories venture into the past or future, they are most often making a comment about the present.[23]

Memory is one of the strongest and most relevant types of modern time travel.[24] Even as we view a narrative linearly, especially on television, which pushes us ever-forward, we also revisit scenes in our memories, or discuss them repeatedly with other fans. We research trivia on the Internet Movie Database, or view continuity on tardis.wikia. Although *Doctor Who*'s narrative might be told from start to finish, our experience of that narrative is continually reinvented through our memory. Memory is also, quite possibly, the most paradox-filled type of time travel. Our memories allow us to remember the past, but it's a past hopelessly filled with the detritus of media, moments, and myths. The confluence of times past manifests within our memories, just as Sardick's experiences with his past, present and future selves influence his life in "A Christmas Carol." This is not to say we forget who we are or what we do, merely to reflect that as a necessary condition of human memory we often forget, re-inscribe, or re-shuffle events in our minds. The mind creates temporal confusion, a veritable apparition of the schizophrenia endemic to the postmodern age, according, at least, to Jameson.[25] The postmodern citizen is not confused as to his/her temporal proximity to events, but rather conflates all levels of temporality into a vague sense of displeasure with non-contemporaneous events.

Such temporal uneasiness is endemic to the Doctor's travels. As he emphatically states in "Blink," "I've got a complex life. Things sometimes don't happen to me in the right order. Especially weddings. I'm rubbish at weddings ... especially my own." Memory, for the Doctor, is an inherently non-linear experience, a truth he must learn to accept as a Time Lord who both creates and encounters time displacement in a variety of places. As viewers, the audience follows the Doctor in a linear manner — we know the first, second, third Doctors as they follow each other chronologically — but the Doctor does not — literally, cannot — live his life in a linear fashion. Yet linearity is the most inherent structure of the human experience. Trying to reconcile the linearity of our life (and the show *Doctor Who*) becomes a struggle when faced with inherently non-linear experiences (the Doctor's life; time travel storytelling).

The result of this reconciliation is a paradox. In theory, the paradox is a logical contradiction, a statement both *true* and *false* at the same time. Perhaps the most well-known time travel paradox, the Grandfather paradox, revels in the instability of time travel: "What would happen," it asks, "if you went back in time and killed your grandfather before you were born?" How were you then born, and able to travel back in time to kill him?[26] It is an inherently unstable situation. As Alec Charles persuasively argues, the new *Who* resolves paradoxes using causal loops, which are in essence the opposite of the Grandfather paradox.[27] Causal loops represent a closed temporal loop; for example, when characters from the future are inspired to go to the past by an event that they themselves cause during their trip.[28] The "Bad Wolf" trope from the first new *Who* series is a quintessential example: Bad Wolf Rose travels back in time to leave the phrase "Bad Wolf" at various temporalities during her travels to spur her past self to become Bad Wolf Rose.[29] Instead of languishing in the instability of time (and the negativity of death), the new *Who* revels in the stability of self-generation (and the positivity of sustaining life).[30]

For the Doctor, such paradoxes are a way of life. Yet for humans, paradoxes are extremely vexing. The only way to reconcile this type of paradox is to think in a dialetheisistic manner, or to see that *both* the thesis and the antithesis of any proposition must be true. As Lewis points out, this dialetheisistic argument is not impossible, merely improbable for our limited worldview.[31] Further, Nahin shows that "paradoxes are often offensive only to human, culturally biased intuitions about how things 'ought to' work, since the classical physical laws are not offended by a reversal in the direction of time."[32] That is, because narrative is a *human* construct, it must be somewhat determined by human characteristics. The resolution of paradoxes, which is central to the New *Who* era, becomes of the utmost concern, because *not* resolving paradox is troubling to conventional narrative theory. Audiences need an explanation, no matter how "gobbledygook" it might be. A perfect example of this comes in "Blink," in which the Doctor explains the complex temporal mechanics of time travel: "People assume that time is a strict progression of cause to effect, but actually from a non-linear, non-subjective viewpoint — it's more like a big ball of wibbly-wobbly, timey-wimey, stuff." Does this make sense? Only sort of ... but it only *sort of* has to in order to make the narrative.

The key example of the narrative resolution of the temporal paradoxes in *Doctor Who* is the new *Who* character of River Song. Just as for the Doctor, time does not move in a linear fashion for River Song. Her appearances, although few, have had momentous effects on the Doctor — the causes of which we have yet to see. Specifically, River Song married the Doctor at some point in time *after* the adventures presented in the fourth and fifth new *Who* series. Yet, chronologically, by the time the audience meets River, she had already married and divorced the Doctor. Indeed, her first appearance in the show is also her last, as she dies at the end of the episode "Forest of the Dead." Given writer/executive producer Steven Moffat's fondness for neatly-tied up time travel narratives (like "Blink" or "A Christmas Carol"), it would come as no surprise if her *last* appearance on the show served/serves as her *introduction* to the Doctor as well.

Yet, unlike the Doctor, River Song is completely human — that is, as "one of us," she tries to reconcile paradoxes into an inherent shape instead of understanding a dialetheisistic answer as the Doctor might. In the penultimate episode of the new fifth series, Amy and River have a conversation that explores this fundamental instability in human thought:

AMY: "This Pandorica thing. Last time we saw you, you warned us about it on the Byzantium."
RIVER: "Spoilers."
AMY: "No, but you told the Doctor you'd see him again when the Pandorica opens."
RIVER: "Maybe I did. But I haven't yet. But I will have."

In fact, River Song ties together these issues of temporal paradoxes within *Doctor Who* and the narrative structure I mentioned earlier in the chapter. By correlating between points in time and points in a temporal structure (which are two different things in the *Doctor Who* universe), River Song bridges the divide between timeframes, between discourse and story, and between memory and paradox.

Ultimately, what River Song's contradictory verb tenses in the previous quotation allude to is the fact that the Doctor himself, and indeed the show *Doctor Who* as a whole, are inherently unstable texts. For example, the Doctor himself has always been an entity in flux. The first producers of the show had an inkling that the narrative of the show could be intrinsically altered by the time travel plots.[33] Such alterations are later made visceral in such "special" shows as "The Three Doctors," "The Five Doctors," and "The Two Doctors" (not to mention the 2007 Children in Need special, "Time Crash"). The presence of multiple Doctors in one show makes little narrative sense — and begs the question, if the first Doctor was present at these events, why does he not later remember them?[34] ("Time Crash" neatly tied that up by allowing the Doctor to create memories as he has/had them).

But if the *Doctor* is unstable, then nothing can be more unstable than the *Doctor Who* text in general. Such instability of narrative is not only inherent in any sort of time travel story, especially when one is so characteristically dependent on paradoxes to maintain narrative consistency, but also one that has such a long and tenured history as *Doctor Who*. Given the nearly fifty-year history of the show,[35] it is natural to revisit and reevaluate central concepts of the narrative. But few shows have engaged so spectacularly and successfully with narrative revision as has *Doctor Who*. From changing the lead actor, to unexplained new interiors of the TARDIS, to revisions of canon information (did the Doctor steal the TARDIS or did he build it?), to completely rewriting the history of the Time Lords: it's surprising there's any stability at all.[36]

The focus on time travel as narrative device serves to hold together the web of unstable elements within *Doctor Who*. As I have alluded to, the paradox at the heart(s) of *Doctor Who* functions as an aesthetic and textual attempt to illustrate a quotidian existence within a networked culture. For example, the narrative of the show *Doctor Who* is inherently networked, as characters like the Doctor and River Song intersect in a variety of ways throughout time. This form of intricate networking is also represented in other contemporary complex television narratives. There is a similar "networkization" of time in other shows, like *Boomtown* (2002–2003), which detailed crimes from multiple perspectives, *Flashforward* (2009–2010), which featured a complex plot made even more complicated by the temporal displacement of character's memories, and *Lost* (2004–2010), which presented a sprawling cast of characters connected via six degrees of separation in both the past and the future.[37] Beyond character, however, television narratives themselves have become more complex and more disjointed.[38] From a narrative point of view, complexity is rapidly becoming one of the most common forms of storytelling on television. According to Jason Mittell, narrative complexity — the intricate dance between seriality and episodic narratives within long form television shows — has become more common and familiar as television storytelling techniques have evolved.[39] David Lavery has also noted this shift, calling it the emergence of "flexi-narratives."[40] In both cases, what each television scholar notes is that there has been a general trend in television narratives to *embrace* complexity. Shows like *Fringe* (2008–), *Dollhouse* (2009–2010), and *The Event* (2010–2011) present episode-long narratives (which begin and end in a single episode of television) coupled with an embracing on-going, serialized narratives through the length of the series. To see the narrative paradox as symbolic of a postmodern networkization is to form a critique of a contemporary media and technology.

Contemporary cyberculture theorists like Manual Castells posit that the flow of information shapes our relationship with industries, communities, and ourselves into a "network" of connections.[41] The network is a mesh of interconnected nodes, presenting many paths through one terrain. It is also the main metaphor we use (and have used in the past) for the hypertextual connections on the web.[42] In the past, hypertextual thinkers visualized the web as a massive network. Now, our contemporary web use doesn't just link *objects,* but also links *users.* We link our Twitter account with our Facebook, which is also connected to Skype and Pandora. It's not that we focus our life online; rather, our multiple *lives* are spread out through our connections online. Thus, the application of this new metaphor harkens back to the very audience that embraces such narrative complexity. The new *Doctor Who* text, by focusing on time travel and exposing of the paradoxes inherent within it, has formed a universal vantage point from which its complex audience can critique and be critiqued.

In the next section of this essay, I will show, using various examples from *Doctor Who*, how the evolution of time travel on the show has highlighted and justified the codes and conventions of narrative, and I will describe the way these conventions remark on the contemporary media user. Further, I will illustrate using examples from both the new *Who* and the classic *Who* that cultural implications of the network/paradox connection appear briefly in the past, but don't fully resonate until the appearance of digital and interactive technology that help revolutionize our limited notions of linearity.

Doctor Who *and Time Travel as Narrative Device:* *"Things can get very complicated"*

As I have mentioned, the cross-cutting at the end of "The Pandorica Opens" seems to indicate that both events — the Doctor being put into the Pandorica and River Song trying to stop the TARDIS from exploding — are happening at the same time. Yet, the seeming-simultaneity of the events indicates not only that peculiar notion that narrative itself can be experienced on two levels, but also that history and memory are both multi-linear as well. As he stands in front of the Alliance of alien ships — Dalek, Cybermen, Sontaran, Judoon, Nestene, Auton, Slitheen, Sycorax, Zygon, and more — the Doctor dares them to approach: "Remember every black day I ever stopped you," he cries, "and then, do the smart thing. Let somebody else try first!" The Doctor's notion of "memory" is evoked here in an odd way, as the uni-directionality of memory (we remember the past in the present, but we have no memories of the future) reverses: the Doctor is counting on *future* memories having equal weight to *past* ones. The ships recede precisely because their memory of the Doctor comes both from their future and from their past.

In fact, memory is key to the Pandorica, as it is constructed from Amy Pond's memories. The Alliance tricks the Doctor by influencing his memories of Amy Pond, and in the end it is Amy's memories of the Doctor that save the universe. Yet, the event that the alien Alliance is trying to prevent — the explosion they all "remember" — is occurring *at the same time*. They create memories in an attempt to prevent them. Their memory, in fact, is triggered by the Doctor's very attempt at uncovering the truth of the myth. The Alliance's attempt to stop the explosion is what triggered it in the first place. The Pandorica becomes a case, as time travel scholar Paul Nahin states, of the *simultaneous causation* at the heart of a causal loop: one event is both the cause and the effect of itself.[43]

In a similar manner indicated by the convergence of timelines of "The Pandorica Opens," the classic series of *Doctor Who* includes at least a couple of stories where two timelines converge on one point in the narrative. The difference between classic *Who* and new *Who*, at least in terms of temporality and narrative, is that when the early stories do deal with time travel paradoxes, their discussion is relatively minor and cursory, while much of new *Who* is preoccupied with a postmodern sensibility of time travel narration. Indeed, *Doctor Who* expert Robert Shearman explains in a documentary, "very few [classic] *Doctor Who* stories ever tackled time travel properly."[44]

The exception that proves the rule is the first episode of "The Space Museum," one of the few stories of classic *Who* that deals with time travel as something primarily more than as a means from getting from (time) point A to (time) point B. The first Doctor and his companions Ian, Barbara and Vicki materialize in an alien museum but on a different "time track" from the rest of the world. To explain this Vicki describes the materiality of time: "Time, like space, although a dimension in itself, also has dimensions of its own."[45] Time as an entity, then, becomes mutable. The four adventurers come face-to-face with themselves as exhibits in the museum, "waiting for time to catch up so they can join the story."[46] The time travelers have landed slightly *ahead* of their own future, and realize that they are actually "out of synch" with the normal timeline, as they leave no footprints, make no sounds, and hear nothing in this alien world. But instead of traveling back in time to correct their error, they merely wait for time to "catch up" with them. They have leapt into a future but are traveling backwards through it, although time for them is also flowing forwards. And the audience is watching them *progress* while time *regresses* until both timelines merge. If they've landed in the future but are traveling backwards through it, how can the audience view them normally? But then why do the *rest* of the characters also move forward? As they watch their new time track intersect with the "correct" time track, the exhibit of them disappears and the two timelines intersect. In contrast to the new *Who* series, though, this rather interesting, but ultimately unstable, time travel plot is quickly dropped and not mentioned in the second, third, or fourth episodes of the serial.

Further, in the ninth season story "Day of the Daleks," the Doctor and Jo must stop a band of guerrillas from coming back in time from the 22nd century and changing history. Yet, in order to do that, the Doctor has to allow the Daleks to intervene in Earth's history — for that's the way it has "always" happened. Contrast this version of time travel with the first season's "The Aztecs," in which the Doctor forcibly declares that no one should change the course of history. It seems as though intervention in history is important sometimes, but not other times, for as Hills reminds us, "if history were always fixed then there would be nothing [narratively] at stake."[47] The Doctor explains the temporal situation to Jo at the end of "The Day of the Daleks":

> Somehow the Daleks managed to pervert the course of history so they could conquer the earth. The guerrillas tried to change things back, but because they were part of history, their intervention just repeated the pattern. I was able to intervene and put history back on its proper tracks.[48]

In the thirteenth season's "Pyramids of Mars," as well, the Doctor and Sarah try to prevent Sutekh, a hostile alien, from destroying Earth in 1911. When Sarah mentions that Earth *wasn't* destroyed and that in her time it is quite verdant, the Doctor travels with her to an alternate "present" of her 1980, a present that emerges from the particular point in time when they *don't* stop Sutekh. The planet is a desolate wasteland; a destroyed planet. Although the classic *Who* cautions against changing history, this is the only time it actually shows us what happens when history is changed.

Yet, for the new *Who* Doctors, there is nothing more dangerous than changing history. Rose encounters this type of paradox in "Father's Day," when she saves her father's life in 1987 by averting his fatal car crash. The paradox affects all of time and space, as changing this event causes temporal disruptions across a range of technologies: Rose's mobile phone picks up messages from Alexander Graham Bell and a 1987 car stereo music plays music from the future. In retaliation for the disruption in time, the Time Vortex (an entity from which time sprang) sends "Reapers," giant dragon-like creatures, to devour all regions of temporal instability.

In tandem, there is also nothing more dangerous to the stability of a coherent narrative than a logical paradox in a discourse. If a narrative doesn't hang together, or doesn't make sense, it can ruin the audience's immersion in the story. The notion of paradoxes as plot devices is eschewed as the instability this brings in the temporal depiction of the discourse clouds narrative stability.

The paradox, in both narrative and time travel, becomes the end result of the interaction with time as the participants explore it. And precisely because paradoxes are narratively untenable, they become adversarial in the *Doctor Who* universe. The quintessential example of this appears within the two-part finale to the fourth new *Who* series, "The Sound of Drums/The Last of the Time Lords." The Master constructs out of the Doctor's TARDIS a "Paradox Machine" that allowed the Toclafane to invade and destroy the "normal" timeline of Earth.

The Toclafane create the paradox through their enslavement of the human race. As the final stage of humanity's evolution, the Tocloafane have regressed to a childlike state. The Master convinces them to travel back to their own past and subjugate the humans in their own past as their slaves. Of course, since this didn't actually happen in their/our past, their invasion becomes a paradox. The Master uses the stolen Doctor's TARDIS to create a paradox machine that keeps this causal loop open, and allows the Toclafane and the Master to rule present-day Earth. Ultimately, this creates an alternate universe, in which the Toclafane enslave Earth, the Master punishes and prematurely ages the Doctor, and Martha rallies humanity together to save the world and reset the timeline so the "year that never was" is removed from the universe. From a narrative theory standpoint, the notion of a "paradox machine" and a reversal of the alternate universe are necessary not only for the plot to conclude, but also in order for narrative coherence to be saved. If the machinery of paradox removal doesn't exist, or if humanity had had to rebuild after the invasion, the world of *Doctor Who* would have been irreconcilable with the narrative events as the audience knows them.

Yet, there remains one paradox, fully articulated in the finale of the new *Who* specials ("The End of Time") that continues to plague the coherence of the overarching narrative of the show: the erasure of the Time Lords and the Daleks in the Time War. The paradox of the disappearance of the Time Lords is vast and problematic from a narrative standpoint.

Namely, it raises the fair and complicated question of, what happened to Susan?[49]

Susan, the Doctor's granddaughter, had been a traveling companion for many years when the series started.[50] If, as the Doctor maintains about the Great Time War, all the Time Lords (and Daleks) had been removed from existence when the war ended, then how does he have a granddaughter? Is the past classic *Who* moot? Or does it exist in an alternate timeframe? Ultimately, the questions are unanswerable, because the *Doctor Who* narrative asks us not to ask them, usually through verbal wordplay or elision that belies the complex narrative confusion underlying the concept. For example, in "The Beast Below," Amy asks the Doctor why he looks human. He responds:

DOCTOR: "No, you look Time Lord. We came first."
AMY: "So there's other Time Lords, yeah?"
DOCTOR: "No. There were, but there aren't ... just me now. Long story. It was a bad day, lots of bad stuff happened."

The Time Lords have disappeared from all of time and space, yet the effect of their existence is still felt in the universe. As an audience, we must accept this fact, while also accepting that, say, the existence of Rose Tyler's father in the universe for a few moments longer than he "should" have existed is cause for the destruction of all. Or that if old Billy contacted young Billy in "Blink" that "two thirds of the universe will be destroyed."

On the one hand, we understand that this is a children's television show, and that such complexities can (and should) be written off so that we can get on with the adventure. But on the other hand, in a show that, at least recently, has spent so much time with time travel explanations and paradox reversals, it appears out of place that this fact remains unexplained. Perhaps part of the confusion over these unexplained elements lies in the fact that so much *is* explained. "Blink" has a fully articulated time travel concept; "Turn Left" and "The Last of the Time Lords" illustrate alternate world theory in a narratively satisfying way. "The End of Time" leaves off with more questions than gobbledygook answers.

Conclusion: "That takes me back. Or forward. That's the trouble with time travel; you can never remember"

As I have argued, I believe that this recent depiction of necessary messiness in temporal mechanics appears at the same moment as the rise of social media in our contemporary context. Media itself is a concept much explored in the new *Who*: in "The Time of Angels," Amy literally has to stare at a television screen in order to survive the Weeping Angel attack (this reflexively works on the audience as well, spurring us to stare intently at the screen). The tenth Doctor travels to the early days of the television in "The Idiot's Lantern." The Jagrafess attempt to take over the minds of humanity via reality television and entertainment/news in "The Long Game." Rose is obsessed with her mobile phone. Sardick watches his past self interact with the Doctor through a home projector. The depiction of media in new *Who* focuses narrative attention on the same things viewers are focusing on: television, mobile phones, and popular entertainment.

We may be the most wired, most visible and most connected beings in our history, but our lives are becoming fragmented into digital segments and our personal life narratives can be rewritten daily. Through a culture of immediacy, we receive our instant media gratification purely digitally. Netflix streaming allows me to watch any new *Who* at any time; much classic *Who* is also available. Postmodern theorists Fredric Jameson and Jean Baudrillard have both argued that our contemporary culture has flattened any distinctions between past, present and future.[51] To these theorists, we live in an extended present made prescient only through our mutual recognition of how the past reflects in the present and how the future springs from it. What *Doctor Who* seems to be interpreting here is what Sean Redmond states about our current culture: "the modern world produces a particularly acute identity crisis and existential schizophrenia"[52] Facebook and other social networks allow us to externalize our selves online.[53] I can, at any time, view my profile and experience a snapshot of my life at a particular moment in time. I am, in effect, seeing myself as I want to be perceived, in a time frame of my choosing. Similarly, in fifth series' "The Hungry Earth," the Doctor, Amy and Rory arrive in 2020 and see the future Rory and Amy standing across a field from them. The future Rory and Amy seem to be visiting the location where they know their past selves have been (where the current Rory and Amy now stand). The future Rory and Amy tour a moment from their past, revisiting their former selves, as if I were to search through my Facebook posts from 2006 and revisit my life then.

Therefore, narratively complex shows like *Doctor Who* are characterized by a type of complex *audience* that similarly finds narrative enjoyment out of the duality of off-line and online life. This focalization plays off the schizophrenic zeitgeist of the era. The end result of this audience reflection is that narrative reflects life just as life reflects narrative. Previous

Doctor Who series played off the cultural factors when they were made.[54] The difference today is that these new series of *Doctor Who* rely on storytelling *as* a structure in order to relate the ideology; in the classic series, such ideology was related through elements within the plot. The new *Who* episodes review today's cultural issues, which often revolve around technology and media use.

To highlight and focus on these issues as structural elements is not to say that the elements within the plot aren't important today, but that the structure of *Doctor Who*— the form the show itself takes — is equally important to analyze. Time travel gives us the narratological tools necessary to investigate the way discourse and story play out in a narratively complex flex-narrative. In a complex world, audiences need both stimulation and familiarity. Mittell references this in the dialogue between episodic and seriality, as the most complex narratives are those that maintain an episodic familiarity but generate serial speculation.[55] Time has to function in two paradoxical, but related, ways in *Doctor Who*. On the one hand, time has to be fixed and constant. The Doctor must be able to travel back to the cliff face in "The Pandorica Opens" that has writing on it, and importantly must also be aware that the cliff has writing on before he goes. On the other hand, time has to be more mutable and less constant than anything else. Events have to be able to happen in the past that have not yet happened before, even if participants in those events have no memory of them happening (that is, that they happen *for the first time* in the past even if the past events have already transpired to the point that they have become legend).

This temporal complexity may appeal to audiences not just because of *Doctor Who*'s history, but also because of its relation to our everyday life. We watch *Doctor Who* to help linearize our non-linear lives; to give meaning to the meaningless; to see solutions to what we perceive as paradoxes. Ultimately, the time travel narrative on television becomes a way to look both at and through our contemporary lifestyle of hypermediation.[56] Only by reconciling the paradox and the multi-linear narrative can we see the quotidian life experience of the contemporary digital citizen. Returning to my original example from the start of this essay, we can see how *Doctor Who* becomes a way to reify this concept: it is this type of reconciliation that emerges from the interplay of Rory and the doubled Doctor in "The Big Bang." When the Doctor appears and speaks to Rory, even though he is also still trapped in the Pandorica, he has doubled his own time line, folding himself back on himself. Two of him now exist, one encased in a mythological box created out of someone else's memory, the other one about to show Rory how to release himself. It's as if the Doctor is able to adjust, change, or avert his own personal history; much like we can adjust, change, or respond to our other "selves" online. And just as we can recover pieces of ourselves from our memory, or from our digital archives, so too can time travel help us here. As the Doctor earlier (later?) says in "The Big Bang":

> People fall out of the world sometimes, but they always leave traces. Little thing we can't quite account for. Faces in photographs, luggage, half eaten meals. Rings. Nothing is ever forgotten, not completely. And if something can be remembered, it can come back.

The Doctor will always come back, because he always has come back. Time travel is wonderful like that.

NOTES

1. "Big Bang." For program details see Videography.
2. See Matt Hills, *Triumph of a Time Lord: Regenerating Doctor Who in the Twenty-First Century* (London: I.B. Tauris, 2009).

3. "Genesis of the Daleks."

4. See Paul J. Nahin, *Time Machines: Time Travel in Physics, Metaphysics, and Science Fictio* (New York: Springer, 1993): p. 134.

5. "Effect," *Dictionary.com* (accessed 03 Dec 2010).

6. Thomas Suddendorf and Michael C. Corballis, "Mental Time Travel and the Evolution of the Human Mind." *Genetic, Social & General Psychology Monographs* 123.2 (1997): pp.133–68 (http://staff.science.uva.nl/~michiell/docs/MentalTime.html).

7. Ibid., p. 136. They are speaking here of using the mind to think of the past and future, not of *actual* time travel; but the general idea that the concept of time travel can be a trope that aids our human development mirrors the relationship between time travel and narrative development nicely.

8. Hills, *Triumph,* pp. 88–9.

9. Richard Walsh, *The Rhetoric of Fictionality: Narrative Theory and the Idea of Fiction* (Columbus: Ohio State University, 2007).

10. Jason Mittell, "Narrative Complexity in Contemporary American Television," *The Velvet Light Trap* 58 (2006): 29–40.

11. See Rob Shearman and Toby Hadoke. *Running Through Corridors: Rob and Toby's Marathon Watch of Doctor Who* (Des Moines: Mad Norwegian Press, 2010).

12. Walsh, *Fictionality,* p. 6.

13. See Seymour Chatman, *Story and Discourse: Narrative Structure in Fiction and Film* (Ithaca: Cornell University Press, 1978); Gérard Genette, *Narrative Discourse: An Essay in Method,* Jane Lewin, trans. (Ithaca: Cornell University Press, 1980).

14. Walsh, *Fictionality,* pp. 53–4. Walsh agrees that the discourse should be privileged.

15. Paul Ricoeur, "Narrative Time," *Critical Inquiry* 7.1 (1980): p. 170.

16. In "Blink" the audience does follow a linear character, Sally Sparrow, but the narrative's complexity increases with her non-linear interaction with the Doctor.

17. Hills, *Triumph,* p. 105.

18. Ibid., p. 91; also Marc Edward DiPaolo, "Political Satire and British-American Relations in Five Decades of *Doctor Who,*" *Journal of Popular Culture* 43.5 (Oct 2010): pp. 964–87.

19. Alec Charles, "The Ideology of Anachronism: Television, History, and the Nature of Time," in David Butler, ed., *Time and Relative Dissertations in Space: Critical Perspectives on Doctor Who* (Manchester: Manchester University Press, 2007): pp. 108–22.

20. Nahin, *Time Machines,* p. 7.

21. Andrew Gorman, "*Back to the Future*: Oedipus as Time Traveller" in Sean Redmond, ed., *Liquid Metal: The Science Fiction Film Reader* (London: Wallflower Press, 2007): p. 116.

22. Walsh, *Fictionality,* p. 6.

23. See Redmond, *Liquid Metal,* p. 113.

24. Nahin, *Time Machines,* p. 7.

25. Fredric Jameson, *Postmodernism: Or, the Cultural Logic of Late Capitalism* (Durham: Duke University Press, 1991).

26. See Nahin, *Time Machines,* pp. 193–201; and Hills, *Triumph,* p. 88.

27. Charles, "Ideology of Anachronism," quoted in Hills, *Triumph,* pp. 87–9.

28. See Nahin, *Time Machines,* pp. 205–14.

29. "Bad Wolf Rose" is the name for Rose after she absorbed the Time Vortex in "The Parting of the Ways."

30. Charles, "Ideology of Anachronism," quoted in Hills, *Triumph,* pp. 87–9.

31. David Lewis, "The Paradoxes of Time Travel," *American Philosophical Quarterly* 13.2 (1976): p. 145.

32. Nahin, *Time Machines,* p. 135.

33. See "The Aztecs," "The Space Museum," and "The Chase" for early examples.

34. Such questions end up being superficially answered within the show itself— usually the Time Lords wiping the experience from his memory. How horrendous, then, that in "The Five Doctors" the Doctor as a character must engage in the same events *five times* over the course of his life. And poor second Doctor, who is roped not once, not twice, but *three times* into meeting himself [to date, he is the earliest incarnation to know the latest incarnation].

35. Do you have plans yet for 23 Nov 2013?

36. See Lance Parkin, "Truths Universally Acknowledged: How the 'Rules' of *Doctor Who* Affect the Writing," in Pat Harrington and Noah Wardrip-Fruin, eds., *Third Person: Authoring and Exploring Vast Narratives* (Cambridge: MIT Press, 1999): pp.13–25.

37. Steven Johnson, *Everything Bad Is Good for You* (New York: Riverside, 2005): pp. 65–100.

38. See Mittell, "Narrative Complexity"; Paul Booth, *Digital Fandom: New Media Studies* (New York: Peter Lang, 2010).

39. Mittell, "Narrative Complexity."

40. David Lavery, "*Lost* and Long Term Television Narrative," in Pat Harrigan and Noah Wardrip-Fruin eds., *Third Person: Authoring and Exploring Vast Narratives* (Cambridge: MIT Press, 2009): pp. 313–22.

41. Manuel Castels, *The Internet Galaxy: Reflections on the Internet, Business, and Society* (New York: Oxford University Press, 2001).

42. See George Landow, *Hypertext 3.0: Critical Theory and New Media in an Era of Globalization*, rev. ed. (Baltimore: Johns Hopkins University Press, 2006).

43. Nahin, *Time Machines*, p. 129.

44. Rob Shearman, "Defending the Museum: Re-Evaluation," *Doctor Who: The Space Museum* DVD, London: BBC, 2010.

45. "The Space Museum."

46. Shearman, "Defending the Museum."

47. Hills, *Triumph*, p. 95.

48. Quotation is taken from the novelization of the episode, Terrance Dicks. *Doctor Who and the Day of the Daleks* (New York: Pinnacle Books, 1982): p. 137.

49. I am indebted to my student Courtney Neal for first voicing this question to me.

50. While it has been hypothesized that Susan is *not* the Doctor's blood granddaughter, there is little in the canon to support this assertion. Thus, I believe that unless it is directly stated in the show that she was not family, she is his relation.

51. Jameson, *Postmodernism*; Jean Baudrillard, "The Ecstasy of Communication," in Hal Foster, ed., *The Anti-Aesthetic* (Port Townsend, WA: Bay Press, 1983): pp.126–34.

52. Redmond, *Liquid Metal*, p. 115.

53. See Booth, *Digital Fandom*, pp. 151–80.

54. See DiPaolo, "Political Satire."

55. Mittell, "Narrative Complexity."

56. Jay David Bolter and Richard Grusin, *Remediation: Understanding New Media* (Cambridge: MIT Press, 1999).

7

Narrative Conflict and the Portrayal of Media, Public Relations and Marketing in the New *Doctor Who*

RACHELINE MALTESE

Despite the degree to which *Doctor Who* and its live-action spin-off series, *Torchwood* and *The Sarah Jane Adventures*, journey in time and space, all three programs are strongly rooted in the here and now. This grounding in contemporary Earth is achieved not only through the familiarity of an only slightly alternate now, but through all three series' use of news media to frame and drive narrative. This presence and portrayal of the news media, however, is deeply conflicted on the subjects of fact and fiction and serves to ground the story arcs in the familiar and plausible, while also, ultimately, arguing for the truth of the shows' fictions.

Even as the media serve as a common narrative tool of all three programs (exemplified by the consistency of actors portraying television journalists across the series),[1] their functions vary in each of the program's narratives, based, in part, on the target audiences. Journalists, or at least an ideal of journalists, are held up as heroes on child-oriented *The Sarah Jane Adventures*. However, on general audience program *Doctor Who*, journalists' societal role and general skill is presented as more suspect. Finally, on adult audience *Torchwood*, journalists are an afterthought, presented as of little value beyond as a tool of active disinformation and manipulation. Taken together, these three perspectives don't just offer age-level appropriate commentary on the media; rather, they form a coherent map of how the *Doctor Who* universe values story.

This centrality of media in the *Doctor Who* universe, it should be noted, is not just limited to journalism. Reality television,[2] marketing[3] and public relations[4] — all media-related endeavors that blend fact and fiction — are repeatedly used to advance the narratives both of individual episodes and of the larger arcs of the series that often stretch across the multiple programs. This underscores the unique way in which *Doctor Who* and its companion shows use media to set up conflict both within the narratives and for their reception. This essay will outline that dynamic by focusing on how *Doctor Who* universe narratives rely on viewer credulity for the fantastic while presenting plots that feature unreliable narrators who are often framed as explicitly malicious in that unreliability. Additionally this dynamic will be examined in light of the shows' requirement that the audience accept truth and revelation as ideals for news media real and imagined, even as that news media is presented as consistently vulnerable to manipulation.

Six Little Words

In the 2005 special, "The Christmas Invasion" (December 25, 2005), the tenth Doctor brings down the administration of Prime Minster Harriet Jones, with six little words: "Don't you think she looks tired?" He murmurs it in the ear of one of her aides after she has effectively shot a retreating enemy in the back against the Doctor's wishes. While this remark is often highlighted as evidence of sexism in the show's treatment of women,[5] I believe where that remark steers Jones's narrative arc speaks strongly to *Doctor Who*'s perception and use of the news media. Jones is next seen in the episode on a television news report being questioned by multiple journalists as to her health and fitness for office; she is ultimately ousted from her position in a vote of no confidence.

Those six words that the Doctor uses to bring down Jones and her administration arguably reflect not, as previously mentioned, on the position of women in the *Doctor Who* universe, nor on the often speculated about power of a Time Lord as compared to a mere human. Rather, these can be seen as a criticism of the modern scandal-obsessed news media, both for *Doctor Who*'s home audience in the United Kingdom, but also as regards the news media of the program's secondary markets. This criticism of the media is not just general, but, in fact, specific, as Andrew Pixley notes in the BBC-authorized *The Doctor Who Companion: Series 2.*[6] Pixley tells us that the Doctor's strike against Jones is a reference to media discussions about Margaret Thatcher at the end of her term in 1990, and thus suggests that any sexist intent in the remark is a reflection of the societal context it references and its main agenda is thus firmly indicated as one of media and political criticism.[7]

In this view, the suggestion of a scandal is all it takes for the news media to pounce and bring a politician down. Certainly, the Doctor makes quite a big show of just how little it takes, first informing Jones that he can bring her down with a single word, before acknowledging that it will take as many six and reiterating what a trivial matter it is. Jones seems incredulous, and as the Doctor's question and its ramifications play out, it's clear that it's not the Doctor or the now-shown-to-be-naive prime minister who have the most power in this scenario, but the media. This power is predicated on a commonality shared by both news and drama to create narrative and rewrite events so as to make them comprehensible.[8] In the matter of Harriet Jones, this occurs not just in an extradiegetic way where the character of the news media is used to help the audience interpret other narrative event, but in an intradiegetic way, wherein the media's preoccupation with the state of Jones's health forces her out of power, simply because of the media's drive to make narrative sense of the rumor started by the Doctor.

However, taken in isolation, especially by that part of the general audience viewership too young to remember Margaret Thatcher, this moment remains ambiguous as to whether the power of that suggestion lies with the Doctor's inhuman persuasiveness or the media's gullibility and venality. But this lack of clarity exists only when that moment with Jones is without the broader context of the *Doctor Who* universe's narrative arc, where the news media is a central world-building element. Rather, the narrative of new *Doctor Who* points the way towards this type of media moment since its very first episode, and the tenth Doctor's takedown of Jones is foreshadowed in the adventures of the ninth.

When the Familiar Is Reassuring but Unreliable

Beginning with the first episode of the new series, news media is used repeatedly throughout *Doctor Who* to locate specific episodes of the show in time and space and to help make its frequently fantastical settings more relatable to its less temporally mobile audience. This media presence within the narrative is gradual and starts with the familiar — one character flips through a tabloid newspaper; another watches a news report of a building fire that is devoid of any reference to or awareness of alien involvement — before taking a more central role in the two-part story comprised of episodes "Aliens of London" and "World War Three."

These two episodes, the fourth and fifth of the new series, serve to introduce two recurring character groupings to the *Doctor Who* universe — the first is the Slitheen family from Raxacoricofallapatorius; the second is the media. Arguably, these two introductions happening in tandem serve as further media criticism and satire. How much difference is there, we are asked to consider, between flatulent (as a descriptor relevant to bodily functions) aliens that masquerade as human and the media (as subject to the same descriptor, in this case indicating pomposity and dubious usefulness) whose humanity is often questioned?

However satirical these episodes are, this presentation of the news media to the *Doctor Who* audience is still fairly within the bounds of the familiar. Even as the media is made the target of the show's humor, it is with these episodes that the series also begins to use news media to structure its narrative and as a tool that increases the audience's ability to suspend its disbelief and invest in the truth of the program's heroes.

The fictionally portrayed media — which represent both broadcast and print — are representations of and responses to the media as we currently experience it: television reporters breathlessly repeat how little they know about a situation; photographers descend upon and gang up on visitors to 10 Downing Street; and the print media provide delayed commentary on the accuracy of broadcast coverage that takes their status as competitors into consideration; thus the media are used in the narrative not just to provide what Matt Hills terms "fictionalised moments of news-shock merely as narrative devices to indicate a diegetic sense of international threat," but to advance the idea of a familiar setting preoccupied with the murky spaces between fact and fiction.[9] The concluding episode in this initial Slitheen story arc also preserves one of the key narrative tropes of new *Doctor Who*, that of early 21st century humanity existing in a moment on the cusp of great change it may not be ready for. These episodes use the actions of the news media to illustrate this, while also providing us with the program's first explicit opinion on the industry.

At the end of "World War Three," with the Slitheen repelled and the Doctor and Rose readying to leave in the TARDIS once again, the Doctor and Mickey (Rose's on-again, off-again boyfriend who functions as a sort of Earth-bound companion) have a brief conversation about what this alien invasion means for Earth. Not very much, it turns out, as Mickey, in disgust, holds up a newspaper that declares the recent invasion and related coverage a hoax. The Doctor is unsurprised, saying that the human race just isn't ready yet, and that it's remarkably easy not to see what's right in front of you. Here we are presented with a media that isn't having trouble catching up on a world-changing story. Rather, this is a media ignoring the truth and retracting its previous reporting on that truth, not for nefarious purposes, but because a truth like this is beyond their ability to recognize.

This is not the only time in the new *Doctor Who* and its spinoff shows that we see the media question or invalidate itself in this manner. Episodes with present-day Earth-based settings with large scale invasions frequently feature news media revision that ultimately frames the events as some kind of hoax or mass hallucination. In the first episode of *Torchwood*, "Everything Changes," soon to be Torchwood agent Gwen Cooper, struggling to come to grips with the presence of aliens, says the Christmas invasion and the battle of Canary Wharf[10] can't have been real, that it's "like a sort of terrorism, like they put drugs in the water supplies," although in this case she attributes the theory to her boyfriend as opposed to the news media.[11]

This instance of journalistic failure in "World War Three" would be damning enough even without the Doctor's reaction. But his lack of surprise and narrative positioning as an expert on, and, arguably, a fan of, human culture tells the audience that this sort of thing happens all the time and that news audiences in the show, and program audiences watching at home, should not to expect too much from their information sources. This judgment of the media helps the program's characters as well as the viewing audience sign on for the adventures that follow; these are less terrestrially focused (even the series' episode 2, "The End of the World," is Earth-focused, despite taking place off-planet). The familiar and comfortable news media, called into question, have now served to make the fiction of the Doctor more plausible. The gap between fiction and non-fiction has narrowed for both the audiences in the narrative and those observing from outside of it, because of a news media inadequate to the task.

Doctor Who *and Agenda Setting*

The next critical use of media in Series 1 comes in episode seven, "The Long Game." Just as the first major use of media by the show came in an episode critical to its longer arc, not just of Doctor Who, but of the spin-off programs,[12] "The Long Game" introduces a locale that is critical to the rest of the season and the development of the Jack Harkness character, who later serves as the center of the *Torchwood* series. Additionally, it is "The Long Game" that points the way to, and arguably instructs, the tenth Doctor's six-word destruction of Harriet Jones' career.

This episode finds the Doctor, Rose, and Adam picked up during the previous episode "Dalek" on Satellite 5, a space station orbiting Earth, now supposedly the center of the Fourth Great and Bountiful Human Empire, nearly 200,000 years in our future. The business of the station is entirely news gathering and broadcasting, and while the technology involved — chips and jacks implanted in the human brain — may have changed, the ubiquity and purpose of the news media hasn't. In the brief scenes of news gathering and dissemination to the station's 600 channels stories focusing on natural disasters, celebrity gossip[13] and politics are presented. Despite the locations and protagonists in these news stories being essentially unfamiliar to us, the nature of these stories and their purpose in a news cycle that is constantly refreshing is clear.

The problem with Satellite 5, however, is not immediately apparently from its news stories, but from the Doctor's assertion than the culture of the space station and the empire it is broadcasting to seem not to match his recollection of history. Eventually this leads him and his companions to Floor 500, the much talked about site of Satellite 5's editorial control. There, they meet the human editor-in-chief of Satellite 5, as well as that editor's boss, a massive alien blob that consumes journalists as a convenient food source. This creature, the Jagrafess of the Holy Hadrojassic Maxarodenfoe, serves as a personification and representation of the nameless, faceless, collective "media" that so often serves as a non-specific target for audience displeasure.

Upon the Doctor's seeing the Jagrafess, the editor-in-chief, explains his work that uses Satellite 5 as a tool in the maintenance of a life-support system for the creature:

> For almost a hundred years, mankind has been shaped and guided, his knowledge and ambition strictly controlled by its broadcast news.[14]

The time-frame described in this speech is particularly notable. Not only does it coincide with the Doctor's assertion earlier in the episode that this future version of the human race seems to be approximately ninety years behind where he believes it should be, but this time frame also corresponds roughly with the time passed since the dawn of broadcast media in our non-fictional world, with the first radio news broadcast believed to have transpired in 1920,[15] eighty-five years before the initial broadcast of this episode. The implication is that news media has always been a danger to the human race's advancement and curiosity, not just in fiction, is clear.

The Doctor does nothing to refute this statement on the power of the news media and makes no speeches about the nobility journalism, and so the editor-in-chief continues, making the previous implication even more clear:

> If we create a climate of fear ... then it's easy to keep the borders closed. It's just a matter of emphasis. The right word in the right broadcast repeated often enough can destabilize an economy ... invent an enemy ... change a vote....[16]

In this statement, not only do we see the suggestion of what the tenth Doctor later does to Harriet Jones, underscored by that future Doctor's initial assertion that it will take only a single word to bring her own, but we see the *Doctor Who* universe's understanding of agenda setting theory and salience.

Agenda setting theory tells us that the news media does not reflect reality, but, rather, creates a filtered version of it through news selection. These news selection choices, often referred to as agenda cutting, then elevate the seeming importance of these subjects for the viewing audience. Agenda setting theory at its most basic level does not imply that the media has a direct control on what opinion audiences have on news topics, but does suggest that the news media is able to control what topics people are focused on, potentially elevating certain concerns to levels disproportionate with their actual occurrence in a way that dictates emotional response to the story in question.[17]

One excellent example of the ability of the news media to set the agenda in a way that's also reflective of Ellis' assertions about the media's habit of examining facts until narrative emerges, came in 2001 as reporting on shark attacks in the U.S. and around the world increased. This "summer of the shark" as *Time* magazine called it,[18] put a new fear on the agenda for news viewers as shark attacks were portrayed as an increasingly common occurrence. However, there was no statistically significant increase in recorded unprovoked shark attacks in the U.S. in this period of time, even as everyone was suddenly talking about a rash of shark attacks, a fact which CNN acknowledged in 2003[19] and *Time* commented on in 2009.[20]

Here, the media did not have to tell people to be afraid of shark attacks. The viewing audience were able to come to that conclusion on their own, thanks to the media's agenda directing them to be preoccupied with the idea of shark attacks, something the audience was able to evaluate for itself as a negative. Once they audience was thinking more about shark attacks, they assumed that more shark attacks must be transpiring. Why else would the media report on it?

Of course, the news media in the "summer of the shark" had no explicit anti-shark agenda. Rather, they had found a news story that was just quirky, alarming and connected with the familiar (i.e., trips to the beach and *Jaws*) enough to help keep audiences tuning in to and discussing their broadcasts. The editor-in-chief of Satellite 5 and the Jagrafess, however, make it clear they are engaging in agenda setting in a far more nefarious way. Their actions are not about generating ratings, but creating control. Satellite 5 has an easier time of creating this control, not just because of its fictional basis, but because it is clear that the marketplace of ideas that normally produces competing media views is absent here.[21] Satellite 5 may produce 600 channels of news content, but each of those channels is subject to the same centralized editorial control and, therefore, the same agenda setting goals. Satellite 5 seems to provide what is effectively the propaganda of a state-run media, without being state-run. The Jagrafess supersedes the state (the Doctor having made clear its impact on the empire) and embodies the horror of the idea of mass media conspiracy as it controls every network and the minds of its viewers, not only for its own gain, but for its self-sustenance at the price of the lives of others.

Certainly, this vision of the media is often a staple of sci-fi and fantasy television, but normally such narratives are restricted to dystopian stories such as U.K. TV movie *Max Headroom: 20 Minutes Into the* Future and a subsequent U.S. television series' central villain, the media conglomerate Network 23.[22] *Doctor Who* and its spinoff shows differ from programs like *Max Headroom* in that these programs are not resolutely dystopian. While many standalone episodes do revolve around dystopias, the Doctor's presence is often a catalyst to restore such dystopias if not to utopia, than to something akin to the middle ground in which we live; even *Torchwood*, which presents a very dark view of our world, ultimately ends on a hopeful note for the world, if not for all of the show's protagonists. Yet, even as *Doctor Who* is described as being about "intellect and romance over brute force and cynicism" by U.S.–based late-night TV host Craig Ferguson,[23] an unconquerable darkness often remains.

Torchwood: *Fictional Records and Recording Fiction*

Of *The Sarah Jane Adventures* and *Torchwood*, the two live-action spin-off shows linked to *Doctor Who*, *Torchwood* is the one that spends less time exploring that explicit connection to its source program. In fact, while the Doctor has appeared on *The Sarah Jane Adventures* and characters from both that show and *Torchwood* have appeared on *Doctor Who*, only the Doctor's companion Martha Jones has ever appeared on *Torchwood*. Multiple characters from the other shows do receive passing mention on *Torchwood* however. With *Torchwood*'s production shift to a BBC collaboration with U.S. pay network Starz, it is likely that this distance of *Torchwood* from the rest of the *Doctor Who* universe will be maintained not just because of concerns regarding pre- and post-watershed content, but because of narrative accessibility for U.S. television audiences that are generally less familiar with the source program.

These factors, as well as a focus on Earth-bound interpersonal relationships (i.e., the aliens come to Torchwood and not the other way around) provide *Torchwood* not just with a different narrative tone than the other live-action *Doctor Who* universe programs, but also with a different perspective and focus when it comes to the news media. Torchwood, the organization, is an insular and secretive world in the early 20th century version the show focuses on.[24]

Keeping Torchwood, its mission and actions secret is a constant source of conflict in the show, not just in its narrative, but in its design. While Jack yells at his medic Owen for ordering pizza under the Torchwood name[25] the fact remains that team Torchwood is also driving around Cardiff in a van labeled with their secret identity. Yet, despite these inconsistencies, that are arguably meant to indicate just what a haphazard organization Jack's Torchwood is, secrecy and cover-ups are a central part of Torchwood's daily business.

Yet, just who Torchwood is lying to is often unclear. While there is frequent discussion about faking suicides and switching bodies and the mechanics of these deceptions, just who is being deceived is rarely explicitly stated. The police, with whom Torchwood have a clear friction from the first episode, are the most obvious choice. But it's not just the police that need to be fooled, but anyone who pays attention to what the police are doing. This, by implication, is the media.

However, while this implication further extends the *Doctor Who* universe's treatment of the media as a powerful tool vulnerable to manipulation, it is not the central way in which news media is used in *Torchwood*. Instead, just as *Doctor Who* shows us a fictional future media that is familiar enough to illuminate our present while also helping us to accept the fantastical in the narrative; *Torchwood* shows us a fictional past media that serves a similar purpose. But, where *Doctor Who* comments on the society through the narrative's use of news media, in *Torchwood*'s first two seasons, this use of media largely comments on the personal.

In the episode "Captain Jack Harkness" (2007), Jack and Torchwood team member Toshiko Sato wind up transported to 1941 as they investigate strange goings on at an old dancehall, resulting in their falling out of touch with the rest of the team. As the team members remaining in the present try to get in touch with Jack and Toshiko, Ianto Jones and Owen Harper discover their missing comrades' whereabouts thanks to a file of old newspaper records on the dancehall, one of which contains a photograph of their colleagues at the location in 1941.

Here, the news media has been used to embed a fact in the narrative's past. The episode further plays with temporality in that the audience does not see this photograph taken until the next scene: at the moment of Ianto's discovery, the past according to *Torchwood* has not yet happened for the viewer. In the scene in which the photo is snapped, we see that it is actually the second of two. The one appearing in the newspaper Ianto has discovered in the now includes the photographer, who we see hand his camera off to a member of the dancehall staff before stepping into the photograph with the request "One more. For the record."[26]

This emphasis on the record, while also including a character serving in a journalistic capacity (he's actually, in typical *Doctor Who* fashion, a non-human who can manipulate time and space and happens to be the manager of the dancehall), speaks to the core of the *Doctor Who* narrative's uneasy relationship with news media and journalistic practice. News media are supposed to represent the reporting of the truth, yet their appearance in a fictional narrative immediately distorts their role. That they are then additionally used by the narrative to manipulate other characters' understanding of facts in the story world, while also serving to help the viewing audience connect to this narrative through a suspension of disbelief, gives the news media in the *Doctor Who* universe an essentially Shroedinger's Cat-like function: they serve both intradiegetic and extradiegetic purposes simultaneously and on multiple levels.

Later, in *Torchwood*'s five-episode third season, "Children of Earth," the media seemingly revert to a more typical role within the narrative; they report the news of a global alien invasion and the political response. Here there are no clever lines or odd personal interactions aimed at using news media characters to establish the events of the narrative as among the *Doctor Who* universe's deeply mutable facts. Rather, this media just reports and filters the very story the audience is already watching. This straightforward reportage is all they have to do to serve their purpose for the audience as the gatekeepers of fact and fiction, because the newscasters in "Children of Earth" include the previously noted faces we've seen before. In particular, it is American newsreader Trinity Wells, played by Lachele Carl, which is particularly familiar to program audiences. At the time of "Children of Earth"'s U.K. and U.S. premiers, the character had already appeared on both *The Sarah Jane Adventures* as well as multiple episodes of *Doctor Who*. Despite not representing a media organization that actually exists, Wells serves as a trusted news face, not just for the characters existing inside of the *Doctor Who* universe, but for the audience watching at home, and the character's nationality helps this cause.

U.K. audiences are, of course, going to be the most familiar with U.K. news and news faces. Even in an era of satellite TV, Internet broadcasting and global distribution that gives us networks like BBC America, Al Jazeera English and CNN International, most viewers of televisions news are viewing news produced, packaged and presented by the country in which they reside. By making the news broadcaster character the audience spends the most time with foreign to the program's main, home audience, it becomes easier for that audience to accept her broadcasting role as true, because it is not as obviously false as a fictional British newsreader from a fictional British network would be. This strategy has also been used to a lesser effect in *Doctor Who* and *The Sarah Jane Adventures*. It receives greater time in "Children of Earth" because of its global narrative and marketing as a global television event. No matter where the audience was located, "Children of Earth" provided them with a foreign, and at times, non–English speaking, newscaster to believe in. When U.K.–based journalist characters have been used in the *Doctor Who* narrative, they have, at times, been portrayed by actual U.K. broadcasters, such as Huw Edwards,[27] playing themselves.

Yet Trinity Wells and her colleagues around the *Doctor Who* universe's version of planet Earth are neither the most trusted, nor the most familiar, journalists in that world. That honor belongs to Sarah Jane Smith, and it is, in fact, her interactions with her profession and the Doctor that make the strongest case for *Doctor Who*–based journalists as advocates for the idea that all stories, or at least all stories about the Doctor, are real.

Love, Truth, and Stories

In *The Sarah Jane Adventures* we learn early and often that the Doctor's former companion from the original series is a journalist. She regularly informs people that she's a journalist who works from home, and occasionally mentions that she is a freelancer. Despite these frequent assertions as to her career, we don't actually see Sarah Jane engage in a great deal of journalism. We don't see her receive story assignments, deal with editors, get published, or, in fact, even sit down to write.

Mostly, the representations of Sarah Jane as a member of the news media are largely limited to a more basic concept of the act of journalism — that is, the recounting of a story that is true and has news value. This act of journaling is performed regularly in the form of a monologue at the opening moments of each story comprised of two episodes. While it is not always Sarah Jane that presents this "Dear diary" moment, where the audience is effectively the diary silently receiving the words, it remains a constant reminder that part of Sarah Jane's mentorship of her young charges revolves around teaching them how to tell the true and secret stories of the universe.

As such, in many ways, Sarah Jane's status as a journalist is difficult to forget, but yet can seem like a front for her tendency to investigate situations that may involve aliens in case her heroism is required. This perception, however, may speak to my biases as someone who works in and about the media; the show makes clear that those around Sarah Jane readily accept her statements about her profession. This becomes somewhat clear in the show's second series when Rani Chandra, an aspiring journalist who becomes friends with Sarah Jane's son, moves in next door and befriends Sarah Jane as well, looking to her often as a journalistic mentor.

The vagueness present in the narrative regarding the logistics of Sarah Jane's journalistic work, helps, however, to extend the *Doctor Who* universe's thematic treatment of journalists as powerful, vulnerable, and not always reliable in ways that are useful, not just for plot development, but for the fate of the universe. While Sarah Jane's moments of clear journalistic activities often demonstrate questionable practices either for ethical reasons or for sheer efficacy (such as flipping through a stack of ID cards before choosing which to use to reach her object of curiosity), the show leaves us with little doubt that she is one of the heroes of her story. The moral ambiguity that surrounds the Torchwood organization and, at times, even the Doctor (as in such episodes as "Family of Blood" and "Waters of Mars" where he is portrayed as vengeful and hubristic), rarely touches Sarah Jane.

Because of this, Sarah Jane is in a unique position to serve as an arbiter of truth in the *Doctor Who* universe. While her profession makes her corruptible by the tradition of the show's narrative, it also makes her an enforcer of reality, both within that narrative and for the viewing audience that engages with media representations in *Doctor Who* as part of its path to a suspension of disbelief. Thus, to return to the idea of agenda setting, because of the salience of news media as a topic in *The Sarah Jane Adventures* both in general, and in regard to Sarah Jane in particular, this program and its central character has the greatest influence on the viewing audience's decisions regarding realities both within its narrative and outside of it. It is *The Sarah Jane Adventures* that lets the audience know whether stories about a Time Lord and his blue box and all the places and times he's been are true. This truth-telling function in regard to the narrative and central figure of the *Doctor Who* universe is most explicitly on display in the story "The Wedding of Sarah Jane Smith" (2009).

In these episodes, Sarah Jane becomes engaged after a whirlwind courtship involving an engagement ring with mind control properties that stunt her normal, journalistic tendency to question and examine everything. It seems like nothing will stop the wedding until the officiant asks if there are any objections and the tenth Doctor rushes onto the scene to declare his, instantly throwing Sarah Jane, her teenaged investigatory team, and the wedding attendees all into different moments in time, trapped by a recurring villain, the Trickster.

While *Doctor Who* audiences had previously seen the tenth Doctor and Sarah Jane interact in "School Reunion" (2006), this event marks the Doctor's first appearance on *The Sarah Jane Adventures* despite the frequency with which he has already been discussed in the narrative. The Doctor is a familiar character to viewers of *The Sarah Jane Adventures* even if they have never seen him before. When questioned by Sarah Jane's teen friends as to whether he's the man they've heard so much about and whether he'll really be able to save the day, he tells them, "Well, you know journalists, always exaggerating, but yeah, I'm pretty amazing on a good day."[28] With that one sentence he establishes his identity, but also Sarah Jane's identity — journalist, yes, but flawed — along with the show's general attitude towards journalists. However, the Doctor's proclamation casts doubt on journalists in a more positive way than on the other two programs. By framing their reportage not as wrong, but as exaggerated over an essential and even constant truth, the Doctor acknowledges that journalists provide at least a kernel of truth. This double-edged remark lays the groundwork for the program's most significant discussion of and advocacy for, what is and is not real.

As the episode continues, and Sarah Jane realizes she's been tricked and her fiancé is not what he seems, she says, "I thought I loved you, but you're not even real."[29] This comment, coming after she struggles to remember the existence of the Doctor as she mumbles about this other man to her fiancé, has multiple implications tied into both Sarah Jane's personal history and her profession. First, she indicates an inability to love that which she believes to be not real. This, coupled with her profession that has just received some moderate degree of approval from the Doctor suggests to us that Sarah Jane is a woman who, due to her nature as a journalist, only loves the truth.

The remark also implies, particularly when coupled with Sarah Jane's frequent wistfulness about the Doctor and her explanations that there is no partner in her life, that she loves the Doctor, if not romantically, then at least to the exclusion of romantic relationships which do not seem as significant to her as that platonic connection. Once she is aware of the deception surrounding her marriage, the Doctor is certainly more real to Sarah Jane than her fiancé, and this, by extension, also gives the audience permission to believe in the Doctor in a mode other than that of ironic belief, despite the fantastical nature of the show suggesting that a more naïve belief, in which the Doctor is really real, is simply not possible.

Yet, engagement by fans is, as suggested by Vera Tobin's examination of naïve and ironic believers in her "Ways of Reading Sherlock Holmes: The Entrenchment of Discourse Blends," often deeply driven by these types of narrative acceptance.[30] In this mater of the reality of the Doctor as argued for by the narrative of episode and Sarah Jane's status as a truth-loving journalist, a third type of potential believer emerges. This believer, an enchanted believer, that I theorized in my work on audience mourning in response to fictional characters' deaths,[31] draws from the idea of Sherlockian ironic believers "re-enchanting the world," as put forth by Michael Saler in "'Clap if You Believe in Sherlock Holmes': Mass Culture and the Re-Enchantment of Modernity, c.1890–c.1940," may be what is most encouraged by the text.[32] Enchanted believers serve an extradiegetic role as a bridge between fact and fiction, much as the news media serves the same role on an interdiagetic basis.

This matter of Sarah Jane's vouching for the truth of the Doctor through her own storyline continues as the scene progresses. The fiancé, it turns out, is not, as Sarah Jane has first surmised, unreal. Instead, he is merely dead. Or rather, someone who is supposed to be dead, and currently exists between states; he will only become fully alive again if he can succeed in getting Sarah Jane to marry him and give up her alien-focused investigatory pursuits. This status revelation serves to confirm the Doctor's initial assessment of journalists in the episode (generally correct, but always exaggerating — the fiancé isn't completely unreal, after all). It also designates the fiancé as something of a ghost, a shade, a half-truth; he is a shadow of the living world and his former self, a non-existent reflection of the truth that is, therefore a fiction. Sarah Jane's perfect relationship with him, it turns out, wasn't entirely a lie; the man who he once was would have truly loved it. But it wasn't entirely true either, the circumstances of the Tricker's intervention being what they are. What the relationship was was a nice story Sarah Jane was able to tell herself, thanks to the influence of that villain.

This attempt on Sarah Jane's part to measure what is and is not real strikes at the heart of the essential conflict created by the pervasive presence of news media in the narratives of the *Doctor Who* universe. How trustworthy are those who make truth into convenient stories that serve (e.g., the Jagrafess's editor-in-chief) or generate agendas (e.g., the journalists that helped to generate the "summer of the shark") that do not necessarily respond to the public good? And, how false are stories, that, however fictional, reflect the world as it actually is? *The Sarah Jane Adventures* does not only ask those questions but seeks to answer them both for its characters and for its audience.

After the fiancé relinquishes his half-life in order to save Sarah Jane and restore the order of the universe such that she continues to protect Earth by gathering information (as journalists do) on suspicious events, the Doctor and she must part ways yet again. The Doctor says to her, "Don't forget me."[33] This line is layered, as this scene also represents the last material David Tennant shot as the tenth Doctor, although the episode aired prior to his final appearance on *Doctor Who* in the two-part story "The End of Time."

Here, the audience is encouraged to remember a fictional character they know they are about to lose before the characters are aware of what is coming. This atemporality of narrative is typical of the *Doctor Who* universe. The order in which events — and episodes — transpire for one character is not necessarily the same for other characters (i.e., the Doctor, Jack, and River Song all experience the events of episodes they appear in, in a different order, not just from each other, but also from the audience). The inclusion of the audience in this atemporality of narrative thus reinforces the message of the *Doctor* Who universe's unreliable, yet tethered-to-reality, journalists: the Doctor is not just a story; he and the vast universe he explores is just as true as any other story journalists select, report on, and elevate to importance.

As the Doctor departs after his farewell to Sarah Jane, the scene transitions from the fantastical set of the TARDIS (as emblematic of story as Narnia's wardrobe) to Sarah Jane's attic, which, though littered with alien artifacts, a robot dog, and a talking supercomputer, looks more or less like any other well-furnished attic. It, like the journalist Sarah Jane Smith, herself, serves as a bridge to the real.

Conclusion

The *Doctor Who* universe is unique in pop-culture properties because of the length and breadth of its canon. It is so vast that even the significant body of content in the new series and its spinoffs can seem dwarfed by the sheer size of classic *Doctor Who* material, especially when one considers not just the original television episodes, but also the tie-in novels and audio adventures that sustained fans during the "wilderness years"[34] when the show was not in production. Yet, even to do a full survey of the new *Doctor Who* universe, all three currently running series, as well as tie-in novels, audio books, short stories appearing in licensed magazines dedicated to the shows, comics, an animated series, several BBC radio plays; and a number of almanac-style books delineating character back stories, would need to be taken into account, and none of these exist free of the influence of, or reference to, the classic series. It is partly the size of the *Doctor Who* universe that enables its narratives to argue so effectively for the reality of its fictions.

But it is not just that this size allows for such detail and layering. Rather, the scale of the *Doctor* Who universe returns us yet again to the principles of McCombs's and Shaw's agenda setting and salience and Ellis's work on the formation of narrative. While a full statistical accounting in the name of agenda setting research is beyond the scope of this article, a statement-by-statement analysis of those remarks attributable to *Doctor Who* universe characters affiliated with the news media across all licensed stories connected to new series narratives, would show not just aliens like the Slitheen, the Daleks, the Cybermen and the Doctor rising to the top of the agenda, but also highlight a split as to the reality of such extraterrestrial life in an intradiegetic context due to the ways the news media is doubted within the narrative, both by itself and others. This then pushes the audience to choose from its extradiegetic position an intradiegetic truth, siding, necessarily, with those fictional news sources that show the least skepticism for the fantastical narratives the broader *Doctor Who* stories present.

Ultimately, however, the key agenda setting question in the *Doctor Who* universe is not whether or not its present-day Earth characters believe in aliens, but whether those characters believe more in aliens than in the news media. By emphasizing the less-than-true components that can exist in news media, whether presented in a fictional context or not, the *Doctor Who* programs do not discredit the media, but rather, use the conflict generated by their presence in the narrative to suggest to both intradiegetic and extradiegetic audiences that all stories are true and that all times and possibilities are now.

NOTES

1. Anthony Debaeck and Lachele Carl both play French and U.S. newsreaders respectively on each of the three new series *Doctor Who* programs.

2. Most notably, in "Bad Wolf." For program details see Videography.

3. Most notably, in "Invasion of the Bane" *SJA*, "The Sound of Drums" *DW*, "Partners in Crime" *DW*, and "Planet of the Ood" *DW*.

4. Most notably, in "Children of Earth" *TW*, and coupled with episodes like "Invasion of the Bane" *SJA* and "Partners in Crime" *DW*.

5. A comment on gay entertainment news site, AfterElton.com in a discussion mainly about the death of character Ianto Jones in *Torchwood* typifies how significant the Harriett Jones moment has become in discussions of how marginalized characters are treated on *Doctor Who*. This comment was made three and a half years after "The Christmas Invasion" was initially broadcast (http://www.afterelton.com/blog/stunt double/torchwood-coe4-facebook-recap#comment-83702).

6. One of the many BBC tie-in products to *Doctor Who*, a new edition of this publication was put out with each season of the new series to provide behind-the-scenes looks and detailed information about each episode.

7. "The Christmas Invasion."

8. John Ellis, *Seeing Things: Television in the Age of Uncertainty* (London: I.B. Tauris, 2000): p. 79.

9. Matt Hills, *The Dispersible Television Text: Theorising Moments of the New Doctor Who*, Science Fiction Film and Television, Volume 1, Issue 1, Spring 2008: p. 38

10. This battle is a reference to reference to *Doctor Who* episode "Doomsday," which aired on July 8, 2006, and has narrative significant to *Torchwood* due to one of its staff members, not seen in the *Doctor Who* episode, being one of the few survivors of that battle.

11. "Everything Changes" *TW*.

12. The Slitheen introduced in "Aliens of London," reappear not only in Series 1, episode 11 "Boom Town," but are also a reoccurring menace on *The Sarah Jane Adventures*.

13. The Face of Boe, an alien first encountered in "The End of the World," appears briefly here as the subject of celebrity gossip on the subject of his pregnancy. The creature is said to be the oldest living thing in the galaxy, and as such is a celebrity figure that is used across episodes to provide familiarity within the

world and to help the viewing audience connect with the recognizable format of celebrity news and gossip.

14. "The Long Game" *DW.*

15. John C. Abell, "Aug. 31, 1920: News Radio Makes News," *Wired.com*, August 31, 2010.

16. "The Long Game" *DW.*

17. M.E. McCombs, and D.L. Shaw, "The Agenda-Setting Function of Mass Media," *Public Opinion Quarterly*, Vol. 36, 1972: pp. 176–187.

18. Terry McCarthy, "Summer of the Shark," *Time*, July, 30, 2001, http://www.time.com/time/2001/sharks/cover.html.

19. Jeordan Legon, "Survey: 'Shark summer' bred fear, not facts," *CNN.com*, March 14, 2003, http://www.cnn.com/2003/TECH/science/03/13/shark.study/.

20. James Poniewozick, "Media Freak-outs: Every Week Is Shark Week," *Time*, August 10, 2009, http://www.time.com/time/magazine/article/0,9171,1913750,00.html.

21. M.E. McCombs, and D.L. Shaw," The Evolution of Agenda-Setting Research: Twenty-Five Years in the Marketplace of Ideas," *Journal of Communication*, Volume 43, Issue 2, 1993: pp. 58–67.

22. While no explicit links exist between *Doctor Who* and *Max Headroom,* the theme for the 23rd annual Gallifrey One convention, the largest Doctor Who convention in North America is, in fact, "Network 23," implying an awareness of the shared focus on media in the two narratives.

23. This description comes from a skit scheduled to be performed on *The Craig Ferguson Show* on November 16, 2010. However, because of difficulties in clearing the music rights, it was not aired, but a tape of a rehearsal of it was leaked onto the Internet on December 1, 2010 (http://blogs.wsj.com/speakeasy/2010/12/02/craig-ferguson-posts-unaired-doctor-who-cold-open/). This tape was then aired on January 6, 2011, when the rights were finally cleared (http://blogs.wsj.com/speakeasy/2011/01/06/craig-fergusons-doctor-who-cold-open-to-see-light-of-day/).

24. Torchwood as an institution is mentioned repeatedly throughout new *Who*, including in episodes "Bad Wolf" *DW*, "The Christmas Invasion" *DW*, "Tooth and Claw" *DW*, "The Impossible Planet" *DW*, "The Satan Pit" *DW*, and the season finale arcs of Series 2, 3 and 4, and the narrative indicates that its existence spans hundreds of thousands of years.

25. "Everything Changes" *TW.*

26. "Captain Jack Harkness" *TW.*

27. "Fear Her" *DW.*

28. "The Wedding of Sarah Jane Smith" *SJA.*

29. Ibid.

30. Vera Tobin, "Ways of Reading Sherlock Holmes: The Entrenchment of Discourse Blends," *Language and Literature*, 2006: p. 83.

31. Racheline Maltese, "Tangible Reality of Absence: Fan Communities and the Mourning of Fictional Characters."

32. Michael Saler, "Clap if You Believe in Sherlock Holmes: Mass Culture and the Re-Enchantment of Modernity, c.1890–c.1940," *Historical Journal*. (2003): p. 606.

33. "The Wedding of Sarah Jane Smith" *SJA.*

34. Kyle Anderson, "Doctor Who for Newbies: The Eight Doctor & The Wilderness Years," December 31, 2010, http://www.nerdist.com/2010/12/doctor-who-for-newbies-the-eighth-doctor-the-wilderness-years-2/.

8

Nostalgia for Empire, 1963–1974

Maura Grady *and* Cassie Hemstrom

Doctor Who is a British TV institution and has been on the air (with a few breaks) since 1963. The show follows the Doctor, a mysterious alien from a race called the Time Lords. The Doctor travels through space and time in a ship called the TARDIS (Time and Relative Dimensions in Space) with various human companions. His race can regenerate their bodies at death, enabling different actors to portray the title character. Currently, the show is up to its eleventh Doctor. Our analysis will focus on the first three Doctors in the years 1963–1974.

Nostalgia for empire has been foundational to *Doctor Who*, but the work and role of nostalgia, as well as the way it engages with and invokes viewers' perceptions of both *Doctor Who*, and of Britain, shifted over the course of the tenure of Doctors one through three. Episodes in the early years fluctuate between historically-themed narratives, monster-driven stories, and outer space adventures, that are thinly-veiled allegories reflecting British politics, the anxieties of the British viewing audience and the BBC's mission to act as a cultural repository and guardian.

As Matthew Kilburn argues, *Doctor Who* was a product of "a working environment at the BBC shaped by the corporation's quest to sustain its role in the cultural life of the United Kingdom in a transformed broadcasting environment."[1] While television had replaced radio as the dominant form of media, the government-funded BBC's monopoly in Britain was under threat from the channel ITV. In defining its media role, according to Hugh Greene, director-general of the BBC, the channel should continue to strive "to hold a mirror to what was going on in contemporary British society."[2]

And "what was going on in contemporary British society" was a shift in national identity, coupled rising tensions about declining British power and the overt retreat from empire. The structure of *Doctor Who* allowed the show's writers and directors to not only project images of what the future might be like and offer commentaries on the present, but also to re-imagine the past, and reshape their viewer's understanding of it. In her book, *The Future of Nostalgia* (2001), Svetlana Boym explains a "cinematic image of nostalgia is a double exposure, or a superimposition of two images—of home and abroad, past and present, dream and everyday life."[3] The Doctor, and his TARDIS, make it possible for these contrasting images to co-exist, for British viewers to recreate a sense of the golden age of British Empire by "Britishizing" the past, and to journey to an alternative present and future in which Britain, though stripped of its imperial standing, nonetheless maintains centrality. Boym writes that nostalgia is "[t]he border zone between longing and reflection, between native land and exile," and argues that, when "explored by the Nabokovian passportless spy," an apt if unintentional description of the Doctor, and his (usually British) companions, nostalgia "opens up spaces of freedom. Freedom in this case is not a freedom from memory but a freedom to remember, to choose the narratives of the past and remake them."[4] A nostalgia for the power and centrality of the British Empire informed the consciousness of the creative teams of the first three Doctors, and the general British television audience, and made certain storylines dealing with anxieties about the end of colonialism necessary.

Boym argues that nostalgia "had not only to do with dislocation in space but also with the changing conception of time,"[5] a claim that is not only a fitting description of the Doctor's adventures, but also draws attention to the ideological needs of *Doctor Who*'s British audiences in the mid–1960s to early 1970s. In the words of Dean Acheson (Truman's secretary of state), in 1962, one year before *Doctor Who* premiered, "Great Britain ha[d] lost an Empire and ha[d] not yet found a role."[6] The show's audience's sense of self was shifting: from defining itself as subjects of the British Empire to members of a country on the periphery of a fractured and loose collection of nations. The audience likely sought reassurance that this change did not diminish their individual or national significance, or endanger their existence as Britons. Boym clarifies that nostalgia is "a longing for a home that no longer exists or has never existed. Nostalgia is a sentiment of loss and displacement, but it is also a romance with one's own fantasy."[7] *Doctor Who* episodes in the years of the first three Doctors sustains the fantasy of "Britain," and demonstrates to its audience that political, sociological, economic and population changes do not signal an end to Britain or Britishness. The Doctor's adventures enact and display possible permutations of Britain's new place in the Commonwealth and role in the world.

In searching for a role, its audience may have found comforting reassurance in the Doctor's relatively unfettered exploration of time and space, even as he moved non-chronologically through history. But even as the Doctor and his fundamentally British companions move from place to place, we need to keep in mind that their adventures are never an accurate representation of "their" past nor ours. As Boym argues: "There should be a special warning in the side view mirror: The object of nostalgia is further away than it appears. Nostalgia is never literal, but lateral. It looks sideways. It is dangerous to take it at face value."[8] *Doctor Who*'s location within the genre of sci-fi serial adventure dictates that it too should not be taken literally. Defining such thorny terms as "colonialism," "imperialism," and "postcolonialism" is challenging because of the subjects' interdisciplinary, international, and transhistorical natures. Dr. Ania Loomba, in her book *Colonialism/Postcolonialism* argues that a useful way to distinguish between imperialism and colonialism may be "to not separate them in temporal but in spatial terms" so that we remember that that the imperial country is the center "from which power flows and the colony or neo-colony is the place which it penetrates and controls."[9] Moreover, she summarizes postcolonialism as the complex study of those various groups destroyed/erased, still oppressed ("so that nothing is 'post' about their colonisation"), or empowered by collaboration with colonizers (as with "elite creoles," in the words of Mary Louise Pratt). Loomba notes that "white settlers were historically the agents of colonial rule, and their own subsequent development — cultural as well as economic — does not simply align them with other colonised people" since they were not subject to the "genocide, economic exploitation, cultural decimation and political exclusion felt by indigenous peoples."[10] In describing the undeniable complexity of sorting out postcolonial power dynamics among the peoples of formerly colonized nations, she notes that even "anti-colonial movements have rarely represented the interests of all the peoples of a colonized country. After independence, these fissures can no longer be glossed over."[11] The challenge for members of the former colonial powers, therefore, would seem to be how to make peace with any implicit cultural complicity with the violence of the British colonial project, especially as Britain's direct colonial grip was all but at an end by the time *Doctor Who* premiered.

In summary, we view colonialism as an inherently nostalgic endeavor, since British colonials inevitably attempted to recreate their "home" environment and customs in the new countries they colonized. This was not only because of a longing for home, but as a means of justifying their colonial project by reiterating that civilization was by default British.

Our analysis focuses on the stories of the first three Doctors, played from 1963 to 1974 by William Hartnell, Patrick Troughton and John Pertwee. We argue that immediately following these foundational years, the show (and persona of the Doctor) underwent a marked shift in character. Joining actor Tom Baker as the Doctor with the creative team of Robert Holmes (story/script editor) and Philip Hinchcliffe (producer), the show began to focus on the Doctor's nature as an alien, albeit an alien who becomes a fan of British people and culture ("Jelly baby, anyone?"). Moreover, during the Tom Baker years, according to Louis Niebur, author of *Special Sound: The Creation and Legacy of the BBC Radiophonic Workshop*, "the primary shift is that we're talking about [changing the intended audience] from kids to adults ... [the program] abandoned the idea of politics in favor of the Gothic."[12] With the exception of the Dalek-focused Terry Nation scripts in Tom Baker's years, Niebur notes: "it's essentially Hammer horror, melded into *Doctor Who* and I think Tom Baker has a lot to do with that, because he plays the character as an alien ... he says things like 'I'm not human. I'm an alien. You can't expect me to behave like a human.' John Pertwee would never have said that; he was doing Karate chops and talking about Horatio Nelson all the time."[13]

Audiences did not see the kind of political story in the years after the first, second and third Doctors "partially because *Doctor Who* stops being political" in the mid–1970s and "just becomes sort of action-adventure or horror, partially because I think it was unfashionable."[14] The BBC's mission as a whole changes in the 1970s, "not because the BBC is too scared [to comment on contemporary political issues], but [because] there is a real dynamic shift in what television [means to audiences]."[15] Niebur explains that "the kinds of commentaries in, for example, [non–*Doctor Who* telefilm] *The War Game*[16] ... would never have happened after 1970." While *Doctor Who* became "adult-genre television" for children, it is not "adult *political* television" [original emphasis] after the Pertwee years, according to Niebur. This retreat from political stories may also have been due to the increasingly heated debate about politics in the 1970s in Britain as the economic situation declined.

The very first Doctor's trips to the past (1963–66) allow the show to use what Boym calls "restorative nostalgia" to rewrite contemporary British cultural values onto viewer's perceptions of past events. In the next two Doctors' adventures in 1960s Britain, and on futuristic alien worlds, the writers and directors espouse "reflective nostalgia" through which the show could present metaphors meant to assuage viewers concerns about cultural change. By focusing on the threat of alien invasions of Earth, Troughton's Doctor's adventures rehearse and reveal contemporary fears about the influx of colonials into Britain. Pertwee's Doctor's journeys into the future similarly expose and negotiate anxieties about the implications of British colonialism and its effects on the development and future of the nation and its people.

Nostalgia is not an easily reducible term; the creators, writers and directors of *Doctor*

Who engage in a complex use of the desire for a home place and time that is lost. Boym suggests that we think of nostalgia as one of two branches: restorative nostalgia, which draws on visible collective symbols, oral culture, and the reconstructed emblems and rituals of "home" to evoke national past and future; and reflective nostalgia, which is more about individuals narratives, rich with details and memorial signifiers, is more oriented towards individual and cultural memory, and perpetually defers "homecoming itself."[17] The two types of nostalgia take different forms, and have different senses of ethos: while restorative nostalgia, often aligned with state productions, "takes itself dead seriously," reflective nostalgia, which is self-consciously aware of gaps between resemblance and identity, "can be ironic and humorous."[18] As Boym explains, "[t]he two might overlap in their frames of reference, but they do not coincide in their narratives and plots of identity."[19] In addition to taking different forms, restorative and reflective nostalgia have different effects, so that, "if restorative nostalgia ends up reconstructing emblems and rituals of home and homeland in an attempt to conquer and spatialize time, reflective nostalgia cherishes fragments of memory and temporalizes space."[20] Reflective nostalgia additionally "reveals that longing and critical thinking are not opposed to one another, as affective memories do not absolve one from compassion, judgment, or critical reflection."[21]

Close readings of the political implications of *Doctor Who* vis-à-vis colonialism in the years of the first three Doctors; demonstrate an unwillingness or inability of restorative nostalgics, such as long-time script supervisor Terrence Dicks, to divorce loyalty to Britain from its colonial past. The restorative nostalgic view eventually conflicts with the emerging reflective nostalgia that is the result of changing social and cultural ideologies. This reflective nostalgia is illustrated by other creative contributors to the series, who critically engage with the negative and long-lasting effects of the British Empire while still honoring Britain through a show and a character that has become emblematic of all that is good, and should be sustained, in "Britain."

We will argue through readings of the episodes "An Unearthly Child" (001), "The Aztecs" (006) with the first Doctor, "Tomb of the Cybermen" (037) with the second Doctor, "Colony in Space" (058), "The Mutants" (063), and "Frontier in Space" (067) with the third Doctor that the show shifts in tone from 1963 to 1974 from sustaining a sense of restorative nostalgia to cautiously espousing reflective nostalgia. This shift can also be seen in the changes of the doctor's characterization under the first three actors to play the role (William Hartnell, Patrick Troughton, and Jon Pertwee). The show begins in the restorative mode, in the Hartnell years, and slowly shifts towards the reflective mode in the Troughton and lands there more definitively in the later Pertwee years.

The assertions of British superiority in *Doctor Who* are central to the plot and structure of the premiere episode, "The Unearthly Child." In this, the first *Doctor Who* story, the Doctor and his granddaughter Susan have traveled to 1960s Britain in their time-and-space machine, the TARDIS. Susan attends a London secondary school, and her vast knowledge of history and science attracts the attention of two of her teachers, Ian and Barbara. The Doctor, Susan, Ian and Barbara travel to the Year Zero, where the group is separated from the TARDIS by a community of Neanderthals.

The cave dwelling Neanderthals — non-contemporary and non–British — are savage, unorganized and aggressive, a representation that contrasts with British civilization, "logic and reason," as the Doctor says. The show restructures the actual, historical record in order to show the superiority of twentieth century British values. Old Mother, the superstitious matriarch of the cave dwellers, who later in the story becomes the first character to die in

Doctor Who, is afraid of the dangerous new ideas the Doctor and companions bring and therefore helps them escape. The other prominent female Neantherthal, Hur, Old Mother's daughter-in-law repeatedly says that the Doctor and his companions act towards the cave men like "a mother guarding her baby," a statement that demonstrates how the Neanderthals, backwards in time and primitive in culture, are the figurative children of their own descendants. Humans, the episode implies, have reached their potential in the twentieth-century, and have become what they are meant to be — logical, reasoning, egalitarian, and British. The Doctor and his companions go back to a time when humans were still developing, and can help direct and encourage their development along the correct path towards contemporary British values.

> National memory reduces this space of play with memorial signs to a single plot. Restorative nostalgia knows two main narrative plots — the restoration of origins and the conspiracy theory.... The conspiratorial worldview is based on a single transhistorical plot, a Manichaean battle of good and evil and the inevitable scapegoating of the mythical enemy. Ambivalence, the complexity of history and the specificity of modern circumstances is thus erased, and modern history is seen as a fulfillment of ancient prophecy. "Home," imagine extremist conspiracy theory adherents, is forever under siege, requiring defense against the plotting enemy.[22]

The choice to make this distinction between backwards, primitive societies and advanced, rational British civilization the focus of the first episode is significant. It asserts the centrality of white British culture (in contrast to the dark-haired, ethnically indiscriminate cave people), and reassures viewers that British rationality, logic and civility is the proper way for humans to be, and is, in fact, the destiny of humanity. According to historian J.H. Plumb, "the past" is "always a created ideology with a purpose, designed to control individuals, or motivate societies, or inspire classes." The job of history, therefore, "[is] to 'dissolve' and 'weaken' the past, and to replace its 'simple, structural generalisations' with properly disciplined understanding."[23]

Two final factors support a reading of this episode of a primitive past/rational present dichotomy. The Doctor's TARDIS is supposed to change its appearance to fit into the setting and culture in which it lands, but in this episode, after traveling to 1960s Britain, it retains the imprint of that culture, in an outward appearance of a British Police Box, as though British superiority retains primacy even over technological advancements from other cultures. James Chapman, in his text *Inside the TARDIS*, explains that the TARDIS' unchanging exterior can "be seen as a metaphor for the persistence of mid-twentieth century Britishness within the series."[24] Thus the TARDIS, stuck as of the first episode in the shape of a uniquely mid-twentieth century British artifact, represents not only a means of moving in time and space, it also is a reassurance that although the interior and the people riding in it may change over the years, its British appearance cannot ever be altered again, not even by the Doctor.

The Doctor's granddaughter, Susan's, desire to stay in 20th century England in this episode[25] also underscores that the 1960s British viewing audience's own home and time is the "right" one — anything older is too primitive and anything newer is too far ahead.

> BARBARA: Susan, listen to me, can't you see that all this is an illusion? It's a game that you and your grandfather are playing, if you like. But you can't expect us to believe it.
> SUSAN: (Very upset.) It's not [a game]! Look, I love your school. I love England in the 20th century. The last five months have been the happiest of my life....

Susan's love of "England in the 20th century" and her willingness later in this episode to "leave the TARDIS" to stay in 1960s London show that despite the audience's desire to explore those other times and places from the safety of their living rooms, their feeling that England is the "right" place is never challenged. Even Susan, an alien and a member of an advanced civilization, sees that England is the best place to be.

Additionally, in "The Aztecs"[26] Barbara, who has been mistaken for the re-incarnation of the Aztec high priestess Yetaxa, decides to use her position in the Aztec culture to attempt to interject contemporary British Cultural values into the Aztec belief system by thwarting the tradition of human sacrifice. She tells the Doctor, "There'll be no sacrifice this afternoon, Doctor, or ever again. The reincarnation of Yetaxa will prove to the people that you don't need to sacrifice a human being to make it rain.... This is the beginning of the end of the sun god." When the Doctor protests, and warns her against getting involved, Barbara argues that she should be able to intervene because the native population is making poor choices.

> BARBARA: Oh, don't you see? If I could start the destruction of everything that's evil here, then everything that is good will survive when Cortez lands.
> THE DOCTOR: But you can't rewrite history, not one line ... Barbara, one last appeal. What you are trying to do is utterly impossible. I know, believe me, I know.
> BARBARA: Not Barbara. Yetaxa.

The Doctor and Barbara fail to interrogate the flaw in this reasoning, namely their assumption that any action or change to the native religious practices could stop Cortez's destruction of the Aztecs. They leave Cortez's colonial project un-critiqued because these characters still in a colonial mindset. It seems deeply misguided to assume that Cortez would have changed his agenda to conquer the Aztecs as a result of encountering a more "civilized" native culture. Barbara's own desire to protect the native population from their own ignorance and backward practices echoes the ideological justification of the colonial project very clearly — namely that a country unable to defend itself through superior technology needs to be overtaken by a stronger, more advanced culture who can then profit by exploiting the natural resources that the native peoples are too unsophisticated to properly value.

Economic historian Niall Ferguson, who has been called a "nostalgist for empire,"[27] argues that even at the height of the colonial project in India, Britain had to recognize similar failings in their attempts to export their own cultural values to their colonized subjects. The Indian Rebellion of 1857 (then called the Indian Mutiny by the British) illustrated that the missionary "project to modernize and Christianize India had gone disastrously wrong ... interfering with native customs had meant nothing but trouble."[28] The Doctor's advice seems to echo the now ridiculous-sounding beliefs of Queen Victoria and her government in India that they renounced "the right and desire to impose Our convictions on any of Our subjects."[29] British official Charles Raikes noted that the Mutiny had shown "the fatal error of attempting to force the policy of Europe on the people of Asia." This view puts the Doctor's advice in rather a more conservative light, and indeed the result of Barbara ignoring that advice (the object of human sacrifice throws himself to his death despite Barbara's interference) seems to echo the colonial conclusion that native groups will insist on their own beliefs, even if those beliefs are destructive to themselves or others.

This conversation and the failure of Barbara's efforts reveal the tension of such an undertaking, as the cultural values of the intended victim win out, and he chooses to carry through with the sacrifice to keep his honor. The Doctor, warning Barbara that she shouldn't interfere, here acts as a reminder that part of the enterprise of maintaining British cultural values will necessarily involve times when they simply will not suffice, and will not be able to supplant the cultural views of the native, or foreign, people, a lesson the compatriots of the British Empire learned the hard way.

In the second-season finale, "The Time Meddler,"[30] the time-traveler Monk describes to the Doctor how much his superior knowledge (read contemporary British values) can benefit the ancient Britons echoes a colonial belief in Western and modern superiority. As the Monk says, "I want to improve things ... King Harold, I know he'd be a good king. There wouldn't be all those wars in Europe, those claims over France went on for years and years. With peace, the people would be able to better themselves." This Monk is presented as misguided, so on the one hand the program could be advocating an anti-colonialist view (the primitives need to be left to sort out their own problems on their own terms, guided by their own cultural values) but yet, the show puts the audience in the position again and again to view the British viewpoint and value-set as the "correct" one. The British characters in the show therefore have to "hold back" from providing their wisdom and the benefit of their superior values. In this way, the program is shown wrestling with the change in world-view that emerging postcolonial movements would demand.

The British audience at this period may have recognized that colonial power is no longer theirs to wield — the show points out that this is not the thinking of an advanced culture like that of the Time Lords — but the characters and the audience are just unable to help themselves from reiterating that THEY are in the right, even as they recognize that it is their duty to step aside, despite their better judgment. The show seems to be suggesting, therefore that although the British recognize that letting go of their colonial power is the "right thing to do," they nonetheless still believe that if the colonized people would only listen to them, they would be much better off. In what represents a shift in thinking, the Doctor reminds his companions and the audience what their motto should be going forward:

THE DOCTOR: You know as well as I do the golden rule about space and time travelling. Never, never interfere with the course of history.

THE MONK: And who says so? Doctor, it's more fun my way.

To complicate the Monk's vision of a playful mix of histories coming together, there was the historical reality of increased emigration by members of the former colonies, such as the British West Indies, who arrived in Britain in the '50s and '60s in search of better economic opportunities. The White British population had to recognize that Empire was not merely a patriotic concept but a political and historical fact that had an immediate effect on the people in colonized places. Thus, for the average Briton, Empire is now not just "out there," in some mystical exotic place that England can lay claim to and define itself against; it has come to England to stay, where it was not warmly welcomed.[31]

In the Troughton years, 1966–69, themes of nostalgia in *Doctor Who* reveal and respond to anxieties about the decentralization of power and continental, colonial, and other foreign peoples. The show's engagement with nostalgia reflects the beginning of a shift in national consciousness, as the nostalgia in *Doctor Who* moves away from being entirely based in restorative nostalgia and edges closer to reflective forms. "Tomb of the Cybermen" appears to espouse reflective nostalgia, by valuing individual memory, which the Cyborg race the Cybermen are trying to erase by assimilating the humans and their individual minds. The Cybermen's process forms a race with a *collective memory*, a less desirable state. But there are two stories being told here — one showing the dangers of succumbing to a dangerous colonizing force (the Cybermen) and one showing the oppression that even individual thinkers can force. Individual selective memory is a narrative that only works for the white, British-associated characters. This contrast is amplified as a result of the choice to cast Roy

Stewart, a Jamaican-born stuntman, in the critical role of Toberman. Toberman, a nearly silent, hulking character, represents in our reading the subaltern colonized minorities who must sacrifice in order for the homogeneity of British culture to remain intact.

Boym notes the need for cultures to find a scapegoat for their misfortunes, preferably somebody different. "They" conspire against "our" homeland's integrity; hence "we" have to conspire against "them" in order to restore "our" imagined community. In this way, conspiracy theory can come to substitute for the conspiracy itself. Indeed, much of twentieth-century violence, from pogroms to Nazi and Stalinist terror to McCarthy's Red scare, operated in response to conspiracy theories in the name of a restored homeland."[32] "The Tomb of the Cybermen" disrupts and challenges the narrative of a benevolent British Empire. The episode juxtaposes the negative totalitizing logic of the Cybermen empire, with the beneficient knowledge and humanity of British culture. When the Cybermen convert Toberman, and threaten to convert the rest of the (white) expedition members, they repeat the imperialistic assertion "YOU BELONG TO US. YOU WILL BECOME LIKE US." Companion Jamie counters, "We're humans, we're not like you." The Doctor appeals to Toberman's humanity, ostensibly freeing him from the Cybermen's control. But Toberman never becomes free as an autonomous human being, even after he breaks from the Cybermen's control. Instead, he is forced to sacrifice his life to save the white characters. As a result, the character Toberman remains an unnerving symbol of *Doctor Who*'s complicated relationship with the colonial project.

The nature of *Doctor Who* allows for potentially disturbing ideas such as these while simultaneously offering comfort to the audience with what Boym calls "restorative nostalgia," to make whole what might seem fractured in changing times. As Boym argues:

> Nostalgia is an ache of temporal distance and displacement. Restorative nostalgia takes care of both of these symptoms. Distance is compensated by intimate experiences and the availability of a desired object. Displacement is cured by a return home, preferably a collective one. Never mind if it's not your home; by the time you reach it, you will have already forgotten the difference. What drives restorative nostalgia is not the sentiment of distance and longing but rather the anxiety about those who draw attention to historical incongruities between past and present and thus question the wholeness and continuity of the restored tradition. Even in its less extreme form, restorative nostalgia has no use for the signs of historical time — patina, ruins, cracks, imperfections.[33]

Boym could even be describing the character of the Doctor in this passage — as a character, he is at home everywhere and nowhere, not even his home planet.[34] The Pertwee years continue and extend the shift from restorative to reflective nostalgia that began in the Troughton years. While potential gaps in the cohesiveness and continuity of British national culture and power leaked into Troughton episodes such as "Tomb of the Cybermen," these gaps seem to be made overt only to also demonstrate how they might be, or already always had been, dealt with. In the Pertwee years, these tensions reappear, and are at first, again summarily dismissed, but later become more nuanced and insistent, and the shift in the show's use of nostalgia in "Colony in Space," "The Mutants," and "Frontier in Space" show that, ultimately, a restorative sense of nostalgia which upholds an unquestioned, superior Britain is unsupportable and flawed. Instead, what emerges as an alternative is a nostalgia based on individual engagements with time and history, which lingers in or foregrounds the ruins, or the complications of social history and culture, and which reveals to the watcher the anxieties and tensions inherent in not-quite-post-Imperial Britain. This reflective engagement with nostalgia creates moments in the show which counter the narrative of still pro–Empire voices and create a site for elided British colonial peoples and concerns to be made visible.

The six episode 1971 story "Colony in Space" critiques the brutality of Empire while at the same time reaffirming British centrality through portraying the necessity of the paternal British presence needed to safely monitor the transition of the colony This story depicts a "native" presence in the form of the non-white, tribal Primitives and the white colonists who arm themselves against the Primitives as well as Earth's central government. The white colonists, who have displaced the native Primitives, defend their claim against later white arrivals.

Moreover, this story represents not only the "native" presence in the form of the Primitives but also the earlier colonizing Europeans who arm themselves not only against the Primitives but also against Earth's government who may move in to take over and re-colonize for material gain (the minerals on the planet are very valuable). A colonist says, "We don't want our planet gutted. You've no right to be here." When asked by the Doctor whether they have laws to protect them, they reveal that they too see the planet for its use-value: "We can complain to Earth's government, just like all the others. By the time we get a final decision, the planet's useless." The first primitive to appear is a humanoid alien carrying a spear, is dark-skinned and has exaggerated lips and nose, wears a loincloth and appears to be coated in mud paint. These primitives, though they do not talk, show native shrewdness by hauling off the TARDIS — they can recognize its intrinsic value.

The White colonists express their desire for freedom, room to move and access to a clean, unspoiled (and mineral-rich) environment. In their speech and clothing, they resemble (white) Britons of the 1970s, though they come from the 2470s. The Primitives, on the other hand, are green-skinned, dressed in loincloths, carry spears, do not speak, and at one point actually make off with the TARDIS. Inside the colonists' space, the setting is recognizable, if sparse. Outside, there are gigantic and frightening lizards as well as the native Primitives, drawing audience sympathy for the more familiar-looking and familiar-sounding colonists.

The narrative structure of the episode — in which the Doctor and Jo are thrown together with the white colonists — also leads the audience to identify with the White colonists. The white colonists have assumed a dominating yet paternalistic role with the Primitives, employing them as servants and providing them constant, gentle instruction on not stealing and not attacking the colonists or their friends. The Doctor shows no reaction or outrage to the white colonists claiming ownership of a planet already inhabited by a humanoid civilization. He does not question the morality of the colonists' use of the natives nor their taking possession of a land already occupied. The Doctor instead advises Ashe, who seems worried about a Primitive revolt, to "just play for time." We soon discover the colonists have only inhabited the planet for one year. But, as the Doctor says, "there's no reason that this planet cannot support a thriving colony." In the end, all conflicts are resolved to eliminate all barriers to the colonists' profitable establishment on the planet. So, although there are undercurrents in the story of criticism of the colonial project, the episode more or less endorses it, offering its establishment as a satisfying conclusion to the story.

Later Jon Pertwee stories engage explicitly with the anxieties involved in the reaffirmation of British centrality, but begin to ponder the dangers of nostalgia for empire. The 1973 six-episode story "Frontier in Space," written by Malcolm Hulke, signals a shift in the show, as it moves from dealing with historical topics to contemporary political issues represented through thinly-veiled metaphors. Hulke's episodes reveal the varied complicated perceptions about colonization and the role Britain in the world (and in the galaxy). Whereas previous depictions of colonial situations relied on the sense of restorative nostalgia to reposition and implicitly suggest to British viewers that they were the height of human civility, and later that British colonialist intentions were noble, this series instead suggests that the story of the history of British colonialism is not about defining good or bad, but instead should be about adjusting to the needs and actualities of a changing world order so that Britain and her people could survive.

"Frontier in Space" is an obvious metaphor for the Communist threat to democracy, explicitly addressing the transition of colonies from being under the power of the ruling government, and instead moving to their own autonomous government. The Doctor describes "two great Empires spreading their way through the galaxy ... both expanding and colonizing one planet after another and they're sitting on a powder keg."[35] Earth's president is a woman with a noticeably "foreign" accent (actress Vera Fusek was born in Czechoslovakia), indicating a genuine threat to the British Empire — not only is the leader non–British and a woman, but the enemy she fights are the Draconians. Their costumes and masks suggest Asian styling to evoke the contemporary fears about the Communist threat in Southeast Asia: the Draconian leader has a cloak resembling the peaked roof of a Chinese pagoda, a textured mask with slanted eyes, similar to the masks worn by dancers in traditional Thai dance. The president is reasonable and even-tempered when dealing with crisis, embodying the best of civilian government, whereas General Williams represents the military mindset, which the episode suggests is flawed.

The episode that is perhaps the most roundly critical of violent enforcement of colonial power is the 1972 Pertwee story "The Mutants." This story has already been widely discussed as a metaphor for the colonial project and has been criticized (notably by Salman Rushdie) for racist undertones. However, we feel it useful to consider this story's take on colonialism in the context of nostalgia. The conflicting positions towards colonialism in the episode illustrate the conflicts that existed in the creative team producing it. In some moments, the story seems to support and sympathize with the British colonial ideal, and at other moments, the story is explicitly critical of the racism, oppression and environmental destruction wrought by colonialism.

In many ways, the episode suggests that colonies are formed as a result of nostalgia for a perceived lost homeland. The colonists in this episode sought out the metaphorical and literal greener pastures when their own homeland's resources had been used up. And rather than adapt to the native environment, the colonists attempt to change the planet to more closely resemble their homeland. This is a search for an imagined past, i.e., the colonists hoped to form a new Earth (echoing historical desires for a New England, New Amsterdam, New York or New Orleans, Nova Scotia, New Brunswick, etc.) in a new environment, since resources in the old homeland are inaccessible or depleted. Boym defines nostalgic longing as the "loss of the original object of desire, and by its spatial and temporal displacement."[36] Those seeking to establish a "new" version of their home in the colony had hoped to re-make their lost, idealized home nation.

The desire to re-create a lost home is the basis for the foundation of the Earth colony on the planet Solos in "The Mutants." Earth people, having used up the resources on their own planet, seek to alter the environment on Solos to make it more like the Earth they remember. The Doctor tries to explain this to Jo, but even though Jo lives in a time where colonialism is a very recent memory, she is unable to understand what happens when a colonial power is in decline:

> DOCTOR: Well, your empire — Earth's empire. Yes, great colonists — Earthmen — you know, Jo. Once they'd sacked the solar system, they moved onto pastures new. Solos is one of them — one of the last. Do you ever read Gibbon's "Decline and Fall"?
>
> JO: (Naively.) No, is it good?
>
> DOCTOR: (Patiently.) Jo, this is like that, you see?
>
> JO: No.
>
> DOCTOR: Oh, well empires rise and empires fall. And if this [hostile welcome] is their idea of a reception, this one has obviously crumbled!

Jo, an "everyman" of contemporary society, is unfamiliar with critical conceptions and histories of imperialism. But, despite her initial ignorance, Jo learns the lesson of colonial decline very well in this episode, and aligns herself closely with Ky, the head of a colonial rebellion. Jo gains sympathy for Ky's position when he explains his view of what Earth must be like and explains what the Earth colonists have done to his home.

> KY: I have seen pictures of Earth. No one lives on the ground. The air is too poisonous. And soon Solos will be the same. The Overlords only promise independence so they can go on plundering our resources, turning our green fields into their grey slagheaps. Am I not right? Is it not true?
>
> JO: I don't know. It's rather a long time since I left Earth.
>
> KY: Once, my people were farmers and nomads. Now look at them. Slaves in factories and mines. Already the pollution is causing mutations. The Mutts, as the Marshal calls them. Mutts!

Even the alien Ky, in expressing his view of Earth's greener past, holds nostalgia for Earth as it once was. An audience in the environmentally-aware 1970s could absolutely understand this longing to engage in Boym's restorative nostalgia and "rebuild the lost home and patch up the memory gaps."[37] Reflective nostalgia is more about savoring a sad memory of the past. Boym notes: "the first category of nostalgics do not think of themselves as nostalgic; they believe that their project is about truth. This kind of nostalgia characterizes national and nationalist revivals all over the world."[38] The Doctor advocates neither of these, preferring to always look forward.

A conflict between these two types of nostalgia is made manifest in the conflicting worldviews within "The Mutants." The Marshal, dedicated to sustaining the Imperial project, and through it, to sustaining his own personal power, is a restorative nostalgic who wants to create a "new Earth," eradicating the native population on Solos and reproducing the atmospheric elements of Earth, but the doomed administrator lingers over sad memories and mourns the end of the Earth Empire.

> ADMINISTRATOR: I take it you've been too busy with security to study the latest reports from Earth? We can't afford an empire any more. Earth is exhausted, Marshal — finished. Politically, economically and biologically — finished.

The Administrator's nostalgic vision is starkly contrasted with the ruins of the native population, and of their sacred places, the location and significance of which has been lost. The production team was as conflicted, with Terrance Dicks holding to a pro-colonial view and the episode's writers and director holding a more critical view. Still, the conflicts surrounding the devastated planet and crumbling empire are mediated for the audience through White male authority figures, the Doctor, the ethnographer, Dr. Sondegaard and Ky.

The Doctor's views on colonization have clearly changed since "Colony in Space." As the Doctor has said to Jo, this is an empire in decline. The emphasis in Pertwee's delivery is on the decline, then end of the empire. This exchange may also be suggesting that the British audience was not educated about, or had a simplistic understanding of, British colonial history and contemporary British Imperialism.

One of colonialism's effects is to erase the colonized peoples' histories and cultural traditions and replace it with that of the colonizers. British colonials tended to also bring with them elements of British culture (styles of dress, eating, manner), transplanting them to the colonial context and then claiming them as "natural" for that place. Moreover, they frequently also sought a sense of adventure, power, room to move and breathe which they then became accustomed to and did not wish to give up. These traits are represented in the episode by the character of the Marshal, who refuses to surrender the colonial dream of remaking the planet into a new Earth, and then murders numerous natives and overlords in order to hang on to power.

As with "Tomb of the Cybermen," what might have been a fairly superficial exploration of political ideas is infused with additional layers of subtext as a result of the casting choices. Many have noted that Rick James, the black actor who plays the enlightened Overlord named Cotton, gives (at best) an unusual performance. At worst, he is described as wooden and with an "apparent inability to deliver his lines"[39] though most commentators (such as Dallas Jones)[40] seem to appreciate the decision to cast a black actor in this serial so explicitly an allegory of colonialism. The creative team was undoubtedly trying to strengthen their critique of the apartheid nature of the colony in the episode ("Overlords" and "Solonians" use separate transmats), but the apparent decision to encourage Rick James to suppress his Caribbean accent renders his performance inauthentic and distracting. This could suggest to the audience that ex-colonials will be integrated fully into the mainstream British culture, losing distinctive accents along the way. This choice is disappointing in that *Doctor Who* had for several years featured White actors using regional accents, yet could not allow this Black actor to speak in his usual accent. The characters of Dr. Sondergaard, and Dr. Jaeger speak English with non–British accents, so the need to suppress James' accent is all the more unnerving. In the end, however, James's character, Cotton, plays a pivotal role in the story — assisting the Doctor, Joe and Ky and the other natives. After Cotton's partner, Stubbs, is killed, James continues in a complex and nuanced role, even if his acting skills seem insufficient to carry it off successfully. Cotton, who in the very beginning of the story stated that the planet should be given back to the natives, is infallibly moral and competent, and ultimately is the only just survivor of the empire, who then is given dominion over the transition back to native Solonian control. However questionable James' performance, the story ends with Cotton assuming command, providing an onscreen example of a black man in a government leadership position.

"The Mutants" seems to suggest that colonial suppression of and interference with native cultures gives rise to genocide, environmental destruction and war. Had the native Solonians not been disconnected from their native language and history, they would have undergone their natural life cycle mutation without incident. But precisely because the Overlords do not understand this natural part of the planet's 500-year rotation, they unfairly and unwisely fear the natives in their metamorphosis. Had the natives been left to their own devices, there would have been no crisis. The misunderstanding by the colonial Overlords creates a panic that nearly leads to the extinction of the native Solonians, who have simply adapted to survive the seasonal increase in radiation by changing form and hibernating. The episode is fair warning to colonial powers that, no matter how well-intentioned, interference with indigenous cultures can have dangerous and far-reaching consequences.

Though the quest to recreate a lost home elsewhere may be appealing, the entire premise of such a quest is flawed. In *Dangerous Liaisons: Gender, Nation, and Postcolonial Perspectives*, Aamir Mufti and Ella Shohat, ask whether there was ever such a place as "home." They argue that

> [h]ome and the loss of home constitute a recurring motif of modernity. The post-world war era has seen it return, nourished on fresh historical experiences, imbued with new meanings. In the last decade [1980s–90s], specifically, rearticulated notions of exile and Diaspora have played an important role in a cultural critique that not only charted the history of communities displaced in the postindependence era but also employed that history as a condition and a trope for cultural criticism itself. In the repeated mutual impacting of divergent trajectories, claims, and memories that constitute the cultural landscape of late capitalism, the loss of home and the struggle to reclaim and reimagine it are experiences fraught with tension.[41]

The production history of "The Mutants" encapsulates this tension, as well as the shift from post-war to independence-era anxieties about the collapse of the Empire, as well as anxieties about the migration of post-colonials to England and post-independence-era cultural critiques of Britain's colonial history. Terrance Dicks had a strong creative influence over the show throughout the 1970s, and was able to choose and edit the direction of *Doctor Who* stories. His pro–Imperial position was at odds with the position of the script writers and director of "The Mutants," who wanted to explicitly engage with the negative and long-lasting effects of imperialism on colonized lands and people. As Dicks remarks:

> They [the Bristol Boys] wanted to do something about the evils of Empire, which I think I didn't necessarily agree with because I was rather pro the British Empire. My view was, and I suppose still is to some extent, that it would be a lot better if it was still there, you know. If you have a look at Africa or Asia or the rest of the world, if the Brits were still in charge, you know, it would all be running smoothly.[42]

Dicks' yearning for a British Imperial past as it never existed in the real world is representative of collective British anxieties of the 1960s–70s about the end of the Empire and the removal of Britain from the center of power. It also functions, on a deeper level, as a reflection of the British colonial project, as driven by the desire to recreate and sustain an image and production of "home" abroad in an idealized, ritualized, and cohesive form that had never actually existed in England.

The references to colonialism were explicitly undertaken by the creative team, as writer Baker relates: "We picked up the theme of racism by having the segregation in the skybase between the Earth people and the aboriginals of the planet. Because at that time there was this kind of segregation in South Africa, for instance." Baker explains that his co-writer Dave Martin had a particular interest in South Africa because he knew someone who was going to go out to South Africa to farm and "to be a kind of master."[43] As McKee noted, there is (even among this creative team) a resistance to too much overtly political content, but Baker disagreed, arguing that "personally, I think it's the best one we ever did. I think it's particularly important that a family show should take on these big themes."[44]

It is now a far more widely accepted idea that the paternalism of Empire has been sadly misguided. Bidisha, an Oxford- and London School of Economics-educated writer and BBC presenter comments:

Something which has been part of the argument against colonization, is no matter what the benefits are, it's not the right of the colonizer to colonize. It's not okay for them, ever, to look at another territory and say, "these people are in a mess. They need our help. We are going over to reform, to bring order, to civilize, to educate. What we're doing is we're being the good guys. This is a nation, a territory, a planet which is crying out for some kind of help" and of course you have the colonized saying, "Well, that's none of your business."[45]

"The Mutants" addresses such apologist arguments directly through the main plot, and in the reactions presented by The Doctor and Jo to the form of imperialism enacted by the Overlords, a form which directly echoes late-stage British imperialism. Actor Garrick Hagon, who played Ky, says that looking at the show 40 years later, "I think it stands up more as a metaphor ... I think it was a very brave thing to do, especially for a young audience because a lot of the characters are pretty angry."[46] The anger surrounding colonial oppression is something that the story does give voice to, without trying to discount the reasons for it. It might have been tempting to have the Doctor or Jo try to convince Ky that the colonizers were well-meaning, but the writers refuse to justify that position. In fact, by the end, "The Mutants" argues that not only is there no excuse for colonization, there is also no excuse for rationalizing or refusing to rectify such situations after they have occurred. While their responses are complex and at times problematic, the Doctor and Jo involve themselves in the fight, and support the Solonians in their attempt to achieve independence and to reconnect with their own history.

Conclusion

While Britain is now firmly in a post–Empire stage,[47] the "new" *Doctor Who* series (2005–) can still be seen as wrestling with Britain's colonial past, and a great deal of the nostalgia for Empire filters in to the series in the form of nostalgia for the original run. The creative team of the new series, notably the two show-runners Russell T. Davies (2005–10) and Steven Moffat (2010–), are fans of the original series. Several of the writers, such as Gareth Roberts,[48] Chris Chibnall,[49] Mark Gatiss,[50] Robert Shearman,[51] and Paul Cornell,[52] came to writing as a career through their love of *Doctor Who*. This team uses creative nostalgia to address continuing British national anxieties within their stories, often projecting into the future resolutions to tensions about gender roles, class, race, homosexuality, and, particularly, colonial and imperial tendencies. While the depictions of characters and situations which respond to these cultural anxieties often contain problematic elements, they represent a move to the future, through a re-visioning of the past. Such creative nostalgia, Boym argues, "reveals the fantasies of the age, and it is in those fantasies and potentialities is that the future is born. One is nostalgic not for the past the way it was but for the past the way it could have been. It is this past perfect that one strives to realize in the future."[53]

Doctor Who continues to engage with concepts of colonization and imperialism specifically because, despite the lessons offered by *Doctor Who* in its early years, Britain still finds itself intervening politically and militarily around the world and using very similar arguments to the ones described by Bishida. New *Doctor Who* series storylines which center upon or contain elements of British Imperialism, such as "The Beast Below," therefore engage at once with Britain's past, *Doctor Who*'s past, and the continuing anxieties which have had such a strong effect on the direction and creation of the program.

Chibnall's 2010 story "The Hungry Earth/In Cold Blood" is a notable example of the new series' nostalgia for the old. Essentially a revisiting and revision of the 1970 Pertwee story "Doctor Who and the Silurians," Chibnall's story repeats the central conflict and numerous plot elements as well, but much more strongly endorses a pacifist solution to the conflict. While Pertwee's Doctor was opposed to the destruction of the Silurians, he was over-ruled by the Brigadier's military solution. Thus the new series is able to engage with the concerns of Britain and with the older series by responding to the same situations with updated, progressive strategies that can give Britain a path to the future.

The new *Who*'s references to its own past have been widely noted, and indeed, the attention to the program's legacy has earned praise from fans and critics. As Kim Newman writes in *Doctor Who: A Critical Reading of the Series*:

> The newest incarnation ... inevitably commands attention. Sometimes, *Doctor Who* (2005–) is fascinating for the way it comments on its predecessors in a manner which suggests writer-producer Russell T. Davies is mounting a critical project as much as refreshing a still-potent concept to suit the demands of twenty-first century television. It is as if every Davies-stamped episode feels obliged to work in some bit of business that the old show should have got to years earlier but somehow overlooked. Deeply engaged with its previous incarnation, it can still stand as a working definition of a useful, creeping prefix by being "not your father's *Doctor Who*."[54]

The structure of the show itself serves the same function as the TARDIS — by creating a show in which the main character can be portrayed by different actors, and where companions can come and go but the essential structure of the show remains the same, the creators and writers have constructed a vehicle that can continue into the future, adapting as necessary to address changing needs and anxieties of the viewing audience, while portraying the continuity and significance of British culture and history.

The anxiety about loss of imperial power continues even in the 2005–series, so that characters, even while acknowledging that England is no longer the world's ruler can be reassured that it is still the focus of most of the *Doctor Who* stories. As Alec Charles notes in "The Ideology of Anachronism: Television, History, and the Nature of Time":

> When Russell T. Davies finally allows the programme's protagonists to take the reins of government (or at least control of Downing Street's Cabinet Room), they can't pass up the chance to make a few sarcastic comments about contemporary British foreign policy, but at the same time ... the programme seems secretly to relish the idea that Britain still boasts a missile defense system that might prove the envy, and the downfall, of extraterrestrial life.[55]

So while the new series continues its predecessor's agenda of processing the end of British centrality as a world power, it has trouble letting go of a nostalgic vision of Britain at the center of things. And its ever-growing American audience doesn't seem to mind. For the first time in its history, episodes of *Doctor Who* were shot outside the U.K. (in Monument Valley, Utah).[56] It will be intriguing to see whether the series will continue to explore the notion of Britain as a fading power even as this quintessentially British *Doctor Who* continues to demonstrate its power over the changing television landscape and its new audiences.

NOTES

1. Matthew Kilburn, "Bargains of Necessity? *Doctor Who, Culloden* and Fictionalizing History at the BBC in the 1960s," *Time and Relative Dissertations in Space*, ed. David Butler (Manchester: Manchester University Press, 2007), p. 69.

2. Ibid., p. 69.

3. Svetlana Boym, *The Future of Nostalgia* (New York: Basic Books, 2001), p.xiv.

4. Ibid., p. 354.

5. Ibid., p. 7.

6. Niall Ferguson, *Empire: The Rise and Demise of the British World Order and the Lessons for Global Power* (New York: Basic Books, 2003), p. 358.

7. Boym, *The Future of Nostalgia*, p. xiii.

8. Ibid., p. 354.

9. Anita Loomba, *Colonialism/Postcolonialism* (London: Routledge, 2005), p. 6.

10. Ibid., pp. 9–10.

11. Ibid., p.11.

12. Louis Niebur, personal interview, 22 February 2011.

13. Ibid.

14. Ibid.

15. Ibid.

16. "The War Games."

17. Boym, *The Future of Nostalgia*, p. 49.

18. Ibid.

19. Ibid., p. xviii.

20. Ibid., p.49.

21. Ibid., pp. 49–50.

22. Ibid., p. 43.

23. Patrick Wright and Andrezej Krause, *On Living in an Old Country: The National Past in Contemporary Britain*, 2d ed. (Oxford: Oxford University Press, 2009), p. ix.

24. James Chapman, *Inside the TARDIS: The Worlds of Doctor Who, a Cultural History* (London: I.B. Tauris, 2006, p.8.

25. Susan will eventually leave her grandfather's TARDIS in 2164's London, after she falls in love with a Dalek-resistance fighter, David Campbell ("The Dalek Invasion of Earth").

26. "The Aztecs." For program details see Videography.

27. http://www.bbc.co.uk/radio4/factual/starttheweek_20060612.shtml.

28. Ferguson, *Empire*, pp. 152–3.

29. Ibid., p.155

30. "The Time Meddler."

31. Enoch Powell's 1968 speech noted that although people should be equal under the law, this does not mean that the immigrant and his descendants should be elevated into a privileged or special class or that the citizen should be denied his right to discriminate in the management of his own affairs between one fellow-citizen and another or that he should be subjected to an inquisition as to his reasons and motives for behaving in one lawful manner rather than another.

32. Boym, *The Future of Nostalgia*, p. 43.

33. Ibid., pp. 44–5.

34. "The Deadly Assasin."

35. "Frontier in Space."

36. Boym, *The Future of Nostalgia*, p. 38.

37. Ibid, p. 34.

38. Ibid.

39. http://www.bbc.co.uk/doctorwho/classic/episodeguide/mutants/detail.shtml.

40. http://www.bbc.co.uk/doctorwho/classic/episodeguide/mutants/detail.shtml.

41. Anne McClintock, Amir Mufti and Ella Shohat, *Dangerous Liaisons: Gender, Nation, and Postcolonial Perspectives* (Minneapolis: University of Minnesota Press, 1997).

42. "Mutt Mad," "The Mutants" DVD.

43. Ibid.

44. Ibid.

45. "Race Against Time," "The Mutants" DVD. Narration written by Simon Guerrier and researched by Jim Sangster.

46. "Mutt Mad."

47. Mike Gapes, HC Paper 147–II House of Commons Foreign Affairs Committee: Overseas Territories, Volume II, The Stationery Office, ISBN 0–215–52150–1, http://books.google.com/?id=HhsZSMEH5DoC (22 July 2009).

48. Roberts wrote the *Doctor Who* episodes "The Shakespeare Code" (2007), "The Unicorn and the Wasp" (2008) and "The Lodger" (2010). Roberts was also a contributor to numerous *Doctor Who* spin-off novels.

49. In addition to *Doctor Who* episodes "42" (2007) and "The Hungry Earth/Cold Blood" (2010), Chibnall wrote a number of episodes for the *Doctor Who* spin-off series *Torchwood* and is a long-time fan of the original series.

50. Gatiss, an author of several *Doctor Who* novels, wrote the episodes "The Unquiet Dead" (2005), "The Idiot's Lantern" (2006) and "Victory of the Daleks" (2010), and appeared in roles in the episodes "The Lazarus Experiment" (2007) and "Victory of the Daleks" (voice only, 2010).

51. Author of several *Who* radio dramas, Shearman wrote the episode "Dalek" (2005).

52. Cornell has authored several *Who* novels, as well as the episodes "Father's Day" (2005), and "Human Nature/Family of Blood" (2007). The latter of these is a two-part, Hugo Award–nominated story and a fan favorite, likely due to its incorporation of numerous elements of the *Doctor Who* mythology.

53. Boym, *The Future of Nostalgia*, p.351.

54. Kim Neman, *Doctor Who: A Critical Reading of the Series,* (London: BFI, 2005), p. 7.

55. Charles, Alec. "The Ideology of Anachronism: Television, History and the Nature of Time," *Time and Relative Dissertations in Space*, ed. David Butler (Manchester: Manchester University Press, 2007), p. 116.

56. "The Impossible Astronaut/Day of the Moon."

9

A Needle Through the Heart

Violence and Tragedy as a Narrative Device

Lindsay Coleman

British television has in previous decades contained series marketed towards children which nevertheless have contained imagery and plot details of disturbing physical and emotional violence. Not the least of these is the classic *Doctor Who* series. Stretching from 1963 through to 1989, the series was viewed by children, but not technically part of children's programming for the BBC.[1] It was a series produced for the family, inclusive of the parents and older siblings.[2] What this specifically resulted in, especially between the early 1970s and its final production in 1989, was a raft of imagery which was troubling to the censors, in the form of critic Mary Whitehouse, children themselves, as their correspondence to the series has reflected, and even the series' producers.[3] Ambivalence on the subject has persisted even to this day on what boundaries were pushed, and whether the series' producers, writers and directors could indeed justify the choices they made over this period.[4] The charges laid by the likes of Mary Whitehouse as to the narrative model the series presented, one which favored heightened emotions of terror experienced empathetically throughout the global viewing community, have stuck as a part of its legacy.[5]

The explicit inclusion of horror imagery and sadistic violence in visual texts whose audience may include children has always been a part of television and film production. One need only watch the celebrated final Harry Potter film to note lurid, horrific images of the serpentine Valdemort wading barefoot through the blood of slaughtered goblins, or the evil wizard's latter appearance as a panting, bloody fetus. At times these images receive scant attention. Certainly, in *Harry Potter and the Deathly Hollows Part 2*,[6] the wider spectacle of battling wizards has doubtless obscured the inclusion of such deeply disturbing imagery in what is an adaptation of a book written primarily for children.[7] Historically the series of *Doctor Who* has not always been so fortunate as to escape criticism. From its early beginnings, gaining strength during the era of producer Phillip Hinchcliffe, subsiding slightly during the era of producer Graham Williams, and returning ferociously during the tenure of script editor Eric Saward, the series has had to withstand criticisms from politicians and pressure groups alike, even the BBC, over its use of violent, horrific imagery and narrative elements.[8]

The application of such criticism has been sporadic in its intensity. Just as Harry Potter's latest adventure has arrived heralded for its dramatic intensity rather than its horror, it is equally likely that the conspiring forces behind a given cultural moment in the case of *Doctor Who* may have emphasized or occluded its own violent, horrific content. Of course to make definitive pronouncements on the fear factor of the classic series of *Doctor Who* can be problematic when considering the vast array of characters, villains, and scenarios the series has come up with. Often the series' antagonists have varied in their respective levels of threat from the deadly Sontarans, to the more cerebral, sympathetic Omega. Likewise the tone of the series has swung from gothic to camp, and every attitude in between in the narrative span between its beginnings in 1963 to its current resurrection. The Doctor himself, while always the series' hero, has likewise oscillated between being a figure of danger and comfort. William Hartnell's Doctor attempts to dash out the brains of a vulnerable, non-villainous caveman in the episode "Forest of Fear" of the serial "The Unearthly Child." Here, in his first incarnation, he reveals a ruthless and violent streak. In contrast the very recent serial "The Beast Below" has companion Amy Pond noting the Doctor, as embodied by Matt Smith, as a figure of essential decency and kindness, altogether more recognizably human. Yet while the title character may be benevolent at times, the adversary's threat level only mild, or a given narrative arc comparatively free of tension, the series has nevertheless developed a reputation for scares, particularly for young children.

The series' fear factor might not perhaps be classified as pervasive, yet it manifests nevertheless in a unique atmosphere, a sense of dread which can be heightened by terror and shocking violence at surprising moments along the Who narrative continuum. It is the ongoing possibility of violence, rather than its frequency, which may be thought to enhance this reputation. When such scares and violence do appear they are indelible in their impression. The fact that the series has often placed such memorably horrific moments in its most highly praised stories has further gone to define the series' reputation for scares wrapped in a powerful narrative, both enhancing and defining a serial's central narrative drive. Storylines which evidence this quickly spring to mind: "Terror of the Autons," "Genesis of the Daleks," "The Deadly Assassin," "The Pyramids of Mars," "Seeds of Doom," "Revelation of the Daleks" among others. From the series' pervasive atmosphere of dread and tension spring these powerful, definitive stories which are composites of narrative clarity, humor, and terror.

The cliché of kiddies hiding behind the couch when *Doctor Who* was on has persisted since its inception. I myself was a ridiculous coward when watching the series as a child, going so far as to actually turn the television off during terrifying moments, followed by a three minute stroll outside of the house, followed by my return to the show when I knew that, more or less, all horrific or terrifying elements had dissipated. To watch the series as a child was to engage with things which frightened. There were monsters which possessed superhuman strength, psychic abilities, and shape-shifting abilities. Naturally these creatures, even without menacing the Doctor and his companions, were intrinsically frightening. As a child, the potential to be physically or mentally outmatched, or to have one's faith in appearances tested, are all ongoing fears, whether in the schoolyard, or in the company of those older. Not only were these creatures frightening in their abilities, but they also were a constant threat to the Doctor throughout his adventures. One of the series' greatest successes was in its ability to place the Doctor and his allies in hundreds of hours' worth of plots and counter-plots, all of which evidenced a constant tension in the viewing experience. When and how, the question on children's minds, would the Doctor next be menaced.

Horror permeates the series. But the question must be asked, on what basis should its presence even be contested? Certainly media watchdogs have been active throughout the series' classic run in criticizing the presence of violent, horrific images, and horrific narrative content. While this atmosphere is an ongoing appeal of the series, in its darker manifestations it has provoked much in the way of the critical consternation and disapproval on the part of television critics such as Mary Whitehouse, and even local British journalists.[9] The often horrific, sadistic nature of the series has disturbed these groups, specifically the National Viewer's and Listener's Association (NVLA). The precise moral justification for entertainment, particularly entertainment seen by young children, inevitably enters the debate. The NVLA founder, Whitehouse, contended that much BBC television violence in the 1960s was effectively normalized in its representation.[10] This was troubling to her in that this might in turn affect public attitudes, the viewer, often a child, interpreting screen violence as a kind of license to commit actual violence.[11] Clearly, the expectation is that the series maintain a wholesome nature, that its thrills continue within the bounds of what might otherwise be judged as "decent." Storytelling as a medium is often agreed to exist to uphold such decency to ward off the iniquitous aspects of human experience. Indeed the tales children have engaged with for generations in fairy tales are described in *The Uses of Enchantment* to teach children "about the inner problems of human beings, and of the right solutions to their predicament in any society."[12] In short, tragedy and evil are a part of life, and they must deal with these problems, upholding social values.[13]

Further, perhaps implying a broader, more adult-inclusive definition of content, American literary critic Wayne C. Booth wrote that "[a]lmost all writers until quite recently have claimed to teach virtue while giving pleasure."[14] What Booth thus implied is that the excitement of narrative, historically, was often balanced by a concern for the espousal of ethically untainted acts and the heroes who fulfill them. Such models would, inevitably, inspire conduct becoming to a society, in particular to its children. The Doctor himself is thus most commonly identified as a figure who promotes such a social order. The Doctor has been noted to be perceived by young viewers as "non-violent, practical, intelligent, logical yet resourceful ... helper of the underdog, the underprivileged, and all those who are being discriminated against ... general human good guy."[15] In a respect the concerns of censorious individuals such a Mary Whitehouse and the NVLA are based on the desire that such models be encouraged in television programming. Not only under such a production regimen would children be given the type of stories which would foster a positive, problem-solving approach to life, in keeping with the "resourceful" nature of the Doctor, but also the viewers in general would have modeled for them narratives championing the path to becoming a "general human good guy."[16] Representation of powerful figures espousing positive values represented the standard expected of programmers, and in turn it was expected that such programming would inspire corresponding models of conduct.

Before this argument is further pursued, the question of the relative decency and age-appropriateness of *Doctor Who*, certain contextual data must be acknowledged. Whitehouse was on record with respect to her opposition. In a technical respect this disapproval was justified. Whitehouse wrote in 1975 "in anger and despair ... because at a time when little children would be viewing, you showed violence of quite unacceptable kind."[17] Violence permeated the program, specifically the third episode of "The Deadly Assassin" which contained a climax; she felt that it "could only be described as sadistic."[18] The finale did contravene the BBC network's guidelines. The specific choice the episode's producer, Phillip Hinchcliffe, had supervised saw the doctor being drowned, his grimacing face forced beneath water. This sudden interruption of the story saw the Doctor's apparent demise; young audiences had to wait a full week to discover if this were the case. The duration of this wait did indeed test narrative limits the broadcaster had set. "For young children even a week may be too long to wait for reassurance that the characters with whom they identify are safe."[19] However, Whitehouse was misguided in her belief that children made up a particularly high portion of the audience. Rather, they were a moderate one. Only 15 percent of viewers were under seven, 18 percent eight to eleven, 11 percent twelve to fourteen; the show was for families rather than children.[20] What this data clarifies is that while in terms of pure viewing figures *Doctor Who* was not a program watched by a majority of children, unlike for example *Teletubbies*, Whitehouse was technically correct in her intuition as to the series' infringement of narrative models set forward by the BBC.

What these models present is an intuitive structure in which the sympathies and emotional responses of an audience are in some way quantified. This is one of the essential means of in fact determining the impact of a fantastical series such as *Doctor Who*. The content of such a series is difficult to monitor, in its imagination, in means other than limiting guidelines of narrative and behavior. Such guidelines aid in the formation of narrative form. The BBC's effective brief to producers would translate as "always be certain to present the world in a form devoid of too great an element of suspense, where beloved characters do not suffer extended periods between life and death." In a respect Whitehouse's observations, rooted as they may have been in a strident moralism, nevertheless intuit a group of theories on narrative impact. Marxist literary theorist Pierre Macherey observed on the nature of narrative content: "A text exists as much by *what it cannot say*, by what necessarily produces fissures and strains within it, destroying its internal harmony...."[21] Indeed contemporary philosopher Michael Novak asserts that people "seldom, if ever, act according to principles and rules stated in words and logically arranged. They act, rather, according to models, metaphors, stories and myths."[22] Anthropologist Clifford Geertz observes that rather "than beginning with the set of observations and attempting to subsume them under a governing law," cultural analysis "begins with a set of (prescriptive) signifiers, and attempts to place them within an intelligible frame."[23] Such a model would be the kind of narrative the BBC promoted in relation to *Doctor Who*: a world in which people the audience cares about are generally safe. This model would provoke greater calm than perhaps a written disclaimer utilizing language to assure viewers of the Doctor's fate. Will Wright, in discussing the mythical structures found in a genre noted for them, the Western, further analyzes "Myth as a conceptual response to the requirements of human action in a social situation."[24] Further to this, "myths reconcile deep social conflicts through models of action."[25] Such myths effectively live up to models in which the tension of sickness, decline, and death is resolved. Indeed the Doctor's ongoing regenerations, or perhaps even those of James Bond, or Sherlock Holmes, present in their own right a mythic resolution of the troubling reality of death as they are characters rendered ageless by the many actors who play them.

Television represents what Novak would typify as an imitative model, a metaphorical structure upon which notions of life are grafted specific to the way in which they stimulate the audience's emotions. It is thus a medium upon which powerful emotions may be projected. Whitehouse's response to the episode, her concern over its impact, exemplifies the varied emotional responses the series' violent/horrific narrative can provoke. The surge of emotions which the sight of the drowning Doctor might provoke as the image is experienced collectively by the viewing public in a simultaneous bundle of sentiments: concern, horror, excitement. In fact emotion is essential to the communal experience which is storytelling. Vernon Lee, celebrated writer on the subject of art, wrote that artistic representation involves "the awakening, intensifying, or maintaining of definite emotional states."[26] In this respect to appreciate the conventions of narrative representation found in *Doctor Who* may be judged, as per Novak's descriptions, to rest upon engagement with models of affectivity rather than "principles and rules." What is so significant about these emotions is that they may be experienced communally through storytelling, through shared empathy. Groups learn about life through the models Novak promotes, yet do so through sharing in the emotional experience of that storytelling. Lee believes empathy to enter into "imagination, sympathy, and also into that inference from our own inner experience which has shaped all our conceptions of an outer world, and given to the intermittent and heterogeneous sensations received from without the framework of our constant and highly unified inner experience, that is to say, of our own activities and aims."[27] This view in turn is reinforced by the writings of the 20th century psychoanalyst D.W. Winnicott, who located the imagination, a force which might be likened to the "interference" Lee describes, as a phenomenon occurring neither within the "inner psychic reality," nor in "external reality," but in between, in the paradoxical space "neither inside nor outside."[28] What Lee's description quantifies is the experience of narrative in the communal sphere, becoming a representative model in which our collective emotions engage. Emotions of fear or horror are of course not a necessity, but in the case of the Doctor's adventures they are certainly one of the prominent strains.

Doctor Who, as a narrative, represents for its audience the specific intensifying of emotions already present within each of us. Indeed television, and particularly television which produces fear, is supported by research as exerting a powerful empathetic effect, one which can in turn influence the young viewer's sense of what constitutes the real world.

From the 1970s, researchers have known that young children who view a lot of television see the world as a more dangerous place than children who don't watch lots of television.[29] In particular support of this is the research of sociologist Karen Cerulo. Media, she argues, is indeed responsible for the formation of the impression of a violent world in its viewers.

> When it comes to violence, media stories may unintentionally form public images of right and wrong.... [S]tory-tellers must consider the very real possibility that the routine formatting of violent accounts may be constructing social opinion rather than re-enacting it. Thus, the role of story sequencing in violent accounts must enter discussions of media responsibility.[30]

Effectively, the world is modeled to children through television, and often represents the emotional "state" of fear in its interface between their internal condition and its dialogue with the outer world.

Fear on television does not necessarily arrive in the form of the likes of which Whitehouse believed it to. Rather the shocks of violence, coupled to a mythic structure, may in fact provoke a far greater desire to imitate rather than to fear.[31] In the first instance screen violence, rather than suggesting a netherworld of death, may in fact present a model which is seen to estimate reality. By many children violence is judged inherently realistic. In this sense the emotions which arise from viewing a story which contains violence directly speak to the child's, or even adult's, sense of the world in which they live. What is an intriguing aspect of this is that violence itself is what suggests the realism of the scenario, the degree to which it speaks to the interface of the individual with the outer world. The Doctor is a clearly fantastical figure, a Time Lord, yet it is still found that the terror, and violence, of a scenario determine the measure of its accessibility to the real world. In April 1975 the correspondent for the *Radio Times* found "Genesis of the Daleks"

> brutal, violent and revolting — totally without plot or point — yet convincingly enough done to be really terrifying for many normal children... Does the producer of this unpleasant effort really expect a not-too-bright child to know the [difference]?[32]

What the series thus simultaneously offers is a figure engaging in conflict that may also possess qualities which, while existing in a fantastical scenario, prove to be highly attractive to an audience, provoking imitation. When a group of eight- to ten-year-olds were asked in a study who they wanted to be like, they named unrealistic characters from television series that they had seen, more often than the characters from television who were closer to people they might encounter in their daily reality.[33] The common reason for their choice was that less realistic characters were brave and strong.[34] This certainly makes sense in that children of this age are often struggling to achieve mastery and competence in their own lives. Notably they seek to imitate powerful characters on the television screen, those who often choose violence as a means of resolving conflict.

Significantly, the Doctor and his allies dealt with foes through violent means. The soldiers of UNIT in the Doctor's second, third and fourth incarnations, were armed soldiers engaging in armed combat. A companion such as Sarah Jane in "Terror of the Zygons" dispatched the titular alien in an act of self-defense. The Doctor himself could be a character who used force. Regardless, the series presented fantastical narratives in which non-realistic characters such as the titular Time Lord exemplified such behavior. Given children's belief that this could be representative of the real world, and their attraction to the Doctor's demonstrations of power and strength, the series was doubly effective, in my view, as an imitative model.

The series represents a unique matrix of the clearly fantastical enmeshed with the integration of these anxieties, with a child's understanding of the real world. By the age of eight, the level of violence in children's play increases if they feel the violence they have seen on television reflects some imitative standard applicable to the real world.[35] While children may not see that actions of Superman or the X-Men as real because they are clearly physically impossible, they may regard the scenarios which contain real world elements as potentially plausible, an element consistent to the production of *Doctor Who* particularly in its '70s heyday in UNIT storylines. The imitative approach of children is validated by research in this respect. If violence is seen onscreen, and seems to be exacted by powerful character which, while being fictional, nevertheless exist in a fictional world comparable to our own, it is deemed worthy of imitation. If the UNIT commandos of the Jon Pertwee era utilize weaponry and physical force to subdue an alien or human adversary, then the viewing child will judge such action as worthy of duplication.

This relationship of the viewing child to on-screen violence alters gradually with age. By the time the children reach the age of ten, "real" is more likely to mean "possible in real life."[36] While they may understand that what they are seeing is occurring in a contrived dramatic scenario they nevertheless observe violence on television which might occur in everyday life as equally real. The actor portraying the fourth Doctor, Tom Baker, believed, similarly, that a power and plausibility would exist for the series so long as it remained terrestrial: "I had a great belief that it was much more frightening to stay on Earth — that all the threats should come to Earth, rather than us going off to other planets."[37]

What this opinion also stresses is the aid which a connection between the real world and television violence and terror might bring to that crucial articulation of the communal sensation of fright, the possibility that the terror emanating from the cathode ray might also exist in your very own living room.

The plausibility of the setting of violence or its enactors is equally influential.

After in-depth interviews with Toronto children in grades four and five, one researcher elaborated:

> What the children describe as scary are those incidents when the familiar and safe, like the home and parents and loved one, are negatively transformed. Home becomes a killing ground, parents are powerless to protect, dolls become killers.[38]

Violence originating from familiar figures, located in familiar settings, is especially upsetting. The inherent threat such images present to the young finds particular relevance in the Barry Letts–produced Jon Pertwee serial "Terror of the Autons." In this serial, and its prequel "Spearhead from Space" the violence which terrifies children originates from familiar figures of comfort, a child's doll, and authority, the police. Likewise in "Autons" a plastic couch smothers a character, the ultimate rendering of the child's refuge from *Doctor Who* terrors as an object of terror itself. Berry Letts commented:

> When we made "Terror of the Autons," there were big leading articles in several newspapers complaining bitterly about what we'd done. We even had a letter from Scotland Yard about the policemen who turned out to be Autons, saying, "Don't do it again." I think we did go over the top, but when you think of it, the most terrifying things are ordinary things that can't be trusted. If it's a monster, it's a monster, you know where you are. But if a toy comes to life and tries to kill you, it's not so funny.[39]

The perceived reality of the violence experienced by the child, and the transfer of that violence into their understanding of the real world, springs from its simple co-opting of basic household items and neighborhood figures to a terrifying sci-fi scenario.

As the series evolved, this model for fear evolved. The wonderful innovation of what became known as the series golden, that of Philip Hinchcliffe, was an increased commitment not to the reality of the violence, the domestic natures of the series thrills, but rather its growing emotional reality. What subsequent producer Philip Hinchcliffe himself noted was that his productions offered was in fact a specific power and psychological reality of fear and violence. The series, he believed, offered in fact a vivid chance to engage with children's imaginations, with their ability to place themselves within the reality of a scenario, within its plausible emotional world. On the television program *Pebble Mill* Hinchcliffe observed:

> It fires the imagination. It's a very vivid program. The reason why it is so popular with children is because it is one of the few programs which deals with the world of the imagination, which is a very powerful world for a child.[40]

In such a world, the infection of Noah by the insectoid Wirrn, in the first televised Hinchcliffe serial "The Ark in Space," need not see its plausibility undone by laughable prosthetics and a wobbling insect costume. Rather, Kenton Moore's moving, tragic performance captures a pathos and torment which predates a similar famous tale of bodily transformation, David Cronenberg's *The Fly* (1986), by more than a decade. The skill and dramatic intensity of the performance transcended easily the numerous production limitations of the scenario, and suggests the possibility that scares may originate from sources other than the brushes with the familiar Letts utilized in some of his more famous serials. What precisely this emotional and imaginative engagement could lead to, this communal empathy, was a narrative space in which the responses of characters to outlandish situations seemed increasingly human and plausible in their scale. Numerous other famous examples of the kind of terror the classic *Doctor Who* could inspire easily spring to mind. Viewers were highly upset by the fourth Doctor adventure "The Seeds of Doom," in which a man was physically transformed into a plant. The progress of the infection played out over the episode, and children complained of the sight of a human life becoming a vegetative creature.[41] In an interview with the *Doctor Who Magazine* Hinchcliffe offered a detailed critique of his own serial:

> Similarly, with "The Seeds of Doom" we had another scene we had to chop down where the guy is being turned green by a plant infection. You see, it all has to do with the portrayal of human

pain which, curiously enough, does not worry many children but does worry a lot of adults. If you have a good actor who is made up to look horrible and who is really putting everything into portraying pain, anguish and torment then it does convey very strong across to the audience. So you have to be a bit careful.[42]

Such instances were numerous in Hinchcliffe's tenure. One need only thing of the suffering of Chang following his encounter with a giant rat in "The Talons of Weng Chiang." Or perhaps the chilling inspection Styre conducts of the humans he has tortured to death in "The Sontaran Experiment." Horror in Hinchcliffe's time was confronting the reality of violence's consequences.

The classic series, as has been already noted, appealed to more than just children. Just as it engaged children in models, myths and narratives whose content would appeal to their young psyches, so too did it appeal to their elder siblings, even parents. "By its tenth anniversary, *Doctor Who* had evolved. The original child viewers of the serial were now in their teens."[43]

In so doing it created new species of communal fear and approbation. Sometimes the series' terror was so disturbing that it transferred its agency to this darker realm. While the use of a couch as an object of menace might be judged effective, its greatest impact would be on children. Adults and teens would understand that while the object was familiar, its inherently inanimate nature would preclude it from doing harm. Yet, just as the discourse of fear has developed with children, so too, had it become pervasive with adults. Producer Philip Hinchcliffe developed a formula for scares in which both children, adolescents, and even adults, would derive equal levels of anxiety. Robert Holmes in fact criticized Gerry Davis' script for "Revenge of the Cybermen" as insufficiently sophisticated for its audience. "You have written it only for children. It's too straightforward (particularly in characterization) and therefore rather dull ... we find our audience is ready to accept quite sophisticated concepts."[44] Fifty-six percent of the show's audience, at the time Holmes wrote this, were over the age of fifteen.[45] In discussing his choices for the narrative elements of a classic episode such as "The Deadly Assassin," Hinchcliffe explained this episode had more mystery, horror, disturbing elements rather than a monster. "There was the younger children and the older children, and I was worried about how they might stick with this."[46] What such a new model crucially represented, though, was an elaboration from the progressively more imitative parallels found in the terror of Letts' era. Unease would increasingly not originate from dangerous objects, or unreliable authority figures as in "Terror of the Autons." Rather it was now to be found in the increasingly grown-up ambiguities of character, in the Doctor's encountering the world of adult emotions.

What must be accepted though is that although the series was incredibly popular with children, they were never considered its sole audience. *Who* director David Maloney observed, in reference to the era of Tom Baker's Doctor, that as the series peaked in popularity there was, at a less official level, an equal amount of interest on the part of adults. On "The Pyramids of Mars," a fourth Doctor story, fratricide is explicitly depicted, moral horror and all, as a zombie convert kills his own brother. The theme of genocide and Nazism is central to "The Genesis of the Daleks," another adventure of the fourth Doctor.[47] Nazism, at the time of the release of this specific Dalek narrative, was a reality in the childhood of most viewers' parents, rather than the youth of that day. These narratives manifest an emotional maturity, a dedication to examining the genuine emotional impact of violence and atrocity.

Returning again to "The Deadly Assassin," the episode which so upset Mrs. Whitehouse, it is worth observing the critical attention paid to this Hinchcliffe serial. The sadism Whitehouse noted was evident, yet there is more to the scenes in the Matrix than just hatred. The scenes are dedicated to both physical and emotional realism. "Thus the 'real' world of Gallifrey is a stylized studio set whereas the 'unreal' dreamscape of the Matrix is shot on location and on film and includes the grittiest and most realistic action scenes ever staged in *Doctor Who*, as [the Doctor and Goth] fight each other to the point of death."[48] The entity who hunts the Doctor in "The Deadly Assassin" is an all-purpose villain, and he menaces the Doctor via numerous means. Yet the confrontation in the swamps is primal, close combat nearly resulting in the Doctor being drowned. Dramatically this close-quarters, muscular violence is confrontational to say the least, a personal element of hatred suffusing the scene. This most ironic of Doctors effectively confronts a most un-ironic of death scenes. While the series passes on from such a cliffhanger image, the emotional violence of the scene remains.

Mary Whitehouse found the explicit near-drowning of the Doctor (Tom Baker) in "The Deadly Assassin" offensive, and asked that the cliffhanger shot be cut to a shorter length. In making such a request her alarm was not unfounded. Admittedly it must be communicated that the Doctor, while inside the Matrix, is being menaced by Chancellor Goth. Numerous violent incidents occur previous to this attempted drowning, but this specific episode constitutes perhaps the most barbaric form of war, hand-to-hand combat. A competition in which one opponent will force the life out of the other with his bare hands, it offers little conceptual respite, no magic dart, or brightly colored laser blast to distract from the act's intent.

Whitehouse's complaint was about the ghoulish quality of the scene, the camera floating about the Doctor's submerged, anguished face for a protracted period of time, dwelling on his demise. Yet the scene is more than this final image. It must be remembered that "a text exists as much by *what it cannot say*, by what necessarily produces fissures and strains within it,"[49] and the scene is a confrontation involving more than might otherwise be expected, by what is implied in the intervening moments before and after its final image. Hinchcliffe himself attests to the elusive quality he and screenwriter Robert Holmes sought to evoke.

> Personally, I felt those two scenes in "The Ark in Space" and "The Seeds of Doom" were far more frightening than the one which did create the big fuss with Mrs. Whitehouse where, in "The Deadly Assassin" cliff-hanger to part three, we held the Doctor's head under water that bit too long. So what Bob and I discovered was that, having made the series more adult and more realistic, we had to run up against the thin dividing line between what is acceptable to Saturday tea-time family viewing and what is not. I felt we steered a pretty good line and I would suggest that most of Mrs. Whitehouse's criticisms were somewhat over-hysterical.[50]

This "good line" he succeeded in straddling is best understood when the scene is considered as a whole, as more than its final image. What perhaps has escaped mention in the scene is the sweating, vicious face of Goth seen in close-up, urging the Doctor to expire. There is certainly hatred in his aspect, arguably the sadism Whitehouse describes. But there is also desperation, the physical contest between the two Time Lords having reached its most desperate. The scene is as much about the physical reality of the force and effort required to drown a human being as it is the complex emotional state an individual must enter to engage in such an act. Fear for one's self, desperation, and pure aggression combine. Such a thesis drove Hinchcliffe's choices as a producer, and created a legacy he is generally eager to defend.

This vectorization of violent intent, the investment of violence with distinct purpose, might well have been what Whitehouse was so disturbed by, and arguably represents a narrative model in its own right, admittedly not imitative in nature. The Doctor, frequently depicted as the ultimate outsider, existing entirely outside of any specific context in terms of time or place, is in the episode reintroduced to his home world, to the planet of his socialization, and to the beings who are his peers. The subtext of Goth's desire to destroy the Doctor is rooted in the Doctor's alternate rejection of the Time Lords and their rejection of him, the ultimate physical manifestation of social ostracism, with a figure of social significance seeking to erase the Doctor from the social equation. This certainly has meaning for children as they engage with the process of their own socialization; learning what talents and qualities they possess will inspire respect and affection in those around them. Certainly it speaks to their aforementioned desire to achieve some level of mastery in the world, in this case social mastery. The violence, even as it occurred in a fantasy sci-fi realm such as the Matrix, attained relevance in this evocation of recognizable social patterns — or their negation — as the base motive of violent acts, and vectorization in the distillation of violent intent into an act such as drowning your rival.

It is of course significant that in the next Gallifrey adventure, "The Invasion of Time," the fourth Doctor becomes president of the Time Lords, a position Goth had seemed primed to occupy in "The Deadly Assassin." In such a narrative context the aspects of personal competition, jealousy, and other powerful emotions play well to an ongoing subtext of personal enmity in the Time Lord's dealings with the Doctor. Now the threat is displaced onto a recognizable villain, the Sontaren. Notably this was a serial found early in the tenure of Graham Williams, a producer noted for shepherding the series into a more humorous, parodic narrative style. Indeed there had been a gradual slide to this new position.

> The generally horrific, genuinely nightmarish feel of Tom Baker's first year on the show did not carry on, though the next two seasons represent the show's most sustained debt to horror as a genre since the run of 'scary monster' stories in the middle of Troughton's tenure.[51]

In short the series began to less and less evoke power narrative models which might inspire fear.

The qualities of human emotional realism found during the Hinchcliffe era were to return, albeit in a less comprehensive manner. During the tenure of script editor Eric Saward in the 1980s the series once again expressed explosive emotion. Malice need not be the only human quality vectorized in the context of violence and terror. Physical violence is arguably intensified in the presence of malice, envy, frustration, or worst of all guilt and grief. My own childhood experience of this occurred in the sixth Doctor's adventure "Revelation of the Daleks." The sight of the character of Tasambeker, spurred on by a combination of Davros's manipulation and sexual jealousy, plunging a giant syringe into the heart of her superior Jobel was sufficient to provide more than a few child nightmares. Sometimes the appearance of such moments seemed inexplicable. The exploding brain-like organism, which was once in Arthur Stengos, in the same episode as Jobel's death was fitting to the nihilistic tone of "Revelation of the Daleks," a storyline which saw civil war among the Daleks. Yet Tasambekar is shown to be, at the very least, infatuated with Jobel. Her murder of him in response to his sadistic abuse of her is emotionally charged, almost an act of sexual frustration in its subtext. It is an adult moment. Her subsequent grief and execution by the Daleks resembles a desperate suicide.

"Revelation" likewise featured a narrative which writer Saward and director Grahame Harper both confess fell into the realm of the absurd, perverse, nihilistic and superlatively dark. In a tight hundred minutes grave robbers are tortured, two hearts are pierced with needles, a transparent Dalek containing the remains of a human is exploded, Davros' good hand is blown off, and the character Orsini's bionic leg is similarly blown off. "Revelation" takes a detour into exquisite sadism before just skirting complete annihilation. Indeed it is remarkable that, given its suffusion of adult level bizarre imagery, more do *not* die, what with the mortuary theme of the serial featuring so prominently and luridly. What similarly creeps in, as a result of these permutations of suffering, is the theme of transgressive sexuality. Jobel intimates that Tasambekar has contemplated, or committed, necrophilia, and comments that he would rather run away with his mother than sleep with her. In this context it is clear that he is expressing a euphemism for incest. As in the case of Goth's desperate, sadistic, hate-filled attempt to extinguish the Doctor's life, the specific emotional context of Tasam-beker's dispatching of Jobel is gloriously fraught, the emotional violence of the scene as pal-pable and sharp as the syringe which penetrates his chest. The specific model which allows for this, the narrative vehicle of this horrific moment, has in fact been theorized in detail by Fiona Moore and Alan Stevens.

In the era of producer Barry Letts, critical consensus places the Autons as among the pre-eminent horrific villains. Their particular brand of terror was to be distilled from the prosaic and everyday. Yet the greatest series villain is certainly the Daleks, certainly the most famed. In turn they are also the most fear-inspiring.

> The Daleks symbolize a unity. Their history and their actions are the distillation of a common fear for us as well as for the fictional characters they torment. They are a lurid representation of evil; death in pantomime garb. We need them.[52]

What must be considered in the case of Tasambeker is the infectious quality of this evil, how the noted complexity of her motives in stabbing Jobel are in fact essentially instigated by the presence of the Daleks within the narrative. Tasambeker is an example of the "Evil Human," prompted to commit horrific acts by her proximity to the Daleks, her alliance with them. Moore and Stevens posit that the "Evil Human" represents the human potential for corruption.[53] This figure, they further suggest, is an ongoing one in the series and effec-tively represents, in its own right, a narrative model for the integration of evil, and the attendant horror it precipitates.

Indeed the "Evil Human," as noted by Moore and Stevens, represents an educative model of much the kind hypothesized in fairy tales in *The Uses of Enchantment*. But it also represents the kind of modeling found in Hinchcliffe's era, which favored the presentation of the complexities and darker aspects of human nature.

> The Dalek/Evil Human relationship fulfils different functions with different audience members. While its purpose ... is partly to educate children in the values of their culture, highlighting the social concerns of the day and presenting a cautionary tale.... In particular, the more complex and/or challenging Evil Human figures, such as the Controller and Lytton, encourage older viewers into consideration of what "evil" is.[54]

"Revelations" in general presents a narrative devoid of pat endings, or the morally pre-deter-mined fates of characters. The sleazy, conniving characters of Takis and Lilt, who collaborate with the Daleks in Revelation, are unpunished, a fact which contemporary reviewer Jackie Marshall was quoted as saying was "unfair to young viewers."[55] What this observation evi-dently suggests is that the concern of young viewers would have been piqued, their awareness of the wrongness of Takis and Lilt's conduct woven into the narrative, while simultaneously the message was broadcast to older members of the audience that no one can truly benefit in a serial which contain Daleks.

This paradigm allows for the infection of evil, for the disquieting loss of moral compass by average figures in the Who universe. "Again in the 1980s, the Evil Humans are less the subject of morality tales than explorations of different ways of being amoral."[56] Takis and Lilt, according to the model presented by Moore and Stevens, exemplify a certain moral horror. These are characters that neither cower before the ultimate evil of the Daleks, nor find themselves coerced into service. Rather, engaging with their pragmatism, they choose to conspire with the series' ultimate villains. The character of Lytton, seen in "Resurrection of the Daleks," is a similar kind of "Evil Human."

> He is a type of Evil Human that is particular to the 80s; he does not ally himself to the Daleks through the temptation to achieve power or become rich ... but, as we are repeatedly informed in the sequel story "Attack of the Cybermen," simply to make a living. In this, he is very much in keeping with the 1980s celebration of the money-making anti-hero...[57]

Saward's fascination with the character came from an interest in people who kill for a living, for whom "evil is a part of everyday business," and indeed what is troubling about such characters to adults is equally troubling to children.[58] Lytton, Takis, and Lilt all represent average human beings nevertheless capable of acquiring the monstrous qualities of the creatures with which they consorted.

The specific horror this produces is a narrative in which, due to their engagement with such villains, characters expose themselves to greater extremities of behavior. Tasambeker is offered by Davros himself the opportunity to become a Dalek. Her murder of Jobel is in fact at the urging of Davros, and this clarifies the horror and tragedy of her choice. Like Judas Iscariot she betrays Jobel, and is driven suicidal with guilt by the knowledge of this. In turn while Lytton is not directly punished in his Dalek narrative his next encounter with a monster prompts his own horrific conversion to the monster. Not only is Lytton gorily tortured by the Cybermen, but they also attempt to transform him into a cyborg. Like the disturbing vision of Arthur Stengos as a converted Dalek in "Revelation," Lytton's susceptibility to the Daleks, then Cybermen, sees him the subject of exquisite sadism. In compromising to the demands of monsters Lytton and Tasambeker subject themselves to emotional and physical torment because, as humans, they still are able to demonstrate human sentiments of regret and conscience. This deepens the horror for all parts of the audience, adult and child alike.

Saward, it can be said, presented a unique contribution to the classic series, not the least of which was the bleakness of "Revelation." The horrific elements of his period represent, in respects, an elaboration on the dramatic intensity of Hinchcliffe's era. Yet the series was once again under attack during his tenure. The adventure "Vengeance at Varos," a satirical commentary on the "video nasties" of the period, was assumed a variant on the same.[59] The sight of Cybermen crushing Lytton's hands such that blood dripped from them caused a likewise furor. Saward's successor Andrew Cartmel offered scenarios in which violence and horror, when presented, were contextualized by a stern moral perspective. Violence, and violent imagery, could at times be justified as instructional, even moral, in their use on the series.

The subject of the seventh Doctor's adventure "Survival" is the effect which violence may have upon those who succumb to the frantic mania it can produce in those it infects. Unlike the unmediated look at Goth's bloodlust, commentary now could intervene mid-action. Caught on a planet which literally transforms its inhabitants into feral beasts, the Master and the Doctor engage, much like the scene in "The Deadly Assassin," in brutal hand-to-hand combat in the fourth episode. In this final episode of the classic series the Doctor suppresses his murderous rage and notes the anathemas which their equally deadly desires represent. The Doctor offers an alternative to violence. Yet this is only after he has shown himself capable of it, and thus capable of making a moral choice. It is perhaps notable that this serial was the last of the classic series and, in terms of horror content, it is neither fish nor fowl. The lesson is no longer to be found in the subtext. Rather, contrary to Novak's hypothesis, the Doctor articulates rather than demonstrates an imitative model. So, in its abrupt conclusion, the series offered threat and violence, while in the same moment pandering to its detractors.

While it cannot be said that the series ended on a classic storyline, the rise and fall of *Doctor Who*'s reputation as a frightening, scary series must be recalled in context. Following Michael Grade's notorious attempts to cancel the series, it had arguably muddled towards its frustrating conclusion. The serials which have most cemented the series' reputation purely in terms of scares were as a majority found in the 1970s. On the question of the series' fear factor it must be noted that during what is often recognized as the classic series' golden era, producer Hinchcliffe was likely most responsible for offering a cogent methodology to the development of these scares. As he noted in the audio commentary to the Tom Baker serial "Planet of Evil": "There's a sort of moral balancing in stories and audiences know when it is not right. They sense it."[60] By such reckoning he determined that the ongoing debates about violence in the series were ultimately best determined by the intuitive response of the audience, seeking both thrills, a level of reality, and the reassurance of the world's longest running science fiction serial. In such calculations, he argued in the commentary for "The Deadly Assassin," the Doctor was the hero and could not really die. Hinchcliffe merely wanted good cliffhanger, and believed his audience would indulge him in the Doctor's near drowning. Suicide, as contemplated in "Planet of Evil" by Sorenson, was more serious than the potential drowning of the Doctor to Hinchcliffe. His period as producer might be judged the most complete in its delivering of thrills and scares to all ages effectively.

"It is a period memorable for its extremes of emotion, characterization and villainy, representing a Manichean universe of good and evil ... a form of individual psychological evil that expresses itself through insanity and megalomania."[61] Corresponding to this balancing was the "the Doctor's alienness becoming more apparent" during the period.[62] He shows little sympathy for Laurence Scarman's death in "Pyramids of Mars," much to Sarah Jane's horror. In this respect inhumanity in narrative content was often complemented by a hero who was himself clearly not human. The series periodically attempted to address this aspect of balance in individual narratives of the producing era of Jonathan Nathan-Turner.

> Christopher Bailey's Kinda is one of the series best scripts... Kinda eerily uses the show's limbo status between adult and children's programme by disturbingly having grown-up characters under an alien influence act like kids and tackling serious political and religious issues.[63]

More frequently, though, this era would place narratives of powerful subtext such as "Revelation" in overlit sets, the actors — especially Colin Baker — being forced to emote in retina-damaging costumes. The balance the audience sought, one which had seen children frightened so effectively in the Barry Lett era, and the whole family petrified in Hinchcliffe's classic Gothic period, was gone. The ephemeral nature of scares, hitherto so transcendent of the series' production limitations, had passed. What Hinchcliffe had effectively identified was a certain narrative causality which insisted that the emotional consequences of action and the corresponding emotional needs of the audience could be met simultaneously. While this may not have been a model which Whitehouse could easily identify in its moral balancing act it is, I believe, one which profoundly fulfills Lee's insistence that art be "the awakening, intensifying, or maintaining of definite emotional states" for an audience.[64]

NOTES

1. J. Chapman, *Inside the TARDIS: The Worlds of Doctor Who: A Cultural History* (London: I.B. Tauris, 2006): p. 6.

2. Ibid., p. 99.

3. "The Pyramids of Mars": "The Two Doctors." For program details, see Videography.

4. "The Brain of Morbius."

5. J. Brown, http://www.independent.co.uk/news/uk/home-news/mary-whitehouse-to-some-a-crank-to-others-a-warrior-617910.html (retrieved 23/09/11).

6. Dir. David Yates, 2011.

7. R. Ebert, http://rogerebert.suntimes.com/apps/pbcs.dll/article?AID=/20110713/REVIEWS/1107199 94 (retrieved 23/09/11)

8. Chapman, *Inside the TARDIS*, p. 154.

9. F. Hope, "Doctor When," *New Statesman*, 22 March 1968.

10. D. Oswell, *Television, Childhood, and the Home: A History of the Making of the Child Television Audience in Britain* (New York: Oxford University Press, 2002): p. 146.

11. M. Whitehouse, *Cleaning Up TV: From Protest to Participation* (London: Blanford Press, 1967): p. 71.

12. B. Bettelheim, *The Uses of Enchantment: The Meaning and Importance of Fairy Tales* (London: Penguin, 1978): p. 5.

13. Ibid., pp. 7–8, 25.

14. W.C. Booth, *The Company We Keep: An Ethics of Fiction* (Berkeley: University of California Press, 1988): p. 3.

15. J. Tulloch and H. Jenkins, *Science Fiction Audiences: Watching Doctor Who and Star Trek* (London and New York: Routledge, 1995) p. 98.

16. Ibid.

17. Chapman, *Inside the TARDIS*, p. 113.

18. Ibid.

19. A. Milne, *The Portrayal of Violence in Television Programmes: Suggestions For a Revised Note of Guidance* (London: British Broadcasting Corporation, 1979): p. 23.

20. Chapman, *Inside the TARDIS*, p. 113.

21. D. Buxton, *From The Avengers to Miami Vice: Form and Ideology in Television Series* (Manchester: Manchester University Press, 1990): p. 13.

22. M. Novak, *The Experience of Nothingness* (New Brunswick: Transaction, 2009): p. 19.

23. Clifford Geertz, *The Interpretation of Cultures* (New York: Basic Books, 1973): p. 26.

24. W. Wright, *Six Guns and Society: A Structural Study of the Western* (Berkeley: University of California Press, 1977): p. 17.

25. Ibid., p. 191.

26. Vernon Lee, *The Beautiful* (London: Cambridge University Press, 2011): pp. 99–100.

27. Ibid., p. 68.

28. D.W. Winnicott, "The Location of Cultural Experience," in *Playing and Reality* (New York: Routledge, 1971): p. 96.

29. G. Gerbner, L. Gross, M.F. Eleey, M. Jackson-Beeck, S. Jeffries-Fox, and N. Signorielli, "Sex, Violence, and the Rules of the Game: TV Violence Profile no. 8: The Highlights," *Journal of Communication*, 27 (1977): pp. 171–180.

30. K. Cerulo, *Deciphering Violence: The Cognitive Structure of Right and Wrong* (New York: Routledge, 1998), p. 141.

31. D. C. Chaney, "Involvement, Realism and the Perception of Aggression in Television Programmes," *Human Relations*, No. 23 (1970): pp. 373–381; D. Buckingham. *Children Talking Television: The Making of Television Literacy* (London: The Falmer Press, 1993): p. 224.

32. Chapman, *Inside the TARDIS*, p. 112.

33. H. Kelly "Reasoning About Realities: Children's Evaluations of Television and Books," in H. Kelly and H. Gardner, eds., *New Directions for Child Development: Viewing Children through Television* (San Francisco: Jossey-Bass, 1981): p.67.

34. D. E. Fernie, "Ordinary and Extraordinary People: Children's Understanding of Television and Real Life Models," in H. Kelly and H. Gardner, eds., *New Directions for Child Development: Viewing Children through Television*, p. 53

35. L. D. Eron, L. R. Huesmann, P. Brice, P. Fischer, and R. Mermelstein, "Age Trends in the Devel-

opment of Aggression and Associated Television Habits," *Developmental Psychology*, No. 19 (1983): pp. 71–77.

36. Kelly, "Reasoning About Realities," p. 202; A. Dorr, "No Shortcuts to Judging Reality," in J. Bryant and D. R. Anderson, eds., *Children's Understanding of Television: Research on Attention and Comprehension* (New York: Academic Press, 1983): p. 202.

37. J. Pertwee, The Doctor Who Story, 2003.

38. S. Campbell "A Report On Children's Experience of Televisual Media Today," *The Federation of Women Teachers' Association of Ontario*, Fall 1992, p 24.

39. B. Letts, http://drwhointerviews.wordpress.com/category/barry-letts/.

40. P. Hinchcliffe, http://drwhointerviews.wordpress.com/category/philip-hinchcliffe/ (retrieved 23/09/2011).

41. "Pyramids of Mars."

42. Hinchcliffe.

43. L. Parkin, "Canonicity Matters: Defining the Doctor Who Canon," in D. Butler, ed., *Time and Relative Dissertations in Space: Critical Perspectives on Doctor Who*, (Manchester: Manchester University Press, 2007):p. 253.

44. Chapman, *Inside the TARDIS*, p. 99.

45. Ibid.

46. "The Deadly Assassin."

47. Chapman, *Inside the TARDIS*, p. 102.

48. Ibid., p. 111.

49. Buxton, *From the Avengers to Miami Vice*, p. 13.

50. Hinchcliffe.

51. K. Newman, *Dr. Who* (London: BFI, 2005): p 99.

52. N. Pegg, "Review: The Sontaran Experiment/Genesis of the Daleks" *Doctor Who Bulletin*, No. 93 (2005): p. 15.

53. Fiona Moore and Alan Stevens, "The Human Factor: Daleks, the 'Evil Human' and Faustia Legend in Doctor Who" in D. Butler, ed. *Time and Relative Dissertations in Space: Critical Perspectives on Doctor Who* (Manchester: Manchester University Press, 2007): p. 139.

54. Ibid., p. 156.

55. Ibid., p. 153.

56. "Audiences and References," *In-Vision*, No. 84 (1999): p. 26; Moore and Stevens, "The Human Factor," p. 152.

57. Moore and Stevens, "The Human Factor," p. 152.

58. Richard Marson, "Eric Saward Interview," *Doctor Who Magazine*, No. 94 (1984): p. 24.

59. Newman, *Dr. Who*, pp. 157–158.

60. "Planet of Evil."

61. Chapman, *Inside the TARDIS*, p.117.

62. Newman, *Dr. Who*, p. 82.

63. Ibid., p. 99.

64. Whitehouse, *Cleaning Up TV*, p. 71; Lee, *The Beautiful*, pp. 99–100.

10

Everything Dies

The Message of Mortality in the Eccleston and Tennant Years

KRISTINE LARSEN

In his introduction to *M Is for Magic*, Neil Gaiman reminds us that "there's nothing like spending some time inside an alien head to remind us how little divides us, person from person."[1] One of those universal truths that bind all living creatures together is that we are all mortal. In short, everybody dies. From the tiniest microbe to the mightiest elephant, the humblest household servant to the most powerful emperor, none of us lives forever. This truism also holds for individual species (Darwinism at its finest), entire planets and stars, and even the universe as a whole. Some lives are long and full, while others are all too brief, cut short before their time and without fulfilling their potential. In a world filled with violence, the latter is unfortunately more common than not. Despite the fact that the world of *Doctor Who* revolves around a 900-plus year-old Time Lord who has the ability to regenerate into a brand-new body when needed, death is ever-present in the *Who*-universe.

As Mickey Smith explains to the Rose Tyler's mother, Jackie, everywhere the Doctor goes, death and destruction seem to follow. The Doctor and Rose are trapped in the cabinet room at 10 Downing Street, faced with the impossible choice of launching nuclear weapons at the prime minister's residence in order to stop the Slitheen plan to take over the world, or do nothing. Jackie Tyler admonishes the Doctor, "Don't you dare." The Doctor explains, "if I don't dare, everyone dies."[2] The Doctor is often faced with the impossible task of acting despite the fact that he knows someone may die as a result, and is also sometimes faced with the equally hard task of remaining inactive and allowing someone to meet their fate. His hands are tied by the sacrosanct laws of time. This explains the Doctor's absolutely giddy response to the resolution of the episode "The Doctor Dances" (2005) because "just this once, everybody lives."[3] Death is therefore an uncredited guest star on many episodes of *Doctor Who*.

Death is a natural part of life, and the untimely death of any individual or species is to be avoided at all cost, and lamented when inevitable. However, accepting this inevitability is often easier said than done, both in the primary world and in the universe of *Doctor Who*. In both the televised episodes and tie-in novels of the ninth and tenth incarnations of the Doctor (portrayed by Christopher Eccleston and David Tennant, respectively), we see this bitter lesson played over and over again, as otherwise intelligent creatures — be they Humans, Daleks, Gappa, and even (one might say especially) Time Lords — refuse to swallow this bitter pill. Some appeal to technology as their personal savior, in a vain attempt to forestall the inevitable, an attempt which never leads to a positive end in the *Who*-universe. Others appeal to the Doctor's time-traveling abilities to save those who were ordained to die. For example, in "The Fires of Pompeii" (2008) Donna Noble pleads with the Doctor to save the doomed citizens of Pompeii. Although he acknowledges that he can sometimes change events, this was not one of those times. As a Time Lord he has the burden of knowing "what was, what could be, what must not."[4] The volcanic eruption at Pompeii is a fixed point in time, and the Doctor knows he cannot prevent the large-scale death and devastation (although at Donna's request he does save a single family). In "Father's Day" (2005), Rose Tyler convinces the Doctor to take her back to the moment when her father, Pete Tyler, died in a traffic accident, and temporarily manages to prevent his death. However, the rift in the timeline causes the Reapers to try to sterilize the wound in time by devouring the earth. Pete Tyler willingly walks into the path of the speeding car in order to set the timeline aright. Therefore the Eccleston and Tennant years of *Doctor Who* offer the viewer much to reflect upon concerning the very human fear of death and our obsession as a culture with postponing death and old age beyond nature's prescriptions.

Humanity's desire to avoid death is as old as literature itself. In the nearly 5000-year-old Sumerian Epic of Gilgamesh the title character searches for his ancestor, Utnapishtim, the survivor of a great flood, who is rumored to possess the secret to immortality. Fast-forward five millennia, and today's culture is likewise obsessed with the elusive fountain of youth, now assumed to be in the form of creams, pills, herbal potions, and plastic surgery. As Olshansky and Carnes describe, "The life extension industry begins with a grain of truth but quickly gets mixed with a tablespoon of bad science, a cup of greed, a pint of exaggeration, and gallon of human desire for a longer, healthier life — a recipe for false hope, broken promises, and unfulfilled dreams."[5] Celebrities deny their constant diet of Botox injections, despite the fact that their frozen faces betray them. Some in the scientific community argue that our obsession with looking young fuels ageism, as it is based on the idea that normal aging is a disease which needs to be cured.[6] Others among their colleagues focus on the improvements in overall health and quality of life promised decelerated aging, and come to the conclusion that we must pursue research into this area "energetically."[7] As with many things, perhaps a balanced approach is best; however, it is the wild swings of the pendulum which often gain the most press.

In the ninth Doctor's second episode, "The End of the World" (2005), we meet a character who (dis)embodies the obsession with youth, the Lady Cassandra O'Brien. More than five billion years in the future, Cassandra claims to be the last "real" human, but is nothing of the sort. Over 700 plastic surgeries have left her reduced to a grotesque translucent trampoline of skin that requires constant moisturizing, hosting a parody of a face, and accompanied by a brain in a jar. Rose Tyler jokingly refers to her as "Michael Jackson," a reference to the singer's repeated plastic surgeries. After the Doctor halts Cassandra's nefarious plan to destroy the Platform One space station (in order to collect enough insurance money to pay for even more plastic surgeries), Cassandra's skin begins to dry out and she begs for Rose and the Doctor to save her. The Doctor reminds Cassandra that "everything has its time, and everything dies," and with a final agonized cry of "I'm too young," she explodes.[8]

However, Cassandra does not go to her demise without a fight, and in "New Earth" (2006), the second episode of the tenth Doctor's adventures, he discovers that she is hiding out in the basement of a hospital in New New York City on New Earth. Chip, an assistant

Cassandra had previously cloned, saved his mistress's brain and a skin sample from Platform One and had reconstructed her. Using a psychograph, Cassandra desperately inserts her consciousness into several bodies, including Rose and the Doctor, before settling into Chip's body. Unfortunately for her plans, Chip is dying, and she must finally face her mortality. She admits to the Doctor that it is indeed time to die, but the Doctor allows her to die with some dignity, transporting her to visit her past self and allowing her to be the one who tells herself how beautiful she looks before she embarks on the dehumanizing plastic surgeries.

Numerous characters in the *Who*-universe attempt to use advanced technology to turn back the hands of time and in some cases attempt to achieve immortality. In "The Lazarus Experiment" (2007) the titular character, a 76-year-old scientist, uses genetic manipulation technology to "perform a miracle" and provide a "chance for humanity to evolve, to improve." While he does indeed appear decades younger when he emerges from his machine, there has been a malfunction, and over the course of the episode he mutates into a terrifying monster that must ultimately be destroyed. Several episodes later in "The Sound of Drums/ The Last of the Time Lords" (2007) the Doctor's nemesis the Master has concentrated the Lazarus technology into his laser screwdriver, and uses it to temporarily age the Doctor, first by a century, and then suspends his ability to regenerate, turning him into a 900-year-old shriveled shell of a creature, who looks similar to Tolkien's Gollum. While the Doctor is ultimately restored to his hale self, the abuse of technology is horrifying and its effects unpredictable.

A similar abuse of technology appears in the ninth Doctor novel *Only Human*. The work opens with the diary entry of Chantal Osterberg, a seven-year-old from the distant future who attempts to improve her pet cat Dusty through some rather gruesome genetic engineering. The main body of the novel introduces us to the humans of Chantal's generation, who have successfully engineered the human body to live for centuries, but at the expense of their nature emotions (which they keep in check through medication). Although all the humans are physically attractive, Rose finds them repulsive, explaining that they're "not human anymore.... They're like androids. What's the point of them being alive?"[9] Near the end of the novel, Jacob pleads with the Doctor to save his wife, Lena, who is dying at the age of 387. The Doctor explains that there is nothing he can do — "Her life's been massively prolonged by genetic restructuring. She's had her ageing mechanism switched off. She's had about 400 transplants. But every system, no matter how hard you try, wears out in the end."[10]

Living for centuries can lead to a desire to live for millennia, and beyond. But as the Doctor noted, bodies are not designed to live indefinitely. Immortality is not natural. After all, immortal cells are generally cancer cells.[11] Even the Time Lords are not immortal, but rather enjoy a sort of serial morality, living one life and then another, dying each time only to be painfully reborn into another form. Even this regeneration process has its limits, as a Time Lord can usually only regenerate a dozen times over his or her existence.[12] Twelve lifetimes, each lasting for perhaps centuries or longer, would certainly be more than enough for many people; not so for the Master. Throughout the run of the series, the Master has cheated death by gaining additional incarnations, for example by stealing the body of another[13] or being resurrected by the Time Lord High Council during the Time War.[14] In the tenth Doctor's final episode, the Master cheats death once more, as a group of acolytes uses his ring, the "potions of life," his "biometrical signature" (wiped from the lips of his human wife, Lucy Saxon), and their own life forces to resurrect his previous form.[15] However,

Lucy disrupts the process (sacrificing her own life in the process), and the Master's new incarnation is unstable, possessing superhuman powers yet burning itself out despite the Master's voracious appetite for devouring both food and life-forces. "This body was born of death," the Master acknowledges to the Doctor. "All it can do is die."[16] Thus any attempt to truly cheat death and achieve immortality is doomed to failure.

Throughout the ninth and tenth Doctors' adventures, character after character learns the important lesson that the search for immortality leads to ill ends. In "The End of Time" (2009/2010), the Master is able to take over the earth by using the so-called Immortality Gate, alien technology which millionaire Joshua Naismith had procured in the hopes of bestowing everlasting life on his beloved daughter Abigail. In the novel *The Deviant Strain* Rose, Jack, and the Doctor watch in horror as Russian scientists and villagers are turned into zombie-like creatures as they attempt to harness the power of an alien spacecraft and the life-force of their fellow humans (termed "mutagenic revivification enhancement energy"),[17] in a vain attempt to achieve eternal life. The Russians believe that they are in control of the situation, when in reality they are being tricked by the symbiotic spirit of the crippled spacecraft and its dead pilot to procure sufficient energy for the ship to be repaired. The Russians' ultimate plan (which is predictably thwarted by the Doctor) is to set off an old nuclear missile, providing sufficient energy to give them at least a thousand years of life in one fell swoop, at the expense of the lives of millions of their fellow citizens.

Another plan to aspire to immortality through technology (and at the expense of one's humanity) is found in the desperate scheme of scientist John Lumic, creator of the Cybermen in the alternate universe termed Pete's World.[18] Lumic's Cybus Industries created a metallic exoskeleton to house a human brain "indefinitely within a cradle of copyrighted chemicals."[19] When presented with the results of Lumic's research, the president calls the work "not just unethical; it's obscene" and reminds Lumic that he is "not God." Lumic counters that he is "governed by greater laws" than those of society, namely "the right of a man to survive."[20] Lumic has created the Cybermen technology to house his own brain, once his crippled body finally gives out, but when the time arrives, he resists being "upgraded." After his transformation, he explains to the Doctor that the "age of steel" has arrived, with Lumic as its creator. "I have an army. A species of my own."[21] But the Doctor (and the audience) are reminded of the horror of Lumic's Frankenstein-like creation when one of the Cybermen is wounded and its emotion inhibitor deactivated. The Doctor talks to the frightened and confused human brain inside, and in an act of mercy, the Doctor puts her out of her misery.

The horror of another type of artificial existence is vividly described in "Silence in the Library/The Forest of the Dead" (2008). In this *Matrix*-like storyline, there had been a mysterious event in the universe's largest library a century prior to the episode's start. The planet's computer system had sent the cryptic message "4022 [library patrons] saved — no survivors" and the planet had been sealed off until the episode's current timeline.[22] When the Doctor, Donna Noble, and an investigation team lead by Professor River Song enter the library, they are attacked by a swarm of the Vashta Nerada, resulting in the deaths of several of the team's members. In a chilling scene, the first victim's spirit continues to communicate for several minutes; a process called "ghosting," as the neural relay in her communicator briefly holds an impression of her consciousness. River Song calls it "just a freak of technology" while Donna has a more visceral reaction, terming it the most horrible thing she'd ever seen.[23] When the Doctor tries to teleport Donna to the safety of the TARDIS, she is instead "saved" by CAL, the computer system, and lives a virtual existence inside the hard drive of the system. In the climax of the narrative, the audience learns that CAL stands for Charlotte Abigail Lux, a young girl whose consciousness was saved within the computer when she died. The library was built to house and entertain her mind for eternity. "This is only half a life," her nephew explains, "but it is forever."[24] When River Song gives her life to stabilize the computer system and return all 4022 library patrons (plus Donna) to normal life, the Doctor uses an imprint of her consciousness (saved in the sonic screwdriver his future incarnation had given to her) to upload her to the computer, thus giving her a new life within the fake reality. While CAL assures River Song that she'll "always be safe"[25] within the main frame, it is indeed "only half a life," no matter its duration.

In those rare instances when immortality is actually achieved within the *Who*-universe, the point is unequivocally made that such an event is an abomination. When Rose looks into the heart of the TARDIS and takes on the Bad Wolf persona, she uses her powers to destroy the menacing Daleks with a wave of her hand, turning them to dust. "Everything must come to dust," she calmly explains, "All things. Everything dies."[26] Yet when the Doctor warns her to let go of the Time Vortex, she brings Jack Harkness back to life, explaining, "How can I let it go? I bring life!" The Time Lord tries to bring her to her senses, warning, "This is wrong — you can't control life and death," but Rose resists. "I can see everything. All that is, all that was, all that ever could be," she explains, before succumbing to the excruciating pain of the Time Vortex burning her alive.[27] She may be able to control life and death, but she cannot hope to control the power that temporarily gave her those godlike powers, and the Doctor sacrifices his ninth incarnation by drawing the power into himself through a kiss.

Several seasons later, the audience learns that Jack has not only been brought back to life, but has been made immortal. When he asks the Doctor why he was abandoned on the space station, the Doctor explains what an abomination he feels his friend to now be:

> It's not easy even just looking at you, Jack, cause you're wrong. You are, I can't help it. I'm a Time Lord, it's instinct, it's in my guts. You're a fixed point in time and space.... Even the TARDIS recognized it, tried shaking you off. She went all the way to the end of the universe just to get rid of you.[28]

Jack is doomed to be the "man who can never die," and throughout the episode "Utopia" (2007) is put into situations where he is mortally and painfully wounded by exposure to radiation and electricity, only to revive (until the next time he is forced to "die" for his friends). Therefore with immortality comes not only limitless life, but limitless opportunities for pain and death. This lesson is even more vividly taught in "Human Nature/The Family of Blood" (2007). The Doctor uses the Chameleon Arch to become human in an attempt to thwart the Family of Blood's ill-thought-out plan to use the Time Lord's regeneration powers to achieve immortality. The Doctor eventually grants the family their wish, but the take-away lesson is that one should be very careful what one wishes for. The family's father is wrapped in unbreakable chains, while the mother is imprisoned in the event horizon of a collapsing galaxy. Their daughter is trapped inside every mirror, and appears to the eye as something briefly moving behind one's reflection. Their beloved son, for whose benefit the original scheme was hatched, was suspended in time and turned into a scarecrow. "We wanted to live forever," the son explains in a final voiceover. "So the Doctor made sure that we did."[29] The horror of immortality is thus both cruelly and clearly demonstrated in the fate of the Family of Blood.

No individual can live forever, nor can any species. One of the fundamental tenets of modern biology is the concept that species evolve in response to stresses in their environment, and when a species cannot adapt, it must, of necessity, perish. But despite the fact that we are all taught this from our grade school years, how many of us secretly wish that *Jurassic Park* was a reality? Currently scientists in Japan are attempting to clone a woolly mammoth,[30] and in 2009 scientists were able to successfully clone an extinct subspecies of wild goat from skin samples frozen from the last living specimen in 1999. The clone had defective lungs and died a few minutes after birth, but the researchers consider the results a success.[31]

With increased attention to the effects of global climate change, as well as the threats of asteroid impacts, pandemics, nuclear war, bioterrorism, and other threats to life on earth (both well-founded and imagined),[32] the human species has begun to contemplate its own eventual demise. The History Channel series *Life After People* illustrates the inevitable destruction of all remnants of human civilization if humans were to suddenly disappear (although a cause for the extinction of humanity is left to the viewers' imagination), and an entire 2009 special issue of *Futures* journal was devoted to the topic of human extinction. An article in that issue details the results of a 2004 web-based poll of nearly 600 people that examined beliefs about the extinction of humanity. Forty-five percent of the respondents believed that humans would eventually become extinct, with over a third of the respondents unable to suggest a possible timescale for such extinction. When asked for a cause for a future human extinction, more than half had no answer, while the two most commonly selected answers (at roughly 7 percent each) were "environmental degradation" and the simple Darwinian idea that "all species eventually become extinct."[33]

While the ultimate fate of the humanity is probably currently best confined to realm of science fiction (including *Doctor Who*), humanity has certainly played a role in the extinction of myriad fellow terrestrial species. Untold numbers of species have been driven to extinction through human intervention (hunting and loss of habitat), with at least 132 species of birds alone known to have been driven to extinction since 1600 (including such iconic animals as the dodo and the carrier pigeon).[34] Our closest living relatives are currently the chimpanzees, but from approximately 300,000 to 30,000 years ago, a much closer relative, the Neanderthals, flourished in many parts of Eurasia. Their disappearance from the fossil record (a few thousand years after modern humans arrived in Europe) has long been a subject of controversy. Many scientists have placed the blame for the extinction of our "sister species" squarely in our laps, accusing modern humans of everything from merely out-competing to openly hunting Neanderthals to extinction.[35] In more recent years a more palatable (i.e., guilt assuaging) theory has emerged, explaining that the "more effective social networks" of modern humans simply allowed our direct ancestors to better compete against the "highly stressed Neanderthal populations" during a time of "fluctuating climate and environment."[36] In Darwinian shorthand, the environment changed, we adapted better, so the Neanderthals simply lost the battle of survival of the fittest.

However, the Doctor is not so quick to let our ancestors off the hook. In the novel *Only Human*, the Neanderthals are depicted as far more human than either the humans of the future, or our human ancestors with which they briefly co-existed. When the ninth Doctor and Rose Tyler travel back to the England of 26,185 B.C., Rose is sorrowed to think that the peaceful Neanderthals she meets are doomed to soon die out. However, her sorrow turns to anger when the equally melancholy Doctor explains that "it wasn't so much that they died out as they were weakened. The climate changed and they couldn't compete." Rose asks, "With humans? Humans finished them off?" The Doctor confirms her fears.[37] Later in the novel, Rose watches a Neanderthal tribe celebrate the birth of a baby, and she feels "pangs of regret and shame burned in her heart. She had never felt more ashamed of being human. Because it was humans who were going to slaughter these people — and they were people — to extinction."[38]

But not only do the Neanderthals have to worry about the dangers posed by the humans of their time period (who are depicted as war-like and prejudiced in the novel), but the humans of 400,000 years in the future, who, under the leadership of Chantal Osterberg, travel to the past with the supposed purpose of observing how the Neanderthals became extinct. In reality, Osterberg, who, as described earlier, had begun her nefarious experiments with genetics engineering on her pet cat while still a child, was testing her new genetically engineered breed of predatory humanoids — the Hy-Bractors — in competition with both past populations of humans. In an eerie throwback to John Lumic's Cybermen, Chantal refers to her creation as an "upgrade of the human race,"[39] a species that she believes deserves to take over the earth from its natural residents because, unlike mere humans, the Hy-Bractor race — "ruthless in its dispatch of inferior human competitors" — can not merely adapt as a species to the environment, but "adapt themselves."[40]

In typical *Doctor Who* style, the Time Lord and his companion defeat the mad scientist, but the Doctor is powerless to stop the genocide of the Neanderthals. However, the end of the novel leaves us with the hope that something of them lives on in us, as several humans fall in love with Neanderthals[41] and, it is suggested, there might be children as the result of those unions. Scientists have argued amongst themselves for many years whether or not anatomically modern humans and Neanderthals interbred, and the same evidence has been interpreted as supporting both sides of the argument at one time or another. In 2010, an analysis of the Neanderthal genome, and subsequent comparison to the DNA of modern humans, suggested that limited interbreeding did take place in Eurasia, contributing only one to four percent of the modern human genome.[42] Several months later, a highly publicized analysis of infamous rock star Ozzy Osbourne's genome found "a little segment on Ozzy's chromosome 10 that very likely traces back to a Neandertal forebearer," a finding that amused many of the television pundits reporting the story. We therefore find *Doctor Who* leading the way in rehabilitating the stereotype of the Neanderthals from brutish cavemen to being *Only Human*. Through the novel's pages we are encouraged to ponder — and to momentarily mourn — the loss of this sister species, and rejoice in the thought that a bit of them still lives within the human genetic code.

If the actions of humans, combined with a changing environment, led to the downfall of the Neanderthals, what does the current human impact on the ecosystems of the world herald for the future of our own species? As previously stated, a significant segment of the population believes that our days as a species are numbered, even though most people do not have a specific prediction as to the timing of our eventual demise. What if an alien species landed on Earth and did unto us what we possibly did unto the Neanderthals? Certainly a feeling of species superiority would make such genocide justifiable in the minds of that invasive species. We need look no further than our own human history for similar examples, with the plight of Native Americans being one of the best publicized. The adventures of the Ninth and Tenth incarnations of the Doctor include several examples of just such a possibility.

In the tenth Doctor novel *SnowGlobe 7*, Beth Cowley, the director of SnowGlobe 7, a research facility, and SnowGlobe 6, a leisure facility, is at her wit's end over the treatment of these precious remains of Earth's polar ice caps. The SnowGlobe project is a series of dozen giant domes which house the remains of the Arctic and Antarctic ice sheets, after global warming had progressed far enough to threaten their very existence. As economics took its inevitable toll on the science, nine of the domes had been changed into tourist attractions hosting a variety of winter sports, leaving Cowley bitter and with a rather negative view of her own species, and therefore susceptible to the telepathic influence of the spider-like Gappa. The alien species had laid dormant within the ice of SnowGlobe 7, the last survivors of a dying planet who had been saved from impending extinction by another alien species. While the Doctor lauds the noble intentions of the unnamed interstellar conservationists (evidence that the "universe is not all about killing and conquest, war and death"),[43] in actuality their meddling in the natural order of evolution and extinction nearly led to the destruction of all terrestrial life forms when their spacecraft crashed onto Earth. Using their new discovery of fire-making, human ancestors were able to repel the Gappa, who took refuge by hibernating in the Arctic ice, until they were awakened by human activity in their transplanted home in SnowGlobe 7.

While Martha and the Time Lord ultimately thwart Cowley's efforts to help the alien Gappa take over the world (the creatures' intent is to use all living creatures as hosts for their young), the Doctor momentarily laments the fact that he cannot save the Gappa in the process: "I wanted to try and stop another race from vanishing from the universe, but the universe had already decided that it was their time to die." He further explains to Martha the futility of the attempt of the alien conservationists to preserve the Gappa, noting that the species "should never have survived" as they were "a biological dead end, an aberration of evolution."[44] Once again, the audience is reminded that everything dies in its due time, including species. Since the Gappa had reached the point of extinction without the intervention of another species, their demise is simply a reluctant inevitability in a Darwinian universe. We may mourn their loss, but any attempt to intervene is doomed to failure (or more regrettable outcomes, such as our own destruction).

In the televised episodes of the series, alien species often consider humanity to be primitive and hence expendable in any attempt to foster their own species' procreation and prosperity. An example is the Sontarans, a warrior species that expands its population by mass cloning. In "The Sontaran Stratagem/The Poison Sky" (2008) the Doctor and Donna come to the aid of Martha Jones and UNIT when the Sontarans plot to turn Earth into a clone planet by poisoning our atmosphere with a clonefeed-laden gas. In A.D. 79 the Doctor and Donna intervene in a plot by the Pyrovilles to harness the power of Mount Vesuvius to turn humans into a new hybrid species after their home planet is lost to them. The Doctor must make the gut-wrenching decision to explode the volcano and sacrifice 20,000 citizens of Pompeii in order to save millions from being converted into Pyroville hybrids.[45]

As already noted, millionaire Joshua Naismith intended to use the so-called Immortality Gate in order to make his daughter Abigail immortal. In reality, the gate was a medical device to repair the bodies of an entire species across an entire planet at a single time. All that is needed is the proper medical template for that species. The Master uses the machine to send his bio-signature across the planet, turning the entire human species into Masters (a rather ingenious yet obviously immoral way for a single individual to in effect commit mass genocide and simultaneously take over an entire planet with little effort). The renegade Time Lord cackles in delight, "There is no longer the human race; there is only the Master race!"[46] But the Master himself is but a pawn in an even greater game of intra- and interspecies warfare. The drumbeat in his head (which has helped to drive him mad over the centuries) is revealed to be a homing signal implanted in his mind by the Time Lord High Council when he was just a child. During the Time War, the doomed Time Lords debated the eventual outcome of their battle with the Daleks. A sole council member admitted the futility of trying to fight against their imminent extinction as a species:

> "Perhaps it's time. This is only the furthest edge of the Time War. But at its heart, millions die every second, lost in bloodlust and insanity, with time itself resurrecting them, to find new ways of dying over and over and over again. A travesty of life. Isn't it better to end it?"

For her honesty she is vaporized by the Lord President Rassilon, who refuses to accept the death of his species (or his own, for that matter): "I will not die! Do you hear me? A billion years of Time Lord history rides on our backs. I will not let this perish. I will not!"[47] The Doctor well understands the desperation of his fellow Time Lords, and how much the Time War has changed them, and it is partially for this reason that he destroys his own home planet during the Time War and his fellow Gallifreyans as well as the Daleks (or so he thought).

Indeed, the Daleks provide perhaps the ultimate example of a species whose inherent belief in their own superiority allows them to perpetrate a seemingly endless litany of atrocities on "lesser" species in the name of their own survival. When the Daleks appear in the ninth Doctor episode "The Parting of the Ways" (2005), their emperor explains to the horrified Time Lord that he was able to survive the Time War, and fell through time to the outer edge of Earth's solar system. Once there he was able to rebuild his army by harvesting the dispossessed of Earth, and nurturing the purest cells to create new Daleks. Although the concept of creating Daleks from human tissue is not a new one to the *Who*-universe (for example, having been done by Davros, the species' creator, in the sixth Doctor episode "Revelation of the Daleks" [1985]), in this specific case, Rose Tyler invokes the ire of the Dalek Emperor by claiming that the new Daleks are in actuality human–Dalek hybrids. The Emperor declares this to be blasphemy, and decrees that their flesh is instead "pure and blessed Dalek."[48]

This selective concept of racial purity stands in direct opposition to that of many real world racists, most especially the "one-drop rule" of the antebellum United States. In this case, anyone with one drop of African American blood was automatically considered to being classified as African American, both legally and culturally. This concept that one drop of blood could taint a person and relegate them to a "lesser" racial/social classification has been largely internalized by the African American community over time.[49] In the case of the Daleks, rather than allow their species to become extinct, they instead redefined what it means to be a pure member of that species — possessing a single drop of Dalek "blood" trumps the presence of any other biological tissue, at least in the minds of some.

Throughout the ninth and tenth Doctors' adventures this rather arbitrary definition of what it means to be Dalek is challenged. For example, in the earlier ninth Doctor episode "Dalek" (2005), a Dalek who had been kept in a private collection becomes "tainted" by some of Rose's DNA when she touches it out of concern for its well-being. The reactivated creature considers itself to be an abomination and commits suicide rather than existing as a hybrid creature. Even though it (and the Doctor) believes it to be the last remaining member of its species, the Dalek prefers its own death (and therefore the death of its species) to existing as a lesser being. In the tenth Doctor novel *I Am a Dalek* it is revealed that, as in the case of the Dalek Emperor, another Dalek had escaped the Time War and landed on Earth centuries prior. Before dying, the Dalek had managed to spread its "Dalek factor" to the environment, introducing a tiny bit of Dalek genetics into an even tinier segment of the human population. The goal was to use the life force of genetically altered humans to create a new Dalek race. "How embarrassing for you," the Doctor taunts upon hearing this plan. "The mighty race of Daleks, so weakened they needed help from the humans they despise. A last, desperate gamble."[50]

The division between the Daleks themselves as they attempt to balance racial purity against racial extinction is most clearly explored in "Daleks in Manhattan/Evolution of the Daleks" (2007). The four members of the Cult of Skaro were created by Davros to find new ways of surviving as a species. Dalek Sec interprets this to mean that they should evolve (as any typical natural species would), and therefore genetically engineers himself to become a human/Dalek hybrid. Dalek Thay argues that they must instead remain "pure," but Sec reminds him that "our purity has brought us to extinction."[51] Dalek Sec's ultimate plan is to use his hybridized DNA as a genetic template in order to convert thousands of imprisoned human into new Dalek hybrids and give birth to a new, more genetically "fit" Dalek species which is not only better adapted but can reproduce more easily and hence is less likely to become extinct. While Dalek Sec embraces the concept of hybrid vigor (heterosis), his companions see this is as an abomination, and not only kill Dalek Sec, but the hybrids he has created. In the end there is a single Dalek left — Dalek Caan — whom the Doctor shows mercy upon, explaining, "I've just seen one genocide. I won't cause another."[52] Dalek Caan transports away before the Doctor can take any action.

When the audience next sees Dalek Caan, he has survived the Time War at the apparent expense of his sanity, and with Davros, his creator, is a virtual prisoner aboard the new Dalek war ship, the Crucible. The new Dalek army was created by Davros from cells of his own body, what he calls "true Daleks."[53] Although Dalek Caan is called insane, in truth is the only Dalek to have a clear understanding of the atrocities his kind have perpetrated on the universe. Behind the scenes he has helped to bring the Doctor and Donna Noble together, in order for them to thwart Davros's latest attempt at universal domination. In the words of Dalek Caan, "I saw the Daleks, what we have done through time and space. I saw the truth of us, Creator, and I decreed no more!"[54] In the chaos created by the Daleks' kidnapping of a number of planets and moons (including Earth) in order to create the ultimate weapon, the Doctor's amputated hand is activated by Donna's human DNA to create a Time Lord/human hybrid called the Meta-crisis. Like the Doctor before him, Dalek Caan realizes that his own species had (de)evolved into a threat to the universe itself, and no longer deserved to exist. Dalek Caan did not have the means to directly commit racial suicide, so he manipulates the situation so that the Meta-crisis achieves the end for him, by destroying the Crucible and committing genocide against the Daleks. In his dying breath, Davros curses the Doctor, naming him "the destroyer of worlds."[55]

The Doctor had indeed destroyed Skaro, the home world of the Daleks, several incarnations prior, in "Remembrance of the Daleks" (1988). But as noted, the Dalek race had not been destroyed in the process. One could argue that Skaro was already dead, having been turned into a wasteland in the racial war between the Kaleds and Thals that had resulted in Davros's creation of the Daleks by genetically engineering his own Kaled race.[56] Throughout the adventures of the Ninth and Tenth incarnations the audience is faced with the destruction of Earth and other inhabited worlds, some through natural events (after all, not even a planet lasts forever), some through the intervention of alien profit-seekers. In "World War Three" (2005), the Slitheen intend to cause a nuclear war in order to turn Earth into a dead, radioactive slab of rock which they could then sell off bit by bit as fuel for spacecraft from other planetary systems. In the novel *The Monsters Inside* (2005) a similar plan is hatched by the Blathereen, who attempt to hijack a new technology to create "the biggest flamethrower in the universe" in order to "burn up any number of worlds anywhere" to reduce them to marketable fuel stockpiles.[57]

The natural (and inevitable) end of planet Earth is highlighted in the ninth Doctor's second adventure, "The End of the World." The Doctor takes Rose five billion years into the future, to the year 5.5/Apple/26, to witness the sun swallowing Earth. The human race had been evacuated to safety some time before, as there had been ample warning. In fact, the destruction of Earth had been staved off for some time, through the use of gravity satellites paid for by the National Trust. When the cash ran out, so did Earth's borrowed time. The event was to be observed from the supposed safety of a specially equipped Earth-orbiting space station, Platform One, and the rich and famous of myriad alien worlds paid good money for a front row seat. To Rose's horror, in the chaos caused by Lady Cassandra's plot to sabotage the event in order to collect insurance money, the actual moment of Earth's demise is not witnessed and it essentially dies alone. "All that history — gone," Rose laments, and her sorrow is only slightly assuaged when the Doctor takes her back to her own time to show her that Earth is still very much alive and well in the past. It is in this context that we first hear of Gallifrey's demise in the Time War, when the Doctor explains to Rose that his planet is also gone. "It burned like the Earth. There was a war and we lost."[58] What is not revealed to the audience at this time is that it was the Doctor himself who decided to destroy both Gallifrey and its inhabitants.

If one leaves out the so-called gravity satellites, the episode does a decent job of summarizing the astronomical community's understanding of our home planet's eventual incineration. According to the most current computer models, in approximately 7.5 billion years the sun will become a bloated red giant and swallow up all three inner planets (with Mercury and Venus being devoured approximately four and one million years respectively before Earth).[59] The astronomical idea of the end of Earth coming at the hands of the same star whose light has sustained our species for billions of years has captured the imagination of a number of science fiction writers. For example, in H.G. Wells' 1895 novella *The Time Machine* the unnamed time traveler extends his journey into the distant future, "watching with a strange fascination the sun grow larger and duller in the westward sky, and the life of the old Earth ebb away."[60] In W. Olaf Stapledon's 1930 fictional examination of the future history of the human species, *Last and First Men*, humans first move to Venus when the Moon begins to move closer to Earth and threatens to shower the planet with meteoritic shrapnel. In the process, the humans commit genocide against the native Venusians. The Venusians are understandably attached to their planet, which is not only invaded by humans, but terra-formed in such a way as to make it uninhabitable to the native species. The humans' response is to kill off the natives as quickly as possible, convincing them that it was a merciful act done "in love."[61] When it is determined that the sun is on its way to becoming a red giant, the humans move to Neptune, which they terra-form to their needs, but in the end it is a moot point because a nearby supernova seals the fate of the entire solar system.

This idea of humanity trying to save their home planet (or at least home solar system) rather than merely moving to more conducive interstellar real estate (as the humanity of *Doctor Who* does, for example founding New New Earth), can also be found in the 2007 British science fiction film *Sunshine*. In this work the sun begins to dim and freezes the earth, rather than frying it, until a group of scientists embarks on a suicide mission to reignite the sun with the largest nuclear weapon ever constructed. But efforts to save our planet from its preordained appointment with fate are no longer only relegated to science fiction. In a 2001 paper, physicists Korycansky, Laughlin, and Adams suggested that with sufficient time it might be possible to move Earth into a more distant orbit, through repeated close encounters with a large asteroid.[62] In a companion article, Korycansky ponders, in the style of the late lunar scientist William K. Hartmann, whether such a desperate engineering project is an example of a "jingoistic boondoggle — the expression of a crazed, technological society that insists on carrying through whatever mad schemes have become technologically feasible."[63] As we have seen, *Doctor Who* is filled with examples of how such schemes lead to ill ends, especially when done in an attempt to cheat death, whether it is the death of an individual, a species, or an entire planet.

All individual things eventually come to dust. But what of the universe as a whole? As the Robert Frost poem "Fire and Ice" correctly notes, "Some say the world will end in fire, Some say in ice."[64] According to Einstein's General Theory of Relativity and the Big Bang model, the universe will either expand to a maximum size and then collapse to form a fiery Big Crunch or it will continue to expand forever. Based on current astronomical observations, the latter is the fate supported by all the evidence. As early as the mid-nineteenth century, physicists realized that because entropy or disorder must always increase in the universe, it will ultimately run down, as the stars burn out and the universe can no longer reorganize material into new sources of energy. This so-called heat death of the universe was the central theme of the 1956 Isaac Asimov short story "The Last Question," which consisted of a series of vignettes in which members of increasingly technological human societies ask their computers if the heat death of the universe can be reversed.

In 1997 Fred C. Adams and Gregory Laughlin used current cosmological theory and observation to map out the distant future of the universe.[65] They termed the current eon of the universe the Stelliferous (star-filled) Era, the period of the universe's existence which is dominated by the births and deaths of stars. But in a hundred trillion years, the last stars will burn out, leaving the universe dominated by stellar corpses such as white dwarfs, neutron stars and black holes. For the next 10^{37} years these dead stars will reign supreme, but all but the black holes will eventually disintegrate as their constituent protons eventually decay. From then on, until the universe is 10^{100} years old, black holes will be the only cosmic citizens, until they, too, decay through the theoretical process known as Hawking decay. This so-far unobserved process is the main scientific claim to fame of the famous British physicist Stephen Hawking, who has persevered in his career despite living with Lou Gehrig's disease for over four decades. Therefore when Frost called the end of the universe "ice," he should have more correctly called it a lonely, empty, absolutely dark, ice.

The end of the universe is therefore nearly beyond comprehension for all but poets and physicists, but the writers of *Doctor Who* dared to tackle at least the end of the Stelliferous Eon in "Utopia." Although they termed it the end of the universe in the episode, it is the certainly the effective end of the universe as far as life is concerned. The TARDIS hurtles 100 trillion years into the future when Jack Harkness — the immortal "impossible thing" — tracks down the Doctor in modern England and hangs on to the police box for dear life. The Doctor is uncertain as to what he and Martha might find when the doors open, as even the Time Lords have not dared to come this far into the future. What he, Martha, and Jack find is the remains of a rock-hewn city on a desolate world on which life is only possible through the intervention of an atmospheric shell and power plants. The Doctor explains to Martha that the city was killed by the ultimate enemy of all things — Time. "This isn't just night," he points out. "All the stars have burned up and faded away, into nothing."[66] The Doctor is impressed when he discovers that anatomically modern humans still exist in this distant time, but there are also humans who have reverted to a more primitive, aggressive state akin to the survivors in the Mad Max series of films — what Professor Yana (the Master in human form) refers to as the Future Kind. Yana launches the remaining humans into space, toward a beacon reported to be from survivors of the Utopia Project, which had been established thousands of years in the past in an attempt to find a way to preserve the human species against the end of the universe. Yana regains his Time Lord identity and body and steals the TARDIS, returning to the present Earth, and in the persona of Harold Saxon rises to power.

In the sequel, "The Sound of Drums," the audience learns that the Master and his human wife, Lucy, had used the TARDIS to visit Utopia, and found it to be anything but a paradise. Lucy describes it as "dying, everything dying. The whole of creation was falling apart."[67] The last humans had cannibalized themselves, eventually engineering themselves into a simple-minded, shriveled head contained within a small metal sphere. The Master uses the TARDIS to create a paradox, allowing these humans — which he calls the Toclafane after the mythical bogeymen invoked to scare Gallifreyan children into behaving — to travel back to the present. His plan is to have the Future humans destroy their Past ancestors, forming a willing army that the Master would use to take over the universe and destroy the Doctor's favorite species in one fell swoop.

The end of the universe is referenced in two other tenth Doctor stories, "Journey's End" (2008) and "The End of Time." In the former, Davros and his new Daleks intend to destroy the universe with a "reality bomb'" which has the power to cancel out the electrical field holding electrons and protons together, resulting in the shredding of every atom in the universe. While the idea is physically impossible as written, it does sound similar to the concept of proton decay to the ears of non-physicists. The Daleks would remain safely inside the Crucible ship, and then rule a matter-less universe (a rather strange idea which seems perfectly sensible to Davros and the Daleks, hence highlighting the general insanity of their species). In "The End of Time," the Time Lords have an even more megalomaniacal plan. They intend to not only destroy the material universe, but time itself. Their species would continue as pure consciousness after destroying all other sentient beings as well as the very fabric of the universe. At last the reason why the Doctor passed judgment on his own people and destroyed both the Time Lords and the Daleks in the Time War is revealed. With the Master's help, the Doctor is able to send the Time Lords back into the Time War to face their fate and in the process saves both Earth and the universe as a whole. In their desperation, the Time Lords tried to doom reality itself (and all sentient beings within it) to the very death which they themselves could not accept. Everything dies, and those who cannot accept it come to no good end.

Throughout the adventures of the ninth and tenth Doctors this important lesson has been made painfully clear. But the tenth Doctor has great difficulty in accepting this bitter pill when applied to his own incarnation. At an age of 900-plus years, the Doctor has "seen more suffering in my life than you can possibly imagine. But that doesn't mean it ever gets any easier. Sometimes I can't help thinking I've lived too long."[68] Given the violence that the Doctor faces in many of his adventures, it seems unlikely that his incarnation's demise would be in his sleep, or some other calm passing, as elderly humans often enjoy in the end. However, the Doctor is granted a vision of such a peaceful death in "The Family of Blood," when he becomes a human named John Smith in an attempt to hide from the Family. He falls in love with a human, Joan Redfern, and when he reassumes his Time Lord form in order to defeat his enemies he is granted a vision of how his life with Joan might have been. Many years in the future, an elderly John Smith, married with children and grandchildren, would have died peacefully in his own bed, his loving wife by his side. "It's time," Smith calmly explains to Joan, and adds, "thank you" before closing his eyes for the last time. Joan sees the Doctor as a complete stranger with her beloved John's face, and notes of the Doctor's human incarnation "he was braver than you in the end, that ordinary man. You chose to change. He chose to die."[69] Joan's statement encapsulates an important theme in the character development of the tenth Doctor, namely how the Time Lord deals with the normal human emotions surrounding his incarnation's impending mortality, with the character passing through many of the stages of the five-stage Kübler-Ross model[70] of the grieving process: shock, denial, anger, despair, and finally acceptance.

The Doctor and the audience are first reminded of the eventual end of the tenth Doctor's incantation in "The Planet of the Ood" (2008), when Ood Sigma tells the Doctor, "I think your song must end soon." When pressed for an explanation, he merely adds "Every song must end."[71] Nine televised adventures later, Carmen, an elderly woman with limited psychic ability, warns the Doctor at the end of "The Planet of the Dead" that he must "be careful, because your song is ending, sir," and adds prophetically "he will knock four times."[72] In the next episode, "The Waters of Mars" (2009), the Doctor is forced to face the mortality of others and his impotence to save their lives, and rather than accepting the eventuality of death, asserts his powers over time itself, momentarily falling into the same megalomaniacal madness which possessed the Time Lord High Council and the Master. In the year 2059 the TARDIS lands on Mars, on the very date that the earth's first Mars base was destroyed for unknown reasons. When he realizes that he has stumbled upon a momentous date in history, he tries to extricate himself from the situation, all the while apologizing to the crew while simultaneously not explaining what he is apologizing for. Adelaide Brooke, the mission captain, eventually forces the Doctor to explain what he means, and the Time Lord complies. According to the historical record, Adelaide initiated the self-destruct mechanism on the base for an unknown reason (revealed to be in order to stop the alien Flood from infecting Earth), and the mysterious destruction of the base sets Adelaide's granddaughter Susie onto the path to becoming the first pilot of a light-speed ship. Thus Adelaide's death becomes the spark which ignites the human race's journey into interstellar space.

"I will not die," Adelaide defiantly argues when faced with her fate, even though the Doctor explains that her death "creates the future." He then explains that despite her pleas for help he cannot change her fate. "Sometimes I can," he offers, "sometimes I do. Most times I can save someone, or anyone, but not you."[73] The destruction of Bowie Base 1 is one of those fixed points in time, like the destruction of Pompeii in A.D. 79, and the laws of time forbid the Doctor from meddling. However, when faced with the imminent destruction of the base, the Doctor finds that he cannot remain impotent, but instead makes a conscious decision to defy the rules of time. "Once upon a time there were people who were in charge of those laws," he explains to Adelaide, "but they died. They all died. Do you know who that leaves? That leaves me. It's taken me all these years to realize the laws of time are mine. And they will obey me!"[74] He offers that their fight is not just against the alien Flood, but against time itself. The Doctor has thus become that which he found so repulsive in "The End of Time"—a Time Lord who feels he is more powerful than time itself.

The Doctor whisks Adelaide and the two other survivors—both of whom, like Adelaide, were supposed to die on Mars—to Earth in the TARDIS. Adelaide protests the Doctor's meddling, concerned that by changing history he might change the future. The Doctor dismisses her concerns, convinced that although the details may have changed, the eventual outcome will be the same. Adelaide is not convinced, however. "You can't know that," she worries, "and if my family changes, the whole of history could change. The future of the human race. No one should have that much power." The Doctor's rather dismissive response is "Tough." "For a long time now, I thought I was just a survivor," he lectures, "but I'm not. I'm the winner. That's who I am — the Time Lord Victorious!" "Is there nothing you can't do?" a horrified Adelaide asks. "Not anymore," the Doctor boasts. While the Doctor prematurely celebrates his seeming victory over time, Adelaide enters her home and kills herself, restoring the most important points of the timeline. The Doctor realizes what he has done, and is visibly horrified — "I've gone too far," he offers, aghast at his actions. Suddenly a vision of Ood Sigma appears and the Doctor asks, "Is this it? My death? Is it time?" When the vision disappears, the Doctor runs into the TARDIS and ignores the cloister bells summoning him, instead firmly stating, "No" and setting off in the TARDIS for points unknown.[75]

At the beginning of the next episode "The End of Time," the Doctor emerges on the Ood planet, dressed for a tropical vacation. When he is chastised by Sigma Ood for delaying his arrival, the Doctor dismissively states, "Last time I was here, you said my song would be ending soon and I'm in no hurry for that." When the Doctor realizes the seriousness of the situation, he rushes back to Earth to try and intercept the Master before he can cause serious harm, and finds himself crossing paths once again with Donna's grandfather Wilf. The Doctor admits to Wilf that he is going to die soon, but the human is confused because he's heard that the Doctor can just assume another body. The Time Lord explains to Wilf that if he is killed before his regeneration is complete he can permanently die. But even when he does successfully regenerate, "it feels like dying. Everything I am dies. Some new man goes sauntering away, and I'm dead."[76]

After defeating the Time Lord High Council's attempt to destroy the universe, the Doctor feels a sense of relief to find himself still very much alive. Then he hears a series of four hesitant knocks. It is Wilf, who is trapped in the control chamber of the Immortality Gate, which is about to be flooded with radiation. Wilf tries to convince the Doctor to allow him to die, since he's an old man who's lived his life. The Doctor bitterly agrees, noting that his tenth incarnation "could do so much more. So much more. But this is what I get. My reward. Well, it's not fair!" After a moment's reflection, the Doctor comes to the rather Buddhist realization that it is his attachment to his current incarnation which is the source of his anger and pain, and accepts his fate, finally completing the grieving cycle. "I've lived too long," he sadly offers, before saving Wilf and exposing himself to a lethal dose of radiation.[77] The Doctor delivers Wilf safely to his home, and then explains he will see Wilf one last time after collecting his reward for his good deeds. The audience then sees a series of vignettes in which the Doctor continues to influence the lives of a number of his companions, such as preventing a Sontaran from killing Martha Jones and Mickey Smith and setting Jack Harkness up with one of the survivors of the spaceship *Titanic*.

The Doctor keeps his word, appearing in the churchyard at Donna's wedding. He gives Wilf a winning lottery ticket to give to Donna, and then says his goodbyes. Wilf's last view of his friend and the TARDIS are from across a graveyard, the symbolism obvious. After a final trip to see Rose at the beginning of the year they first met, time catches up to the Doctor, and his regeneration cannot be stalled any longer. A vision of Ood Sigma appears to the dying Time Lord, and explains, "We will sing to you, Doctor. The universe will sing you to your sleep. This song is ending, but the story never ends." The Doctor stumbles back to the TARDIS, resisting his regeneration to the very last moment, and with a plaintive

"I don't want to go" that is reminiscent of Lady Cassandra's last words aboard Platform One, the energy overtakes him in a violent flash of light which causes damage to the interior of the TARDIS.[78] The eleventh Doctor emerges, no worse for wear, for as the Ood predicted, the story never ends.

The tenth Doctor fights against his own death not only because of his own attachment to that incarnation, but because after living in his various forms for nine centuries, he understands how precious life truly is, in all its forms. While death cannot be defeated, it can sometimes be sidestepped for the time being, and killing others is to be avoided at all cost. One can accept that death is a natural part of life without feeling helpless; one can accept that death will come to us all while still working tireless to preserve life in as high a quality as one can muster for as long as one possibly can. River Song reads from her journal to her cyber children within CAL's dream world:

> "Everybody knows that everybody dies, and nobody knows it like the Doctor. But I do think that all the skies of all the worlds might just turn dark if he ever for one moment accepts it."[79]

As long as the Doctor continues to tirelessly work to right wrongs and preserve the liberties and safety of others, the lights of the universe will continue to shine. Not forever, mind you, but just long enough.

This essay is dedicated to Casper. Everything dies, but you died far too soon.

NOTES

1. Neil Gaiman, *M Is for Magic* (New York: HarperCollins, 2008): p. x.
2. "World War Three." For program details see Videography.
3. "The Doctor Dances."
4. "The Fires of Pompeii."
5. S. Jay Olshansky and Bruce A. Carnes, *The Quest for Immortality* (New York: W.W. Norton, 2001): p. 13.
6. Robert Butler, "Is There an 'Anti-Aging' Medicine?" *Generations* 25, no.4 (2001): p.64. In the tenth Doctor episode "New Earth" the ancient Face of Boe is said to be dying of "an incurable disease: old age."
7. David Gems, "Tragedy and Delight: the Ethics of Decelerated Ageing," *Philosophical Transactions of the Royal Society* B 366 (2011): p. 108.
8. "The End of the World."
9. Gareth Roberts, *Only Human* (London: BBC Books, 2005): p. 104.
10. Roberts, *Only Human*, 248.
11. Mark Benecke, *The Dream of Eternal Life* (New York: Columbia University Press, 2002): p.9.
12. See, for example, "The Deadly Assassin."
13. "The Keeper of Traken."
14. "The Sound of Drums."
15. "The End of Time, Part 1."
16. "The End of Time, Part 2."
17. Justin Richards, *The Deviant Strain* (London: BBC Books, 2005), p. 136.
18. In this reality, Rose's father, Pete Tyler, was very much alive, but Rose had never been conceived.
19. "Rise of the Cybermen."
20. Ibid.
21. "The Age of Steel."
22. "Silence in the Library."
23. Ibid.
24. "Forest of the Dead."
25. Ibid.
26. "The Parting of the Ways."
27. Ibid.

28. "Utopia."

29. "The Family of Blood."

30. Judith Ryall, "Mammoth 'Could Be Reborn in Four Years,'" *The Telegraph*, January 13, 2011 (accessed February 10, 2011) http://www.telegraph.co.uk/science/science-news/8257223/Mammoth-could-be-reborn-in-four-years.html.

31. J. Folch, M.J. Cocero, P. Chesne, et al., "First Birth of an Animal from an Extinct Subspecies (*Capra pyrenaica pyrenaica*) by Cloning," *Theriogenology* 71 (2009): p. 1026.

32. Much of the current hysteria about the supposed December 21, 2012 end of the world scenario is fueled in the media by concerns for hypothetical threats, such as the non-existent planet Nibiru, the erroneous idea of an alignment with the central black hole of our galaxy, and unfounded fears that the Large Hadron Collider will create a black hole in the laboratory which will swallow up the earth. For more information, see Kristine Larsen, "Chichén Itzá and Chicken Little: How Pseudosciences Embraced 2012," in *2012: Decoding the Countercultural Apocalypse*, ed. Joseph Gelfer (London: Equinox, 2011).

33. Bruce Tonn, "Beliefs About Human Extinction," *Futures* 41 (2009): p. 770.

34. "Grebe from Madagascar Extinct After Introduction of Carnivorous Fish," *The Telegraph*, May 26, 2010 (accessed February 21, 2011) http://www.telegraph.co.uk/earth/wildlife/7765868/Grebe-from-Madagascar-extinct-after-introduction-of-carnivorous-fish.html.

35. Katerina Harvati, "Neanderthals," *Evolution: Education and Outreach*, (accessed February 10, 2011) (doi:10.1007/S12052-010-0250-0), p. 1.

36. Ibid., p. 7.

37. Roberts, *Only Human*, p. 35.

38. Ibid., p. 134.

39. Ibid., p. 214.

40. Ibid., pp. 215–16.

41. One of those unions is actually in the present time, as Das, one of the Neanderthals, is trapped in modern England and Jack Harkness spends several weeks helping Das adapt to his new environment. Our final view of Das is at his wedding, to a modern woman, Anna Marie O'Grady.

42. Richard E. Green, Johannes Krause, Adrian W. Briggs, et al., "A Draft Sequence of the Neanderthal Genome," *Science* 328 (2010): p. 716.

43. Mike Tucker, *SnowGlobe 7* (London: BBC Books, 2008): p. 212.

44. Tucker, *SnowGlobe 7*, p. 249.

45. "The Fires of Pompeii."

46. "The End of Time, Part 1."

47. "The End of Time, Part 2."

48. "The Parting of the Ways."

49. Wendy D. Roth, "The End of the One-Drop Rule? Labeling of Multiracial Children in Black Intermarriages," *Sociological Forum* 20 (2005): p. 36.

50. Gareth Roberts, *I Am a Dalek* (London: BBC Books, 2006): p. 84.

51. "Daleks in Manhattan."

52. "Evolution of the Daleks."

53. "The Stolen Earth."

54. "Journey's End"

55. Ibid.

56. "Genesis of the Daleks."

57. Stephen Cole, *The Monsters Within* (London: BBC Books, 2005): p. 206.

58. "The End of the World."

59. K.-P. Schröder and Robert Connon Smith, "Distant Future of the Sun and Earth Revisited," *Monthly Notices of the Royal Astronomical Society* (2008), January 25, 2008 (accessed February 10, 2011) http://arxiv.org/PS_cache/arxiv/pdf/0801/0801.4031v1.pdf.

60. H.G. Wells, *The Time Machine*, ed. Patrick Parrinder (London: Penguin, 2005): p. 84.

61. W. Olaf Stapledon, *Last and First Men* (1930; Oxford: Benediction Classics, 2007: p. 225).

62. D.G. Korycansky, G. Laughlin, and F.C. Adams, "Astronomical Engineering: A Strategy for Modifying Planetary Orbits," *Astrophysics and Space Science* 275 (2001): pp. 349–66.

63. D.G. Korycansky, "Astroengineering, or How to Save the Earth in Only a Billion Years," *Revista Mexicana de Astronomia y Astrofísica* 22 (2004): p. 120.

64. Robert Frost, "Fire and Ice," *Harper's Magazine* 142 (December 1920): p. 67.

65. Fred C. Adams and Gregory Laughlin, "A Dying Universe: the Long-term Fate and Evolution of Astrophysical Objects," *Reviews of Modern Physics* 69 (1997): pp. 337–72.

66. "Utopia."
67. "The Sound of Drums."
68. Mark Morris, *Ghosts of India* (London: BBC Books, 2008): p. 51.
69. "The Family of Blood."
70. Elizabeth Kübler-Ross, *On Death and Dying* (New York: Scribner, 1997).
71. "The Planet of the Ood."
72. "The Planet of the Dead."
73. "The Waters of Mars."
74. Ibid.
75. Ibid.
76. "The End of Time, Part 1."
77. "The End of Time, Part 2."
78. Ibid.
79. "Forest of the Dead."

11

"Ready to outsit eternity"
Human Responses to the Apocalypse[1]

ANDREW CROME

Arriving in the late sixteenth century, the tenth Doctor is keen to demonstrate to new companion Martha Jones that life four centuries before her own time is not as unfamiliar as she might presume. The shoveling of dung thus prefigures recycling; the gathering around a barrel "a water cooler moment"; and a preacher proclaiming that Earth will be destroyed in flames "global warming." Towards the end of the episode, as the majority of Londoners flee in panic as the sky rips open, the same preacher approaches the travelers with jubilant expressions of triumph: "I told thee so! I told thee!"[2] Besides the (entirely accurate) implication that the sixteenth century was an apocalyptic age,[3] his outburst is suggestive of some of the complexities of apocalyptic form. While apocalyptic judgment is proclaimed so that hearers might escape it (through reform of self or society), paradoxically it is that same judgment that serves to vindicate those who make the apocalyptic pronouncements. The question this raises is whether apocalyptic judgment is to be averted through a program of reformation, or embraced as an inevitable and purifying vindication of the persecuted. While "The Shakespeare Code" does not set out to provide an answer to this question, the complexities of the apocalypse nonetheless have a long provenance in the Doctor's adventures in time and space. Having witnessed both the start and the end of the universe and countless threats to its existence in-between, both the Doctor himself and the show's producers have been forced to wrestle with what the apocalyptic means for the Time Lord and the humans he encounters.

With this in mind, here I aim to interrogate the way in which humans have responded to apocalyptic scenarios throughout *Doctor Who*'s long history. The purpose of this examination is twofold. Firstly, it will highlight the way in which the ambiguities of apocalyptic discourse can be interrogated in the show in a surprisingly complex fashion. While *Doctor Who* has always aimed to entertain as its first priority,[4] we will see that several episodes feature sophisticated examinations of the apocalyptic form. Secondly, this study will trace the way in which the Doctor's role in resolving apocalyptic tension has evolved and developed increasingly messianic undertones. However, as we will see, these were not presented in a simplistic manner, but rather portrayed the Doctor as a problematic messiah.

"The end of time itself": Defining the Apocalyptic

At its roots, apocalypse is merely an unveiling, a revelation of that which is hidden (as in the biblical book of Revelation). Speaking more broadly, "apocalyptic" can be seen to have an essential eschatological element as a specific revelation of "the end." As sociologist John Hall notes, the apocalyptic is "centered on [the] cultural disjuncture concerned with 'the end of the world'" manifested in a variety of forms.[5] An apocalyptic event, then, is one that threatens the destruction of the society it is menacing — a scenario in which life will become unrecognizable from its pre-apocalyptic form. This means that the apocalyptic, while having elements of the catastrophic about it, cannot merely refer to a local disaster (a major earthquake, a tsunami, etc.): by its very nature it is a global phenomenon that demands a response of some kind from humanity *as a whole*. The form of apocalypse itself might vary but, as Stephen D. O'Leary has pointed out, it is always concerned with the central psychic concern of modernity: the fear of the destruction of the society that produced the apocalyptic work.[6] This might be expressed in terms of obliteration through a demonic other, collapse through the internal breakdown of the familiar world, or the self-destructive impulses of society itself.

For a deeper appreciation of the apocalyptic it is therefore necessary to move beyond the cataclysmic events themselves and onto the roles that humans are expected to play as actors within those events. As Peter Scott has noted, the apocalyptic takes the "future of the human" as its central theme. This poses fundamental questions about how humans should act in the face of the apocalypse. These questions broadly address human destiny (and our contribution to it) and the guarantor of that destiny (and our participation in it).[7] Science fiction, in that it regularly examines the way in which individuals or communities respond to apocalyptic events, is therefore an ideal lens through which to examine these questions. As John Tulloch and Manuel Alvarado realized, science fiction (and *Doctor Who* in particular) is built on the "anthropocentric principle." That is, the continual struggle between humanity's degeneracy and potential to be good: "something between the brutish beasts and the angels."[8] If this is correct, then we might expect apocalyptic events to act as a form of judgment, allowing science fiction characters to demonstrate either their "brutish" or "angelic" characteristics.

Yet while there is certainly something to this conception, in the face of the apocalypse fictional protagonists are left with a number of options. Firstly, characters can resign themselves to an inevitable apocalypse. As the end must come, it can be accepted passively. Such an idea might be linked to the concept of judgment: whether through a divine response to sin, or as the "revenge" of nature against man. In terms of science fiction this can lead to characters resigning themselves to the certainty of the events which will inevitably overwhelm them. For example, Neville Shute's 1957 novel *On the Beach* portrays an Australian population passively preparing for suicide as they await the arrival of fallout that has already destroyed the Northern hemisphere. Alternatively, characters, while still accepting the inevitability of events can choose to flee from them, a scenario in which they survive the apocalypse and are responsible for rebuilding Earth (for Hall, a key apocalyptic fantasy).[9] This involves finding ways to preserve a remnant of humanity against the apocalypse while accepting that its effects will destroy the majority. A variant of this finds humans taking a number of survivors to "begin again" on a new planet, as at the conclusion of Walter M. Miller's 1959 novel *A Canticle for Leibowitz*. In opposition to these approaches, characters can also fight *against* the apocalypse itself, holding out (a vain?) hope for salvation and the preservation of their threatened society. These contrasting approaches are evidenced in two 1998 movies dealing with the possibility of an asteroid colliding with Earth. While *Armageddon* depicts a successful attempt to destroy an incoming asteroid, *Deep Impact* shows humanity preparing for extinction with a select few protected underground.[10] The option of fighting back against apocalyptic events particularly applies to narratives of alien invasion, especially those in the "threat and disaster" school of science fiction. The template for these remains H.G. Wells' 1898 *The War of the Worlds,* with its descriptions of Martians disrupting and destroying the patterns of everyday life. In such stories, however, resistance can take on many forms — whether an organized military assault (as in the 1996 film *Independence Day*), the efforts of resistance fighters in an already occupied world (as in television series *V*), or humans fighting for survival (as in the latter parts of *War of the Worlds*).

There is a final human approach to the apocalypse not touched upon above — the idea of humans not just welcoming but *causing* the apocalypse. On the one hand, this might be through human foolishness; e.g., the impact of global warming in *The Day After Tomorrow* (2004). On the other hand, apocalyptic events might be deliberately instigated by a particular group of humans as a way of "cleansing" a fallen world. This idea is present in more radical streams of millenarian thought. The apocalyptic event then acts as a form of vindication for those who have instigated it — both as a judgment on the "sinful" world destroyed and as an opportunity to create a new society in their own image. This inevitably raises the question of the role of the savior within apocalyptic myth. Here the question becomes whether it is possible for humankind to escape apocalyptic events themselves, or whether supernatural intervention is required to free them from the situation they find themselves trapped within.

Doctor Who has featured all of these human responses, sometimes even within single episodes. It thus represents an ideal lens through which to examine both the ways in which humans can respond to the apocalypse and the ambiguity of the apocalyptic form itself. This leads us naturally to questions of how to view the problematic role of the Doctor and his relationship with humanity. The Doctor emerges at moments of human crisis offering superhuman wisdom and knowledge of the "correct" timeline. In other words, the Doctor's position allows him to fulfill the apocalyptic role traditionally attributed to Christ — a fact that is coded both overtly and subtly (and sometimes denied outright) in various eras of the show. Examining human responses to the apocalypse therefore allows us to focus on both the portrayal of humanity favored by the show and the way in which its lead character has been presented.

In the following I have divided the material thematically and limited the episodes examined to those that focus upon direct threats to Earth (or human responses to such threats). Unfortunately this means that some areas and episodes will be examined in more detail than others. The Troughton era (1966–69), for example, had a large number of similar "threat and disaster" or "base under siege" stories[11]; Jon Pertwee's early years in the role were marked by a string of alien invasions of the Home Counties; and Davison's and Colin Baker's runs featured few "alien invasion of Earth" stories.[12] The following could certainly be expanded by references to other episodes, but for reasons of space I focus on those exhibiting particularly interesting examinations of the apocalyptic.[13] I will begin by looking at the way in which human attempts to survive the apocalypse have been portrayed, before moving on to look at the ways in which humans have attempted to bring about the apocalypse, and finally examining how humans have "fought back."

"What an inventive, invincible species!": Surviving the Apocalypse

The specter of Earth's destruction raises certain critical questions. Stories in which humanity is dislocated (perhaps permanently) from Earth can deal with the problem of displacement and the question of what it is that makes humans "human" (as it is clearly something other than reliance on the home planet). Different stories across *Doctor Who*'s history offer a variety of answers to this question. Here, I want to focus on three examples of humanity attempting to escape (and thus survive) the apocalypse: the 1966 story "The Ark," the 1974 Tom Baker adventure "The Ark in Space" and the 2007 David Tennant story "Utopia."

Set in the far future, "The Ark" presents humanity as fleeing their home planet for a new colony world (Refusis) after the earth is threatened by the sun. The TARDIS materializes aboard a large ship controlled by the Guardians, rulers of humanity who watch over the whole Earth's population, placed in stasis in miniaturized form. The Ark (a name applied by the Doctor's companion Dodo rather than the humans themselves) is also home to another race — the Monoids — that function as slave workers for the humans. "The Ark" serves as an opportunity to explore the challenges of protecting the species against outside influence in a manner that suggests a response to McCarthyism and contemporary concerns on immigration. When Dodo infects both humans and Monoids with the cold that she is carrying, the travelers are placed on trial by the distrustful security chief, Zentos, who suspects that they represent a disguised infiltration force sent by the inhabitants of Refusis. The Doctor's companion Stephen, representing the TARDIS crew, is placed before a tribunal led by the supposedly neutral Zentos and made up of a majority of the people. Zentos is clear — the travelers' alterity is a sign that they are not really human:

> ZENTOS: Are we to be fooled by such tricks?
> CROWD: No!
> ZENTOS: Are we to be taken in by such nonsense? Because these creatures have the outward appearance of human beings?
> GUARDIAN: They are our enemies! They should be punished.[14]

The fear of alien infiltration in human form recalls the paranoia of *Invasion of the Body-Snatchers*, while Zentos's concern that the appearance of difference in the sealed environment of the Ark must be representative of enemy infiltration is a clear parallel to the way in which fear of the unknown is evoked in nationalist discourse. While "The Ark" might work as a conventional morality play about overcoming small mindedness (by the end of the second episode the Doctor has cured the crew and secured an apology from Zentos) the final two episodes destabilize this simple moral by taking the TARDIS crew seven hundred years into The Ark's future. Here they discover the Monoids have risen against the Guardians and reduced them to slavery. For the Doctor, this was caused by the Guardians' attitudes towards the Monoids. They were conquered because they were "extremely selfish and intolerant"; "[the Monoids] were treated like slaves. Is it any wonder that when they got the chance, they repaid you in kind?"[15] Besides the unsettling fact that the Doctor was untroubled by the initial slavery of Monoids (while he was immediately willing to help the Humans rebel),[16] the story also contains the disturbing suggestion that there were other reasons behind the downfall of the Guardians. Indeed, the Monoids themselves suggest that Zentos was right: The Ark *was* under threat from infiltration, but not from external alien forces. Rather, it was the Monoids, willingly taken aboard, who presented the greatest danger to man's survival. Indeed, it is the fact that later Guardians *lacked* Zentos's fear of the Other that led to humanity's defeat. According to Monoid leader "One" the "main reason" for the revolt was "the Guardians themselves. They were a simple people. They actually encouraged the research that led to our voice box and heat rod. They were totally unprepared for the conflict when it came."[17]

It was thus the overly trusting nature of the Guardians which led to their downfall. A healthy suspicion, it is suggested, would have protected them from the danger of Monoid revolt. Zentos's worries are proved further justified when the Monoids land on Refusis. As the Guardians had initially believed, the planet appears uninhabited. However it transpires that the Refusians are creatures who have lost bodily form — who are able to move unnoticed amongst the humans. Given that Zentos's greatest fear was that the Refusians "would be able to pass, to mingle amongst us"[18] this is profoundly ironic. The story ends with the Monoids and the Humans agreeing to live in harmony on Refusis, but with the Refusians hovering ominously (and invisibly) over the future of their relationship. Neither race will have "any future on Refusis" if they fail to meet the standards of their hosts.[19]

"The Ark" therefore uses the idea of apocalypse as a construct to build a remarkably complex story about the concerns of humanity facing its future. The new world is to be marked not by freedom, but by a complex series of interrelated infiltrations and dislocations, the Monoids are strangers in the human domain fearful of infiltration, a situation reversed in later episodes, while both Humans and Monoids are strangers in a Refusian world in which it is impossible to avoid infiltration by their invisible hosts. The message of "The Ark" is that surviving the apocalypse will never lead to a recreation of human society as it was in its pre-apocalypse days (the Guardians, after all, aimed to transplant human life wholesale from Earth to Refusis). Rather, continuing life after the apocalypse leads inherently to the creation of new communities and new trials, with dislocation bringing its own ominous challenges — it is only total oversight and the threat of retribution that will allow the two communities to work together. In the context of national debates on immigration following the 1965 Race Relations Act, this suggestion might seem particularly worrying for the future unity of the British state.

While on paper possessing a similar plotline to "The Ark," the 1975 adventure "The Ark in Space" presented a very different attempt to survive the apocalypse. Arriving on the seemingly abandoned Space Station Nerva, the Doctor and companions Harry and Sarah discover that they have landed on a cryogenic storage facility for the last survivors of an Earth ravaged by solar flares. At the same time, it becomes clear that the facility has been infiltrated by the Wirrn, an insect race who are seemingly consuming the crew.

Where "The Ark" wore its biblical influence lightly (it is Dodo who named the spaceship, with the crew claiming never to have heard the Genesis story), the "Ark in Space" explicitly attempts to construct intertextual links with its source material. As Tulloch and Alvarado have pointed out, this is expressed as much in terms of difference as it is in similarity. Thus the fact that Nerva's commander has been nicknamed Noah is something of a joke, "a name from mythology."[20] Whereas Noah in Genesis presided over a microcosm of perfect order, with man and beast co-existing harmoniously, Nerva's Noah becomes a site of internal conflict as he is slowly transformed into a Wirrn and sees the station degenerate into an elemental conflict between the human and the alien.[21] Indeed, biblical allusions continue to be used throughout the serial in an unusual manner. For while the apocalyptic events which ended life on Earth are shown to have been natural, there is the unsettling suggestion that they were not entirely unwelcome. The recorded voice of the Earth High Minister that greets those about to enter cryogenic storage thus uses recalls discourses of martyrdom: "I salute you who are about to make the supreme sacrifice. In a few minutes you will pass beyond life. In case there is any fear in your heart or mind at this awesome moment, let me remind you, that you take with you all our pasts. You carry the torch that has been handed down from generation to generation."[22] When a similar message is relayed to those awakening from cryogenic storage, it becomes clear that their mission has been constructed as a chance to form a utopian community. Apocalypse becomes an *opportunity* to purge the unwanted elements of human life. In Genesis 1:28, God addressed man: "Be fruitful and increase in number; fill the earth and subdue it. Rule over the fish in the sea and the birds in the sky and over every living creature that moves on the ground." The echoes of this passage in the High Minister's speech are unmistakable:

> You will return to an Earth purified by flame — a world that we cannot guess at. If it be arid, you must make it flourish, if it be stony, you must make it fertile. The challenge is vast, the task enormous, but let nothing daunt you. Remember, citizen volunteers, that you are the proud standard bearers of our entire race. Of the millions that walk the world today, you are the chosen survivors. You have been entrusted with a sacred duty — to see that human culture, human knowledge, human love and faith shall never perish from the universe. Guard what we have given you with all your strength.[23]

The irony of this pronouncement of humanity's survival is that it is intercut with shots of Noah recoiling in horror as he realizes the extent of his own transformation into a non-human form. Indeed, while the Doctor gives a famous speech about humanity's greatness in the story ("Homo sapiens. What an inventive, invincible species ... ready to outsit eternity. They're indomitable") and proclaims the cryogenic chamber "an amazing sight.... The entire human race in one room. All colors, all creeds, all differences finally forgotten,"[24] he is soon shown to be wrong. Far from forgetting their differences, humanity has moved to emphasize them to a greater extent. Thus Noah and medical technician Vira describe the risk that is posed by the presence of "regressive" factors such as the Doctor and his companions. The Nerva crew have been specially selected from a limited gene pool so as to preserve only the best of humanity, a group used to thinking in crudely utilitarian terms (for example, Vira wants to know if Sarah is "of value" before resuscitating her).

In the case of "The Ark in Space," apocalyptic events therefore play a very different role to the destruction of Earth in "The Ark." The earlier episode presented an (inherently disorientating and disturbing) opportunity for humanity to attempt to forge a new society on an alien planet. In the later story, however, apocalyptic events have a purgative function for the humans involved. They grant the survivors the chance to construct a "pure" society in the image of the dominant members of their own "in group." In this way, the humans in "The Ark in Space" embrace the typical millenarian dream of a world divested of difference. That this is problematized by the intervention of the Wirrn underlines the difficulties with this form of thinking. For the "in-group" can easily be compromised from within, as Noah finds as he slowly loses his humanity. Indeed, it is not entirely surprising to find that the Wirrn's aggressive method of procreation (like many wasps, the Wirrn incubate within other creatures, consuming them from the inside out) is a parodic reimagining of what the Wirrn see humans as doing to colony planets.[25]

In closing this section we can turn to a more recent example of humanity's attempted survival post-apocalypse, Russell T. Davies's "Utopia" (2007). The first part of Davies's "Master Trilogy" (a series of stories reintroducing the Doctor's arch nemesis), "Utopia" is concerned with the last survivors of humanity who aim to travel to Utopia so as to escape the end of the universe. For the Doctor, this is an opportunity to reassert the inherent strength of humanity as a species. Recalling the fourth Doctor's panegyric in "The Ark in Space," the tenth Doctor praises: "The ripe old smell of humans — you survive... You always revert to the same basic shape. The fundamental human. End of the universe, here you are. Indomitable, that's the word!"[26]

Yet like Tom Baker before him, David Tennant's words here are undermined by the presentation of humanity throughout the story. In this episode, as in Thomas More's original pun, Utopia is quite literally "no place"; it is simply an imaginary construct embraced by humans hoping to postpone their own inevitable destruction. Recalling themes from "The Ark," "Utopia" thus revolves around a fear of infiltration and of humanity's limits being compromised. The human base is thus surrounded by the savage Futurekind who represent the possibility that, quite against the Doctor's original statement, it might be possible to be something less than "the fundamental human" ("It is feared they are what we will become — unless we reach Utopia"). The irony of this is made manifest in the remainder of the episode and the following stories in the trilogy, in which the claim that humans retain a fundamental essence and form (as the Doctor believes) is repeatedly undermined. While the Futurekind are inherently "Other," they are shown to have been able to infiltrate the human base with ease — their difference (shown mainly through animalistic teeth) is not as deeply ingrained as the humans had presumed. Professor Yana, in charge of getting humans to Utopia (and thus the quintessential example of humanity), is revealed to be the amnesiac Master disguised in human form. When the Doctor's visit helps triggers memories of his true Time Lord status, it is revealed not only that humanity's defender was not even human, but also that he was well aware that escape from the end of the universe was nothing more than an illusion. Whereas humanity had viewed Utopia in terms of the traditional millennial kingdom ("the skies are made of diamonds"), when the Master describes its reality he appropriates dystopian terms to create an increasingly ironic description: "You should have seen it, Doctor. Furnaces burning. The last of humanity screaming at the dark." This is made manifest when the newly regenerated Master allows his new wife to explain what Utopia really was:

> Dying, everything dying. The whole of creation was falling apart and I thought ... there's no point, no point to anything ... not ever.... There was no solution. Just the dark and the cold.[27]

The true future of humanity is revealed to be the murderous Toclafane. While humans *have* survived, they are not, as the Doctor originally claimed, consistent with "the same basic shape." Instead, mentally regressing to the most violent of childhood urges, they are reduced to shrunken heads in small spheres, killing others simply "because it's fun!" As the Master tells the Doctor: "human race, greatest monsters of them all."[28]

The act of escaping the apocalypse is therefore never an uncomplicated affair. Instead, throughout the show's history, *Doctor Who* has problematized the issue of humanity escaping its own end. Whereas "The Ark" calls for tolerance as the means for human continuity, at the same time it points to the very limits of that tolerance — the value of suspicion and the need for an invisible disciplinary presence to maintain the supposedly "accepting" society. While "The Ark in Space" seems to evidence the Doctor's belief in the survival of humanity, in reality it serves only to show that even a society in which all colors and creeds have been eliminated still views the apocalypse as a necessary purge of the undesirable elements of their culture. Davies's "Utopia" shows not only that the utopian dream is little more than a regressive nightmare, but that the "fundamental" essence of humanity that the Doctor presumes is a good thing may, in fact, point instead to humanity's corruption. While each of these elements obviously reflects contemporary concerns of the eras in which they were produced, each episode nonetheless remains important in its ability to deconstruct the complexities of apocalyptic narrative. Different problems are raised when *Doctor Who* examines those who appropriate apocalyptic rhetoric for their own ends. Thus, we can move on to look at how "constructed" apocalypse has worked in the show.

"It's all become too complicated and corrupt": Creating the Apocalypse

The notion of a constructed apocalypse might initially seem incoherent. After all, if the apocalypse should reflect God's judgment on man, the expectation might be that events will be brought about through natural phenomenon or supernatural "signs and wonders." However, the millenarian element of apocalyptic thinking has often privileged direct action in bringing about the kingdom of God on Earth — whether through disastrous attempts at Münster in the sixteenth century, or the nerve gas attack on the Tokyo subway in 1995. This also raises the conspiracy theory, recently reiterated in conjunction with 9/11, that apocalyptic events can be falsified so as to justify the unjustifiable. Again, *Doctor Who* has been a rich source in examining this theme.

The idea of a fictional apocalyptic scenario first raised its head in the Patrick Troughton serial "The Enemy of the World," which found the actor playing both the Doctor and his double, the twenty-first century dictator Salamander. While this might suggest that the story play out as a standard morality play on the dangers of totalitarian power, the narrative is in fact considerably more complex and subversive than it first appears, working to highlight the danger of governments presenting the figure of a monolithic enemy to their people. The story is notable for having no alien menace, instead focusing on Salamander's despotism, as he maintains his personal power through a series of artificially created natural disasters. It transpires that these are being produced by a small team of scientists hidden in a nuclear shelter. Having been convinced by Salamander that the outside world has been rendered unrecognizable due to nuclear warfare, they create the disasters so as to rid the surface of the mutated and wild survivors. It is notable that Salamander, in his speeches to the shelter's inhabitants, clearly appropriates Cold War rhetoric in describing their mission: "We have to ... fight for a while longer ... creating natural disasters, monsoons, earthquakes, volcanic eruptions, always in the places where the enemies of truth and freedom gather together."[29]

When the leader of the scientists, Swann, discovers a recent newspaper clipping amongst a food delivery, he is brought to challenge Salamander's presentation of a dystopian surface world. Freely admitting that he has lied, Salamander nonetheless claims that he had the community's best interests at heart: "They have a kind of society [on the surface], but it's evil! Corrupt! You don't think I could expose you to that sort of thing? Think of Mary and the other women." When Swann worries that he is therefore responsible for the deaths of innocent human beings, Salamander returns to the millennial dream, attempting to reassure the scientist with the promise of a purified Earth:

> SALAMANDER: Swann, they're not fit to live.
> SWANN: You're murdering them, killing them off!
> SALAMANDER: I want you and others to inherit the earth, make a new world.[30]

Salamander is therefore engaging in a two stage process of deception. Firstly, he presents a monolithic, inhuman Other that must be destroyed. When Swann realizes that the supposed enemy differs little from the "survivors" in the bunker, Salamander changes tack. While the enemy is now recognizable, their society is inherently "evil" and particularly threatening to established gender roles ("Think of Mary..."). There is no opportunity for co-operation: it is a case of destroy or be destroyed. Salamander's thinking here parallels the presentation of the USSR in popular propaganda as either an inhuman, destructive force or as a society so radically different from our own that it deserves destruction for its own sake ("It's not murder ... It's an act of mercy.") Salamander thus moves to placate the consciences of scientists involved in the creation of weapons of mass destruction by appealing to a millenarian hope for a purified world. He is therefore engaging in multiple layers of deception: the "enemy" that the scientists fight against is their own population, the same people that Salamander deceives into viewing him as a benevolent ruler. This adds an extra layer of complexity to the character, and works as a destabilizing influence on what could have been a simplistic story. Salamander's actions here find a parallel in Davies's 2005 episodes "Aliens of London/World War Three," in which the alien Slitheen fake the crash landing of a space craft into Big Ben so as to provoke a war for fuel — again, the deception relies on the falsified belief in a non-existent threat, although on this occasion the deception is taken from the micro to a macro level. The 9/11 parallels should be, as Marc DiPaolo has pointed out, readily apparent.[31]

Perhaps the most interesting example of a created apocalypse is found in Malcolm Hulke's final script for the show, "Invasion of the Dinosaurs," which features a group of idealistic humans attempting to literally reverse time and return Earth to "a golden age."[32] Their aims necessitate both the evacuation of London (caused by the arrival of several rather dubious looking dinosaurs) and the complete destruction of human civilization — which will be erased from history. Yet those behind the scheme, a group of environmentalists disgusted at the way in which humans have damaged the earth, are working from complex motives. While the ring leaders (including the government minister, Charles Grover) are aware of the details of the plan, the majority of the group is hidden in a bunker mocked up as a spaceship, believing themselves to be on a journey to a new colony world.

Two major apocalyptic motifs stand out in the story. The first deals with the destruction and abandonment of the normal way of life in London. The very first shots of the serial focus upon a city bereft of life. The shots of streets devoid of people, empty roads and abandoned landmarks are here interspersed with images that suggest a sudden and catastrophic destruction has been visited upon the capital. An abandoned car sits in the middle of the road, doors open — when the camera pans back it reveals a row of semi-detached houses partially destroyed, the streets strewn with rubble; another shot finds a crashed milk cart and a purse abandoned, money scattered on the road. In the next scenes we find a looter stealing from a jeweler's shop while the recently arrived Doctor attempts to make sense of the situation. Things are made clearer for the viewer when the action switches to UNIT HQ — here we learn both that London has been evacuated and that General Finch, in charge of the still mysterious operation, orders looters shot on sight. The effect of the mysteriously evacuated city, the presence of looters and the sudden destruction appear intended to bring to mind the results of a sudden nuclear attack. In this regard it is interesting to draw parallels between the presentation of the first part of "Invasion of the Dinosaurs" and Peter Watkin's un-broadcast (but well-known) 1965 docudrama "The War Game," which pictured both the widespread evacuation of urban centers and the military shooting civilians in the aftermath of an atomic attack. While this is only a casual connection it is nonetheless a significant one, especially when it was clear that the audience were meant to be kept in the dark about the nature of the threat.[33]

The second point of interest concerns the apocalyptic discourse employed by the environmentalists behind the time shift. They are initially introduced in uniformly positive terms: they include the "brilliant" scientist Whittaker and the minister, Sir Charles Grover, the author of the suitably apocalyptic environmental tome "Last Chance for Man."[34] Indeed, the Doctor is initially impressed by Grover, telling him that "this planet needs people like you."[35] However, the aim of destroying civilization so as to create what is in effect a millennial state on Earth proves abhorrent to the Doctor. Indeed, the "chosen" group upon the "space-ship" deliberately appropriate apocalyptic language to describe the fate of the planet. This is not always in the context of merely condemning pollution. Thus Ruth, an aristocratic member of the crew, describes humans as having abandoned themselves to judgment. When Sarah criticizes Ruth's attack on freedom of choice, she is dismissive: "People on Earth were allowed to choose. And see what kind of a world they made! Moral degradation, permissiveness, usury, cheating, lying, cruelty."[36] The mocked-up ship also features a re-education suite, in which the would-be colonists are constantly reminded of the inevitable judgment facing their home planet.

Against this apocalypticism, the Doctor represents a voice of progress. While he sympathizes with the aims of the environmentalists, he nonetheless deplores their primitivist assertion that it might be possible to return to a prelapsarian state of innocence:

> YATES: The world used to be a cleaner, simpler place. It's all become too complicated and corrupt...
> DOCTOR: Do you realize what will happen if they succeed?
> YATES: We shall find ourselves in the golden age!
> DOCTOR: There never was a golden age, Mike. It's all an illusion.[37]

From the Doctor's point of view, the alternative is not a naïve millennialism. Instead, he issues a call to recognize the reality of the situation and to operate within it. While Yates claims that there is "no alternative" to the plan, the camera slowly zooms in for a close-up of Pertwee's face as he solemnly intones: "Yes there is. Take the world that you've got and try and make something of it. It's not too late." Indeed, this might be seen as the central theme of the Pertwee years; neatly encapsulated in the Doctor's recognition, after returning to our world after viewing the destruction of a parallel Earth in "Inferno" (1970), that "free will is not an illusion after all. The pattern can be changed!"[38]

A similar criticism of those who would bring about apocalyptic events for their own ends occurs in 1989's "The Curse of Fenric." Set in the later parts of World War II, the story details attempts by British commander A.H. Millington to develop chemical weapons which he will use to destroy what he fears will be a resurgent USSR. Millington reads events through a filter of Norse mythology, and is goaded into raising an ancient evil ("Fenric"—an Anglicized version of the great wolf Fenrir) whom the Doctor had imprisoned in the distant past. Fenric is working with "The Ancient One," the vampiric leader of a future evolution of humanity living in a world destroyed by chemical waste, who has been forced back in time (a figure Millington sees as "The Great Serpent" who will poison the world). To survive, the Ancient One plans on using Millington's weapons to re-make the world as a chemical wasteland.

What makes "The Curse of Fenric" such an interesting story, is in the way in which it reveals the inherently circular and self-perpetuating nature of apocalyptic thought. As convinced as he is by the Norse predictions of destruction, Millington believes that he is the one to bring them about through the chemical weapons he has developed. Indeed, in using the Ancient One, Fenric creates an historical paradox: it is the Ancient One's actions in using chemical weapons in the present that will bring about his own apocalyptic future. Millington sees his weapons as at one and the same time redemptive (in the destruction of the Soviet threat) and of symbolizing the destructive forces of Ragnarok. Fenric's arrival is thus viewed as a sign of the destruction of the established order ("The Gods have lost the final battle!").[39] The question raised by "The Curse of Fenric" is the extent to which apocalyptic events are predetermined and the extent to which they are contingent happenings. For Fenric shows that all the seemingly random events which have brought the Doctor and companion Ace to the 1940s were part of his carefully mediated plan to create the apocalyptic moment. However, the fallacy that all history is predetermined (whether by God or by an evil entity such as Fenric) is undermined in the final moments when the Ancient One kills both himself and Fenric with chemical weapons. Even when evil manipulates humans like pawns (chess is an important motif running throughout the serial) apocalyptic events are not preordained. Change is always possible even in the darkest of situations. Thus the apocalyptic keeps humans prisoners—whether literally in the case of the scientists in "The Enemy of the World" and environmentalists of "Invasion of the Dinosaurs," or metaphorically, as for Millington who feels he must play his predetermined role in end times events.

"Doctor, if you're out there, we need you": Human Resistance and the Role of the Doctor

The most common portrayal of apocalyptic threats in *Doctor Who* has featured attempts by humanity to resist invading forces. Such events, often hinging on the intervention of the Doctor for their resolution, are a suitable conclusion to this examination of the apocalyptic in the show. An analysis of their central themes allows us to ask *how* humanity can resist the apocalypse and whether such events presume the necessity of the Doctor's presence.

The first story to present a major alien invasion, 1964's "Dalek Invasion of Earth," examined what Britain would look like under enemy occupation. According to the BBC's Audience Reaction report, some viewers were taken by the realism of the episode: "They made the impossible (I hope) seem credible."[40] The viewer's "hope" that the conditions portrayed in the serial would not come to pass was an acknowledgment of the show's success in the clear "Daleks as Nazis" subtext that was encoded throughout. As James Chapman has recognized, images of Daleks with sucker arms raised in fascist salutes parading in front of Westminster were clearly designed to horrify.[41] Allusions proliferate throughout the narrative. For example, the shots of the Dalek labor camp are framed in the same way as newspaper photographs of the V2 Mittelwerk complex, with the Black Dalek described as the camp's "commandant." The Daleks' discussion of how to deal with the remaining human prisoners makes the parallel clearer still:

> BLACK DALEK: Have all work tasks been completed?
> DALEK 1: They have.
> BLACK DALEK: Then arrange for the extermination of all human beings.
> DALEK 2: The final solution, clean up this planet.
> DALEK 1: Kill! Kill! Kill! Kill![42]

Human resistance here has been reduced to small bands of disorganized rebels, attempting piecemeal opposition. Other humans have been converted into "Robomen" (slaves for the Daleks) or survive through black marketeering or collaboration ("Oh well, they'd have been captured anyway," reasons an old woman after betraying the Doctor's companion Barbara).[43]

Here the Doctor plays the part of rabble rouser. While his role in the narrative is important, his presence is not central to the resolution of events (the defeat of the Daleks). Instead, he enables the rebels to fight the Daleks through his encouragement ("we must dare to stop them!").[44]

Apocalyptic events can therefore serve as tools for writers to hold up mirrors to contemporary societies, demonstrating the fragility of the status quo and the way in which a seemingly stable society can potentially shatter. "The Dalek Invasion of Earth" perhaps remains the best example of this, although a similar visit to a post-apocalyptic Dalek ruled future (again featuring humans as collaborators) is featured in the 1972 "Day of the Daleks." As a commentary on totalitarianism the serial aims to show the Daleks' paranoia and complacency in occupation, in contrast to the resourcefulness of the human resistance ("For every guerilla cell you destroy another springs up," notes the Controller, a human collaborator). Indeed, in many ways its vision of the future is bleaker than that shown in "Dalek Invasion of Earth": the Controller's collaboration in "Day" extends to willingly enslaving others in comparison to the informants and black marketeers of the earlier story, a point that the Doctor takes up forcefully when he confronts him: "Then what's you're saying is, that the entire human population of this planet, apart from a few remarkable exceptions such as yourself, are really only fit to lead the life of a dog."[45] Where the Doctor argues that it is necessary to fight the occupation (or at least resist in such a way that the essential humanity of the individual might be reasserted) the Controller claims that only collaboration can preserve his race in the face of apocalyptic danger. The Controller's position privileges his role as a survivor ("You don't understand. No one who didn't live through those terrible years can understand") and views his collaboration in distinctly redemptive terms — ensuring that humanity was not destroyed or reduced to an "inhuman" state: "There were hundreds of years of nothing but destruction and killing. Nearly seven eighths of the world's population wiped out. The rest living in holes in the ground, starving, almost reduced to the level of animals." Thus the Controller claims that "we have helped make things better for the others! We have gained concessions, I have saved lives."[46] Against such thinking, "Day of the Daleks" proclaims the necessity of human resistance and reassertion of humanity in the face of apocalyptic threats, particularly in its sympathetic portrayal of resistance fighters. It is through a reassertion of his own humanity in the face of the Daleks that the Controller is eventually redeemed, although he is exterminated for his pains.

These two examples of stories on post-apocalyptic Earth are relatively rare for the series, although humans on plenty of other planets have found themselves oppressed by either human (i.e., "The Sun Makers" [1977]; "The Happiness Patrol" [1988], "New Earth" [2006]) or alien threats (i.e., "The Macra Terror" [1967], "Frontios" [1984], "The Long Game" [2005]). In considering how humans should react to the challenge of post-apocalyptic conditions, it becomes increasingly clear that the Doctor plays a key role in encouraging or engineering a victory for humanity. After all, the Doctor can play an apocalyptic role in and of himself. Hall's work has emphasized that apocalypse works in a distinct way upon human understandings of time. Everyday life is conducted along a dual axis of "strategic" and "diachronic" time. Diachronic time refers to the packing of time into neatly delineated units, represented by the modern use of clock and calendar. While this sort of time is inherently arbitrary (for example, an hour could just as easily contain 36 minutes consisting of 100 seconds as 60 minutes of 60 seconds), diachronic time comes to be considered "natural," indeed, to be an obvious part of the revealed order. Strategic time is the time in which human beings, using their experiences, pursue particular goal-orientated ends in the present with the aim of influencing the future. To use an example that might not always reflect contemporary student behavior, an undergraduate might attend a lecture as they know (from the previous year's study) that attendance will boost their chances of passing their course. When there is a shift from focusing on "an end" to "the End" strategic time can become an important part of the apocalyptic. In Hall's work, apocalypse thus irrupts into our normal world of diachronic time, orientating our strategic time towards the End.[47] This is precisely the role that the Doctor plays — a force, suddenly irrupting into the regular world of diachronic time, helping oppressed groups (as in the Dalek stories examined above) regroup around new strategic goals. The Doctor is "apocalyptic" in the sense that he is quite literally the "unveiler"; pulling back the curtain of the established world to reveal the true nature of the societies that he visits.

We can therefore ask about the role that the Doctor plays within these apocalyptic moments. For the danger of any apocalyptic movement (besides the move towards an earthly millenarianism) is that of direct messianism: particularly when a charismatic individual takes charge (e.g., Jim Jones or David Koresh). As a highly charismatic and other worldly figure, the Doctor certainly has the potential to represent such a messianic figure. Indeed, it can be argued that (at times) the Doctor has been increasingly coded as a Christ figure in both the way in which he has been presented on screen and in his actions.

Such implicit coding might be detected in the later 1980s, when script editor Andrew Cartmel attempted to inject greater mystery into the character. It was repeatedly suggested that the Doctor was more than simply another Time Lord. In "The Curse of Fenric" it is suggested that the Doctor represents a Manichean force of primal good to Fenric's force of primal evil.[48] Similarly, Lady Pienforte laughs at Ace's suggestion that the Doctor is merely a Time Lord in "Silver Nemesis" (1988). Yet the Christic coding of the Doctor came into its own in the 1996 TV movie.[49] This is sometimes explicit — the eighth Doctor's emergence from a morgue wrapped in a shroud is not the show's most subtle allegorical moment. In the TV movie, the Doctor now appears to possess a near omniscience. He knows, for example, the fate of individuals he meets, telling a security guard which question to answer on an exam he will take in the future, and having to be forced by de-facto companion Grace Holloway to avoid revealing her own future to her. Grace's greatest wish is "to hold back death" a power the Doctor explicitly claims for himself ("I came back to life before your eyes. I held back death").[50] At the story's conclusion, the Doctor is able to literally resurrect both Grace and the Master's reformed associate Chang Lee by unspecified means. In addition to these messianic traits, in preventing the apocalypse that the Master is attempting to bring about, the Doctor has to undergo his own crucifixion. He is tortured as the Master attempts to steal his body — suffering, arms outstretched, wearing headwear that appears modeled on a crown of thorns.

Where Chapman could describe the TV movie as drawing "explicitly on biblical allusion,"[51] the revived BBC series has generally taken a more subtle approach to religious subtexts. Two examples might serve as particularly notable, however. The first is marked not by the Doctor's presence but rather by his absence. Centering on the Doctor's companion Donna, "Turn Left" (2008) imagines an alternative universe in which the Doctor was killed in the midst of the events of "The Runaway Bride" (2006). Without the Doctor to preserve Britain from apocalyptic threats there is a radical deterioration in national life. Indeed, the nation quickly slips into dystopian mode, as we are given glimpses into a Britain that rounds up immigrants and inters them at "labor camps." Donna's bemusement in the face of the apocalypse might be taken as symptomatic of the wider response of the West to post 9/11 reality. While her grandfather, Wilf, calls for "wartime spirit," Donna can only offer her own confusion at the status quo: "But there isn't a war. There's no fight. There's just ... this." It is perhaps noteworthy that when Wilf claims, "America, that'll save us! It was on the news...."[52] the next scene cuts to a news report covering the destruction of the United States.

Within the Britain of "Turn Left" the Doctor represents the only factor that is holding the nation back from a slide into a dystopian fascist regime. Apocalyptic events are therefore never seen as a threshold that must be crossed in order to pass into a redeemed world, but are rather highlighted only as destructive and degrading. It is the figure of the Doctor who allows characters to survive apocalyptic events and the Doctor who serves to limit the impact of these events themselves. It is therefore possible, in 2005's "The Christmas Invasion," for Prime Minister Harriet Jones to publicly appeal for the Doctor's help: "Doctor, if you're out there, we need you ... help us, please Doctor."[53] This is why it is important that "Turn Left" remains just a glimpse at the sort of world that would exist without the Doctor — with his presence the possibility of any slide toward dystopia is quickly arrested. To use Scott's terms, the Doctor himself has become the "guarantor" of our destiny; specifically of the characteristics that he sees as "fundamentally" human against emotionless Daleks and Cybermen.[54] Thus the world after the potential apocalypse is not remade in any significant sense in the revived series — rather the Doctor, when he works on contemporary Earth, works precisely to maintain the status quo.[55] This perhaps evidences Geoff King's assertion that Hollywood representations of apocalypse avoid portrayals of a radically re-imagined world order: "sufficient destruction is achieved to offer cleansing or redeeming potential for any survivors, but any threat of annihilation usually recedes."[56] We could think of the destruction of Downing Street and Big Ben ("Aliens of London"), London's "Gherkin" ("The Christmas Invasion") and New York itself ("The Stolen Earth" [2008]) as examples of this. In addition to this, however, *Doctor Who*'s appeal may rest in the reassurance offered by the spectacle of watching apocalyptic events devoid of their transformative power. While Matt Hills argues that the revived series opens up a space in which change is conceivable (and the present recognized "as history"), it seems to me that this is only ever presented as a possibility rather than as a tangible reality.[57] Indeed, as Hills recognizes, the future is often coded directly in terms of an abstract representation of present reality[58] — a position which argues against the show's recognition of the likelihood of fundamental change in society or of the historicity of our own present. The series thus helps reassure contemporary viewers of the unbroken continuity of the current world-historical situation. *Doctor Who* thus supplies further evidence for Peter Y. Paik's recent hypothesis that while postmodern society is fascinated with the apocalyptic destruction of society, this is combined with "an inability to imagine change on the more modest scale of history."[59] The society that follows the averted apocalypse of the Slitheen ("Aliens of London/World War Three"), Sycorax ("The Christmas Invasion"); Daleks and Cybermen ("Army of Ghosts/Doomsday" [2006]); Racnoss ("The Runaway Bride"); Daleks again ("The Stolen Earth/Journey's End"), and the Master/Time Lords ("The End of Time" [2009]) is fundamentally the same as that which first experienced the apocalyptic events. Indeed, after the apocalyptic events of "Last of the Time Lords" time is literally wound back to a pre-apocalyptic moment in "the year that never was."[60]

I want to turn to "Last of the Time Lords" in more detail now, to examine the second example of this salvific concern in revived *Doctor Who*. To set the scene, the Doctor has been dramatically aged and weakened by the Master. The method of his revival is of particular interest here. The Doctor's companion, Martha Jones, is sent across the world with the task of spreading the Doctor's story. What is interesting about this is the way in which her language is couched in explicitly evangelistic terms. As with John the Baptist, Martha proclaims that she merely acts as a servant of a higher power:

> But if Martha Jones became a legend then that's wrong, because my name isn't important. There's someone else. The man who sent me out there, the man who told me to walk the Earth. And his name is The Doctor. He has saved your lives so many times and you never even knew he was there. He never stops. He never stays. He never asks to be thanked. But I've seen him, I know him ... I love him.[61]

The Doctor's restoration to (comparative) youth and vitality is achieved through the combined mental energy of those on Earth expressing their hope in salvation through his name. While this is couched in science fiction terms, the method of the Doctor's restoration seems uncomfortably religious. Indeed, the Master is prepared to mockingly dismiss it as "prayer"— while the anguished cries of the masses calling on the Doctor by name are intercut with shots of his shimmering levitation and restoration. This image is at least implicitly reliant on religious imagery for its impact, an observation which is also true of the Doctor's ascension, borne aloft by robotic angels in "Voyage of the Damned." Of course, this is not to suggest that Davies directly coded the Doctor as Christ, an idea he explicitly (and often angrily) denies.[62] His work often delights in subverting conventional religious tropes,[63] so as Vincent O'Brien suggests, the Doctor's fallibility means that he is "simultaneously the deceiver and the gift, the saviour [sic] and the destroyer."[64] Yet at the very least, the use of such religious imagery invites viewers to draw such conclusions.[65]

Nonetheless, it is interesting that Davies did not take the Christic parallels to their logical conclusion. While I cannot fully support Una McCormack's claim that Davies used the figure of the Doctor primarily to critique claims of religious authority in the series,[66] it is certainly true that the Doctor's messianic traits are presented as problematic. As Alec Charles has noted, the Doctor is always presented as a figure who, despite his power, must avoid the temptation to fully claim the messianic mantle for himself—a claim recently reiterated by Ruth Deller and proven in Davies' "Waters of Mars" (2009) when the Doctor's attempts to overcome the "laws of time" prove disastrous.[67] This is a manifestation of the phenomenon Paik recognized, in which contemporary films often pull back from the full implication of drawing their lead characters as Christic figures.[68] In Davies's vision of the show, while the Doctor represents a savior figure, he is not usually portrayed in a redemptive mode. Thus, when the Doctor sacrifices his own life, it is not in the expectation that his sacrifice will ensure universal redemption. Instead, the Doctor offers his own life for *individuals*— to save Rose in "Parting of the Ways"; his desperate wish to die for River Song in "Forest of the Dead," and in freeing Wilf (at the cost of his tenth incarnation) in "The End of Time."

It is perhaps ironic, then, that Steven Moffat's first series as executive producer saw a finale that hinged on the necessity of the Doctor's sacrifice as a resolution. In the first part of the story, "The Pandorica Opens" (2010), River Song deliberately played down the connection of the Doctor with the divine in a conversation with a Roman centurion: "You've been a soldier for too long to believe that there are gods watching over us. But there is a man..." Despite this, the resolution again draws clear Christic parallels. With all of time and space in the process of being destroyed by an explosion of the TARDIS, the only hope for the universe rests on the Doctor flying the Pandorica (a prison designed for the Doctor, containing elements of the "normal" universe) into the heart of the explosion, thus sacrificing himself for the restoration of all creation. As in the TV movie, this is a literal resurrection of the dead, portrayed in striking fashion through the return to life of companion Amy's parents. Creating, in the Doctor's words "Big Bang II," his act mirrors that of God in creation — turning aside destruction and overcoming the threat of formless chaos. Indeed, there is even an element of propitiation in the form of the Doctor's sacrifice — it is only he who is capable of turning aside the destructive wrath of the TARDIS through the offering of his life. Examining the ninth and tenth Doctors, Melody Green has suggested that while the Doctor might "occasionally exhibit Messianic qualities, his sacrifice is never once for all."[69] Yet this sacrifice *is* presumed to be unique — it is anticipated as the final act of the Doctor's life and will result in a universal restoration. For the philosopher Slavoj Žižek, this kind of Christic portrayal represents an inherent regression in contemporary thought, a move towards a more simplistic and (on the surface) unproblematic ideological mode.[70] While I find it hard to uncritically support this notion in what was in many ways a more explicitly complex and intellectual season than any which preceded it,[71] Žižek's assertion may be useful when examined against upcoming seasons of the show.[72] As the series continues it will no doubt be useful to trace the continuing role of human agency when compared to the way in which the Doctor acts in the face of the apocalyptic.

Conclusion

The purpose of this chapter has been to trace the way in which the complexities of apocalyptic thought have emerged across *Doctor Who*'s history. The fact that the show spans the best part of five decades makes generalizations impossible. Nonetheless, what has been demonstrated here is that the program, while providing "good entertainment," can nonetheless analyze and debate the contradictions, challenges and ambiguities of apocalyptic discourse: whether this is through examining the difficulties of maintaining our society in a post-apocalyptic world ("The Ark"), dealing with the problematic potential of apocalyptic rhetoric in environmentalism ("Invasion of the Dinosaurs"), touching upon contemporary political anxieties ("Dalek Invasion of Earth"; "The Curse of Fenric") or examining the ambiguities of the Christ-figure ("The TV Movie"/"Last of the Time Lords"). The important differences that have been traced above notwithstanding, some broad suggestions can be made. Firstly, there is an essential shift between the treatment of the apocalyptic in the original series (1963–1989) and its recent reworking. In the "classic" series the apocalypse is often presented as an opportunity for change and the construction of new societies. This is invariably a society built on liberal-tolerationist values — in this sense *Doctor Who*'s use of apocalyptic has always represented Žižek's recognition of the Western inability to imagine an alternate future to the present political order. However in the revived series, especially under Davies, apocalyptic events serve primarily as an opportunity to restore contemporary society to the status quo.

A second point can be made in terms of the way in which the apocalyptic in the show reminds us that the Doctor's representation as the Christ figure (as Charles has argued) must always be problematic. Nonetheless, I suggest the Doctor is increasingly understood in Christic terms as the series has progressed — through the "more than a Time Lord" pronouncements of the late-eighties, the overt coding of the TV movie, the troubled Christ figure of the Davies era and the near propitionary sacrifice of Steven Moffat's latest finale, the Doctor increasingly acts as a knowing savior. Humanity now survives *because* of the Doctor.

This need not be a regressive step. Instead, perhaps such considerations allow us to explore the way in which we, as a "postmodern" society, react to the apocalypse. In a recent article, Christopher McMahon has argued that the apocalyptic in science fiction can serve as a particularly useful tool through which to understand the challenges of the twenty-first century, through presenting a discursive space in which the real and fantastic mingle — the ideal space, in other words, to understand the abstractions of theology.[73] If McMahon is right, *Doctor Who*'s reinvention provides just such a creative space in which to examine the complex relationship of religious ideas and reaction to apocalyptic threats facing contemporary society; even more, a lens through which to examine what it means to be human in the face of our own apocalypse. As the show develops in the Steven Moffat era, whatever direction it takes, it will continue to provide further reflections on the hopes of our race to, in the Doctor's words, "outsit eternity."

NOTES

1. I would like to gratefully acknowledge the support of the Irish Research Council for the Humanities and Social Sciences in funding my research.

2. "The Shakespeare Code."

3. See Crawford Gribben, *The Puritan Millennium* (Milton Keynes: Paternoster, 2008).

4. This is made clear by a number of producers: i.e., John Nathan-Turner noted, "There's no substitute for a good story" (John Tulloch and Manuel Alvarado, *Doctor Who: The Unfolding Text* [London: MacMillan, 1983], p.146) and script editor Eric Saward responded to the Buddhist allegory of 1983's "Kinda," "The symbolism ... is there if you can get it... But when children are sitting there, they want a bit of something that will help them along" (Tulloch and Alvarado, *Unfolding Text*, p.267).

5. John R. Hall, *Apocalypse: From Antiquity to the Empire of Modernity* (Malden, MA: Polity, 2009): p.2.

6. Stephen D. O'Leary, *Arguing the Apocalypse: A Theory of Millennial Rhetoric* (Oxford: Oxford University Press, 1994): p.31.

7. Peter Manley Scott, "Are We There Yet? Coming to the End of the Line, a Postnatural Enquiry," pp.265–9 in Stefan Skrimshire, ed., *Future Ethics: Climate Change and the Apocalyptic Imagination* (London: Continuum, 2010): pp. 265–9..

8. Tulloch and Alvarado, *Unfolding Text*, p.77.

9. Hall, *Apocalypse*, p.201.

10. It is worth noting that *Deep Impact* also features the last minute, miraculous destruction of the asteroid. However, the focus of the film, after initial prevention has failed, is on the survival of a minority.

11. "The Invasion" (1968), which features an attempted occupation by the Cybermen and the threat of nuclear destruction, is perhaps the key apocalyptic story of the Troughton era.

12. Some of the more relevant stories, such as 1983's "Warriors of the Deep" (a Cold War allegory) or 1985's "Attack of the Cybermen" (a mess of a story involving Cybermen threatening Earth, among many other plot strands) have been omitted on grounds of space. I am also aware that I have also skipped over a large period of Tom Baker's tenure — the apocalyptic threats of "The Hand of Fear" (1976) and "Logopolis" (1980) both contain interesting ideas but there is not room to discuss them here.

13. It is impossible to disagree with Matt Hills' claim that *Doctor Who* now presents "a multiplatform megatext from which fans and academics can only ever consume a cross section" (Matt Hills, *Triumph of a Time Lord*, [New York: I.B. Tauris, 2010]: p.4).

14. "The Ark."

15. Ibid.

16. Alec Charles, "The Ideology of Anachronism: Television, History and the Nature of Time," in David Butler, ed., *Time and Relative Dissertations in Space* (Manchester: Manchester University Press, 2007), p.115.

17. "The Ark," Episode 3.

18. Ibid., Episode 1.

19. Ibid., Episode 4.

20. "The Ark in Space," Episode 2.

21. A point made by Tulloch and Alvarado, *Unfolding Text*, p.150.

22. "The Ark in Space," Episode 1.

23. Ibid., Episode 3. There is also an allusion here to Paul's command to Timothy to "Guard the good deposit" of faith in 2 Tim. 1:14.

24. Ibid., Episode 1.

25. Tulloch and Alvarado note that this is a distinctly Wellsian inversion (*Unfolding Text*, p.123).

26. "Utopia."

27. "Last of the Time Lords."

28. Ibid.

29. "The Enemy of the World," Episode 4.

30. Ibid., Episode 5.

31. Marc Edward DiPaolo, "Political Satire and British-American Relations in Five Decades of *Doctor Who*," *Journal of Popular Culture* 43:5 (2010), pp.974–7.

32. Hulke was a former Communist party member and was animated by pacifist and environmental concerns. Initially he had wanted to write an allegorical narrative based on Churchill and appeasement (James Chapman, *Inside the TARDIS* [New York: I.B. Tauris, 2006] p.91). For more on Hulke see DiPaolo, p.968.

33. The first episode is titled only "Invasion," a decision that managed to irritate Hulke, and was undermined when the *Radio Times* printed the full title.

34. The sixties and early seventies produced a large number of apocalyptically tinged books on the environmental crisis — for example, Paul Ehlrich's *The Population Bomb* (1968). For more on this see Frederick Buell, "A Short History of Environmental Apocalypse" in Skrimshire, ed., *Future Ethics*, pp.13–36.

35. "Invasion of the Dinosaurs," Episode 2.

36. Ibid., Episode 4.

37. Ibid., Episode 6.

38. "Inferno," Episode 7.

39. "The Curse of Fenric," Episode 3.

40. BBC Archives R9/7/72. I am grateful to Fallon Lee at the BBC Archives for her kindness in providing copies of audience research reports.

41. Chapman, *Inside the TARDIS*, pp.42–44.

42. "The Dalek Invasion of Earth," Episode 6.

43. Ibid., Episode 4.

44. Ibid., Episode 5.

45. "Day of the Daleks," Episode 3.

46. Ibid., Episode 3.

47. Hall, *Apocalypse*, pp.9–17.

48. The Manichean creation narrative is explicit: "Two forces, only good and evil. Then chaos! Time is born, matter, space; the Universe cries out like a new born. The forces shatter as the universe explodes outwards. Only echoes remain. Yet somehow ... somehow, the evil force remains. An intelligence, pure evil." Chapman has commented on similar Manichean representations of evil in the Philip Hinchcliffe (1974–77) and Graham Williams (1977–80) eras (Chapman, *Inside the TARDIS*, pp.117–25).

49. See also Chapman, *Inside the TARDIS*, pp.180–1.

50. *Doctor Who: The Movie*, Matthew Jacobs (W), Geoffrey Sax (D), 1996.

51. Chapman, *Inside the TARDIS*, p.181

52. "Turn Left."

53. "The Christmas Invasion."

54. For more on the link between essential humanity and emotions in the revived series see Anne Cranny-Francis and John Tulloch, "Vaster than Empire(s) and More Slow: The Politics and Economics of Embodiment in *Doctor Who*," in Pat Harrigan and Noah Wardrip-Fruin, eds., *Third Person: Authoring and Exploring Vast Narratives* (Cambridge: MIT Press, 2009), pp.351–55.

55. Tulloch and Alvarado suggest that the hero's role in conventional narrative is "to restore the precious object, to re-establish the consensus" (*Unfolding Text*, p.130). Taken in terms of society as a whole, this is a very limiting role and ignores the possibility for the hero to instigate change in a given situation.

56. Geoff King, *Spectacular Narratives: Hollywood in the Age of the Blockbuster* (New York: I.B. Tauris, 2003):, p.146.

57. Hills, *Triumph*, p.102.

58. Ibid., p.91.

59. Peter Y. Paik, *From Utopia to Apocalypse: Science Fiction and the Politics of Catastrophe* (Minneapolis: University of Minnesota Press, 2010):, p.124.

60. This forgetfulness was commented upon by the seventh Doctor in "Remembrance of the Daleks." Steven Moffat has used this device on a wider scale, with "cracks" in time leading to human forgetfulness about the apocalyptic events they have experienced. The theme has been further used by Moffat in his creation of "The Silence," creatures that are instantly forgotten when seen by humans.

61. "Last of the Time Lords."

62. Russell T. Davies and Benjamin Cook, *Doctor Who, The Writer's Tale: The Final Chapter* (London: BBC Books, 2010):, pp.55–56.

63. See, for example, the "death of God" in *The Second Coming* (2003) or the ironic conclusion to *Torchwood: Miracle Day* (2011) that serves to reverse the usual motif of salvation. Captain Jack Harkness literally sheds his blood to redeem the world; but not, in this case, to defeat death and usher in human immortality, but to allow mortality to return.

64. Vincent O'Brien, "The Doctor or the (Post)Modern Prometheus," in Anthony S. Burdge, Jessica Burke and Kristine Larsen, eds., *The Mythological Dimensions of Doctor Who* (Crawfordville: Kitsune, 2010):, p.197.

65. Dee Amy-Chin has made a persuasive case for the use of Roland Barthes' work in reading the religious imagery and themes found within Davies's *Who*. This is certainly useful in moving us away from an overt focus on intentionality (and thus Davies himself) and exploring the range of meanings contained within the program. See Dee Amy-Chin, "Davies, Dawkins and Deus ex TARDIS: Who finds God in the Doctor?" in Christopher J. Hansen, ed., *Ruminations, Peregrinations, and Regenerations: A Critical Approach to Doctor Who* (Cambridge: Cambridge Scholars, 2010):, pp.22–34.

66. Una McCormack, "He's Not the Messiah: Undermining Political and Religious Authority in New *Doctor Who,*" in Simon Bradshaw, Antony Keen and Graham Sleight, eds., *The Unsilent Library: Essays on the Russell T. Davies Era of the New Doctor Who* (London: The Science Fiction Foundation, 2011): pp.45–62. McCormack's critique of the series is valuable, particularly in highlighting the ambiguity created by the Doctor's intervention in historical events.

67. See Alec Charles, "War Without End? Utopia, the Family, and the Post–9/11 World in Russell T. Davies's *Doctor Who,*" *Science Fiction Studies* 35 (2008): pp.456–9 and Ruth Deller, "What the World Needs Is ... a Doctor," in Courtland Lewis and Paula Smithka, *Doctor Who and Philosophy: Bigger on the Inside* (Chicago: Open Court, 2011): pp.239–48. In "The Waters of Mars" the Doctor takes on the mantle of "Time Lord Victorious," claiming that "the laws of time are mine and they will obey me!" This is shown to have a disastrous impact upon the lives of individuals, with the Doctor eventually admitting that he had been in the wrong. Nonetheless, a parallel could be made with the Doctor's limitation on what he *could* do and a similar self-imposed limitation followed by Christ in his temptation by Satan (i.e., Mt. 4:1–11).

68. Paik, *Utopia to Apocalypse*, pp.126–9.

69. Melody Green, "'It Turns Out They Died for Nothing': *Doctor Who* and the Idea of Sacrificial Death" in Burdge, Burke and Larsen, eds., *Mythological Dimension*, p.118.

70. Slavoj Žižek, *Living in the End Times* (New York: Verso, 2010): pp.61–66. Žižek is writing specifically of the simplification across a series of remakes (*I Am Legend* and *3:10 to Yuma*)—both of which he sees as displaying a move from more complex moral and philosophical position to a simpler (and in terms of *I Am Legend*) specifically Christic representations.

71. These include an episode in part inspired by Hobbes' *Leviathan* ("The Beast Below"); an allegorical exploration of the Middle East peace process that (uniquely) ended without clear resolution ("The Hungry Earth/ Cold Blood"); a sensitive meditation of depression ("Vincent and the Doctor") and the often mind-boggling uses of time travel as a narrative device in the finale itself. Themes explored in Moffat's second season (on going at the time of writing) have included questions on the nature of identity ("The Rebel Flesh/The Almost People") and the humanity ignorance of the true nature of their society ("The Impossible Astronaut/Day of the Moon").

72. The 2011 episode "The God Complex" explored both the dangers of holding too strong a faith in the Doctor and the title character's desire to dictate events. Interestingly, while the Doctor admits that he is "no hero" he is nonetheless responsible for saving companion Amy Pond, defeating a rampaging monster and for making major life decisions for both Amy and husband Rory.

73. Christopher McMahon, "Imaginative Faith: Apocalyptic, Science Fiction Theory and Theology," *Dialog* 47:3 (Fall 2008): 275.

FILMOGRAPHY

Armageddon. John Hensleigh and J.J. Abrams (W), Michael Bay (D). (1998).
The Day After Tomorrow. Roland Emmerich and Jeffery Nachmanoff (W), Roland Emmerich (D). (2004).
Deep Impact. Bruce Joel Rubin and Michael Tolkin (W), Mimi Leder (D). (1998)
Independence Day. Dean Devlin and Roland Emmerich (W), Roland Emmerich (D). (1996).
The War Game. Peter Watkins (W, D). (1965).

A Country Made from Metal?

The "Britishness" of Human-Machine Marriage in Series 31

KATE FLYNN

Robots, cyborgs and automata have made regular appearances in *Doctor Who* over the television program's long history. But the thirty-first series[1] (3 April–26 June 2010) shows a fresh interest in using human-machine relationships to demarcate the culturally approved subject. This essay will analyze one such relationship: Amy Pond's romantic involvement with Rory Williams and his Nestene duplicate.

Amy and Rory are the most recent in a long line of characters to travel as the Doctor's companions. Like most of her female predecessors, Amy provides a point of identification for younger audiences while also offering titillation "for the dads."[2] However the dramatic centrality of her wedding to Rory, followed by her express intention to continue traveling with the Doctor, alters this established dynamic and provides the program with its first pair of married companions. As a consequence, *Doctor Who*'s long standing thematic concern with difference (usually allegorized, as Lindy Orthia points out, as conflict with the alien)[3] is situated anew, within the culturally inflected sites of marriage and family.

Rory's yearning for marriage, family and a domestic space with Amy is marked through dialogue and mise-en-scène as "British." When Amy shows ambivalence to his fantasy of family life she concomitantly shows ambivalence towards "Britishness." I use the terms "British" and "Britishness" here to denote a specific co-construction of nationhood, landscape and history, rather than to invoke an essential identity. Namely, my concern is with the rural idyll as a symbol of nationhood linked to industrial, colonial, and military projects.

The significance of the machine to Britain's industrial and military development informs *Doctor Who*'s visual and linguistic imagery. Both Rory and Amy, in different ways, fail to comply with the idealized "British" subject; their subsequent acculturation is expressed through metaphorical and literal mechanizations of the body, in ways that I will analyze by drawing on Paul Connerton's concepts of embodied memory and forgetting. I have used the word "marriage" with a double meaning—it applies to the socio-legal contract made by Rory and Amy at their wedding, but also applies to the merging of human and machine forms that recurs throughout the series. With regard to Amy, the mechanization is a metaphorical one, and takes the form of pregnancy in a group hallucination sequence central to the episode "Amy's Choice." In Rory's case, the mechanization is literal. He is annihilated in the episode "Cold Blood," but subsequently returns as a mechanical duplicate modeled on Amy's memories by an alien race called the Nestene Consciousness. It will be shown that the program equates both transformations to compliance with "British" ideals.

I enclose "Britishness" in quotation marks to acknowledge the contested nature of the term; there are many alternative constructions of "Britishness," including celebrations of the urban landscape,[4] which could be related fruitfully to the program. These alternative constructions do not, however, fall within the scope of this essay. My main focus is on Series 31's relationship to the ideological assumptions of idealized rurality. The historical influences upon this relationship, as manifest in the program's portrayal of Leadworth village, will be our starting point.

Leadworth — A Rural Idyll?

Rory's home of Leadworth is first named thirty minutes into "The Eleventh Hour," when the Doctor, freshly regenerated and unsure of how to thwart an imminent alien attack, expresses frustration with the local amenities. The Doctor rushes to Leadworth's center, giving us the opportunity to glimpse stone houses, a half timbered pub, and the local post office. Birdsong plays on the soundtrack. We see a passing cyclist, an ice cream seller, and a duck pond on the village green. Amy informs the Doctor that Gloucester is "half an hour away by car,"[5] locating the action in the South West of England. Despite this snippet of geography, the Doctor leaves us in no doubt that Leadworth is archetypal — it is "the"[6] English village, complete with a definite article.

Leadworth is a far cry from Rose Tyler's council estate. On the original air date the contrast seemed particularly striking, perhaps because Rose had recently — albeit briefly — returned to the program. "The Eleventh Hour" is the opening episode for Series 31. It was preceded by 2010's New Year Special "The End of Time," wherein Rose's concrete tower block loomed large during the tenth Doctor's final scenes.[7] Foregrounding rural iconography at the start of the thirty-first series thus signals a thematic departure from Russell T. Davies' period as executive producer. *Doctor Who*'s newly incumbent producer, Steven Moffat, explicitly promoted the program's potential to "teach our children that there are things in the world that might want to eat them."[8] His desire to permeate supposedly safe places with horror is well served by a village setting. Depictions of the pastoral in art and literature have a long history, stretching back to Theocritus' *Idylls* in the third century B.C.E.; but positive associations between, specifically, childhood and English rurality have more recent origins.

The idealization of English rural landscapes saw particular intensification with the emergence of an urban middle class during Britain's industrial revolution. Christine Berberich attributes the intensification to nineteenth century industrialists, who constructed the countryside as a refuge from urban living and sought to emulate the English gentry by relocating to country estates at the earliest opportunity.[9] Middle-class responses to growing separation between family and working life saw rural spaces simultaneously constructed as a safe, domestic, feminine idyll in which to raise children. According to the ideology of the rural idyll, a woman alone in a "big, empty house" doesn't, as the Doctor pronounces of Amy, "make any sense."[10] Leonore Davidoff argues that nineteenth century constructions of the idyll legitimated certain gendered power relations; women's proper place was deemed to be a safe "interior," to which the male head of household could return from worldly tribulations.[11] I would add that intersecting power relations positioned children as subordinate, and the family as heteronormative, in this hierarchical cordoning of rural and domestic space.

Via the fiction of George MacDonald, Frances Hodgson Burnett, Kenneth Grahame, Enid Blyton, Arthur Ransome and Richmal Crompton — not to mention their twentieth and twenty-first century television adaptations — associations between the rural idyll and idyllic childhoods have been perpetuated. Leadworth, with its interdimensional parent-swallowing crack in time, escaped alien prisoner, and risk of obliteration by the Atraxi, instills a safe space with threat: to paraphrase Moffat, the village is peopled with creatures that might want to eat you. The potency of the threat relies on prior assumptions regarding the idyll's qualities as a refuge. As such, Leadworth can be related to David Bell's "anti-idyll" in which the cozy "armchair countryside" constructed by tourist leaflets and Sunday night historical dramas is contested by a horrific "behind the sofa countryside."[12]

Doctor Who's relocation to a rural setting serves a second thematic purpose entwined with Leadworth's threat to the young. Unlike Bell's anti-idyll, Leadworth does not position victims as urban and the aggressor as rural. Rather, Leadworth is positioned as a symbol of nationhood, and its horrors allow ambivalence to be expressed towards "Britishness" as a collective identity. Prior to the airing of Series 31, Moffat's Scottish origins were regularly mentioned both in the press and online,[13] typically with reference to his pursuit of a "Scottish agenda." Most incarnations of the Doctor have presented as English. The seventh Doctor was played by Sylvester McCoy with his own Scottish accent, but more recently David Tennant was dissuaded from doing so. Tennant reported that Davies did not want the Doctor's accent to "tour the regions"[14] after Christopher Ecclestone's distinctive Lancashire delivery in Series 27. The casting of Matt Smith marked a return to received pronunciation, but Moffat expressed excitement in pre-publicity at the casting of Inverness-born Karen Gillan as Amy; she would be, he speculated, the program's "secret weapon."[15]

Such a context makes the thirty-first series uniquely interesting in its ambivalence towards an implicitly Anglocentric, classed "Britishness." Orthia[16] has argued that earlier series of *Doctor Who* adopt an essentialist view of humanity, within which harmonious cosmopolitanism is presented as the default; structural oppression is largely ignored; and racism assumes the status of a correctable blip. I would suggest that Series 31 continues in this tradition, and does so with an associated Eurocentrism. However, the series expresses unease with "Britishness" by focusing on what might be thought of as internal others. Scotland is implicated as an aggressor in Britain's colonialist history, but is simultaneously marginalized within cultural and political constructions of "Britishness"; thus, like several of the subject positions explored in this chapter, to be Scottish is to be both inside and outside the culturally approved norm.

Why is Leadworth a suitable setting for pursuing Moffat's "Scottish agenda"? We may answer this question by addressing how previously local, class-based constructions of rural England acquired greater currency. To be clear, Scotland has its own rural myth, which Annie Morgan James traces to the marginalization of Highlanders after Scotland's union with England in 1707. She argues that the highland landscape was thereafter represented in art and literature as "the last great wilderness"[17] — a space associated with enchantment, and the resurrection of legendary heroes, which was appropriated for pleasure by British imperialists (including lowland Scottish elites). Scottish landscapes are conspicuously absent from Series 31, but *Doctor Who* shows the continued influence of Scotland's rural myth in at least one recent example of spin-off material.

Stephen Cole's *The Ring of Steel*,[18] the second of as yet five audio stories to include

Amy and the eleventh Doctor, is set in the Orkney Islands.[19] Though rural, Orkney has none of Leadworth's misleading gentility. The terrain is described as "wild" and "bleak,"[20] in compliance with stereotypes of Scotland as a wilderness. Intriguingly, Orkney is positioned as a liminal place of uncertain nationhood. The Doctor makes a disparaging comment that the island is "not even sure if it's Scottish or Norwegian,"[21] effacing, in the process, the degree to which any national identity is mutually constitutive of other identities. Series 31 questions the validity of such effacements while, to some extent, still enacting them. Leadworth is a potent setting for problematizing "Britishness" precisely because of historical tendencies to singularly equate British nationhood with English nationhood. The English rural idyll's ascent as a symbol of "Britishness" was facilitated by the Victorian landed classes. Their role in colonial administration, Michael Woods argues, was characterized by nostalgia for the English estates they had left behind; in practical terms their involvement in establishing the British Empire lent aristocratic, Anglocentric constructions of "Britishness" a global reach.[22] By imbuing the archetypal English village with threat, Moffat expresses ambivalence towards century-old constructions of "Britishness." He expresses ambivalence, rather than hostility, insofar as Series 31 perpetuates the cultural invisibility of non–English Britain. For one thing, the fictional Leadworth is not really "half an hour" from Gloucester at all; filming took place in Llandaff, Wales.

Nearly all the action of Series 31 takes place in English[23] settings. Only two episodes deviate from pattern—"The Hungry Earth" and "Cold Blood." Both installments, which form a two-part story, transplant the action to Cwmtaff in Wales. Appropriately enough the plot concerns conflicting claims to land. Negotiations between the human villagers above ground, and the reptilian or Silurian race below, end in failure; the latter group is placed in stasis for a thousand years in hope of "future harmony."[24] Such a pessimistic allegory is consistent with the series' questioning of what is concealed, and what is emphasized, in a collective identity where constituent communities may not be equally powerful or visible; we might surmise that someone, in allegedly unifying constructions of "Britishness," is kept "underground."

Unlike "the" English village of Leadworth, Welsh villages have explicit industrial connotations for viewers in Britain. The drill that disturbs the Silurians is initially identified by the Doctor as a "big mining thing,"[25] consistent with Wales' historical involvement with coal mining. "The Hungry Earth" thus incorporates geographically specific industrial discourses. This trait is shared by *The Ring of Steel*, wherein Orkney's landscape is ravaged by a species of steel creatures known as the "Caskelliac." When the Caskelliac overturn the roads, traces of bitumen leak from the earth,[26] and the creatures themselves share their biological makeup with oil[27]; such imagery implicitly evokes Orkney's proximity to the oil rigs of the North Sea. It is interesting, furthermore, that the machines in both texts are military, as well as industrial constructs; the Silurians perceive the drill as a "weapon"[28] while the Caskelliac claim to have been originally created as "weapons of war."[29]

References to weaponry are pertinent to the merging of humanity and the machine that we see elsewhere in the thirty-first series. Martin J. Weiner points out that, although the first and second world wars helped to drain imperialist fervor in the twentieth century, the English rural idyll remained a powerful symbol of "Britishness" because it came to be opposed in the public imagination against experience of "martial horrors."[30] Whether in war poetry, recruitment posters or political speeches, the country that "British" soldiers fought for was made synonymous with rural England. The English rural idyll, constructed as a refuge from industry and, later, from war, has an oppositional relationship to machinery that the aforementioned Welsh and Scottish landscapes do not. While machines may provoke fear in the Silurians or the residents of Orkney, machinery is also, literally, part of the scenery.

The oppositional pairing of martial horror and English rural idylls still informs media representations of the first and second world wars today. It informs the characterization of Edwin Bracewell, whose ambiguous relationship to the rural idyll foreshadows, in microcosm, the negotiations Amy (as a fellow Scot) and Rory (as a fellow machine) must make when resisting or complying with particular cultural norms. In "Victory of the Daleks," Bracewell is initially introduced as a Scottish professor of science. When he is also revealed to be a cyborg, he reacts with shock. "I can remember things," he cries out. "So many things. The last war. The squalor and the mud and the awful, awful misery of it all. What am I? What am I?"[31]

In fact, he is a Dalek bomb implanted with another person's memories of war. The Doctor deduces that Bracewell must adopt these false memories as his own; if Bracewell believes he is human, he will not detonate. He is encouraged by the Doctor to recollect a childhood in surroundings closely comparable to Leadworth: "My family ran the Post Office. It's a little place just near the Abbey. Just by the ash trees."[32] This attempt to deactivate Bracewell fails, unsurprisingly. For why would reiterating the symbolism of Anglocentric rural idylls and military machines humanize Bracewell, rather than reinforce his mechanization? Even as a stand-alone image, the ash trees of Bracewell's recollection are a curious conflation of rural and military associations; their name derives from the Old English word *æsc*, meaning spear.

Bracewell is finally saved by Amy — who, significantly, is also Scottish. "Hey ... Paisley," she asks, using a nickname that refers to his Scottish origins; "Ever fancied someone you know you shouldn't?"[33] Her mode of address favors their common Scottishness over the Anglocentric recollections the Doctor tries to elicit, and her question prioritizes memories one "shouldn't" have, over a socio-culturally approved narrative of ash trees, Post Offices and the trenches. Bracewell is thus able to contain the military function that co-constructions of rurality and martial endeavor would have him fulfill.

Nevertheless, Amy's question does not fully circumnavigate the values of the rural idyll. Bracewell "proves"[34] he is human by yearning for a woman with eyes "like the last touch of sunset on the edge of the world."[35] The image constructs links between femininity, the landscape and refuge, which are situated in a narrative of heterosexual desire. When, subsequently, Rory's Nestene duplicate must "prove" his humanity by loving Amy, comparable links are constructed between gender role conformity, the land and heteronormativity. In the remaining sections of this chapter I will analyze how these links relate to "Britishness."

Rory: Soldier, Machine, Man

The discovery that Edwin Bracewell is not human prompts a response from Winston Churchill. "I don't give a damn if you're a machine," he states. "Are you a man?"[36] His question assumes that the two categories are not mutually exclusive. I would suggest that the program's co-construction of masculinity and cultural memories of combat makes the two categories, if anything, interdependent. This is highly relevant to Rory's mechanization, masculinization and militarization.

Rory is initially introduced as a local nurse. In the first episode of the series he appears as Amy's "kind of" boyfriend[37]; four episodes and two diegetic years later, he is re-introduced to the audience as her fiancé.[38] The plot of "Amy's Choice" concerns a group hallucination in which Amy, Rory and the Doctor envision their lives five years hence. As the title indicates, the hallucination clarifies Amy's aspirations, but Rory's hopes are also foregrounded. He fantasizes of expecting a child with Amy, and working as a doctor in the community of "Upper Leadworth." The cottage where Amy awaits the birth of their child is a source of great contentment to him: "We relax, we live, we listen to the birds."[39] He considers Upper Leadworth to be "a sweet little village,"[40] and when confronted with the unreality of their hallucination, protests: "I want the other life. You know, where we're happy and settled and about to have a baby."[41] He indicates the interrelation of idealized landscapes and idealized family life when he repeats "I just wanted a nice village and a family."[42]

Inevitably, Rory's choice of fantasy job implies a sense of competition with *the* Doctor. But the gap between his fantasy and his day-to-day life also indicates how greatly Rory's character departs from the masculinities constructed elsewhere in the programme. When the Doctor comments that Rory has imagined "Your dream wife, your dream job, probably your dream baby,"[43] the familial role that Rory aspires to is implicitly linked to his work role, and both are implicitly linked to a regulation of his gender performance. Nursing in Britain has not, traditionally, been seen as a masculine profession.[44] Rory is not an adventurer, like the Doctor, with all the imperialist trappings that might imply; nor is he a soldier, as Bracewell recollects himself to be. He is a nurse, and therefore fulfils a nurturing role — quite at odds with the gender ideology of the rural idyll, wherein the man of the household is aligned with the public sphere, and the emotional interior is a refuge to be returned to rather than his proper place.

The waking, un-fantasizing Rory seems wary of public influence. He is, for instance, distrustful of the Doctor's authority: "It's not that you make people take risks," he observes. "It's that you make them want to impress you. You make it so they don't want to let you down. You have no idea how dangerous you make people to themselves when you're around."[45] This wariness does not exclude physical bravery — Rory shows no hesitation in helping the volatile Restac,[46] or in protecting the Doctor from a murder attempt at his own expense.[47] And yet his timidity is the butt of humor throughout Series 31, in scenarios that reify troubling gender stereotypes of shrill women and emasculated men. At the hospital where Rory works, the female doctor supervising him dismisses his concerns about patients with exasperated phrases such as "For God's sake" and "Yes, I know"[48]; Amy undermines him with her refusal to acknowledge their relationship[49]; and when he must don a disguise in Venice, her insistence that he pretends to be her eunuch brother while the Doctor impersonates her partner is made with demeaning overtones.[50] The program thus alternates between validating Rory's nurturing qualities and positioning him through intended humor as the henpecked boyfriend to Amy's shrew. This vacillation persists in the depiction of Rory's wish to be a doctor. On the one hand, to be a doctor accommodates his nurturing characteristics while endowing him greater authority; on the other, his masculinity continues to be mocked by Amy and the Doctor. Either way, *Doctor Who* suggests that the fantasy role of husband in the rural idyll demands greater public status than Rory-as-Nurse possesses.

Amy's assessment of the village's reality is portrayed as partly dependent on Rory's gender performance (and the consequent likelihood of her marrying him). The Dream Lord, a projection of the Doctor's psyche, attempts to encourage Amy's doubts by asking, "You ran away with a handsome hero. Would you really give him up for a bumbling country doctor?"[51] Although she winces at the question, she has previously joined the Doctor's mockery of Rory in, for instance, laughing at the ponytail Rory wears.[52] The crux of the humor is that Rory's ponytail is neither "cool"[53] nor "interesting"[54] when he believes it to be so. In short, his hairstyle is an inadequate gesture of nonconformity. Their mockery is based on class markers, for Rory's ponytail represents the pretension of an affluent man effecting rebellion; but intersecting associations between femininity and long hair endow the removal of his ponytail with additional meaning. After he cuts his hair[55] the resultant short-back-and-sides complies more closely with "British" middle class masculinity. His explanation that he wants to cut his hair "for"[56] Amy foreshadows another, more serious gendered sacrifice. The principle of laying down one's life as a tenet of military masculinity was established in "Victory of the Daleks"; no sooner has Bracewell's humanity been "proven" by his recollections of lost love, than one of the incidental characters, Miss Breen, appears crying because "her young man didn't make it."[57] Rory's compliance with this protective masculine role is secured by his death in Upper Leadworth. Just as the ponytail's removal prompts Amy's protestation that she "was starting to like it,"[58] Rory's mortal sacrifice elicits another change of heart. "I didn't know," Amy tells the Doctor. "I didn't, I didn't, I honestly didn't, till right now. I just want him ... I love Rory."[59]

The development of Amy and Rory's love story complies with the gendered ideology of the rural idyll — so how are we to interpret Upper Leadworth's *anti*-idyllic qualities? Do they mean we should view Amy and Rory's burgeoning relationship with suspicion? Rory initially believes Upper Leadworth is "just so tranquil and relaxed. Nothing bad could ever happen here"[60]— but as in "The Eleventh Hour," we are ultimately led to fear the village. Far from comprising an idyllic setting to raise a family, all the village children are incinerated by the Eknodines, an alien race residing parasitically in the bodies of old people.

There are extra-textual references, too, which undermine the desirability of the rural idyll. "Amy's Choice" was written by Simon Nye, creator of *How Do You Want Me*—a sitcom in which the Irish comedian Dylan Moran experiences various trials, including death threats, when forced to relocate to a small English village by his country wife. Predictably, given the demonstrable failings of the "idyll," Amy soon re-expresses skepticism at the likelihood of a lasting relationship with Rory. Despite realizing she loves him, she is shocked to see their future selves holding hands on a distant hill at the start of "The Hungry Earth." "We're still together after ten years?" she asks. "After everything we've seen, we just drop back into our old lives, the nurse and the kissogram?"[61]

The catalyst for her change of heart is Rory's transformation into a mechanical duplicate. In a second mortal sacrifice — which this time is not undone by waking up from a "dream"[62]— Rory protects the Doctor from an assassination attempt. Rory is shot, and the wound prevents his escape from an inter-dimensional crack in time which wipes his existence from the universe. In an attempt to trap the Doctor, the Nestene Consciousness recreates Rory as a cybernetic Roman Centurion. Possessing Rory's memories and a conviction of his own human nature, he tries to remind Amy of his previous role in her life.

As with Edwin Bracewell, Rory's "humanity"[63] is contested by his new physical form — they are both built to be weapons, and possess debatable bodily autonomy. As with Bracewell, Rory's "humanity" is proven by his love for a woman. This is made clear when the Doctor voices exasperation and grudging admiration of Rory's "human"[64] wish to ensure Amy's safety. However, Rory and Bracewell have subtly different relationships with the rural idyll, and this is expressed through the details of their mechanization. Anglocentric recollections don't halt the countdown to Bracewell's detonation, but nor do they trigger it. For Rory, the idyll plays a much more active role in his dangerousness. Against Rory's will, the Nestene

Consciousness use a gun concealed in his hand to shoot Amy. The gun is a fairly obvious phallic symbol, and in this scenario constructs relationships between male embodiment, heterosexual desire and military masculinity. Crucially, when Rory kneels before Amy in his armor, she identifies him as "Rory Williams from Leadworth."[65] Her reference to the village where he grew up indicates that his machine form, by militarizing him, correctly orientates him to the rural idyll: the idyll is the safe space the soldier comes from, which sustains what Bracewell would call the "misery" of war. Recollections of the idyll reassert that Rory occupies the oppositional sphere of martial horror, and his role is to kill. His gun fires at exactly the point Amy states, "You remember. This is you. And you are staying."[66] His gender performance is thus brought into compliance, via mechanization, with the "British" culturally-approved subject.

The Doctor places Amy's corpse in a restorative box called the Pandorica. As an act of penance and devotion, Rory guards her for the two thousand years that must elapse before she is revived. His mechanized body consequently facilitates strength and endurance that his human body could not accommodate. The earlier use of sexist humor regarding Rory's status as a "eunuch" and the fact he is rewarded with Amy's final capitulation to a village marriage (despite his shooting her) suggest this is a celebratory fantasy of military masculinity. Certainly it might be enjoyed as such by an implied male viewer strongly aware of "British" cultural memories of war but with no personal experience of combat. Bracewell's experience of possessing "someone else's stolen thoughts"[67] could be said to reflect the experience of an audience long familiar with other people's images of "the Great War." Nevertheless there is little to envy in the experience of Series 31's military men. The death of the soldiers aboard the Byzantium, for instance — which also involves a mechanization of their bodies, this time by the Weeping Angels — emphasizes that they "died afraid, in pain and alone."[68]

An alternative interpretation might treat the series' sexist humor as grist to the mill of challenging "Britishness." Understood this way, marriage to Amy is no reward at all, but simply another marker of compliance with "British" values to be questioned. The close relationship between the rural idyll, marriage and the nuclear family as "British" institutions is mirrored by a distrust of all three constructs that the program expresses, problematically, through gender stereotyping. This is not to suggest that Amy's portrayal is one-dimensional. Far from it; her dramatic trajectory is considerably more complex than Rory's. While his transformation finally leads to consequences he has long sought, Amy is shown to have more to lose by conforming to the idyll.

Amy is Scottish rather than English, and is not portrayed as fully adult, in addition to being disadvantaged by the rural idyll's gender binary. Rory is relatively unencumbered in comparison. Mechanization brings Rory privileges, albeit with a loss of autonomy, whereas Amy must abdicate key aspects of her identity and forgo her original aspirations to comply with the ideology of the idyll. In the next section, I will examine Amy's relationship to the rural idyll as a non–English character, how this relationship is implicated in Series 31's narrative development as Amy's coming of age story, and how her coming of age is portrayed as an acculturation through metaphorical mechanizations of her body.

Amy: Record and Replicate

At the opening of "The Beast Below," the Doctor looks over a vast starship emblazoned with a Union Jack and remarks, "It's Britain, but metal."[69] This is the only explicit reference to "Britain" made throughout the series, and it hinges on the presence of the flag. The ship resembles an oval landmass beneath a cluster of grey buildings, several of which are labeled with the names of English counties. Welsh and Scottish counties are conspicuously absent.[70] Without the Union Jack, the Doctor's certainty in proclaiming, "It's Britain" would seem misplaced — he might more accurately state, "It's England" (although note that the ship's Anglocentrism does contain some ambiguity, for none of the English place names are specific to the British Isles: Yorkshire, Surrey, Devon, and Kent can also be found in former British colonies). We might therefore take the Union Jack as a nodal point for understanding how this series of *Doctor Who* constructs "Britishness."

Patriotic displays of the national flag are relatively rare in Great Britain compared to countries such as the United States. By way of explaining this tendency, Susanne Reichl's examination of ambivalence towards the Union Jack cites an appropriation by hooligans and racist far right groups.[71] I would add, however, that the Union Jack has a long history of serving colonial strategies abroad[72] which may also contribute to contemporary reluctance to wave the flag. The reluctance seems specific to overt displays of patriotism. At the time of writing, mainstream retailers in Britain such as Marks and Spencer and Tesco continue to stock a wide range of goods decorated with the Union Jack, including fridges, rugs, dresses, pencil cases, hair straighteners and guitars amongst other items; this would suggest a continued public identification with the flag, in the ostensibly less controversial arena of consumer choice. Within such a context, *Doctor Who*'s use of the Union Jack must carry multiple meanings. Are we to read the flag as an expression of patriotism or does its presence signify that the *Doctor Who* franchise, like fridges, rugs, and pencil cases, is regarded as an innocuous consumer good? Both and neither; I would argue that the flag is used to place questions of nationhood at the forefront of the program's visual language, in full knowledge of the Union Jack's contradictory meanings. One advantage of this interpretation is its consistency with "The Beast Below's" ambivalence towards imperialist trappings. After all, Amy learns that Scotland has departed on its own ship,[73] and by the end of the episode, the British Queen is forced to abdicate.[74] Alongside such plot developments it is hard to read the flag's presence as a patriotic statement.

Patriotic symbol or no, the flag is ubiquitous. When Amy and the Doctor board Starship U.K. — as this "country made from metal" is known — the interior is festooned with Union Jacks. What's more, certain photographic choices make the flag hard to ignore. In particular, I wish to comment on the color grading that characterizes the ship's interior, which is both drawn from and accentuates appearances of the Union Jack.

Scenes set in the TARDIS are usually color graded in warm shades of orange; conversely, the village of Leadworth, Starship U.K. and the wartime bunkers in "Victory of the Daleks" are shot in cooler blue shades, with deeply saturated red accents. Amy herself tones into this environment. She typically dresses in scarlet and navy blue. The palette allows Amy to be related to several seemingly disparate cultural archetypes. Our first glimpse of Amy — as a seven-year-old, parentless child referred to by the more formal name Amelia — shows her praying at her bedside.[75] She is posed as a supplicant. A cheat shot allows us to see a shaft of moonlight on the wall behind her, rather than the bedstead that should be rightfully there. The moonbeam appears to fall from Amelia's forehead, and this, in combination with the scene's red and blue hues, is strongly suggestive of Renaissance images of the Madonna. Amelia is also associated with the folkloric: for instance when she first emerges from the trees outside her house, dressed in a red cardigan, she evokes Red Riding Hood.[76] As she ages the iconography associated with her grows more sexualized. The teenage Amy becomes a kissogram, and her reported guises of nurse, nun and police woman[77] continue to comply with the color scheme: nurses, nuns and police women are recognized by their blue clothing. Of course Amy's off-screen adoption of such personae is also, we can assume, "blue" in the sexual sense. Finally, while undergoing the rite of passage that is her wedding, dressed in a white bridal gown and surrounded by red balloons, she is prompted, at the Doctor's prior arrangement, to remember him by the rhyme "something old, something new, something borrowed, something blue."[78] The phrase is explicitly used to describe the TARDIS, but might equally describe the cultural iconography surrounding Amy.

These varied guises inform Series 31 as a coming of age story,[79] in which Amy must "grow up"[80] by "choosing"[81] from a range of potential identities. Amy is variously depicted as a hypersexual teenager who is "still such a child inside,"[82] a young adult resistant to pressure to "grow up" and start a family in a "nice village,"[83] a willing rural bride, and a potential mother—all in a visual palette drawn from the Union Jack. The color grading connects her seemingly individual negotiation of identity to questions of nationhood, by accentuating icons of "Britishness" from pillar boxes[84] to telephone booths,[85] and London Underground signs[86] to, of course, numerous appearances of the national flag.[87]

Amy's contiguity with the Union Jack palette emphasizes that she is "British." Yet there are repeated references to her outsider status, for—unlike the rural idyll of Leadworth or the counties that float atop of the Starwhale—she is not English. When the Doctor looks around Leadworth and complains, "Where's the rest of it?"[88] he tacitly refers not only to the insularity of the village, but to the absence of other "British" landscapes, and, by implication, of other "British" identities. Unsurprisingly, the Doctor interprets Amy's accent as a sign that she does not belong in Leadworth any more than he does: "You're the Scottish girl in the English village, and I know how that feels."[89] The conflict is also suggested by her appearance: her red hair, while in harmony with the color grading, is also a stereotypical marker of Scottishness. Amy is simultaneously dislocated from, and in keeping with, her environs.

The disjoint is further emphasized by Amy's ongoing memory loss. The Doctor expresses horror[90] that she cannot recall any of the alien invasions with which the world[91] has been afflicted. A crack in the fabric of time is said to be the cause; yet Amy's capacity to remember events is always out of synchronization with others who might be similarly affected. A comparison of her memory loss with Rory's is indirectly illustrative of this point. When the Doctor "resets" the universe, Amy's memories are used to restore Rory to what we assume is his human self. The distinction between human Rory and his Nestene duplicate seems clear enough, until, in a passing comment at their reception, Rory indicates he remembers when he "was plastic."[92] The fabula does not indicate why he should recall this. Assuming the distinction between Rory and his duplicate is meaningful—and that future episodes will not deny he has ever been human—his continuity of consciousness indicates that Rory remembers considerably more than he should be able to. By contrast, Amy's memories are repeatedly unavailable to her, even when they are experienced by her at a bodily level. Her grieving for Rory,[93] and latterly for the Doctor,[94] is embodied without being retained in her conscious recollection: she cries and feels sadness without knowing why.

But Rory, of course, is English, and Amy is not. Amy's centrality to the drama makes it difficult to detach what the Doctor calls a "collapse" of history from her particular cultural position.[95] Indeed, a child on Starship U.K. demonstrates the link between being an approved cultural subject and articulating an approved history when she asks the Doctor, "How do you not know about this? Are you Scottish too?"[96] As a result, Amy's memory loss seems symptomatic of a cultural disconnect. Her coming-of-age tale must therefore track not only her progress from Amelia the orphaned child to Amy the bride and prospective mother. Her coming of age must also involve a cultural assimilation, in which she comes to possess an approved history. It is here that the image of the machine becomes highly relevant.

In the episode of Amy's first appearance, "The Eleventh Hour," earthly machines are used primarily to survey, record and replicate. The Atraxi, a galactic police force of aliens resembling giant eyeballs, circle the Earth with the intention of destroying the planet if an escaped prisoner is not found. In thwarting them, the Doctor commandeers a laptop to hack into a conference call of world leaders; expresses disdain for the villagers' rush to video-phone the aliens' arrival; and attracts the Atraxi's attention by replicating a figure zero (the prisoner's name) across every functioning screen in the world.[97] These images derive much of their force from concerns about surveillance and civil liberties surrounding Britain's Labor government, who at the airdate were preparing for a general election. Nonetheless they also provide a context for considering Amy's transformation into the approved subject.

According to Connerton, machines of this type allow information to be stored, replicated and retrieved without our continued involvement: they are used for "inscribing practices,"[98] as opposed to "incorporated practices" where memory is embodied in culturally inflected postures and behaviors. Amy's incorporated practices are constructed by the programme as foreign to the Southern English rural idyll of Leadworth: this is implied in comments made by the Doctor regarding "that accent"[99] and imperatives to act out particular stereotypes such as "You're Scottish — fry something."[100] As a corollary the pressure to assimilate is suggested through Amy's bodily vulnerability; like the machines that store, replicate and retrieve, she becomes a site for "inscribing practices."

First, she is a site for storage. The Weeping Angels "climb inside"[101] her eye as a means of preserving their image, in a process that leads the Doctor to describe her as a machine from which he must "pull the plug."[102] (To my English eyes, this metaphor seems culturally inflected because the statues' design is reminiscent of Anglican rather than Catholic or Scottish Presbyterian churches.) The Doctor, too, does his fair share of inscribing. When Amy is revived from death during the series finale, Amy comments that he has left "a message in [her] head like [she's] an answer phone"[103]: a seemingly benign invasion on the Doctor's part, the meaning of which is nevertheless shaped by this incarnation of the Doctor presenting as English. The Doctor also makes use of her inscrutability when he recounts the "Something Blue" rhyme during her sleep.[104] Amy is not the only internal other to show this bodily vulnerability. The soldier Bob, one of few characters in the entirety of the series who speaks with a regional accent rather than Received Pronunciation, has his cerebral cortex stripped and reanimated so that the Weeping Angels might use his voice to address the Doctor through walkie-talkies.[105]

Second, Amy is a site for retrieval. Her memories are ransacked at two key points in the narrative. At the end of "The Pandorica Opens," River Song discovers that material generated from Amy's own inscribed practices — in the form of photographs, pictures and writing — has been manipulated by the Nestene Consciousness to duplicate Rory.[106] An episode later, when the Doctor "resets" the universe, Amy's memories are used to restore Leadworth.[107] The centrality of her memories to ending or saving the world might constitute a position of power, but in neither situation is Amy aware that her memories have been drawn upon. In both cases the retrieval processes are thus most fruitfully read as an example of cultural and gendered erasure: her contribution is made invisible, to herself and to the other characters if not to the audience.

Finally Amy is a site for replication. Her hallucinatory pregnancy is constructed as reproductive — not only biologically, but culturally. Prospective motherhood is emblematic of her embodied acculturation to English village life. She asserts her pregnancy's unreality in terms of her resistance to the domestic interior, and the rural idyll: "Not really me, is it? Would I be happy settling down in a place with a pub, two shops and a really bad amateur dramatics society?" The degree to which pregnancy is constructed as a mechanization of her body, and the relationship of that mechanization to "Britishness," forms the focus of the next section.

"A thing in the belly of that ship"

Amy describes her pregnant body as a "boat,"[108] evoking River Song's warning about the Byzantium in "The Time of Angels": "there's a thing in the belly of that ship."[109] The Byzantium is not the only ship to carry a "thing" in its "belly." Starship U.K. bears the tortured Starwhale who "British" inhabitants repeatedly choose to "forget."[110] These two associations help to illuminate how Amy's pregnancy embodies her cultural position.

First, both associations imply her body is a machine harboring an alien. If she is aligned with, specifically, the Byzantium harboring Weeping Angels in its "belly" — the "thing" that, according to River, "can't ever die"[111] — Amy can be read as carrying an English child, perpetuating the values of the British Empire, and thus fulfilling her role in the rural idyll. In support of this interpretation, the "boat" reference aligns Amy with foundation myths in which boats, and pregnancy, figure as motifs. One salient example is the story of Albina, which was deployed with political intent in opposition to Scottish foundation myths that circulated during strained Anglo-Scottish relations in the thirteenth century.[112] Albina, who is characterized as a promiscuous woman, arrives in an uninhabited England after being cast out on the ocean. Her fraternization with demons leads her, alongside her sisters, to give birth to a race of giants that populate Britain. This chronologically remote text gains immediacy when we examine the pseudo-mythology surrounding the Nestene Consciousness in *Doctor Who* spin-off material.

In the novel *Synthespians*, Nestene duplicates (or Autons) are engineered by the progeny of a Lovecraftian character known as Shub-Niggurath. The Doctor recounts what he calls "a universal race memory"[113] of her arrival: "At the dawn of time — and by that, I mean the beginning of the universe — a creature known only as Shub-Niggurath emerged into our universe.... She manifested herself on a planet trillions of light years from here, and gave birth before the end."[114] It is the Nestene Consciousness she gives birth to. Shub-Niggurath's narrative of migration, pregnancy and birth shares motifs with the Albina myth, but mechanizes Albina's monstrous offspring. In novels such as *Doctor Who and the Terror of the Autons*, the Nestene Consciousness attempt to colonize other planets by inhabiting, variously, telephone cords[115] and radio waves.[116] The Nestene also, of course, animate humanoid autons[117]; Rory's mechanization and militarization is Series 31's example of the same process, placing Rory's duplicate in a genealogy of migrant mothers, founders of nations, and colonizers.

Inserting Amy into a comparable narrative arc imbues her pregnancy with questions of nationhood. Her pregnant body comprises an example of English inscription; but the possibility of pregnancy as an incorporated practice is also raised, when Amy encounters Vincent Van Gogh. The TARDIS endows him with a Scottish accent, and he, conversely, takes Amy to be Dutch.[118] He proposes marriage, suggesting that if they marry they "will have children by the dozen!"[119] Although smitten, she declines the offer.[120] Despite the conservative gender role her acceptance would place her in, Van Gogh's offer accommodates the complexity of her own national identity, implies there are commonalities across different cultures and, moreover, does so without suggesting national identities are essential. But the reason for her refusal — an embodied grief for Rory's death that she does not, consciously, remember — testifies to the split nature of her national identification and the complexities of its articulation.

There is a further, fruitful interpretation of Amy's pregnant body available. By connecting Amy's body to Starship U.K., rather than the Byzantium, we can align her with the "country made from metal" that relies on unseen, "alien" labor. We may thus view the "thing" in her belly as a colonized other. This seems counter-intuitive, given the range of previous images that position Amy as an outsider, but may be contextualized by Scotland's substantial role in extending the British Empire. Heidi J. Nast argues that the co-emergence of industrialization, the nuclear family, and colonization in Africa and Asia, is suggestive of a nostalgic desire to rescue the remnants of a declining monarchical order with colonial royal subjects who were structurally infantilized through "race."[121] In a family-state analogy, this would position Amy's pregnant body as "Mother Britain." But who is the colonized, infantilized other upon whose labor she relies? Here the reference to the "country made from metal" becomes newly useful. The Doctor observes of another Mother Britain, Starship U.K., that the machine is not just a ship but "an idea. That's a whole country, living and laughing and" — he pauses — "shopping."[122] Shopping is an incongruous addition to his index of the country's defining characteristics, unless consumerism is acknowledged as the site of "British" neo-colonialism. The commodification of "Britishness," exemplified in the earlier examples of consumer goods marked with the Union Jack, is underpinned by an exploited labor force in the global East.[123] That exploitation involves not only what Nast would call structural infantilization, but the extensive use of child workers.[124]

The advantage of this reading is its consistency with the terms used by the Doctor to justify intervening, or not, in the lives of the peoples he visits. "You never interfere in the affairs of other people or planets, unless there are children crying," Amy speculates.[125] But at over nine hundred years of age, the Doctor has considerable latitude in whom he considers "children," and he favors a flexible interpretation. When Amy informs him that she has "grown up" since his last visit, he responds, "Oh, you never want to do that."[126] The Dream Lord certainly implies there is a power dimension in the Doctor's sentimentality towards children: "Your friends never see you again once they've grown up. The old man prefers the company of the young, does he not?"[127] It would seem, from *The Sarah Jane Adventures*, that at least one of his former assistants would agree; when the eleventh Doctor encounters Jo Grant, the assistant of his third incarnation; she expresses sadness at his lack of contact:

JO: So you've a married couple in the TARDIS?
DOCTOR: Mr. and Mrs. Pond!
JO: I only left you because I got married. Did you think I was stupid?
DOCTOR: Why do you say that?
JO: Well, I was a bit dumb. Still am, I suppose.
DOCTOR: Now what in the world would make you think that? Ever, ever, ever?
JO: We'd been travelling down the Amazon for months, and we reached a village in Cristalino, and it was the only place in thousands of miles that had a telephone, so I called you. I just wanted to say hello. And they told me that you'd left, left UNIT, never came back. So I

waited, and waited. Because you said you'd see me again. You did, I asked you and you said yes, you promised.[128]

Leaving because she "got married" might, in other contexts, suggest the Doctor was a romantic rival for Jo's attentions, but her tone and word choice here indicate a father-daughter relationship. Jo's fears of inadequacy, references to waiting, and the plaintiveness of "you promised" are all evocative of an abandoned child. Amelia, we might recall, was literally an abandoned child — and one for whom "waiting" was a source of distress leading to psychiatric treatment.[129]

Sentimentality towards children in the program repeatedly signals a facile morality; the Starwhale, for instance, is described as "old and really kind"[130] because it doesn't eat human children, even though it has willingly eaten adults, and similarly, Malokeh the Silurian meets with the Doctor's approval for not experimenting upon human children, even though he had dissected numerous human adults without anesthetic.[131] In the Doctor's case, invoking the needs of children is a mark of his privileged position, not to be undertaken by lesser mortals — hence his lack of sympathy when Ambrose, motivated by fear for her young son, fatally wounds the Silurian Restac.[132] The flexibility of his moral code in this regard rather suggests the Dream Lord is right to question his intent. The dynamic between the Doctor and the (usually British) humans he encounters suggests humanity is the infantilized other, to his subject. Yet the eleventh Doctor, for all his Gallifreyan origins, presents as a White, affluent, southern English man, speaking BBC English and wearing a bow tie. Rory, Amy, and their unborn child may be the mechanized "British" family unit — but the Doctor requires no mechanization to fulfill the role of "British" patriarch.

Beyond Series 31

At the close of Series 31, Amy marries Rory; yet in an apparent renegotiation of what their marriage signifies, they bid farewell to the rural idyll. On the day of their wedding they depart in the TARDIS with the Doctor, deciding it is "definitely goodbye" to Leadworth.[133]

It is not clear if, in their marriage, they have brought the ideology of the rural idyll with them; or whether their departure indicates a suspension of the identity conflicts "Britishness" involves. The 2010 Christmas special, "A Christmas Carol," dispensed with the rural idyll for urban winter scenes, with Rory and Amy featuring only briefly. Shown honeymooning aboard an endangered space liner, the interiors of which looked suspiciously similar to the Starship *Enterprise*, the pair made momentary appearances in Amy's kissogram police uniform, and Rory's Centurion outfit. The scenario suggested an ongoing play with identity temporarily loosened from Amy and Rory's cultural moorings.

At the time of writing, the first trailers for Series 32 have aired in the U.K. Intriguingly the new footage include images of Monument Valley, the White House, and Roswell, suggesting that "A Christmas Carol's" tongue-in-cheek *Star Trek* reference will not be an isolated nod to American pop culture. The impact that this change in locale will have upon the program's construction of "Britishness" remains to be seen. But if there is to be a family unit, it looks as though Amy and Rory will still play the infantilized other to the Doctor's paternal subject. Unless, that is, Amy's hallucinatory pregnancy is realized in waking hours — to finally complete the assimilation of the "Scottish girl in the English village."

NOTES

1. A note on terminology: throughout this chapter I make occasional references to *Doctor Who* texts that predate the program's revival in 2005. To acknowledge continuity between pre–and post–2005 texts, I use the old series numbering system, according to which Steven Moffat's first series as executive producer is the thirty-first overall.

2. James Chapman, *Inside the TARDIS: The Worlds of Doctor Who: A Cultural History* (London: I.B. Tauris, 2006): p. 6.

3. Lindy Orthia, "'Sociopathic Abscess' or 'Yawning Chasm'? The Absent Postcolonial Transition in Doctor Who," *The Journal of Commonwealth Literature* 45 (2010): p. 207.

4. See Woods for an example of class-based and cultural differences in expressions of national identity. He suggests that while many countries identify rural landscapes with the peasant working class, in Britain progressive movements have tended to celebrate industrial society. Michael Woods, *Contesting Rurality: Politics in the British Countryside* (Aldershot: Ashgate, 2006): p. 89.

5. "The Eleventh Hour." For program details see Videography.

6. Ibid.

7. "The End of Time."

8. Charlie Jane Anders, "Doctor Who's Steven Moffat: The io9 Interview," *io9* (18 May 2010).

9. Christine Berberich, "This Green and Pleasant Land: Cultural Constructions of Englishness," *Landscape and Englishness*, eds. Robert Burden and Stephan Kohl (Amsterdam: Rodopi, 2006): p. 209.

10. "The Big Bang."

11. Leonore Davidoff, Jeanne L'Esperance and Howard Newby, "Landscape with Figures: Home and Community in English Society," *Worlds Between: Historical Perspectives on Gender and Class*, ed. Leonore Davidoff, (Cambridge: Polity, 1995): p.52.

12. David Bell, "Anti-Idyll: Rural Horror," *Contested Countryside Cultures: Otherness, Marginalisation, and Rurality*, eds. Paul J. Cloke and Jo Little (London, Routledge, 1997): p. 95.

13. See Whitelaw and Martin for examples. Paul Whitelaw, "A Heartfelt letter to Doctor Who producers," *Scotland on Sunday* (14 March 2010); Daniel Martin, "Doctor Who: Matt Smith's Debut in The Eleventh Hour — the Verdict," Blog, *The Guardian* (3 April 2010).

14. "Press Launch Transcript," *David Tennant: The Site* (28 March 2006).

15. Adrian Lourie, "Interview: Steven Moffat, Doctor Who Screenwriter," *The Scotsman* (22 March 2010).

16. Orthia, "'Sociopathic Abscess' or 'Yawning Chasm?'" p. 211.

17. Annie Morgan James, "Enchanted Places, Land and Sea, and Wilderness: Scottish Highland Landscape and Idenity in Cinema," *Representing the Rural: Space, Place, and Identity in Films About the Land*, ed. Catherine Fowler and Gillian Hellfield (Detroit: Wayne State University Press, 2006): p. 187.

18. Stephen Cole, *The Ring of Steel*, BBC/*The Observer* (20 February 2011).

19. The Orkney Islands are a Scottish archipelago, off the north coast of Britain.

20. Cole, *The Ring of Steel*, p. 12.

21. Ibid., p. 19.

22. Woods, *Contesting Rurality*, p. 89.

23. Although episodes such as "The Vampires of Venice" and "Vincent and the Doctor" are ostensibly set in other European countries, the majority of characters present as English in their dialect and accent.

24. "Cold Blood."

25. "The Hungry Earth."

26. Cole, *The Ring of Steel*, p. 12.

27. Ibid., p. 16.

28. "Cold Blood."

29. Cole, *The Ring of Steel*, p. 16.

30. Martin J. Weiner, *English Culture and the Decline of the Industrial Spirit, 1850–1980* (Cambridge: Cambridge University Press, 1981): p. 63.

31. "Victory of the Daleks."

32. Ibid.

33. Ibid.

34. Ibid.

35. Ibid.

36. Ibid.

37. "The Eleventh Hour."

38. "Flesh and Stone."
39. "Amy's Choice."
40. Ibid.
41. Ibid.
42. Ibid.
43. Ibid.
44. The most recent gender breakdown provided by the Nursing and Midwifery Council indicates that 89 percent of nurses registered in the U.K. are female. *Statistical Analysis of the Register 1 April 2007 to 31 March 2008*, NMC (23 February 2010) 5.
45. "The Vampires of Venice."
46. "Cold Blood."
47. Ibid.
48. "The Eleventh Hour."
49. Ibid.
50. "The Vampires of Venice."
51. "Amy's Choice."
52. Ibid.
53. Ibid.
54. Ibid.
55. Ibid.
56. Ibid.
57. "Victory of the Daleks."
58. "Amy's Choice."
59. Ibid.
60. Ibid.
61. "The Hungry Earth."
62. "Amy's Choice."
63. "The Big Bang."
64. Ibid.
65. "The Pandorica Opens."
66. "The Pandorica."
67. "Victory of the Daleks."
68. "The Time of Angels."
69. "The Beast Below."
70. Ibid.
71. Susanne Reichl, "Flying the Flag: The Intricate Semiotics of National Identity," *European Journal of English Studies* 8:2 (2004): p. 206. Reichl examines the Union Jack in tandem with the St. George's Cross; she notes how projects that seek to reconsider Englishness and to reinforce British nationalism have developed side by side. Her premise is that the Union Jack and St. George's Cross have seen numerous ideological de- and re-contextualizations in recent years because the individual and collective associations of both flags are at stake. Conversely, the Welsh dragon, St. Andrew's Saltire and St. Patrick's Saltire have not seen equivalent efforts at reinvention.
72. For examples of its use in Jamaica and Ireland respectively, see Brian L. Moore and Michele A. Johnson, *Neither Led Nor Driven: Contesting British Cultural Imperialism in Jamaica, 1865–1920* (Kingston: University of the West Indies Press, 2004): p. 296, and Ewan Morris, *Our Own Devices: National Symbols and Political Conflict in Twentieth-Century Ireland* (Dublin: Irish Academic Press, 2005): p. 112.
73. "The Beast Below."
74. Ibid.
75. "The Eleventh Hour."
76. Ibid.
77. Ibid.
78. "The Big Bang."
79. Amy's coming of age has an interesting counterpoint in the story of Elliot, the Welsh boy who features in "The Hungry Earth" and "Cold Blood." Elliot responds skeptically to the Doctor's comment that Cwmtaff must be a "lovely place to grow up" ("The Hungry"). Unlike Amy, Elliot associates "growing up" with moving away: "I want to live in a city one day. Soon as I'm old enough, I'll be off" ("The Hungry"). The difference is partly gendered. For girls, "growing up" means assuming their domestic role in the idyll, while for boys, it means assuming a public role in the world beyond. However Elliot's intention

to leave also shows a rotated symmetry with Amy's expected cultural trajectory; he could not be assimilated into an Anglocentric "Britishness" if he remained in his Welsh, childhood village.

80. "The Eleventh Hour."
81. "Amy's Choice."
82. "The Eleventh Hour."
83. "Amy's Choice."
84. "The Eleventh Hour."
85. Ibid; "The Beast Below."
86. "The Beast Below."
87. Ibid; "Victory of the Daleks."
88. "The Eleventh Hour."
89. Ibid.
90. Ibid.
91. The invasion he refers to is only nominally of the "world." Both "Victory of the Daleks," and the incidents that Amy fails to recall from the Series 28 episode "Doomsday," are diegetically London-centric. In fact London settings and characters are the default for New Who. Episodes such as Series 30's "The Stolen Earth" are relatively unusual in depicting invaded cities across the globe; and unsurprisingly London is still featured as a proxy for England (though Cardiff at least features as another British city). On a related point, Brett Mills notes that despite being filmed in Wales, the post–2005 *Doctor Who* "requires its audience to assume that stories are set in London unless told otherwise" (384). London's dramatic centrality to the program means we might read Amy's blank response as a tongue-in-cheek comment on her cultural position vis-à-vis *Doctor Who*'s diegetic geography. As a Scot in a Gloucestershire village, why should she have witnessed the Battle of Canary Wharf?
92. "The Big Bang."
93. "Vincent and the Doctor."
94. "The Big Bang."
95. Ibid.
96. "The Beast Below."
97. "The Eleventh Hour."
98. Paul Connerton, *How Societies Remember*, Cambridge, Cambridge University Press, 1989, p. 73.
99. "The Eleventh Hour."
100. Ibid.
101. "Flesh and Stone."
102. Ibid.
103. "The Big Bang."
104. Ibid.
105. "The Time of Angels."
106. "The Pandorica Opens."
107. Ibid.
108. "Amy's Choice."
109. "The Time of Angels."
110. "The Beast Below."
111. "The Time of Angels."
112. Gordon McMullan, and David Matthews, *Reading the Medieval in Early Modern England* (Cambridge: Cambridge University Press, 2007): p. 110.
113. Craig Hinton, *Doctor Who: Synthespians* (London: BBC Books, 2004): p. 133.
114. Ibid. pp. 133–134.
115. Terrance Dicks, *Doctor Who and the Terror of the Autons* (London: Target, 1979): p. 38.
116. Ibid., p. 40.
117. Hinton, *Doctor Who*, p. 158.
118. "Vincent and the Doctor."
119. Ibid.
120. Ibid.
121. Heidi J. Nast, "Mapping the 'Unconscious': Racism and the Oedipal Family," *Annals of the Association of American Geographers*, 90 (2000): p. 218.
122. "The Beast Below."
123. For further details of *Doctor Who*'s rare attempts to recognize postcolonial economic arrangements as exploitative, see Orthia, "'Sociopathic Abscess' or 'Yawning Charm?'" pp. 218–9.

124. For an extended consideration of factors in the child labor crisis, including the role played by colonialism, see Cathryne L. Schmitz, Elizabeth KimJin Traver, and Desi Larson, *Child Labor: A Global View* (Westport, CT: Greenwood, 2004).

125. "The Beast Below."

126. "The Eleventh Hour."

127. "Amy's Choice."

128. "Death of the Doctor,."

129. "The Eleventh Hour"; "The Big Bang."

130. "The Beast Below."

131. "Cold Blood."

132. Ibid.

133. "The Big Bang."

13

"Whatever you do, don't blink!"

Gothic Horror and the Weeping Angels Trilogy

DAVID WHITT

In the interest of full disclosure I have a confession to make — I am not particularly a fan of the horror genre. The only "slasher" films I have ever seen in theaters were *Friday the 13th Part 3 in 3-D* (1982), *Scream* (1996) and *Scream 2* (1997); my DVD collection only has one movie that could be considered horror, Ridley Scott's science fiction classic *Alien* (1979); and I read Mary Shelley's *Frankenstein* only because it was a seminal text for my doctoral dissertation on cyborgs. Perhaps my aversion to horror can be traced back to my youth, a subconscious byproduct of watching *The Omen* (1976), *The Amityville Horror* (1979) and *Poltergeist* (1982) ad nauseam with my sisters on cable television. Or perhaps it is my general dislike for blood, psychotic and/or supernatural villains, formulaic plots, and predictable twists. On a more basic level, maybe I am just afraid of "things that go bump in the night." Regardless of the reason, I tend to purposefully and adamantly avoid all things that may make me feel anxious or scared. So, this naturally begs the question, why am I writing about horror? I blame the Doctor and his ominous warning, "Don't turn your back, don't look away, and don't blink!"

Until 2007, my favorite David Tennant *Doctor Who* episode had been "The Girl in the Fireplace," a love story (of sorts) whose plot shifts between 18th century France and a seemingly abandoned spaceship in the 51st century. However, later that year the Doctor-lite episode "Blink" left a profound impression upon me. "Blink" featured an alien race called the Weeping Angels, ancient hunters who had the appearance of stone statues with large wings, but could not move while being observed. When not seen the Angels can move impossibly fast, attacking prey by touch, and sending their victim into the past. The Steven Moffat script received critical acclaim including the 2008 British Academy of Film and Television Arts TV Craft[1] and Cymru awards for Best Writer,[2] and the 2008 Hugo Award for Best Dramatic Presentation — Short Form.[3] It also received a Fear Factor rating of 5.5 out of 6 from four children on the BBC *Doctor Who* Fear Forecasters website placing it in the category above "Terrifying."[4] The note for parents on the site states, "This is one of the scariest episodes of *Doctor Who* yet.... The parents suggest that, if you're concerned, then tape the episode and watch it with children during the daytime, or, at least, a long time before bedtime." One of the Fear Forecasters, Harry (age 8), provides perhaps the most astute and concise observation about "Blink," enthusiastically proclaiming, "This is brilliant!" Doctor Who fans obviously agreed with Harry's assessment as "Blink" was named the second best episode ever according to a poll published in *Doctor Who Magazine* September 2009.[5]

Considering my general dislike of horror I was surprised by how much I enjoyed "Blink" and began thinking more critically about how Moffat used elements of Gothic horror to create such a memorable and terrifying episode. Consequently, I became interested in learning more about Gothic horror, not only to deconstruct "Blink," and its 2010 follow-up Steven Moffat penned episodes "The Time of Angels" and "Flesh and Stone,"[1] but also to become more informed about a genre that began centuries ago in literature, and has evolved to include television programs such as *Twin Peaks* (1990–1991), *American Gothic* (1995–1996) and films including Tim Burton's *Batman* (1989), Francis Ford Coppola's *Bram Stoker's Dracula* (1992*)*, and Martin Scorsese's *Shutter Island* (2010). Perhaps through this process I can confront my own reservations about Gothic horror and have a better appreciation for this popular and influential genre.

The Origins of Gothic Horror

The word Gothic has been used in a variety of different fields to define history, art, architecture, and, of course, literature, where its subject matter has ranged from romance to detective fiction.[6] However, Gothic literature is perhaps best known in relation to horror, tapping into the fear or anxiety of the reader. Jason Colavito states, "Gothic horror is the name usually given to a group of novels and stories composed between 1764 and 1820 that used supernatural elements and spooky settings to generate an atmosphere of terror."[7] He explains that novels such as Horace Walpole's *The Castle of Otranto* (1764), Ann Radcliffe's *The Mysteries of Udolpho* (1794), and Mary Shelley's *Frankenstein* (1818) were products of the "Romantic Movement," which was a reaction against the rationalism of the Enlightenment. Colavito describes how writers of this era "turned to the supernatural as a critique of rationalism and an expression of the emotional truths the Romantics sought to explore."[8]

Clive Bloom examines the history of Gothic horror over the past several centuries emphasizing the works of Edgar Allan Poe, Henry James, and Robert Louis Stevenson. Bloom argues these authors "developed and perfected the horror/ghost genre, placing it now in contemporary fashion and setting,"[9] and that Poe's *The Fall of the House of Usher* (1839) and James's *The Turn of the Screw* (1898) elevated the genre to a popular art form. Indeed, Bloom contends that *The Fall of the House of Usher* is "probably the most interpreted short story ever written,"[10] and that *The Turn of the Screw* is "a moment in the formal evolution of horror."[11]

Horror in the twentieth century, Bloom explains, was influenced by "the radiation-storm mixture of the 1930s pulp science fiction, H-Bomb hysteria, B Movie radioactive mutation, and UFO delirium."[12] H.P. Lovecraft (1890–1937) is perhaps the most celebrated name of early twentieth century horror, with Stephen King, Anne Rice, and Clive Barker taking up the literary mantle a few decades later. Because of its influence and appeal since the 18th century, Gothic has been labeled a trans-historical genre, responding to important events of the time such as the French Revolution, developments in science and technology, racism, sexism, and postmodern alienation.[13]

While the works of Edgar Allan Poe and Stephen King are separated by over one hundred years, they, and other Gothic horror authors, have relied on well-established tropes of the genre to tell their terrifying tales. A brief summary of these character and plot devices is provided by David Punter, who states that Gothic literature "is the fiction of the haunted house, of heroines preyed on by unspeakable terrors, of the blackly lowering villain, of ghosts, vampires, monsters, and werewolves."[14] Martin Tropp provides a more detailed review of the "classic Gothic pattern," which he argues became a literary standard of this type of storytelling. He writes,

> The most familiar of these [Gothic horror stories] was told and retold with few variations. It takes place in an ancient abbey or castle, liberally supplied with ghosts and gruesome sights, cursed by an ancient prophecy, and run by a tormented villain. To this sinister setting comes a young woman who ends up pursued by the villain with equally sinister plans; along the way she is frightened by real or imagined brushes with the supernatural while lost in the intricate maze of passages, what [Horace] Walpole called the "long labyrinth of darkness" underlying the castle. Somehow, amid a tangle of subplots, flashbacks, false turnings and dead ends, the heroine emerges unscathed, the curse hanging over the castle is fulfilled, the villain overthrown, and the poor but honest hero (who has been hanging around from the start) is revealed as the true heir to the gloomy pile of masonry that has housed them all.[15]

In contrast to Tropp, Cyndy Hendershot has a deceptively simple definition of the genre, stating, "The Gothic disrupts. It takes societal norms and invades them with an unassimilable force."[16] Hendershot's examples of this unassimilable force include a vampire in 1890s London (*Dracula*), a beast-man in London who is actually a doctor (*Dr. Jekyll and Mr. Hyde*), and a man who murders people after adopting the personality of his dead mother (*Psycho*). Consequently, this tension between societal norms and an unassimilable force impacts the emotional and psychological state of the reader/viewer, creating fear and anxiety.

In addition to its narrative elements, Gothic horror is also defined by its visual aesthetic. Several authors have written in similar ways about the various atmospheric elements of the Gothic world describing them as "rife with ruins, castles, vast landscapes and subject to violent storms, in tune with the labyrinthian nature of decaying interiors"[17]; "The Gothic has made us familiar with such paraphernalia as claustrophobic castles"[18]; "Everything in the Gothic world is exaggerated ... the seemingly infinite corridors of castles, the dimness of moonlit landscapes, the ferocity of storms, the ruggedness of mountains."[19] Certainly, this imagery creates a world where darkness and shadow dominate, hiding unknown terror around the next corner of a cold stone hallway or in fog covered forest. After providing this rather brief description of Gothic horror, attention will now shift to its use in *Doctor Who* and the Weeping Angels trilogy.

Doctor Who *and Gothic Horror*

Although *Doctor Who* is traditionally recognized as a science fiction program, it has relied on other genres such as historical drama, mystery, romance, comedy, western, and horror for its narratives. For example, the third Doctor (Jon Pertwee) fought his nemesis The Master and supernatural beings in "The Daemons" (1971), the fourth Doctor (Tom Baker) battles the Osiran Sutekh in a Victorian Gothic mansion in "Pyramids of Mars" (1975), while the seventh Doctor (Sylvester McCoy) has a "good old fashioned haunted house story"[20] in "Ghost Light" (1989), to name but a few. Arguably the Weeping Angels trilogy of "Blink," "The Time of Angels" and "Flesh and Stone" "ups the ante" when compared to previous horror themed *Doctor Who* episodes. Each Weeping Angels episode will be reviewed individually in terms of its plot, characters, and imagery and then discussed collectively to analyze and trace the Gothic overtones within the trilogy. With respect to

Doctor Who purists, and for the sake of brevity, some episode details that are not essential to this critique have been cut or condensed.

"Blink"

It is nighttime and rain is falling. A young woman climbs over a tall iron gate fence with a sign that says, "Danger. Keep Out. Unsafe Structure." She next approaches an old house, kicks in the door, and walks inside. The house has old, dusty furniture and vines are growing on the walls and inside a fireplace. The woman begins to take pictures of the interior, but then stops, becoming curious about a piece of blue wallpaper peeling off the wall, partially hiding the letter B. She pulls back more wallpaper and uncovers the warning "Beware" and "The Weeping Angel." She removes more wallpaper revealing the warning, "Oh, and duck! Really Duck! Sally Sparrow. Duck now." She ducks just as a rock crashes through the window hitting the wall. She looks outside with her flashlight and sees a large marble statue in the shape of woman with wings covering its face with its hands. She turns away to once again look at the mysterious words on the wall and tears off a final piece of wallpaper to find "Love from the Doctor (1969)."

Escaping whatever danger threatened her at the abandoned house Sally goes to her friend Kathy's apartment. In the living room she sees a man (the Doctor) on a television screen looking as if he is having a conversation with someone on the other side of the monitor, saying, "Your life could depend on this. Don't blink! Don't even blink. Blink and you're dead. They are fast, faster than you can believe. Don't turn your back, don't look away, and don't blink. Good luck." She then meets Kathy's brother Larry, who, much to his horror, is not wearing pants.

That morning Kathy returns with Sally to the abandoned house to investigate what happened the night before. However, a few minutes later Kathy has the unfortunate fate of being touched by a Weeping Angel and is instantly transported back to Hull, England, in 1920. However, shortly before Kathy disappears a man named Malcolm shows up at the house and surprises Sally with a letter from Kathy. In the letter there are pictures and a note from Kathy explaining her disappearance in 2007, with details about her new life in the past with a husband and children. Sally is disgusted at the seemingly bad joke being played on her and runs upstairs trying to find Kathy, still believing she is in the house. At the top of the stairs Sally sees three Weeping Angels, each covering its eyes. She then hears the sound of wings flapping, and turns to see one of the statues holding a thin piece of string with a key attached. Sally grabs the key, studies it a moment, and then runs outside as she hears Malcolm leaving, just escaping the outstretched arms of an Angel. As Sally leaves the house the Weeping Angels watch her through the windows. An Angel later observes Sally as she leaves the cemetery after having visited Kathy's gravestone.

The scene then shifts to the DVD store where Kathy's brother Larry works. Obviously, Larry does not know that his sister has suddenly disappeared ninety years into the past and is now dead. Larry takes Sally into the back room of the store where she again sees the man (the Doctor) on the television from the night before having a conversation with someone about time and not blinking. Larry explains that the person is a DVD Easter egg, an extra hidden feature that, in this case, is on seventeen different DVDs. Larry does not really understand what the man is saying, but that he and his friends have been trying to figure out what the other half of the conversation is all about.

Later, it is raining when Sally arrives at the police station to explain the strange incident she experienced the night before at the abandoned house, revealed as Wester Drumlins. While waiting for assistance Sally looks out a window and across the street sees two Weeping Angels outside of a church. She looks away and instantly the two Angels are outside the police station. Detective Inspector Billy Shipton, the officer assigned to the Wester Drumlins case, talks to Sally. Billy takes Sally to the station's underground garage where there are several cars parked. He tells her that over the past two years all of the cars were found at Wester Drumlins, each had personal items inside, and some were even still running, but the owners had mysteriously disappeared. Sally then inquires about the large blue police box also in the garage (the TARDIS). Billy explains it is not a real one and that despite it having an ordinary Yale lock, the police have not been able to open it. Billy then asks Sally out for a drink. She gives him her phone number and then leaves the garage. Billy turns around to see four Weeping Angels surrounding the blue police box, walks up toward one of the Angels studying it, and blinks. Meanwhile, Sally leaves the station, but then in her coat pocket finds the key she took from the Weeping Angel. Thinking the key perhaps could open the police box, she returns to the garage only to discover both the blue box and Billy are gone.

At approximately the halfway mark of the episode the Doctor (David Tennant) finally makes his non–Easter egg appearance. Accompanied by Martha (Freema Agyeman), the Doctor welcomes Billy to 1969 and informs him that he was touched by an Angel, explaining,

> Fascinating race, the Weeping Angels. The only psychopaths in the universe to kill you nicely. No mess, no fuss, they just zap you into the past and let you live to death. The rest of your life used up and blown away in the blink of an eye. You die in the past, and in the present they consume the energy of all the days you might have had, all your stolen moments. They're creatures of the abstract. They live off potential energy.

The Doctor then tells Billy he has an assignment for him, to give a message to Sally Sparrow, but then sincerely apologizes because Billy will have to wait a long time before it can be delivered.

Sally then receives a cell phone call from Billy. The scene then shifts to a large hospital room with an old man lying in a bed near a window. It is Billy. He tells Sally that a man from 1969 called the Doctor has a message for her — to "look at the list," meaning the list of the seventeen DVDs with the Easter eggs Larry discovered. Billy tells Sally that he did not stay a policeman, instead getting into video and DVD publishing and it was he who was responsible for adding all the DVD Easter eggs. However, now that Billy has delivered the message he has been holding onto for forty years he tells Sally that he will die when it stops raining. Sally stays with him until the end.

Sally then calls Larry and tells him that the seventeen DVDs on the list are all the DVDs she owns. Larry grabs a portable DVD player and they meet at Wester Drumlins that night. In the room with the wallpaper message to Sally they watch one of the DVDs. The Doctor comes on the screen and he and Sally have a conversation, which Larry is transcribing. From a transcript he is reading the Doctor tells Sally that he is talking to her from 1969 and begins to tell her about the "big ball of wibbly-wobbly, timey-wimey stuff" that defines our concept of time. He then asks Sally if the Angels have taken blue box, and then provides additional information about these creatures from another world, the Weeping Angels.

> DOCTOR: Lonely assassins, they used to be called. No one quite knows where they came from. They're as old as the universe, or very nearly and they've survived this long as they have the most perfect defense system ever evolved. They are quantum-locked. They don't exist when

being observed. The moment they're seen by any other living creature they freeze into rock. No choice. It's a fact of their biology. In the sight of any living thing, they literally turn to stone. And you can't kill a stone. Course, a stone can't kill you either. But then you turn your head away, then you blink, and oh, yes it can!

SALLY [to Larry]: Don't take your eyes off that! (looks at the Weeping Angel behind him).

DOCTOR: That's why they cover their eyes. They're not weeping, they can't risk looking at each other. Their greatest asset is their greatest curse. They can never be seen. The loneliest creatures in the universe.

The Doctor then tells Sally that the Angels want to feast on the time energy inside the blue box, his time machine, and that she must send it back to him. It is then that the Doctor ends the conversation since the transcript he was reading from has ended. The Doctor accurately concludes the Angels must be coming and warns them "Don't blink! Don't even blink. Blink and you're dead. They are fast, faster than you can believe. Don't turn your back, don't look away, and don't blink! Good luck!"

Unfortunately, Larry has stopped looking at the Angel he was supposed to be watching and it us almost upon him. The Angel has its arms extended and mouth open exposing its sharp teeth like a feral animal ready to strike. Larry thinks there is only one Angel, but Sally tells him there are three more. They frantically try to leave Wester Drumlins, but the Angels have locked the front door. Sally believes they want the key she took the last time she was there; the key to the blue box. Every escape route from the house is blocked so Sally and Larry try the cellar. There, they see the blue box the Doctor spoke of along with three Angels covering their eyes. One Angel then begins pointing at a light bulb trying to turn it off. As the light in the cellar flickers Sally frantically tries to use the key to open the blue box and each time the light goes off and on the Angels get closer, their arms extended and mouths open. Sally finally unlocks the door, and she and Larry go inside. A hologram of the Doctor appears saying that an authorized control disc has entered the vehicle and to insert it and prepare for departure. As the Angels outside begin to rock the blue box Larry inserts the now glowing DVD into the control panel. The blue box begins to dematerialize, but Sally and Larry are left in the middle of the cellar floor surrounded by now inanimate Weeping Angels. Sally concludes that the Doctor tricked the Angels and that they looked at each other as the blue box disappeared, in effect, immobilizing the creatures forever.

One year later, Sally and Larry are running a book and DVD shop. At the front desk Sally is putting in a large enveloped pictures of Weeping Angels and the transcript of her conversation with the Doctor. Suddenly, she sees the Doctor and Martha get out of a taxi armed with bows and arrows. Sally runs outside to talk to the Doctor, but he has no idea who she is. Sally tells him that someday he will be trapped in 1969 and gives him the envelope with the pictures and transcript. The Doctor asks for Sally's name, and then runs away with Martha to complete their adventure. The episode ends with various images of marble and metal statues on buildings and streets, interspersed with the Doctor's warning, "Don't blink! Blink and you're dead! Don't turn your back. Don't look away. And don't blink! Good luck!"

"The Time of Angels"

It would be three years until the Weeping Angels would make their return to *Doctor Who.* However, this time the Eleventh Doctor (Matt Smith) and his companion Amy Pond

(Karen Gillan), along with some help from the enigmatic River Song (Alex Kingston), and a squad of very well armed clerics, must do battle with a colony of Angels in the back-to-back episodes "The Time of Angels" and "Flesh and Stone."

Again, for the sake of brevity I will summarize the details of how the Doctor and River Song reunite in the beginning of "The Time of Angels." In short, Song was conducting a covert mission on a spacecraft called the *Byzantium*, was discovered, escaped, and is now in the TARDIS with the Doctor. The *Byzantium* crash lands into a large temple on the planet Alfava Metraxis, which according to Song, has been "unoccupied for centuries." Despite everyone on the *Byzantium* dying in the crash Song states there is "one survivor. There's a thing in the belly of that ship that can never die." Song then receives a call from a ship in orbit above the planet and provides her coordinates.

Several men in combat gear and weapons materialize on Alfava Metraxis led by Father Octavian who tells the Doctor he has with twenty soldier-clerics at his command. Song then asks the Doctor what he knows about the Weeping Angels. It becomes clear that the objective of the soldiers is to neutralize the Weeping Angel that was being transported by the *Byzantium*. However, to get to the Angel they must first negotiate the catacombs that lead up to the temple known as the "Maze of the Dead." The Doctor informs Amy that a Weeping Angel is "the deadliest, most powerful, most malevolent life form evolution has ever produced." River Song calls the Doctor and Father Octavian inside what looks to be a communications facility, and on a television monitor see a recording of a Weeping Angel in a *Byzantium* storage compartment, turned away from the camera and covering its eyes. The same image repeats every four seconds.

Outside the communications facility the Doctor says that the area where the *Byzantium* crashed is going to be filled with radiation that is deadly to humans, but will make the Angel stronger. Meanwhile, inside the facility Amy notices the recording of the Angel on the monitor is now slightly different — its hands are no longer covering its face. Amy goes outside and asks Song if she had any other images of the Angel, but Song says no, only those four seconds. Amy walks back in and the Angel on the monitor is now facing the security camera, its arms extended and palms up. Amy looks at the time marking on the recording and it is the same repeated four-second sequence. When she looks up the Angel has moved closer to the camera. As she continues to stare at the Angel the door behind her suddenly closes. Amy anxiously tries to shut off the monitor, but it keeps turning back on. She looks down to unplug the monitor and then looks up to see the Angel's face in full view of camera. Amy yells for the Doctor and attempts to open the door, but it refuses to open. She looks back at the monitor and the Angel now has its mouth open, its pointed teeth exposed.

Nearby the facility the Doctor and Song are studying a book written about the Angels. The Doctor notices the book does not contain any pictures, but there is a passage that states, "That which holds the image of an Angel becomes itself an Angel." Meanwhile, the Angel is beginning to materialize in front of Amy. She again tries to switch off the monitor with the remote, but the Angel flickers back on. The Doctor, now realizing Amy is in danger, and unable to open the outside door to the facility, tells her to continue looking at the Angel, but not into its eyes. Unfortunately, she has already done so. Amy desperately uses the remote control one last time and manages to stop the Angel at the exact moment when the four-second image is recycled on the screen. The door to the facility unlocks, and Amy is now safe. The Doctor says that the image was the projection of the Angel reaching out to get a look at everyone.

Now inside the catacombs a gravity globe is launched, a ball-shaped device that hovers high inside the cavern providing light. The illumination from the globe reveals dozens, if not hundreds, of statues, but their faces are worn down. Amy pauses a moment to rub her eye and a bit of sand comes out. Song tells Amy that the Maze of the Dead is a labyrinth with dead people buried in the walls. Meanwhile, two clerics, Christian and Angelo, are exploring a side chamber, seeing more faceless statues. Suddenly, Christian's flashlight goes out, he hears a noise, and an Angel appears. Angelo then hears Christian telling him to come and see something. The Angel appears again and Christian is killed.

As the group inside the Maze of the Dead continues walking toward the *Byzantium* the Doctor and Song notice something about the statues. The native race of the planet, the Aplans have two heads, but the statues in the catacombs only have one. The Doctor immediately moves everyone to the side of the passage and tells them to turn off their flashlights. The Doctor turns his flashlight off then quickly back on. The statues have turned and are now facing the group, with some having even moved slightly toward them. The Doctor announces, "They're Angels. All of them." Meanwhile, a cleric named Bob receives a message from Angelo to come and see something. Bob goes to investigate, and is killed by an Angel.

There is now discussion among the group as to how these statues are Angels. The Doctor surmises that because of their decaying form they must have been in the Maze for centuries starving, but are now drawing power from the *Byzantium*'s radiation. The Doctor also believes the crash was not an accident, but a rescue mission for the Angels. Father Octavian contacts cleric Bob to let him know the statues are active and have killed Angelo and Christian. The Doctor asks Bob how he managed to escape. Bob replies that he did not escape — the Angel killed him too.

On the way out of the labyrinth the Doctor passes Amy who cannot move her hand believing it is made of stone. The Doctor tries to convince her it is all in her head, but Amy tells him she looked into the eyes of the Angel earlier when she was trapped. The Doctor bites Amy's hand, she screams, sees that her hand is not stone, and they run. The hull of the *Byzantium* is then seen, lodged at the top of the cavern. As the statues continue to advance from all directions the Doctor tells everyone to prepare to jump on his signal, then shoots the gravity globe high above them. Roll credits, end of Part One.

"Flesh and Stone"

The beginning of Part Two finds the Doctor, Amy, Song and the clerics standing upside down on the *Byzantium*'s hull. The destruction of the gravity globe allowed the *Byzantium*'s still active artificial gravity well to pull everyone upward to the ship's exterior. The Doctor opens a hatch into the ship with his sonic screwdriver and then locks it after everyone goes inside. However, their escape route it quickly thwarted as the door to the secondary flight deck becomes sealed. The corridor lights flicker, the hatch opens, the lights go out, and the Angels move inside. The Doctor manages gets turn the lights in the corridor back on, momentarily freezing the Angels. However, to open the door behind them he will need to transfer power from the lights for a split second, which will darken the corridor. Father Octavian gives instructions to his clerics to begin shooting when the lights go out. The machine gun fire illuminates and freezes the Angels when seen, but they quickly advance in-between shots when it is dark. The Doctor manages to open the locked door and they escape into the control room of the secondary flight deck. Adjacent to the control room they discover a thick forest of trees, or what Song calls the "oxygen factory." The Doctor explains the forest is "trees plus technology ... sucking in starlight and breathing out air.... A forest in a bottle on a spaceship in a maze." At the other end of this forest is the *Byzantium*'s main flight deck and their only means of escape from the ship.

After a quick reconnaissance of the forest, a path to the main flight deck is discovered. Angel Bob then contacts the Doctor and tells him the Angels are feasting on the ship's radiation and getting stronger. Meanwhile, for the past several moments Amy has been inexplicably blurting out numbers counting down from ten, which initially does not draw much attention. However, when Amy says "six" the Doctor asks Bob what the Angels have done to her. Bob informs him, "There's something in her eye." The Doctor asks, "What's in her eye?" to which Bob replies, "We are."

Above the door to the control room the Doctor sees the crack in time, first seen in Amy's room from when she was a young girl in the Series 5.1 episode "The Eleventh Hour." Everyone runs into the forest except for the Doctor who is analyzing the crack with his sonic screwdriver. Suddenly, several Angels are inside the control room. As the Doctor attempts to maneuver past the Angels one grabs his jacket, but he escapes when the Angels become distracted by the crack in time. In the forest Amy is beginning to succumb to whatever the Angels have done to her. The Doctor tells Amy she is dying, and realizes there is an Angel in her mind from when she stared into the eyes of the one earlier in the communications facility. A close-up of Amy's eye shows an Angel in her pupil. Meanwhile, Angels are beginning to quickly descend on their location in the forest.

The Doctor contacts Angel Bob and asks why Amy is counting down. The Angels are doing it to make her afraid. The Doctor realizes Amy's vision center in her brain needs to be shut down, tells her to close her eyes, and that she is not allowed to open them, not even for a second. The Doctor tells Father Octavian and his clerics to stay and protect Amy while he and Song go find the primary flight deck, but Octavian insists in joining them.

The Doctor, Song, and Father Octavian walk through the forest and eventually find the primary flight deck. After Father Octavian opens the entrance to the flight deck the light in the forest flickers and an Angel grabs him around the neck. Octavian tells the Doctor he cannot trust River Song, explaining that she was a prisoner and killed someone, but does not reveal who. The Doctor reluctantly leaves Octavian, who is then killed by the Angel. Both the Doctor and Song are safely inside the primary flight deck and Song believes she can get the ship's teleporter to work.

Meanwhile, the Angels are closing in on Amy and the clerics when suddenly a bright white light is seen in the distance — the crack in time, but much larger than in the forest control room — and the Angels surprisingly disappear. Each of the clerics protecting Amy leave to investigate this phenomenon, but do not return. The Doctor contacts Amy and tells her to walk to him, but still keeping her eyes closed, adding that if the time energy — the white light in the forest — catches up with her she will have never lived. Amy, with eyes closed, begins to walk through the forest and is soon surrounded by Angels. The Doctor transmits a proximity detector to Amy's communicator which signals when she gets close to an Angel. The Doctor then tells Amy she should "walk like she can see" as the Angels are more concerned with their survival, running scared from the time energy rather than attacking her. Amy successfully navigates through the Angels, but trips and falls, dropping the communicator. Just as one of the Angels is about to touch Amy she is teleported to the flight deck.

Moments later, the Angels drain the last of the ship's power and an exterior door on the primary flight deck opens revealing dozens of Angels. Angel Bob tells the Doctor that the time field — the white light in the forest — is coming and will destroy their reality unless the Doctor throws himself into this rupture in time. However, because the Angels have been draining all the power from the *Byzantium* the gravity on the ship begins to fail and all Angels fall backwards into the time field, disappear, and the crack in time is sealed. The Angel in Amy's mind is now gone and can no longer harm her. The Doctor tells Amy that because she is now a time traveler it changes the way she sees the universe. Later, on the shore outside the temple, Song tells the Doctor they will meet again soon and then is transported to a prison ship.

Discussion

The opening two minutes of "Blink" establish the story clearly within the realm of Gothic horror. The setting is dark and dreary (the abandoned house at night in a rainstorm), there is a dangerous unassimilable force (the Weeping Angels) and the female protagonist (Sally Sparrow) becomes a woman in distress. Similarly, much of "The Time of Angels" and "Flesh and Stone" takes place inside a darkened setting (a labyrinth underneath a temple and a spooky forest), the unassimilable force is even more powerful (an army of Weeping Angels), and the female protagonist (Amy Pond) experiences distress on several occasions. Certainly the Angels themselves are cut from the classic Gothic pattern of vampire stories, creatures that upon first glance appear harmless, even beautiful, but when attacking, become ferocious hunters unsheathing their sharp teeth and long nails. Additionally, the Angels are frequently shown advancing on their prey through the darkness and shadows, highlighted by a dim or flickering light, a standard horror trope. While the Angels are perhaps the most obvious example of Gothic horror in the trilogy a closer analysis of the episodes reveals other similarities and distinct differences from traditional Gothic themes.

Gothic Ambiance

According to David Huckvale, eighteenth-century Gothic romance "had little to do with actual horror. It was far more concerned with evoking extremes of emotions (particularly terror) by means of architectural and scenic setting."[21] In other words, an essential component to generating terror was a story's location, which, as discussed earlier, would typically take place in an abbey or castle, some of which had an underground labyrinth. Huckvale discusses how elements such as thunderstorms and ruins create an atmosphere of fear and dread. For example, in Gothic literature storms are an essential part of Charles Maturin's *Melmouth the Wanderer* (1820) and Percy Bysshe Shelley's poem *A Vision of the Sea* (1820) and in films such as *Frankenstein* (1931) and *Dr. Jekyll and Mr. Hyde* (1931). Ruins, such a decrepit abbey overrun with foliage or a cathedral with pointed arches, ribbed vaulting and broken stained glass, provide a unique atmosphere to such Gothic tales as Ann Radcliffe's novel *The Romance of the Forest* (1791), and the film *Dracula* (1931). Each of these Gothic architectural and scenic components is evident within the Weeping Angels trilogy.

As stated earlier the opening scene of "Blink" contains several Gothic elements. The setting is at night in the rain, and Sally Sparrow ignores the "Danger Keep Out Unsafe Structure" sign, climbing a locked iron gate to enter Wester Drumlins. However, instead of a decaying abbey Sally is in a home with vegetation growing inside the fireplace, peeling wallpaper, and old furniture, a modern variation on the Gothic ruin. When Sally and her friend Kathy return to Wester Drumlins the next day the general disrepair of the house becomes even more evident with broken windows, leaves scattered on the floor, and a dilapidated garden. Toward the end of the episode the house even becomes a labyrinth of sorts when the Weeping Angels lock Sally and Larry inside. The two eventually end up in a dimly lit cellar with columns and pointed arches, as if they were inside a Gothic structure.

Two other locations that reflect Gothic atmospherics are the police station and, to a lesser degree, Billy's hospital room. When Sally walks into the police station to report the disappearance of Kathy it is raining quite heavily outside. Then, as Sally looks out the police station windows, she notices two Weeping Angels across the street on the wall of what looks to be a Victorian cathedral, a primary example of Gothic architecture. Soon after, Billy takes Sally into an underground parking garage filled with several cars and a blue box all abandoned at Wester Drumlins. The garage is old, with chipped paint and broken cement, and a ceiling covered with large plastic sheets, some of which are hanging down, as if the area is being remodeled. Later, when Sally returns to the station to try the key she took from the Weeping Angel, the blue box is gone as the hard wind and rain blow in through the now open garage door. When compared to Wester Drumlins the police garage can perhaps be characterized as something of a minor ruin. The garage is certainly not as gloomy or menacing as the house, but its underground locale, poor condition, and dark lighting suggest a less than safe environment. Similarly, the hospital room where Sally visits the much older Billy later that day is bleak and dreary, with old and worn tile, and empty beds. The rainstorm outside is also an ominous sign for Billy as has been told by the Doctor that he will die when the rain finally stops.

In "The Time of Angels" the obvious Gothic motif is the "Maze of the Dead" labyrinth underneath the temple on Alfava Metraxis, with its ruins, columns, side chambers, and countless Weeping Angel statues. What makes the Maze unique is that, according to River Song, it has six levels, which creates a potentially more terrifying environment for the Doctor, Amy, Song, Father Octavian and his clerics. It is only when the group moves deeper into the Maze that the Doctor realizes the statues are actually Angels and that they are in great danger. Their escape route now blocked by numerous Angels the group has no choice but to move further up the levels of the Maze eventually finding the *Byzantium*, with its exterior hull protruding from the top of a cavern. Having successfully navigated the "Maze of the Dead" the group's next challenge is the labyrinth of corridors and compartments onboard the *Byzantium*, the primary location for the next episode "Flesh and Stone."

Once onboard the *Byzantium* the group discovers an unusual escape route, the ship's "oxygen factory" or what the Doctor calls "a forest in a bottle on a spaceship in a maze." This vast terrain provides different challenges to the group. The Doctor, Song, and Father Octavian try to find the ship's main flight deck while Amy, her mind now inhabited by an Angel, and the clerics stay in the forest as the Angels slowly advance on their position. Eventually each cleric is drawn to a bright light in the distance (the "crack in time") soon leaving Amy alone to negotiate this artificial labyrinth with her eyes closed. Like Theseus of Athens in Greek mythology who used thread to find his way out of the labyrinth of Daedalus, Amy is guided by a proximity detector to help her avoid the Angels surrounding her, until being safely transported by the Doctor to the flight deck.

From Wester Drumlins to the "Maze of the Dead" to the interior of the *Byzantium*, the Gothic motifs of ruins, the labyrinth, and to a lesser degree storms are evident throughout the Weeping Angels trilogy. While the analysis of the visual or atmospheric elements is an important part of the trilogy's Gothic tone, it is also necessary to discuss how the characters of Sally Sparrow and Amy Pond reflect, or more interestingly diverge from, traditional female Gothic roles.

Sally and Amy as Gothic Heroines

From Emily St. Aubert in Ann Radcliffe's *The Mysteries of Udolpho* (1794) to Elizabeth Lavenza in Mary Shelley's *Frankenstein* (1818) the female protagonist in Gothic literature often experiences intense psychological and sometimes even physical trauma. Howells explains,

> The Gothic heroine.... Constantly threatened by emotional and physical assault, she is so delicately elusive that she deprives aggression of its reality and her sufferings impinge on her no more than the events of nightmare. Her experiences in no way lead to the growth of her self-awareness or modification of any of her attitudes; at the end she emerges with sensibility intact, even if on rare occasions physically violated. She is the familiar figure in women's fiction of any age, embodying all the fashionable feminine fantasies and neuroses.[22]

An even more candid assessment of the Gothic heroine is provided by Susan Wolstenholme, who contends, "[a]ll Gothic fiction might be said to employ a kind of sadomasochism. Both film and literary criticism have recognized this dynamic in suggesting some degree of continuity between Gothic novels and contemporary narratives of violence to women, particularly slasher films."[23] This is not to suggest that male protagonists in Gothic fiction do not experience their fair share of terror, but when compared, there is perhaps a disproportionate amount of fear and suffering with female characters.

The Weeping Angels trilogy both reflects the sadomasochistic claim of Wolstenholme while directly challenging Howells belief that Gothic heroines are incapable of personal growth, self-awareness or modification of attitudes. In "Blink" Sally Sparrow is immediately introduced as an adventurous individual, breaking into Wester Drumlins at night and even returning the next day after having a rock thrown at her by an unknown assailant. Although Sally becomes hunted by the Weeping Angels because she has the key to the TARDIS, she exhibits great courage and resilience in the face of this danger. Additionally, any fear Sally experiences does not prevent her from trying to uncover the mystery of Kathy's disappearance. Even during the episode's third act Sally exhibits more rational thinking than Larry does regarding how to escape the Angels inside Wester Drumlins. Sally's behavior throughout the episode reflects a strong and smart female protagonist, without exhibiting any of the neuroses described by Howells.

In contrast to Sally Sparrow, Amy Pond experiences arguably more emotional, and certainly more physical trauma. First, in "The Time of Angels" Amy is locked inside the communications facility as the Weeping Angel on the television monitor begins to materialize in front of her. While the Doctor tries to unlock the door Amy is feverishly attempting to turn off the monitor until she is finally successful. The fear experienced by Amy in regard to the Angel is hers alone, the consequences of which are soon felt in the seemingly innocuous act of rubbing her eye. Because Amy looked at the Angel in the eyes it is now inside her mind, eventually influencing her thoughts and words. The first instance of this control is in the "Maze of the Dead" when Amy believes her hand is made out of stone and cannot move. The next is in "Flesh and Stone" as Amy inexplicably begins counting down from ten, the purpose of which, Angel Bob explains, is to make her afraid. Perhaps the most traumatic example is when Amy must close her eyes and not open them, even for a moment, to keep the Angel's influence in check. Later, when the clerics leave her in the forest to investigate a mysterious light, she must try to stay calm in the face of the advancing Angels.

When compared to the Doctor, River Song, Father Octavian and his clerics, no other character in "The Time of Angels" or "Flesh and Stone" experiences as much fear and torment as Amy. However, despite Amy becoming the target of great emotional and physical suffering, she has grown as an individual, becoming more self-aware. In fact, the Doctor tells her at the end of "Flesh and Stone" that because Amy is a now a time traveler, the way she sees the universe has changed. Amy's transformation from terrestrial tourist to intergalactic time traveler is perhaps the ultimate antithesis of the traditional Gothic heroine; a woman not defined, or in this case, confined by her earthly roles and responsibilities, but one with a larger sense of purpose and being.

Conclusion

Hendershot argues "while the Gothic may have been a genre at the end of the eighteenth century, it increasingly became a mode in the nineteenth and twentieth centuries."[24] It is easy to extend this statement to the twenty-first century as Gothic has influenced modern literature, television, and film. The fact that *Doctor Who* has tapped into this popular genre should not be surprising as Gothic has been an integral part of previous episodes. However, what distinguishes the Weeping Angels trilogy from other Gothic-style *Who* episodes is the darker atmospheric tone and higher level of terror of the stories. Certainly this could be a matter of personal taste as those *Who* fans who grew up on "The Daemons" or "The Pyramids of Mars" in the 1970s may prefer these episodes and their Gothic overtones to the Weeping Angels trilogy. Still, generational and personal opinions aside, it is obvious *Doctor Who* has evolved over the decades in terms of its narrative tone. Indeed, William Hopper of the *Doctor Who* fanzine *Enlightenment* argues that the modern *Doctor Who* is no longer a family show, as the writing today expresses more adult themes and its 1960s monsters such as the Daleks and Cybermen are out of place generating more "bemused laughter instead of the fear they once elicited."[25] Hopper also contends what made "Blink" so scary was the writing, not the visuals (I expect he would also include "The Time of Angels" and "Flesh and Stone" in his argument). While I respectfully disagree with Hopper regarding the visuals of "Blink" not being scary, especially in terms of reflecting Gothic motifs, his overall point is well taken. The modern Doctor is not your parents' or grandparents' Doctor. The twenty-first century *Doctor Who* reflects a more sophisticated and perhaps impatient viewing audience wanting tighter narratives, realistic special effects, and emotionally honest stories. In this way the Weeping Angels trilogy and its use of Gothic horror is perfect for today's television audience craving a more visceral viewing experience.

June, 2010. I am taking an early morning bicycle ride through a housing development near my home. As I turn the corner to attack a hill, I notice out of the corner of my eye a gray angel statue, approximately three feet high, decorating the entryway to a house. My mind immediately remembers the end of "Blink" and the Doctor's warning — "Don't blink!" — as numerous images of statues, large and small, metal and stone are shown on the screen. Since then, I have memorized the location of every type of porch and lawn statue on my bike route, instinctively looking away at each at the last second, the Doctor's words echoing in my mind. Granted, this behavior is as illogical as the premise of the Weeping Angels, but that is not the point. Despite my well-documented aversion to horror, its power to invoke fear and terror in the form of the Weeping Angels has impacted my psyche, forever changing how I see my environment. If that was Steven Moffat's intention, he was successful. Damn you, Mr. Moffat. Damn you!

NOTES

1. British Academy of Film and Television Arts, "Winners 2008," http://www.bafta.org/awards/television-craft/television-craft-nominations-in 2008,363,BA.html.

2. British Academy of Film and Television Arts, "Awards database," http://www.bafta.org/awards-database.html?sq=steven+Moffat.

3. World Science Fiction Society, "2008 Hugo awards announced," http://www.the hugoawards.org/2008/08/2008-hugo-award-results-announced (2010).

4. BBC Home Doctor Who Fear Forecast, http://www.bbc.co.uk/doctorwho/episodes/2007/fear/f-10.shtml.

5. Lester Haines, "Doctor Who Fans Name Best Episode," *The Register,* September 17, 2009, http://www.theregister.co.uk/2009/09/17/ best_who_ever/.

6. David Punter, *The Literature of Terror: A History of Gothic Fictions from 1765 to The Present Day* (New York: Longman, 1980): p. 1.

7. Jason Covalito, "Oh, the Horror," *Skeptic Magazine,* 15 (3) 2010: p. 21–23, www.skeptic.com.

8. Ibid., p. 22.

9. Clive Bloom, *Gothic Horror: A Guide for Students and Readers* (New York: Palgrave Macmillan, 2007): p. 3–8.

10. Ibid., p. 3.

11. Ibid., p. 6.

12. Ibid., p. 8.

13. Diane Long Hoeveler and Tamar Heller, *Approaches to Teaching Gothic Fiction: The British and American Traditions* (New York: The Modern Language Association of America, 2003): p. xi.

14. Punter, *The Literature of Terror,* p. 1.

15. Martin Tropp, *Images of Fear: How Horror Stories Helped Shape Modern Culture (1818–1918)* (Jefferson, NC: McFarland, 1990): p. 15.

16. Cyndy Hendershot, *The Animal Within: Masculinity and the Gothic* (Ann Arbor: University of Michigan Press, 2001): p. 1.

17. Tropp, *Images of Fear,* p. 26.

18. Hoeveler and Heller, *Approaches to Teaching Gothic Fiction,* p. xi.

19. Coral Ann Howells, *Love, Mystery, and Misery: Feeling in Gothic Fiction* (London: The Athlone Press, 1978): p. 27.

20. Byron Bonsall, personal interview, July 1, 2010.

21. David Huckvale, *Touchstones of Gothic Horror: A Film Genealogy of Eleven Motifs And Images* (Jefferson, NC: McFarland, 2010): p. 5.

22. Howells, *Love, Mystery, and Mystery,* p. 9.

23. Susan Wolstenholme, *Gothic (Re)visions: Writing Women as Readers* (Albany: State University of New York Press, 1993): p. 11.

24. Hendershot, *The Animal Within,* p. 1.

25. William Hopper, "Absolutely Not A Family Show," *Enlightenment,* 160, November 2010, p. 8–9.

14

Doctor Who's Women and His Little Blue Box

Time Travel as a Heroic Journey of Self-Discovery for Rose Tyler, Martha Jones and Donna Noble

ANTOINETTE F. WINSTEAD

The new *Doctor Who* series exemplifies the use of travel as a means of self-discovery for the Doctor's[1] female companions Rose Tyler (Billie Piper), Martha Jones (Freema Agyeman), and Donna Noble (Catherine Tate). The series combines Joseph Campbell's heroic journey, as modified by Maureen Murdock, to include the unique internal/psychological aspects of a heroine's journey, with what Miriam F. Polster terms "Eve's Legacy," turning the once strictly male driven heroic journey plotline of the original show into a heroine's journey. In its current incarnation, the *Doctor Who* series serves as the perfect model of the heroine's journey. As will be shown, the plotlines of the series include many of the elements discussed in Polster's *Eve's Daughters: The Forbidden Heroism of Women*, elements crucial to a heroine's journey of self-discovery. Also illustrated is the use of travel in *Doctor Who* as a means for the Doctor's female companions to escape the pressure to conform to the roles and standards dictated to them by society, thus giving them the freedom to be themselves without fear of judgment or condemnation.

Virginia Woolf laments in *A Room of One's Own* that unless a woman's "parents were exceptionally rich or very noble" the possibility of a woman having "a room of her own, let alone a quiet room or a soundproof room" in which to think or create "was out of the question" before or during the time in which Woolf wrote.[2] Moreover, while Woolf's treatise explores the state of women in the late nineteenth and early twentieth century, it is still unusual for the average woman to have her own dedicated space, separate from the world at large, wherein she is free to be herself, to create and to think without fear of being judged by outside forces, be they family or friends. Woolf also describes how her "Mary" character roams from place to place, looking for a quiet spot, one from which she will not be told to leave because she is female, one in which she is truly welcomed. It is a fruitless search, leading her to become increasingly disheartened by the circumstances inflicted upon her because of her gender. One can see a similarity between Mary's quest and that of *Doctor Who*'s female companions who are also searching for "a room of their own," one in which they will not be dominated, judged, or criticized, which they, fortunately, find through their travels with the Doctor.

The use of travel in the new *Doctor Who* series (2005–) goes beyond the superficial expectations of the science fiction genre, which is usually to explore and conquer strange lands and worlds. Travel, instead, serves as a symbolic representation of a heroic journey of self-discovery for the Doctor's female companions, who are given a chance to grow and expand in ways they never would have without the freedom the TARDIS[3] (the Doctor's "Time and Relative Dimension in Space" traveling machine) gives them. Their newfound freedom allows them to explore "regions of the unknown" and develop as individuals.[4] In many ways, the TARDIS becomes "a room of their own," a room in which they can be themselves without the constraints of societal norms that have superficially classified them. Rose, Martha, and Donna, with the help and guidance of the Doctor, face seemingly insurmountable obstacles, leading them to make important self-discoveries that leave them independent and confident, more willing to step out of the box constructed for them by others; the freedom that Woolf's "Mary" so desperately sought. Because of their epic heroic journeys, all three women find something in themselves that they never realized existed, a confidence to be strong, independent individuals without apology or compromise.

In many ways, the new *Doctor Who* series mirrors aspects of the travels and explorations of women in the nineteenth century. These were intrepid women who sought to escape the "restrictive concepts of home life and women's domestic duty" by setting out on journeys into the unknown.[5] The journeys these female explorers embarked upon were considered risky, but for them it was "a risk well worth taking," because it served as "a means of self-transformation and self-discovery."[6] Rose, Martha, and Donna are 21st century versions of these 19th century female travelers and explorers and, likewise, seek the same freedom and self-transformation. In their travels with the Doctor, they find what they seek and much more, including confidence.

The confidence that the Doctor's companions develop through their travels is exactly what Polster speaks of in *Eve's Daughters: The Forbidden Heroism of Women*. In her text, Polster analyzes the circumstances that lead women to step outside the confines of their ordinary lives to take on heroic roles. These are challenging roles that often involve personal sacrifice and struggle. However, despite whatever foreseen or unforeseen hardships they may encounter, the women who consciously make this leap into heroism do so believing "that [it] is the birthright of energetic, hardworking women to earn, by their own efforts, the right to make informed decisions about the conduct of their own lives," what Polster terms as "Eve's legacy."[7] The fact that "Eve's legacy" requires conscious, active decision-making is where Polster's description and analysis of the heroine's journey differs substantially from the heroine's journey as outlined by Katherine Phelps.[8]

Phelps' heroine's journey is based on fairy tale and myth structures, which requires a Prince Charming/Sir Lancelot/god-type figure to rescue the damsel in distress, a plot structure often used in the old version of the *Doctor Who* series (1963–1989). Polster, however, bases her heroine's journey on an active heroine who has decided to chart her own path, much in the way the female companions in the new *Doctor Who* series do. Likewise, one also finds the idea of the active heroine expressed in Murdock's *The Heroine's Journey*, wherein Murdock acknowledges the heroine's "struggle to separate both physically and psychologically" from societal constraints, which includes breaking free "from her own mother and from the mother archetype."[9]

The longing to separate from mother is something that Rose, Martha, and Donna each experience. However, each is conflicted "between wanting a freer life than their mother and wanting their mother's love and approval."[10] What helps them break free is the "geographical separation" offered by traveling with the Doctor, which serves to "resolve the tension between a daughter's need to grow up and her desire to please her mother."[11] Although separation from mother is part of Rose, Martha, and Donna's quest, it is only a minor part.

The true quest for Rose, Martha and Donna is one of self-discovery, which proves "more internally complex than the hero's quest" used in the original series; because, as Linda S. Griggs points out, the hero's quest, as outlined by Joseph Campbell, "'only' involves battling real-world demons."[12] In contrast, the heroine's journey also includes battling inner demons — such as low self-esteem — that keep her from reconciling her personal desires with those imposed by outside forces. This is particularly true of the Donna Noble character who embodies, what Carol S. Pearson terms the "Caregiver" archetype.[13]

Each of the heroines in the new *Doctor Who* series embodies a particular archetype, as outlined by Carol Pearson in *Awakening the Heroes Within*. Pearson lists twelve archetypes, noting the role of each through the stages of the heroine's journey, which she labels as "Preparation," "The Journey," and the "The Return."[14] The archetypes represented by Rose, Martha, and Donna are Seeker, Warrior, and Caregiver, respectively. The Seeker, Rose, is in "search of a better life," one that does not call for "conformity," which she is "flee[ing] from."[15] The Warrior, Martha, is driven to "win" and does not accept any "weakness" in herself.[16] Instead, whenever there is a problem, she courageously "confront[s] it," exhibiting her greatest strength, "discipline."[17] Donna as noted earlier is the Caregiver. She is always willing to "help others" with complete "selflessness," displaying her unbiased "compassion and generosity."[18] While Rose, Martha and Donna each have a dominant archetype characteristic, it should be noted, they each eventually grow to encompass the characteristics of all three archetypes. And, by the end of their journeys, the merging of the Seeker, Warrior, and Caregiver helps create in each a balanced, more confident individual, a very important by-product of their heroines' journeys. The merging of archetypical traits is not commonly found in the typical monomyth, which is something that helps distinguish the heroine's journey from the hero's journey.

It is important to note that as originally conceived, the *Doctor Who* series mirrored the typical monomyth, wherein the hero battled and won against evil and saved the damsel in distress. It was not until its new, post–9/11 incarnation in 2005 that the heroine's journey took center stage in the *Doctor Who* series, reflecting a 21st century sensibility toward the role women play in not only science fiction, but also the horror and action-adventure genres.

The science fiction heroines in the new *Doctor Who* series are the 21st century descendents of Ripley (played by Sigourney Weaver in *Alien*), the first female protagonist in a science fiction film who did not "rely on a man" to save her and who "was [not] finally crushed by evil forces plotting against her."[19] While *Doctor Who's* heroines are like Ripley in that they are independent agents who survive seemingly insurmountable obstacles placed in their paths, there are some major difference between Rose, Martha, and Donna and their predecessor. First, Ripley was originally written as a male character; therefore, many of Ripley's actions and reactions are decidedly masculine — cold and calculating. In contrast, Rose, Martha, and Donna, are very feminine and respond to situations accordingly, with thoughtful, careful consideration. Secondly, Ripley represents a desexualized female, with a boyish figure and very few feminine traits. *Doctor Who's* heroine's are "Cosmo Girls," shapely and fashionable, who embrace both their femaleness and their commodity culture. Finally, Ripley is the feminist ideal of the single girl: equal to "the boys," career focused, and completely independent, with no need for a man or children in her life. Rose, Martha and Donna represent the neo-feminist ideal of the single girl, which means they strive for independence, and "want to achieve on [their] own," but they are not averse to men, marriage and children.[20] In fact, all three of the *Doctor Who* heroines eventually get engaged once their exploits with the Doctor conclude, which aligns perfectly with the heroine's journey. After all, one of the main reasons for the heroine's journey is to venture back with a balanced sense of self, which allows for better more loving relationships with others, as one finds in the *Doctor Who* series.

Originally conceived and produced as a children's educational program for the BBC (British Broadcasting Corporation), the *Doctor Who* series premiered on November 23, 1963, the day after President John F. Kennedy's assassination in Dallas, Texas.[21] The producers envisioned the series as a way to "enlighten children about various historical time periods" while at the same time incorporating the idea of space and time travel as used in the very successful adaptation of H.G. Wells's *The Time Machine* by George Pal in 1960.[22] Another important aspect of the series was the "quest concept," which firmly established the Doctor within the pantheon of mythic heroes, serving to relegate his companions to sidekicks.[23] The *Doctor Who* series had an unprecedented run of twenty-six years before succumbing to an unofficial cancellation in 1989.

During the twenty-six year run of the series, the Doctor had thirty companions of which only nine were males. However, it should be noted that all the companions, regardless of gender, were individuals that at one time or another needed the Doctor to rescue them. The Doctor, in other words, was the consummate hero, riding in on his white horse — the TARDIS — to save the day. It is a heroic role to save the damsel in distress (whether male or female) that fits in perfectly with the heroine's journey as outlined by Phelps.

In the early years of the series, the female companions often had an "adolescent charm and naïveté"; although, in Season 7, the innocent female type was briefly replaced by "an intellectual Cambridge scientist" who proved "more than a match for the Doctor's wit and brain."[24] However, the intellectual female role was short lived, and in Season 8 was "replaced by a more traditional female lead," the "daffy, helpless damsel" type.[25] Not until Season 11, with the introduction of "Sarah Jane Smith,"[26] does one find another female lead in the *Doctor Who* series that matches the wit and intelligence of the Doctor. In contrast, the resurrected version of the series has had an impressive cast of female companions, each able to competently match the Doctor's wit and intellect with her own brand of streetwise, common sense.[27]

Russell T. Davies, the producer behind the 2005 resurrection of the *Doctor Who* series (a.k.a. Nu Who[28]), is responsible for breaking away from the stereotypical roles first issued to the Doctor's female companions in the original series. Davies, instead, presents a 21st century version of women who are capable of not only thinking for themselves, but also of rescuing themselves and others, and, when necessary, the Doctor. His female characters are shown as "[un]willing to settle for obscure satellite or accessory roles" in the Doctor's life.[29] In fact, they often openly "rebel against" the "subordination" that Polster describes as being what has forced women to focus "their energies to the service of other people's goals" at the expense of their own.[30] The world Davies has created is an equal opportunity, post-modern construct that speaks to both dystopian and utopian ideologies in which traditional roles take on an androgynous quality. The androgyny of roles allows the female companions to expand beyond the relegated boundaries of gender performance[31] assigned them in the original series, which, in turn, allows them the freedom to embark on personal quests of self-discovery, quests that leads each of them on heroic journeys of epic proportions.

As noted earlier, the journeys that Rose, Martha, and Donna embark upon resemble the journeys taken by women explorers and travelers in the mid– and late 1800s. According to biographer Marion Tinling in *Women into the Unknown: A Sourcebook on Women Explorers and Travelers*, these 19th century women chose to travel in order "to escape stultifying Victorian social restrictions."[32] Likewise, Rose, Martha and Donna are looking to escape the ordinariness of their mundane lives and the roles forced upon them by society. They are also "drawn by curiosity and attracted by the color and excitement of foreign lands," worlds, and times that travel with the Doctor promises.[33] The same curiosity compelled the three companions' 19th century nonfiction counterparts to explore uncharted lands. The reward for Rose, Martha, and Donna's curiosity is a new sense of self-worth and confidence that can only come from stepping out into the unknown just as the women travelers of the 19th century dared to do, resulting in real life heroic journeys.

The basic structure of the classic "heroic journey," as described by Campbell in *The Hero with a Thousand Faces*, follows twelve stages beginning with "The Ordinary World," wherein one finds the "hero in his [her] own element"[34] and ending with the "Return with the Elixir" wherein "the hero returns to the ordinary world with the treasure that will heal his world and restore the balance which was lost."[35] One finds Campbell's basic monomyth formula used in the new *Doctor Who* series; however, because of Davies's unique approach to the roles played by the female companions, the formula deviates to include the internal/spiritual "quest that women/heroines undergo," as introduced by Murdock.[36] The inclusion of the internal/spiritual quest is what makes the heroine's journey, utilized by Davies, uniquely feminine.

The heroine's journey begins with an internal "search for identity,"[37] which is necessary because the heroine's identity has been sublimated by societal and familial demands, leading to an "internal split that tells [her] to override the feelings, intuitions, and dream images that inform [her] of the truth of life."[38] Before the journey begins, the heroine lives in a fog of a daily mundane routine. The journey lifts her out of the fog and serves as "an initiation into the realities of the Soul journey," which requires that she relinquish "control over [her life]" and "put aside [her] horror of confronting death, pain, and loss to experience life's wholeness."[39] Once she lets go of the need to control everything around her, she is free to search for her own truth and, in turn, grow spiritually without any inhibitions. Typically, this internalized journey is mistaken for depression, because of the solitude sought by the heroine, who may seek a return to nature as a way to rejuvenate her spirit and find her purpose.

The heroine's internalized journey represents a major contrast between her journey, as delineated by Polster, Murdock and Pearson, and hero's journey as outlined by Campbell. Campbell's heroic journey is primarily physical and mental. The heroine's journey incorporates both the physical and mental with the spiritual. In doing so, the heroine emerges from her journey with a deeper wisdom that often eludes the hero. With this newfound wisdom, she is able to "serve not only the needs of others, but can value and be responsive to her own needs as well," something she was unable to accomplish before her journey began.[40]

The heroine's journey, as incorporated into the new *Doctor Who* series, recognizes a "richer diversity of and complexity in spiritual [and personal] development than the images of the heroic, singular journey" typically allowed in the original series.[41] The diversity and complexity of growth is directly linked to the "developmental patterns and interpretive paradigms that are communal and relational throughout the life course" of an individual, which again is ignored by the monomyth, because its primary focus is on the solitary figure, be it male or female, whose quest is decidedly physical rather than mental.[42] The heroine's journey, however, incorporates the mental and physical quest resulting in a complete self-transformation, leading to more harmonious relationships with those she returns to at the end of her journey, as one finds illustrated through the female heroines in the *Doctor Who* series under the stewardship of Davies.

When the viewer first encounters *Doctor Who*'s heroines, they are shown as living typical, mundane lives. Rose works as sales clerk in a department store, Henricks. She wakes up at the same time every morning, gets ready for work, goes to work, has lunch with her boyfriend, and then returns to work until closing time. Martha is an intern working in a hospital, where she is shown being continually "overruled" by her supervisor. Donna, when she first encounters the Doctor, is about to get married. Unfortunately, her fiancée turns out to be a villain who is murdered by his evil alien accomplice, leaving Donna to live a rather boring, uneventful life.

Martha, though the most educated of the three women, is still within that class of women Woolf alludes to as not being able to afford their own "space." Even though she has her own flat, the "space" she lacks is independence from her family and the demands of being a "good" daughter. These demands require that she serves as a mediator between her divorced, bickering parents. In the role of mediator, she effectively becomes parent to her siblings and to her parents. Rose, likewise, plays parent to her rather "wild" mum, Jackie, who assumes the role of daughter, going so far as to behave and dress like a teenager. Donna, in contrast, is yoked to an overbearing mother, Silvia, who refuses to recognize Donna as an adult. Instead, Silvia continually nags and badgers Donna as if she were a teenager, and not a middle-aged woman. Martha, though decidedly upper middle class, with her own flat, is no better off than Rose and Donna, both still residing at home with their mothers. All three women, despite class and ethnicity, are limited and constrained by their assigned familial roles — roles they wish to escape. It is into this mundane, paint-by-numbers world that the Doctor appears, offering these three women the adventure of a lifetime, which is where the heroine's journey, again, deviates somewhat from the heroic journey.

In the classic heroic journey structure, "the hero balks at the edge of adventure," but one finds that Rose and Martha, so desperate to escape their lives, take little convincing to join the Doctor, and, spontaneously, agree to take a ride on the TARDIS, unlike Donna, who hesitates briefly before embarking on her path to adventure.[43] This path begins when Donna encounters the Doctor on her wedding day. Their brief adventure opens Donna's eyes to a world that she has been happily oblivious to, a world of deceivers and monsters. However, it is not the fear of the monsters, but rather the Doctor's rage and vindictive nature that repel Donna and cause her to decline his initial invitation to join him. Instead, Donna opts to retreat to the comfort and routine of her "normal" life. However, she quickly discovers that her brief encounter with the Doctor — despite his anger — has rendered her "normal" life mundane and meaningless and that she will never find fulfillment unless she can break free from it and join him, and in joining him, perhaps help "tame" his inner demons. Now hungry for the freedom of adventure, Donna packs her bags (at least half a dozen), and searches for the Doctor in hopes of encountering him, which, after a year, she eventually does. Of the three, Donna, the only middle-aged companion in the Nu Who, is the most active and relentless in her pursuit of adventure. She is a woman who has been looking for the right opportunity to spread her wings and break free. With this driving desire to follow "The Call to Adventure" with little or no hesitation, the heroine's response to adventure in *Doctor Who* significantly diverges from the standard male response when offered the opportunity to embark on heroic journey.

One reason for this divergence is that, as Polster has observed, "the heroic woman experiences the flux of existence; she senses the pulse of change and is hospitable to it, rather than immobilized."[44] This hospitability is perhaps due to her longing to escape the restrictive norms of society that dictate what she can and cannot do, which is certainly the case for Rose, Martha and Donna. Because these heroines are not immobilized by fear of the unknown, they are "free to [readily] create new institutions and new alliances."[45] Their first and most crucial alliance is, of course, with the Doctor, who provides the "missing link in the circle of [the heroines'] self-relation" which releases "the desire to live" and experience life to its fullest.[46]

The Doctor, without question, is the "Wise Old Man" figure or in heroic journey parlance, the Supernatural guide. He resembles a human male, but is, actually, "an incredibly old alien who has been knocking around the universe for more than 900 years."[47] The Doctor also has two hearts and the uncanny the ability to "'regenerate'[48] into a new, younger body" when necessary.[49] And although he is supposedly this figure of wisdom and experience, his insights and reasoning are sometimes slightly flawed, reminding one of Merlin, or Gandolph, or even Dumbledore. However, despite his flaws, he serves as the heroine's mentor and guide. And while traditionally the mentor "helps the hero make the right decision[s]," in the case of the Doctor, he often sets the stage for the heroine to decide for herself what should or should not be done, thus providing for her the freedom of choice she craves.[50] It is unclear if the Doctor's reluctance to breach the rules of certain situations is sincere or merely a means of testing and strengthening heroine's resolve. Whichever the reasoning, the Doctor's reluctance to intervene clearly helps the heroine grow more confident and independent in her own decision-making, as demonstrated when Donna insists in Episode 2 of Season 4, "The Fires of Pompeii," that the Doctor save a Pompeii family from being consumed by the molten lava.

The Doctor's reluctance to intervene on the family's behalf is based on a creed not to interfere with the course of history. However, Donna's insistence leads the Doctor to relent and save the family. Throughout Season 4, Donna serves as the persistent voice of reason for the Doctor, demanding that he relinquish his rigid, set beliefs, and, instead, show compassion and empathy. Donna consistently exhibits a heroine's resolve to right wrongs at her own expense, which in turn makes her a stronger, more confident individual. As Polster states, "The heroic woman believes, and reminds others, that common experience and accepted opinion can be changed, and she is willing to be the catalyst, even though she may confront opposition."[51] Repeatedly, the heroines in the *Doctor Who* series exhibit a willingness to step up to the plate and take a swing at whatever comes their way, regardless of their personal wellbeing. However, they do so with an understanding of their tenuous relationship with the Doctor, noting that their quest for freedom and for exploration is contingent upon his goodwill, which continually fluctuates.

Traditionally, the Supernatural Guide is secretive, with emotions that are in constant flux, as exemplified by the Doctor, who sees himself as a superior being, sent to protect earthlings from alien forces, which leads to an arrogance that, at times, distances him from his companions. Both benevolent and volatile, the Doctor is a war veteran suffering from posttraumatic stress disorder. Because of his trauma, he harbors many secrets, the biggest of which is his name. Unable to share neither his name nor past, he is also incapable of sustaining a long-term relationship. The Doctor is a loner in need of companionship; although, once his companions get too close, they are forced to move on, either by "divine" intervention or, in the case of Martha, by choice. Their quest, after all, is to heal their own soul, not his; although, because of their sensitivity and compassion for others, especially for him, they each attempt to mend his soul as well, to no avail. From this volatile environment, they learn how to balance their own needs with those of others, understanding eventually that it is possible to be both independent and connected without feeling guilty.

One finds that a woman's heroic journey or "quest is to balance her independence with her sensitivity to relationships and connections."[52] It is a higher burden of expectation than one finds with the male hero, who is often an independent agent of action, willing to strike out on his own, regardless of ties to family or friends. The hero may be reluctant at first to embark on an adventure, but it has little to do with relationships and more to do with "his fears concerning the unknown."[53] In contrast, the heroine seems to have little fear of embarking on an adventure, because, usually suffering from crisis of despair, anywhere would be better than where she currently finds herself. However, unlike her male counterpart, she does have a problem with resolving the impact her departure will have on her relationships. Moreover, this is her biggest struggle. One might even call their struggle the "dramatic question" for *Doctor Who*'s women: Will they be able to "resolve ... how to distinguish [themselves] as individual[s] within familiar environmental pressures"?[54] In fact, the entire reason for the quest that *Doctor Who*'s women embark upon is to "achiev[e] this equilibrium" within their relationships.[55] It is a fine line to walk, but like all successful heroines, *Doctor Who*'s women face and eventually overcome this challenge, thus returning to "the land of the living [as it were] with a vengeance."[56]

The reason for Rose, Martha, and Donna's success in overcoming not only the stress and complication of relationships, but also the many obstacles encountered during their journeys, is due to "five shared characteristics of heroism."[57] These characteristics are the backbone of every effective heroine and as are follows:

1. All heroes are motivated by a profound respect for human life.
2. Heroes have a strong sense of personal choice and effectiveness.
3. Their perspective on the world is original, going beyond what other people think is possible.
4. They are individuals of great physical and mental courage.
5. Heroes are not measured by publicity.[58]

These combined characteristics serve as the prototype for every heroine. Moreover, they are characteristics that each of the Doctor's three companions possess, which is demonstrated throughout the first four seasons of Nu Who.

Rose and Martha continually demonstrate "profound respect for human [and alien] life," which by Season 4 wears off on the Doctor, making him more susceptible to Donna's urgings to be more compassionate towards others. In fact, of the three companions, Donna exhibits the most respect for others, perhaps because she has a greater understanding of what it is like to be misunderstood and "abused." She demonstrates this understanding best in Season 4, Episode 3, "Planet of the Ood," where in she encounters the Ood, an enslaved alien race. She internalizes their pain and upon hearing their song of grief, weeps openly for their plight, and seeks to personally avenge and free them. She also seems to be the companion with the greatest impact on Doctor's overall behavior, in regards to respecting life. As noted earlier, Donna forces the Doctor to intervene and save a family from the volcanic eruption in Pompeii; however, her first cry for sympathy actually comes in Season 3, Episode 1, "Runaway Bride," wherein she begs for him to have mercy on the Empress of the Racnoss, a giant alien spider he is bent on killing. She proves ineffective in this instance, but eventually her insistence on preserving life has a substantial impact on the Doctor.

Each of the Doctor's three companions, despite the limitations imposed on them by their families and society, "have a strong sense of personal choice and effectiveness." For example, Rose and Martha are "willing leave the safety of [their] parents' home[s]" to go "in search of" self-fulfillment and adventure.[59] In taking this step to leave, they can "no longer ... blame parents, siblings, friends, lovers ... the outcome of [their] live[s]."[60] They are independent agents of action and change, with solid moral groundings, willing to risk everything for what they perceive as right.

Likewise, Rose, Martha, and Donna share a unique "perspective on the world," one that allows for the impossible, which is born from their inner Seeker. They are, thus, more open to adventure and chance than the average individual. Without this perspective, they would never venture onto TARDIS with the Doctor. They also would never break free of the perception that they are "lacking in competence, intelligence, and power," a condemnation they all face at some point before they join the Doctor.[61] For Rose it is a lack of power to rise above her "station," reinforced by her mother; for Martha it is a lack of competence inferred by her boss; and for Donna, it is a lack of intelligence, opined by everyone in her life, including her mother. Because they can envision something more for themselves, something beyond the routine of their lives, they are open to the "Call to Adventure" offered by the Doctor.

In addition, like every great hero, who ventures onto the path of adventure, Rose, Martha and Donna show tremendous physical and mental courage, reflecting their Warrior spirit. Rather than running from danger, they run towards it as demonstrated in the episodes in which each character is introduced. In Season 1, Episode 1, Rose, curious to learn more about the Doctor, seeks out information on him despite the warning that death is his constant companion and that by pursuing him, she is pursuing possible annihilation. She also shows no fear in her confrontations with the Plastic people, often leading the charge against them. In Season 3, Episode 2, Martha, intrigued by the Doctor's odd behavior, also pursues him. She even risks her life for the Doctor, literally using her last breath to save him. However, the intrepid Donna is by far the most vocally courageous, willing to challenge the Doctor and anyone else she feels is in the wrong. Beginning with her brief debut in Season 3, Episode 1, "Runaway Bride," Donna shows a feisty, tough spiritedness, equal to that of the Doctor's. She is in fact, on many levels, the Doctor's peer, a quality that foreshadows her most significant feat of courage. And, like her fellow travelers, she exhibits tremendous physical and mental bravery, confidently confronting each new obstacle thrown in her path.

Like all truly brave, heroic figures, none of the Doctor's three companions performs any deed for fame or fortune. They act from a place of moral obligation, not personal gain, willing to sacrifice themselves for the good of others. The urge to help and protect others stems from their Caregiver instincts and points to a "willingness to care and be responsible for people ... beyond [their] own immediate family and friends" for the good of the universe, not just themselves.[62] Their selflessness does not allow for the glory of recognition; it serves instead as another a means of personal development, learning how "to care for [themselves] so that caring for others is enriching not maiming" or burdensome.[63]

Because Rose, Martha, and Donna possess these five special traits, they are able to step onto the "Road of Trials" and enter "The Inmost Cave," which is "the place of greatest danger" wherein their enemies reside.[64] While in this "Inmost Cave," they each face "The Supreme Ordeal," which in all three cases means facing death/annihilation, not merely their own, but humankind's. One finds that "The Supreme Ordeal" is where the hero's journey intersects with the heroine's journey. In both cases, the hero/heroine "must face crucial failure, an apparent defeat, out of which he/she will achieve the wisdom or ability to succeed in the end," a success upon which many depend.[65] Knowing that so many are depending on her success, the heroine taps into "her desire to live," releasing a powerful force of strength in herself, not just for "her own advantage" and preservation, but "for others as well."[66]

Rose delves into "The Inmost Cave" in Episodes 12 and 13 of Season 2 of the Nu Who. In "Army of Ghosts" and "Doomsday," Rose must face down the combined forces of the Cybermen[67] and the Daleks.[68] Likewise, Martha confronts another great threat to humankind, the Master,[69] in the final three episodes of Season 3: "Utopia," The Sound of Drums" and "The Last of the Time Lords." While the battles these two heroines fight are truly epic with catastrophic implications for humankind, should they lose, it is Donna Noble who faces the greatest danger and challenge and, in turn, ultimately loses the most, making her heroine's journey by far the most tragic of the three.

Once the heroine has entered the "Inmost Cave," faced "The Supreme Ordeal," and has gained a newfound "knowledge or greater capability, [she] can now defeat the hostile forces" of the enemy.[70] "Seizing the Sword" of knowledge, truth and/or power strengthens the heroine, emboldening her, giving her those invincible qualities long associated with the hero. With the sword of knowledge, truth and power in hand, she is able to forge "the path of her destiny," and confidently face anything or anyone who crosses her path.[71]

Because this is a heroine's journey, taking on these superhuman qualities is usually in opposition to what she is ultimately seeking, a way to balance the expectations of the world with her personal dreams and aspirations. Leaning too far to either side of these conflicting roles will cause the boat to tip. Her quest is "to balance her independence with her sensitivity to relationships and communication."[72] According to Polster, it is only

> when she has achieved this equilibrium, when she perceives what she can accomplish through her own independent action, [that] she is free to move from her personal center and relate to her world with a firm sense of agency, independence, and choice.[73]

One clearly sees *Doctor Who*'s women finding their equilibrium, especially in the character of Martha Jones, who, of the three, seems to be the one that most embodies the transformation from dependent to independent. Martha's independence is clearly demonstrated in the final episode of Season 3 when she makes the decision to walk away from the TARDIS and the Doctor. Of the three women, Martha is the only one who makes a conscious, deliberate decision to leave the Doctor.

While Rose gains as much independence and confidence as Martha, she is forced to part ways with the Doctor. Likewise, Donna, the woman who hunted the Doctor down for adventure, is no willing partner in her separation from the Doctor. This is not to say that Rose and Donna are weaker women than Martha is or less noble in their quest. Rather, what their reluctance points to are myriad aspects of growth and development the heroine's journey enjoys, which in turn make it uniquely feminine. It is not a one-size-fits-all "Call to Adventure," although the results are the same: a break from the greater influence of the society at large and a renewed sense of confidence in the ability to determine one's own path, for better or worse. As noted, Donna makes the same progressive strides towards independence and confidence as Rose and Martha; however, her quest ends tragically — not in death, exactly, but close to it.

The final three stages of the heroine's quest/journey are "The Road Back," the "Resurrection," and the "Return with the Elixir." The first of the final three stages is "The Road Back," which is heralded by an "urgent yearning to reconnect with the feminine," her family and friends[74] and "to be comforted, held and nurtured."[75] The connections and nurturing sought by Rose, Martha and Donna are beyond the Doctor's capabilities, because of his many secrets and barriers, which fuel his alienation and isolation. Because the Doctor is unable — unwilling — to provide them with the "love" they need, Rose, Martha and Donna seek someone who can, which in all three cases is family — specifically their mothers. The "Resurrection," the second of the three final stages, requires that the heroine heal what Murdock terms "the mother/daughter split," the separation between "feelings and ... spiritual natures."[76] Once the heroine mends the split, she is then able to fully understand and recognize "that everything is connected to everything else."[77] The comprehension of this universality, signals a rebirth. Thus reborn, the heroine is able to "Return with the Elixir," which in the case of Rose, Martha, and Donna is independence and confidence. Of the three stages, the "Resurrection" proves the most fascinating when analyzing the role it plays in determining how *Doctor Who's* women will fair when they return to the "ordinary" world.

During the "Resurrection," the heroine "is spiritually or literally reborn and purified by [her] ordeal as [she] approaches the threshold of the ordinary world.[78] Rose's rebirth occurs in Season 2, Episode 14, "Doomsday." After a Cyberman and Daleks invasion, she is "reborn" in another dimension, leaving the Doctor behind. Her rebirth requires that she cope with being separated from the Doctor — a man she deeply loves — and with beginning anew with a reconstructed family and career as a secret agent with Torchwood. It is literally a fresh start, which her adventures in the TARDIS leave her more than capable of handling.

In the last episode of Season 3, "The Last of the Time Lords," Martha is spiritually reborn and purified by a yearlong quest. On her quest, she circles the globe, spreading the word about the Doctor's plight, as a doomed prisoner of the Master. Her trek around the world is perilous, but she endures in order to save the Doctor's life. Although, she gains worldwide recognition for her journey, she refuses to acknowledge her status as a folk hero. Instead, she continues to put the focus on the Doctor. Elevating the Doctor above herself in the same selfless manner as Rose and Donna proves empowering for Martha, who finds a greater independence in letting go of the need to control. In doing so, she develops a psychological and physical toughness that, as a comfortable, middle-class, professional woman, she lacked before embarking on her journey with the Doctor. As a result of her new empowerment, like Rose, she embarks on a new career as a secret agent, but with the Unit, working with the government to combat alien and terrestrial forces, something she is more than qualified to do thanks to her adventures with the Doctor.

Unlike her predecessors, Donna is reborn twice, once in Season 4, Episode 11, "Turn Left" and then again in Episode 13, "Journey's End." Her rebirths are spiritual, psychological and mental. Donna, the street-smart, stubborn, yet compassionate adventuress, is on a quest to find her self-worth and her place in the wider-world where she is, unfortunately, perceived as being flaky and dimwitted, not only by outsiders, but by her mother and friends, as well. Her rebirths bring her closer to eradicating these perceptions. However, for Donna, the "Resurrection," while life altering, also proves the most devastating.

Donna's first resurrection occurs in Season 4, Episode 11, "Turn Left." In this episode, she must decide, as noted earlier, between life and death. She chooses death and, in doing so, saves the universe from annihilation. With this choice, she comes to understand her interconnectedness to everything around her. She also begins to comprehend the "multiplicity and complexity of truth," and that "all truth" is ultimately "relative."[79] Her selfless sacrifice affords her a "second" chance at life and the opportunity to see the universe as a realm of infinite possibilities and choices. In other words, she finds the freedom to break free of the negative labels assigned to her by others. Moreover, her newfound freedom brings her closer to capturing the sword of knowledge and truth.

Donna's second resurrection occurs in Episode 13, "Journey's End," in which she gets the opportunity to "Seize the Sword" of knowledge and truth. However to capture this sword, Donna must merge her brain with the Doctor's. Melding their brains together creates a super Donna — infinitely wise and knowledgeable. The merger resembles what Murdock calls the "integration of masculine and feminine," an ideal state in which the "dualistic culture which values, creates and sustains polarities — an either/or stratified mentality which identifies and locates ideas and people at opposite ends of a spectrum" is dissolved.[80] With this newfound super knowledge, she is able to save not only planet Earth, but also the universe from Davros, the Doctor's ultimate nemesis. In doing so, she becomes an interstellar hero, far surpassing the accomplishments of the Doctor's former companions. Moreover, while she does not perform her heroic acts for the adulation of others, the resulting fame helps Donna conceptualize a stronger sense of self-worth. Sadly, this moment of self-realization and glory is short lived.

The melding of minds with the Doctor proves too much for Donna's mortal body and the only way to save her is to separate their combined knowledge, leaving her with total amnesia. Her year of adventure and development is wiped from her memory. Through the "Resurrection," she is literally reborn with a clean slate. The universe celebrates her accomplishments, but in order to protect her from a certain death, she can never be allowed to remember all she has accomplished. All her growth and newfound independence is erased. Fortunately, her mother and grandfather are keenly aware of her contribution to humankind. In lieu of their knowledge, there is hope that they will treat Donna with the respect she craves and help support her in rediscovering her independence, should the old/new Donna care to embark on such a quest again.

In many ways, Donna's journey comes the closest to mirroring what Virginia Woolf's "Mary" was seeking and what so many women seek, that "precarious balance between independence and despair," a despair resulting from the overwhelming pressure of being squeezed between society's expectations and one's own.[81] As Laurie Brands Gagne states in *The Uses of Darkness: Women's Underworld Journeys, Ancient and Modern*, "To despair is to have no program," no purpose in life, which can cause one "to lose the future."[82] The pressure of societal expectations combined with the despair over having no future is clearly illustrated in the eleventh episode of Season 4, "Turn Left" wherein Donna must make a literal life or death decision by turning either left or right. One way leads to the future, the other to death. What one finds in Donna's quest is a "search for a personal sense of direction and significance that would give [her] a unique life of dignity and purpose."[83] She eventually finds dignity and purpose, and gets to "Return with the Elixir" that "will heal [the] world and restore balance"; however, she does so at great cost.[84] Donna represents women who "have historically been on the forefront of the insistence on humane principles and treatment" even though these same courtesies were denied to her by all but her grandfather and the Doctor.[85] Her willingness to sacrifice herself for others makes her true heroic figure.

The heroine's journey begins with a quest for a room of her own, resulting from "a greater struggle to separate herself from the intense pull of home and family.[86] The Doctor, uniquely positioned to offer his companions the freedom and ability to escape, provides the means by which Rose, Martha, and Donna can grow and develop as independent women through literal and symbolic travel. Though all the companions eventually return home, they do so as women determined to "choose the way [they] will be involved" with their families "and what [their] contribution[s] will be" to the greater community.[87] Being able to make this choice is best represented by Donna, who makes the decision to erase her memories and live in obscurity — the ultimate sacrifice for one seeking the approval and validation of others. In the end, Rose Tyler, Martha Jones, and Donna Noble find something deep within themselves that they never realized existed, a confidence to be strong, independent individuals without apology or compromise thanks to the Doctor and his little blue box.

NOTES

1. In Season 1, Christopher Eccleston played the Doctor. In Seasons 2–4, David Tennant played the Doctor. For program details see Videography.

2. Virginia Woolf, *A Room of One's Own, Selected Works of Virginia Woolf* (Ware: Wordsworth Editions, 2005): p. 595.

3. The TARDIS is a space ship disguised as blue police box.

4. Joseph Campbell, *The Hero with a Thousand Faces*, 3d ed. (Princeton: Princeton University Press, 1973): p. 79.

5. Bonnie Frederick, and Susan H. McLeod, eds., *Women and the Journey: The Female Travel Experience* (Pullman: Washington State University Press, 1993): p. xix.

6. Ibid., p. xxiii.

7. Miriam F. Polster, *Eve's Daughters: The Forbidden Heroism of Women* (San Francisco: Jossey-Bass, 1992): p. 6.

8. Katherine Phelps notes that the "heroic journey" has limited applicability and is only "useful for working within the genre of heroic myths," which is why it is necessary to expand the definition of the hero's journey to include aspects of the heroine's journey. Phelps has done this with her 1998 creation of "The Heroine's Journey," a chart that outlines Psyche's as well as four other female fairytale characters' journeys.

9. Maureen Murdock, *The Heroine's Journey* (Boston: Shambhala, 1990): p. 17.

10. Ibid., p. 17.

11. Ibid.

12. Linda S. Griggs, "Hero Quest Cycles," *Quest Cycles: Life-After-Treatment Support for Breast Cancer Survivors,* http://www.questcycles.com/hqcycle.html (25 June 2009), par. 8.

13. Carol S. Pearson, *Awakening Heroes Within: Twelve Archetypes to Help Us Find Ourselves and Transform Our World* (New York: HarperOne, 1991): p. 10.

14. Ibid., pp. 10–12.

15. Ibid., pp. 10–11.

16. Ibid., p. 10.

17. Ibid., p. 11

18. Ibid., pp. 10–11.

19. Ximena Gallardo-C and C. Jason Smith, *Alien Woman: The Making of Lt. Ellen Ripley* (New York: Continuum, 2004): p. 17.

20. Hilary Radner, *Neo-Feminist Cinema: Girly Films, Chick Flicks and Consumer Culture* (New York: Routledge, 2011): p. 24.

21. John Kenneth Muir, *A Critical History of* Doctor Who *on Television* (Jefferson, NC: McFarland, 1999): p. 1.

22. Ibid., p. 9.

23. Ibid., p. 20.

24. Ibid., p. 21.

25. Ibid.

26. Sarah Jane Smith was the most popular of the original companions and, in 2007, reemerged in her own television series, *The Sarah Jane Adventures.*

27. The new version of *Doctor Who* has featured three male companions, two of which (Mickey and Adam) served as the "daffy, damsel in distress" figure, and one (Captain Jack Harkness) who was clearly bi-sexual. The role of the male companions has changed substantially from the original series, thus demonstrating Davies's commitment to broader more liberal interpretations of gender roles.

28. Avid *Doctor Who* fans refer to the resurrected 2005 version of *Doctor Who* as Nu Who.

29. Polster, *Eve's Daughters*, p. 17.

30. Ibid.

31. Gender performance in this case refers to the traditional roles of daughter, wife, and mother imposed on the female companions by society.

32. Marion Tinling, *Women into the Unknown: A Sourcebook on Women Explorers and Travelers* (New York: Greenwood Press, 1989): p. xxiv.

33. Ibid., p. xxvi.

34. Robin U. Russin and William Missouri Downs. "Historical Approaches to Structure," *Screenplay: Writing the Picture* (Los Angeles, Silman-James Press, 2003): p. 94.

35. Ibid., p. 95.

36. Griggs, "Hero Quest Cycles," par. 3.

37. Murdock, *The Heroine's Journey*, p. 4.

38. Ibid., p. 11.

39. Pearson, *Awakening the Hero Within*, p. 39.

40. Murdock, *The Heroine's Journey*, p. 11.

41. Ruth E. Ray, and Susan H. McFadden, "The Web and the Quilt," *Alternatives to the Heroic Journey Toward Spiritual Development, Journal of Adult Development*, 8.3 (2001): p. 203.

42. Ibid., p. 202.

43. Russin, "Historical Approaches to Structure," p. 94.

44. Polster, *Eve's Daughters: The Forbidden Heroism of Women*, p. 178.

45. Ibid.

46. Laurie Brands Gagne, *The Uses of Darkness: Women's Underworld Journeys, Ancient and Modern* (Notre Dame, University of Notre Dame Press, 2000): p. 26.

47. Muir, *A Critical History of Doctor Who on Television*, p. 3.

48. The idea to add the ability to "regenerate" as one of the Doctor's alien qualities was incorporated as a characteristic in order to allow a new actor to assume the Doctor's role without disrupting the flow of the show.

49. Muir, *A Critical History of* Doctor Who *on Television*, p. 16.

50. Russin, "Historical Approaches to Structure," p. 94.

51. Polster, *Eve's Daughters*, p. 25.

52. Ibid., p. 20.

53. Russin, "Historical Approaches to Structure," p. 94.

54. Polster, *Eve's Daughters*, p. 20.

55. Ibid.

56. Gagne, *The Uses of Darkness*, p. 28.

57. Polster, *Eve's Daughters*, p. 22.

58. Ibid.

59. Murdock, *The Heroine's Journey*, p. 46.

60. Ibid.

61. Ibid., p. 29.

62. Pearson, *Awakening the Heroes Within*, p. 115.

63. Ibid.

64. Russin, "Historical Approaches to Structure," p. 94.

65. Ibid.

66. Gagne, *The Uses of Darkness*, p. 28.

67. Cybermen were first introduced to the *Doctor Who* series in Season 4 of 1966. Cybermen are silver plated robots with human brains, but no emotions.

68. The Daleks were introduced in Season 1 of 1963. They are non-humanoid mutants that reside inside salt/pepper shaker type armor.

69. Treacherous and rebellious, the Master is one of the last Time Lords and is set on destroying humankind and the Doctor.

70. Russin, "Historical Approaches to Structure," p. 95.

71. Murdock, *The Heroine's Journey*, p. 47.

72. Polster, *Eve's Daughters*, p. 20.

73. Ibid.

74. Murdock, *The Heroine's Journey*, p. 5.

75. Ibid., p. 122.

76. Ibid., p. 131.

77. Pearson, *Awakening the Heroes Within*, p. 205.
78. Russin, "Historical Approaches to Structure," p. 95.
79. Pearson, *Awakening the Heroes Within*, p. 212.
80. Murdock, *The Heroine's Journey*, p. 167.
81. Polster, *Eve's Daughters*, p. 22.
82. Gagne, *The Uses of Darkness*, p. 26.
83. Polster, *Eve's Daughters*, p. 22.
84. Russin, "Historical Approaches to Structure," p. 95.
85. Polster, *Eve's Daughters*, p. 24.
86. Ibid., p. 181.
87. Ibid.

15

Spoiled for Another Life

*Sarah Jane Smith's Adventures with
and Without Doctor Who*

SHERRY GINN

"There's nothing 'only' about being a girl"
— Sarah Jane Smith, "The Monster of
Peladon," Story #73

Doctor Who, according to Steven Moffat (qtd. in Lacob), has always been about the companion. The companions who travel with any given Doctor serve as a substitute for the viewer and a person with whom the viewer can identify, the person who will be transported into the past or into the future to share the Doctor's adventures.[1] These companions may be male or female, human or alien, young or old, but they must always be ready and willing for the adventure of a lifetime. During that adventure the companion will face danger and terror and learn about their strengths and weaknesses. Each will grow as a person and the assumption is that each will leave the Doctor's company better for having made the journey.[2] However, Lynnette Porter notes that each companion pays a price for travel with the Doctor. "They lose their innocence, and quite often they become physically or emotionally injured as a result of their travels.... The Doctor, however, seldom follows up to 'heal' the wounds his companions suffer."[3]

Such is the case with one of the most popular of the Doctor's companions, Sarah Jane Smith, who traveled with both the third and fourth incarnations of the Doctor (1973–1976).[4] Portrayed by Elisabeth Sladen, Sarah Jane figured in 18 adventures before "retiring" from further travel. Attempts were made briefly to revive Sarah Jane, but those efforts were unsuccessful.[5] Sarah Jane was reunited with the tenth Doctor in three episodes — "School Reunion" (from which the CBBC launched *The Sarah Jane Adventures* [*SJA*] in 2007), "The Stolen Earth," and "Journey's End." Highly-acclaimed and award-winning, three episodes of series five of *SJA*[6] had yet to air when Elisabeth Sladen's death from cancer was announced in April 2011. The series will not continue without her.

Sarah Jane provides a unique view of the effects of travel with the Doctor as we are able to examine the life of this woman during those travels as well as afterwards. Despite the laments of various companions, notably Rose Tyler, as to how she could ever live without the Doctor,[7] SJ did have a life after she left the Doctor, as we learned during her reunion with the tenth Doctor and her subsequent adventures on Bannerman Road. The purpose of this chapter is to examine Sarah Jane's life, with a view toward situating her within the times in which she lived, examining how her character lived in that time, and how Sarah Jane changed from our first meeting with her in 1973 to our last in 2011.

The Adventures of Sarah Jane Smith

We first meet Sarah Jane in the episode "The Time Warrior." SJ is masquerading as her Aunt Lavinia, a device she will continue to employ periodically throughout her time in the Whoniverse.[8] SJ is an investigative reporter, she tells the Doctor, and she is quite suspicious of him during the course of this episode, thinking that he might be behind the mysterious events which are occurring in both the present and the past. Having decidedly different views of the character and how she should be portrayed, Barry Letts, Terrance Dicks, and Elisabeth Sladen provided insights into the type of character expected of the Doctor's new companion in the "Beginning to End" Special Feature for the DVD of "The Time Warrior." Dicks for example did not want to address feminism, preferring instead that Sarah Jane's character continue the traditional pattern with respect to the Doctor's companions, i.e., the damsel in distress who can scream loudly and wait to be rescued by the Doctor.[9] Letts was willing to allow a new type of companion to emerge, yielding to the social and political realities of the 1970s. Sladen provided a glimpse into her own thinking about SJ when she produced a note from her copy of the script of the story, with a list of characteristics that she believed were important to SJ's character. These included: impulsive; ready for anything new; everything very obvious; and righteous indignation. Sladen's portrayal of Sarah Jane, in both the 1970s and the 2000s, was true to her vision of the character.[10]

Sarah Jane proved to be a new type of companion for the third Doctor, one who, although impressed by his brilliance and joie de vivre, nevertheless insisted that he never condescend to her or treat her differently simply because she was female. From their first meeting, she refused to prepare coffee for him, to allow him to protect or coddle her, and to remain on the sidelines when the action commenced. Based upon both her beliefs and her actions, Sarah Jane would be labeled a feminist, someone who believes that women and men should be considered equal, socially, economically, and legally. According to Matlin, a feminist "is a person whose beliefs, values, and attitudes reflect a high regard for women as human beings."[11] Sarah Jane embodied the new woman, the woman arising out of the Women's Liberation Movement of the 1960s, referred to today as the second-wave of the women's movement, or as liberal feminism.[12]

Liberal feminism places feminism firmly within the bounds of political liberalism. These feminists believe that women should be given equal access with men to educational and vocational opportunities. They believe that legal barriers to women's rights must be destroyed, but they also believe that such destruction should come within the system via political activism. In addition, liberal feminists recognize that sex and gender are not synonymous, and that traditional gender roles are stultifying for men as well as women. Thus, liberal feminists would advocate that men and women become more androgynous. This view was condemned by other feminists who argued that liberal feminism was too white and too middle-class; that is, it was too exclusive of women who differed from the founding mothers of the Women's Movement. Nevertheless, we owe liberal feminists many laws that now protect women and their rights, although the job is far from done. Although there are other types of feminism, such as Marxist feminism, radical feminism, psychoanalytic feminism, and eco-feminism, Sarah Jane's youth and education would coincide with liberal feminism, and she served as one of the first feminist role models for young men and women watching *Doctor Who* during the 1970s, including the author, who was first introduced to *Doctor Who* during the Tom Baker/fourth Doctor years, which are also frequently referred to as the golden age of *Doctor Who*.[13]

As the story proceeds, Sarah Jane demonstrates that she is willing to do whatever is necessary to fight for the cause. Indeed, she insists upon being thick in the action and refuses to stay behind when a man named Hal tells her that she should not attempt to rescue the Doctor because she is a girl. Later when working in the kitchen at Irongron's castle, the better to drug him and his men, Sarah Jane tells Meg, the cook, that she is not afraid of men; that women are equal to men and they should not be subjected to slavery just because they are women. While these statements are very much in keeping with 1970s feminist philosophy, and continue to inform the viewer as to the type of person the new companion will be, the statements also seem quite condescending and "chauvinistic" in their own right. Sarah Jane, having no idea of the times in which she is situated (rather surprising in a woman who is supposed to be an investigative reporter), is able to tell everyone what they should do and should think just because she, the young, smart, white, English woman says so. Thus, in our first meeting with her, Sarah Jane shows us that she is inquisitive, is willing to help out, will not take "no" for an answer, and will stand up for herself and what she believes is right. We also see that her impulsivity can lead to danger and that she possesses the arrogance of youth, if not a completely Anglocentric view. After all, *Doctor Who* has always been written from the British point of view, reflecting a

> contradictory sense of national awareness. On the one hand, it expresses a sense of paranoia and insecurity: the nation is vulnerable to alien (for which read foreign) invasion and proves unable to resist a technologically superior force until it is saved by the advanced scientific knowledge of the Doctor. One the other hand, it also suggests a perverse sense of national self-importance and prestige: as long as alien invaders deem it necessary to take over the British Isles as a prelude to their conquest of Earth, the illusion of Britain as a great power is maintained.[14]

The next two adventures find the Doctor attempting to return Sarah Jane to Earth; she is not yet the Doctor's companion at this point. However, they are sidetracked, arriving at an Earth far into the future ("The Invasion of the Dinosaurs") before actually leaving Earth and visiting another planet, Exxilon, where SJ meets the Daleks for the first time ("Death to the Daleks"). Sarah Jane's feminism is put to good use in the next story "The Monster of Peladon." The Doctor attempts to help the daughter of his deceased friend, the King of Peladon. Queen Thalira is a young woman, ruling a world that has never had a female ruler. Her people are dismissive of females, including her. This is also true of the various Federation ambassadors who refer to Sarah Jane as just a female or a girl. Naturally SJ does appreciate being dismissed so handily and having to sit around, waiting for the Doctor. At one point the Doctor tells her that she needs to have a talk with the Queen. Sarah Jane does so, telling Thalira about "women's lib." Sarah Jane says that one reason Thalira is so ignored is because she does not act "queenly." Only by acting like a Queen, can one become a Queen, SJ tells her. This feminism subplot is a little silly, as Wood points out: SJ and Thalira are the only females in the entire episode, with the sole exception of "The Women in Purple," who never speaks and is never identified.[15] Sladen herself recalls that the "irony of the male writers getting a male character to 'order' a woman to talk about feminism wasn't lost on me."[16]

Sarah Jane's feminism continued throughout her time with Pertwee's third Doctor. His manner toward her was courtly and, given her history, he was a father-figure for her.

However, that did not stop him from teasing her, usually in such a way as to imply she was "just a girl," so that he could watch her reaction. Sarah Jane was retained as companion after Tom Baker's introduction in "Robot," primarily to provide continuity for fans that might be leery of a new actor in the role of the Doctor. Unfortunately, she was increasingly relegated to a damsel in distress type of companion.

Sarah Jane's relationship with the fourth Doctor was slightly different than her relationship with the third Doctor. As indicated, DW3 was much more of a father-figure for SJ, whereas DW4 was closer in age to her, at least as far as his physical appearance was concerned. Although DW4 could be short with her and was sometimes annoyed with her questions, their relationship was friendlier than was the relationship between DW3 and SJ. As a matter of fact, DW4 referred to Sarah Jane as his best friend in the episode "Seeds of Doom."

His tenure was referred to as the golden age of *Doctor Who* by many,[17] but there were also a number of fans and critics who were disappointed with Tom Baker's interpretation of the Doctor. This was especially true in his later years, as his characterization of the Doctor grew increasingly campy and buffoonish. Elisabeth Sladen's decision to the leave the series after three and a half years led the way for a more feminine and less overtly feminist type of companion ("The Hand of Fear"). To her credit Sladen was never critical of Baker, or the direction in which her character had been written during her last two years on *Doctor Who*.

Sarah Jane was "revived" in 1981 for an adventure entitled "A Girl's Best Friend." Proposed as a pilot for a new children's television series, *K-9 and Company*, only one episode was filmed, although a number of stories were published. In this episode we learn that Sarah Jane has been working for Reuters, and has come to Moreton Harwood to spend the Christmas holidays with her Aunt Lavinia and Lavinia's ward, Brendan Richards. Lavinia is scheduled to leave for the U.S. after Christmas but receives a call informing her that she must leave immediately. She is unable to contact Sarah Jane about the change in plans, leading Sarah Jane to wonder about her aunt's "disappearance" when she arrives at the house, especially given the strange events happening in the vicinity of Moreton Harwood. It is in this episode that Sarah Jane finally opens a package that has been stored at Lavinia's various houses for a number of years. She is delighted to discover that the package contains K-9, a Mark III model robotic dog built for her by the Doctor.[18] With the help of Brendan and K-9, Sarah Jane investigates the mysterious events that have been occurring in the village and discloses the nefarious activities of a coven of "witches."[19] Although *K-9 and Company* was not picked up for serialization, a number of stories were published afterwards continuing the adventures of Sarah Jane, K-9, and Brendan.[20] In these stories we learn that Sarah Jane moves to Moreton Harwood ("Powerstone") and lives with Aunt Lavinia for some time (although we do not learn for exactly how long she stays there). Other facts we learn are that SJ has studied martial arts and is very good at it as one of the villains in the story "Horror Hotel" learns. In addition, Sarah Jane loves to vacation in Scotland, although she does not visit as often as she would like ("The Monster of Loch Crag"). Her uncle, Africana Smith, was an archaeologist and died while on a dig ("The Curse of Kanbo-Ala"); however, he died doing what he loved best and that, Lavinia says, is how he would have wanted his life to end.

We lose sight of Sarah Jane at this point in time and do not encounter her again until "The Five Doctors." The implication, when she meets the Doctors, is that they have not seen each other for some time. If we use our standard time, since Sarah Jane is from Earth, then it would be about seven years since they last met. After this adventure we again lose sight of SJ until she encounters the tenth Doctor in "School Reunion." During this episode we learn that SJ has continued to work as a journalist. Indeed her cover story during her investigation of the school is that she is writing an article about the Headmaster for the Sunday *Times*.

During the interim which ranged from the early 1980s to the present time (assuming that *SJA* also occurs during the present time), Sarah Jane establishes herself and her career more thoroughly and continues her mission of protecting Earth from the nefarious intentions of various alien species. Aunt Lavinia eventually dies and apparently leaves Sarah Jane a good deal of money, enough to buy an enormous house at 13 Bannerman Road in Ealing. Along with K-9 Sarah Jane possesses a Xylok, a crystalline alien masquerading as a computer, which she calls Mr. Smith, and a sonic lipstick, another gift from the Doctor. She is apparently quite happy in her life, and then extraordinary things begin to happen — she acquires a son, Luke ("The Invasion of the Bane"), as well as a couple of teen-age "companions," Maria Jackson and Clyde Langer in Series One and Rani Chandra and Clyde in series two through five, and a daughter, Sky, in Series Five ("Sky"). Sarah Jane's protégés ignore her orders to stop and do nothing on their adventures, about as well as she ignored those of the Doctor.

Luke is actually a genius, and although human, he is much more than that. Grown by the Bane from the DNA of over 10,000 people, Luke was created by the Bane as test-subject for their plans to conquer Earth. Sarah Jane had never planned to have children, never trusting anyone long enough to get close, she tells Rani, and she had apparently cared much more for the Doctor than anyone realized, telling Maria that there was ever only one man for her, no other man could ever compare ("Bane"). However, she grows to love Luke deeply over the course of the series. She also becomes closer than she would like to Maria and Clyde, and is very disappointed and upset when Maria's father accepts a transfer to Washington ("The Last Sontaran"), becoming angry when she hears the news. Rani, the new girl, wants to be a journalist and shares many of Sarah Jane's characteristics: nosiness, curiosity, bravery, and impulsiveness. She quickly becomes one of the gang, although she frequently feels that they like Maria more than her, a feeling that gets her into trouble occasionally ("The Mad Woman in the Attic"). Sarah feels the "empty nest" keenly when Luke leaves for university. One morning she opens her door to find a baby on her doorstep. The child — created to be a bomb and thus deliver her species, the Fleshkind, from annihilation by the Metalkind — is first "activated" as a 12-year-old girl and then "defused." She is abandoned by her people and adopted by Sarah Jane.

We learn a good deal about Sarah Jane's life during seasons one through five. A Season One episode shows us what life would be like if Sarah Jane had never grown up. We learn in "Whatever Happened to Sarah Jane" that she had a good friend who died when they were thirteen. The death was accidental; however, an alien named The Trickster offers the girl the chance to live again if SJ dies. Only Maria remembers Sarah Jane's existence, and only then because of an alien device that captures memories. Nevertheless, Maria's memories of SJ are enough to cause her to relentlessly pursue any lead that will help her find Sarah Jane.

The Trickster returns in the Season Two episode "The Temptation of Sarah Jane Smith" in which he gives SJ the ability to travel back in time to answer the question that has plagued her for her entire life: why did her parents leave her on the side of the road just prior to the automobile accident that claimed their lives when SJ was three months old? SJ learns the answer to the question, but not before meeting her parents. In addition, they meet her and learn who she is. In the tradition of all time paradoxes, Sarah Jane learns that they left her behind and drove to their deaths in order for Sarah Jane to live and defeat The Trickster: if Sarah Jane had accepted the bargain, to stop her parents from dying, then the entire world she knew, including Luke, would vanish.

The Trickster's next appearance is in Season Three's "The Wedding of Sarah Jane Smith." Sarah Jane falls in love with a man named Peter Dalton, who is the perfect man for her. They fall in love quickly, and when he proposes, she accepts. Luke is happy for her, but Clyde believes that everything is happening too quickly; he thinks that Peter is an alien. He actually is not, but that does not stop Clyde and Rani from attempting to learn what is happening and why his actions are so mysterious. It is only on the wedding day that the Doctor arrives and attempts to stop the ceremony. The Trickster appears and once again tries to tempt Sarah Jane into accepting a bargain: marriage to the man of her dreams. Sarah Jane is forced to choose life without Peter in order to keep the world and everything and everyone she knows safe. Once again, Sarah Jane must accept her destiny, to keep Earth safe.

The events as mentioned in these few episodes provide us with one major insight into Sarah Jane's psyche and also explain the increasing number of arguments that she has with Luke. He is no longer a young boy, but developing into a young man. Given that he was grown in a lab, he does not know how to be human. Luckily for him, he has Clyde to help him as well as Rani and Maria. Nevertheless, the fact that Luke is growing up, that he is a teenager and trying to be a normal teenager at that, leads to tension and conflict with Sarah Jane, and it all comes to a head in the Series Three episode "Mona Lisa's Revenge." Luke and Sarah Jane are arguing more than usual, and he is angry at the way she is treating him. Because he is angry, Luke does not tell her that Clyde's artwork has won an award or that their class has been invited to the International Museum to view the Mona Lisa, which is on loan from The Louvre. At the museum, the teens learn that the painting has come to life, and Mona Lisa is searching for her brother so that they may wreak havoc on Earth. When Clyde and Rani realize what is happening, they suggest calling Sarah Jane for help, but Luke tells them no, that they can handle things on their own — they do not need her help. However, Sarah Jane learns of trouble at the museum and comes to look for Luke, Clyde, and Rani. Mona Lisa, ever willing to stoke discord, repeats Luke's words to Sarah Jane, who is upset by the anger she hears in his voice. She wonders about the future of their relationship: she knows that Luke is growing up and that he will eventually leave her.

And that, I propose, is at the core of Sarah Jane's relationships: fear of abandonment. We have seen that her parents were the first to abandon her, leaving her beside the road prior to their accident. It does not matter that they died; what mattered to a young girl was that her parents left her in her pram all alone, and then drove off without her. Sixty years later she will learn the truth ("Temptation"), but for the time in between, she had to live with the knowledge that her parents left her. Although Sarah Jane was raised by her aunt, Lavinia had her own life as a well-respected virologist, and Sarah Jane was mostly ignored. Her best friend died when they were young schoolgirls ("Whatever Happened"). The Doctor did not come back for her, as he said he would, when they were forced to separate upon the Doctor's recall to Gallifrey ("The Hand of Fear"). Peter Dalton left her, because it was the only way he could save her life and the lives of the children ("Wedding"). And Luke will eventually grow up and leave her, just as all children leave their parents upon maturity.

Sarah Jane had made the decision when she was a young woman that she would not marry or have children. She tells Rani that there had been men before in her life, but none of the relationships had lasted, because she was unable and unwilling to tell these men about her life ("Wedding"). How could she tell them that she had traveled in space and time? How could she tell them that beings from other worlds regularly visited Earth? She had learned that people could not be trusted. Part of this lesson had been learned by a young girl who was abandoned by her parents. Another part had been learned more overtly as when people she trusted turned out to be traitors or worse, such as Captain Mike Yates of UNIT who turned out to be a traitor (or, at least, a misguided one who was later redeemed) ("Invasion of the Dinosaurs"). These were certainly defining moments in Sarah Jane's life and led to her being the woman we see in *The Sarah Jane Adventures*. What we also see in *SJA* is a woman reassessing her life, wondering about the road not taken, i.e., motherhood, and then choosing to pursue that path. Such a reappraisal of one's life is characteristic of many women in contemporary society, and one theoretical orientation that examines this issue is life-course theory.

Life-Course Theory and the Seasons of a Woman's Life

Two theories that dominated psychology during the twentieth century were Sigmund Freud's Theory of Psychosexual Development[21] and Jean Piaget's Cognitive-Developmental Theory.[22] Freud was particularly interested in elucidating the stages through which the individual's personality developed from birth into adolescence. Piaget, on the other hand, was concerned with the changes that occurred in the way children and adolescents think. Each theory was important for shaping the field of developmental psychology; however, neither postulated development past adolescence, proposing instead that human beings' personality and cognitive structures were molded by childhood experiences. Neither proposed that significant changes occurred beyond adolescence and into adulthood.

One theorist who did propose that human development continued throughout the lifespan was Erik Erikson.[23] In the tradition of Freud and Piaget, Erikson postulated that social development occurred in a series of stages that were heavily influenced by biological and cultural constraints. Erikson believed that development proceeded in eight stages from birth until death, with each stage characterized by a crisis that the individual must overcome in order for development to proceed in a healthy manner. For the purposes of this essay on the life of Sarah Jane Smith, three of the adult stages are important.

During adolescence one confronts the questions "Who am I and why am I here?" The heart of the fifth stage of development, Identity vs. Role-confusion, is the identity crisis.[24] The adolescent must confront the roles that he or she has played in his or her life thus far and incorporate them into a cohesive identity. To this end the adolescent must be allowed to explore new and different roles or different paths in previous roles. Failure to synthesize an identity leads to the inability to find direction in life and pursue a meaningful future.[25] Following identity development the adolescent enters young adulthood, in which the overwhelming social pressure is to find a mate. Increasingly intimate relationships with friends and the drive toward marriage and procreation characterize this stage. Thus, young adulthood is the period of childbearing and childrearing. Generativity vs. Stagnation, the stage encompassing Middle adulthood, is characterized by launching one's children into the world. Some middle-aged individuals may now feel a need to "give back" to the world, and these people become concerned with future generations, a concern that may manifest as charitable work. However, the primary task of this stage is helping younger generations of people develop useful and productive lives.

When we meet Sarah Jane Smith in "The Time Warrior," she is 23 years old and working as a journalist. For some time after that, representing three years in our world, she travels with the Doctor until she is forced to return home. Sarah Jane has apparently resolved her identity crisis and is comfortable with her career choice, which has led to her experiences with the Doctor. As we meet up with her over the next ten years or so, we find that she has continued her work as a journalist and she is apparently quite good at it. She drops names (of very respected journals and magazines), letting us know that her career has proceeded very well. However, the two times we encounter Sarah Jane between her adventures with the Doctor and those on Bannerman Road ("K-9 and Company," "The Five Doctors") we do not learn very much about her private life. Nor will we learn anything about her private life until she meets the Doctor again in "School Reunion." Unlike Rose Tyler or Martha Jones, Sarah Jane never indicated that she harbored romantic feelings for the Doctor. Nevertheless, she expresses the depth of her feelings toward him in "School Reunion," telling DW10 how devastated she was when he never returned for her. She tells him that he was her life, and his cryptic response is that he could not come back for her because everyone died. Before leaving again the Doctor invites Sarah Jane to come along with Rose and him, but she says no, it is time that she stopped waiting for him and found a life of her own. Little does she realize that the new life she finds will include a teen-age son.

When the Doctor asked her about her life and she replied that no, she had no children, she never had time (although why the Doctor would have to ask such questions is a mystery, as shouldn't he already know?), SJ was not contemplating changing her life in such dramatic fashion. Apparently Sarah Jane has not resolved the crisis of Erikson's Stage Six of development, as she does not seem to have developed any close relationships with a person of either the opposite or same sex. She appears to have completely skipped Stage Six. Several theorists, including Erikson, have proposed that women sometimes flip stages five and six.[26] That is, women will sometimes enter into an intimate relationship with another person prior to establishing a clear sense of identity. However, it does not appear that such is the case with Sarah Jane, much as it appears she would have liked a relationship with the Doctor.

Examining Sarah Jane's life in the present, she appears to be in Stage Seven, Generativity vs. Stagnation. Although Sarah Jane does not have biological children, she adopts a son who was created by aliens, and a daughter who is not Human; each was left with no one to take care of them. SJ is clearly mentoring a group of young people, teaching them to question things that are not quite right, how to investigate, and to be brave and resourceful. Much as she was the Doctor's companion for a number of years, she has four teens, five if we count Maria, acting as hers. It is during the time of her adventures on Bannerman Road that we begin to see Sarah Jane re-assessing her life and questioning some of the decisions that she made when younger. This time of reflection, a crisis we could say, is not unique to Sarah Jane. According to Daniel Levinson both men and women have several times in their adult lives when they experience transition points, or shifts, in their developmental trajectories.[27]

Levinson and his colleagues developed this Life-Course Theory based upon extensive and in-depth interviews with men and women at various times in their adulthood, beginning in late adolescence and continuing until late middle adulthood. Based upon the interviews with his sample of women, Levinson separated women into two categories: a homemaker sample, or those with a Traditional Marriage Enterprise, and a career woman sample, or those with an Anti-Traditional Marriage Enterprise. Those women who espouse the traditional marriage enterprise marry at an early age either directly after high school, in college, or shortly after college and begin having children shortly after marriage. They generally do not work outside of the home once their children are born; however, they may seek a job after their children reach school-age. Like their husbands these women believe that a woman's primary responsibility is to her children and therefore she should not work outside of the home. Those that must work outside the home due to financial constraints are generally unhappy. Nevertheless some of the women found that they enjoyed this outside work and transitioned from part-time employment to full-time as their children aged.

The women who espoused the "Anti-Traditional Marriage Enterprise" in Levinson's sample were career women who worked in corporate America or academia. The women in this category were quite diverse as far as their lives were concerned; they were less likely to be married, have children, and be involved in a traditional marriage. They believed in what Levinson called the Successful Career Woman myth, which stated that women could have it all: career, marriage, family, leisure — everything — if they just worked hard enough.[28] However, by middle age, during a period referred to as the Mid-Life Transition (approximately 40–46), these women were questioning this myth, realizing that instead of being a Successful Career Woman, they were actually Jugglers, "who managed to keep several spheres moving at the same time, but who had a very restricted life and little connection to her self and her inner spheres."[29] This is a period of time when career women begin to question and reconsider what it means to have a career or a marriage or a family, perhaps asking the question "Is this all there is?"

Unfortunately Levinson's sample did not study women much older than fifty; however, it is my belief that Sarah Jane, even though she is older than Levinson's sample, fits nicely into the mid-life transition described above. Sarah Jane has had a satisfying career as a journalist; she is apparently well-respected and well-connected. She is good enough at her job that she has been able to continue it for almost forty years. Yet, she also realizes, once she meets Luke, that the decisions she made earlier in life — to have a career and not a family — might not have been the best decision. Hence, her decision to "adopt" Luke and later Sky, her obvious love for Luke, and her continued mentorship of the teenagers Maria, Clyde, and Rani, indicate that Sarah Jane has reached a transition point in her life, where she reassesses her life and decides to follow a different path. As mentioned earlier, Sarah Jane's life would also reflect Erikson's Stage seven of generativity, where she begins to "give back" to the next generation: her knowledge of what is "out there," her curiosity, her refusal to take no for an answer coupled with her refusal to accept anything at "face value." Her life also reflects Levinson's Life Course Theory which proposes that developmental transition points occur periodically throughout one's life, when one examines the decisions made and determines if a new trajectory is called for.

Sarah Jane Smith, although only a fictional character, provides the viewer with many positive exemplars of a woman living life on her own terms. However, those terms include having a large amount of money and teenage children, the first to allow her the luxury of not having to worry about how to pay the bills and the second of not having to worry about diapers and childcare.[30] Obviously intending to appeal to children and adolescents, *The Sarah Jane Adventures* does provide this audience with several positive role models of women: Sarah Jane is an investigative journalist, with a secret life; Rani Chandra is a teenage girl who plans to have a career; and, Rani's mother, Gita Chandra, owns her own flower shop.

Given that over 60 percent of the female population in the U.S., Canada, and Britain work outside the home, even those with young children, a television series that portrays women in the work force does reflect the reality of contemporary life. It is doubtful that the writers of *The Sarah Jane Adventures* meant to create a character that so clearly illustrates concepts from developmental psychology. Nevertheless, Sarah Jane's life can be analyzed using these concepts, providing an example, not of life imitating art, but rather art imitating life.

NOTES

1. Jim Leach, *Doctor Who* (Detroit: Wayne State University Press, 2009): pp. 58–9.

2. David J. Howe, Stephen James Walker, and Mark Stammers, *The Handbook: The Unofficial and Unauthorised Guide to the Production of Doctor Who* (Tolworth: Telos, 2005).

3. Ibid., p. 228.

4. Elisabeth Sladen joined Jon Pertwee during the last year of his tenure as the third Doctor and then remained for approximately three seasons with Tom Baker as the fourth Doctor, for a total of 18 episodes. Five of the earlier Sarah Jane episodes are unavailable on DVD. Much to my delight these episodes (see the Videography for complete information) are available at www.dailymotion.com, although they require patience to watch as each part is generally available in a 5–10 minute block. Elisabeth Sladen's autobiography is an excellent source for her memories of those years. *Elisabeth Sladen: the Autobiography* (London: Arum, 2011).

5. Attempts to create a series called *K-9 and Company* in 1981 were unsuccessful.

6. Sarah Jane Smith will be referred to by name throughout this chapter, as well as by her initials SJ. The series *Sarah Jane Adventures*, will be referred to by name and as well as by its initials *SJA*.

7. Frankly, Rose Tyler is my least favorite of all the companions, and it was absolutely irritating to hear her constantly whine about how bad her life would be without the Doctor. That whining did not make either her mother or her boyfriend feel any better, either.

8. I am using the term Whoniverse to refer not only to the televised *Doctor Who* episodes, but also to *The Sarah Jane Adventures* series, audio adventures, and books for each series, etc. For an interesting discussion of how Sarah Jane Smith was able to gain entry into UNIT headquarters through the third Doctor's years working there, see Tat Wood, *About Time: The Unauthorized Guide to Doctor Who, Expanded Second Edition, 1970–1974, Seasons 7 to 11* (Des Moines: Mad Norwegian Press, 2009). He proposes that Sarah Jane was well known to UNIT, and might even had been an agent, using her journalist credentials as a cover. It would certainly explain a lot of what happened during Season 11 and SJ's adventures with the third Doctor.

9. James Chapman, *Inside the TARDIS: The Worlds of Doctor Who* (London: I.B. Tauris, 2006): p. 7.

10. "Time Warrior" DVD, BBC, 1973–1974.

11. Margaret W. Matlin, *The Psychology of Women, 3ᵈ ed.* (Ft. Worth: Harcourt Brace, 1996):, p. 5.

12. The interested reader is directed to Rosemarie Tong, *Feminist Thought: A More Comprehensive Introduction, 3ᵈ Ed.* (Boulder: Westview Press, 2008). She provides an introduction to the different types of feminism as well as a detailed discussion of the history of feminism. A discussion of the various types of feminism is beyond the scope of this chapter.

13. Chapman, *Inside the TARDIS*, p. 98.

14. Ibid., p. 5.

15. Wood, *About Time*, p. 448.

16. Sladen, *Elisabeth Sladen*, p. 83.

17. Chapman, *Inside the TARDIS*, p. 98.

18. The gift of K-9 from the Doctor is another of those continuity errors for which the program is famous. See Paul Cornell, Martin Day and Keith Topping, *The Discontinuity Guide* (Austin: MonkeyBrain Books, 2004). The Doctor's letter, in which he gives K-9 to SJ, was written/delivered in 1978. However, we know that the Third Doctor and SJ were traveling together in 1980, as SJ says she is from 1980 when the Doctor shows her what will happen to the Earth if they do not stop Sutekh in "Pyramid of Mars."

19. I use the word witches in quotation marks because the people in the story are actually practicing the Dark Arts. That has nothing to do with Wicca.

20. The six *K-9 and Company* stories I have can be found on the DVD of that title. Titles of the other two stories, not mentioned in the text, are: *Hound of Hell* and *The Shroud of Azaroth*. Brendon ages quite rapidly in these stories, from being an adolescent school boy in the television movie, to possessing a full

beard in an illustration of *Powerstone*. Wood would argue that stories such as these are not to be considered factual or true, given that they were not televised stories, nevertheless, "it seems fair to use them to fill the gaps in the ... folklore" (Wood, *About Time*, p. 6).

21. Peter Gay, *The Freud Reader* (New York: W.W. Norton, 1995).

22. Barry J. Wadsworth, *Piaget's Theory of Cognitive and Affective Development: Foundations of Constructivism*, 5th Ed. (Needham Heights, MA: Allyn and Bacon, 2003).

23. Erik H. Erikson, *The Life Cycle Completed: A Review* (New York, W.W. Norton, 1982).

24. Erik H. Erikson, *Dimensions of a New Identity* (New York: W.W. Norton, 1974); Erik H. Erikson, *Identity: Youth and Crisis* (New York: W.W. Norton, 1968).

25. Erik H. Erikson, *Identity and the Life Cycle*, 2d ed., New York: W.W. Norton, 1980).

26. Elizabeth A.M. Douvan and Joseph Adelson, *The Adolescent Experience* (New York: Wiley, 1966); Carol Gilligan, "Joining the Resistance: Girls' Development in Adolescence," paper presented at the Symposium on Development and Vulnerability in Close Relationships, May 1992, Montreal, QC; Serena J. Patterson, Ingrid Sochting and James E. Marcia, "The Inner Space and Beyond: Women and Identity," in G.R. Adams, T.P. Gullotta and R. Montemayor, eds. *Adolescent Identity Formation* (Newbury Park, CA: Sage, 1992); Annie Rogers, *Questions Gender Differences: Ego Development and Moral Voice in Adolescence*, unpublished manuscript, Harvard University, 1987.

27. Daniel J. Levinson, *The Seasons of a Woman's Life* (New York: Ballantine, 1996).

28. Ibid., p. 372.

29. Ibid.

30. When Sky first appears in the episode "Sky" she is a baby, still requiring nappies and bottles. In a nice role-reversal neither Sarah Jane nor Rani know how to take care of a baby, relying instead on Clyde who has cared for young relatives before. Clyde duly entertains Sky with silly jokes and pantomimes. When Sky is "activated" as the bomb and morphs into a 12-year-old girl, she remembers those jokes and the other things that Clyde told her. Obviously a baby would seriously hamper Sarah Jane's ability to chase aliens, hence Sky's transformation into a young girl. Like Luke, Sky does not know how to be human and would have provided the usual alien other against which humanity is measured, a very traditional science fiction plot device, if *SJA* had continued.

16

Chasing Amy

*The Evolution of the Doctor's Female
Companion in the New* Who

LYNNETTE PORTER

Although Russell T. Davies' reboot of *Doctor Who* with the ninth (Christopher Eccleston) and tenth (David Tennant) Doctors revitalized the television series, the companions who graced the TARDIS between 2005 and 2009 also should be credited with increasing the series' appeal to a wider audience. These companions provide new insights about the Doctor and travel in time and space. Rose Tyler (Billie Piper), Martha Jones (Freema Agyeman), Donna Noble (Catherine Tate), and even a returned Sarah Jane Smith (Elisabeth Sladen) develop unique relationships with their Doctor(s) and make the role of companion more dynamic—and more acceptable to adult female viewers. Captain Jack Harkness (John Barrowman) also brings out different aspects of the Doctor's personality, from disapproving to playful, and back again. All these companions find their lives altered by their experiences with the Doctor, who also surprisingly becomes emotionally affected by his companions. Nevertheless, the role of companion clearly means a secondary role, with the Doctor forever being the superior character. He becomes ever more self-sacrificing throughout the Davies era of producing the show, but, even though his sacrifices lead to two regenerations, the Doctor relies on himself far more than on a companion to save the day—or his very existence.

With the shift in producer/lead writer from Davies to Steven Moffat by early 2010, as well as the introduction of the eleventh (and youngest) Doctor (Matt Smith), a second reboot of the companion role also was in order. Although Amelia/Amy Pond (Karen Gillan) has been a controversial figure in *Who* fandom during the first year of the Moffat/Smith series, she is appealing because she blends the best qualities of several previous companions and, like them, provides new insights into the controversial eleventh Doctor. Throughout Amy's first season as a companion, she tries on a number of stereotypical female roles and personas before emerging in the finale as her own woman—and a very different type of companion than has been seen in the series to date.

True to the equal nature of their roles, the eleventh Doctor often chases after Amy as her curiosity leads them into adventure. Certainly, Amy's fiancé Rory Williams (Arthur Darvill) would never have found himself traveling through time if he had not been following his beloved. Even viewers sometimes find it hard to catch up to her—to figure out exactly who she is and why she does what she does. She is the feistiest companion since the 2005 reboot. Her independence, forthrightness (i.e., bluntness), and determination to have her own way have attracted some viewers, but repelled those used to more "acceptable" female companions who defer to the Doctor without quite so much fuss.

The presence of Amy signals the influence of a new producer/lead writer and a new direction for the venerable series, but she also indicates a different direction for female characters within the *Who* franchise. This chapter includes both a textual analysis and an analysis of the media and fan material generated by Amy's often-controversial presence. Amy is compared to recent previous companions, as well as to a female character increasingly important to the Doctor's future, River Song (Alex Kingston). Amy's character growth throughout the 2010 season's episodes illustrates how the *Who* franchise continues to stir up fan and media controversy.

The Companion's Roles in Doctor Who, 2005–2010

From 2005 to 2010, the ninth and tenth Doctors traveled with a series of companions who had more to do than the companions of the earlier era and who developed closer personal relationships with the Time Lord. The most personally important companion, bookending both Doctors' lifespans (as well as Davies' time as executive producer), is Rose Tyler. She not only re-introduces audiences to the Doctor and allows viewers to jump into the TARDIS alongside her — crucial to the success of the rebooted series — but she becomes the Doctor's love interest. She is the first companion of the new series; near the culmination of possibly the longest death scene in television history, she is the last companion the tenth Doctor visits before his regeneration.[1] Although the Doctor visits and tries to "save" his companions one last time before he regenerates, he stands apart from them and observes them; he does not talk with them directly — except for Rose. In many ways, she is always the exception. In his final moments, the Doctor stands in the shadows and tells a teenaged Rose, who has not yet met his ninth self, that the coming year will be very special. Of course, this is the year when she will meet the Doctor.

Throughout her years as companion, Rose dances, flirts, and argues with her Doctor. She sacrifices herself to save the Earth and risks her life crossing dozens of parallel timelines until she can be reunited with him. She loves him but, when he cannot say the words she needs to hear, ultimately takes what she can get — a human clone of the tenth Doctor. The humanized hybrid can provide her both the ordinary (presumably a romantic relationship and family stability) and the extraordinary (the memories of a Time Lord housed within a mortal body).[2] Rose settles for less than the complete Doctor, who is unsettled by his emotional response to her and realizes that he, too, is less than complete without her. He mopes and pines, decides being alone is much better than having a companion, and, for the rest of the Davies era, develops loving friendships but not romantic attachments with his female companions.

Even Sarah Jane Smith does not achieve this type of relationship with her Doctor(s), past or present. As a plucky sidekick, she offers journalistic insights and straightforward devotion in the 1970s episodes. During "School Reunion,"[3] when Sarah Jane meets the Doctor several regenerations after he had dropped her off back home, their spark is rekindled, but both Sarah Jane and the Doctor have moved on. Another of the Doctor's current companions, Mickey Smith, laughingly compares the Doctor's relationship with Rose to that with Sarah Jane as "the missus and the ex." Whatever Sarah Jane's feelings for the Doctor, their on-screen relationship in this episode is that of old friends forever connected by their time together. In a *Sarah Jane Adventures* episode broadcast after Tennant's last *Who* episode but obviously taking place within the *Who* canon before his regeneration, the tenth Doctor even attends Sarah Jane's wedding.[4] Before he regenerates, the tenth Doctor helps his companions one last time, and Sarah Jane merits a visit. This time, however, the tenth Doctor's action indicates his diminished role in her life. He saves Sarah Jane's son from being hit by a car, which, ultimately, "saves" Sarah Jane, before he exits her life.[5] By now, however, Sarah Jane has become used to the Doctor's infrequent but continuing presence in her life. In the Davies-produced *Sarah Jane Adventures,* the eleventh Doctor once again returns for a two-part episode.[6] Nevertheless, Sarah Jane will never have the Doctor's heart quite like Rose does (and, to be fair, if Rose had her own television series written by Davies, the Doctor would most likely be unable to stay away).

Even more than Rose, Donna Noble can get away with greater criticism of the Doctor and outspoken questions or outrageous confrontations during alien encounters. She assumes the role of the Doctor's best friend or big sister — not quite an equal, but a confidante, a sibling playmate, a solid supporter but not always a fan. Her pet names for him include "Dumbo" and "Space Man,"[7] and she often takes him to task for his abrupt behavior. While the Doctor explores a planet, she luxuriates in an alien spa.[8] She may not always share the Doctor's need for danger and adventure, but she provides an important emotional balance that helps deflate his ego at times, while providing companionship and empathy. She names the Doctor's daughter and helps him deal with his grief at her loss.[9] Donna goes well beyond her self-deprecating role as a temp to become the Doctor Donna who saves the universe with her vast knowledge tempered with human spirit.[10]

Nevertheless, Donna's story becomes firmly earthbound when she is forced to live without the realization that she was the Doctor's companion — more important, the one who saved humanity. Instead, the first and last episodes of the Donna story center on her role as a bride. She first meets the Doctor as a runaway bride whose fiancé turns out to be under the influence of a murderous alien.[11] The Doctor last sees her as a bride who settles for a cash-strapped middle-class life, one that, the Doctor assumes, can be improved with the instant infusion of cash from a winning lottery ticket.[12] With this act, the Doctor literally repays Donna's friendship and familial familiarity.

Once Martha Jones meets the Doctor, her talents as a doctor are subverted when she instead becomes a warrior woman/alien fighter. Audiences also see her as a UNIT soldier, a disciple of the Doctor to save the world, and a companion who truly believes in the Doctor but has to find her own path in life. She eventually leaves him because she fears subsuming her personality in light of the Doctor's vast experience and intellect and living a life of unrequited love. She commiserates with Jack, also suffering presumably (at least on screen) unrequited love for the Doctor, that they are not "blonde enough" to keep the Doctor's interest; his love nature remains focused on Rose, long after her disappearance into another dimension.[13] Davies, not the Doctor, surprisingly marries off Martha in the tenth Doctor's final episode; the Doctor saves Martha and husband Mickey Smith (Rose's former boyfriend and, briefly, the Doctor's companion) from death by Sontaran during a firefight.[14]

Davies also introduces River Song, a character who, as episodes during Davies' era and Moffat's stories continue to reveal, plays many important roles in the series: martyr, wise woman, adventurer, spy, time traveler (with her own vortex manipulator, a working model similar to Captain Jack's now-broken one), and, possibly, the Doctor's future spouse and/or his murderer. Fans debate her exact future role in his life, but she clearly knows the Doctor's real name and has intimate knowledge of his past and future habits.[15] She is as close a female version of the Time Lord as audiences have seen in the new series.

In some ways, River's presence around the Doctor mirrors the early, fun days of Captain Jack, back when he was the Doctor's companion. Jack's role begins as a con man that plays fast and loose with others' lives as he travels through space and time. Like River, Jack's past is mysteriously told through snippets of dialogue or brief flashbacks (in Jack's case, primarily illustrated in *Torchwood* episodes). River and Jack seem well acquainted with multiple sides of the law and have had miraculous escapes. They both are devoted to the Doctor and become better people when they are around him. River, however, displays greater confidence around the Doctor and knows exactly who she is, whereas Jack often looks to the Doctor for approval. Of course, River's timeline seems to be backwards from the Doctor's and Jack's; she knows the Doctor's future and refuses to reveal "Spoilers!," as she cheerfully reminds him (and the audience).

This variety of companions established audience expectations for *Who* companions, ones who have distinctive personalities, may provide a bit of controversy (e.g., Captain Jack), but ultimately go along with the Doctor's plans without much fuss. When they divert from the Doctor's plan, as Rose does to save the ninth Doctor from the Daleks,[16] the Doctor soon takes control of the situation again. The Doctor is the most powerful character; although companions assist him or may have more demands placed upon them when he is incapacitated or weakened, they are not the Doctor's equal.

Echoes of Companions Past

Amy often brings to mind several familiar aspects of these companions of the recent past:

- Like River, Amy goes where no companion has gone before and has a natural familiarity with the Doctor: part sexual, part knowing, part exasperated, part superior.
- Like Rose, Amy has a boyfriend in an ongoing but less-than-perfect relationship. When given the opportunity to leave him behind in order to travel with the Doctor, Amy, like Rose before her, ditches him.
- Like Rose, Amy envisions a sexualized relationship with the Doctor and tempts him.
- Like Rose, Amy brings along a former/current boyfriend and creates a rivalry between her human lover and the Time Lord.
- Like Rose, Amy finds a way to leave the safety of home in order to save the Doctor from extinction (i.e., death by Dalek in "The Parting of the Ways" or erasure from Time in "The Big Bang").
- Like Donna, Amy takes no guff from the Doctor and asks the rude or difficult questions that the audience would like to ask or berates the Doctor for less than "human" behavior.
- Like Donna, Amy is a runaway bride who somehow cannot make it to the church on time when she becomes involved with the Doctor. When the respective ceremonies finally take place, the Doctor finds a way to make the event extremely memorable (e.g., Donna wins the lottery, and, at Amy's wedding reception, the Doctor dances ... again).
- Like Donna and Rose, Amy decides that true love is a requirement for her life, not merely settling for (what passes for) a normal life.

- Like Sarah Jane, Amy chooses a domestic life (if one involving aliens and the recurring presence of the Doctor can be termed normal domesticity).
- Like Jack, Amy is often abandoned by the Doctor and has a special relationship with Time.

Amy, however, also distinguishes herself from these familiar touchstones. Whereas Jack is a fixed point in time (at least during the Davies era) and cannot seem to change the events in which he has participated, Amy can will the Doctor back into existence and rewrite time through the power of memory.[17] Whereas River and Donna have maturity on their side and can get away with pointing out the Doctor's less-than-stellar behavior, youthful Amy seems abrupt. She is not a "wise woman" by virtue of age or experience, and her attitude thus seems abrasive and annoying rather than mature and ballsy.

Although journalist Sarah Jane, Doctor Martha, and former Time Agent Jack are proud of their meaningful work lives before they meet the Doctor (unlike shop-girl Rose or temp Donna, who are dissatisfied with their jobs), they all feel these roles somehow lacking in comparison to their "job" as the Doctor's companion, and each struggles to find meaning to her or his societal roles in the aftermath of traveling with the Doctor. Of course, these former companions eventually gain their footing and find a way to balance their occasional interactions with the Doctor with their regular jobs, but they struggle initially before they succeed.

Rose finds a new career as a parallel-world traveler/alien expert and lives a life quite different from what she expected. Jack kills time with Torchwood while waiting for the Doctor and, after learning that his immortality is permanent, returns to Earth as its protector, not simply a stranded refugee. Martha and Sarah Jane turn their skills and personal lives toward Earth's protection, although they maintain a semblance of normal domesticity. Donna's life truly has to return to normal, because she cannot survive if she remembers her travels with the Doctor.

Although all these characters are independent, Amy differs in this regard. She always has created a successful life separate from her experiences with the Doctor. Even as a child, when "abandoned" by the Doctor, she carves out a unique, well-known persona within the village—one not entirely understood or accepted. She forces her playmate Rory to enact stories featuring the "raggedy Doctor" of her childhood fantasies. She knows how to get her way and regularly bullies the village men, who seem rather afraid of her fiery determination. Although her kiss-o-gram role confuses some villagers, such as little old ladies who are unsure whether Amy really is all those people she pretends to be (e.g., nun, police officer, nurse),[18] her personality is fiercely independent. The majority of companions fall into the traditional role of companion by making a spur-of-the-moment decision when the Doctor invites them to travel with him; Amy, however, waits for the Doctor, expects his eventual return, and chooses to travel with him. Hers is a premeditated choice.

Amy's fierce self-determination and her ability to get what she wants by force of personality makes her seem far more controlling and manipulative than previous companions. Although the Doctor has abandoned, disappointed, and been unable to live up the expectations of previous companions (e.g., Rose, Martha, Jack), he does not seem to want to disappoint Amy and expends a great deal of effort manipulating time in order to save her life a few times during the first season. Despite all this attention, Amy clearly succeeds in having a life without the Doctor and often acts on her own without asking for his advice even when she travels with him (e.g., her interaction with stone angels, her introduction to Vincent), but this very independence seems to intrigue the Time Lord. As with Donna, who could be left on her own at times (e.g., the aforementioned spa treatment) and join him later, Amy allows the Doctor to have his own adventures while still being linked to her.

In "A Christmas Carol,"[19] the Doctor spends years (although mere hours of his life) trying to change one man's life so that he makes a decision that ultimately will save hundreds of lives, including Amy and Rory's. The couple finally is spending their honeymoon on a futuristic cruise; they have time away from the Doctor before they join him for more adventures. Although the Doctor's actions during "A Christmas Carol" take place in order to save Amy and Rory (and peripherally others on the same cruise), he nevertheless enjoys himself and has minor adventures (e.g., evading a shark, becoming involved with Marilyn Monroe, spending multiple Christmases in the company of new friends). Amy does not need to be around the Doctor all the time, which is refreshing, given most companion stories.

Even when, for example, Martha travels the Earth for a year in order to thwart the Master's time paradox, every thought and action are focused on the Doctor.[20] Jack spends more than a century simply waiting for the Doctor. When Rose is trapped in a parallel universe, she learns how to span several parallel worlds in order to find her Doctor. Perhaps because Amy seems comfortable on her own, even as a child (having only a seldom-seen aunt as guardian) and already has survived living with and without the Doctor, she more easily develops her own interests and seems comfortable living independently.

Of course, the flip side to this independence is that Amy also seems more easily separated from the Doctor. Her presence is not necessary to stories, even when she is a continuing character in the Doctor's story. In "A Christmas Carol," the Doctor seems equally effective as a character and enjoys his challenges and adventures just as much with new friends. If ratings are a reliable indicator, the audience also finds the eleventh Doctor intriguing and highly watchable in stories in which Amy remains on the sidelines.[21] The pair can have their separate story lines, as in their first Christmas special, but remain linked.

Although Amy often seems derivative of other companions, she manages to separate herself from companions past with her independence and forthrightness, even if she sometimes does so in an annoying way. Her choices and the in-your-face way they are presented may even shock long-time *Doctor Who* viewers who expect companions to be, if not chaste, at least family friendly on screen (no matter what some fans think may be taking place off screen).

Not a Fairy Tale Princess: First Impressions of Amelia/Amy

"The Eleventh Hour" introduces the newly regenerated Doctor and immediately presents him with a future companion, Amelia (later known as Amy) Pond. The little girl who finds the Doctor crash-landed in her back garden and invites him into her home seems to be the heroine of a fairy tale. As in the Grimm-est of stories, however, Amy's story includes monsters, and the Prince (or Doctor) arriving out of the blue (box) to save her almost immediately abandons her for more than a decade. As she grows up, she dreams of her "raggedy Doctor" who will mysteriously take her from her mundane village life and vanquish the monsters in the process. Of course, by the end of this episode, that is exactly what happens, but by the time Amelia has grown into the twenty-something Amy, she has learned to confront her own problems. The fairy tale premise promised by new executive producer Moffat turns into a dark story,[22] one, appropriately, that presents female companion

Amy as less fairy tale princess than modern young woman finding her own identity in a complex story.

In this "fairy tale," Amy and the Doctor develop a shifting power relationship, in which one is responsible for the well-being of the other, but not in the typical "damsel in distress" or "savior hero" roles of most fairy tales. Additionally, both the eleventh Doctor and grown-up Amy are sexual beings who are very much aware of the power of their sexuality — an unexpected aspect of the balance of power now emphasized in the Moffat era. Even the setting of key scenes establishes a different on-screen relationship between the Doctor and his latest female companion.

The eleventh Doctor's first encounter with Amelia (Amy) Pond takes place when she is still a child, even if a highly competent one who is unafraid of the strange man landing in the back garden. She provides him all the comforts of home — shelter, assistance/protection, food, companionship. In many ways this early encounter with precocious Amy sets up their later relationship. Undoubtedly this introduction also presents viewers with the Doctor's perspective of Amy. Whereas all his human companions are much younger than the Time Lord, even romantic interest Rose — who is nearly 900 years his junior, Amy will likely always remind the Doctor of the child she once was. As such, she is "hands off," even when she grows up, expresses very adult interest in him, and seems estranged from her fiancé. Allowing the audience to watch Amy grow up during the first episode makes her an unobtainable, inappropriate sex object — at least from the Doctor's and the audience's perspective.

That perspective, however, is not shared by Amy. Viewers' first look at how attractively she has grown up comes with a series of shocks that foreshadows Amy's role throughout the first season. Her entrance into the scene — the first glimpse of an adult Amy — makes her seem like an authority figure (a police woman), someone trained to deal with unexplained, difficult, life-threatening situations. That role, however, is a ruse. Amy can bluff with the best of them and is naturally courageous, but she is often out of her experiential depth. All too soon she has to admit to the Doctor that she really is not who she seems to be.

As a child, Amelia prays for "a policeman or someone" (an authority figure) to take care of the crack in her wall. Immediately, humorously, the Doctor falls from the sky — in a battered blue police box. Amelia asks the Doctor if he is a policeman; she is clearly looking for a savior, which is not uncommon for a child looking to an adult for help, and Amelia appears to be alone in the house. She does the best she can, but at times she longs for the Doctor's help, a trend that continues throughout the season.

The association of both Amy and the Doctor with the police indicates how equal the two are meant to be perceived, a fact that Gillan often expresses during interviews with comments that Amy will not "just constantly stand around in awe of the Doctor."[23] They both are temporal authority figures of sorts, but they have no real power or jurisdiction. They take the authority they need in order to bluff their way through dangerous situations requiring their intervention. They also can mimic the role of the police; they look like role models or saviors, but they are only role playing. Their approaches make them unconventional heroes; their wardrobe changes to fit the situation. From the beginning, Amy knows how to role play, something the Doctor, in his many regenerations, also has become very good at doing.

During her first adult encounter with the Doctor, Amy is dressed as a policewoman, but this wardrobe is false. In reality, Amy works as a kiss-o-gram enacting the make-believe role of a police officer, a more sexualized real-life role than Rose's shopgirl, Martha's doctor, or Donna's temp secretary roles. In a reversal of their first encounter when Amelia is a child, the Doctor mistakenly thinks Amy is a policewoman, someone able to save the situation.

Amy realizes that she is an attractive woman, although the Doctor may not relate to her as such. She also remembers her "raggedy Doctor." From the beginning, she is comfortable with the Doctor and seems to be his equal, even at times his savior when he is not quite himself. By the end of the first season, she has realized this role as a fully-formed companion (even as an adult, she "grows up" during the first season's travels) who not only remembers the Doctor but is the only one who can truly save him from being lost in time. This back-and-forth tug-of-war in roles of "false authority" and their ongoing game of who saves whom sets the tone for the first season.

Amy's role as the Doctor's caretaker is quite different from Rose's caretaker role during the previous Doctor's troublesome regeneration.[24] Rose is already an adult when she meets the fully-formed ninth Doctor and has been his traveling companion through several dangers before he is regenerated into the tenth Doctor. At the time the TARDIS returns Rose to her home, just in time for Christmas, the still-regenerating Doctor convalesces in her mother's flat. There Rose, assisted by her mother and former boyfriend, looks after an ailing Doctor while dealing with an alien invasion. Although Rose, in effect, is the Doctor's nurse and is in love with him, the raciest dialogue follows Rose's offhand comment that the Doctor has two hearts. Rose's mother lifts an eyebrow, peers around her daughter, and wonders, "What else has he got two of?" Rose may have disrobed the Doctor and put him into pajamas before putting him into bed, but this action takes place off camera. When the Doctor truly becomes himself, he rushes in to save Rose — as well as the rest of Earth's population — from alien invaders and acts like a swashbuckling hero, right down to a sword fight.

In contrast, young Amelia interacts with the Doctor, alternately helping him discover who he is in this new incarnation, and being protected by him from the aliens on the other side of her bedroom wall. Whereas Rose acts alone with a comatose Doctor who must depend on her until he is well, Amelia interacts with the still-regenerating Doctor and basically parents him until he can assume the role of authority figure. In contrast, the tenth Doctor makes a grand entrance to save Rose from the deadly aliens and take back his role as the ultimate authority figure — one who knows how to deal with aliens. Although the balance of power shifts from the Doctor to Rose while he is unconscious and still regenerating, it quickly shifts back so that Rose is a love interest to be saved by the Doctor. During the eleventh Doctor's regeneration, Amelia takes care of him, although she herself is a child — perhaps still an "equal" to the not-yet-fully-developed eleventh Doctor, who acts very childishly when he first meets her. When the eleventh Doctor takes control of the situation, he cannot immediately save Amelia from that troublesome crack in the wall. Neither of them can save the day yet. For all that, at first glance, Rose and Amy are both potential love interests for the Doctor, executive producers Davies and Moffat, who also wrote these episodes' scripts, treat these heroines very differently.

The controversy over whether Amy is merely an independent woman who does what she pleases (and what pleases her may include traditional or highly sexualized female roles) or a female stereotype begins early in "The Eleventh Hour." Although Amelia is a female (child) seeking a savior, the hero sent to her is far from conventional or coolly competent. Instead, she becomes a "parental" figure trying to get her childlike visitor to eat whatever she cooks to please him. That she acts older than the newly regenerated Doctor is illustrated by the choice of camera angles. The camera tilts upward to showcase Amy's superiority early in the Doctor's regeneration. He knocks himself out by walking into a tree and is shown flat on his back, his head upside down to the camera. His view of Amy as he looks up gives her authority — the camera looks up to her. Only when the Doctor has "stopped cooking" enough to regain command of the situation does he look at the temporal crack in Amy's house and become the adult or authority figure in the episode. The camera angle changes appreciably to reflect the shift in power.

When the Doctor opens the crack in Time, his torso is in the foreground, and Amelia peeks around his back. When the huge alien eye looking through the crack from the other side spies the Doctor and Amelia, the camera highlights the Doctor looming in front, the depth of field emphasizing him standing larger and protectively in front of Amelia. This shift in perspective, even in the first episode, when Amy is a child, balances the power between the Doctor and Amy and illustrates a different, equal-from-the-get-go relationship that the Doctor has not immediately had with other recent companions.

The balance of power shifts again in the next scene, although years have elapsed in Amy's world. When the Doctor breaks into her house, Amy knocks him out. Again, Amy, this time a woman, is shown from the perspective of an up-tilted camera to reflect the Doctor's subdued position in the scene and Amy's superior power as his subduer. However, the camera also controversially pans slowly up her legs instead of presenting a simple tilt-up shot. The camera caresses the long, bare legs visible because of Amy's abbreviated police-woman costume. The resonance of this camera movement with earlier camera angles and the repeated shift in power of the scenes between Amy and Doctor indicate character equality, just as Gillan emphasizes in later interviews as she responds to feminist backlash to her character, as discussed later in this chapter.

However, unlike the camera movement used to present earlier companions, this scene emphasizes Amy's physical attributes. At first she seems to be a real authority figure, a policewoman who has called for backup but seems to have the situation under control even as she waits for another officer to arrive. When the Doctor finds himself restrained by hand-cuffs to the radiator (a possibly kinky scenario), the camera again tilts up to show Amy's control of the scene — and of the Doctor. That illusion of control is soon destroyed when Amy sexily reveals her true job: not as a policewoman with hair bundled under her hat, but as a kiss-o-gram. As she explains, she pulls off the police officer's hat and her luxuriant red hair tumbles to her shoulders. This revelation prompts the Doctor to take control of the potential crisis and changes the audience's perception of Amy's role in this scene. The camera, in reality, does only what Amy wants it to do for her customers (now given the audience's perspective). They should appreciate her glorious gams and see her as sexually attractive.

A later scene reveals that Amy also role plays as a nurse and a nun as part of her professional repertoire. She seems to be trying on a variety of personas until she finds out what she wants to be — a partner to Rory and a companion adventurer to the Doctor. Along the way she "role plays" being a pregnant housewife, but she gives up that role because it does not seem real; a whole episode involves a life-or-death game to determine if the time travelers' current reality is, indeed, real. Although Amy may someday choose that real-life role, she ultimately concludes that the motherhood scenario is not her current choice.[25]

Throughout her "growing up" phase to become a fully realized person, Amy does not define herself by her relationships with men, even if the series seems to do so. Instead, she (and Gillan) interprets Amy's choices as those of an independent adult. Amy is the only companion who has her own successful private life separate from the Doctor *while* she travels with him.

Just as Amy tries on different roles and wardrobes before she decides who she really is, in "The Eleventh Hour" the Doctor ultimately decides who this eleventh incarnation is and dons the appropriate clothing. The scene becomes controversial when he changes clothes in front of Rory and Amy. He is tired of being the "raggedy Doctor" of Amy's childhood and becomes the more refined dresser of her adulthood and his new regeneration. The Doctor sheds the persona he tried on around Amy during this episode and becomes the fully formed character with whom she will travel.

The creation of equality between these new characters is more important than their first adventure together and reflects both characters' increased sexual awareness. This Doctor's response to life in general is more sexualized, too, as "The Eleventh Hour" repeatedly demonstrates. He hastily raises his legs to avoid a rather painful personal collision with the top of Big Ben during his descent into London. He comments, "You sexy thing, you! Just look at you!" when he first sees "her" (always feminine pronoun), the revamped TARDIS.[26] Like Amy, the Eleventh Doctor is aware of his sexuality, whether or not he chooses to act on that nature.

Setting is another key to this more sexualized duo. Part of the "is she or isn't she an appropriate role-model" controversy comes from the setting of many of the Doctor's and Amy's earthly encounters: her bedroom. Of course, that is where the temporal crack exists, but it also becomes the place where Amy's memories and primary relationships with the Doctor are forged.

Bedroom scenes, although not sexualized in content, still have a different meaning in popular culture than scenes set in other rooms. The bedroom is a more intimate space and reflects the inner (otherwise hidden) nature or desires of the person who owns the room. A prominent (and controversial) scene takes place when Amy throws herself at the Doctor and passionately kisses him. Although he rebuffs her, not only her impetuous kiss but also the location of the scene — Amy's bedroom — makes her formerly hidden desires all the more obvious to the Doctor and the audience.

"The Eleventh Hour" has several bedroom scenes: Amelia revealing her bedroom's cracked wall, Amy's former boyfriend hiding from his mother in his bedroom, and Amy waking up in her bedroom on the night before her wedding. In a scene closely paralleling her first encounter as a child with the Doctor, adult Amy again is in her bedroom when she hears the TARDIS return. The Doctor returns to spirit Amy away from home in the middle of the night, when she is asleep in bed. In nightclothes, just as when, as a child, she first saw the TARDIS, Amy runs to the window to witness the TARDIS' arrival. According to Disney–style fairy tales, the handsome prince often arrives to spirit the would-be princess away from her troubles. The Doctor arrives years later than planned in this "dark fairy tale," and he turns up in the middle of the night. His arrival is secret, not heralded, and Amy leaves the confines of her bedroom, clad in a less-than-sexy nightdress reminiscent of her childhood nightie. Her white wedding gown hangs on the door. All the symbols of innocence about to be lost, as well as the scene's setting, emphasize the fact that Amy is about to lose her "innocence" to the Doctor. However, the Doctor is not an escape mechanism or a Prince Charming to take Amy away from the normalcy (or dullness) of her upcoming married life.

Instead, he provides a way for Amy to define and refine who she is — just as the Doctor has been doing in this episode. She must decide which of the personas she has tried on and the roles she has played — and will play — are the ones she chooses to become permanent.

Self-discovery and self-determination become the adventure that the Doctor offers Amy. It is a very grown up journey, for all that he tells Amy that she should never really grow up.

In the final episode of the first season, "The Big Bang,"[27] the Doctor tells Amy a bedtime story before he is lost to her memory — and to all of time. Amy has been released from her role as companion in order to begin her role as Rory's partner. Because of his self-sacrifice in this episode, the Doctor also restores the childhood Amy should have had: one with a family to support and guide her. The final bedroom scene sets up an "either/or" scenario, one that has been the choice for most companions. They can choose life with a partner/family/friends (i.e., a normal, grown-up life) or the life of adventure (i.e., the fantasy life). The Doctor puts Amy to bed with a story, as if she is a child. The expectation is that she will wake up as an adult, take up her new life, and forget "childish" things (i.e., the Doctor — self-described as her "imaginary friend" — and all he represents). Amy finds a way both to marry Rory and remember the Doctor, ending the episode (and first season) with a grand farewell to what her parents and community expect her to become. Instead, Amy finds a way to have it all — the lives/roles associated both with Rory and the Doctor.

Perhaps this is part of Moffat's meaning that his era of *Who* is an atypical fairy tale, one for adults as much as for children. Amy, like the Doctor and viewers who want to keep believing in him, must find a way to integrate their inner child within their adult lives. Instead of outgrowing the Doctor — as Martha, Sarah Jane, Donna, and even Rose and Jack eventually do — Amy finds a way to keep the adventure going and to find a way to fit all aspects of her personality into one cohesive whole. Perhaps that is what makes her controversial and different from any other companion to date.

By the end of the first season, as in a traditional fairy tale, the Doctor saves Amy's life, literally and metaphorically, several times. Unlike a traditional fairy tale, Amy also saves the Doctor's life; only her memories of him are capable of restoring him to reality. She remembers/believes in him; therefore, he exists. Amy and the Doctor equally share the responsibility for saving the other.

Amy is able to be such a savior because she does not outgrow her "bedtime stories" as told by the Doctor. The way in which Amy incorporates her memory of the Doctor into her life, from childhood on, despite what others tell her to do or think, is unique among the Doctor's companions and the way they relate to the Doctor. The way Amy's story is told throughout a series of bedroom scenes is not "creepy," but these scenes, uniquely in *Doctor Who*, reflect a female character's growing awareness of who she wants to become. The way Amelia's/Amy's story is told naturally makes her introduction to the Doctor more controversial than introductory scenes involving already-adult companions who meet the Doctor and allow him to change their lives. Throughout the first season's "fairy tale," Amy Pond manages to alienate part of the *Who* audience and invite questions about whether she is a "suitable" companion for the Doctor or role model for younger viewers.

Amy's Sexuality and Feminist Backlash

Amy's sexuality sometimes seems out of place in a children's show. Although the tenth Doctor gets in a bit of innuendo by hinting he got into the Virgin Queen's knickers ("Her nickname is no longer..."),[28] tells Rose that he had been a dad,[29] and even antiseptically fathers a full-grown child in front of Donna and Martha,[30] he is best known for his unrequited love of Rose and a brief asexual liaison (another example of unrequited love) with

Madame du Pompadour.[31] This Doctor may have loved and lost, but he did not lock lips with his companions, even if "fangirls" hoped he would.

In contrast, the eleventh Doctor does not seem interested in sex nearly as much as adventure, but the two sometimes coincide, even if the action takes place off camera. During "A Christmas Carol," the Doctor and his temporary companions attend a Hollywood party where an apparently besotted Marilyn Monroe ropes the Doctor into a quickie engagement. The Doctor's tie is askew, and lipstick is smudged on his cheek. The joke is perpetuated when Marilyn rings the TARDIS later, and an uncomfortable Doctor avoids the call.[32] The Doctor may not choose to become sexually involved with Amy (or Marilyn), but he clearly is a sexual being.

Some viewers initially criticized the eleventh Doctor's first episode ("The Eleventh Hour") because he changes clothes in front of Amy and Rory. Although Rory turns his back and asks if Amy will do the same, she gleefully tells him, "Nope!" and watches the show.[33] The Doctor's nudity is not shown, except for glimpses of his shoulders and chest, but the impression is that Amy gets an eyeful.

Amy undoubtedly picks up on this "possibility of sex" vibe, as well as her own conflicted feelings for much of the first season — she wants to marry Rory, but she does not want to give up her independence. In a last-ditch expression of cold feet, Amy grabs the Doctor and kisses him passionately. He extricates himself, but viewers get the feeling that he does so more because he understands her motivation and he has seen her grow up. Nevertheless, the scene caused a few viewers to complain to the BBC.

One science fiction news site summarized the controversy arising from complaints made soon after the first episode was broadcast in the U.K.:

> One reader said: "Why did she dress up as a tarty policewoman? Surely that's not fitting for a family show." Another said: "They've completely demeaned *Doctor Who* by replacing good episode stories with slutty girls."

In response to this claim, the series' executive producer, Piers Wenger, explained this character development:

> The whole kiss-o-gram thing played into Steven's desire for the companion to be feisty and outspoken and a bit of a number. Amy is probably the wildest companion that the Doctor has travelled with, but she isn't promiscuous. She is really a two-man woman and that will become clear over the course of the episodes.[34]

Amy's interest in the Doctor and his discomfort in dealing with her sexually is a younger, less knowing type of connection than that between the Doctor and River Song. Although River's warnings of "Spoilers!" so far have only hinted at a possibly intimate, but also possibly sinister connection between them in his future/her past, River insists on calling him Sweetie and seems to know a lot about the Doctor's many strengths and personal failings (e.g., driving the TARDIS properly). In many ways, Amy is a younger, less experienced River Song — they both delight in teasing the Doctor and point out his faults, but they steadfastly believe in him, no matter how dire the situation. Amy is the beginning and River the mature culmination of adult female companions who view the Doctor realistically.

Amy's on-again, off-again relationship with Rory makes her possible rejection of him in favor of the rival Doctor more controversial. Much of that controversy centers around Amy's sexual nature, the way in which she expresses it, and the way it is portrayed on camera. Not only does the early-episode kiss but that famous kiss-o-gram police outfit —

brought back as part of her honeymoon role play with Roman-clad Rory in "A Christmas Carol"—make the outfit representative of "the real Amy."

Much like Hugh Hefner explaining how *Playboy* helped women's liberation, Amy as a character is rather controversial because, to some, she is feminist because of her independence and choices, whereas to others she is being packaged by costume and camera angle as a sex object. Is Amy simply a wilder woman than the Doctor's previous companions? Is she less sexualized than, say, Captain Jack, but perceived as a "tart" because she is a woman? According to Gillan, Amy is the most feminist of recent companions because she considers herself equal to the Doctor. Yet the way she is portrayed, in everything from scene setting to wardrobe, creates this duality of feminist/sex object, resulting in controversy. Amy is sexual, demanding, and often illustrative of "typical" female roles, but is that done to illustrate that she is her own woman or to portray her as a sex object created only for the gratification of male viewers?

Feminist viewers denounced the portrayal of Amy as a sex object (similar to the way that Captain Jack is a glorified sex object during the ninth Doctor's brief tenure). The emphasis on costume, innuendo about sexual exploits (or desire to have them), and the possibility of off-camera sex between Amy and the Doctor (or Rory/Amy/Doctor) parallel fan speculation (and fan fiction) about those backroom, off-camera TARDIS exploits between Jack or Rose and the Doctor (or Jack/Rose/Doctor). Fan speculation often trumps the scenes depicted on screen. Nevertheless, some recent viewers found more than Amy's police outfit objectionable.

During a podcast interview, feminist fan Courtney explained the objectification of Amy:

> Part of the reason that there seems to be a contradiction between allowing Amy to celebrate her own sexuality onscreen and not objectifying her is that we have screwed up definitions of women's sexuality. There is no contradiction once we define Amy's sexuality by *her own desires*, not by the display and consumption of her body by heterosexual male viewers. When we allow "Amy reveling in her own sexuality" to be "Amy partaking of and enjoying her own desires," female sexuality is not spectacle, with all the power dynamics inherent in that model, but a model of autonomy and subjectivity, in which women articulate and fulfill their desires in whatever way makes them most happy.[35]

Part of the argument, also summarized in the podcast interview, is that Amy is presented for the objectification of "fanboys" of all ages, who seem to be the most likely viewers of *Doctor Who*.

Gillan was surprised by the feminist backlash. She thinks of Amy as a strong female character wearing clothing typical for her age and being an equal to the Doctor—or to any male character.[36] Her interview with the *Radio Times*, a well-distributed U.K. television publication, was summarized in several in-print and online newspapers throughout the U.K., including BBC news, which helped to get out the word that Gillan, like Amy, is her own woman and does not feel objectified. If anything, Gillan feels she represents her generation of women, adding in the interview that "feminism [is] not the issue anymore." Amy's sexiness is who she is, not a manifestation of what boys or men want to see and not a bad role model for girls or women.[37]

Amy's sexuality has been a hot topic during her first season, which ends with her marriage. Perhaps there is a double standard among *Doctor Who*'s creators and fan perceptions of Amy's fiancé/partner, Rory. He looks fetching in his Roman gladiator costume, which possibly reminds adult viewers of clichéd allusions to male sexuality (e.g., from *Airplane!*'s famous line "Do you like gladiator movies?" to film posters of buff, sweaty *Gladiator* Russell Crowe). Yet no mention is made of Rory's depiction as a Roman soldier, even when he wears this outfit as a stereotypical sexual role-play costume on their honeymoon.[38] Only Amy's attire is mentioned again and again in the press.

Beginning with "A Christmas Carol," Amy can be appropriately sexy in a marriage relationship because she is no longer a potential partner for the Doctor (once she has made up her mind, not because of any legal or moral sanctions against extramarital sexual relationships). In children's TV series etiquette, the lead character — especially the beloved Doctor — will not become the Other Man.

An Uncertain Future

Any time *Doctor Who* makes a significant change in cast or executive producer, some fans will be dissatisfied with the change. Because of the "Amy controversy" and perceived lower ratings for the eleventh Doctor's first season,[39] rumors began that Amy would be killed off (permanently) or the Doctor might regenerate earlier than expected. Neither proved true as the series began filming in late 2010 for a second season. Moffat's critically acclaimed and fan-pleasing ratings winner of "A Christmas Carol" seemed to cement the eleventh Doctor's place within fandom. Nevertheless, it is interesting that Moffat and Smith felt compelled to comment in the press about the show's or companion's future.[40]

Because the executive producer/writer, the Doctor, and his companion all were new in 2010, Moffat, Smith, and Gillan likely faced more criticism than they would have if only one element — producer or cast — had been different. In the Davies era of the ninth and tenth Doctors, once fans became accustomed to a Doctor, the comings and goings of companions was mitigated by the continuing familiar presence of the current Doctor. For example, when Captain Jack becomes a companion, the audience already is familiar with continuing characters Rose and the ninth Doctor. When the ninth Doctor is regenerated into the tenth, Rose provides the character bridge between the former and new Doctors. When companions such as Martha or Donna enter, leave, and re-enter the story, the tenth Doctor is the constant presence that provides continuity. With the shift not only from the tenth to the eleventh Doctors, but from Davies to Moffat as executive producer and from all previous companions to Amy, the audience has a lot of newness to accept, especially when Moffat introduces a more "adult" version of the Doctor and his female companion into the fairy tale format, as well as made the TARDIS sexier. Whether the eleventh Doctor or Amy gains viewer support, attracts more controversy (and thus more press), or departs earlier than expected remains the real cliffhanger to be determined by the second season of the Moffat era. In hindsight, however, Amy likely at least will be one of the most controversial, and therefore perhaps most memorable, companions of Moffat's or any other executive producer's era of *Doctor Who*.

NOTES

1. "The End of Time, Part 2." For program details see Videography.
2. "Journey's End."
3. "School Reunion."
4. *The Sarah Jane Adventures,* "The Wedding of Sarah Jane Smith."
5. "The End of Time, Part 2."

6. *The Sarah Jane Adventures,* "The Death of the Doctor, Parts 1 and 2."

7. "The Runaway Bride."

8. "Midnight."

9. "The Doctor's Daughter."

10. "The Stolen Earth" ; "Journey's End."

11. "The Runaway Bride."

12. "The End of Time, Part 2."

13. "Utopia."

14. "The End of Time, Part 2."

15. "Silence in the Library"; "Forest of the Dead."

16. "The Parting of the Ways."

17. "The Pandorica Opens"; "The Big Bang."

18. "The Eleventh Hour."

19. "A Christmas Carol."

20. "The Sound of Drums"; "Last of the Time Lords."

21. "A Christmas Carol" attracted 10.3 million U.K. viewers, second only to the eleventh Doctor's first episode, "The Eleventh Hour," which had 10.8 million viewers. Other episodes in the first season of the Moffat era regularly attracted 7 to 8 million viewers. "Doctor Who Ratings," *The Mind Robber,* http://www.themindrobber.co.uk/ratings.html; "10.3 Watch A Christmas Carol," *Doctor Who News Page,* December 26, 2010, http://www.doctorwhonews.net/2010/12/dwn261210015912-overnight-ratings.html.

22. Michael Hickerson, "Moffat: 'Doctor Who' Is a 'Dark Fairy Tale,'" *Slice of SciFi,* May 19, 2010, http:/www.sliceofscifi.com/2010/0519/Moffat-doctor-who-is-a-dark-fairy-tale/.

23. "Doctor Who's Karen Gillan Hits Back at Feminism 'Outrage,'" *London Evening Standard,* June 15, 2010, http://www.thisislondon.co.uk/showbiz/article-23844963-doctor-whos-karen-gillan-hits-back-at-feminism-outrage.do.

24. "The Christmas Invasion."

25. "Amy's Choice."

26. "The Eleventh Hour."

27. "The Big Bang."

28. "The End of Time, Part 1."

29. "Fear Her."

30. "The Doctor's Daughter."

31. "The Girl in the Fireplace."

32. "A Christmas Carol."

33. "The Eleventh Hour."

34. Michael Hickerson, "New Season of 'Doctor Who' Raising Eyebrows," *Slice of SciFi,* April 8, 2010, http:www.sliceofscifi.com2010/04/08new-season-of-doctor-who-raising-eyebrows/.

35. "Sexism, Amy Pond, and the Kindness of Podcasters," April 17, 2010, podcast and interview, http://austintotamu.blogspot.com/2010/04/sexism-amy-pond-and-kindness-of.html.

36. *London Evening Standard,* June 15, 2010.

37. "Doctor Who Assistant Denies Being 'Too Sexy' in Role," *BBC News,* June 15, 2010, http://www.bbc.co.uk/news/10316872

38. "A Christmas Carol."

39. Although several online articles described the ratings of Smith and Moffat's first season as lagging far behind the average ratings of previous seasons, the end-of-year tally showed that the ratings were often close, but the most recent season's average was slightly higher than most seasons in the Tennant/Davies years. Stephen Bray. "Doctor Who Ratings: Putting Things Straight," *Den of Geek,* July 4, 2010, http://www.denofgeek.com/television/529040/doctor_who_ratings_putting_things_straight.html.

40. Mathew Wace Peak, "Steven Moffat Insists BBC Is Committed to Doctor Who," *Digital Journal,* September 24, 2010, http://www.digitaljournal.com/article/298065.

Videography

DOCTOR WHO: THE ORIGINAL SERIES

Doctor: William Hartnell
Producer: Verity Lambert

Season One

1. An Unearthly Child, 23 Nov–14 Dec 1963, Anthony Coburn & CE Webber writers, Waris Hussein dir.
2. Daleks, 21 Dec 1963–1 Feb 1964, Terry Nation writer, Richard Martin & Christopher Barry dir.
3. Edge of Destruction, 8–15 Feb 1964, David Whitaker writer, Richard Martin & Frank Cox dir.
4. Marco Polo, 22 Feb–4 Apr 1964, John Lucarotti writer, Waris Hussein dir.
5. Keys of Marinus, 11 Apr–16 May 1964, Terry Nation writer, John Gorrie dir.
6. The Aztecs, 23 May–13 June 1964, John Lucarotti writer, John Crockett dir.
7. The Sensorites, 20 June–1 Aug 1964, Peter R. Newman writer, Mervyn Pinfield & Frank Cox dir.
8. The French Revolution [The Reign of Terror], 8 Aug–12 Sept 1964, Dennis Spooner writer, Henric Hirsch & John Gorrie dir.

Season Two

9. Planet of the Giants, 31 Oct–14 Nov 1964, Louis Marks writer, Mervyn Pinfield & Douglas Camfield dir.
10. Dalek Invasion of Earth, 21 Nov–26 Dec 1964, Terry Nation writer, Richard Martin dir.
11. The Rescue, 2–9 Jan 1965, David Whitaker writer, Christopher Barry dir.
12. The Romans, 16 Jan–6 Feb 1964, Dennis Spooner writer, Christopher Barry dir.
13. The Web Planet, 13 Feb–20 Mar 1965, Bill Strutton writer, Richard Martin dir.
14. The Crusaders, 27 Mar–17 Apr 1965, David Whitaker writer, Douglas Camfield dir.

15. The Space Museum, 24 Apr–15 May 1965, Glyn Jones writer, Mervyn Pinfield dir.
16. The Chase, 22 May–26 June 1965, Terry Nation writer, Richard Martin & Douglas Camfield dir.
17. Time Meddlar, 3–24 July 1965, Dennis Spooner writer, Douglas Camfield dir.

Season Three

18. Galaxy Four, 11 Sept–2 Oct 1965, William Emms writer, Derek Martinus & Mervyn Pinfield dir.
19. Mission to the Unknown, 9 Oct 1965, Terry Nation writer, Derek Martinus dir.

Producer: John Wiles

20. The Myth Makers, 16 Oct–6 Nov 1965, Donald Cotton writer, Michael Leeston-Smith dir.
21. The Dalek Master Plan, 13 Nov 1965–29 Jan 1966, Terry Nation & Dennis Spooner writers, Douglas Camfield dir.
22. The Massacre, 5–26 Feb 1966, John Lucarotti & Donald Tosh writers, Paddy Russell dir.
23. The Ark, 5–26 Mar 1966, Paul Erickson & Lesley Scott writers, Michael Imison dir.
24. The Celestial Toymaker, 2–23 Apr 1966, Brian Hayles and Donald Tosh writers, Bill Sellars dir.
25. The Gunfighters, 30 Apr–21 May 1966, Donald Cotton writer, Rex Tucker dir.
26. The Savages, 28 May–18 June 1966, Ian Stuart Black writer, Christopher Barry dir.
27. The War Machines, 25 June–16 July 1966, Ian Stuart Black & Kit Pedler writers, Michael Ferguson dir.

Season Four

28. The Smugglers, 10 Sept–1 Oct 1966, Brian Hayles writer, Julia Smith dir.
29. The Tenth Planet, 8–29 Oct 1966, Kit Pedler & Gerry Davis writers, Derek Martinus dir.

Doctor: Patrick Troughton

30. Power of the Daleks, 5 Nov–10 Dec 1966, David Whitaker & Dennis Spooner writers, Christopher Barry dir.
31. The Highlanders, 17 Dec 1966–7 Jan 1967, Elwyn Jones & Gerry Davis writers, Hugh David dir.
32. The Underwater Menace, 14 Jan–4 Feb 1967, Geoffrey Orme writer, Julia Smith dir.
33. The Moonbase, 11 Feb–4 Mar 1967, Kit Pedler writer, Morris Barry dir.
34. Macra Terror, 11 Mar–1 Apr 1967, Ian Stuart Black writer, John Davies dir.

Associate Producer: Peter Bryant

35. The Faceless Ones, 8 Apr–13 May 1967, David Ellis & Malcolm Hulke writers, Gerry Mill dir.
36. Evil of the Daleks, 20 May–1 July 1967, David Whitaker writer, Derek Martinus dir.

Season Five

Producer: Peter Bryant

37. Tomb of the Cybermen, 2–23 Sept 1967, Kit Pedler & Gerry Davis writer, Morris Barry dir.

Producer: Innes Lloyd

38. The Abominable Snowman, 30 Sept–4 Nov 1967, Mervyn Haisman & Henry Lincoln writer, Gerald Blake dir.
39. The Ice Warriors, 11 Nov–16 Dec 1967, Brian Hayles writer, Derek Martinus dir.
40. Enemy of the World, 23 Dec 67–27 Jan 1968, David Whitaker writer, Barry Letts dir.

Producer: Peter Bryant

41. Web of Fear, 3 Feb–9 Mar 1968, Mervyn Haisman & Henry Lincoln writers, Douglas Camfield dir.
42. Fury from the Deep, 16 Mar–20 Apr 1968, Victor Pemberton writer, Hugh David dir.
43. Wheel in Space, 27 Apr–1 Jun 1968, David Whitaker & Kit Pedler writer, Tristan de Vere Cole dir.

Season Six

44. The Dominators, 10 Aug–7 Sept 1968, Norman Ashby writer, Morris Barry dir.
45. Mind Robber, 14 Sep–12 Oct 1968, Peter Ling & Derrick Sherwin writers, David Maloney dir.
46. Invasion, 2 Nov–21 Dec 1968, Derrick Sherwin & Kit Pedler writers, Douglas Camfield dir.
47. The Krotons, 28 Dec 68–18 Jan 1969, Robert Holmes writer, David Maloney dir.

48. Seeds of Death, 25 Jan–1 Mar 1969, Brian Hayles & Terrance Dicks writers, Michael Ferguson, dir.
49. The Space Pirates, 8 Mar–12 Apr 1969, Robert Holmes writer, Michael Hart dir.

Producer: Derrick Sherwin

50. The War Games, 19 Apr–21 Jun 69, Malcolm Hulke & Terrance Dicks writers, David Maloney dir.

Season Seven

Doctor: Jon Pertwee

51. Spearhead from Space, 3–24 Jan 1970, Robert Holmes writer, Derek Martinus dir.

Producer: Barry Letts

52. Doctor Who and the Silurians, 31 Jan–14 Mar 1970, Malcolm Hulke writer, Timothy Combe dir.
53. The Ambassadors of Death, 21 Mar–2 May 1970, David Whitaker, Trevor Ray & Malcolm Hulke writers, Michael Ferguson dir.
54. Inferno, 9 May–20 June 1970, Don Houghton writer, Douglas Camfield & Barry Letts dir.

Season Eight

55. The Terror of the Autons, 2–23 Jan 1971, Robert Holmes writer, Barry Letts dir.
56. Mind of Evil, 30 Jan–6 Mar 1971, Don Houghton writer, Timothy Combe dir.
57. Claws of Axos, 13 Mar–3 Apr 1971, Bob Baker & Dave Martin writers, Michael Ferguson dir.
58. Colony in Space, 10 Apr–15 May 1971, Malcolm Hulke writer, Michael E Briant dir.
59. The Daemons, 22 May–19 June 1971, Guy Leopold writer, Christopher Barry dir.

Season Nine

60. Day of the Daleks, 1–22 Jan 1972, Louis Marks writer, Paul Bernard dir.
61. Curse of Peladon, 29 Jan–19 Feb 1972, Brian Hayles writer, Lennie Mayne dir.
62. The Sea Devils, 26 Feb–1 Apr 1972, Malcolm Hulke writer, Michael Briant dir.
63. The Mutants, 8 Apr–13 May 1972, Bob Baker and Dave Martin writers, Christopher Barry dir.
64. The Time Monster, 20 May–24 June 1972, Robert Sloman & Barry Letts writers, Paul Bernard dir.

Season Ten

65. The Three Doctors, 30 Dec 1972–20 Jan 1973, Bob Baker & Dave Martin writers, Lennie Mayne dir.

66. Carnival of Monsters, 27 Jan–17 Feb 1973, Robert Holmes writer, Barry Letts dir.

67. Frontier in Space, 24 Feb–31 Mar 1973, Malcolm Hulke writer, Paul Bernard dir.

68. Planet of the Daleks, 7 Apr–12 May 1973, Terry Nation writer, David Maloney dir.

69. The Green Death, 19 May–23 Jun 1973, Robert Sloman & Barry Letts writers, Michael Briant dir.

Season Eleven

70. The Time Warrior, 15 Dec 1973–5 Jan 1974, Robert Holmes writer, Alan Bromly dir.

71. Invasion of the Dinosaurs, 12 Jan–16 Feb 1974, Malcolm Hulke writer, Paddy Russell dir.

72. Death to the Daleks, 23 Feb–16 Mar 1973, Terry Nation writer, Michael Briant dir.

73. The Monster of Peladon, 23 Mar–27 Apr 1974, Brian Hayles writer, Lennie Mayne dir.

74. Planet of the Spiders, 4 May–8 Jun 1974, Robert Sloman & Barry Letts writers, Barry Letts dir.

Season Twelve

Doctor: Tom Baker

75. Robot, 28 Dec 1974–18 Jan 1975, Terrance Dicks writer, Christopher Barry dir.

Producer: Philip Hinchcliffe

76. Ark in Space, 25 Jan–15 Feb 1975, Robert Holmes & John Lucarotti writers, Rodney Bennett dir.

77. The Sontaren Experiment, 22 Feb–1 Mar 1975, Bob Baker & Dave Martin writers, Rodney Bennett dir.

78. Genesis of the Daleks, 8 Mar–12 Apr 1975, Terry Nation writer, David Maloney dir.

79. Revenge of the Cybermen, 19 Apr–10 May 1975, Gerry Davis writer, Michael Briant dir.

Season Thirteen

80. Terror of the Zygons, 30 Aug–20 Sept 1975, Robert Banks Stewart writer, Douglas Camfield dir.

81. Planet of Evil, 27 Sept–18 Oct 1975, Louis Marks writer, David Maloney dir.

82. Pyramid of Mars, 25 Oct–15 Nov 1975, Stephen Harris writer, Paddy Russell dir.

83. Android Invasion, 22 Nov–13 Dec 1975, Terry Nation writer, Barry Letts dir.

84. Brain of Morbius, 3–24 Jan 1976, Robin Bland writer, Christopher Barry dir.

85. Seeds of Doom, 31 Jan–6 Mar 1976, Robert Banks Stewart writer, Douglas Camfield dir.

Season Fourteen

86. The Masque of Madragora, 4–25 Sept 1976, Louis Marks writer, Rodney Bennett dir.

87. Hand of Fear, 2–23 Oct 1976, Bob Baker & Dave Martin writers, Lennie Mayne dir.

88. The Deadly Assasin, 30 Oct 76–20 Nov 1976, Robert Holmes writer, David Maloney dir.

89. Face of Evil, 1–22 Jan 1977, Chris Boucher writer, Pennant Roberts dir.

90. Robots of Death, 29 Jan–19 Feb 1977, Chris Boucher writer, Michael Briant dir.

91. Talons of Weng Chiang, 26 Feb–2 Mar 1977, Robert Holmes writer, David Maloney dir.

Season Fifteen

Producer: Graham Williams

92. Horror at Fang Rock, 3–24 Sept 1977, Terrance Dicks writer, Paddy Russell dir.

93. Invisible Enemy, 1–22 Oct 1977, Bob Baker & Dave Martin writers, Derrick Goodwin dir.

94. Image of the Fendahl, 29 Oct–19 Nov 1977, Chris Boucher writer, George Spenton-Foster dir.

95. The Sunmakers, 26 Nov–17 Dec 1977, Robert Holmes writer, Pennant Roberts dir.

96. Underworld, 7–28 Jan 1978, Bob Baker and Dave Martin writers, Norman Stewart dir.

97. Invasion of Time, 4 Feb–11 Mar 1978, David Agnew writer, Gerald Blake dir.

Season Sixteen

98. The Ribos Operation, 2–23 Sept 1978, Robert Holmes writer, George Spenton-Foster dir.

99. The Pirate Planet, 30 Sept–21 Oct 1978, Douglas Adams writer, Pennant Roberts dir.

100. Stones of Blood, 28 Oct–18 Nov 1978, David Fisher writer, Darrol Blake dir.

101. Androids of Tara, 25 Nov–16 Dec 1978, David Fisher writer, Michael Hayes dir.

102. The Power of Kroll, 23 Dec 1978–13 Jan 1979, Robert Holmes writer, Norman Stewart dir.

103. The Armageddon Factor, 20 Jan–24 Feb 1979, Bob Baker and Dave Martin writers, Michael Hayes dir.

Season Seventeen

104. Destiny of the Daleks, 1–22 Sept 1979, Terry Nation writer, Ken Grieve dir.

105. City of Death, 29 Sept–20 Oct 1979, David Agnew writer, Michael Hayes dir.

106. Creature from the Pit, 27 Oct–17 Nov 1979, David Fisher writer, Christopher Barry dir.

107. Nightmare from Eden, 24 Nov–15 Dec 1979, Bob Baker writer, Alan Bromly dir.

108. Horns of Nimon, 22 Dec–23 Jan 1980, Anthony Read writer, Kenny McBain dir.

Shada, (never aired), Douglas Adams writer, Pennant Roberts dir.

Season Eighteen

Producer: John Nathan-Turner

109. The Leisure Hive, 30 Aug–20 Sept 1980, David Fisher writer, Lovett Bickford dir.

110. Meglos, 27 Sept–18 Oct 1980, John Flanagan & Andrew McCulloch writers, Terence Dudley dir.

111. Full Circle, 25 Oct–15 Nov 1980, Andrew Smith writer, Peter Grimwade dir.

112. State of Decay, 22 Nov–13 Dec 1980, Terrance Dicks writer, Peter Moffatt dir.

113. Warrior's Gate, 3–24 Jan 1981, Stephen Gallagher writer, Paul Joyce & Graeme Harper dir.

114. The Keeper of Traken, 31 Jan–21 Feb 1981, Johnny Byrne writer, John Black dir.

115. Logopolis, 28 Feb–21 Mar 1981, Christopher H. Bidmead writer, Peter Grimwade dir.

Season Nineteen

Doctor: Peter Davison

116. Castravalva, 4–12 Jan 1982, Christopher H. Bidmead writer, Fiona Cumming dir.

117. Four to Doomsday, 18–26 Jan 1982, Terence Dudley writer, John Black dir.

118. Kinda, 1–9 Feb 1982, Christopher Bailey writer, Peter Grimwade dir.

119. The Visitation, 15–23 Feb 1982, Eric Saward writer, Peter Moffatt dir.

120. Black Orchid, 1–2 Mar 1982, Terence Dudley writer, Ron Jones dir.

121. Earthshock, 8–16 Mar 1982, Eric Saward writer, Peter Grimwade dir.

122. Timeflight, 22–30 Mar 1982, Peter Grimwade writer, Ron Jones dir.

Season Twenty

123. Arc of Infinity, 3–12 Jan 1983, Johnny Byrne writer, Ron Jones dir.

124. Snakedance, 18–26 Jan 1983, Christopher Bailey writer, Fiona Cumming dir.

125. Mawdryn Undead, 1–9 Feb 1983, Peter Grimwade writer, Peter Moffatt dir.

126. Terminus, 15–23 Feb 1983, Stephen Gallagher writer, Mary Ridge dir.

127. Enlightenment, 1–9 Mar 1983, Barbara Clegg writer, Fiona Cumming dir.

128. The King's Demons, 15–16 Mar 1983, Terence Dudley writer, Tony Virgo dir.

129. The Five Doctors, 23 Nov 1983, Terrance Dicks writer, Peter Moffatt dir.

Season Twenty One

130. Warriors of the Deep, 5–13 Jan 1984, Johnny Byrne writer, Pennant Roberts dir.

131. The Awakening, 19–20 Jan 1984, Eric Pringle writer, Michael Owen Morris dir.

132. Frontios, 26 Jan–3 Feb 1984, Christopher H Bidmead writer, Ron Jones dir.

133. Resurrection of the Daleks, 8–15 Feb 1984, Eric Saward writer, Matthew Robinson dir.

134. Planet of Fire, 23 Feb–2 Mar 1984, Peter Grimwade writer, Fiona Cumming dir.

135. Caves of Androzani, 8–16 Mar 1984, Robert Holmes writer, Graeme Harper dir.

Doctor: Colin Baker

136. Twin Dilemma, 22–30 Mar 1984, Anthony Steven writer, Peter Moffatt dir.

Season Twenty Two

137. Attack of the Cybermen, 5–12 Jan 1985, Paula Moore writer, Matthew Robinson dir.

138. Vengeance on Varos, 19–26 Jan 1985, Philip Martin writer, Ron Jones dir.

139. Mark of the Rani, 2–9 Feb 1985, Pip & Jane Baker writers, Sarah Hellings dir.

140. The Two Doctors, 16 Feb–2 Mar 1985, Robert Holmes writer, Peter Moffatt dir.

141. Timelash, 9–16 Mar 1985, Glen McCoy writer, Pennant Roberts dir.

142. Revelation of the Daleks, 23–30 Mar 1985, Eric Saward writer, Graeme Harper dir.

Season Twenty Three

143. Trial of a Timelord

- The Mysterious Planet, 6–27 Sep 1986, Robert Holmes writer, Nicholas Mallett dir.
- Mindwarp, 4–25 Oct 1986, Philip Martin writer, Ron Jones dir.
- Terror of the Vervoids, 1–22 Nov 1986, Pip and Jane Baker writers, Chris Clough dir.
- The Ultimate Foe, 20 Nov–6 Dec 1986, Robert Holmes & Pip and Jane Baker writers, Chris Clough dir.

Doctor: Sylvester McCoy

144. Time and the Rani, 7–28 Sept 1987, Pip & Jane Baker writers, Andrew Morgan dir.

145. Paradise Towers, 5–26 Oct 1987, Stephen Wyatt writer, Nicholas Mallett dir.

146. Delta and the Bannermen, 2–16 Nov 1987, Malcolm Kohll writer, Chris Clough dir.

147. Dragonfire, 23 Nov–7 Dec 1987, Ian Briggs writer, Chris Clough dir.

Season Twenty Five

148. Remembrance of the Daleks, 5–26 Oct 1988, Ben Aaronvitch writer, Andrew Morgan dir.
149. The Happiness Patrol, 2–16 Nov 1988, Graeme Curry writer, Chris Clough dir.
150. Silver Nemesis, 23 Nov–7 Dec 1988, Kevin Clarke writer, Chris Clough dir.
151. The Greatest Show in the Galaxy, 14 Dec 1988–4 Jan 1989, Stephen Wyatt writer, Alan Wareing dir.

Season Twenty Six

152. Battlefield, 6–27 Sept 1989, Ben Aaronvitch writer, Michael Kerrigan dir.
153. Ghostlight, 4–18 Oct 1989, Marc Platt writer, Alan Wareing dir.
154. Curse of Fenric, 25 Oct–15 Nov 1989, Ian Briggs writer, Nicholas Mallett dir.
155. Survival, 22 Nov–6 Dec 1989, Rona Munro writer, Alan Wareing dir.

Doctor: Paul McGann
Producer: Philip Segal

156. Doctor Who: The Movie, 12 May 1996, Matthew Jacobs writer, Geoffrey Sax dir.

Doctor: Christopher Eccleston
Executive Producers: Russell T Davies,
Julie Gardner & Mal Young
Producer: Phil Collinson

Series One

157. Rose, 26 Mar 2005, Russell T Davies writer, Keith Boak dir.
158. The End of the World, 2 Apr 2005, Russell T Davies writer, Euros Lyn dir.
159. The Unquiet Dead, 9–Apr 2005, Mark Gatiss writer, Euros Lyn dir.
160. Aliens of London/ World War Three, 16–23 Apr 2005, Russell T Davies writer, Keith Boak dir.
161. Dalek, 30 Apr 2005, Robert Shearman writer, Joe Ahearne dir.
162. The Long Game, 7 May 2005, Russell T Davies writer, Brian Grant dir.
163. Father's Day, 14 May 2005, Paul Cornell writer, Joe Ahearne dir.
164. The Empty Child/ The Doctor Dances, 21–8 May 2005, Steven Moffat writer, James Hawes dir.
165. Boom Town, 4 Jun 2005, Russell T Davies writer, Joe Ahearne dir.
167. Bad Wolf/ The Parting of the Ways, 11–8 June 2005, Russell T Davies writer, Joe Ahearne dir.

Doctor: David Tennant
Executive Producers: Russell T Davies
and Julie Gardner

Doctor Who: Children in Need Special, 18 Nov 2005, Russell T Davies writer, Euros Lyn dir.
168. Christmas Invasion, 25 Dec 2005, Russell T Davies writer, James Hawes dir.
169. New Earth, 15 Apr 2006, Russell T Davies writer, James Hawes dir.
170. Tooth and Claw, 22 Apr 2006, Russell T Davies writer, Euros Lyn dir.
171. School Reunion, 29 Apr 2006, Toby Whithouse writer, James Hawes dir.
172. The Girl in the Fireplace, 6 May 2006, Steven Moffatt writer, Euros Lyn dir.
173. Rise of the Cybermen/ The Age of Steel, 13–20 May 2006, Tom MacRae writer, Graeme Harper dir.
174. The Idiot's Lantern, 27 May 2006, Mark Gatiss writer, Euros Lyn dir.
175. The Impossible Planet/ Satin Pit, 2–10 Jun 2006, Matt Jones writer, James Strong dir.
176. Love and Monsters, 17 Jun 2006, Russell T Davies writer, Dan Zeff dir.
177. Fear Her, 24 Jun 2006, Matthew Graham writer, Graeme Harper dir.
178. Army of Ghosts/ Doomsday, 1–8 Jul 2006, Russell T Davies writer, Graeme Harper dir.

Series Three

179. Runaway Bride, 25 Dec 2006, Russell T Davies writer, Euros Lyn dir.
180. Smith and Jones, 31 Mar 2007, Russell T Davies writer, Charles Palmer dir.
181. The Shakespeare Code, 7 Apr 2007, Gareth Roberts writer, Charles Palmer dir.
182. Gridlock, 14 Apr 2007, Russell T Davies writer, Richard Clark dir.
183. Daleks in Manhattan/ Evolution of the Daleks, 21–8 Apr 2007, Helen Raynor writer, James Strong dir.
184. The Lazarus Experiment, 5 May 2007, Stephen Greenhorn writer, Richard Clark dir.
185. 42, 19 May 2007, Chris Chibnall writer, Graeme Harper dir.

Producer: Susie Liggat
Executive Producer: Phil Collinson
(episode 186 only)

186. Human Nature/ The Family of Blood 26 May–2 June 2007, Paul Cornell writer, Charles Palmer dir.
187. Blink, 9 Jun 2007, Steven Moffat writer, Hettie MacDonald dir.
188. Utopia/ The Sound of the Drums/ Last of

the Timelords, 16–30 Jun 2007, Russell T Davies writer, Graeme Harper and Colin Teague dir.

Series Four

Time Crash: Children in Need, 16 Nov 2007, Stephen Moffat writer, Graeme Harper dir.

189. Voyage of the Damned, 25 Dec 2007, Russell T Davies writer, James Strong dir.

190. Partners in Crime, 5 Apr 2008, Russell T Davies writer, James Strong dir.

191. The Fires of Pompeii, 12 Apr 2008, James Moran writer, Colin Teague dir.

Producer: Susie Liggat
Executive Producer: Phil Collinson

192. Planet of the Ood, 19 Apr 2008, Keith Temple writer, Graeme Harper dir.

193. Sontaran Strategy/ The Poison Sky, 26 Apr–3 May 2008, Helen Raynor writer, Douglas Mackinnon dir.

194. The Doctor's Daughter, 10 May 2008, Stephen Greenhorn writer, Alice Troughton dir.

195. The Unicorn and the Wasp, 17 May 2008, Gareth Roberts writer, Graeme Harper dir.

196. Silence in the Library/ Forest of the Dead, 31 May–7 Jun 2008, Steven Moffatt writer, Euros Lyn dir.

197. Midnight, 14 Jun 2008, Russell T Davies writer, Alice Troughton dir.

198. Turn Left, 21 Jun 2008, Russell T Davies writer, Graeme Harper dir.

Executive Producers: Russell T Davies
and Julie Gardner

199. The Stolen Earth/ Journey's End, 28 Jun–5 July 2008, Russell T Davies writer, Graeme Harper dir.

Specials

200. The Next Doctor, 25 Dec 2008, Russell T Davies writer, Andy Goddard dir.

201. Planet of the Dead, 11 Apr 2009, Russell T Davies and Gareth Roberts writer, James Strong dir.

202. The Waters of Mars, 15 Nov 2009, Russell T Davies and Phil Ford writers, Graeme Harper dir.

203. End of Time, 25 Jan 2009–1 Jan 2010, Russell T Davies writer, Euros Lyn dir.

Doctor: Matt Smith
Executive Producers: Steven Moffatt,
Piers Wenger & Beth Willis

Series Five

204. The Eleventh Hour, 3 Apr 2010, Steven Moffatt writer, Adam Smith dir.

205. The Beast Below, 10 Apr 2010, Steven Moffat writer, Andrew Gunn dir.

206. Victory of the Daleks, 17 Apr 10, Mark Gatiss writer, Andrew Gunn dir.

207. The Time of Angels/ Flesh and Stone, 24 Apr–1 May 2010, Steven Moffat writer, Adam Smith dir.

208. The Vampires of Venice, 8 May 2010, Toby Whithouse writer, Jonny Campbell dir.

209. Amy's Choice, 15 May 2010, Simon Nye writer, Catherine Morshead dir.

210. The Hungry Earth/ Cold Blood, 22–9 May 2010, Chris Chibnall writer, Ashley Way dir.

211. Vincent and the Doctor, 5 Jun 2010, Richard Curtis writer, Jonny Campbell dir.

212. The Lodger, 12 Jun 2010, Gareth Roberts writer, Catherine Morshead dir.

213. The Pandorica Opens/ The Big Bang, 19–26 Jun 2010, Steven Moffat writer, Toby Haynes dir.

Series Six

214. The Christmas Carol, 25 Dec 2010, Steven Moffat writer, Toby Haynes dir.

Space and Time: Comic Relief, 18 Mar 2011, Steven Moffat writer, Richard Senior dir.

215. The Impossible Astronaut/ Day of the Moon, 23–30 Apr 2011, Steven Moffat writer, Toby Haynes dir.

216. The Curse of the Black Spot, 7 May 2011, Stephen Thompson writer, Jeremy Webb dir.

217. The Doctor's Wife, 14 May 2011, Neil Gaiman writer, Richard Clark dir.

218. The Rebel Flesh/ The Almost People, 21–8 May 2011, Matthew Graham writer, Julian Simpson dir.

219. A Good Man Goes to War/ Let's Kill Hitler, 4 June/27 Aug 2011, Steven Moffat writer, Peter Hoar & Richard Senior dir.

220. Night Terrors, 3 Sep 2011, Mark Gatiss writer, Richard Clark dir.

221. The Girl Who Waited, 10 Sep 2011, Tom MacRae writer, Nick Hurran dir.

222. The God Complex, 17 Sep 2011, Toby Whithouse writer, Nick Hurran dir.

223. Closing Time, 24 Sep 2011, Gareth Roberts writer, Steve Hughes dir.

224. The Wedding of River Song, 1 Oct 2011, Steven Moffat writer, Jeremy Webb dir.

K-9 AND COMPANY

Producer: John Nathan-Turner

A Girl's Best Friend, 28 Dec 1981, Terence Dudley writer, John Black dir.

TORCHWOOD

Executive Producer Russell T Davies

Series One

1. Everything Changes, 22 Oct 2006, Russell T Davies writer, Brian Kelly dir.
2. Day One, 22 Oct 2006, Chris Chibnall writer, Brian Kelly dir.
3. Ghost Machine, 29 Oct 2006, Helen Raynor writer, Colin Teague dir.
4. Cyberwoman, 5 Nov 2006, Chris Chibnall writer, James Strong dir.
5. Small Worlds, 12 Nov 2006, Peter J Hammond writer, Alice Troughton dir.
6. Countrycide, 19 Nov 2006, Chris Chibnall writer, Andy Goddard dir.
7. Greeks Bearing Gifts, 26 Nov 2006, Toby Whithouse writer, Colin Teague dir.
8. They Keep Killing Suzie, 3 Dec 2006, Paul Tomalin & Dan McCulloch, James Strong dir.
9. Random Shoes, 10 Dec 2006, Jacquetta May writer, James Erskine dir.
10. Out of Time, 17 Dec 2006, Catherine Tregenna writer, Alice Troughton dir.
11. Combat, 24 Dec 2006, Noel Clarke writer, Andy Goddard dir.
12. Captain Jack Harkness, 1 Jan 2007, Catherine Tregenna writer, Ashley Way dir.
13. End of Days, 1 Jan 2007, Chris Chibnall writer, Ashley Way, dir.

Series Two

14. Kiss Kiss, Bang Bang, 16 Jan 2008, Chris Chibnall writer, Ashley Way dir.
15. Sleeper, 23 Jan 2008, James Moran writer, Colin Teague dir.
16. To the Last Man, 30 Jan 2008, Helen Raynor writer, Andy Goddard dir.
17. Meat, 6 Feb 2008, Catherine Tregenna writer, Colin Teague dir.
18. Adam, 13 Feb 2008, Catherine Tregenna writer, Andy Goddard dir.
19. Reset, 13 Feb 2008, JC Wilsher writer, Ashley Way dir.
20. Dead Man Walking, 20 Feb 2008, Matt Jones writer, Andy Goddard dir.
21. A Day in the Death, 27 Feb 2008, Joseph Lidster writer, Andy Goddard dir.
22. Something Borrowed, 5 Mar 2008, Phil Ford writer, Ashley Way dir.
23. From Out of the Rain, 12 Mar 2008, Peter J Hammond writer, Jonathan Fox Bassett dir.
24. Adrift, 19 March 2008, Chris Chibnall writer, Mark Everest dir.
25. Fragments, 21 Mar 2008, Chris Chibnall writer, Jonathan Fox Bassett dir.

26. Exit Wounds, 4 Apr 2008, Chris Chibnall writer, Ashley Way dir.

Children of Earth

27. Day One, 6 July 2009, Russell T Davies writer, Euros Lyn dir.
28. Day Two, 7 July 2009, John Fay writer, Euro Lyn dir.
29. Day Three, 8 July 2009, Russell T Davies & James Moran writers, Euros Lyn dir.
30. Day Four, 9 July 2009, John Fay writer, Euros Lyn dir.
31. Day Five, 10 July 2009, Russell T Davies writer, Euros Lyn dir.

Miracle Day

32. The New World, 8 July 2011, Russell T Davies writer, Bharat Nalluri dir.
33. Rendition, 15 July 2011, Doris Egan writer, Billy Gierhart dir.
34. Dead of Night, 22 July 2011, Jane Espenson writer, Billy Gierhart dir.
35. Escape to LA, 29 July 2011, Jim Gray and John Shiban writers, Billy Gierhart dir.
36. The Categories of Life, 5 Aug 2011, Jane Espenson writer, Guy Ferland dir.
37. The Middle Men, 12 Aug 2011, John Shiban writer, Guy Ferland dir.
38. Immortal Sins, 19 Aug 2011, Jane Espenson writer, Gwyneth Horder-Payton dir.
39. End of the Road, 29 Aug 2011, Jane Espenson & Ryan Scott writers, Gwyneth Horder-Payton dir.
40. The Gathering, 2 Sept 2011, John Fay writer, Guy Ferland dir.
41. The Blood Line, 9 Sept 2011, Russell T Davies & Jane Espenson writers, Billy Gierhart dir.

THE SARAH JANE ADVENTURES

Russell T Davies, Producer

1. Invasion of the Bane, 1 Jan 2007, Gareth Roberts & Russell T Davies writers, Colin Teague, dir.

Series One

2. Revenge of the Slitheen, 24 Sept 2007, Gareth Roberts writer, Alice Troughton dir.
3. Eye of the Gorgon, 1–8 Oct 2007, Phil Ford Writer, Alice Troughton dir.
4. Warriors of Kudlak, 15–22 Oct 2007, Phil Gladwin writer, Charles Martin dir.
5. Whatever Happened to Sarah Jane, 29 Oct–5 Nov 2007, Gareth Roberts writer, Graeme Harper dir.
6. The Lost Boy, 12–19 Nov 2007, Phil Ford writer, Charles Martin dir.

Series Two

7. Enemy of the Bane, 1–8 Dec 2008, Phil Ford writer, Graeme Harper dir.

8. The Temptation of Sarah Jane Smith, 17–24 Nov 2008, Gareth Roberts writer, Graeme Harper dir.

9. The Mark of the Berserker, 3–10 Nov 2008, Joseph Lidster writer, Joss Agnew dir.

10. Secrets of the Stars, 20–27 Oct 2008, Gareth Roberts writer, Michael Kerrigan dir.

11. Day of the Clown, 6–13 Oct 2008, Phil Ford writer, Michael Kerrigan dir.

12. The Last Sontaran, 29 Sept 2008, Phil Ford writer, Joss Agnew dir

Comic Relief Special

From Raxacoricofallapatorius with Love, 13 Mar 2009, Gareth Roberts & Clayton Hickman writers, Joss Agnew dir.

Series Three

13. Prisoner of the Judoon, 15–16 Oct 2009, Phil Ford writer, Joss Agnew dir.

14. The Mad Woman in the Attic, 22–23 Oct 2009, Joseph Lidster writer, Alice Troughton dir.

15. The Wedding of Sarah Jane Smith, 29–30 Oct 2009, Gareth Roberts writer, Joss Agnew dir.

16. The Eternity Trap, 5–6 Nov 2009, Phil Ford writer, Alice Troughton dir.

17. The Gift, 19–20 Nov 2009, Rupert Laight writer, Alice Troughton dir.

18. Mona Lisa's Revenge, 12–13 Nov 2009, Phil Ford writer, Joss Agnew dir.

Series Four

19. The Nightmare Man, 11–12 Oct 2010, Joseph Lidster writer, Joss Agnew dir.

20. The Vault of Secrets, 18–19 Oct 2010, Phil Ford writer, Joss Agnew dir.

21. Death of the Doctor, 25–26 Oct 2010, Russell T Davies writer, Ashley Way dir.

22. The Empty Planet, 1–2 Nov 2010, Gareth Roberts writer, Ashley Way dir.

23. Lost in Time, 8–9 Nov 2010, Rupert Laight writer, Joss Agnew dir.

24. Goodbye, Sarah Jane Smith, 15–16 Nov 2010, Gareth Roberts and Clayton Hickman writers, Joss Agnew dir.

Series Five

25. Sky, 4 Oct 2011, Phil Ford writer, Ashley Way dir.

26. The Curse of Clyde Langer, 10–11 Oct 2011, Phil Ford writer, Ashley Way dir.

27. The Man Who Never Was, 17–18 Oct 2011, Gareth Roberts writer, Joss Agnew dir.

References

Abell, John C. "Aug. 31, 1920: News Radio Makes News." Wired.com, August 31, 2010.

Akyuz, Gun. "BBC Sci-fi Thriller Finds Partner." C21Media, http://www.c21media.net/news/detail.asp?area=4&article=29877 (October 27, 2008).

Amy-Chin, Dee. "Davies, Dawkins and Deus ex TARDIS: Who Finds God in the Doctor?" *Ruminations, Peregrinations, and Regenerations*, ed. Hansen, 22–34.

_____. "Rose Tyler: The Ethics of Care and the Limit of Agency." *Science Fiction Film and Television* 1, no. 2 (2008): 231–47.

Anders, Charlie Jane. "Doctor Who's Steven Moffat: The io9 Interview." io9, May 18, 2010, http://uk.io9.com/#!5542010/doctor-whos-steven-moffat-the-io9-interview (February 18, 2011).

Anderson, Kyle. "Doctor Who for Newbies: The Eighth Doctor & The Wilderness Years." http://www.nerdist.com/2010/12/doctor-who-for-newbies-the-eighth-doctor-the-wilderness-years-2/ (December 31, 2010).

"Audiences and References." *In-Vision*, No. 84: 26–27.

Baudrillard, Jean. "The Ecstasy of Communication." *The Anti-Aesthetic*, ed. Hal Foster. Port Townsend, WA: Bay Press, 1983: 126–34.

Beeler, Stan. "*Stargate Sg-1* and the Quest for the Perfect Science Fiction Premise." *The Essential Science Fiction Reader*, ed. J.P. Telotte. Lexington: University Press of Kentucky, 2008: 267–82.

Bell, David. "Anti-Idyll: Rural Horror." *Contested Countryside Cultures: Otherness, Marginalisation, and Rurality*, eds. Paul J. Cloke and Jo Little. London: Routledge, 1997: 91–104.

Berberich, Christine. "This Green and Pleasant Land: Cultural Constructions of Englishness." *Landscape and Englishness*, eds. Robert Burden and Stephan Kohl. Amsterdam: Rodopi, 2006.

Bettelheim, B. *The Uses of Enchantment: The Meaning and Importance of Fairy Tales*. London: Penguin, 1978.

Bolter, Jay David, and Richard Grusin. *Remediation: Understanding New Media*. Cambridge: MIT Press, 1999.

Booth, Paul. *Digital Fandom: New Media Studies*. New York: Peter Lang, 2010.

Booth, W.C. *The Company We Keep: An Ethics of Fiction*. Berkeley: University of California Press, 1988.

Bould, Mark. "Science Fiction in the United Kingdom." *The Essential Science Fiction Reader*, ed. J. P. Lexington: University Press of Kentucky, 2008: 209–30.

Bourne, Craig. *A Future for Presentism*. Oxford: Clarendon Press, 2006.

Boym, Svetlana. *The Future of Nostalgia*. New York: Basic Books, 2001.

Bradshaw, Simon, Antony Keen and Graham Sleight, eds. *The Unsilent Library: Essays on the Russell T. Davies Era of the New Doctor Who*. (London: The Science Fiction Foundation, 2011.)

Bray, Stephen. "Doctor Who Ratings: Putting Things Straight." *Den of Geek*, July 4, 2010.

Brecht, Bertolt. "Alienation Effects in Chinese Acting: The A-Effect," *Twentieth Century Theatre: A Sourcebook*, ed. Richard Drain. London: Routledge, 1995.

British Broadcasting Corporation. "Audience Research Report: Dr Who, 22nd December 1964." R9/7/92.

Britton, Piers D. and Simon J. Barker. *Reading Between Designs: Visual Imagery and the Generation of Meaning in the Avengers, the Prisoner, and Doctor Who*. Austin: University of Texas Press, 2003.

Brooker, Peter. *A Glossary of Cultural Theory*, 2d ed. London: Arnold Hodder Headline Group, 2003.

Buckingham, D. *Children Talking Television: The Making of Television Literacy*. London: The Falmer Press, 1993.

Buell, Frederick. "A Short History of Environmental Apocalypse" in Skrimshire (ed.), *Future Ethics*, ed. Skrimshire, 13–36.

Burk, Graeme. "CanCon Who: Half Canadian, on His Father's Side." *Enlightenment Magazine*, Issue 97 (March/April 2000): *"The Doctor, Eh?"* http://www.dwin.org/article.php?sid=67 (September 30, 2008).

_____. (Interview-2). Doctor Who Information Network (October 2, 2008).

_____. (Interview-1). *The Planet of the Doctor*. Documentary. 2005. Dir. Johnny Kalaingas. Canadian Broadcasting Corporation, http://www.cbc.ca/planetofthedoctor/videos.html# (September 30, 2008).

Burdge, Anthony S., Jessica Burke and Kristine Larsen, eds. *The Mythological Dimensions of Doctor Who*. Crawfordville: Kitsune, 2010.

Butler, David. *Time and Relative Dissertations in Space*. Manchester: Manchester University Press, 2007.

Buxton, D. *From the Avengers to Miami Vice: Form and Ideology in Television Series*. Manchester: Manchester University Press, 1990.

Campbell, Joseph. *The Hero with a Thousand Faces*, 2d ed. Princeton: Princeton University Press, 1968.

_____. *The Masks of God: Primitive Mythology*. New York: Penguin, 1959.

Campbell, S. "A Report On Children's Experience of Televisual Media Today." *The Federation of Women Teachers' Association of Ontario*, Fall 1992, 22–28.

Canadian Broadcasting Corporation. "The Financials 2005–2006." Utopia Communications, Toronto, http://www.cbc.radio-canada.ca/annualreports/2005–2006/pdf/financials-e.pdf (October 4, 2008).

Canadian Radio-television and Telecommunications Commission. "Canadian Content for Radio and Television Fact Sheet," http://www.crtc.gc.ca/public/old_pubs_e/G11.htm (September 30, 2008).

Cartmel, Andrew. *Through Time: An Unauthorized and Unofficial History of Doctor Who*. London: Continuum International, 2005.

Castells, Manuel. *The Internet Galaxy: Reflections on the Internet, Business, and Society*. New York: Oxford University Press, 2001.

Chaney, D. C. "Involvement, Realism and the Perception of Aggression in Television Programmes." *Human Relations*, No. 23, 1970: 373–381.

Chapman, James. *Inside the TARDIS: The Worlds of Doctor Who*. New York: I.B. Tauris, 2006.

Charles, Alec. "The Ideology of Anachronism: Television, History and the Nature of Time." *Time and Relative Dissertations in Space*, ed. Butler. 2007.

_____. "War Without End? Utopia, the Family, and the Post-9/11 World in Russell T. Davies's *Doctor Who*." *Science Fiction Studies* 35 (2008): 450–65.

Cole, Stephan. "Who's Who?" *Canadian Broadcasting Corporation Online — Arts*, http://www.cbc.ca/arts/tv/drwho.html (October 2, 2008).

Cole, Stephen. *The Ring of Steel*. Narr. Arthur Darvill. BBC/*The Observer* February 20, 2011.

Connerton, Paul. *How Societies Remember*. Cambridge: Cambridge University Press, 1989.

Cook, John R., and Peter Wright. *British Science Fiction Television: A Hitchhiker's Guide*. London: I.B. Tauris, 2005.

Cornell, Paul, Martin Day, and Keith Topping. *The Discontinuity Guide*. Austin: MonkeyBrain Books, 2004.

Cranny-Francis, Anne, and John Tulloch. "Vaster Than Empire(S), and More Slow: The Politics and Economics of Embodiment in *Doctor Who*." *Thirdperson: Authoring and Exploring Vast Narratives*, eds. Pat Harrigan and Noah Wardrip-Fin. Cambridge: MIT Press, 2009: 343–55.

Crean, S.M. *Who's Afraid of Canadian Culture?* Don Mills, Ontario: General Publishing, 1976.

Cull, Nicholas J. "'Bigger on the Inside ...': *Doctor Who* as British Cultural History." *The Historian, Television and Television History*, eds. Graham Roberts and Philip M. Taylor. Luton: University of Luton Press, 2001: 95–111.

Culler, Jonathan. *Literary Theory: A Very Short Introduction*. Oxford: Oxford University Press, 1997.

Davidoff, Leonore, Jeanne L'Esperance and Howard Newby. "Landscape with Figures: Home and Community in English Society." *Worlds Between: Historical Perspectives on Gender and Class*, ed. Leonore Davidoff. Cambridge: Polity, 1995.

Davis, G. Todd. "The Eternal Vigil: Captain Jack as Byronic Hero." *Illuminating Tourchwood: Essays on Narrative, Character and Sexuality in the BBC Series*, ed. Andrew Ireland. Jefferson, NC: McFarland, 2010: 79–89.

Deller, Ruth. "What the World Needs Is ... a Doctor." *Doctor Who and Philosophy*, eds. Lewis and Smithka, 239–48.

Dicks, Terrance. *Doctor Who and the Day of the Daleks*. New York: Pinnacle Books, 1982.

_____. *Doctor Who and the Terror of the Autons*. London: Target, 1979.

DiPaolo, Marc Edward. "Political Satire and British-American Relations in Five Decades of *Doctor Who*." *Journal of Popular Culture*, 43.5 (October 2010): 964–87.

Di Rocco, Gian-Luca (John). "Attn: U.K. — Canada Exists!" *The Doctor Who Blog*. http://www.dwin.org/expressionengine/index.php/site/attn_uk_canada_exists/ (January 16, 2006).

_____. (Interview). October 2, 2008.

"Doctor Who Assistant Denies Being 'Too Sexy' in Role." *BBC News*, June 15, 2010, http://www.bbc.co.uk/news/10316872.

"Doctor Who Ratings." *The Mind Robber*, http://www.themindrobber.co.uk/ratings.html.

"Doctor Who's Karen Gillan Hits Back at Feminism 'Outrage.'" *London Evening Standard,* June 15, 2010, http://www.thisislondon.co.uk/showbiz/article-23844963-doctor-whos-karen-gillan-hits-back-at-feminism-outrage.do.

Dorr, A. "No Shortcuts to Judging Reality." *Children's *Understanding of Television: Research on Attention and Comprehension*, eds. J. Bryant and D.R. Anderson. New York: Academic Press, 1983: 199–220.

Douvan, Elizabeth A. M., and Joseph Adelson. *The Adolescent Experience*. New York: Wiley, 1966.

Erikson, Erik H. *Dimensions of a New Identity*. New York: W. W. Norton, 1974.

_____. *Identity and the Life Cycle*, 2d ed. New York: W. W. Norton, 1980.

_____. *Identity: Youth and Crisis*. New York: W. W. Norton, 1968.

_____. *The Life Cycle Completed: A Review*. New York: W. W. Norton, 1982.

Eron, L. D., L. R. Huesmann, P. Brice, P. Fischer and R. Mermelstein. "Age Trends in the Development of Aggression and Associated Television Habits." *Developmental Psychology*, No. 19, 1983: 71–77.

Fernie, D. E. "Ordinary and Extraordinary People: Children's Understanding of Television and Real Life Models." *New Directions for Child Development: Viewing Children through Television*, eds. H. Kelly and H. Gardner. San Francisco: Jossey-Bass, 1981: 47–58.

Feshbach, S. "The Role of Fantasy in the Response to Television." *Journal of Social Issues* 32.4 (1976):71–85.

Fiske, John. "*Doctor Who*: Ideology and the Reading of a Popular Narrative Text." *Australian Journal of Screen Theory*, 14–15 (1983): 69–100.

French, David. "Leaving Home." *Modern Canadian Plays, vol. 1, 4th ed.*, ed. Jerry Wasserman. Vancouver: Talonbooks, 2000.

Frey, J.M., and Karen Wood. *Torchwood 4*. http://www.youtube.com/watch?v=mULMXxztIGw (November 10, 2008).

Gale, Richard M. "The Static Versus the Dynamtic Temporal." *The Philosophy of Time: A Collection of Essays*, ed. Richard M. Gale. Atlantic Highlands, NJ: Humanities Press, 1968: 65–84.

Gay, Peter. *The Freud Reader*. New York: W. W. Norton, 1995.

Geertz, Clifford. *The Interpretation of Cultures*. New York: Basic Books, 1973.

Genette, Gérard. *Narrative Discourse: An Essay in Method*. Jane Lewin, trans., Ithaca: Cornell University Press, 1980.

Gerbner, G., L. Gross, M. F. Eleey, M. Jackson-Beeck, S. Jeffries-Fox, and N. Signorielli. "Sex, Violence, and the Rules of the Game: TV Violence Profile no. 8: The Highlights."*Journal of Communication*, 27, 1977:171–180.

Gilligan, Carol. "Joining the Resistance: Girls' Development in Adolescence." Paper presented at the Symposium on Development and Vulnerability in Close Relationships, May 1992, Montreal, Québec, Canada.

Gorman, Andrew. "*Back to the Future*: Oedipus as Time Traveller." *Liquid Metal: The Science Fiction Film Reader*, ed. Sean Redmond. London: Wallflower Press, 2007: 116–25.

Green, Melody. "'It Turns Out They Died for Nothing': *Doctor Who* and the Idea of Sacrificial Death." *Mythological Dimensions*, eds. Burdge, Burke and Larsen, 105–119.

Gregg, Peter R. "England Looks to the Future: The Cultural Forum Model and *Doctor Who*." *Journal of Popular Culture*, 37, no. 4 (2004): 648–61.

Grey, John, and Eric Peterson. "Billy Bishop Goes to War." *Modern Canadian Plays, vol. 1, 4th ed.*, ed. Jerry Wasserman.Vancouver: Talonbooks, 2000.

Gribben, Crawford. *The Puritan Millennium*. Milton Keynes: Paternoster, 2008.

Gurudata, Andrew. "CanCon Who: Rage Against the Machine." *Enlightenment Magazine,* Issue 147 (September 2008), ed. Graeme Burk. Toronto: Q-Print, 2008: 24–25.

Hall, John R. *Apocalypse: From Antiquity to the Empire of Modernity*. Malden, MA: Polity, 2009.

Hansen, Christopher J., ed. *Ruminations, Peregrinations, and Regenerations: A Critical Approach to Doctor Who*. Cambridge: Cambridge Scholars Press, 2010.

Harrigan, Pat, and Noah Wardrip-Fruin, eds. *Third Person: Authoring and Exploring Vast Narratives*. Cambridge: MIT Press, 2009.

Harvey, C. B. "Canon, Myth, and Memory in Doctor Who." *The Mythological Dimensions of Doctor Who*, eds. Burdge, Burke and Larson. Cawfordville: Kitsune Books, 2010: 22–36.

Heidegger, Martin. *Being and Time*. Trans. Joan Stambaugh, ed. Dennis J. Schmidt. New York: State University of New York Press, 1996.

_____. *The Concept of Time*. Trans. William McNeill. Oxford: Basil Blackwell, 1992.

_____. "The Question Concerning Technology." In *The Question Concerning Technology and Other Essays*. New York: Harper and Row, 1977: 3–35.

Henderson, John. "Doctor Who and the Curse of Fatal Death." *Doctor Who*. London: BBC, 1999.

Hickerson, Michael. "Moffat: 'Doctor Who' Is a 'Dark Fairy Tale.'" *Slice of SciFi*, May 19, 2010, http:/www.sliceofscifi.com/2010/0519/Moffat-doctor-who-is-a-dark-fairy-tale/.

_____. "New Season of 'Doctor Who' Raising Eyebrows," *Slice of SciFi*, April 8, 2010, http:www.sliceofscifi.com2010/04/08new-season-of-doctor-who-raising-eyebrows/.

Hills, Matt. "The Dispersible Television Text: Theorising Moments of the New Doctor Who." *Science Fiction Film and Television* 1, no. 1 (2008): 25–44.

_____. *Triumph of a Time Lord: Regenerating Doctor Who in the Twenty-First Century*. London: I. B. Tauris, 2010.

Hinchcliffe, P. http://drwhointerviews.wordpress.com/category/philip-hinchcliffe/.

Hinton, Craig. *Doctor Who: Synthespians*. London: BBC Books, 2004.

Howe, David J., Mark Stammers and Stephen James Walker. *Doctor Who—The Eighties,* 1st ed. London: Virgin, 1996.

_____, Stephen James Walker, and Mark Stammers. *The Handbook: The Unofficial and Unauthorised Guide to the Production of Doctor Who.* Tolworth: Telos, 2005.

IMDB. "Doctor Who (1996)." *The Internet Movie Database,* http://www.imdb.com/title/tt0116118/.

Jameson, Fredric. *Postmodernism: Or, the Cultural Logic of Late Capitalism.* Durham: Duke University Press, 1991.

James, Annie Morgan. "Enchanted Places, Land and Sea, and Wilderness: Scottish Highland Landscape and Idenity in Cinema." *Representing the Rural: Space, Place, and Identity in Films About the Land,* eds. Catherine Fowler and Gillian Hellfield. Detroit: Wayne State University Press, 2006.

Johnson, Steven. *Everything Bad Is Good for You.* New York: Riverside, 2005.

Johnson, Catharine. *Telefantasy.* London: BFI, 2005.

Kalangis, Johnny, Dir. *The Planet of the Doctor.* Documentary. Prod. Shawn Bailey. Feat. Robert J. Sawyer. Canadian Broadcasting Corporation. 2005. http://www.cbc.ca/planetofthedoctor/videos.html# (September 30, 2008).

Keller, Pierre. "Heidegger's Critique of the Vulgar Notion of Time." *International Journal of Philosophical Studies* 4, no. 1 (1996): 43–66.

Kelly, H. "Reasoning About Realities: Children's Evaluations of Television and Books." *New Directions for Child Development: Viewing Children through Television, eds.* H. Kelly and H. Gardner. San Francisco: Jossey-Bass, 1981: 59–71.

Keohane, Kieran. *Symptoms of Canada.* Toronto: University of Toronto Press, 1997.

King, Geoff. *Spectacular Narratives: Hollywood in the Age of the Blockbuster.* New York: I.B. Tauris, 2003.

Kung, Michelle. "Craig Fergus's Lost 'Doctor Who' Cold Open to Finally Air." Speakeasy, January 6, 2011. http://blogs.wsj.com/speakeasy/2011/01/06/craig-fergusons-doctor-who-cold-open-to-see-light-of-day/.

Lacob, Jace. "The New Doctor Who." *The Daily Beast,* March 31, 2010.

Lambert, Verity. (Interview). *The Planet of the Doctor.* Documentary. Dir. Johnny Kalangis. Canadian Broadcasting Corporation. 2005. http://www.cbc.ca/planetofthedoctor/videos.html# (September 30, 2008).

Landow, George. *Hypertext 3.0: Critical Theory and New Media in an Era of Globalization,* rev. ed. Baltimore: Johns Hopkins University Press, 2006.

Lavery, David. "*Lost* and Long Term Television Narrative." *Third Person: Authoring and Exploring Vast Narratives,* eds. Pat Harrigan and Noah Wardrip-Fruin. Cambridge, MIT Press, 2009: 313–22.

Lawrence, John Shelton. "Introduction: Spectacle, Merchandise, and Influence. " *Finding the Force of the Star Wars Franchise,* edu. Matthew Wihelm Kapell and John Shelton Lawrence. New York: Peter Lang, 2006: 1–20.

Leach, Jim. *Doctor Who.* Detroit: Wayne State University Press, 2009.

Lee, V. *The Beautiful.* London: Cambridge University Press, 2011.

Le Poidevin, Robin. *The Images of Time.* Oxford: Oxford University Press, 2007.

Letts, B. http://drwhointerviews.wordpress.com/category/producers/page/2/.

Levinson, Daniel J. *The Seasons of a Woman's Life.* New York: Ballantine, 1996.

Lewis, Courtland, and Paula Smithka. *Doctor Who and Philosophy: Bigger on the Inside.* Chicago, Open Court, 2011.

Lewis, David. "The Paradoxes of Time Travel." *American Philosophical Quarterly,* 13, no. 2 (1976): 145–52.

Lloyd, Genevieve. *Being in Time: Selves and Narrators in Philosophy and Literature.* London: Routledge, 1993.

Lourie, Adrian. "Interview: Steven Moffat, Doctor Who Screenwriter." *The Scotsman,* March 22, 2010 (February 18, 2011).

Marson, Richard. "Eric Saward Interview." *Doctor Who Magazine,* No. 94: 20–25.

Martin, Daniel. "*Doctor Who*: Matt Smith's Debut in The Eleventh Hour—The Verdict." *The Guardian,* April 3, 2010 Web. November 18, 2010.

Matlin, Margaret W. *The Psychology of Women,* 3d ed. Ft. Worth: Harcourt Brace, 1996.

McCormack, Una. "He's Not the Messiah: Undermining Political and Religious Authority in New Doctor Who." *The Unsilent Library,* eds. Bradshaw, Keen and Sleight, 45–62.

_____. Personal Correspondence. October 12, 2009.

McKee, Alan. "Is *Doctor Who* Australia." *Media International Australia,* no. 132 (2009): 54–66.

_____. "Is Doctor Who Political?" *European Journal of Cultural Studies* 7, no. 2 (2004): 201–16.

McMahon, Christopher. "Imaginative Faith: Apocalyptic, Science Fiction Theory and Theology." *Dialog* 47:3 (2008): 271–77.

McMullan, Gordon, and David Matthews. *Reading the Medieval in Early Modern England.* Cambridge: Cambridge University Press, 2007.

McTaggart, John, and Ellis McTaggart. *The Nature of Existence,* vol. 2. Cambridge: Cambridge University Press, 1927.

Miller, Mary Jane. *Rewind and Search: Conversations With The Makers and Decision-Makers of CBC Tel-*

evision Drama. Montreal, Quebec: McGill-Queens University Press, 1996.

_____. *Turn Up the Contrast: CBC Television Drama Since 1952*. Vancouver: University of British Columbia Press, 1987.

Miller, Walter M. *A Canticle for Leibowitz*. New York: Bantam, 2007.

Mills, Brett. "My House Was on Torchwood! Media, Place and Identity." *International Journal of Cultural Studies* 11 (2008): 379–400.

Miles, Lawrence, and Tat Wood. *About Time: The Unauthorized Guide to Doctor Who, 1975–1979, Seasons 12 to 17*. Des Moines: Mad Norwegian Press, 2004.

Milne, A. *The Portrayal of Violence in Television Programmes: Suggestions for a Revised Note of Guidance*. London: BBC, 1979.

Mittell, Jason. "Narrative Complexity in Contemporary American Television." *The Velvet Light Trap* 58 (2006): 29–40.

Moore, Brian L., and Michele A. Johnson. *Neither Led nor Driven: Contesting British Cultural Imperialism in Jamaica, 1865–1920*. Kingston: University of the West Indies Press, 2004.

Morris, Ewan. *Our Own Devices: National Symbols and Political Conflict in Twentieth Century Ireland*. Dublin: Irish Academic Press, 2005.

Nahin, Paul J. *Time Machines: Time Travel in Physics, Metaphysics, and Science Fiction*. New York, Springer, 1993.

Nast, Heidi J. "Mapping the 'Unconscious': Racism and the Oedipal Family." *Annals of the Association of American Geographers*, 90 (2000): 215–255.

Newman, Kim. *Doctor Who: A Critical Reading of the Series*. London: BFI, 2005.

Novak, M. *The Experience of Nothingness*. New Brunswick, NJ: Transaction, 2009.

O'Brien, Vincent. "The Doctor or the (Post) Modern Prometheus." *The Mythological Dimensions of Doctor Who*, eds. Burdge, Burke and Larsen. 184–97.

O'Leary, Stephen D. *Arguing the Apocalypse: A Theory of Millennial Rhetoric*. Oxford: Oxford University Press, 1994.

Orthia, Lindy A. "'Sociopathic Abscess' Or 'Yawning Chasm'?" The Absent Postcolonial Transition in Doctor Who." *The Journal of Commonwealth Literature* 45, no. 2 (2010): 207–25.

Owens, K. *The World of the Child*. New York, Macmillan, 1993.

Paik, Peter Y. *From Utopia to Apocalypse: Science Fiction and the Politics of Catastrophe*. Minneapolis: University of Minnesota Press, 2010.

Parkin, Lance. *A History: An Unathorised History of the Doctor Who Universe*. Des Moines: Mad Norwegian Press, 2006.

_____. "Truths Universally Acknowledged: How the 'Rules' of *Doctor Who* Affect the Writing." *Third-person: Authoring and Exploring Vast Narratives*, Pat Harrigan and Noah Wardrip-Fin, eds. Cambridge: MIT Press, 2009: 13–24.

Patterson, Serena J., Ingrid Sochting, and James E. Marcia. "The Inner Space and Beyond: Women and Identity." *Adolescent Identity Formation*, eds. G. R. Adams, T. P. Gullotta, & R. Montemayor. Newbury Park, CA: Sage, 1992.

Peak, Mathew Wace. "Steven Moffat Insists BBC Is Committed to Doctor Who." *Digital Journal*, September 24, 2010, http://www.digitaljournal.com/article/298065.

Pegg, N. "Review: The Sontaran Experiment/Genesis of the Daleks." *Doctor Who Bulletin*, No. 93 (1991): 15.

Perryman, Neil. "*Doctor Who* and the Convergence of Media: A Case Study in 'Transmedia Storytelling.'" *Convergence: The International Journal of Research into Media Technologies* 14, no. 1 (2008): 21–39.

Plato, *Timaeus and Critias*. Trans. Desmond Lee. London: Penguin, 1965.

Poniewozick, James. "Media Freak-outs: Every Week Is Shark Week." *Time Magazine*, August 10, 2009. http://www.time.com/time/magazine/article/0,9171,1913750,00.html

Porter, Lynnette. *Tarnished Heroes, Charming Villains, and Modern Monsters: Science Fiction in Shades of Gray on 21st Century Television*. Jefferson, NC, McFarland, 2010.

"Press Launch Transcript." *David Tennant: The Site*, March 28, 2006. Web. February 18, 2011. http://www.team-tennant.com/article/id50.html

Redmond, Sean. *Liquid Metal: The Science Fiction Film Reader*. London: Wallflower Press, 2004.

Reichl, Susanne. "Flying the Flag: The Intricate Semiotics of National Identity." *European Journal of English Studies* 8.2 (2004): 205–217.

Ricoeur, Paul. "Narrative Time." *Critical Inquiry* 7.1 (1980): 169–90.

Rogers, Annie. "Questions of Gender Differences: Ego Development and Moral Voice in Adolescence." Unpublished manuscript, Harvard University, 1987.

Ross, Stephen David. *Un-Forgetting: Re-Calling Time Lost*. New York: Global Academic, 2009.

Salem, Rob. "Some Good News From Who-ville." *The Star.com*, http://www.thestar.com/entertainment/article/501961 (October 3, 2008).

Schmitt, Carl. *Political Theology: Four Chapters on the Concept of Sovereignty*. Trans. George Schwab. Cambridge: MIT Press, 1922.

Schuster, Marc, and Tom Powers. *The Greatest Show in the Galaxy: The Discerning Fan's Guide to Doctor Who*. Jefferson, NC: McFarland, 2007.

Schmitz, Cathryne L., Elizabeth KimJin Traver, and Desi Larson, eds. *Child Labor: A Global View*. Westport, CT: Greenwood, 2004.

Scott, Peter Manley. "Are We There Yet? Coming to the End of the Line, a Postnatural Enquiry." *Future Ethics*, Skrimshire, ed. 260–79.

"Sexism, Amy Pond, and the Kindness of Podcasters." April 17, 2010, podcast and interview, http://austintotamu.blogspot.com/2010/04/sexism-amy-pond-and-kindness-of.html

Shannon Miller, Liz. "'Doctor Who' Honored by Guinness: Sci-Fi Series Considered Most Successful of All-Time." *Variety*, July 26, 2009.

Shearman, Rob. "Defending the Museum: Re-Evaluation." *Doctor Who: The Space Museum* DVD, London, BBC, 2010.

_____, and Toby Hadoke. *Running Through Corridors: Rob and Toby's Marathon Watch of Doctor Who*. Des Moines: Mad Norwegian Press, 2010.

Singer, J. L., D. G. Singer, and W. Rapaczynski. "Family Patterns and Television Viewing as Predictors of Children's Beliefs and Aggression." *Journal of Communication*, No. 34, Spring 1984: 73 89.

Skrimshire, Stefan, ed. *Future Ethics: Climate Change and the Apocalyptic Imagination*. London: Continuum, 2010.

Smith, Steve. *The Friday Night Project—"David Tennant,"* Justin Lee Collins, Allan Carr, Feat. David Tennant. http://www.youtube.com/watch?v=cAYuHbHJmr0&feature=related (September 6, 2008).

Stiegler, Bernard. *Technics and Time, 1: The Fault of Epimetheus*. Trans. Richard Beardsworth. Stanford: Stanford University Press, 1998.

Suddendorf, Thomas, and Michael C. Corballis. "Mental Time Travel and the Evolution of the Human Mind." *Genetic, Social & General Psychology Monographs* 123.2 (1997): 133–168. http://staff.science.uva.nl/~michiell/docs/MentalTime.html.

Statistical Analysis of the Register 1 April 2007 to 31 March 2008. Nursing and Midwifery Council. February 23, 2010. Web. February 18, 2011.

Sullivan, Shannon Patrick. "The Lost Stories." *A Brief History of Time (Travel)*, http://www.shannonsullivan.com/drwho/lostunt.html.

"10.3 Watch a Christmas Carol." *Doctor Who News Page*, December 26, 2010, http://www.doctorwhonews.net/2010/12/dwn261210015912-overnight-ratings.html.

Tong, Rosemarie. *Feminist Thought: A More Comprehensive Introduction*, 3d ed. Boulder: Westview Press, 2008.

Tulloch, John, and Manuel Alvarado. *Doctor Who: The Unfolding Text*. London: Macmillian, 1983.

_____, and Henry Jenkins. *Science Fiction Audiences: Watching Doctor Who and Star Trek*. London: Routledge, 1995.

Wadsworth, Barry J. *Piaget's Theory of Cognitive and Affective Development: Foundations of Constructivism*, 5th ed. Needham Heights, MA: Allyn and Bacon, 2003.

Walsh, Richard. *The Rhetoric of Fictionality: Narrative Theory and the Idea of Fiction*. Columbus: Ohio State University, 2007.

Wasserman, Jerry. "David Fennario." *Modern Canadian Plays, vol. 1, 4th ed.* Wasserman, ed. Vancouver: Talonbooks, 2000.

Wasserman, Jerry. "John Gray with Eric Peterson." *Modern Canadian Plays, vol. 1, 4th ed.* Wasserman, ed. Vancouver: Talonbooks, 2000.

Weiner, Martin J. *English Culture and the Decline of the Industrial Spirit, 1850–1980*. Cambridge: Cambridge University Press, 1981.

Wells, Herbert George. *The War of the Worlds*. London: Gollancz, 2001.

White, Carol J. *Time and Death: Heidegger's Analysis of Finitude*. Aldershot, UK: Ashgate, 2005.

Whitelaw, Paul. "A Heartfelt Letter to *Doctor Who* Producers." *Scotland on Sunday*, March 14, 2010. Web. November 18, 2010

Wikipedia. "Canadian Content." *Wikipedia, the Free Online Encyclopaedia*, http://en.wikipedia.org/wiki/Canadian_content (September 30, 2008).

Wikipedia. "Doctor Who." *Wikipedia, the Free Online Encyclopaedia*. http://en.wikipedia.org/wiki/Doctor_Who (October 4, 2008).

Wikipedia. "I Am Canadian." *Wikipedia, the Free Online Encyclopaedia*. http://en.wikipedia.org/wiki/I_Am_Canadian (October 4, 2009).

Wikipedia. "Sydney Newman." *Wikipedia, the Free Online Encyclopaedia,* http://en.wikipedia.org/wiki/Sydney_Newman (September 30, 2008).

Winick, M. P., and C. Winick. *The Television Experience: What Children See*. Beverly Hills, CA: Sage, 1979.

Woods, Michael. *Contesting Rurality: Politics in the British Countryside*. Aldershot, UK: Ashgate, 2006.

Wolcher, Louis E. *Law's Task: The Tragic Circle of Law, Justice and Human Suffering*. Aldershot, UK: Ashgate, 2008.

Wood, Tat. *About Time: The Unauthorized Guide to Doctor Who, Expanded Second Edition, 1970–1974, Seasons 7 to 1*. Des Moines: Mad Norwegian Press, 2009.

Žižek, Slavoj. *Living in the End Times*. New York: Verso, 2010.

About the Contributors

Paul **Booth** is an assistant professor in the College of Communication at DePaul University. He researches and teaches on new media, technology, popular culture, and cultural studies. The author of *Digital Fandom: New Media Studies,* he has also published articles, journals and edited collections.

Lindsay **Coleman** is a writer and film academic based in Melbourne, Australia. His doctoral thesis explored links between Marcel Proust, Henri Bergson and Joseph Campbell and HBO programming 2000–2010. He is working on two anthologies which explore explicit sexuality, narrative, media and philosophy, and a book of interviews with cinematographers.

Andrew **Crome** is a lecturer in the history of modern Christianity at the University of Manchester. He researches and writes on apocalyptic thought, particularly the history of Christian Zionism in the Western world from the seventeenth century onwards. He is co-editing a volume on religion and *Doctor Who* with James McGrath.

Kate **Flynn** is a Ph.D. candidate with research interests in children's literature and media, comics for girls, and the body. Her dissertation focuses on changing constructions of the fat child in *Jackie* magazine and British juvenile fiction between 1960 and 2010. She is based at the University of Worcester in the United Kingdom.

J.M. **Frey** is a science fiction and fantasy author and pop culture scholar who participates in podcasts, documentaries, and television programs to discuss all things geeky through the lens of academia. Her debut novel *Triptych* won the San Francisco Book Festival award for SF/F, was named one of The Advocate's Best Overlooked Books of 2011, and garnered both a starred review and a place among the Best Books of 2011 in *Publishers Weekly.*

Sherry **Ginn** has published numerous research articles in the fields of neuroscience and psychology, but focuses her extracurricular work on the intersection of popular culture with psychology and neuroscience. She is the author of *Power and Control in the Television Worlds of Joss Whedon* (McFarland, 2012) and co-author (with Michael J. Cornelius) of *The Sex Is Out of this World: Essays on the Carnal Side of Science Fiction* (McFarland, 2012).

Maura **Grady** earned her doctorate in English with emphases in film studies and gender theory at the University of California, Davis. She is an assistant professor of English at Ashland University where she teaches screenwriting, film studies, writing and literature. She is a proud alumnus of the Reno Time Team, whose goal is to watch every extant episode of *Doctor Who*, beginning with 1963's "An Unearthly Child."

Aaron **Gulyas** is an instructor at Mott Community College in Flint, Michigan, where he teaches U.S. and world history courses and consults for the college's professional development office. His latest book, *Extraterrestrials and the American Zeitgeist: Contact Tales since the 1950s,* will be published in 2013 by McFarland.

Cassie **Hemstrom** is completing her doctorate in English with emphases on contemporary ethnic American literature and gender, race and identity theories at the University of Nevada, Reno. Her dissertation focuses on relationships between individuals and local, national, transnational and global communities in contemporary literature by Japanese American, Filipino American and Chicano authors. She is a member of the Reno Time Team, a full series *Doctor Who* re-watch group.

Kristine **Larsen** is a professor of astronomy at Central Connecticut State University. She is the author of *Stephen Hawking: A Biography* and *Cosmology 101* and co-editor of *The Mythological Dimensions of Doctor Who* and *The Mythological Dimensions of Neil Gaiman*. Her research focuses on the intersections between science and society.

Gillian I. **Leitch** is an independent scholar and senior researcher at CDCI Research in Ottawa, Ontario. Her Ph.D. thesis analyzes the public expressions of British identities in British Montreal, 1800–1850. A longtime *Doctor Who* fan, she has given several papers on the topic at the PCA/ACA national conferences. She is the co-chair of the Science Fiction and Fantasy Area of the Popular Culture Association.

Racheline **Maltese** is an independent scholar, storyteller, and performer focused on themes of desire, mourning, and the construction of fame. The author of *The Book of Harry Potter Trifles, Trivias and Particularities*, she has published on topics from ranging from *Buffy the Vampire Slayer* to "peace journalism" in a number of anthologies and journals.

Andrew **O'Day** received his Ph.D. in television studies from Royal Holloway, University of London. His thesis concentrated on metafiction in telefantasy with an emphasis on the classic *Doctor Who* series. He is co-author (with Jonathan Bignell) of the book *Terry Nation* and has contributed to other edited collections on *Doctor Who*. His other research interests include Jack the Ripper in media and popular culture, and LGBT studies and the law.

Lynnette **Porter** is a professor in the Humanities and Social Sciences Department at Embry-Riddle Aeronautical University in Daytona Beach, Florida, where she teaches film, communication, and humanities courses. She is the author of thirteen books, most recently *Sherlock Holmes for the 21st Century* (McFarland, 2012) and *The Doctor Who Franchise: American Influence, Fan Culture and the Spinoffs* (McFarland, 2012).

Kieran **Tranter** is a senior lecturer at Griffith Law School, Griffith University, in Australia. He writes on the cultural intersections of law and technology. He is finishing a book on law, technology and science fiction. With his parents and children he is part of a three generation family of *Doctor Who* aficionados.

David **Whitt** is an associate professor of communication at Nebraska Wesleyan University. He is the co-editor of and contributor to two books on comparative mythology: *Sith, Slayers, Stargates and Cyborgs: Modern Mythology in the New Millennium* and *Millennial Mythmaking: Essays on the Power of Science Fiction and Fantasy Literature, Films and Games*.

Antoinette F. **Winstead** is a professor of mass communications, drama, and English at Our Lady of the Lake University in San Antonio, Texas, where she serves as program chair of Mass Communications and Drama and teaches courses in screenwriting, film studies, and production. Her research interests range from film production in small African nations to the heroic journey in science fiction and horror works.

Index